RINGWORLD

THE GRAPHIC NOVEL   PART ONE

BASED ON THE NOVEL BY
LARRY NIVEN

ADAPTED BY ROBERT MANDELL
ILLUSTRATED BY SEAN LAM

TOR®   Seven Seas

A TOR/SEVEN SEAS BOOK
NEW YORK

RINGWORLD: THE GRAPHIC NOVEL, PART ONE

Copyright © 2014 by Red Sky Entertainment, Inc.

Staff Credits
Adaptation: **Robert Mandell**
Art: **Sean Lam**
Toning: **Ludwig Sacramento**
Lettering: **Cassandra Wedeking**
Production Editor: **Adam Arnold**
Editor: **Jason DeAngelis**

A Tor/Seven Seas Paperback
Published by Tom Doherty Associates, LLC
175 Fifth Avenue
New York, NY 10010

Visit us online at www.gomanga.com
and www.tor-forge.com.

Seven Seas and the Seven Seas logo are trademarks
of Seven Seas Entertainment, LLC.
Tor® and the Tor logo are registered trademarks of
Tom Doherty Associates, LLC.

ISBN 978-0-7653-2462-7

Tor/Seven Seas books may be purchased for educational, business, or promotional use. For information on bulk purchases, please contact Macmillan Corporate and Premium Sales Department at 1-800-221-7945, extension 5442, or write specialmarkets@macmillan.com.

First Edition: July 2014

Printed in the United States of America

D 0 9 8 7 6 5 4 3

RINGWORLD

THE GRAPHIC NOVEL   PART ONE

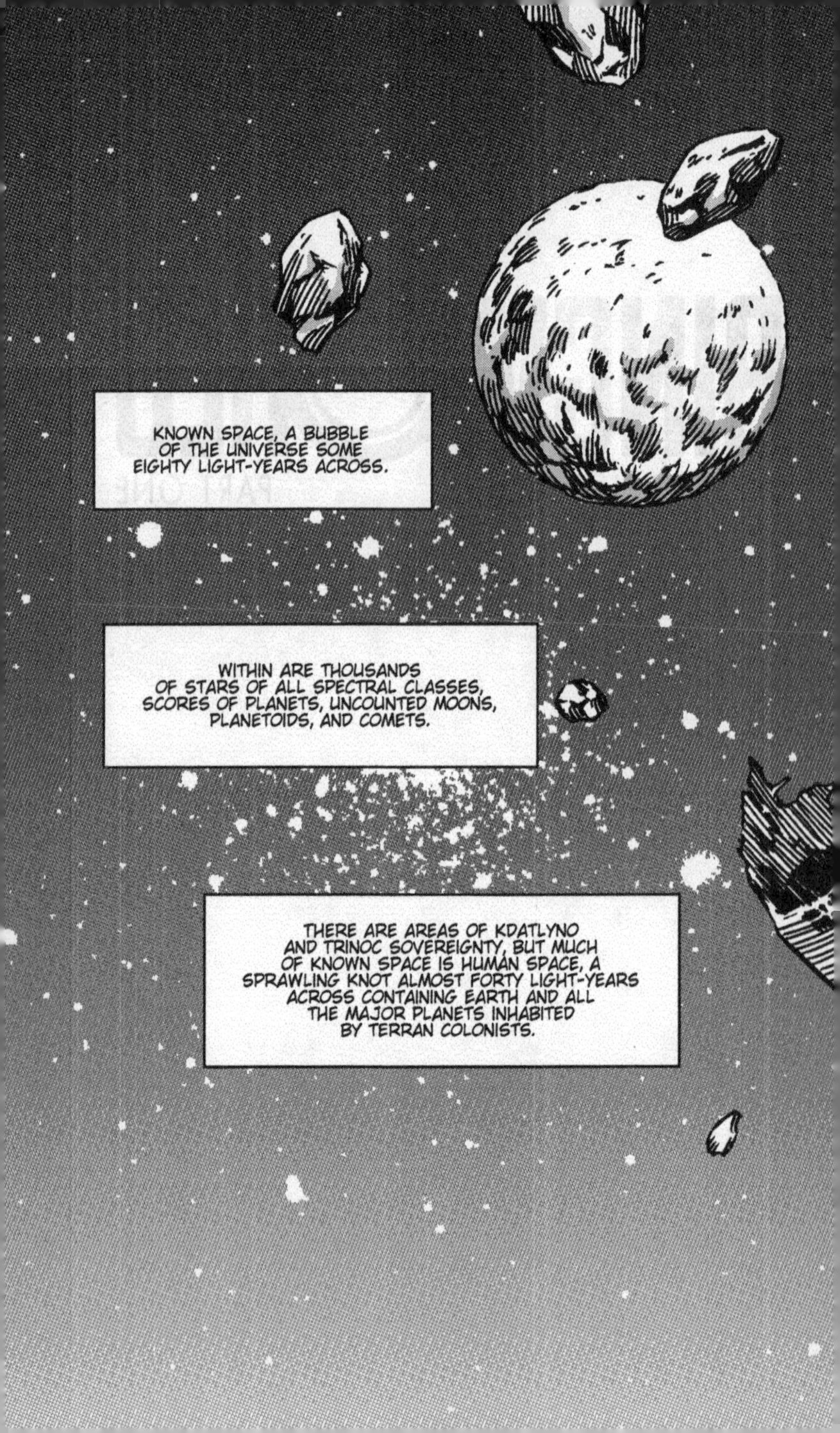
KNOWN SPACE, A BUBBLE OF THE UNIVERSE SOME EIGHTY LIGHT-YEARS ACROSS.
WITHIN ARE THOUSANDS OF STARS OF ALL SPECTRAL CLASSES, SCORES OF PLANETS, UNCOUNTED MOONS, PLANETOIDS, AND COMETS.
THERE ARE AREAS OF KDATLYNO AND TRINOC SOVEREIGNTY, BUT MUCH OF KNOWN SPACE IS HUMAN SPACE, A SPRAWLING KNOT ALMOST FORTY LIGHT-YEARS ACROSS CONTAINING EARTH AND ALL THE MAJOR PLANETS INHABITED BY TERRAN COLONISTS.

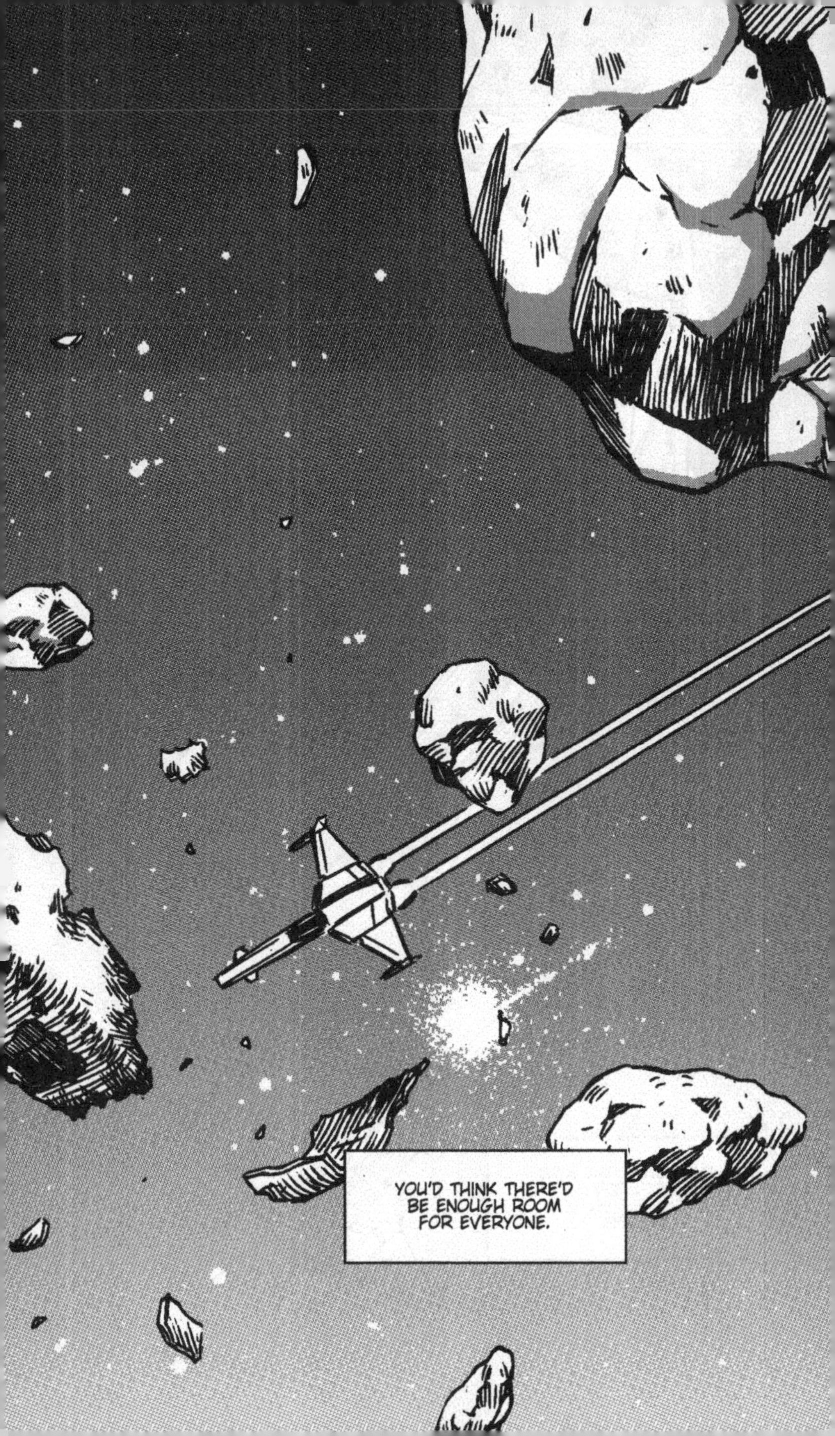
YOU'D THINK THERE'D BE ENOUGH ROOM FOR EVERYONE.

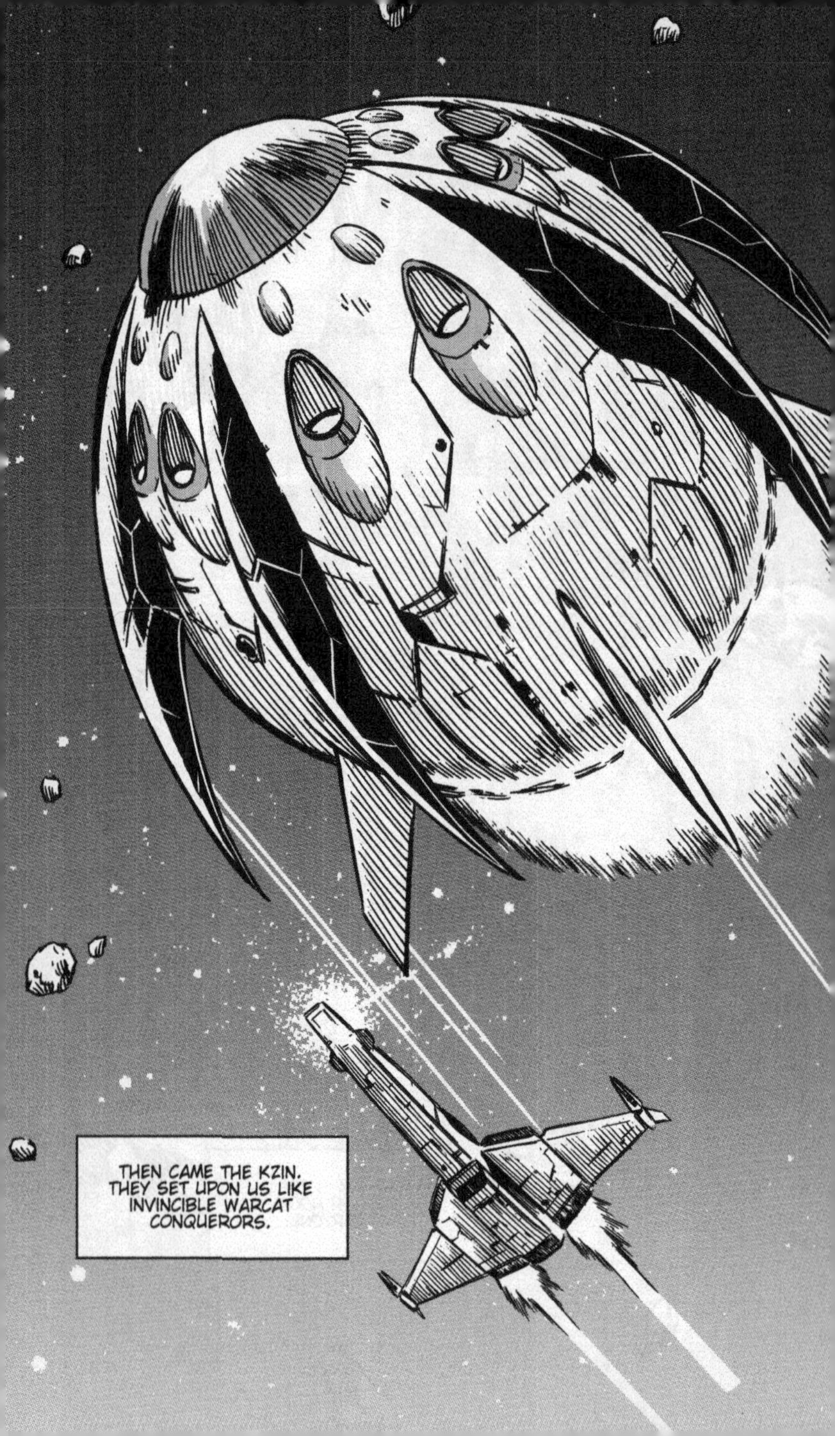
THEN CAME THE KZIN. THEY SET UPON US LIKE INVINCIBLE WARCAT CONQUERORS.

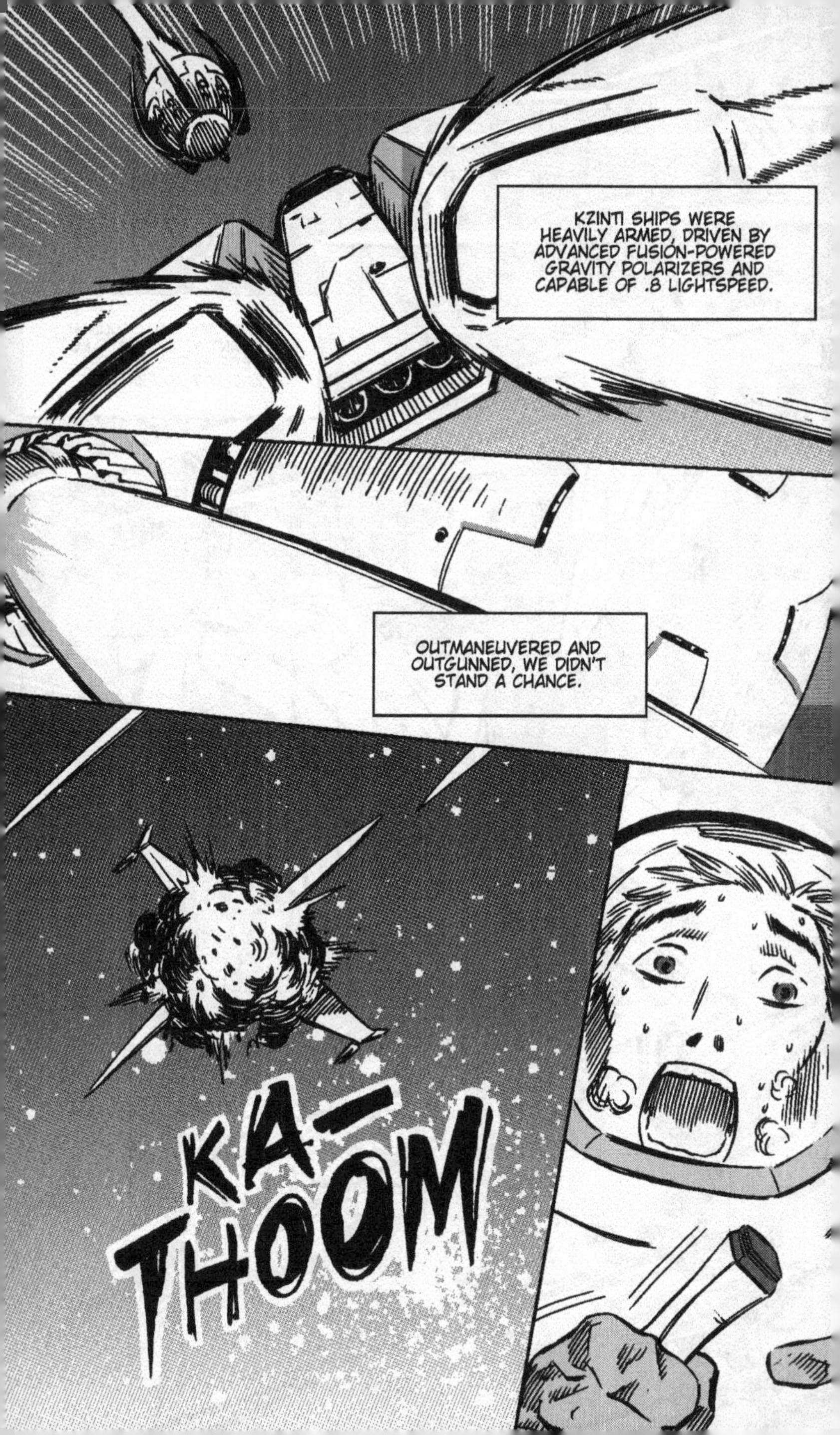
KZINTI SHIPS WERE HEAVILY ARMED, DRIVEN BY ADVANCED FUSION-POWERED GRAVITY POLARIZERS AND CAPABLE OF .8 LIGHTSPEED.
OUTMANEUVERED AND OUTGUNNED, WE DIDN'T STAND A CHANCE.
KA-THOOM

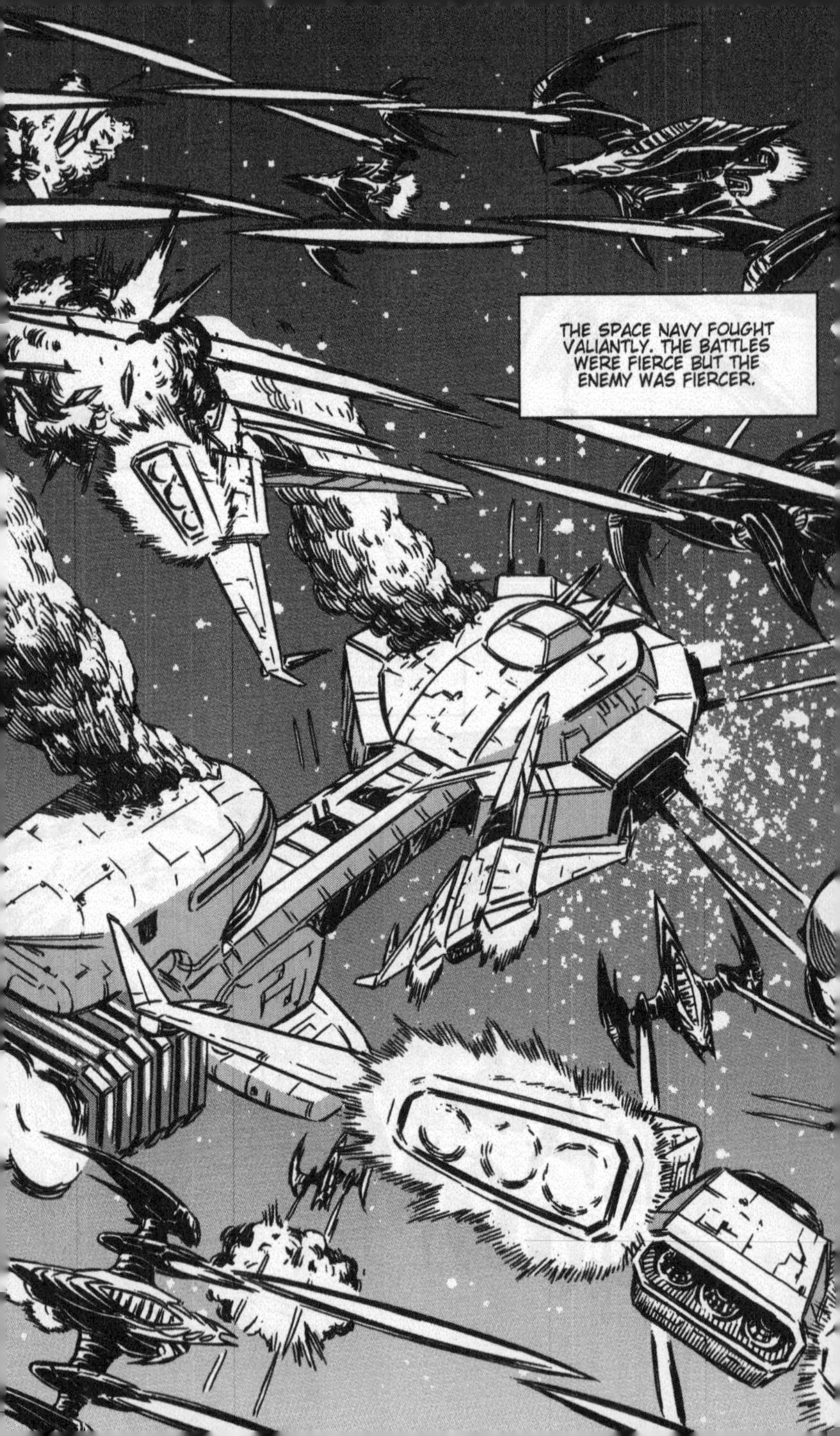
THE SPACE NAVY FOUGHT VALIANTLY. THE BATTLES WERE FIERCE BUT THE ENEMY WAS FIERCER.

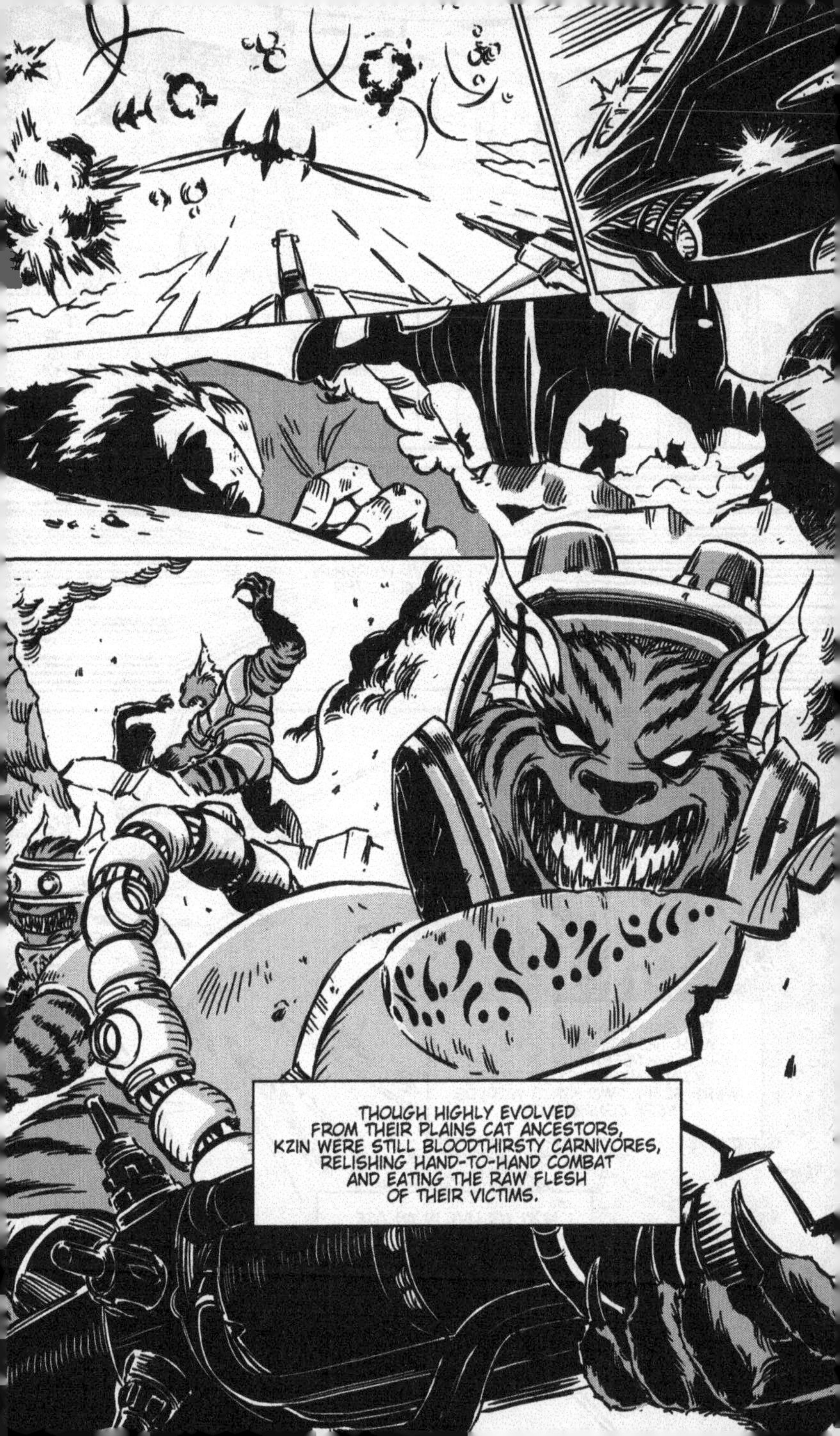
THOUGH HIGHLY EVOLVED FROM THEIR PLAINS CAT ANCESTORS, KZIN WERE STILL BLOODTHIRSTY CARNIVORES, RELISHING HAND-TO-HAND COMBAT AND EATING THE RAW FLESH OF THEIR VICTIMS.

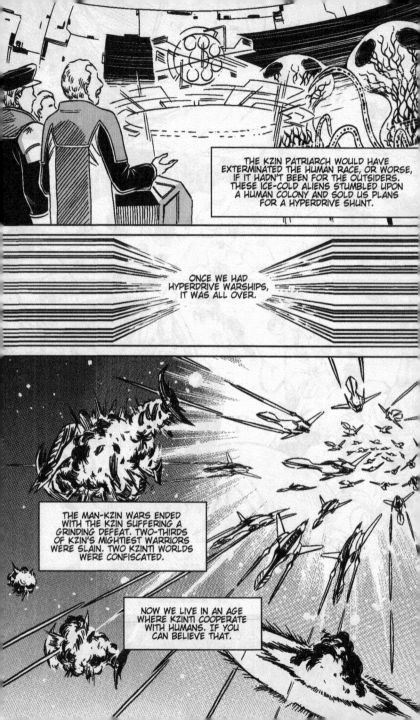

THE KZIN PATRIARCH WOULD HAVE EXTERMINATED THE HUMAN RACE, OR WORSE, IF IT HADN'T BEEN FOR THE OUTSIDERS. THESE ICE-COLD ALIENS STUMBLED UPON A HUMAN COLONY AND SOLD US PLANS FOR A HYPERDRIVE SHUNT.

ONCE WE HAD HYPERDRIVE WARSHIPS, IT WAS ALL OVER.

THE MAN-KZIN WARS ENDED WITH THE KZIN SUFFERING A GRINDING DEFEAT. TWO-THIRDS OF KZIN'S MIGHTIEST WARRIORS WERE SLAIN. TWO KZINTI WORLDS WERE CONFISCATED.

NOW WE LIVE IN AN AGE WHERE KZINTI COOPERATE WITH HUMANS. IF YOU CAN BELIEVE THAT.

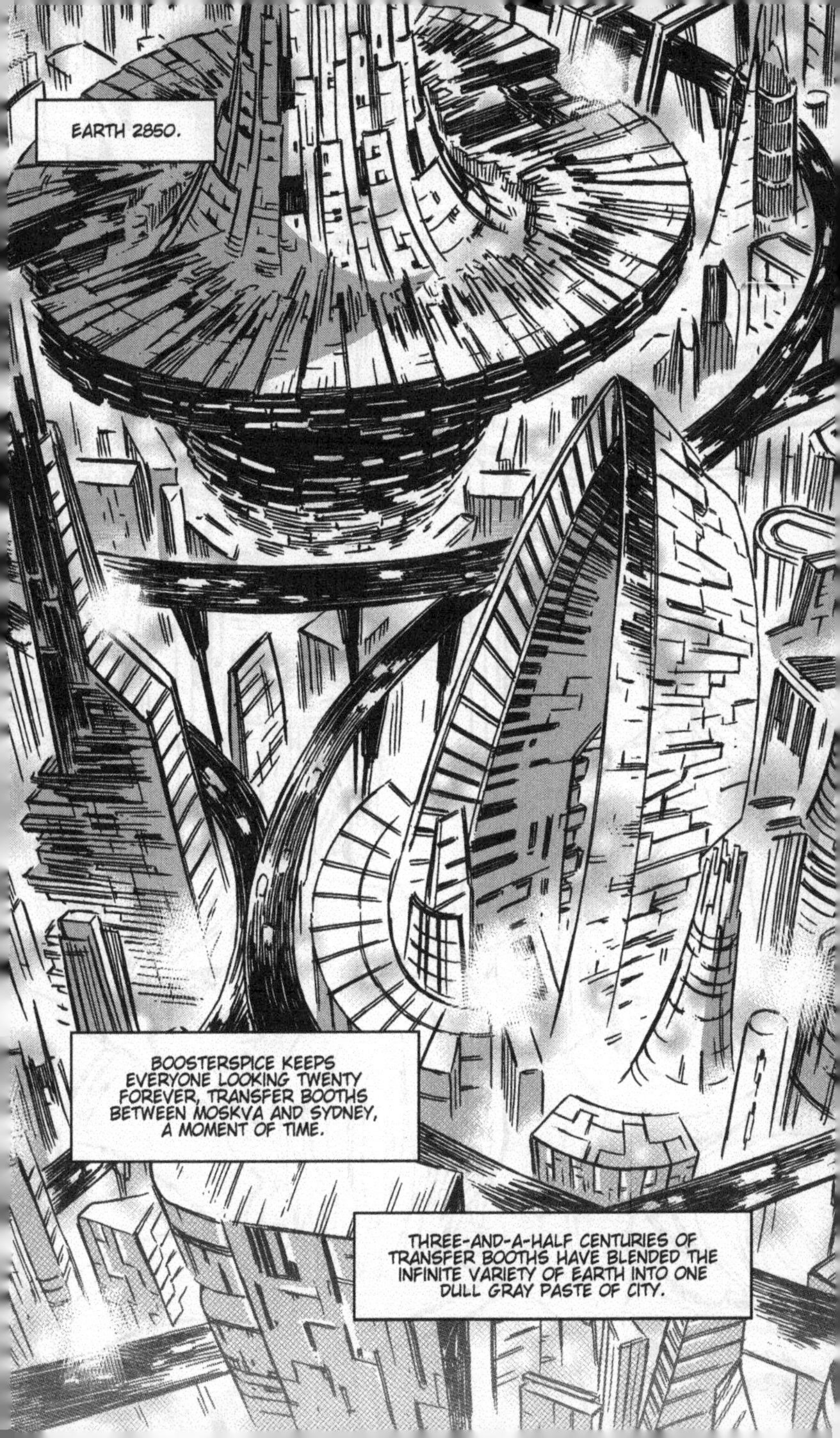
EARTH 2850.
BOOSTERSPICE KEEPS EVERYONE LOOKING TWENTY FOREVER, TRANSFER BOOTHS BETWEEN MOSKVA AND SYDNEY, A MOMENT OF TIME.
THREE-AND-A-HALF CENTURIES OF TRANSFER BOOTHS HAVE BLENDED THE INFINITE VARIETY OF EARTH INTO ONE DULL GRAY PASTE OF CITY.

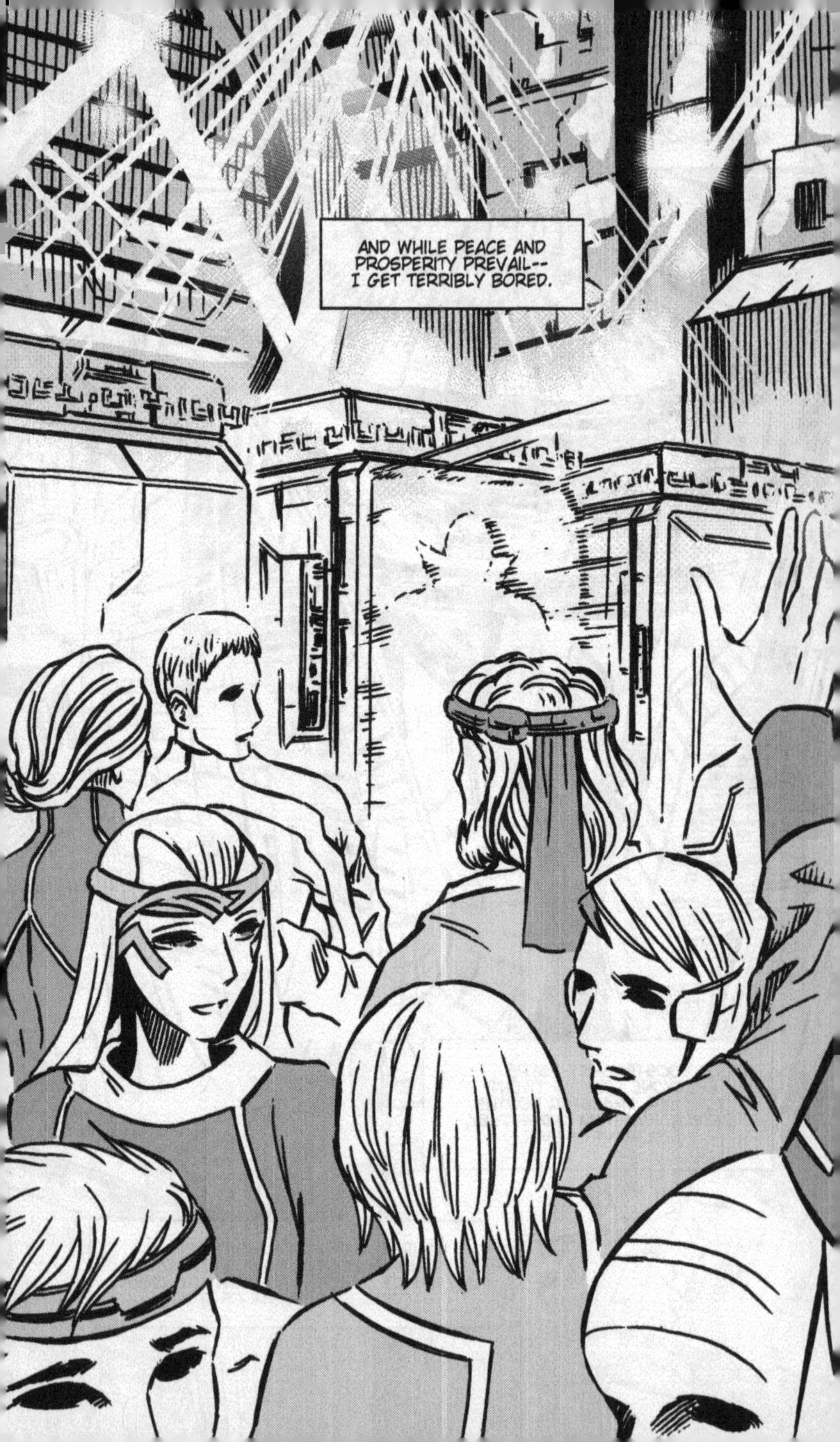
AND WHILE PEACE AND PROSPERITY PREVAIL-- I GET TERRIBLY BORED.

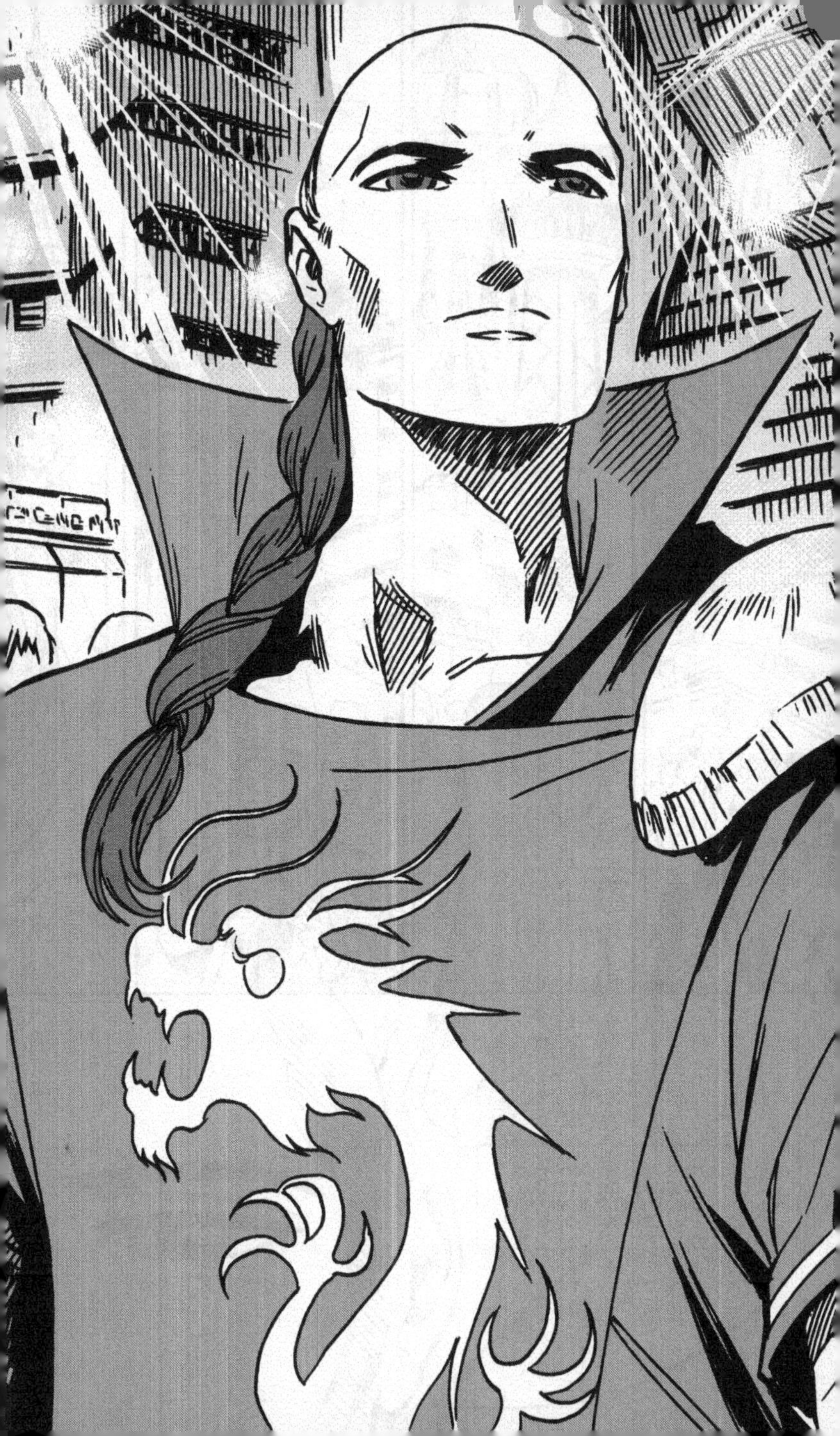

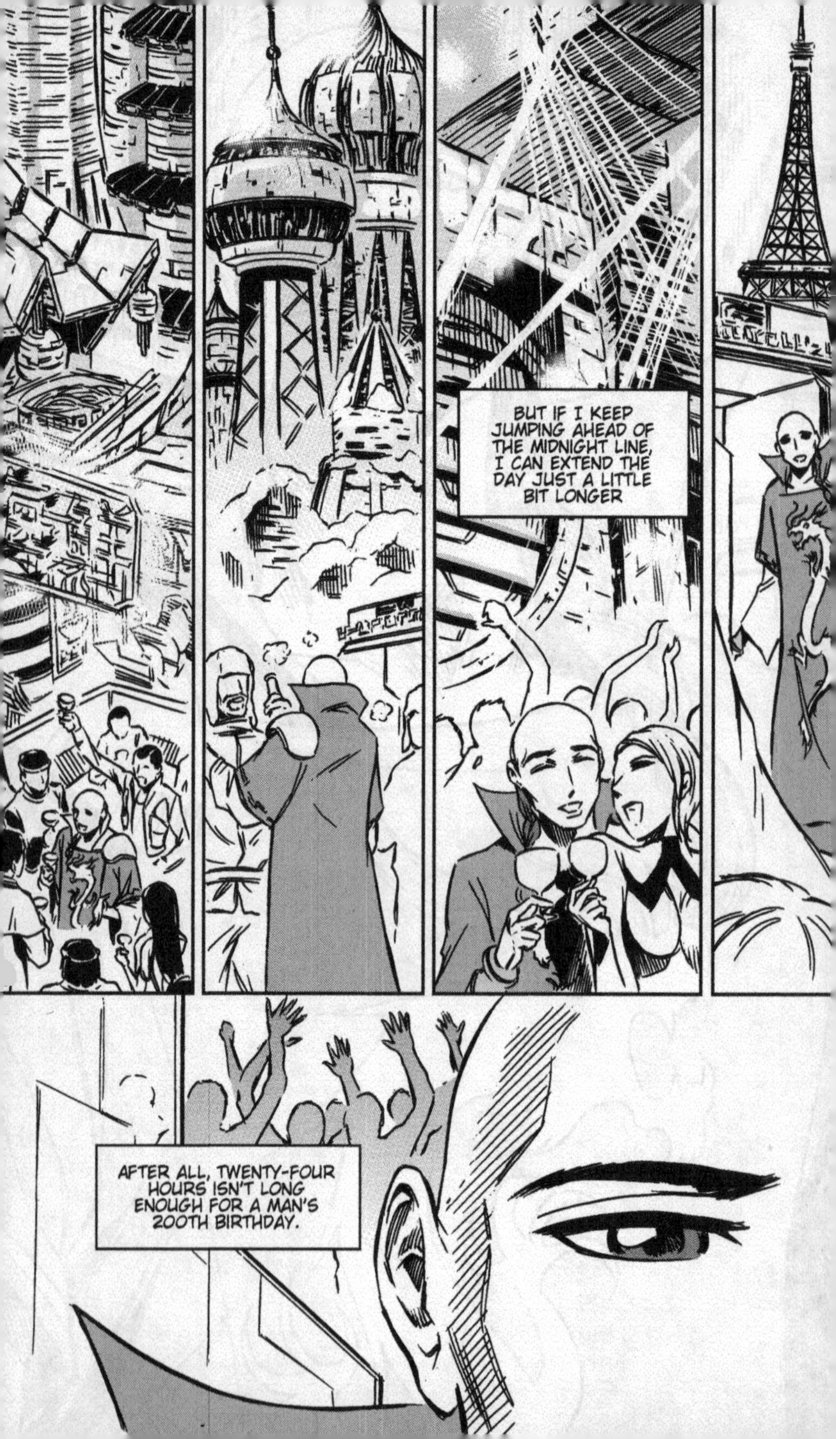
BUT IF I KEEP JUMPING AHEAD OF THE MIDNIGHT LINE, I CAN EXTEND THE DAY JUST A LITTLE BIT LONGER
AFTER ALL, TWENTY-FOUR HOURS ISN'T LONG ENOUGH FOR A MAN'S 200TH BIRTHDAY.

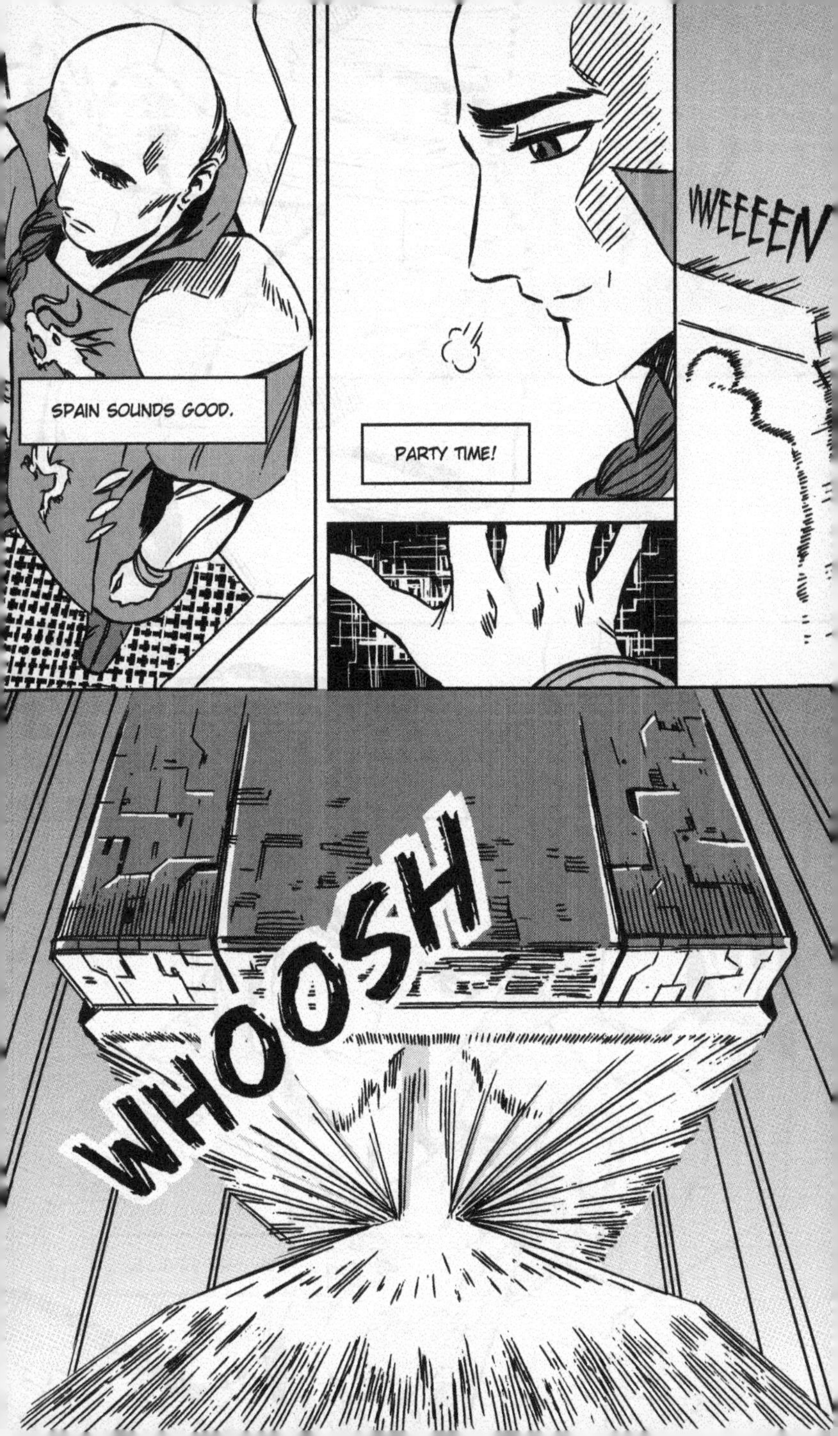
SPAIN SOUNDS GOOD.
PARTY TIME!
VWEEEEN
WHOOSH

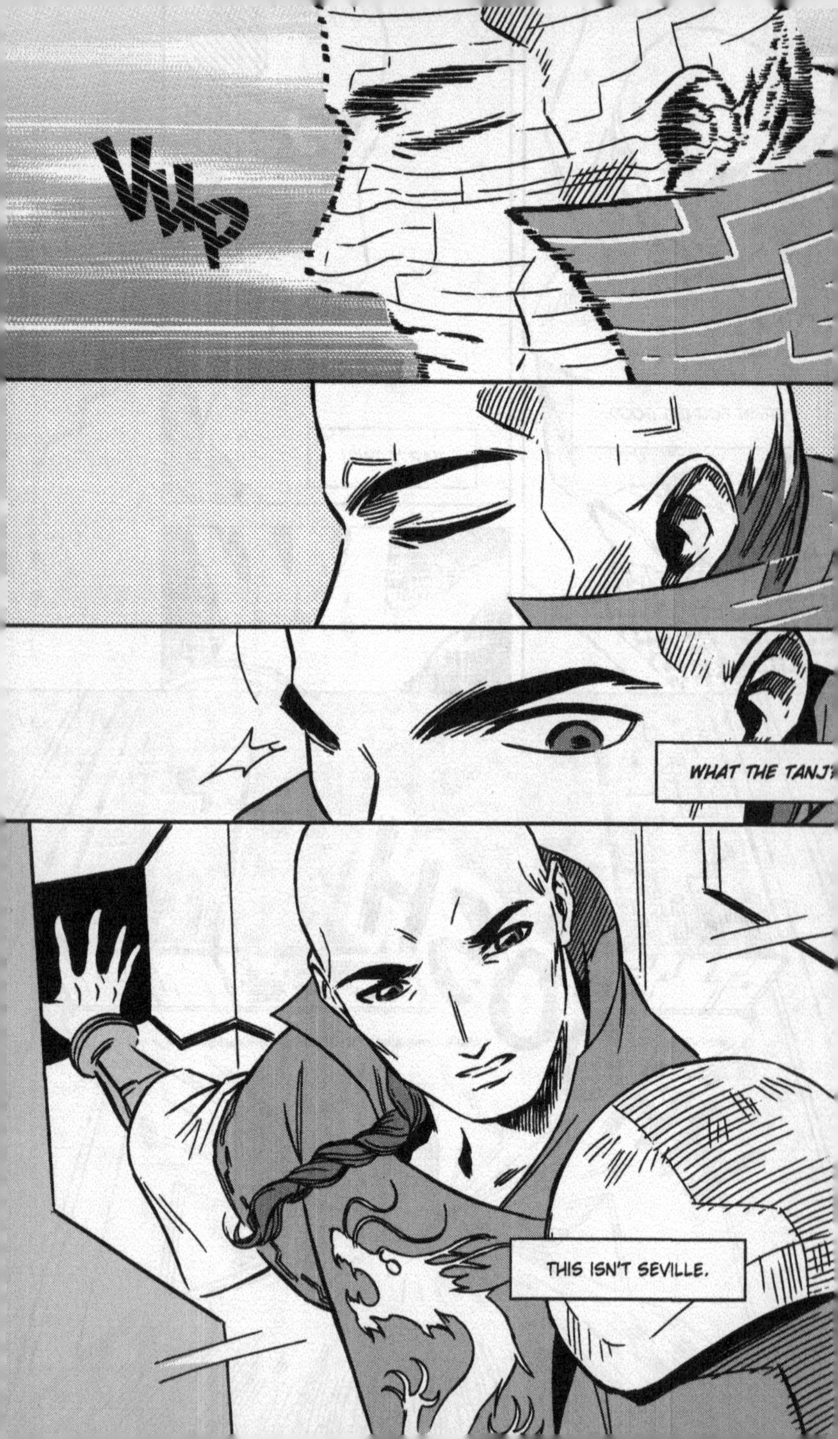
VWP
WHAT THE TANJ?
THIS ISN'T SEVILLE.

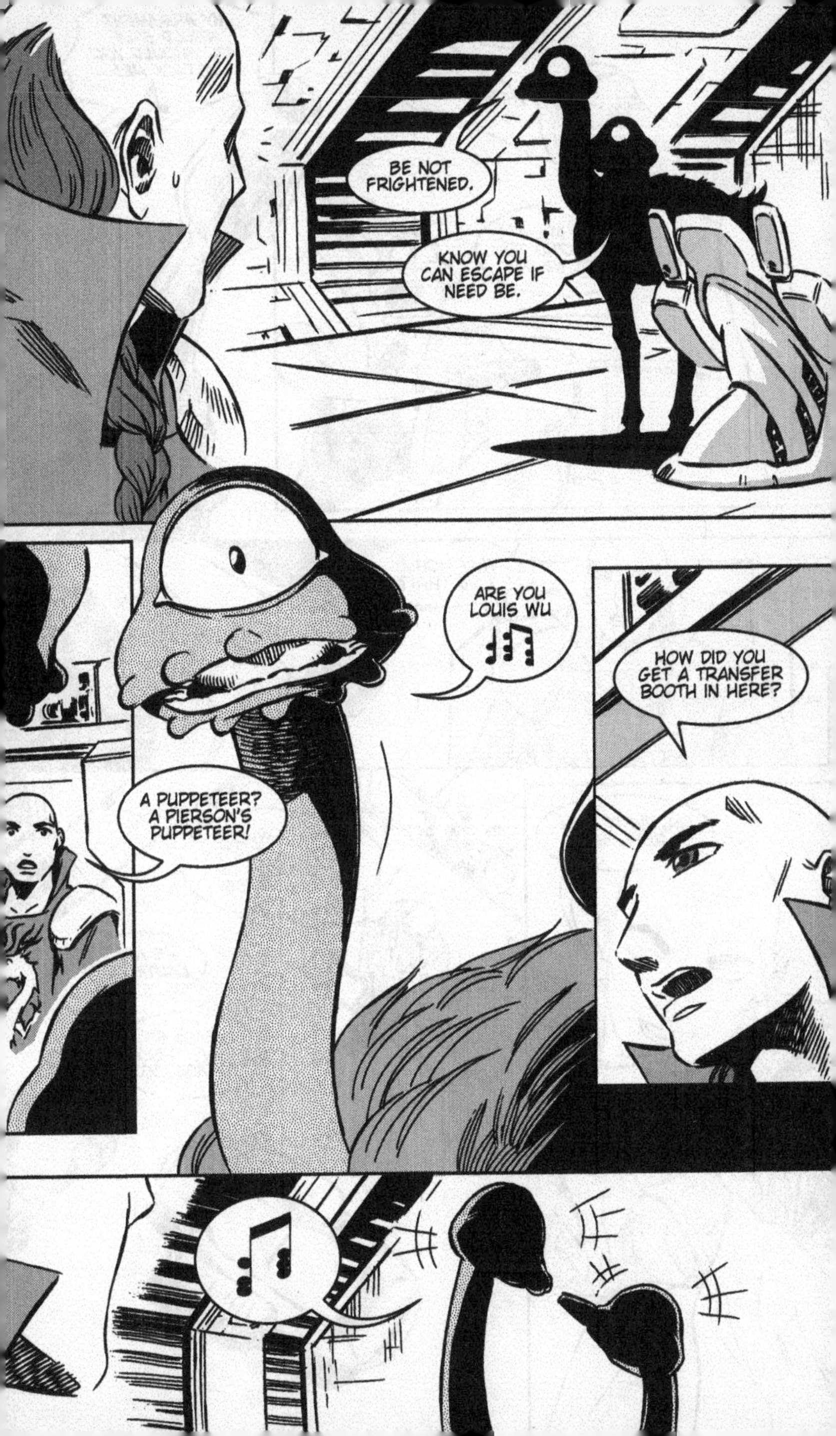
BE NOT FRIGHTENED.
KNOW YOU CAN ESCAPE IF NEED BE.
A PUPPETEER? A PIERSON'S PUPPETEER!
ARE YOU LOUIS WU
HOW DID YOU GET A TRANSFER BOOTH IN HERE?

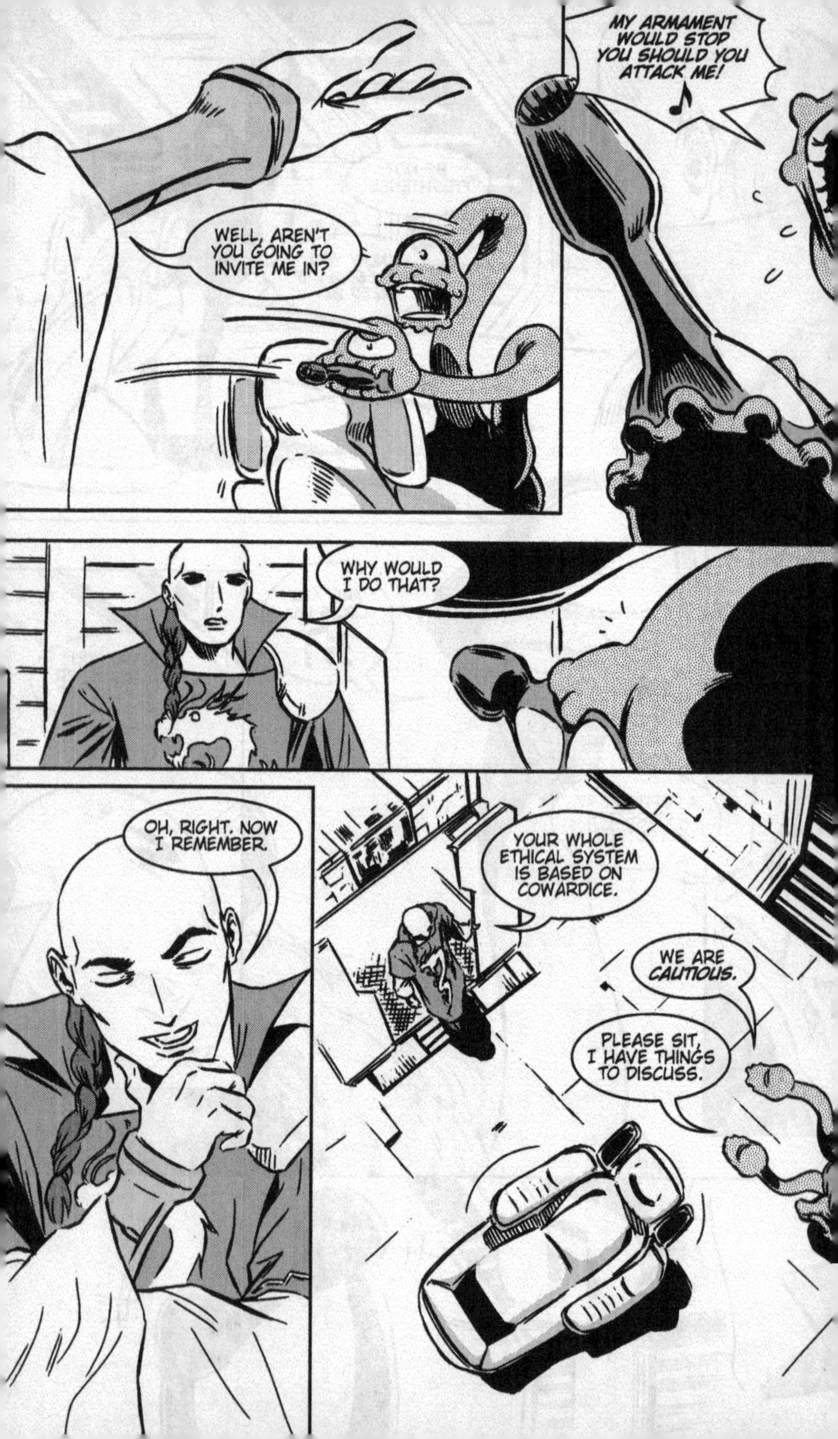
WELL, AREN'T YOU GOING TO INVITE ME IN?
MY ARMAMENT WOULD STOP YOU SHOULD YOU ATTACK ME! ♪
WHY WOULD I DO THAT?
OH, RIGHT. NOW I REMEMBER.
YOUR WHOLE ETHICAL SYSTEM IS BASED ON COWARDICE.
WE ARE *CAUTIOUS.*
PLEASE SIT, I HAVE THINGS TO DISCUSS.

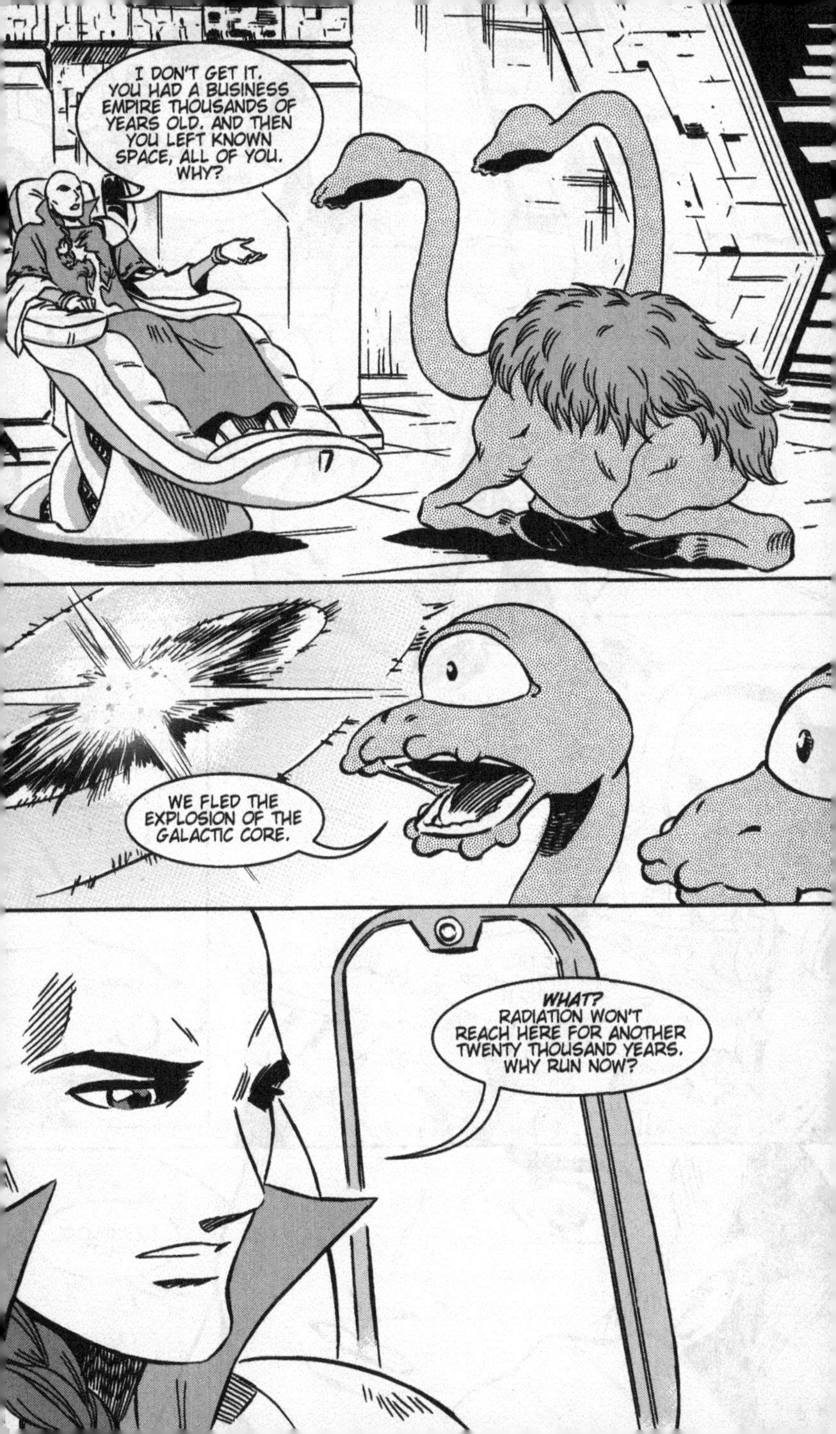
I DON'T GET IT. YOU HAD A BUSINESS EMPIRE THOUSANDS OF YEARS OLD. AND THEN YOU LEFT KNOWN SPACE, ALL OF YOU. WHY?
WE FLED THE EXPLOSION OF THE GALACTIC CORE.
WHAT? RADIATION WON'T REACH HERE FOR ANOTHER TWENTY THOUSAND YEARS. WHY RUN NOW?

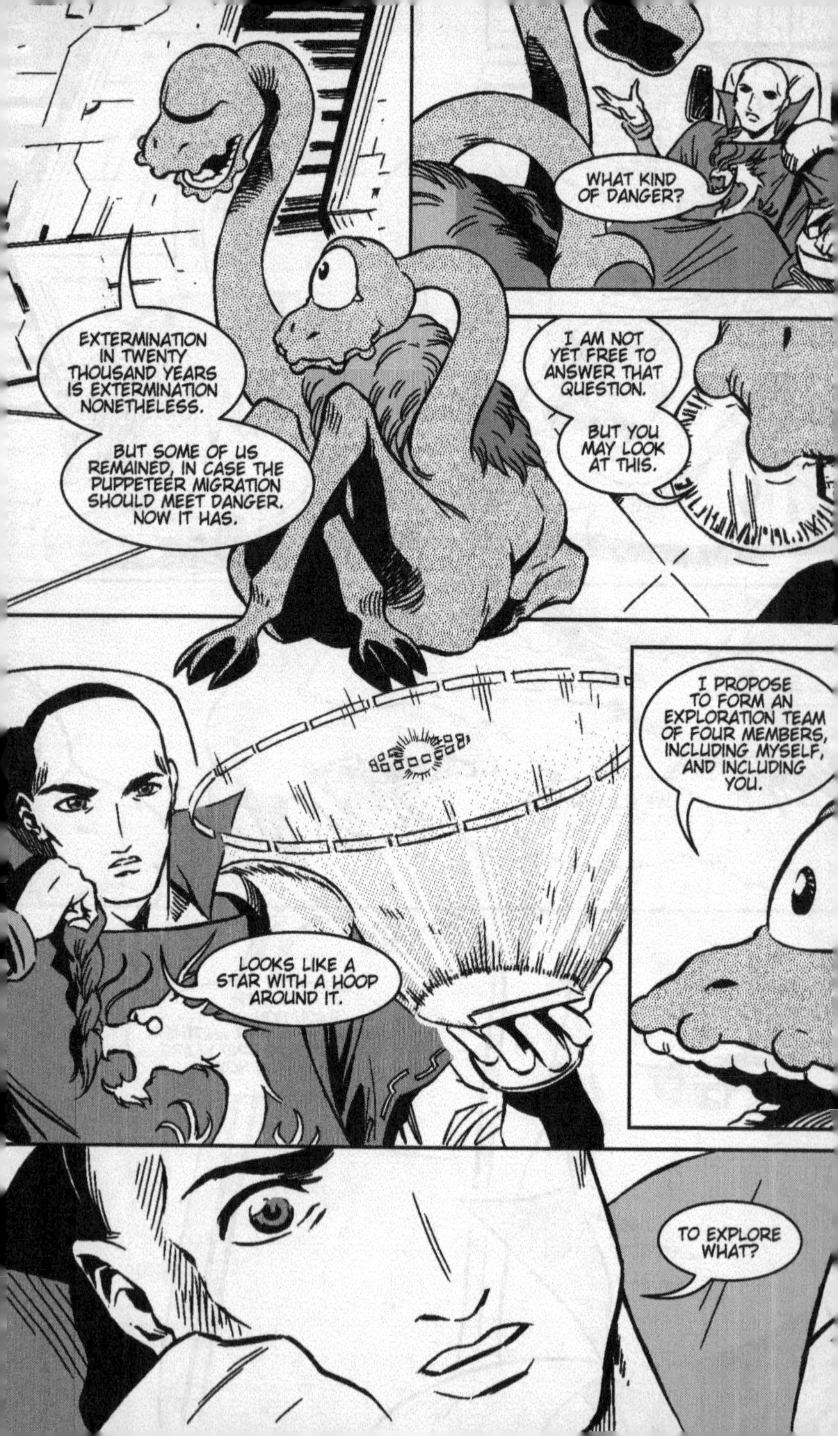
WHAT KIND OF DANGER?
EXTERMINATION IN TWENTY THOUSAND YEARS IS EXTERMINATION NONETHELESS.
BUT SOME OF US REMAINED, IN CASE THE PUPPETEER MIGRATION SHOULD MEET DANGER. NOW IT HAS.
I AM NOT YET FREE TO ANSWER THAT QUESTION.
BUT YOU MAY LOOK AT THIS.
LOOKS LIKE A STAR WITH A HOOP AROUND IT.
I PROPOSE TO FORM AN EXPLORATION TEAM OF FOUR MEMBERS, INCLUDING MYSELF, AND INCLUDING YOU.
TO EXPLORE WHAT?

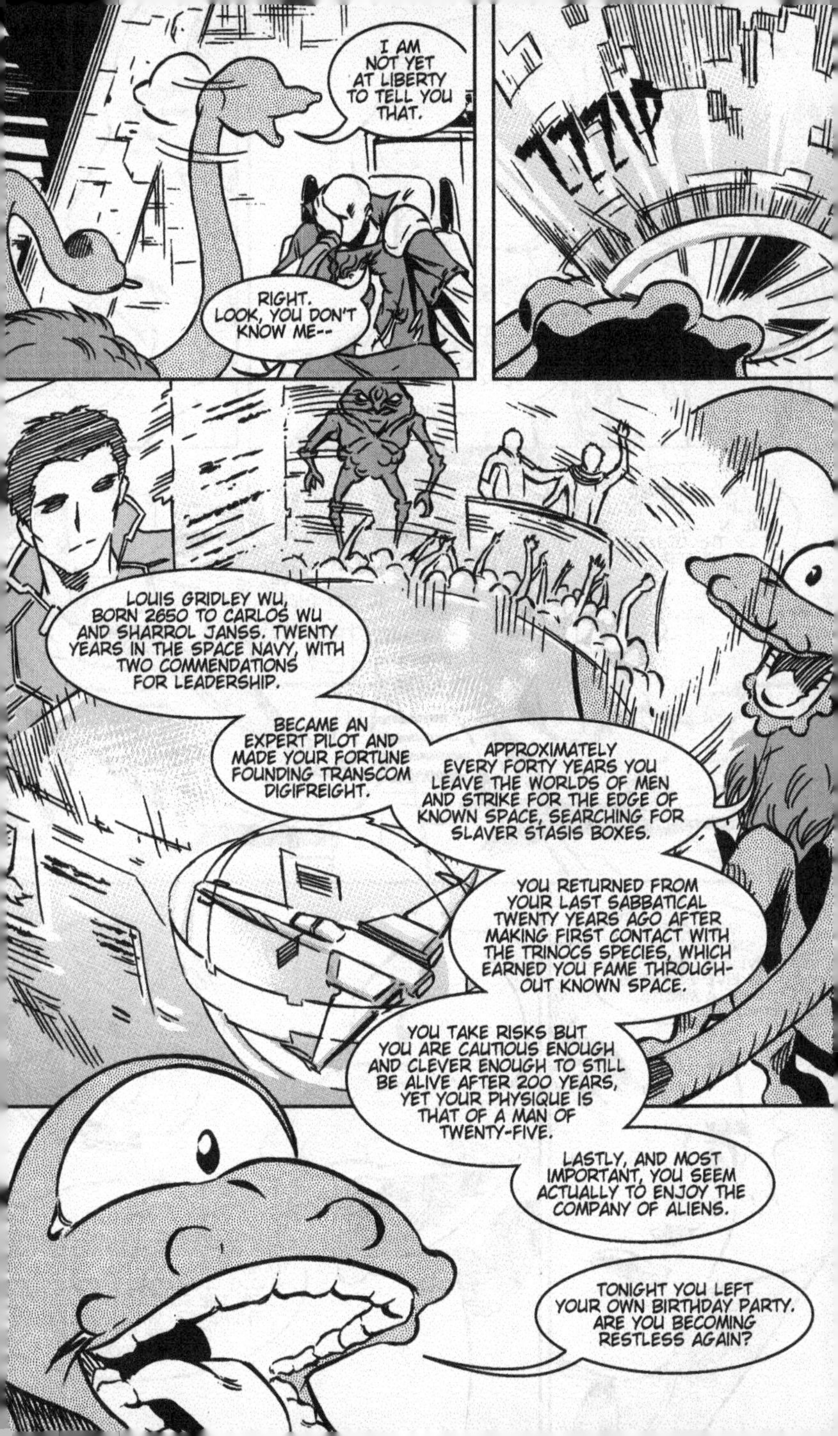
I AM NOT YET AT LIBERTY TO TELL YOU THAT.
RIGHT. LOOK, YOU DON'T KNOW ME--
TZZIP
LOUIS GRIDLEY WU, BORN 2650 TO CARLOS WU AND SHARROL JANSS. TWENTY YEARS IN THE SPACE NAVY, WITH TWO COMMENDATIONS FOR LEADERSHIP.
BECAME AN EXPERT PILOT AND MADE YOUR FORTUNE FOUNDING TRANSCOM DIGIFREIGHT.
APPROXIMATELY EVERY FORTY YEARS YOU LEAVE THE WORLDS OF MEN AND STRIKE FOR THE EDGE OF KNOWN SPACE, SEARCHING FOR SLAVER STASIS BOXES.
YOU RETURNED FROM YOUR LAST SABBATICAL TWENTY YEARS AGO AFTER MAKING FIRST CONTACT WITH THE TRINOCS SPECIES, WHICH EARNED YOU FAME THROUGH-OUT KNOWN SPACE.
YOU TAKE RISKS BUT YOU ARE CAUTIOUS ENOUGH AND CLEVER ENOUGH TO STILL BE ALIVE AFTER 200 YEARS, YET YOUR PHYSIQUE IS THAT OF A MAN OF TWENTY-FIVE.
LASTLY, AND MOST IMPORTANT, YOU SEEM ACTUALLY TO ENJOY THE COMPANY OF ALIENS.
TONIGHT YOU LEFT YOUR OWN BIRTHDAY PARTY. ARE YOU BECOMING RESTLESS AGAIN?

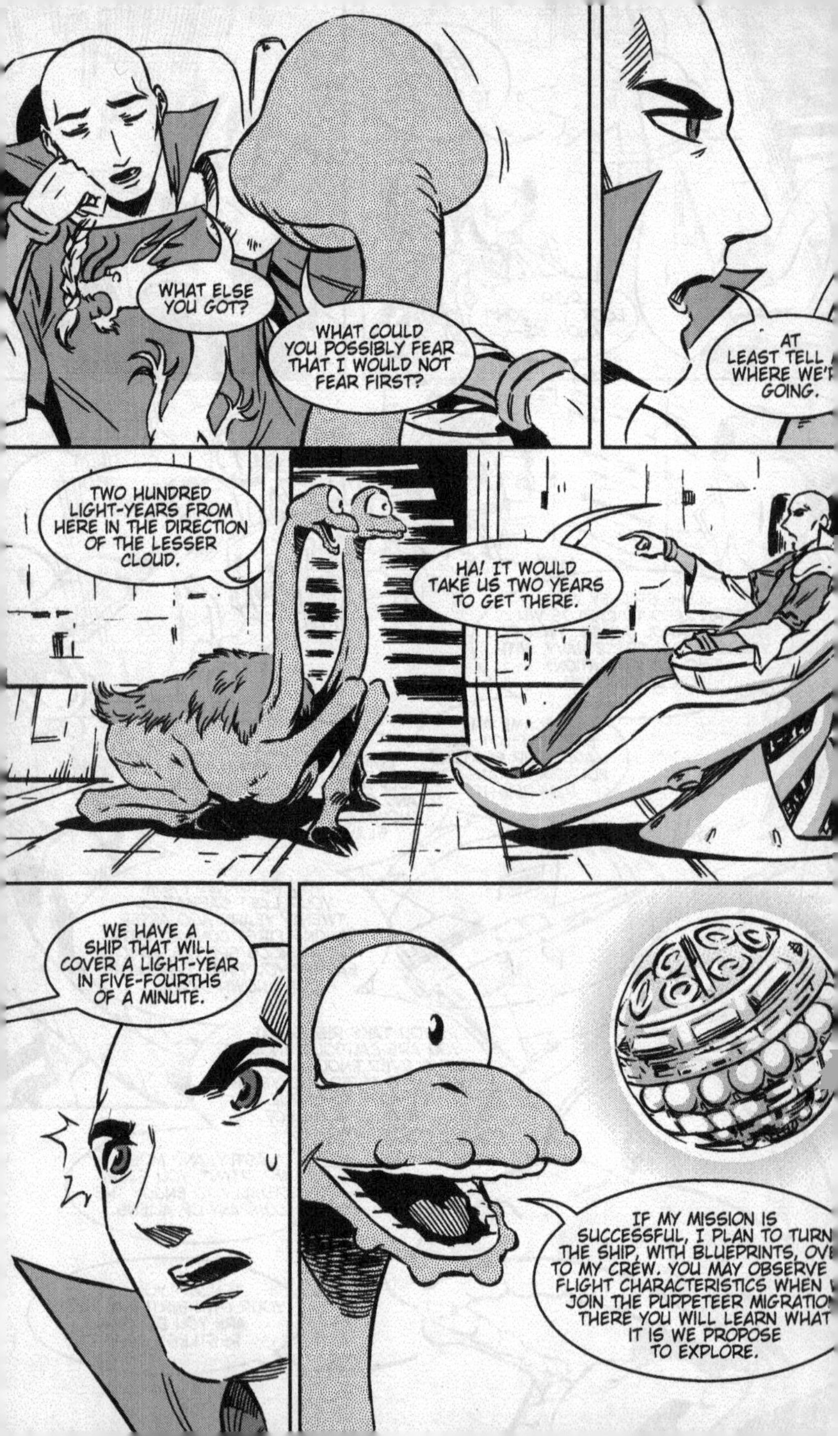
WHAT ELSE YOU GOT?
WHAT COULD YOU POSSIBLY FEAR THAT I WOULD NOT FEAR FIRST?
AT LEAST TELL WHERE WE'
GOING.
TWO HUNDRED LIGHT-YEARS FROM HERE IN THE DIRECTION OF THE LESSER CLOUD.
HA! IT WOULD TAKE US TWO YEARS TO GET THERE.
WE HAVE A SHIP THAT WILL COVER A LIGHT-YEAR IN FIVE-FOURTHS OF A MINUTE.
IF MY MISSION IS SUCCESSFUL, I PLAN TO TURN THE SHIP, WITH BLUEPRINTS, OV TO MY CREW. YOU MAY OBSERVE FLIGHT CHARACTERISTICS WHEN JOIN THE PUPPETEER MIGRATIO THERE YOU WILL LEARN WHAT IT IS WE PROPOSE TO EXPLORE.

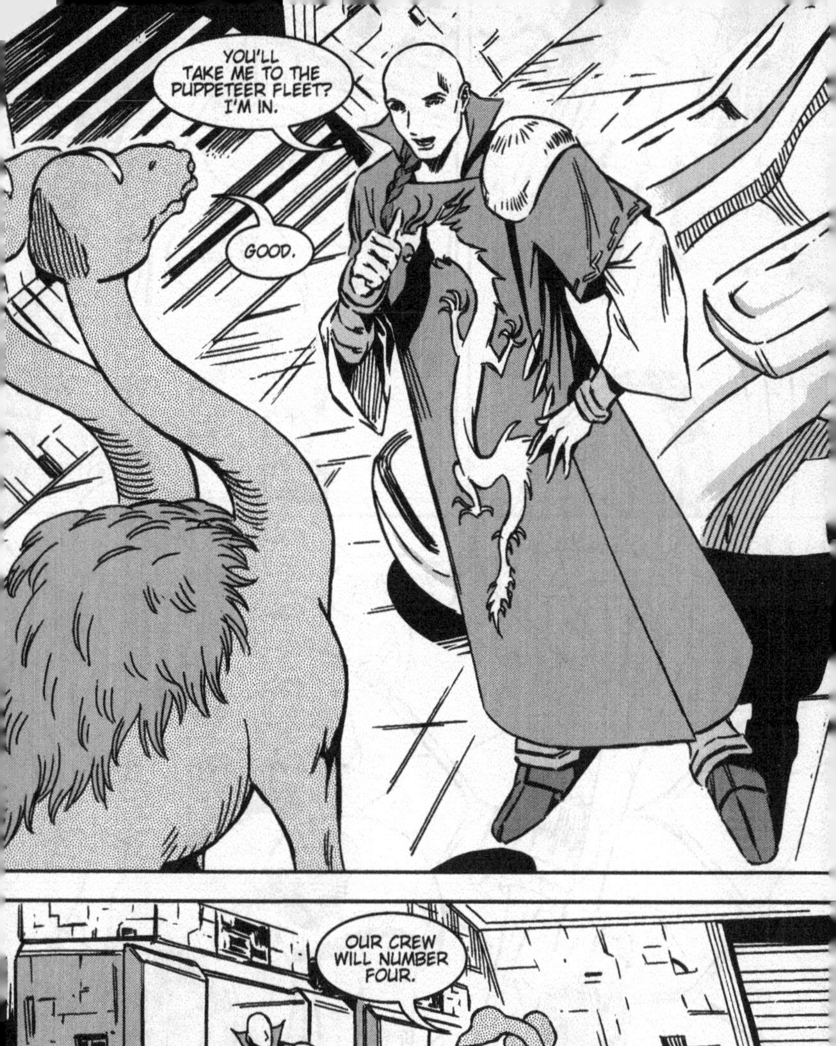
YOU'LL TAKE ME TO THE PUPPETEER FLEET? I'M IN.
GOOD.

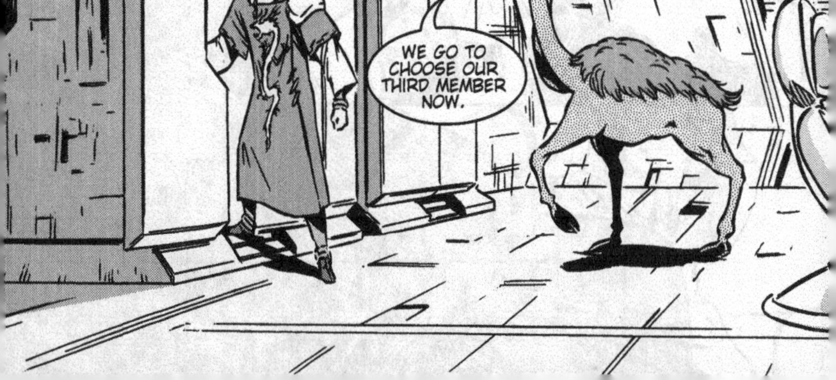
OUR CREW WILL NUMBER FOUR.
WE GO TO CHOOSE OUR THIRD MEMBER NOW.

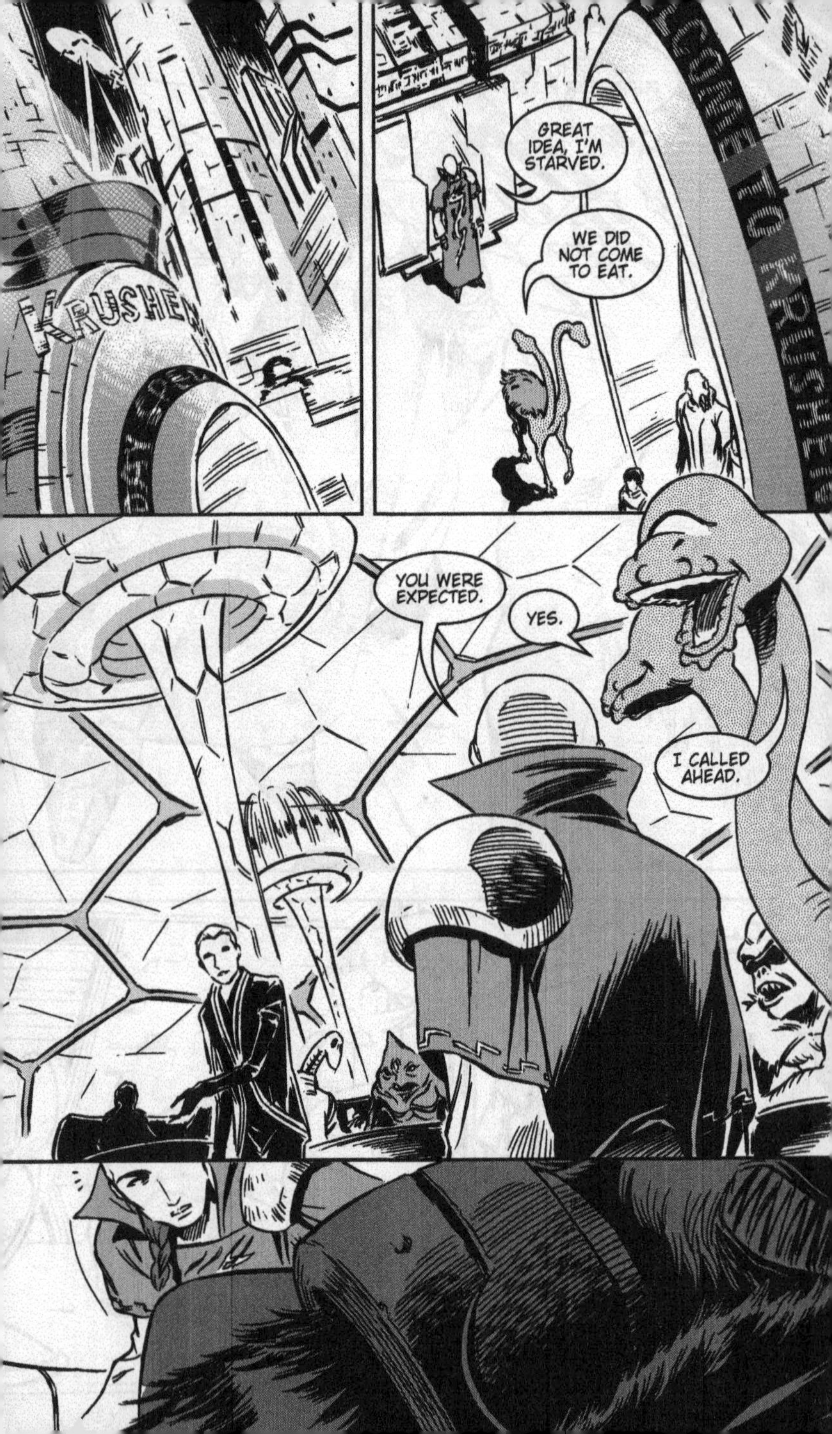
GREAT IDEA, I'M STARVED.
WE DID NOT COME TO EAT.
YOU WERE EXPECTED.
YES.
I CALLED AHEAD.

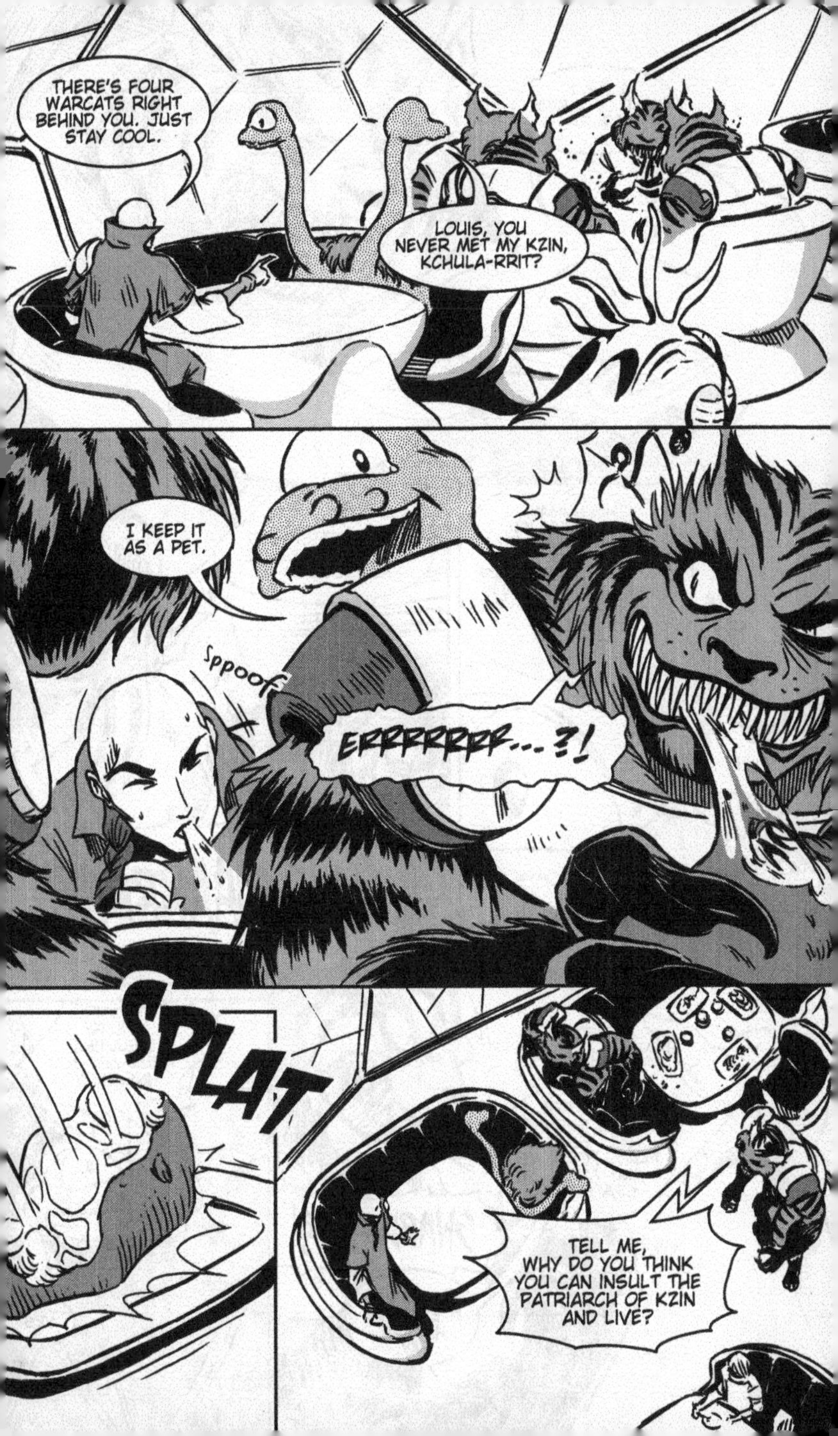
THERE'S FOUR WARCATS RIGHT BEHIND YOU. JUST STAY COOL.
LOUIS, YOU NEVER MET MY KZIN, KCHULA-RRIT?
I KEEP IT AS A PET.
Sppoof
ERRRRRRR...?!
SPLAT
TELL ME, WHY DO YOU THINK YOU CAN INSULT THE PATRIARCH OF KZIN AND LIVE?

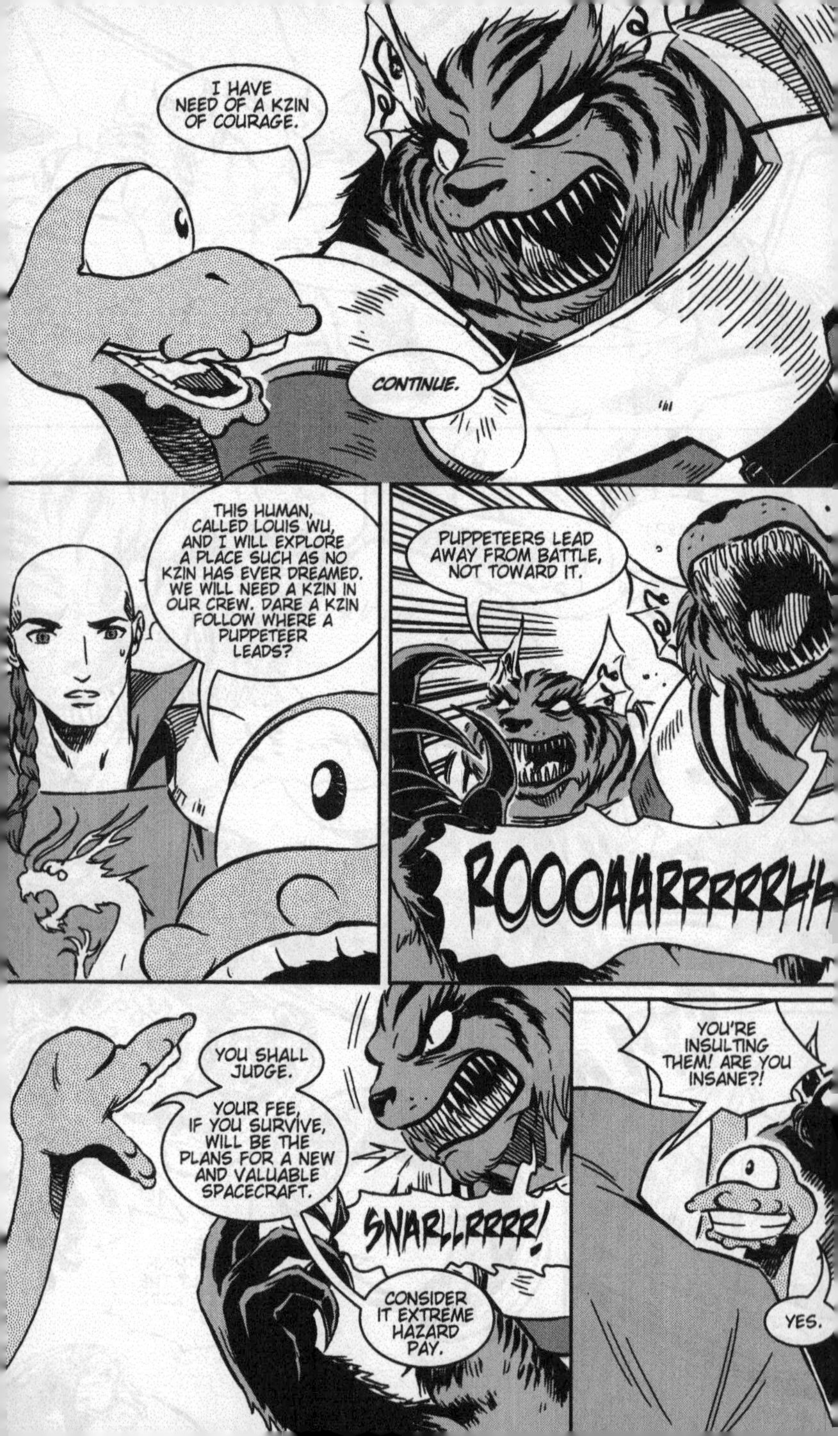

I HAVE NEED OF A KZIN OF COURAGE.
CONTINUE.
THIS HUMAN, CALLED LOUIS WU, AND I WILL EXPLORE A PLACE SUCH AS NO KZIN HAS EVER DREAMED. WE WILL NEED A KZIN IN OUR CREW. DARE A KZIN FOLLOW WHERE A PUPPETEER LEADS?
PUPPETEERS LEAD AWAY FROM BATTLE, NOT TOWARD IT.
ROOOAARRRRRH
YOU SHALL JUDGE.
YOUR FEE, IF YOU SURVIVE, WILL BE THE PLANS FOR A NEW AND VALUABLE SPACECRAFT.
SNARLLRRRR!
CONSIDER IT EXTREME HAZARD PAY.
YOU'RE INSULTING THEM! ARE YOU INSANE?!
YES.

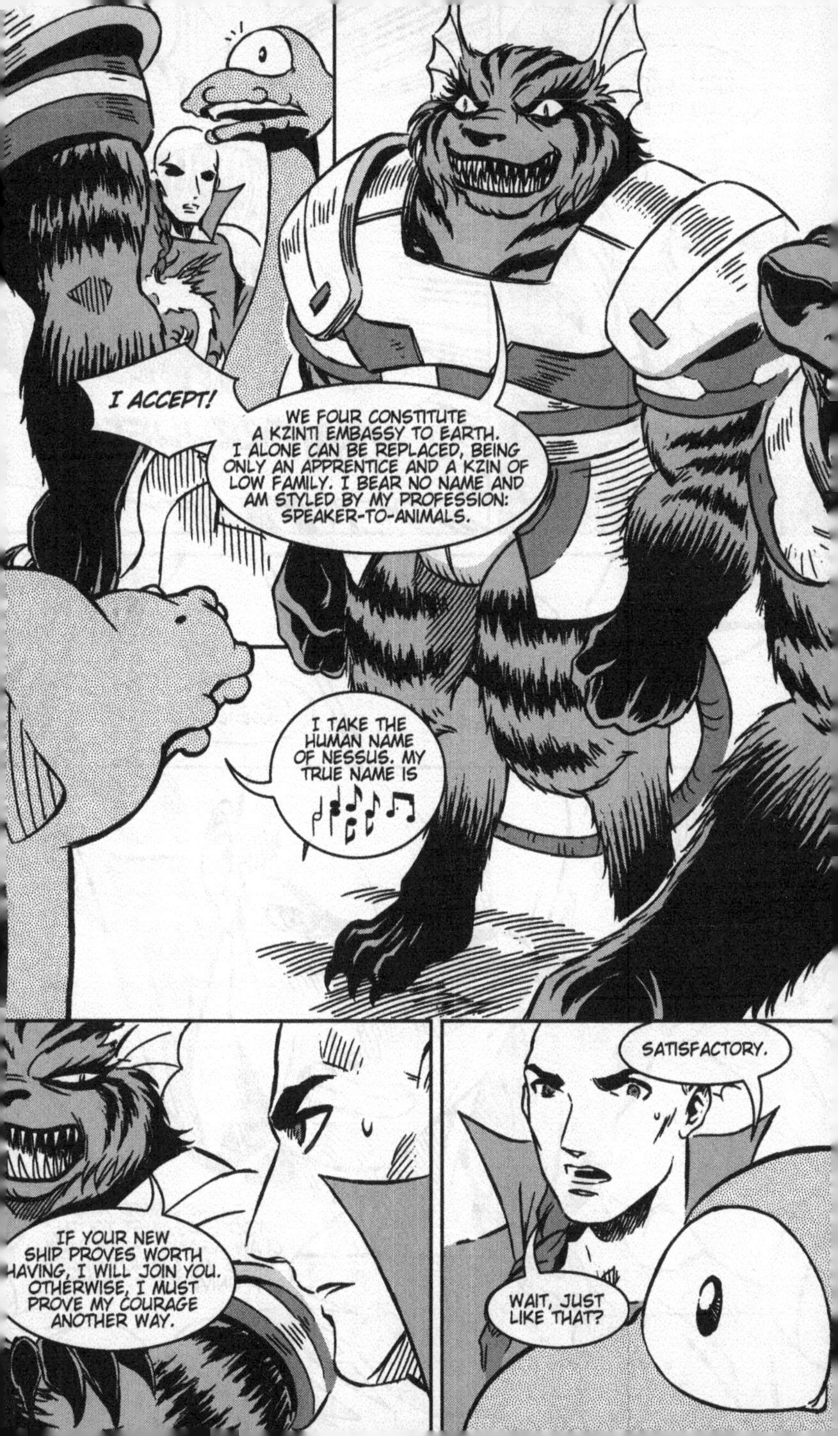
I ACCEPT!
WE FOUR CONSTITUTE A KZINTI EMBASSY TO EARTH. I ALONE CAN BE REPLACED, BEING ONLY AN APPRENTICE AND A KZIN OF LOW FAMILY. I BEAR NO NAME AND AM STYLED BY MY PROFESSION: SPEAKER-TO-ANIMALS.
I TAKE THE HUMAN NAME OF NESSUS. MY TRUE NAME IS
IF YOUR NEW SHIP PROVES WORTH HAVING, I WILL JOIN YOU. OTHERWISE, I MUST PROVE MY COURAGE ANOTHER WAY.
SATISFACTORY.
WAIT, JUST LIKE THAT?

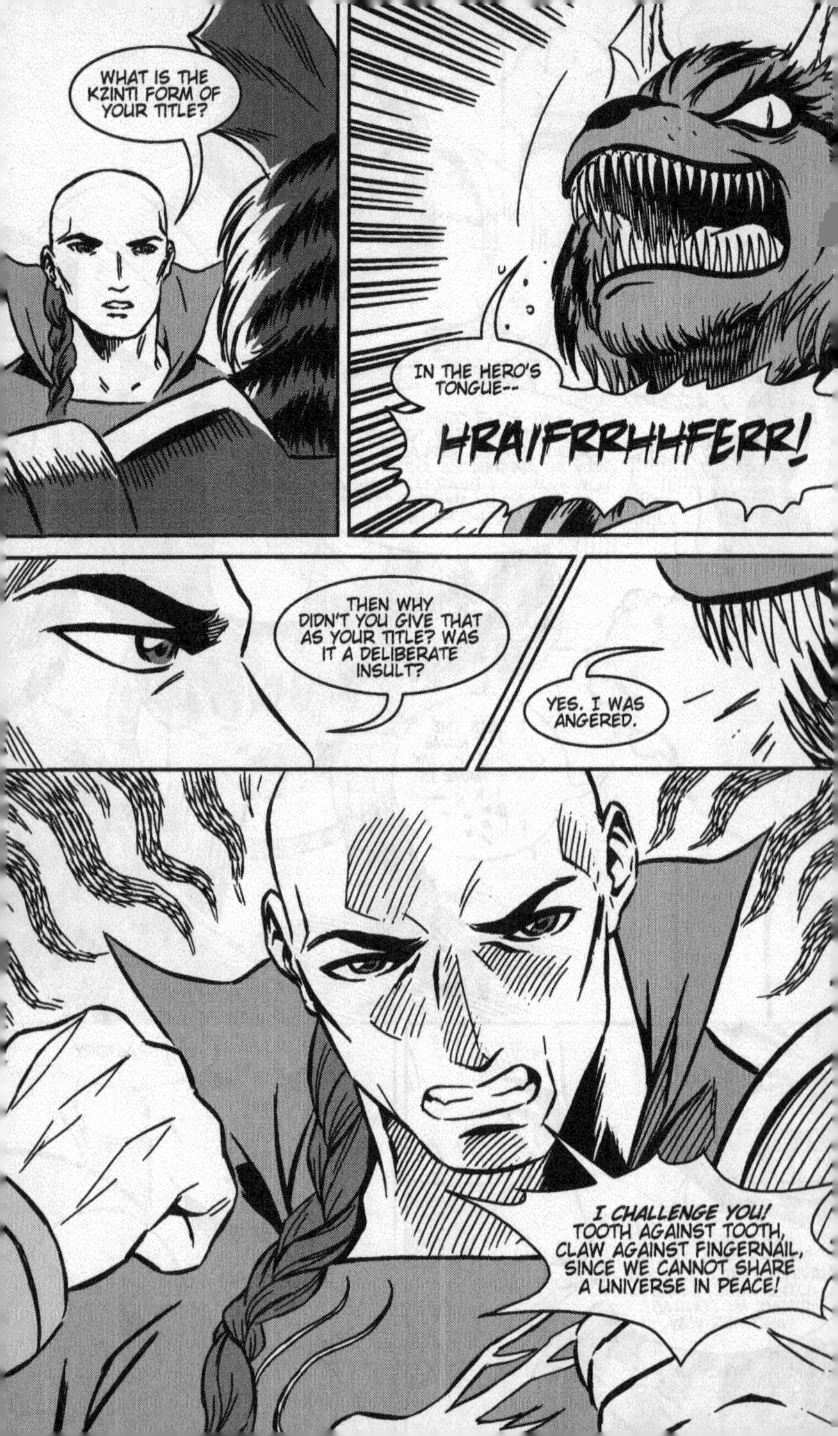
WHAT IS THE KZINTI FORM OF YOUR TITLE?
IN THE HERO'S TONGUE--
HRAIFRRHHFERR!
THEN WHY DIDN'T YOU GIVE THAT AS YOUR TITLE? WAS IT A DELIBERATE INSULT?
YES. I WAS ANGERED.
I CHALLENGE YOU! TOOTH AGAINST TOOTH, CLAW AGAINST FINGERNAIL, SINCE WE CANNOT SHARE A UNIVERSE IN PEACE!

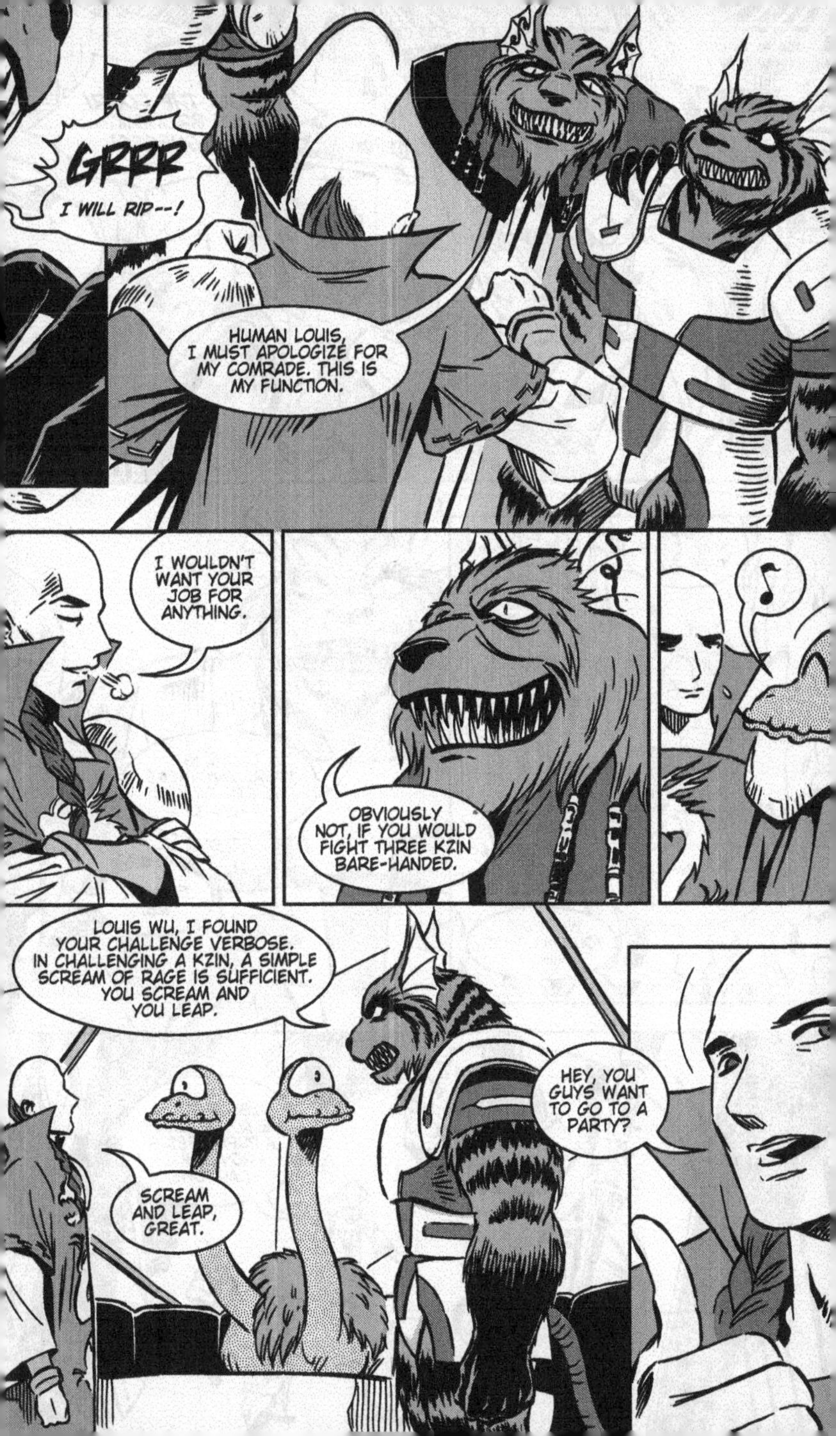
GRRR
I WILL RIP--!
HUMAN LOUIS, I MUST APOLOGIZE FOR MY COMRADE. THIS IS MY FUNCTION.
I WOULDN'T WANT YOUR JOB FOR ANYTHING.
OBVIOUSLY NOT, IF YOU WOULD FIGHT THREE KZIN BARE-HANDED.
♪
LOUIS WU, I FOUND YOUR CHALLENGE VERBOSE. IN CHALLENGING A KZIN, A SIMPLE SCREAM OF RAGE IS SUFFICIENT. YOU SCREAM AND YOU LEAP.
SCREAM AND LEAP, GREAT.
HEY, YOU GUYS WANT TO GO TO A PARTY?

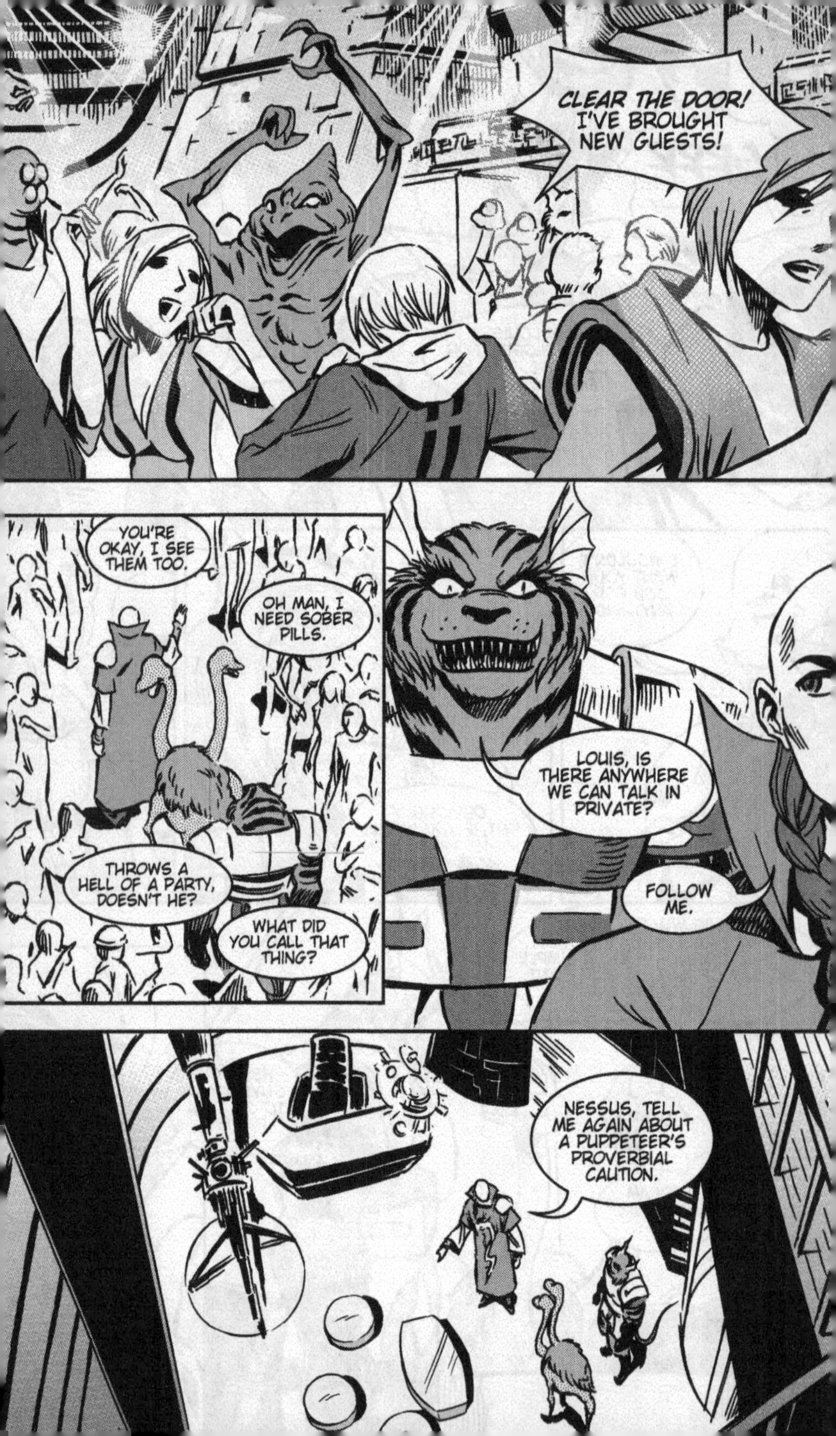

CLEAR THE DOOR! I'VE BROUGHT NEW GUESTS!
YOU'RE OKAY, I SEE THEM TOO.
OH MAN, I NEED SOBER PILLS.
THROWS A HELL OF A PARTY, DOESN'T HE?
WHAT DID YOU CALL THAT THING?
LOUIS, IS THERE ANYWHERE WE CAN TALK IN PRIVATE?
FOLLOW ME.
NESSUS, TELL ME AGAIN ABOUT A PUPPETEER'S PROVERBIAL CAUTION.

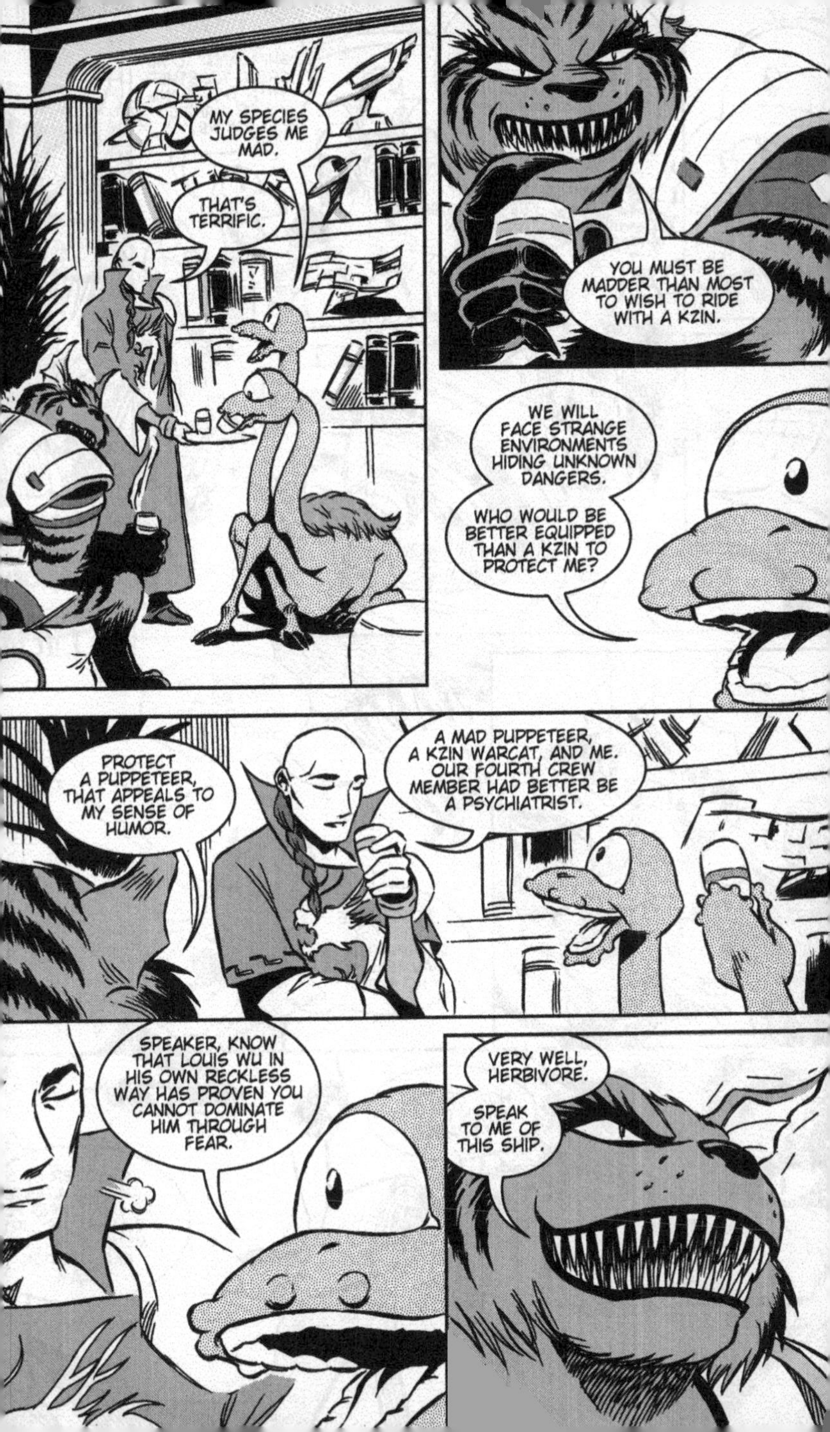
MY SPECIES JUDGES ME MAD.
THAT'S TERRIFIC.
YOU MUST BE MADDER THAN MOST TO WISH TO RIDE WITH A KZIN.
WE WILL FACE STRANGE ENVIRONMENTS HIDING UNKNOWN DANGERS.
WHO WOULD BE BETTER EQUIPPED THAN A KZIN TO PROTECT ME?
PROTECT A PUPPETEER, THAT APPEALS TO MY SENSE OF HUMOR.
A MAD PUPPETEER, A KZIN WARCAT, AND ME. OUR FOURTH CREW MEMBER HAD BETTER BE A PSYCHIATRIST.
SPEAKER, KNOW THAT LOUIS WU IN HIS OWN RECKLESS WAY HAS PROVEN YOU CANNOT DOMINATE HIM THROUGH FEAR.
VERY WELL, HERBIVORE.
SPEAK TO ME OF THIS SHIP.

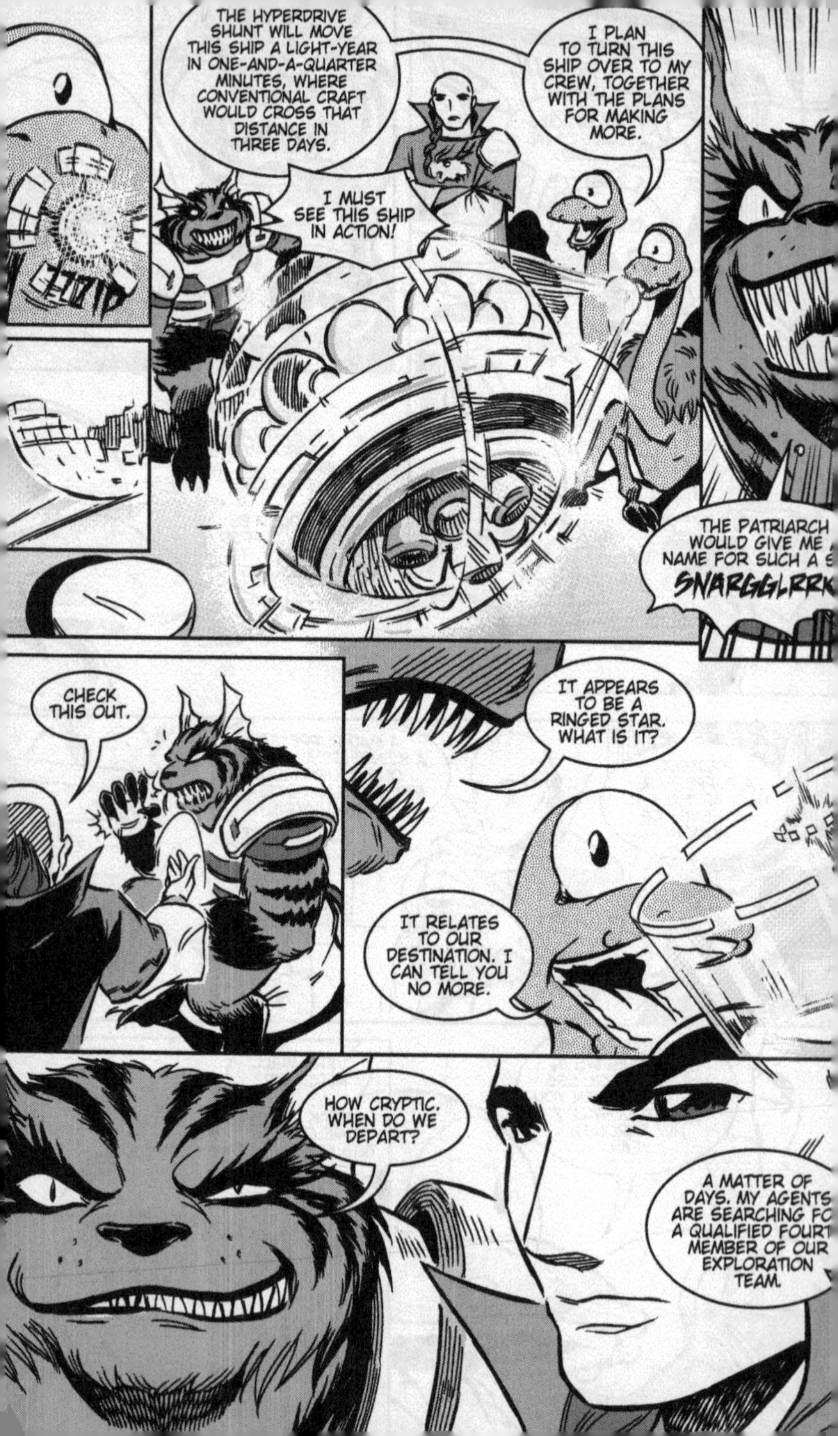
THE HYPERDRIVE SHUNT WILL MOVE THIS SHIP A LIGHT-YEAR IN ONE-AND-A-QUARTER MINUTES, WHERE CONVENTIONAL CRAFT WOULD CROSS THAT DISTANCE IN THREE DAYS.
I PLAN TO TURN THIS SHIP OVER TO MY CREW, TOGETHER WITH THE PLANS FOR MAKING MORE.
I MUST SEE THIS SHIP IN ACTION!
THE PATRIARCH WOULD GIVE ME NAME FOR SUCH A
SNARGGLRRK
CHECK THIS OUT.
IT APPEARS TO BE A RINGED STAR. WHAT IS IT?
IT RELATES TO OUR DESTINATION. I CAN TELL YOU NO MORE.
HOW CRYPTIC. WHEN DO WE DEPART?
A MATTER OF DAYS. MY AGENTS ARE SEARCHING FO A QUALIFIED FOURT MEMBER OF OUR EXPLORATION TEAM.

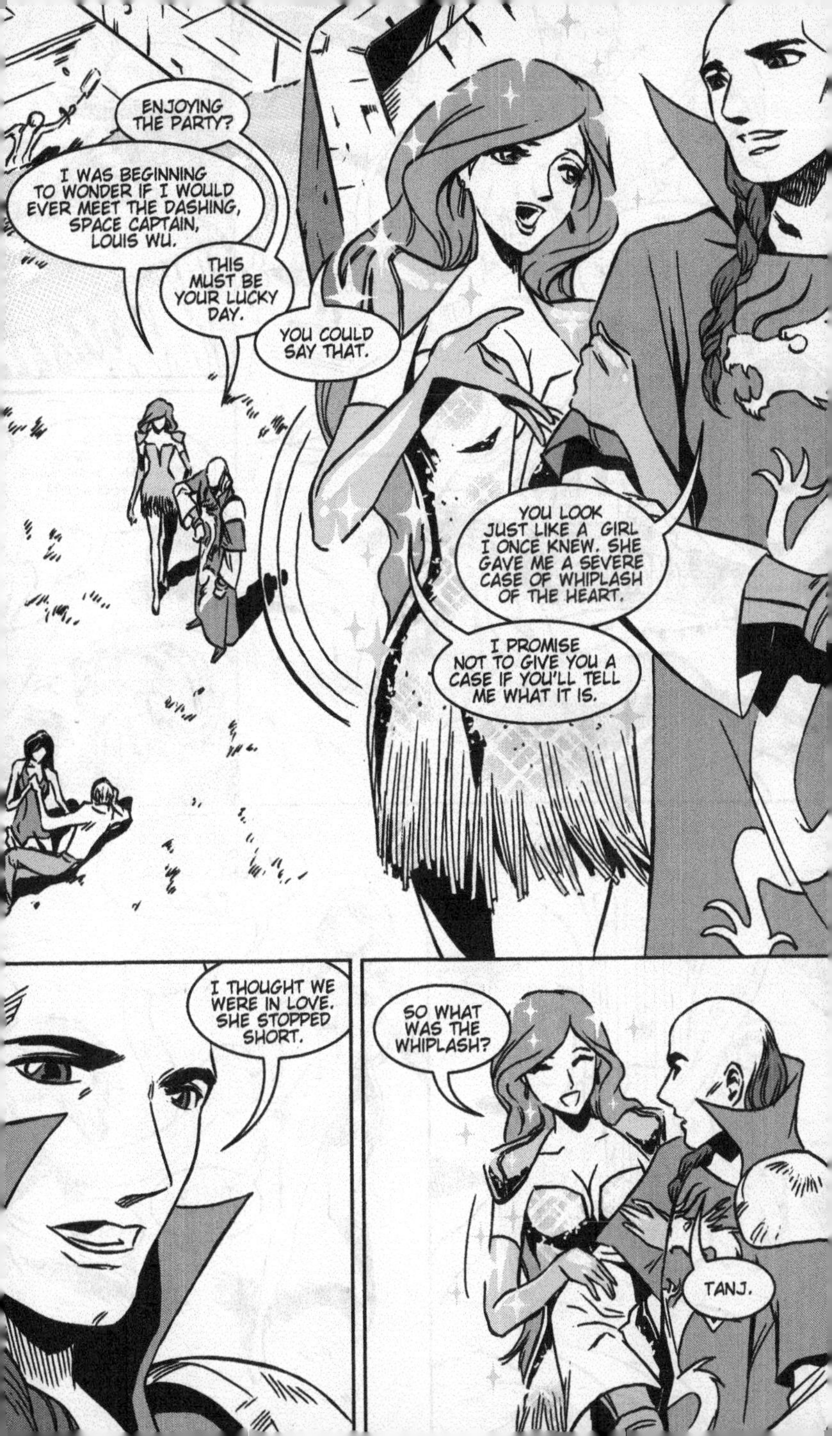
ENJOYING THE PARTY?
I WAS BEGINNING TO WONDER IF I WOULD EVER MEET THE DASHING, SPACE CAPTAIN, LOUIS WU.
THIS MUST BE YOUR LUCKY DAY.
YOU COULD SAY THAT.
YOU LOOK JUST LIKE A GIRL I ONCE KNEW. SHE GAVE ME A SEVERE CASE OF WHIPLASH OF THE HEART.
I PROMISE NOT TO GIVE YOU A CASE IF YOU'LL TELL ME WHAT IT IS.
I THOUGHT WE WERE IN LOVE. SHE STOPPED SHORT.
SO WHAT WAS THE WHIPLASH?
TANJ.

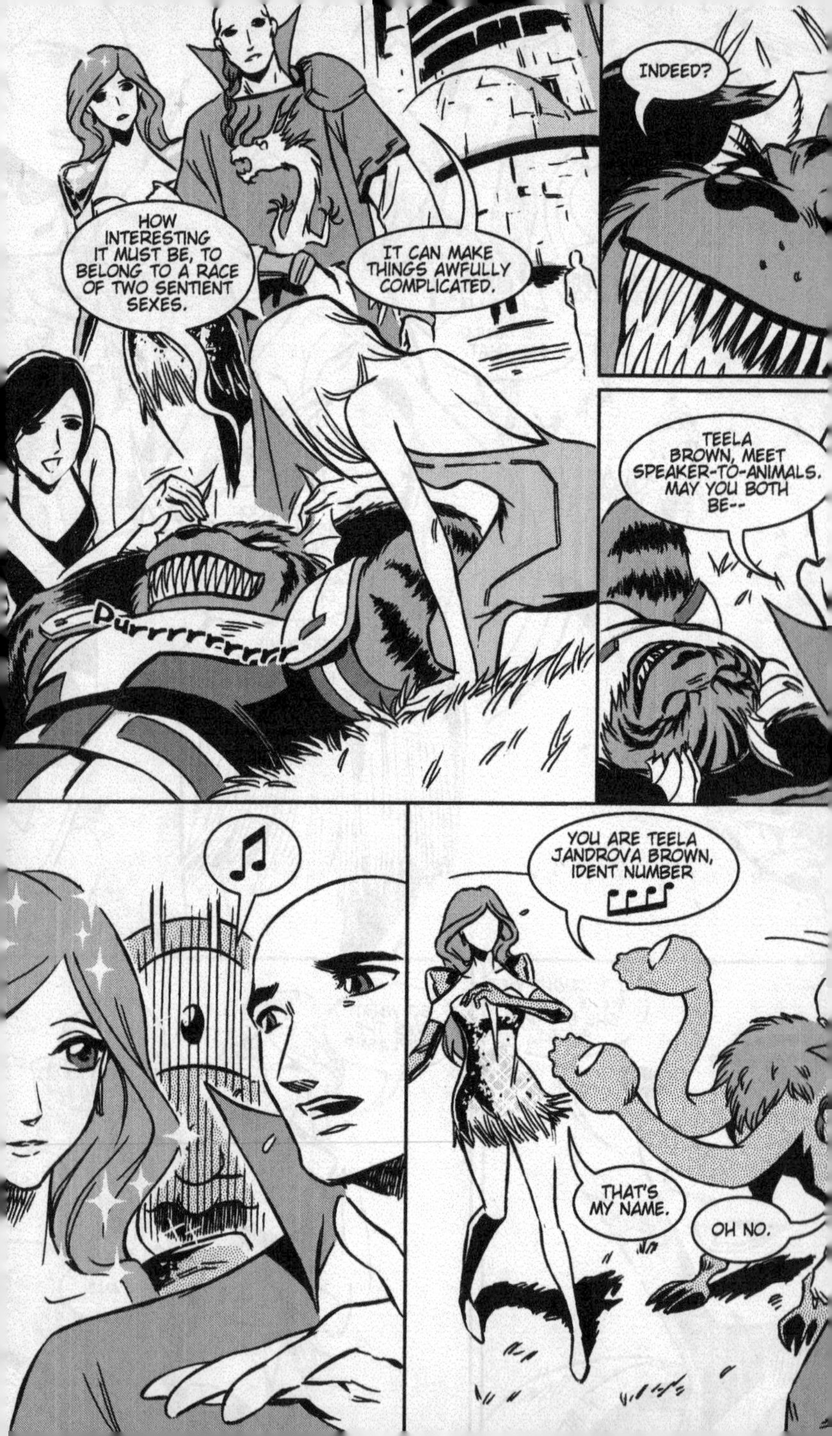
HOW INTERESTING IT MUST BE, TO BELONG TO A RACE OF TWO SENTIENT SEXES.
IT CAN MAKE THINGS AWFULLY COMPLICATED.
Purrrrrrrrrr
INDEED?
TEELA BROWN, MEET SPEAKER-TO-ANIMALS. MAY YOU BOTH BE--
YOU ARE TEELA JANDROVA BROWN, IDENT NUMBER
THAT'S MY NAME.
OH NO.

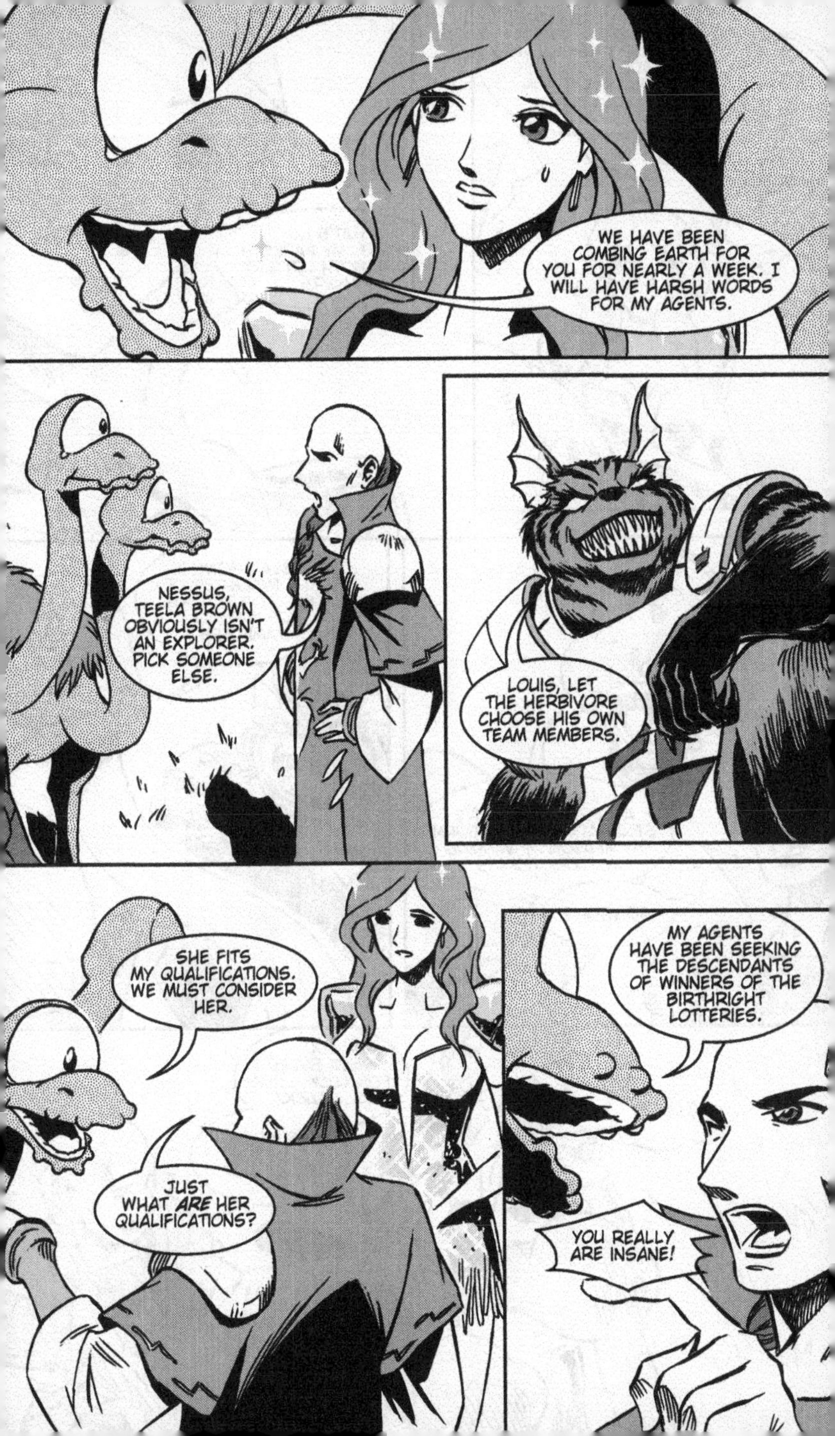
WE HAVE BEEN COMBING EARTH FOR YOU FOR NEARLY A WEEK. I WILL HAVE HARSH WORDS FOR MY AGENTS.
NESSUS, TEELA BROWN OBVIOUSLY ISN'T AN EXPLORER. PICK SOMEONE ELSE.
LOUIS, LET THE HERBIVORE CHOOSE HIS OWN TEAM MEMBERS.
SHE FITS MY QUALIFICATIONS. WE MUST CONSIDER HER.
JUST WHAT *ARE* HER QUALIFICATIONS?
MY AGENTS HAVE BEEN SEEKING THE DESCENDANTS OF WINNERS OF THE BIRTHRIGHT LOTTERIES.
YOU REALLY ARE INSANE!

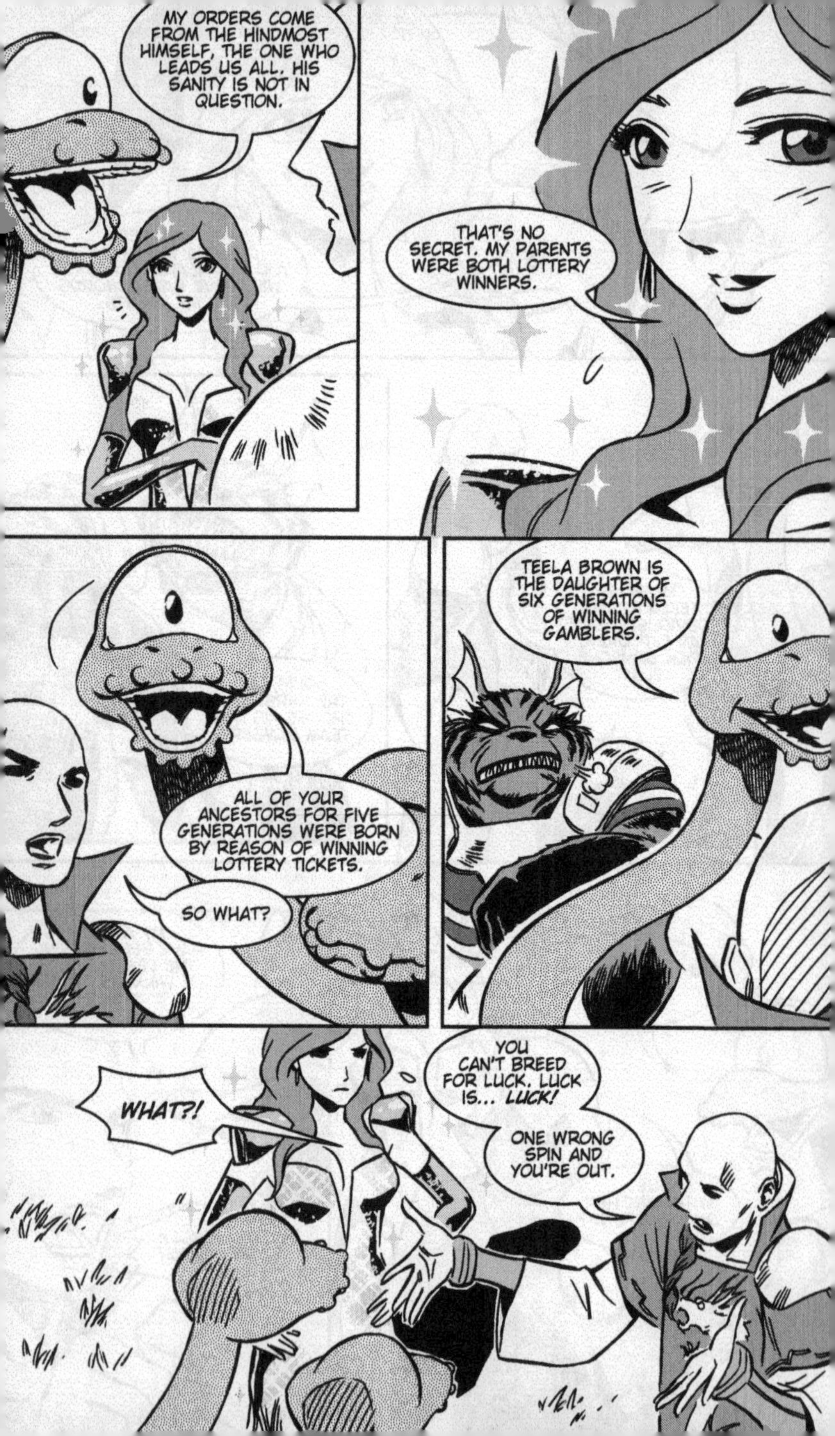
MY ORDERS COME FROM THE HINDMOST HIMSELF, THE ONE WHO LEADS US ALL. HIS SANITY IS NOT IN QUESTION.
THAT'S NO SECRET. MY PARENTS WERE BOTH LOTTERY WINNERS.
ALL OF YOUR ANCESTORS FOR FIVE GENERATIONS WERE BORN BY REASON OF WINNING LOTTERY TICKETS.
SO WHAT?
TEELA BROWN IS THE DAUGHTER OF SIX GENERATIONS OF WINNING GAMBLERS.
WHAT?!
YOU CAN'T BREED FOR LUCK. LUCK IS... LUCK!
ONE WRONG SPIN AND YOU'RE OUT.

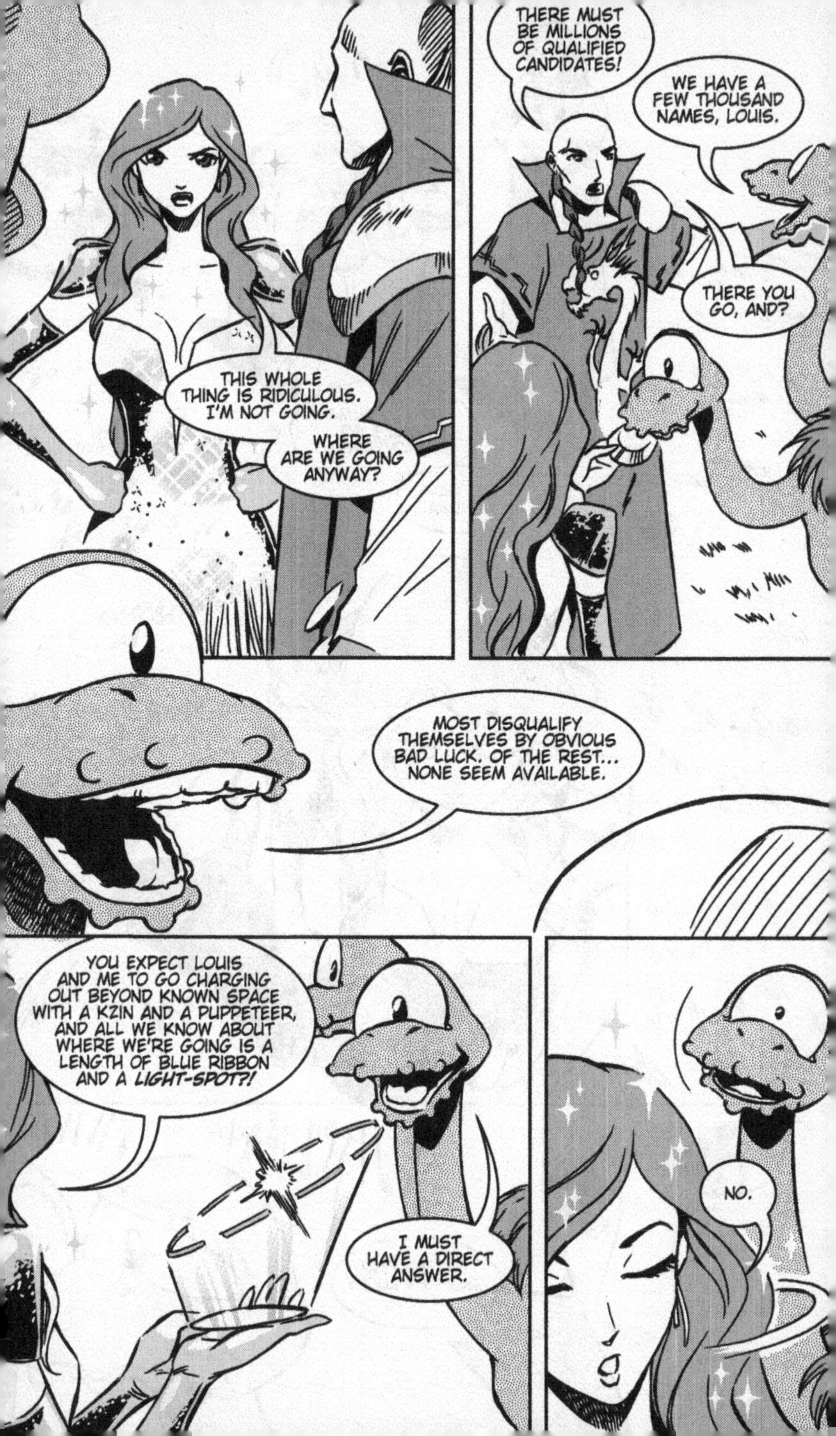
THIS WHOLE THING IS RIDICULOUS. I'M NOT GOING.
WHERE ARE WE GOING ANYWAY?
THERE MUST BE MILLIONS OF QUALIFIED CANDIDATES!
WE HAVE A FEW THOUSAND NAMES, LOUIS.
THERE YOU GO, AND?
MOST DISQUALIFY THEMSELVES BY OBVIOUS BAD LUCK. OF THE REST... NONE SEEM AVAILABLE.
YOU EXPECT LOUIS AND ME TO GO CHARGING OUT BEYOND KNOWN SPACE WITH A KZIN AND A PUPPETEER, AND ALL WE KNOW ABOUT WHERE WE'RE GOING IS A LENGTH OF BLUE RIBBON AND A *LIGHT-SPOT*?!
I MUST HAVE A DIRECT ANSWER.
NO.

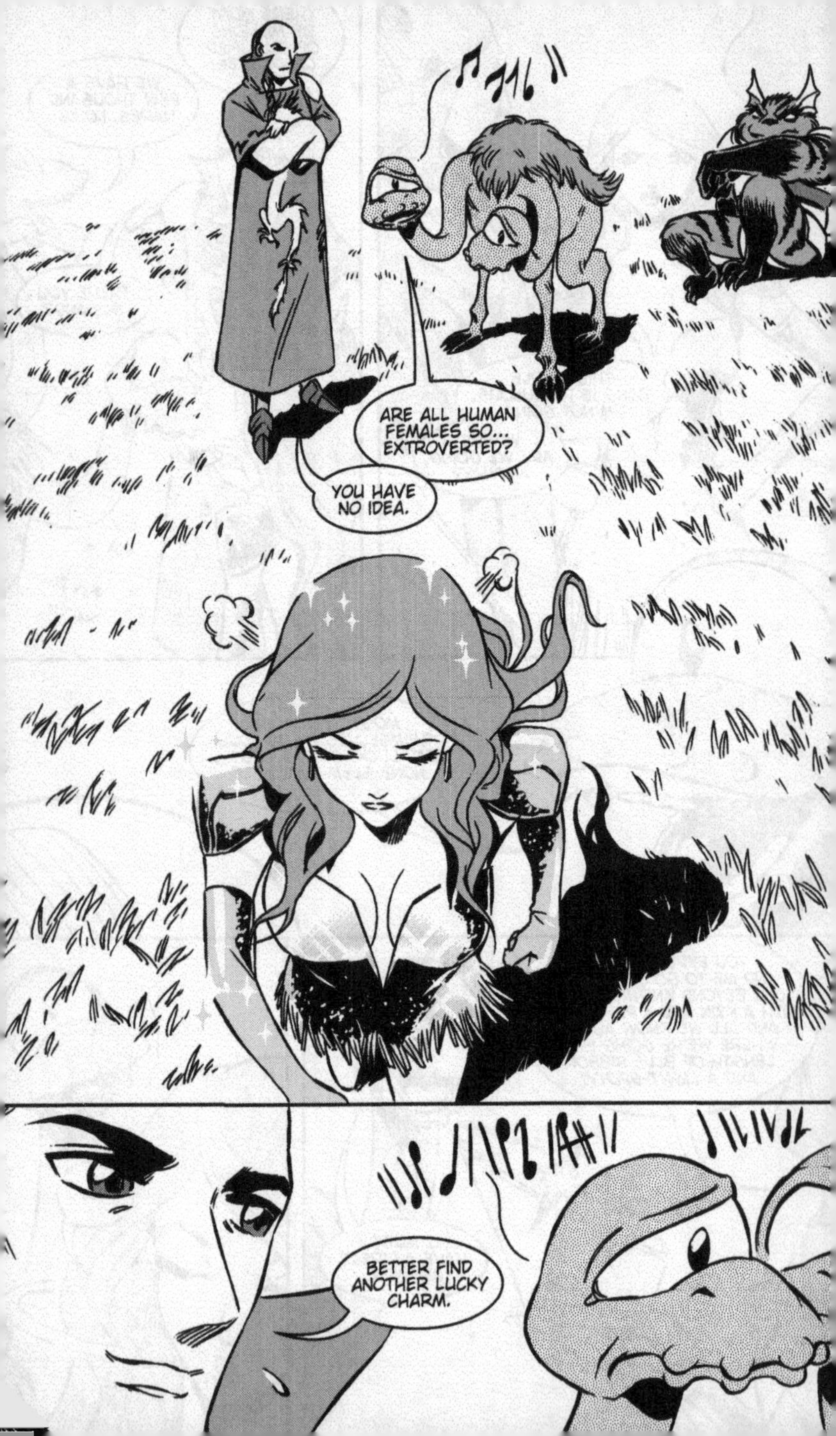

ARE ALL HUMAN FEMALES SO... EXTROVERTED?
YOU HAVE NO IDEA.
BETTER FIND ANOTHER LUCKY CHARM.

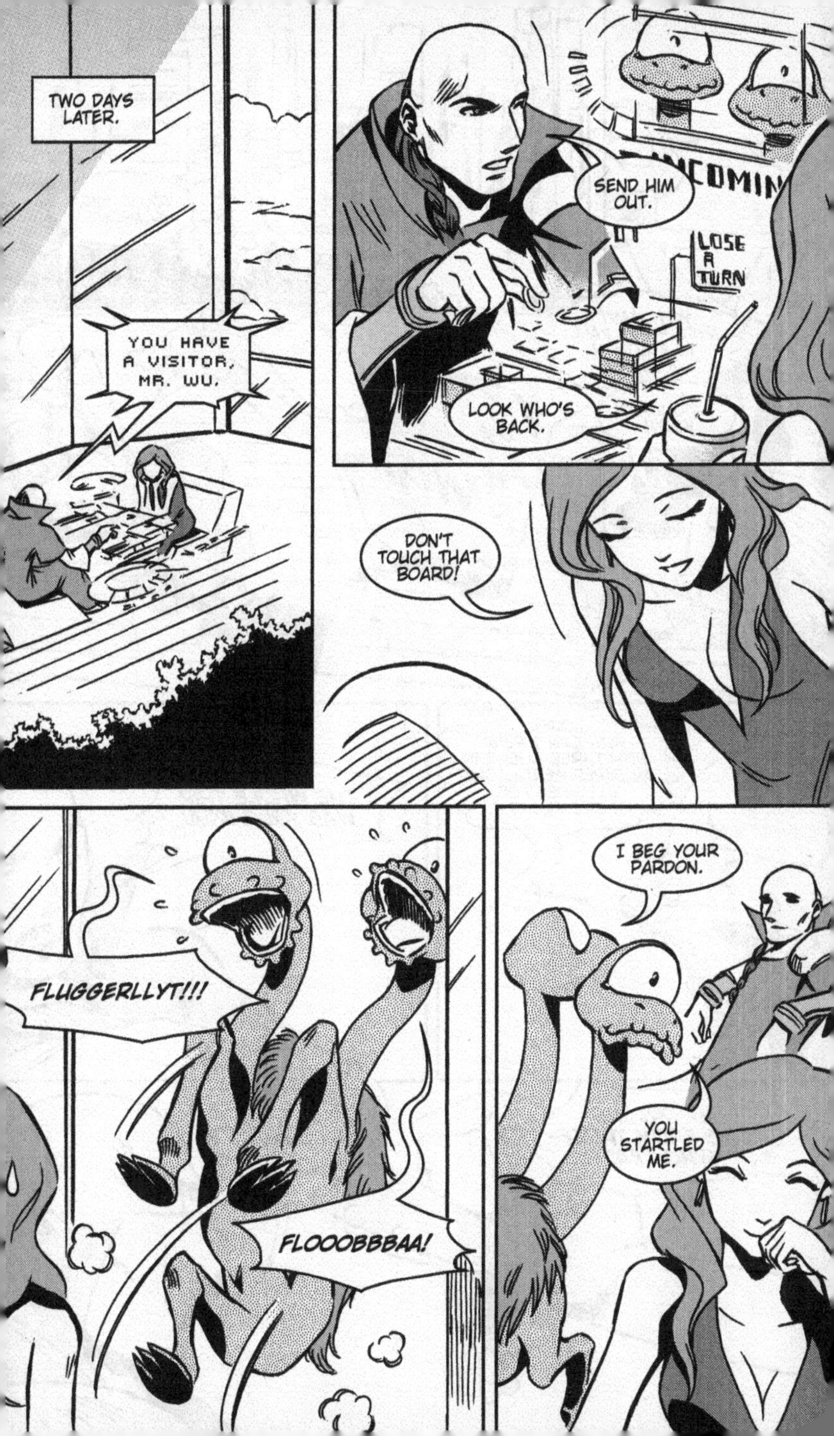
TWO DAYS LATER.
YOU HAVE A VISITOR, MR. WU.
SEND HIM OUT.
LOSE A TURN
LOOK WHO'S BACK.
DON'T TOUCH THAT BOARD!
FLUGGERLLYT!!!
FLOOOBBBAA!
I BEG YOUR PARDON.
YOU STARTLED ME.

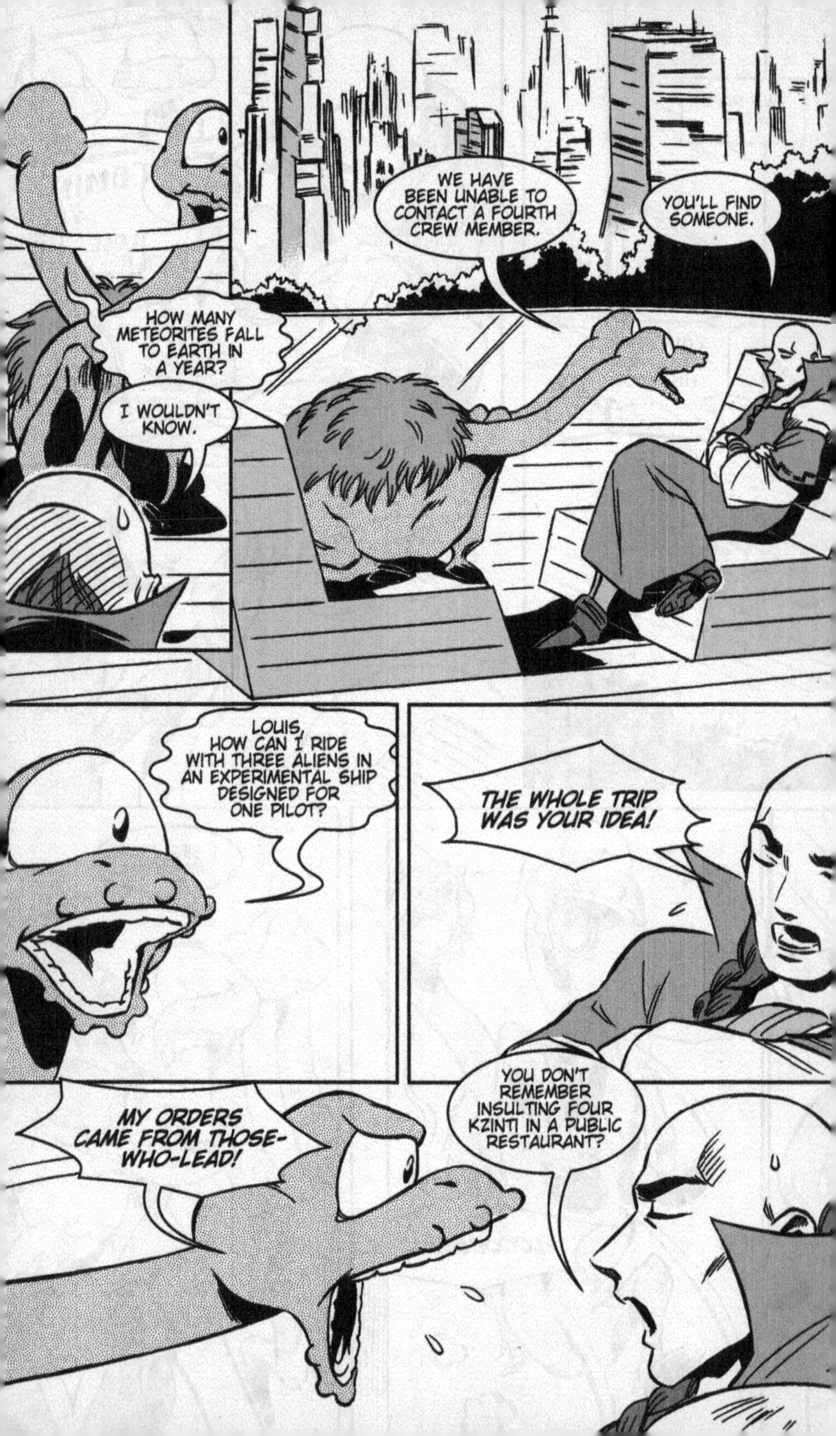

HOW MANY METEORITES FALL TO EARTH IN A YEAR?
I WOULDN'T KNOW.
WE HAVE BEEN UNABLE TO CONTACT A FOURTH CREW MEMBER.
YOU'LL FIND SOMEONE.
LOUIS, HOW CAN I RIDE WITH THREE ALIENS IN AN EXPERIMENTAL SHIP DESIGNED FOR ONE PILOT?
THE WHOLE TRIP WAS YOUR IDEA!
MY ORDERS CAME FROM THOSE-WHO-LEAD!
YOU DON'T REMEMBER INSULTING FOUR KZINTI IN A PUBLIC RESTAURANT?

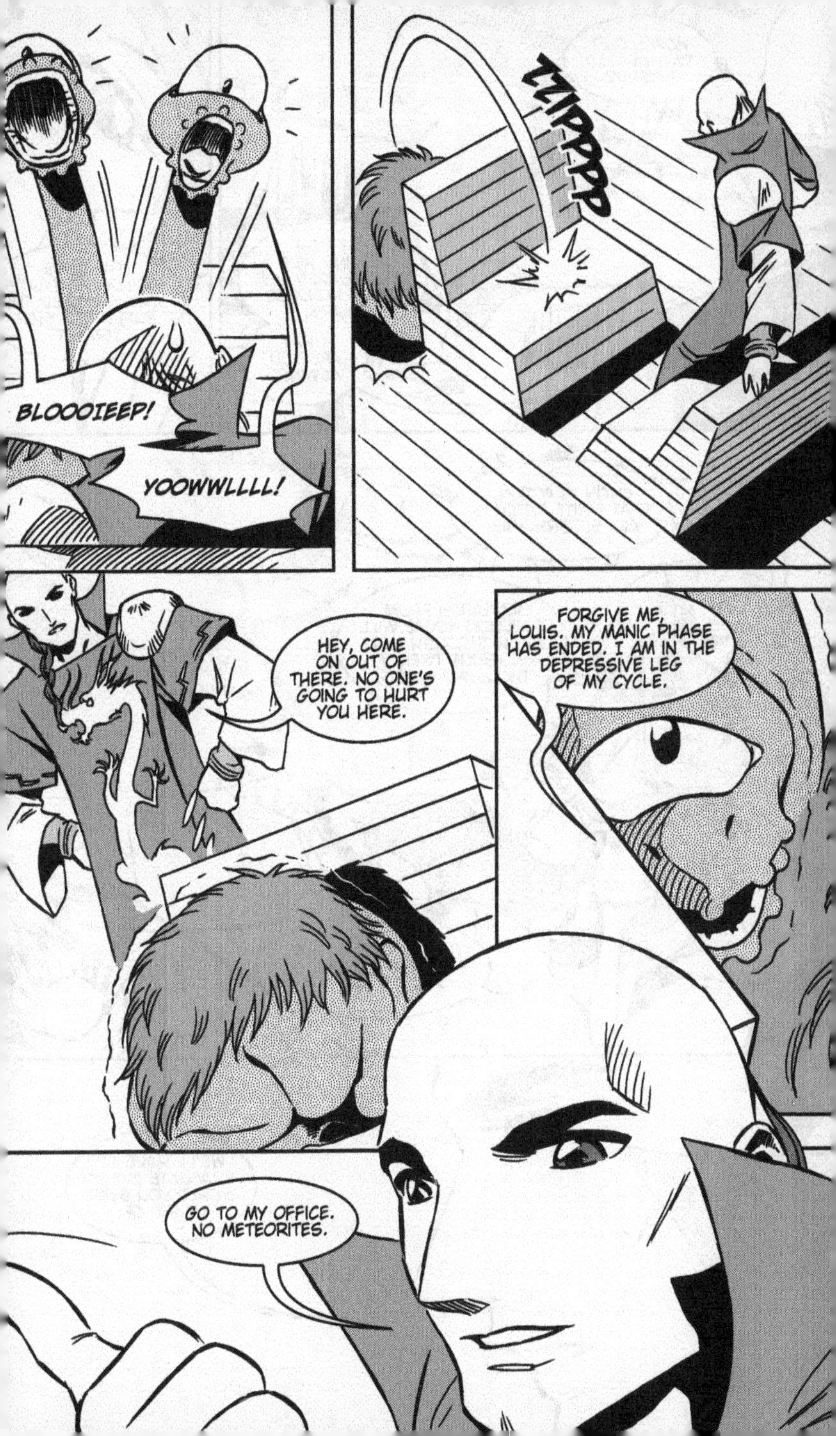
BLOOOIEEP!
YOOWWLLLL!
ZZIPPPPP
HEY, COME ON OUT OF THERE. NO ONE'S GOING TO HURT YOU HERE.
FORGIVE ME, LOUIS. MY MANIC PHASE HAS ENDED. I AM IN THE DEPRESSIVE LEG OF MY CYCLE.
GO TO MY OFFICE. NO METEORITES.

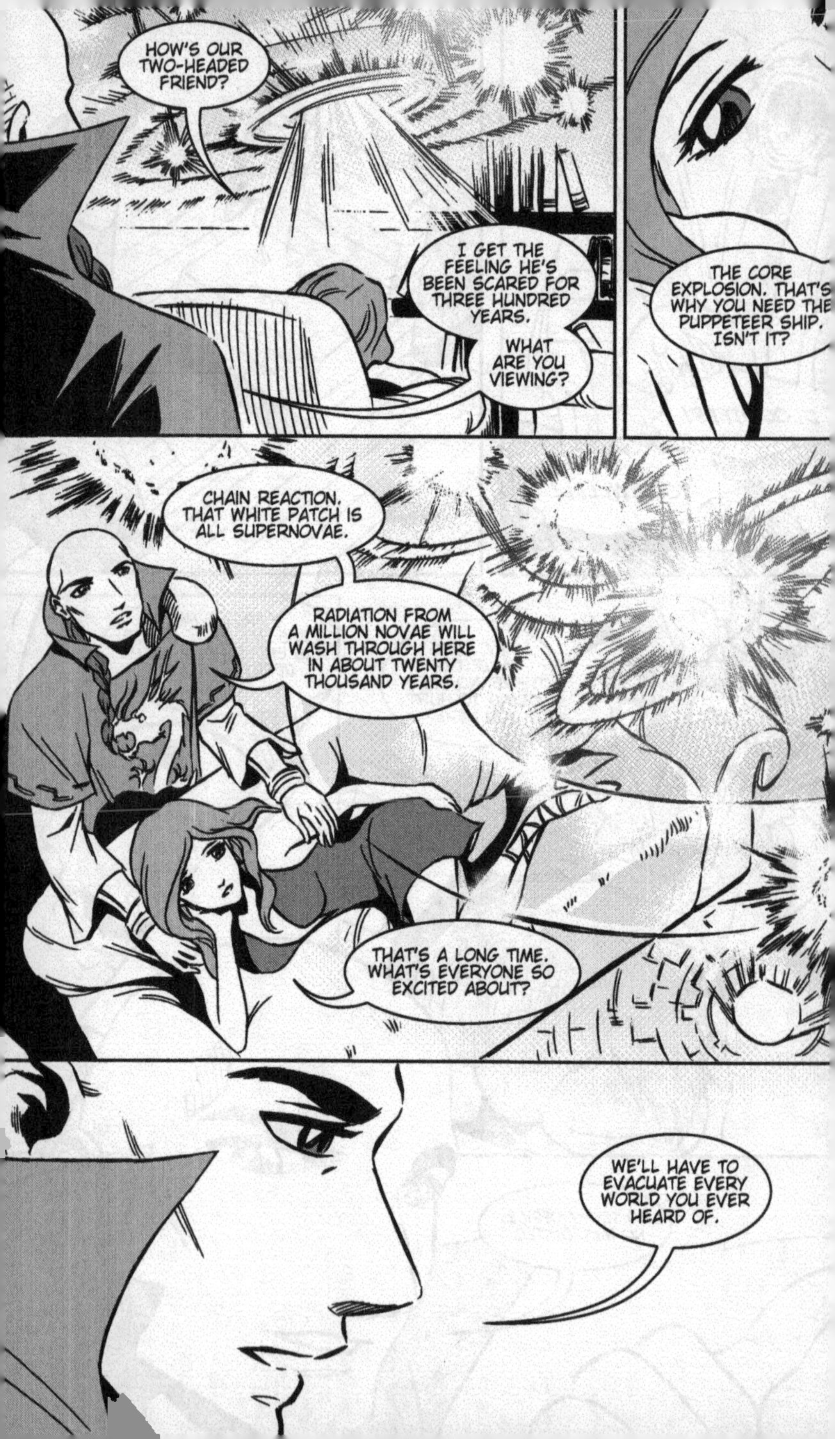
HOW'S OUR TWO-HEADED FRIEND?
I GET THE FEELING HE'S BEEN SCARED FOR THREE HUNDRED YEARS.
WHAT ARE YOU VIEWING?
THE CORE EXPLOSION. THAT'S WHY YOU NEED THE PUPPETEER SHIP. ISN'T IT?
CHAIN REACTION. THAT WHITE PATCH IS ALL SUPERNOVAE.
RADIATION FROM A MILLION NOVAE WILL WASH THROUGH HERE IN ABOUT TWENTY THOUSAND YEARS.
THAT'S A LONG TIME. WHAT'S EVERYONE SO EXCITED ABOUT?
WE'LL HAVE TO EVACUATE EVERY WORLD YOU EVER HEARD OF.

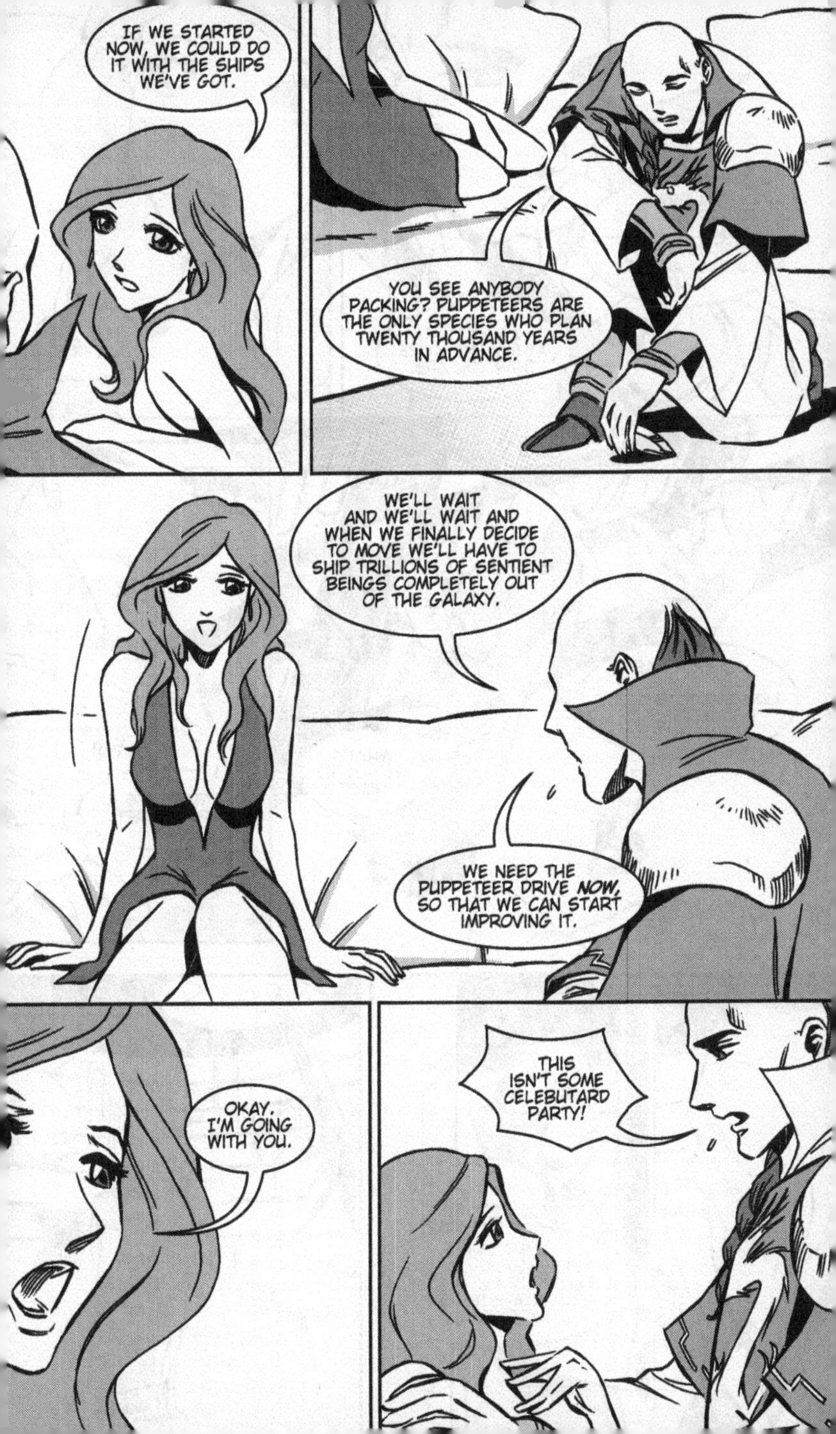
IF WE STARTED NOW, WE COULD DO IT WITH THE SHIPS WE'VE GOT.
YOU SEE ANYBODY PACKING? PUPPETEERS ARE THE ONLY SPECIES WHO PLAN TWENTY THOUSAND YEARS IN ADVANCE.
WE'LL WAIT AND WE'LL WAIT AND WHEN WE FINALLY DECIDE TO MOVE WE'LL HAVE TO SHIP TRILLIONS OF SENTIENT BEINGS COMPLETELY OUT OF THE GALAXY.
WE NEED THE PUPPETEER DRIVE ***NOW***, SO THAT WE CAN START IMPROVING IT.
OKAY. I'M GOING WITH YOU.
THIS ISN'T SOME CELEBUTARD PARTY!

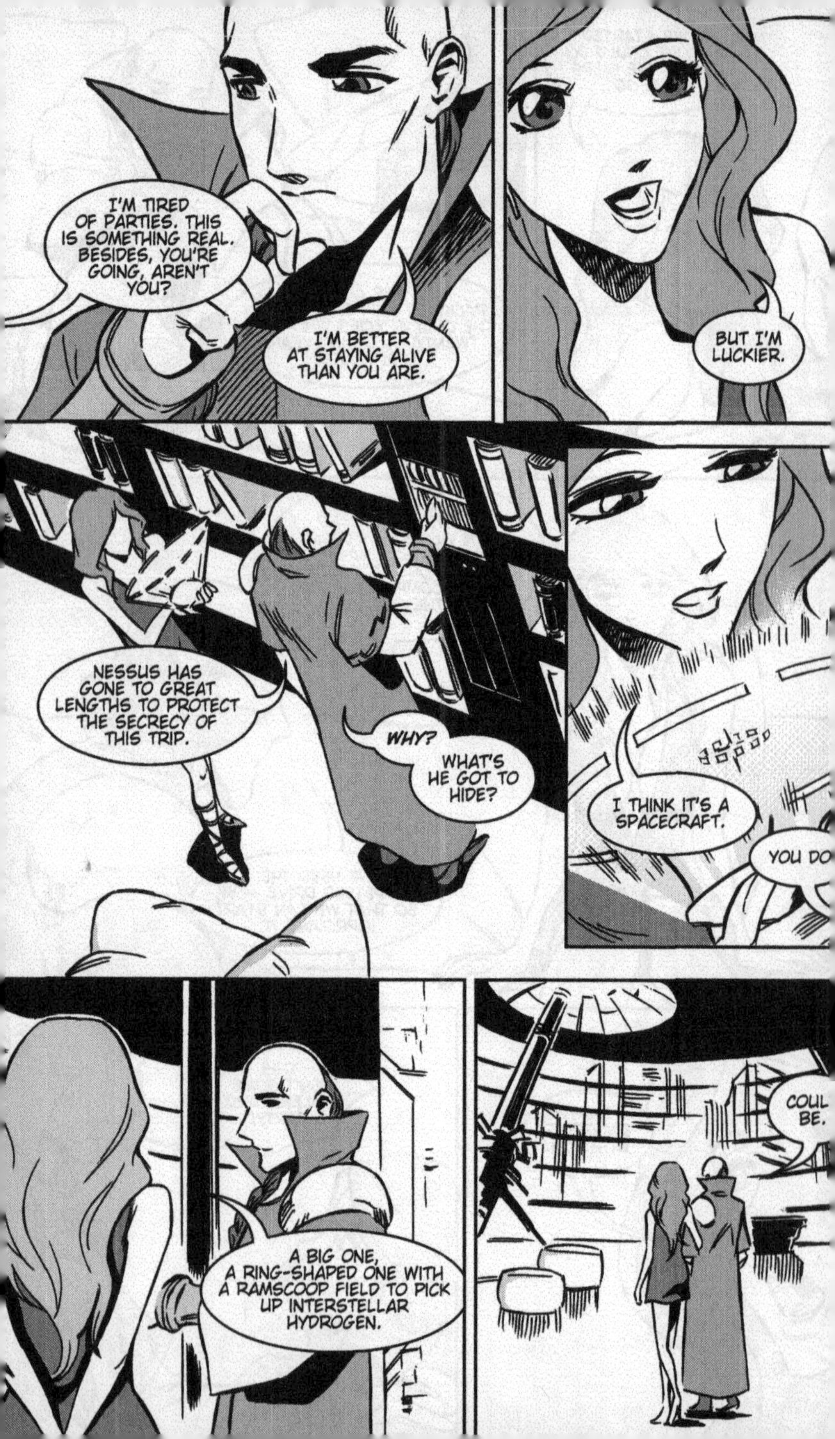
I'M TIRED OF PARTIES. THIS IS SOMETHING REAL. BESIDES, YOU'RE GOING, AREN'T YOU?
I'M BETTER AT STAYING ALIVE THAN YOU ARE.
BUT I'M LUCKIER.
NESSUS HAS GONE TO GREAT LENGTHS TO PROTECT THE SECRECY OF THIS TRIP.
WHY? WHAT'S HE GOT TO HIDE?
I THINK IT'S A SPACECRAFT.
YOU DO
A BIG ONE, A RING-SHAPED ONE WITH A RAMSCOOP FIELD TO PICK UP INTERSTELLAR HYDROGEN.
COUL BE.

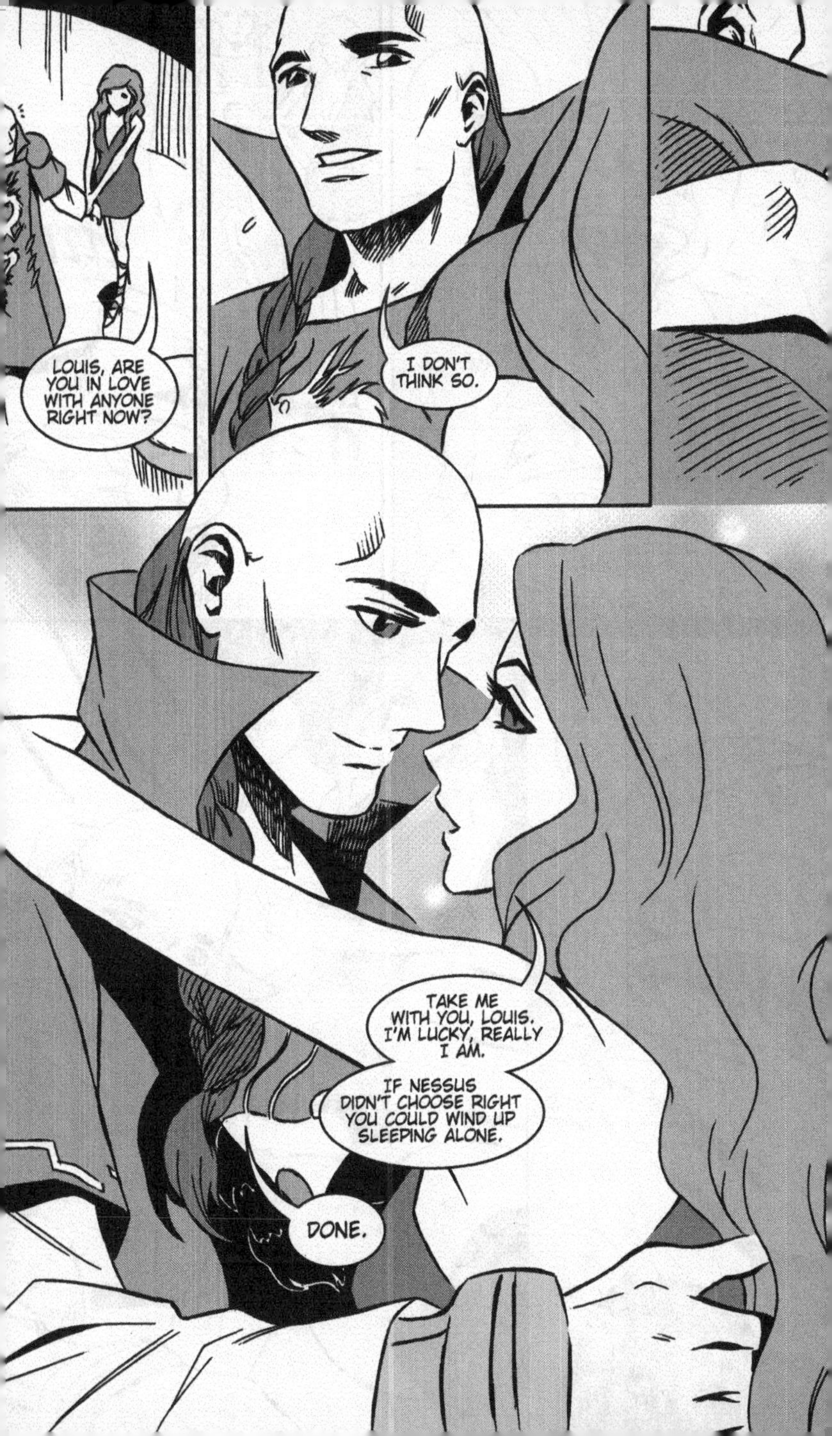

LOUIS, ARE YOU IN LOVE WITH ANYONE RIGHT NOW?
I DON'T THINK SO.
TAKE ME WITH YOU, LOUIS. I'M LUCKY, REALLY I AM.
IF NESSUS DIDN'T CHOOSE RIGHT YOU COULD WIND UP SLEEPING ALONE.
DONE.

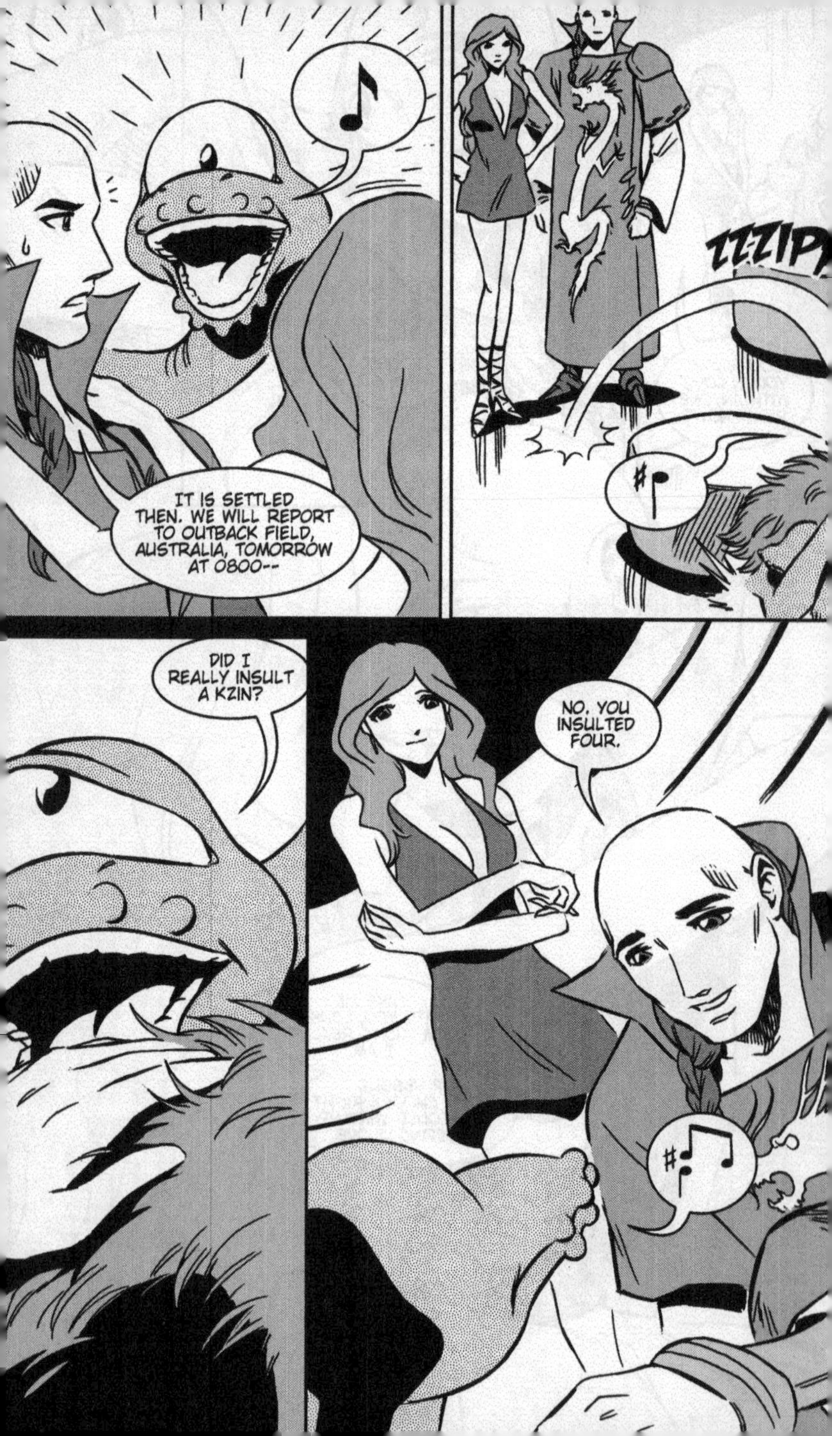
IT IS SETTLED THEN. WE WILL REPORT TO OUTBACK FIELD, AUSTRALIA, TOMORROW AT 0800--
ZZZIPP
DID I REALLY INSULT A KZIN?
NO, YOU INSULTED FOUR.

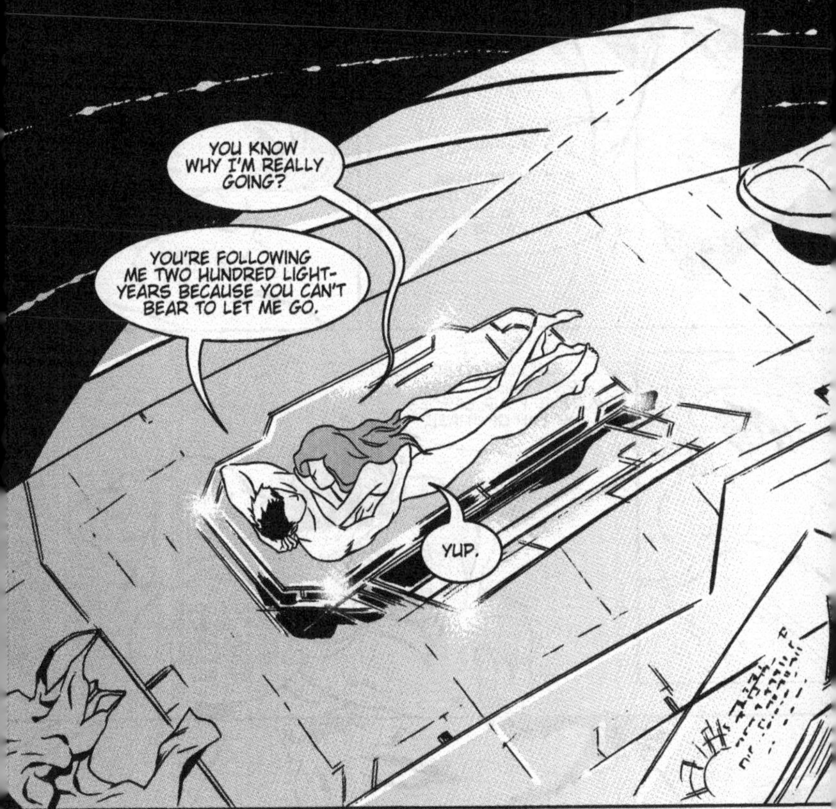
YOU KNOW WHY I'M REALLY GOING?
YOU'RE FOLLOWING ME TWO HUNDRED LIGHT-YEARS BECAUSE YOU CAN'T BEAR TO LET ME GO.
YUP.
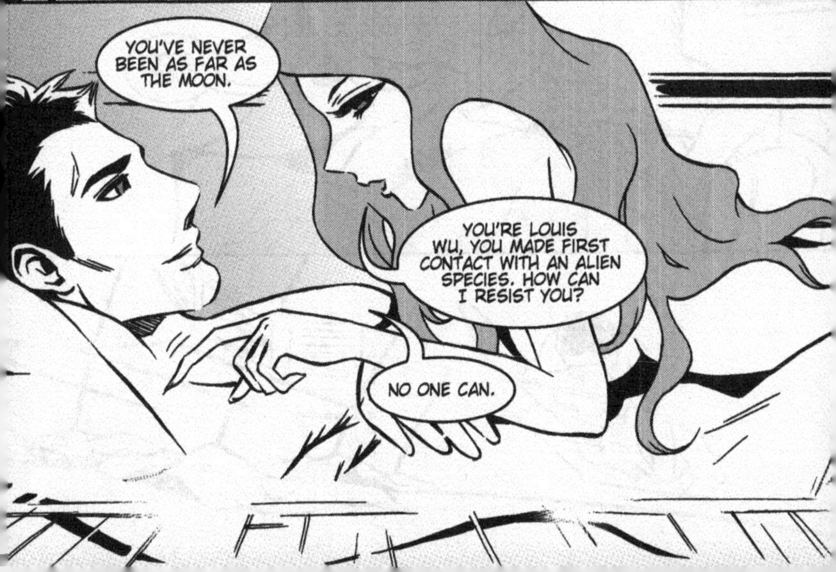
YOU'VE NEVER BEEN AS FAR AS THE MOON.
YOU'RE LOUIS WU, YOU MADE FIRST CONTACT WITH AN ALIEN SPECIES. HOW CAN I RESIST YOU?
NO ONE CAN.

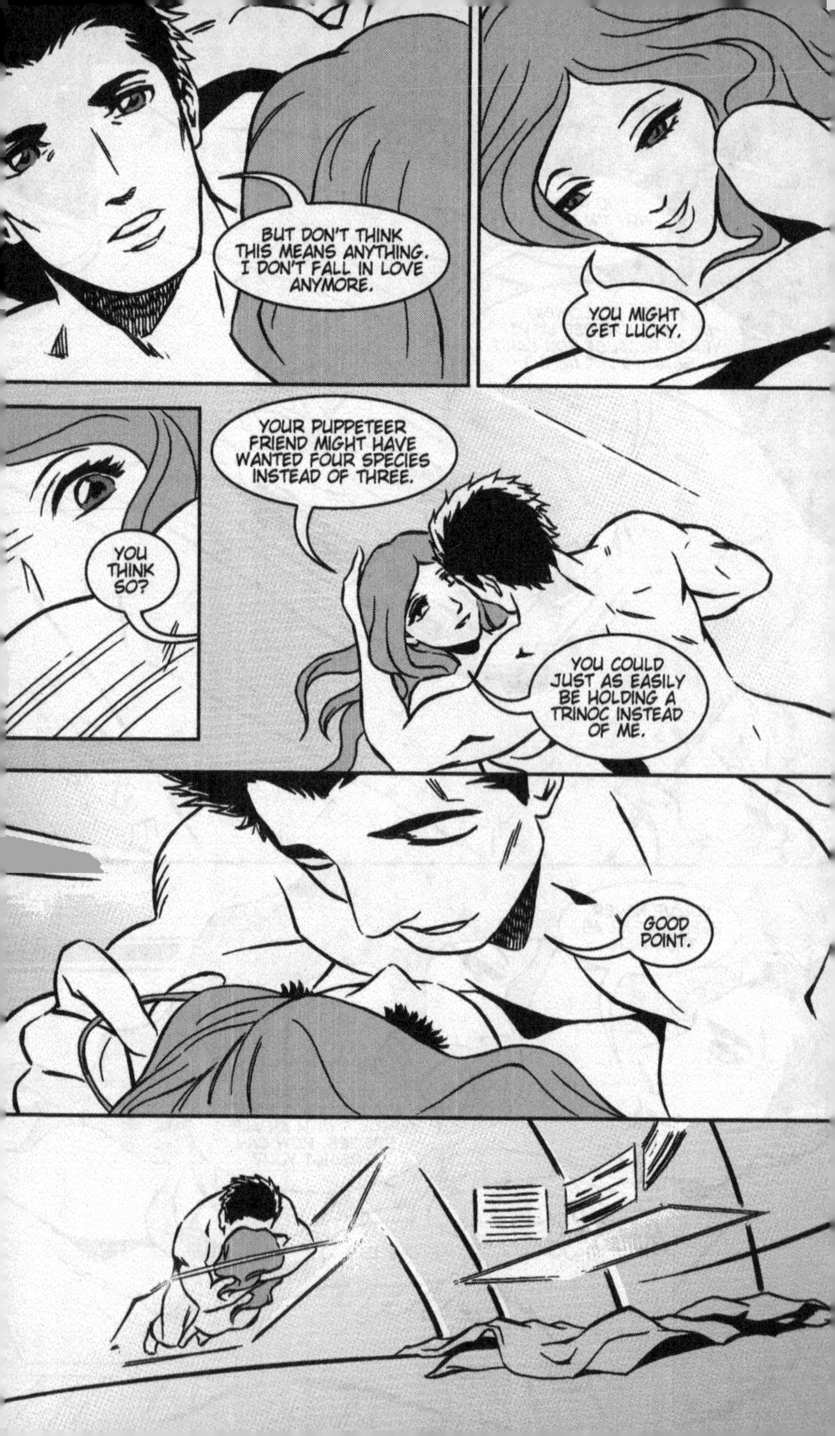
BUT DON'T THINK THIS MEANS ANYTHING. I DON'T FALL IN LOVE ANYMORE.
YOU MIGHT GET LUCKY.
YOU THINK SO?
YOUR PUPPETEER FRIEND MIGHT HAVE WANTED FOUR SPECIES INSTEAD OF THREE.
YOU COULD JUST AS EASILY BE HOLDING A TRINOC INSTEAD OF ME.
GOOD POINT.

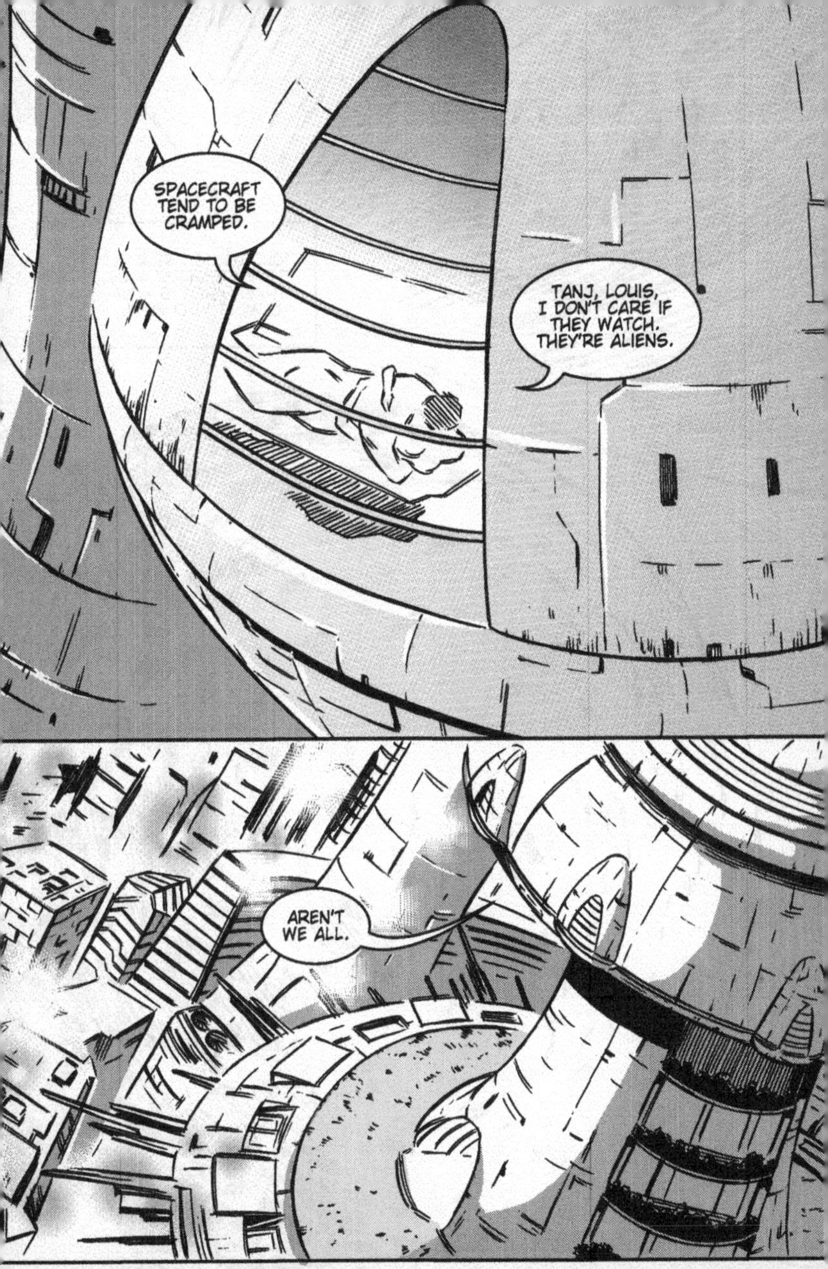
SPACECRAFT TEND TO BE CRAMPED.
TANJ, LOUIS, I DON'T CARE IF THEY WATCH. THEY'RE ALIENS.
AREN'T WE ALL.

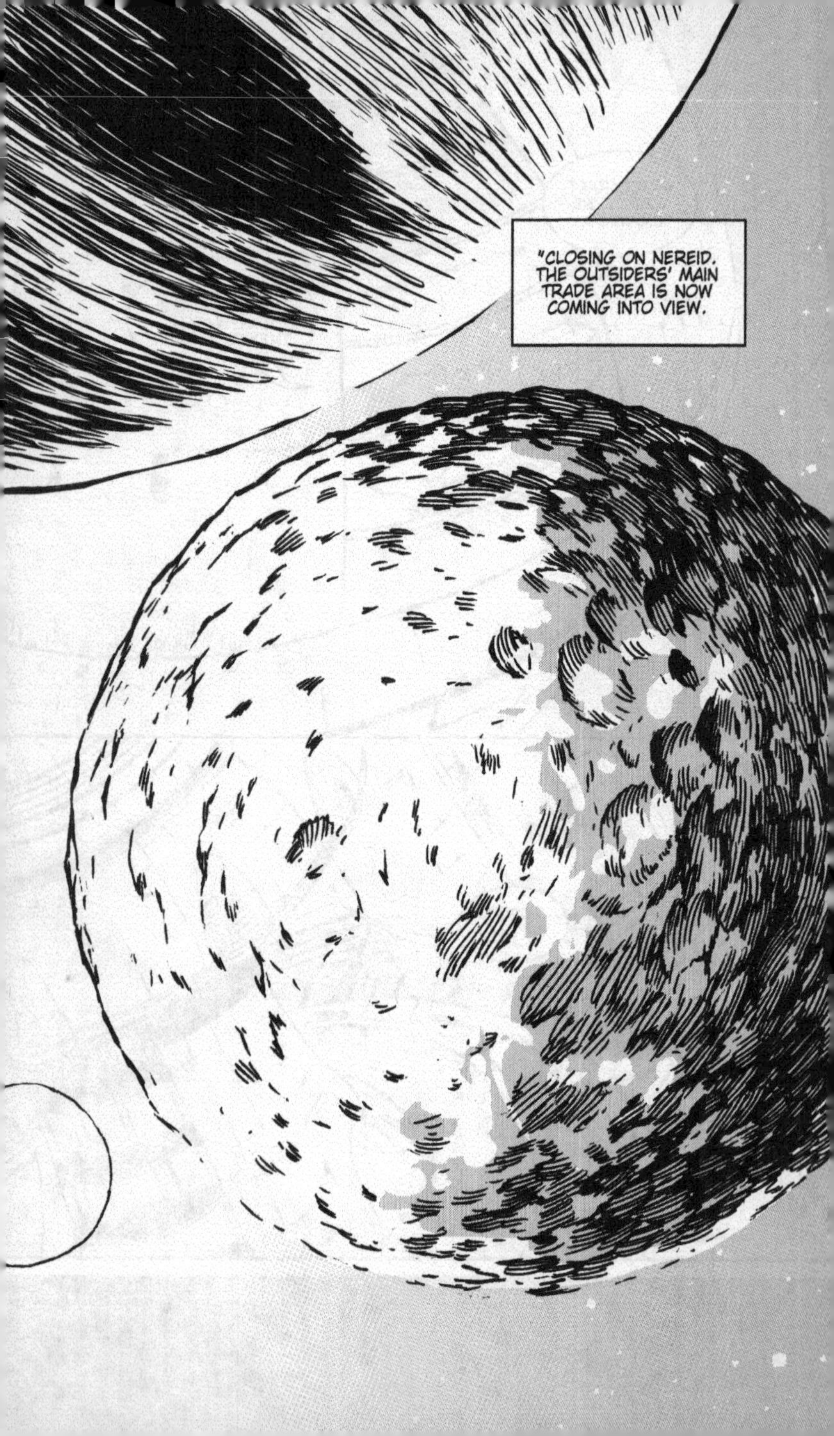
"CLOSING ON NEREID. THE OUTSIDERS' MAIN TRADE AREA IS NOW COMING INTO VIEW.

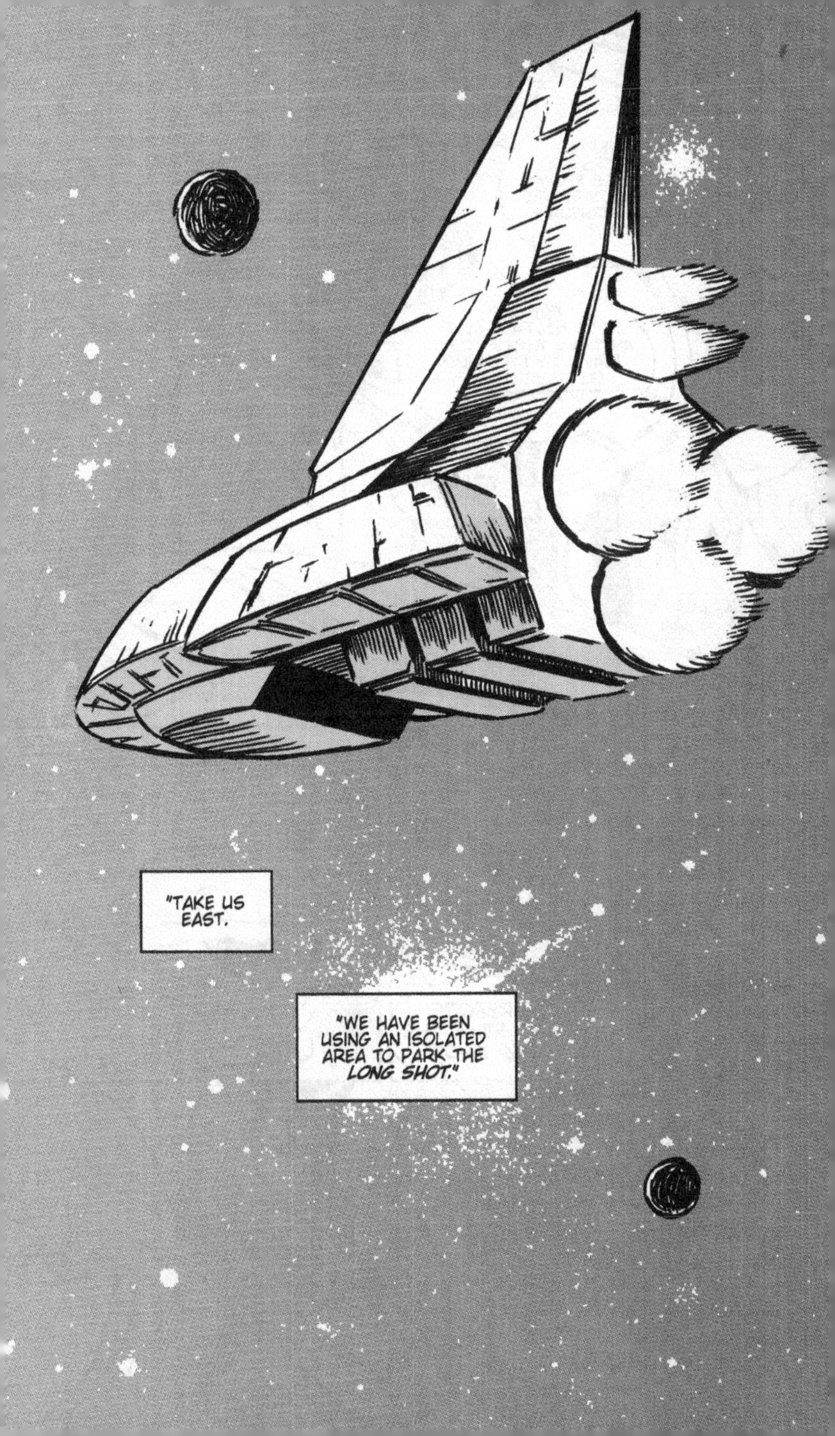
"TAKE US EAST.
"WE HAVE BEEN USING AN ISOLATED AREA TO PARK THE *LONG SHOT*."

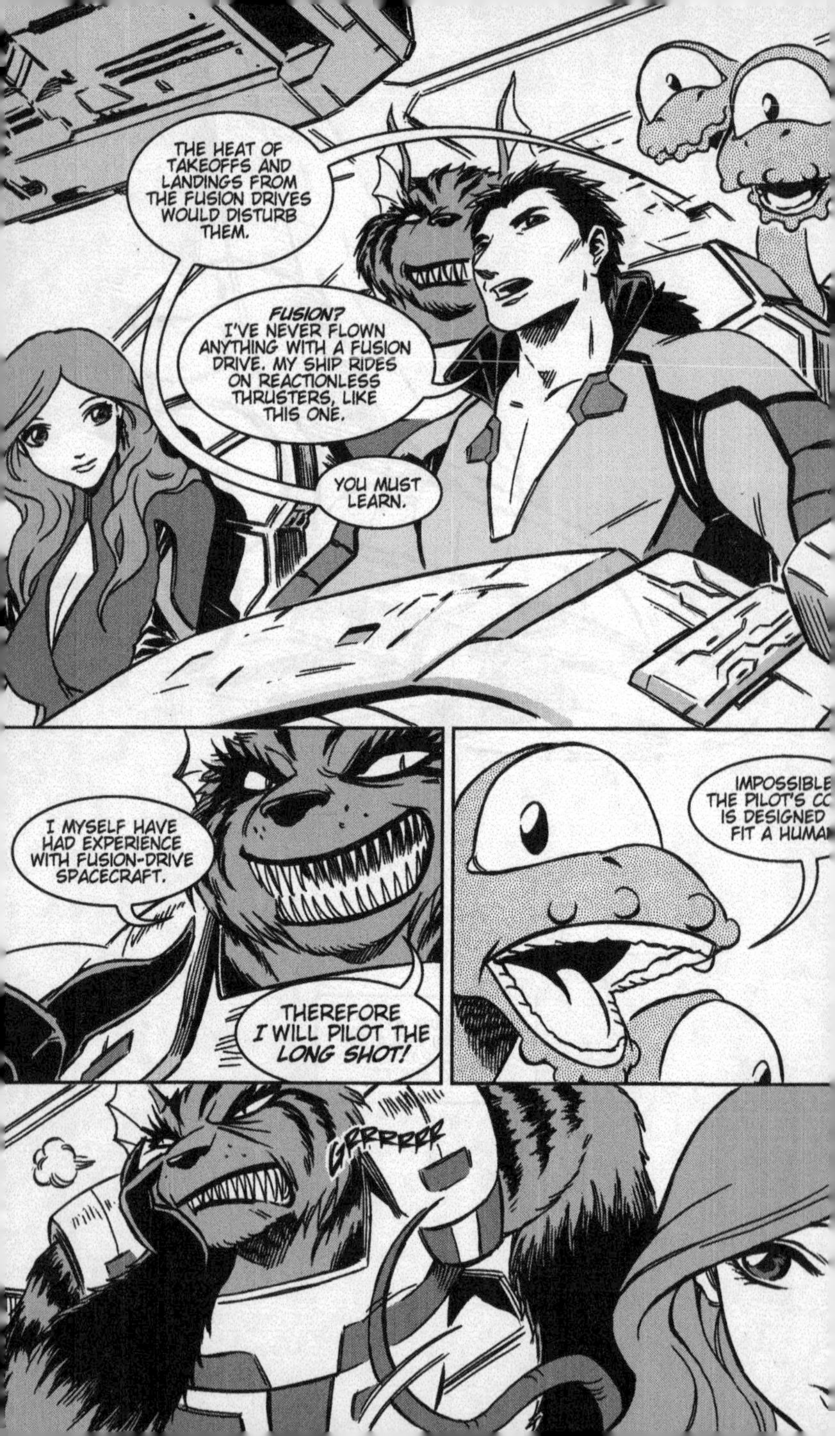
THE HEAT OF TAKEOFFS AND LANDINGS FROM THE FUSION DRIVES WOULD DISTURB THEM.
FUSION? I'VE NEVER FLOWN ANYTHING WITH A FUSION DRIVE. MY SHIP RIDES ON REACTIONLESS THRUSTERS, LIKE THIS ONE.
YOU MUST LEARN.
I MYSELF HAVE HAD EXPERIENCE WITH FUSION-DRIVE SPACECRAFT.
THEREFORE *I* WILL PILOT THE *LONG SHOT!*
IMPOSSIBLE THE PILOT'S CO IS DESIGNED FIT A HUMA
GRRRRRR

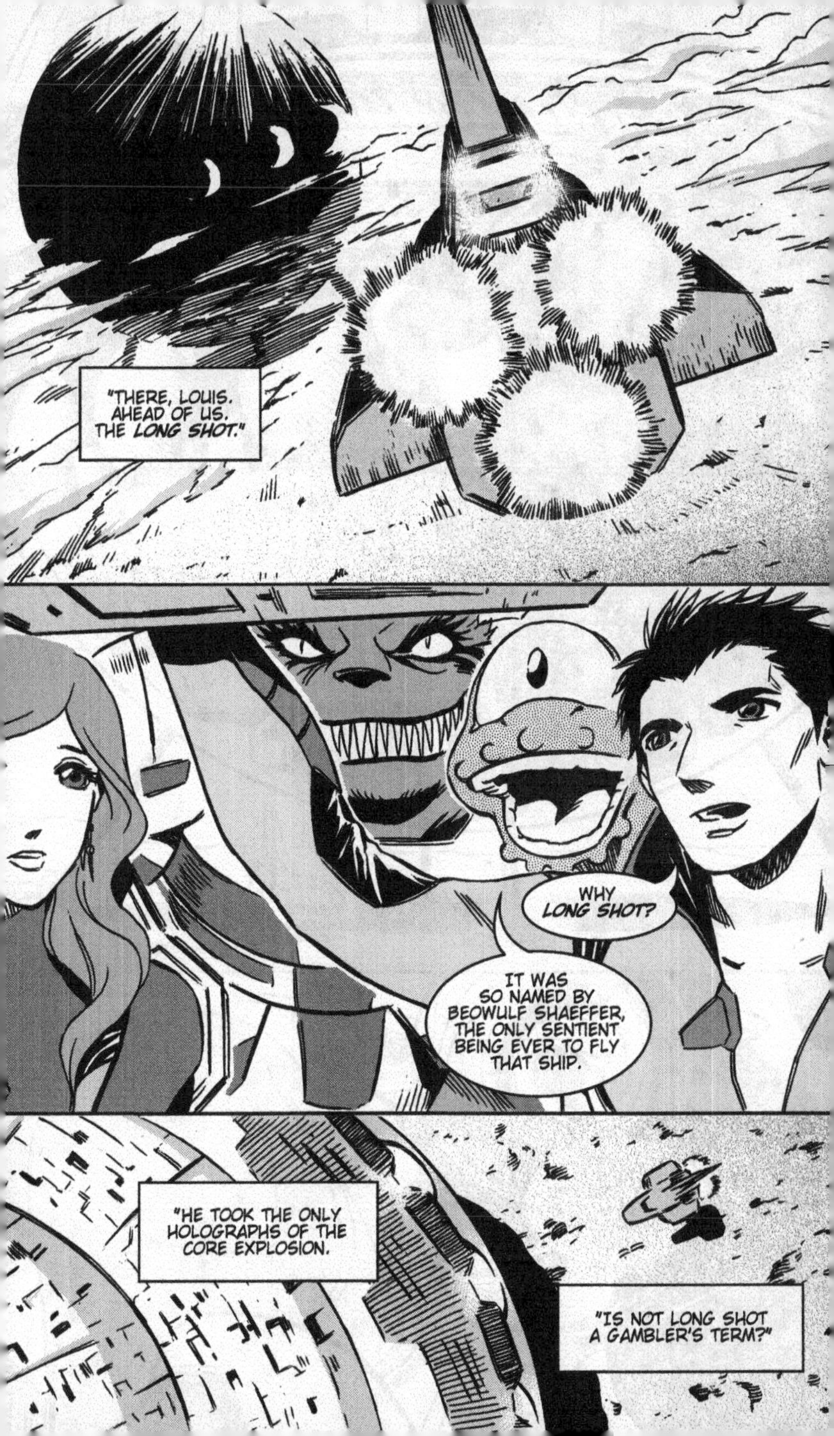
"THERE, LOUIS. AHEAD OF US. THE *LONG SHOT.*"
WHY *LONG SHOT?*
IT WAS SO NAMED BY BEOWULF SHAEFFER, THE ONLY SENTIENT BEING EVER TO FLY THAT SHIP.
"HE TOOK THE ONLY HOLOGRAPHS OF THE CORE EXPLOSION.
"IS NOT LONG SHOT A GAMBLER'S TERM?"

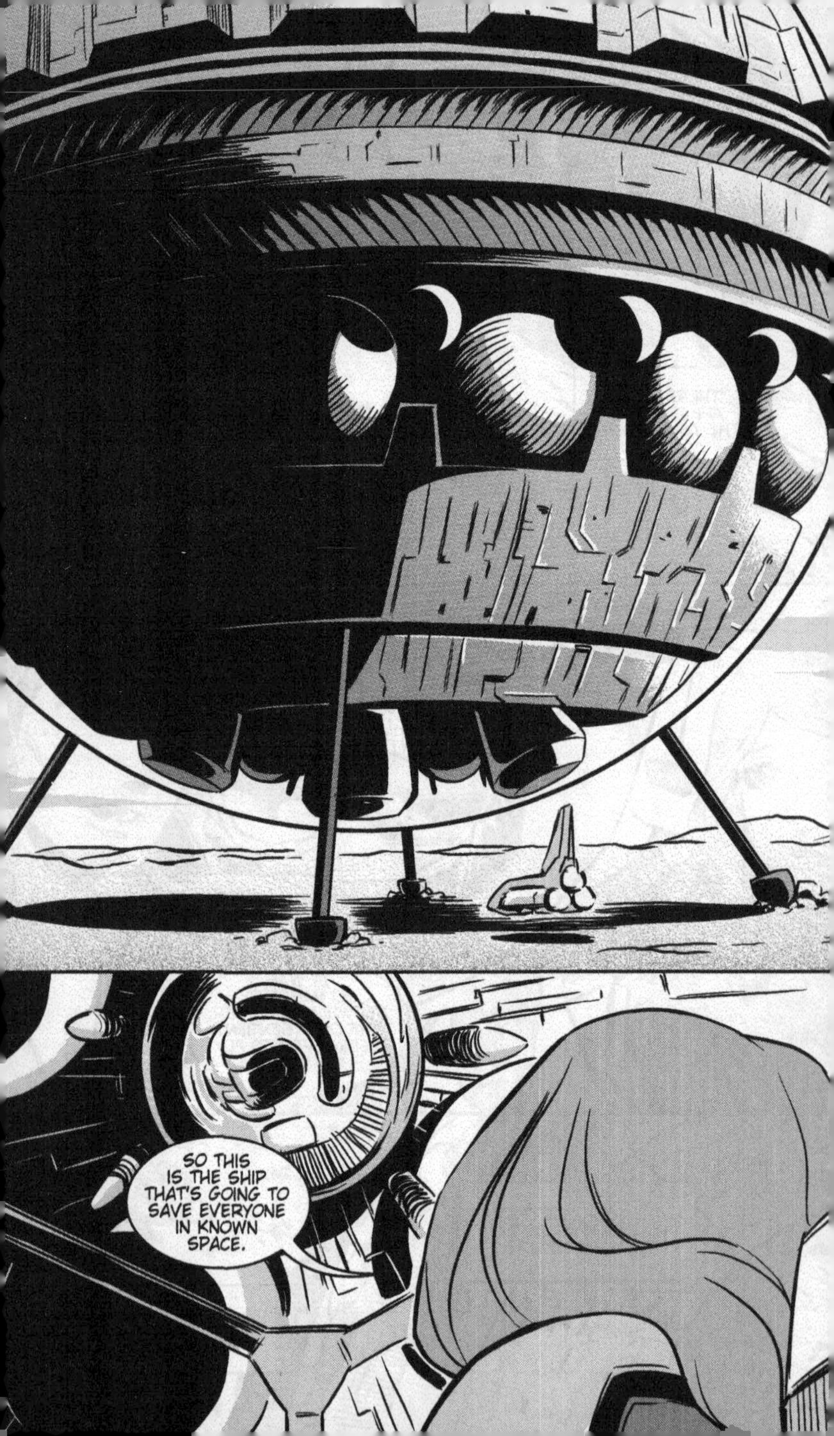
SO THIS IS THE SHIP THAT'S GOING TO SAVE EVERYONE IN KNOWN SPACE.

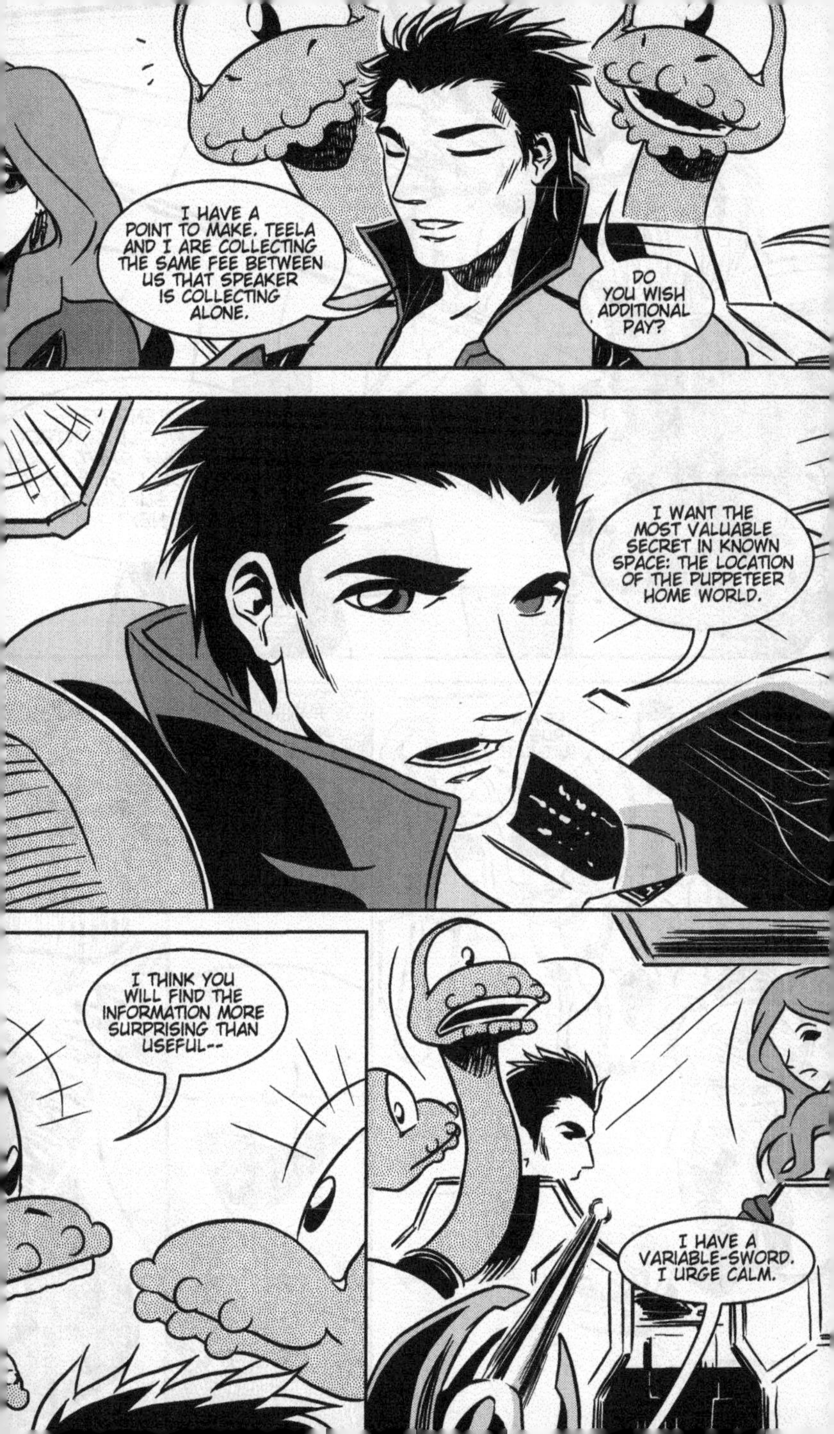
I HAVE A POINT TO MAKE. TEELA AND I ARE COLLECTING THE SAME FEE BETWEEN US THAT SPEAKER IS COLLECTING ALONE.
DO YOU WISH ADDITIONAL PAY?
I WANT THE MOST VALUABLE SECRET IN KNOWN SPACE: THE LOCATION OF THE PUPPETEER HOME WORLD.
I THINK YOU WILL FIND THE INFORMATION MORE SURPRISING THAN USEFUL--
I HAVE A VARIABLE-SWORD. I URGE CALM.

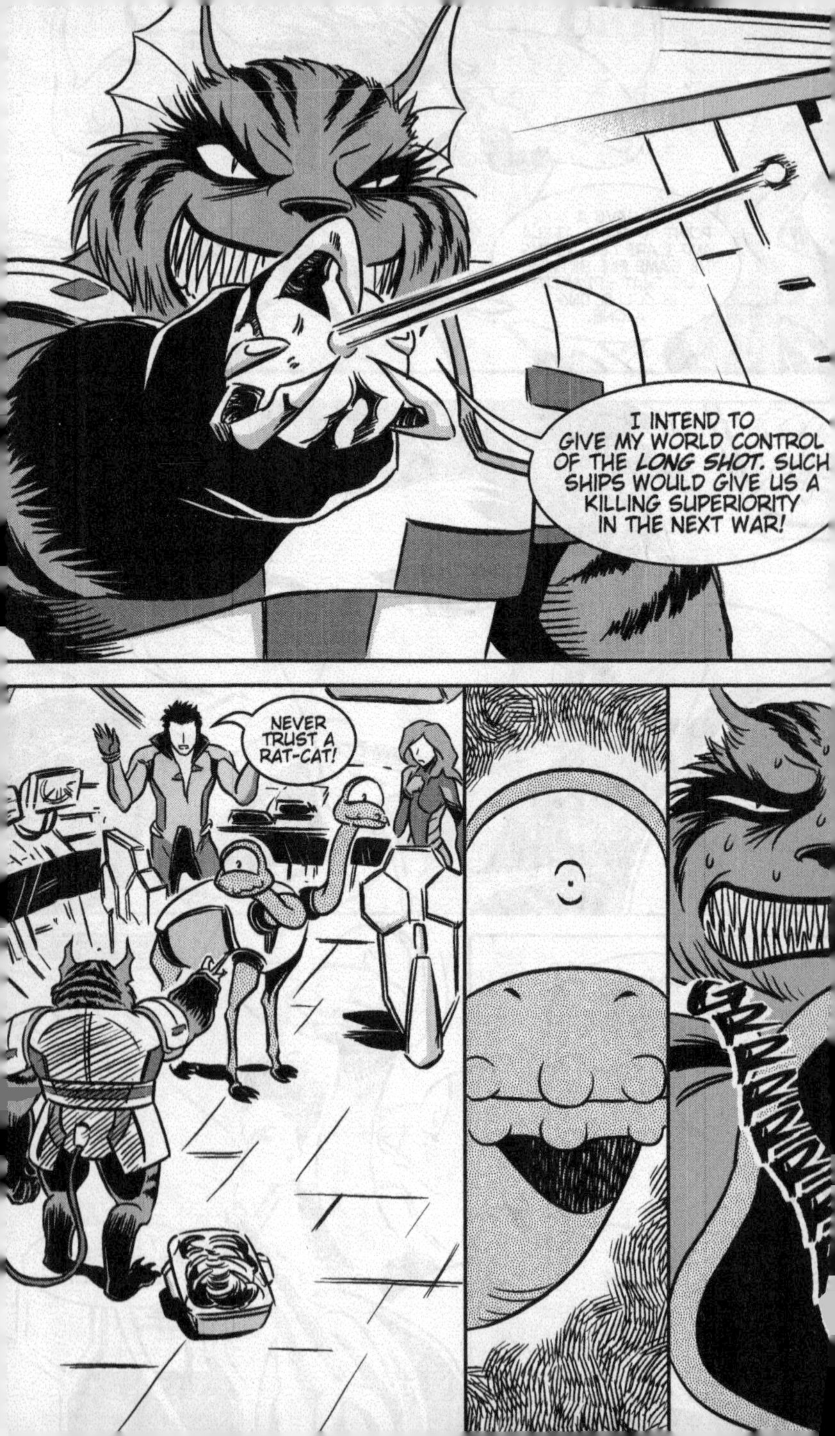
I INTEND TO GIVE MY WORLD CONTROL OF THE *LONG SHOT*. SUCH SHIPS WOULD GIVE US A KILLING SUPERIORITY IN THE NEXT WAR!
NEVER TRUST A RAT-CAT!

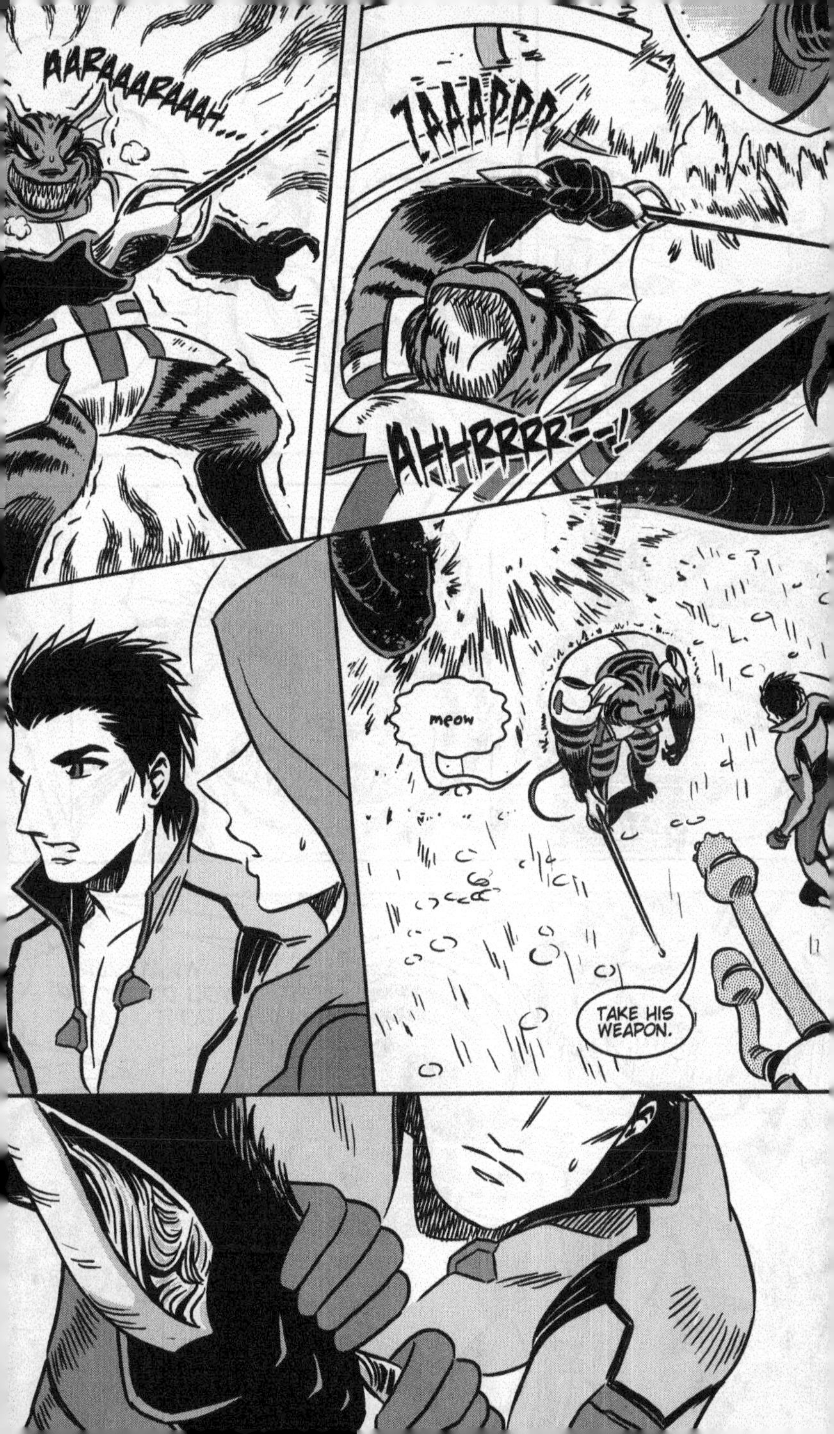
AARAAARAAAH...
ZAAAPPP
AHHRRRR---!
meow
TAKE HIS WEAPON.

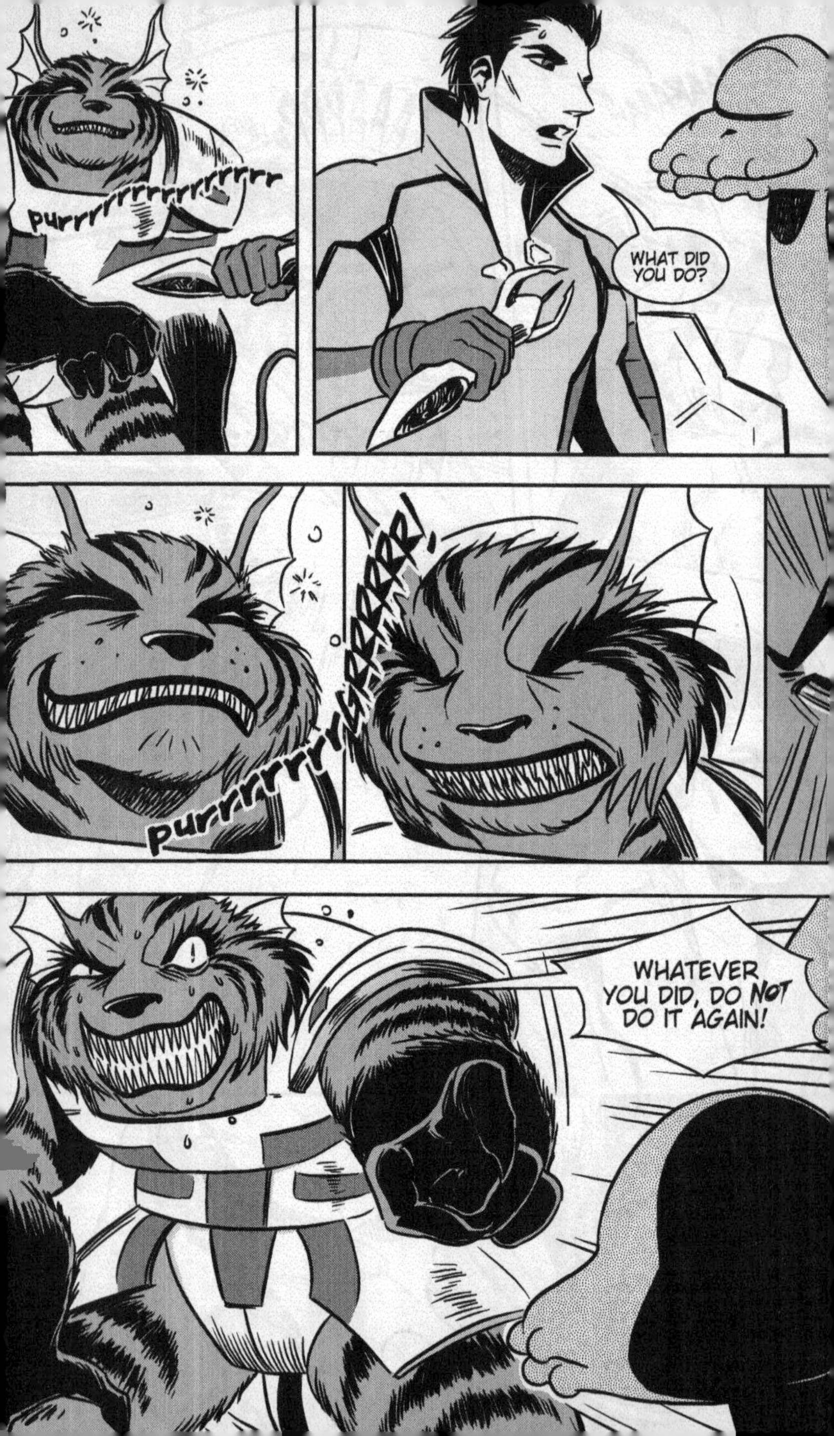
purrrrrrrrrrrrrr
WHAT DID YOU DO?
purrrrrrrrrGRRRRR!
WHATEVER YOU DID, DO NOT DO IT AGAIN!

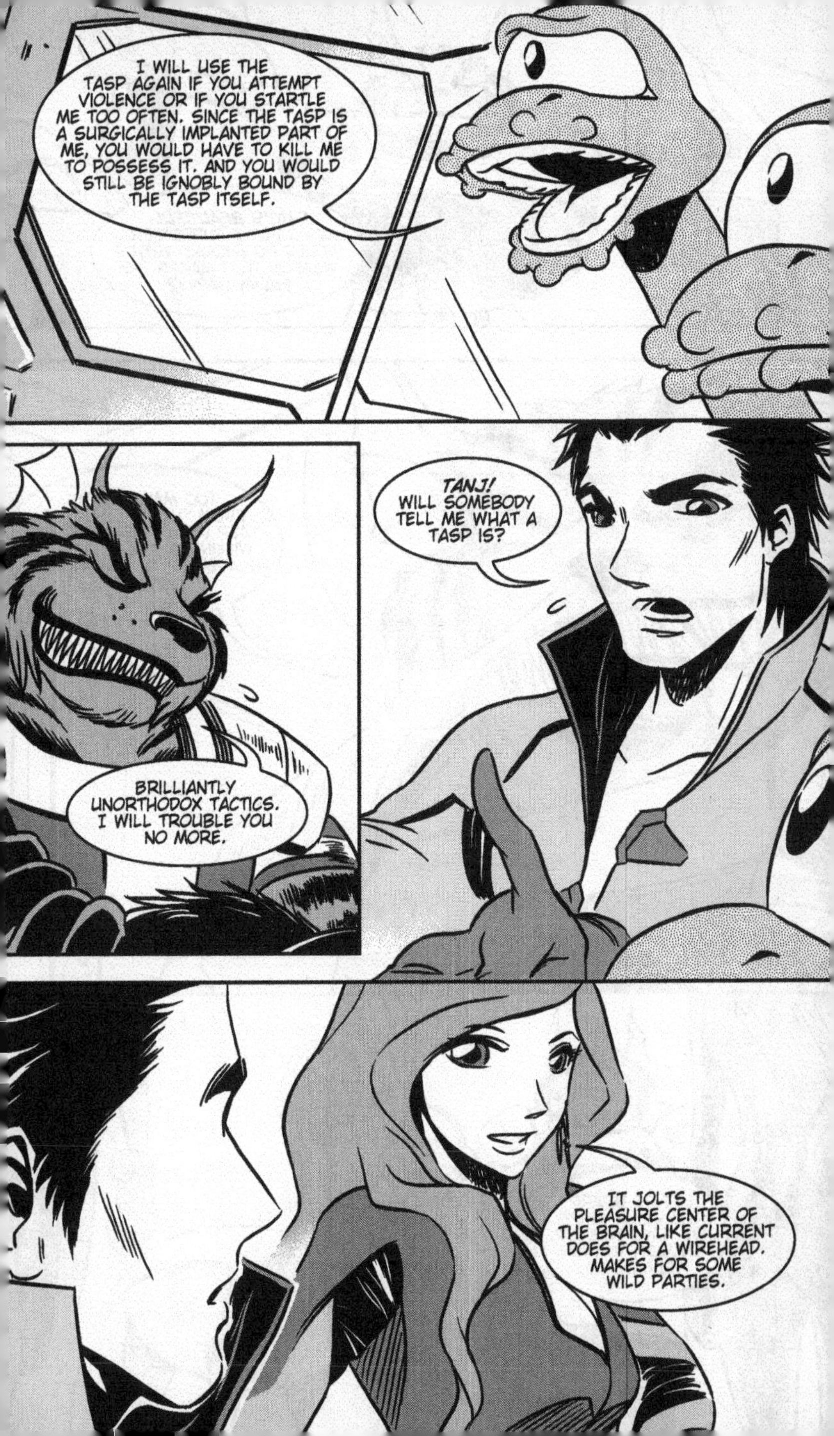
I WILL USE THE TASP AGAIN IF YOU ATTEMPT VIOLENCE OR IF YOU STARTLE ME TOO OFTEN. SINCE THE TASP IS A SURGICALLY IMPLANTED PART OF ME, YOU WOULD HAVE TO KILL ME TO POSSESS IT. AND YOU WOULD STILL BE IGNOBLY BOUND BY THE TASP ITSELF.
BRILLIANTLY UNORTHODOX TACTICS. I WILL TROUBLE YOU NO MORE.
TANJ! WILL SOMEBODY TELL ME WHAT A TASP IS?
IT JOLTS THE PLEASURE CENTER OF THE BRAIN, LIKE CURRENT DOES FOR A WIREHEAD. MAKES FOR SOME WILD PARTIES.

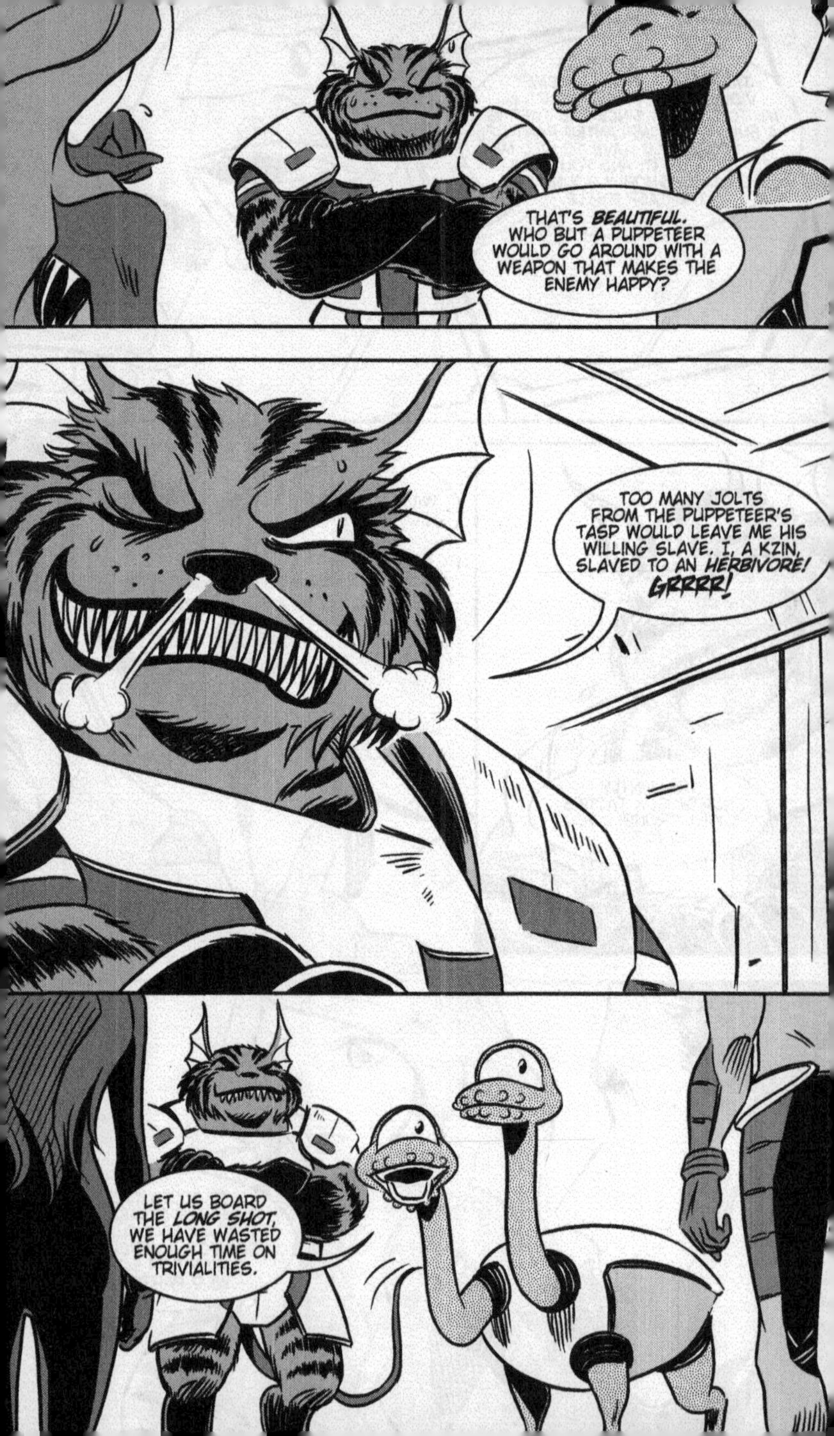
THAT'S *BEAUTIFUL*. WHO BUT A PUPPETEER WOULD GO AROUND WITH A WEAPON THAT MAKES THE ENEMY HAPPY?
TOO MANY JOLTS FROM THE PUPPETEER'S TASP WOULD LEAVE ME HIS WILLING SLAVE. I, A KZIN, SLAVED TO AN *HERBIVORE*! *GRRRR!*
LET US BOARD THE *LONG SHOT*, WE HAVE WASTED ENOUGH TIME ON TRIVIALITIES.

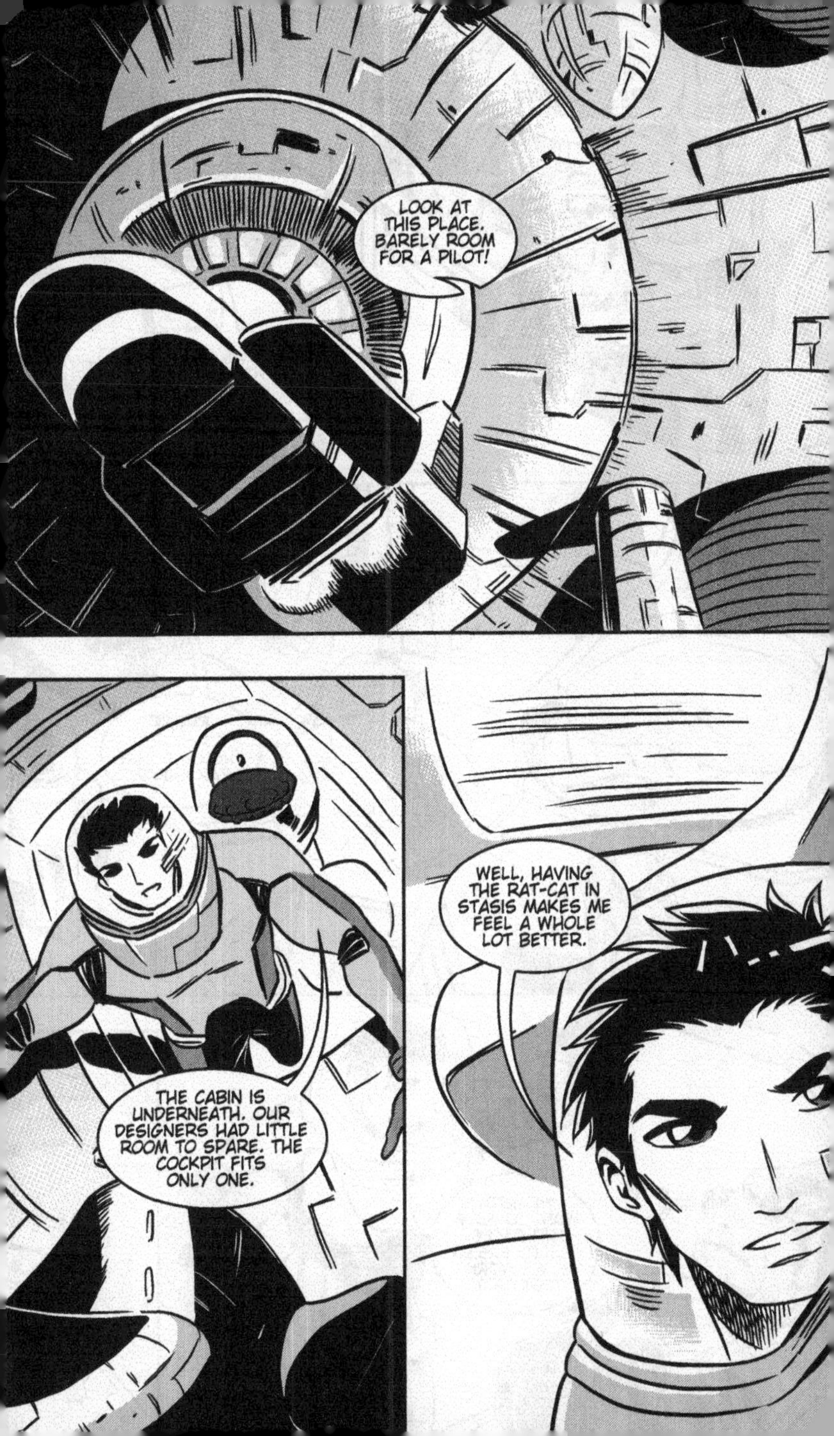
LOOK AT THIS PLACE. BARELY ROOM FOR A PILOT!
THE CABIN IS UNDERNEATH. OUR DESIGNERS HAD LITTLE ROOM TO SPARE. THE COCKPIT FITS ONLY ONE.
WELL, HAVING THE RAT-CAT IN STASIS MAKES ME FEEL A WHOLE LOT BETTER.

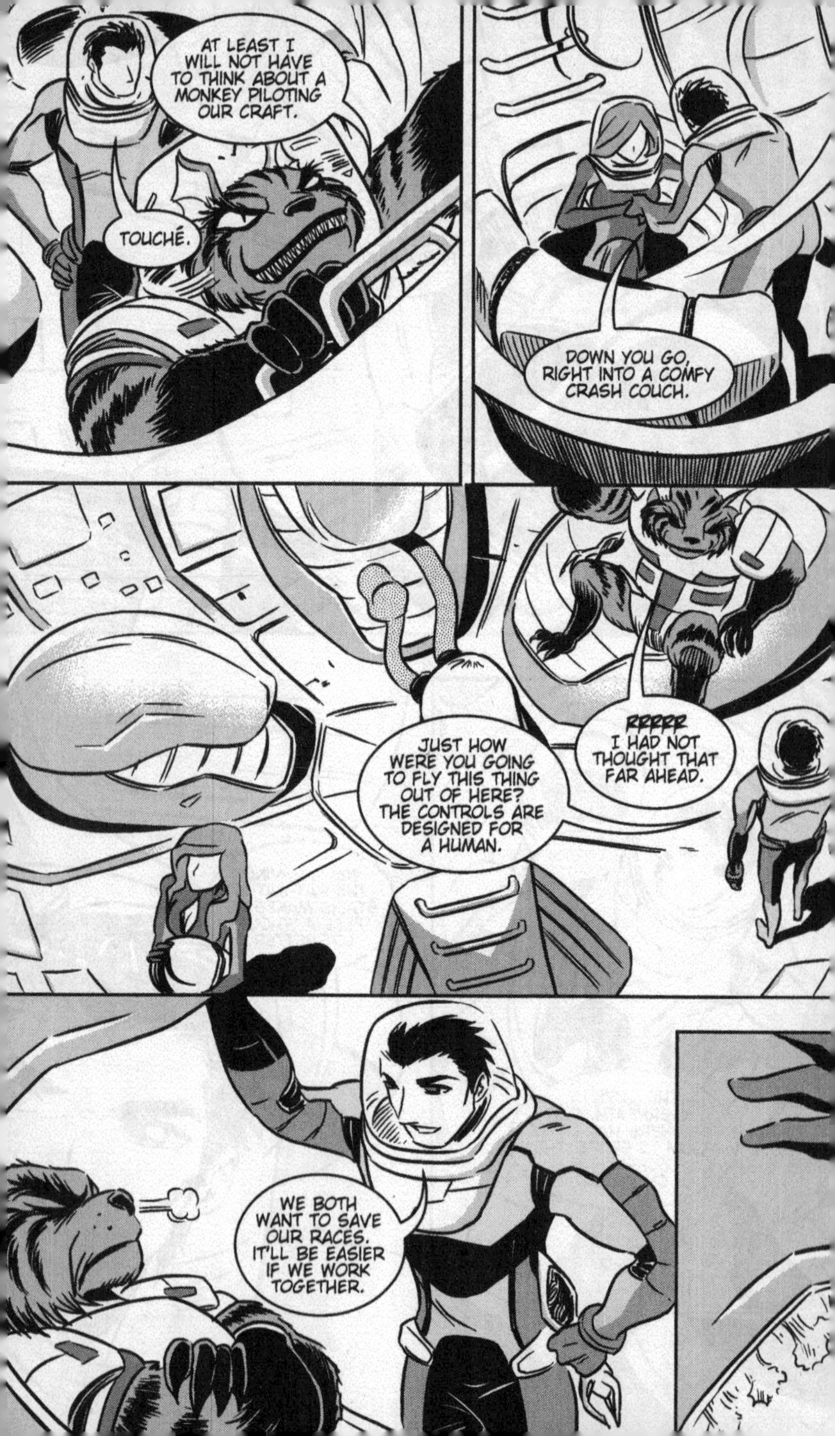
AT LEAST I WILL NOT HAVE TO THINK ABOUT A MONKEY PILOTING OUR CRAFT.
TOUCHÉ.
DOWN YOU GO, RIGHT INTO A COMFY CRASH COUCH.
JUST HOW WERE YOU GOING TO FLY THIS THING OUT OF HERE? THE CONTROLS ARE DESIGNED FOR A HUMAN.
RRRRR
I HAD NOT THOUGHT THAT FAR AHEAD.
WE BOTH WANT TO SAVE OUR RACES. IT'LL BE EASIER IF WE WORK TOGETHER.

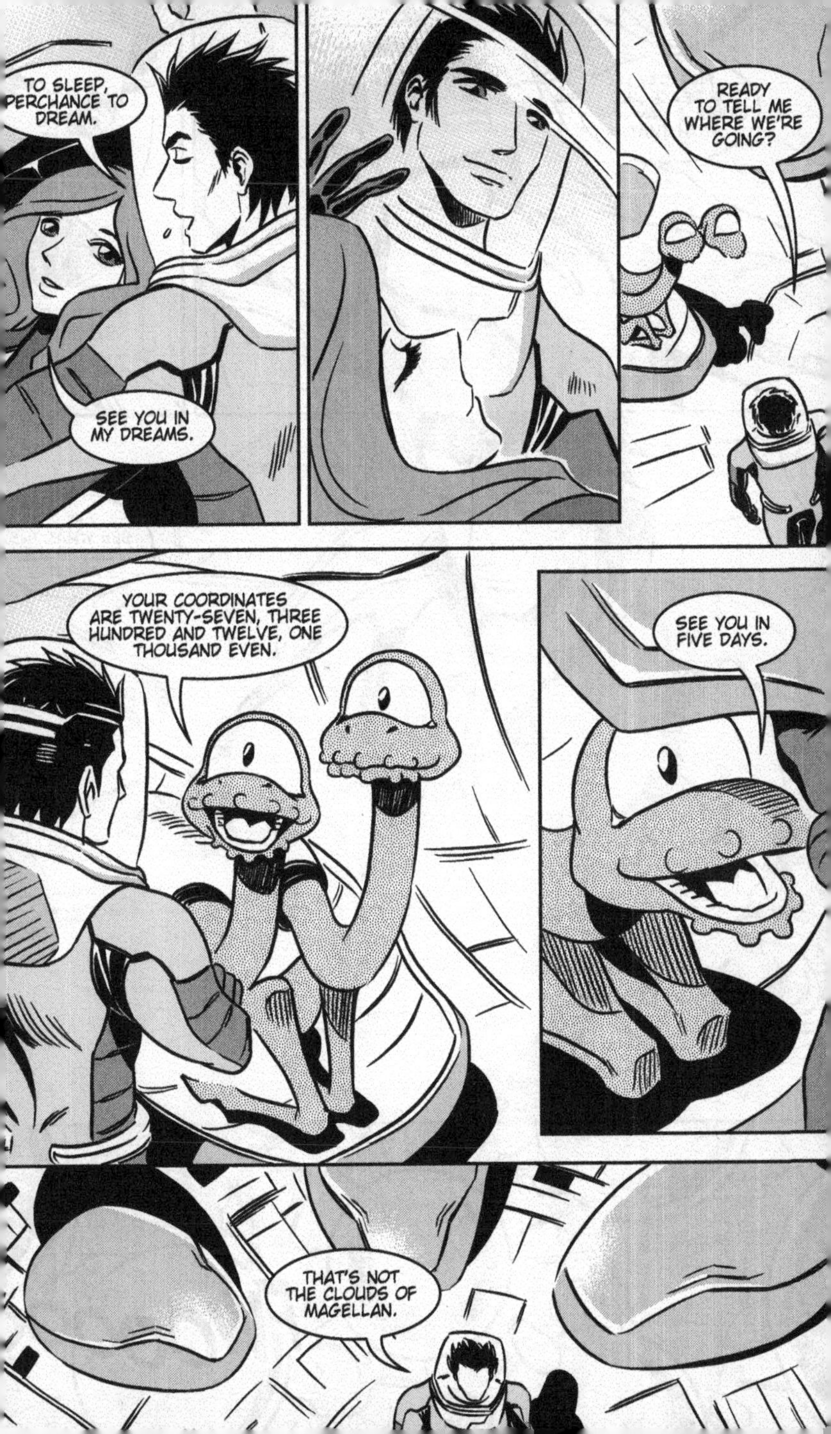
TO SLEEP, PERCHANCE TO DREAM.
SEE YOU IN MY DREAMS.
READY TO TELL ME WHERE WE'RE GOING?
YOUR COORDINATES ARE TWENTY-SEVEN, THREE HUNDRED AND TWELVE, ONE THOUSAND EVEN.
SEE YOU IN FIVE DAYS.
THAT'S NOT THE CLOUDS OF MAGELLAN.

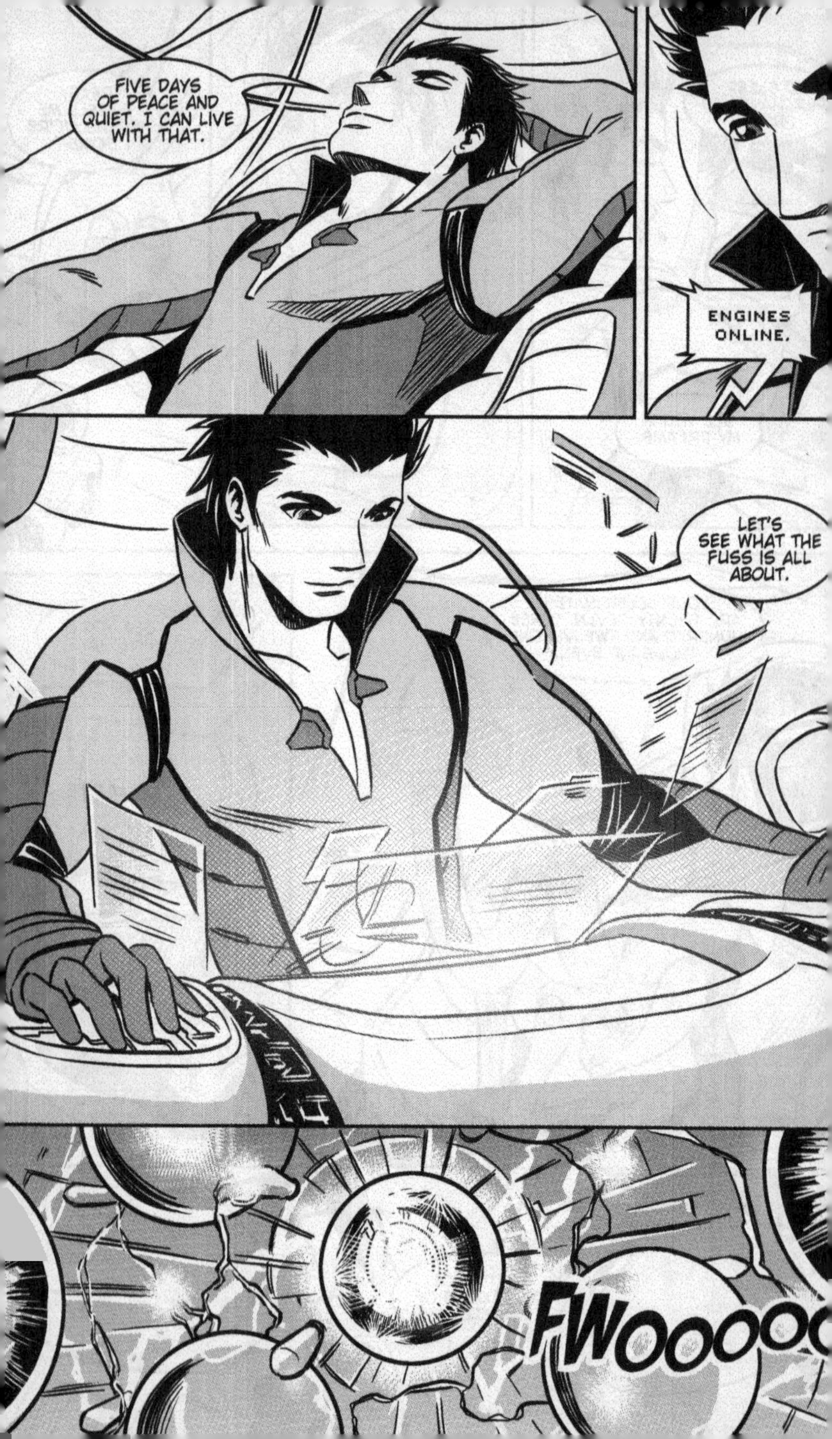
FIVE DAYS OF PEACE AND QUIET. I CAN LIVE WITH THAT.
ENGINES ONLINE.
LET'S SEE WHAT THE FUSS IS ALL ABOUT.
FWOOOOO

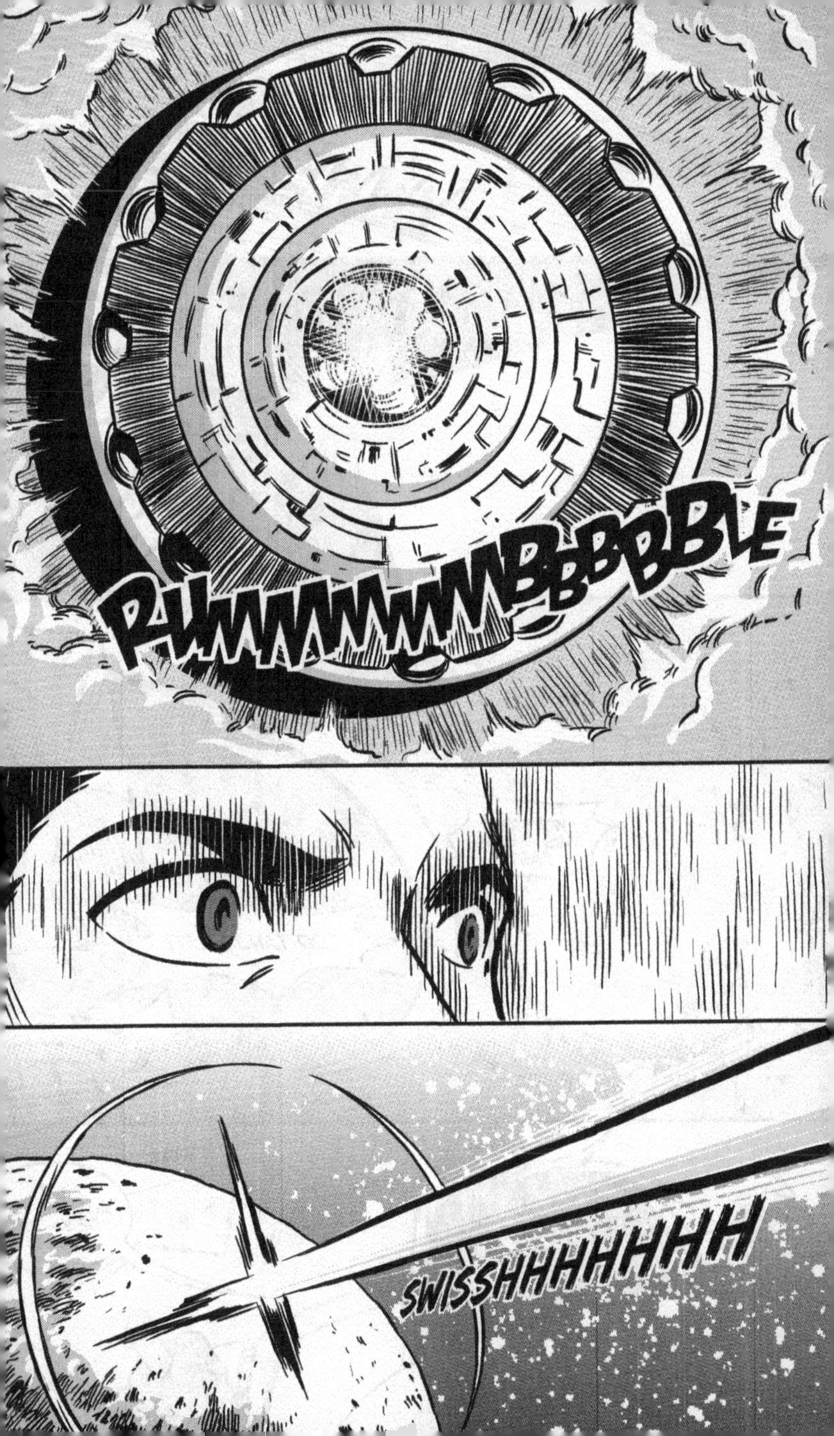
RUMMMMMMBBBBBLE
SWISSHHHHHHHH

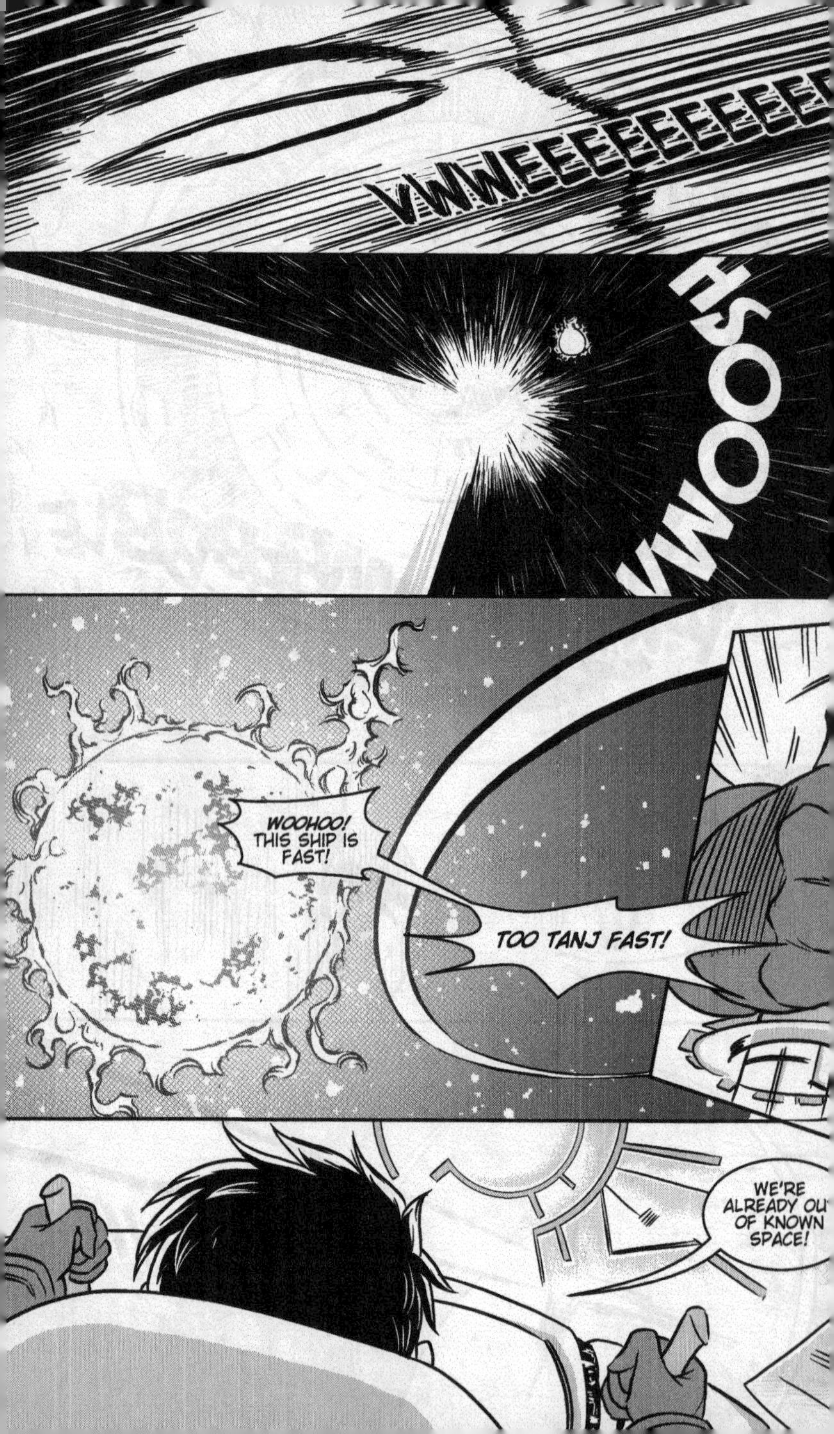
VWWEEEEEEEEEEEE
WOOOSH
WOOHOO! THIS SHIP IS FAST!
TOO TANJ FAST!
WE'RE ALREADY OUT OF KNOWN SPACE!

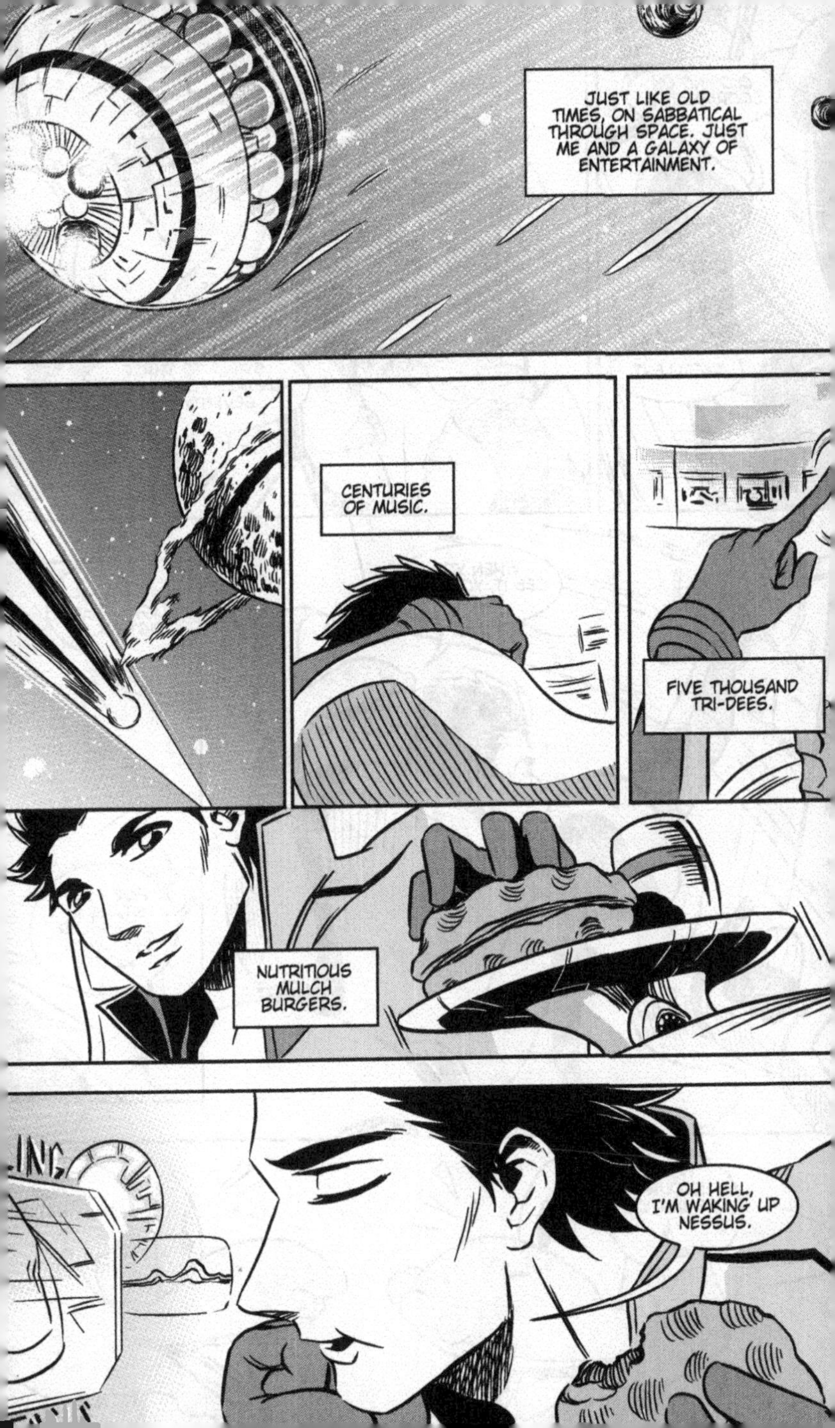
JUST LIKE OLD TIMES, ON SABBATICAL THROUGH SPACE. JUST ME AND A GALAXY OF ENTERTAINMENT.
CENTURIES OF MUSIC.
FIVE THOUSAND TRI-DEES.
NUTRITIOUS MULCH BURGERS.
OH HELL, I'M WAKING UP NESSUS.

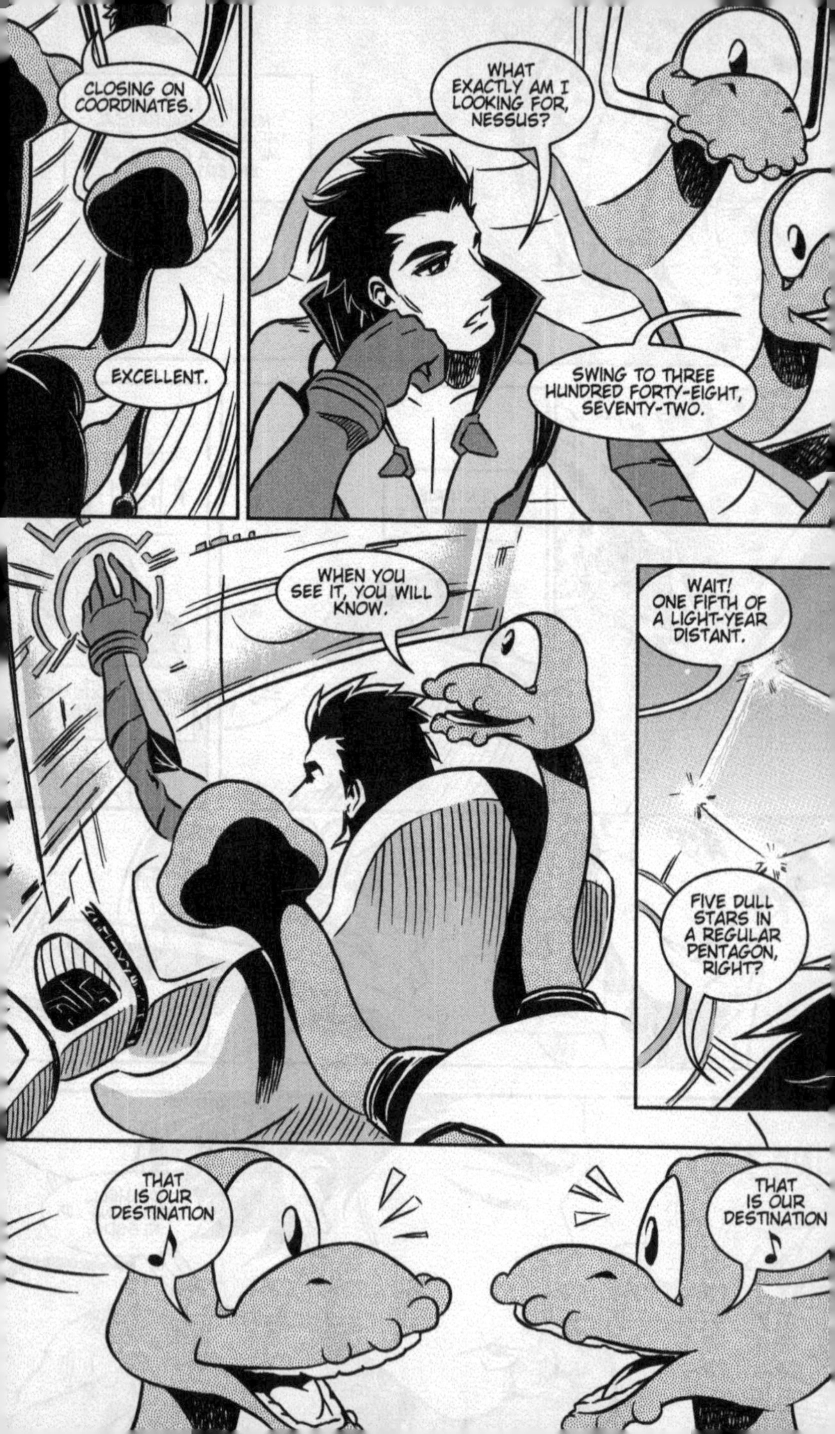
CLOSING ON COORDINATES.
EXCELLENT.
WHAT EXACTLY AM I LOOKING FOR, NESSUS?
SWING TO THREE HUNDRED FORTY-EIGHT, SEVENTY-TWO.
WHEN YOU SEE IT, YOU WILL KNOW.
WAIT! ONE FIFTH OF A LIGHT-YEAR DISTANT.
FIVE DULL STARS IN A REGULAR PENTAGON, RIGHT?
THAT IS OUR DESTINATION ♪
THAT IS OUR DESTINATION ♪

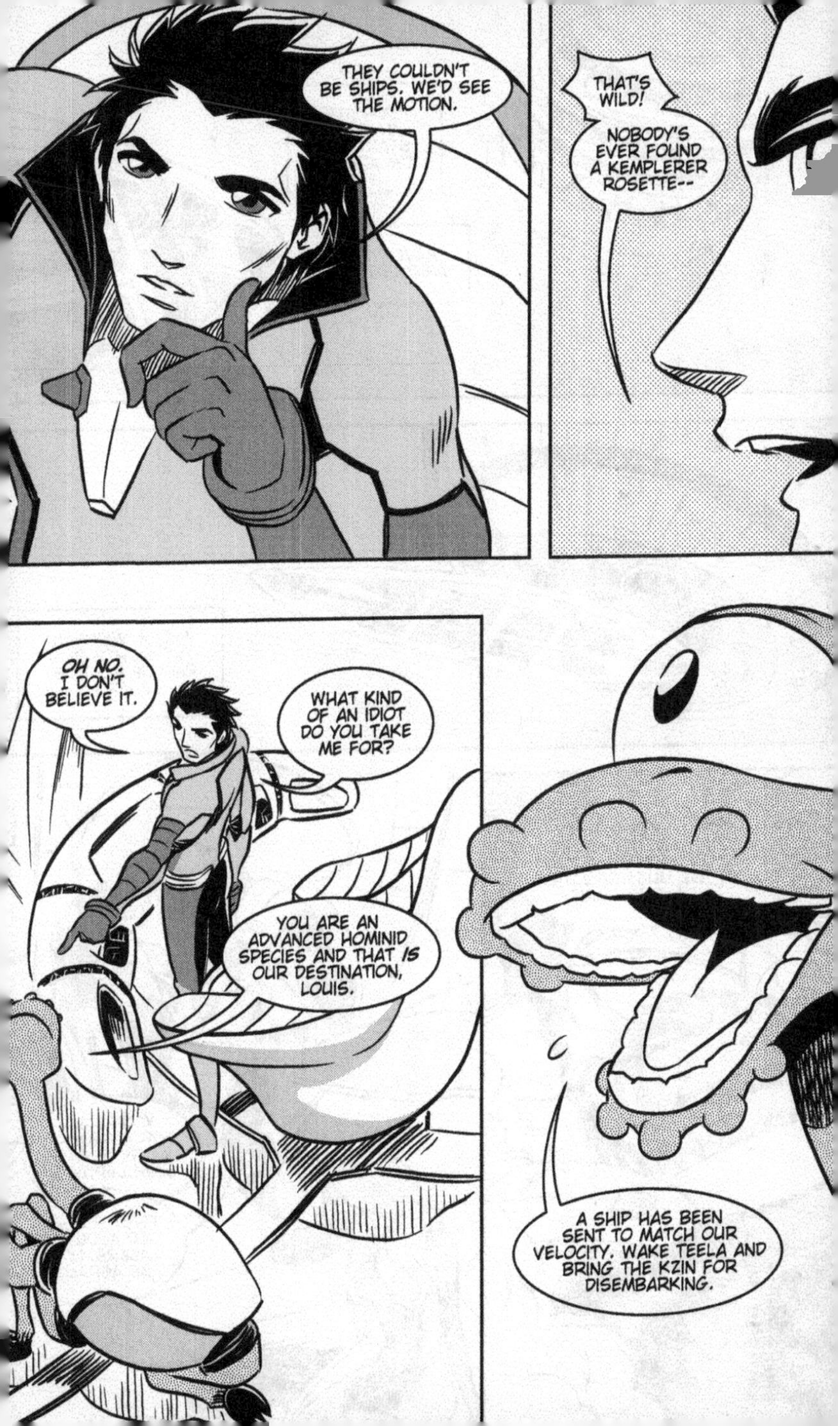
THEY COULDN'T BE SHIPS. WE'D SEE THE MOTION.
THAT'S WILD!
NOBODY'S EVER FOUND A KEMPLERER ROSETTE--
OH NO. I DON'T BELIEVE IT.
WHAT KIND OF AN IDIOT DO YOU TAKE ME FOR?
YOU ARE AN ADVANCED HOMINID SPECIES AND THAT *IS* OUR DESTINATION, LOUIS.
A SHIP HAS BEEN SENT TO MATCH OUR VELOCITY. WAKE TEELA AND BRING THE KZIN FOR DISEMBARKING.

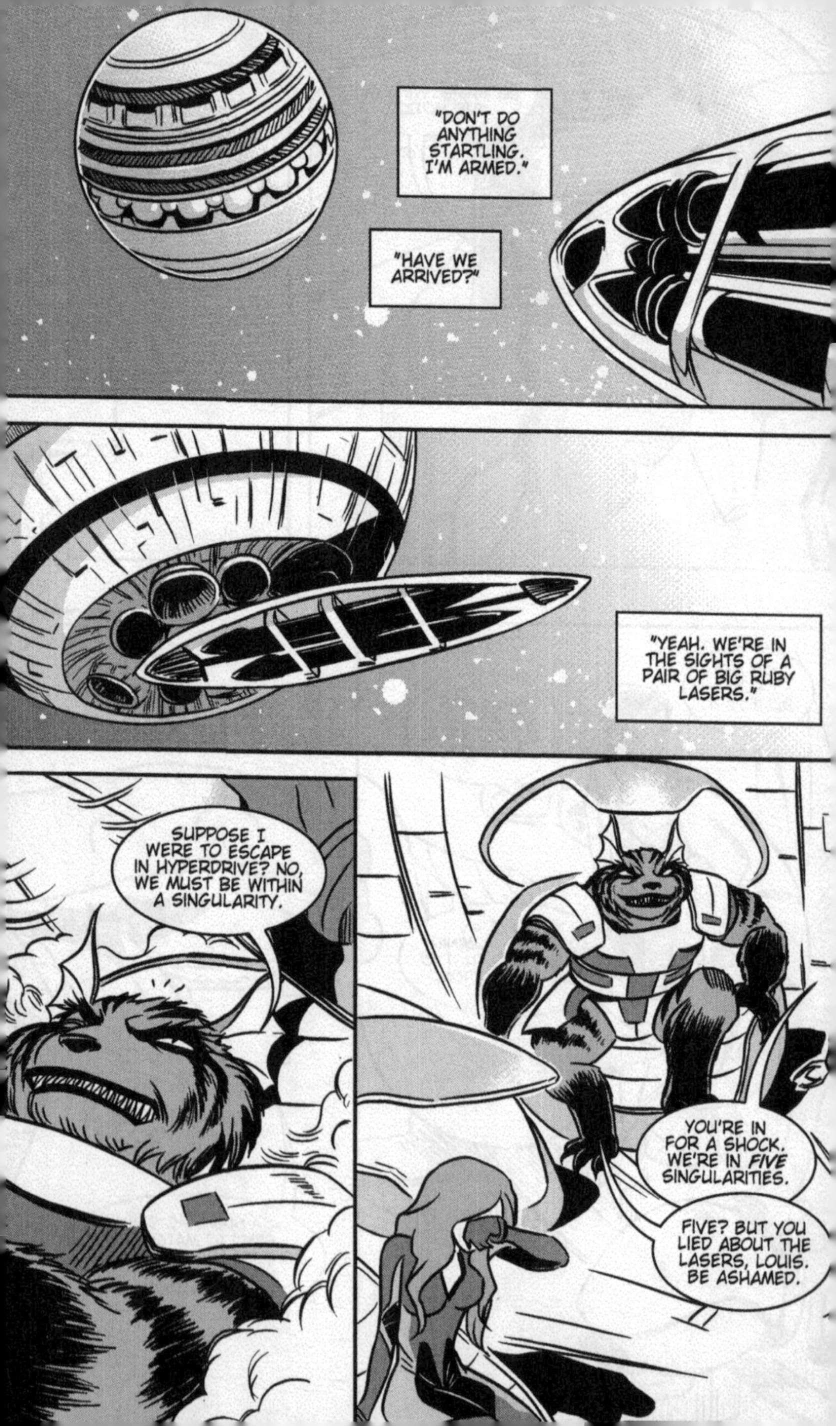
"DON'T DO ANYTHING STARTLING. I'M ARMED."
"HAVE WE ARRIVED?"
"YEAH. WE'RE IN THE SIGHTS OF A PAIR OF BIG RUBY LASERS."
SUPPOSE I WERE TO ESCAPE IN HYPERDRIVE? NO, WE MUST BE WITHIN A SINGULARITY.
YOU'RE IN FOR A SHOCK. WE'RE IN *FIVE* SINGULARITIES.
FIVE? BUT YOU LIED ABOUT THE LASERS, LOUIS. BE ASHAMED.

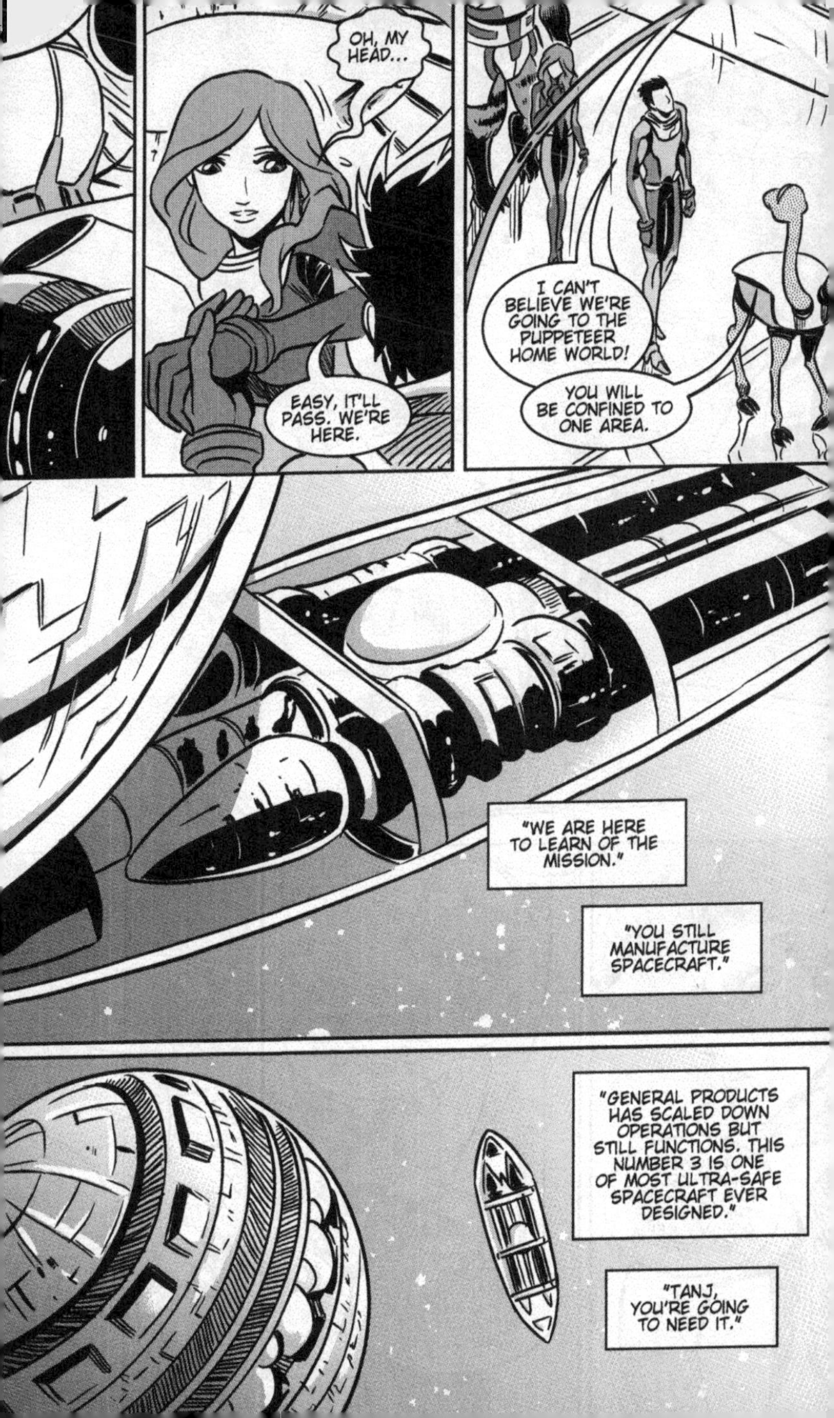
OH, MY HEAD...
EASY, IT'LL PASS. WE'RE HERE.
I CAN'T BELIEVE WE'RE GOING TO THE PUPPETEER HOME WORLD!
YOU WILL BE CONFINED TO ONE AREA.
"WE ARE HERE TO LEARN OF THE MISSION."
"YOU STILL MANUFACTURE SPACECRAFT."
"GENERAL PRODUCTS HAS SCALED DOWN OPERATIONS BUT STILL FUNCTIONS. THIS NUMBER 3 IS ONE OF MOST ULTRA-SAFE SPACECRAFT EVER DESIGNED."
"TANJ, YOU'RE GOING TO NEED IT."

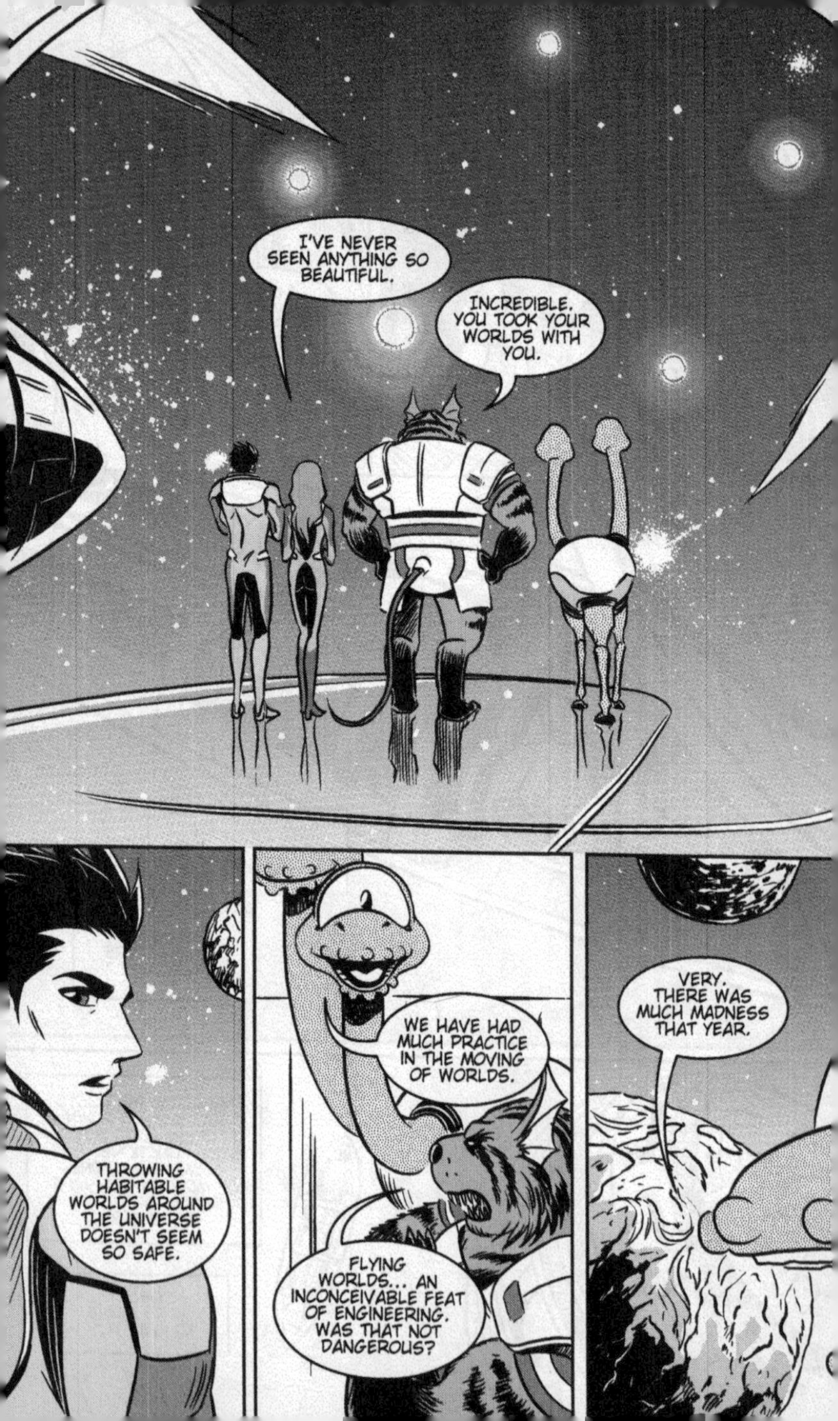
I'VE NEVER SEEN ANYTHING SO BEAUTIFUL.
INCREDIBLE. YOU TOOK YOUR WORLDS WITH YOU.
THROWING HABITABLE WORLDS AROUND THE UNIVERSE DOESN'T SEEM SO SAFE.
WE HAVE HAD MUCH PRACTICE IN THE MOVING OF WORLDS.
FLYING WORLDS... AN INCONCEIVABLE FEAT OF ENGINEERING. WAS THAT NOT DANGEROUS?
VERY. THERE WAS MUCH MADNESS THAT YEAR.

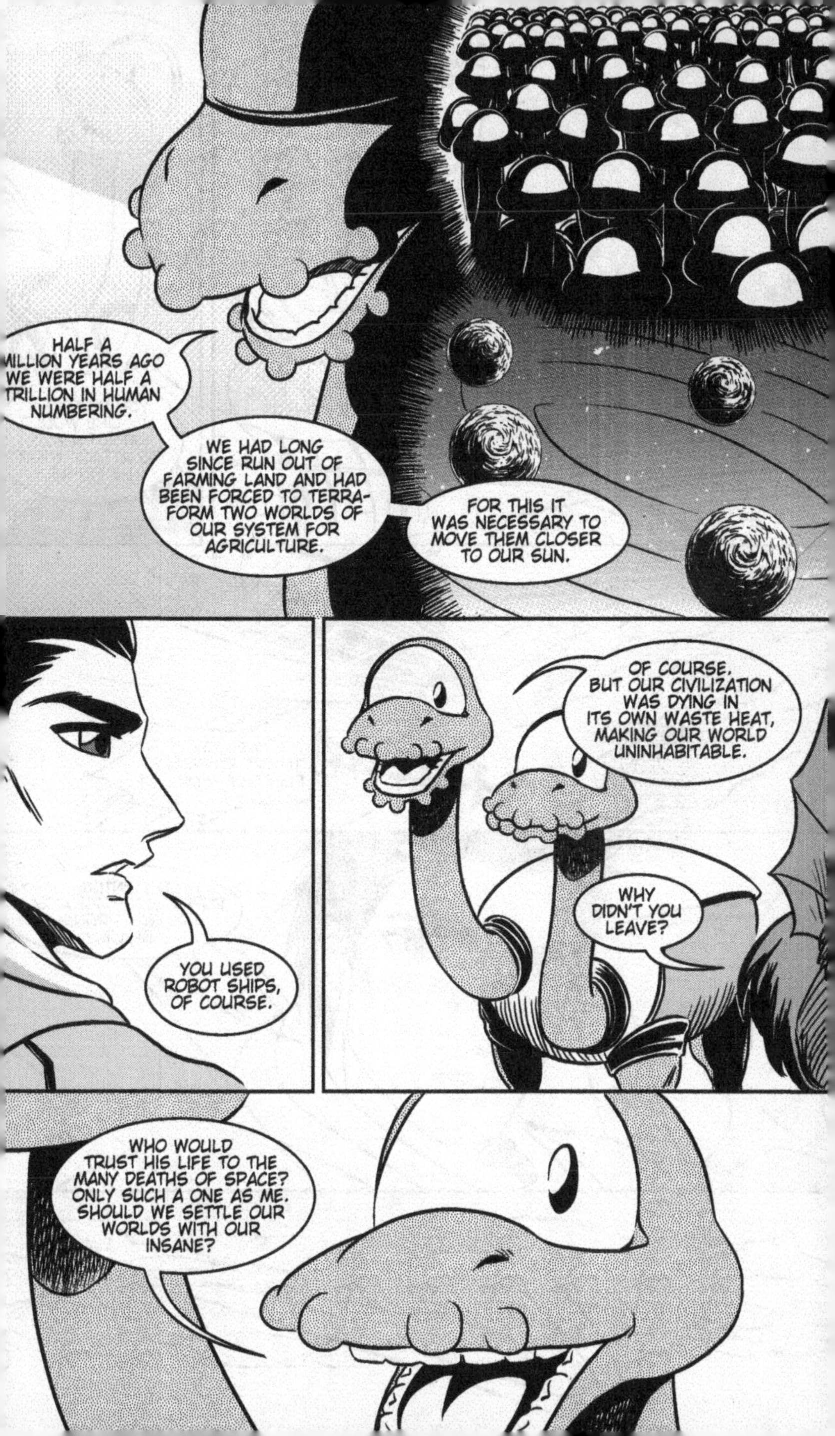

HALF A MILLION YEARS AGO WE WERE HALF A TRILLION IN HUMAN NUMBERING.
WE HAD LONG SINCE RUN OUT OF FARMING LAND AND HAD BEEN FORCED TO TERRA-FORM TWO WORLDS OF OUR SYSTEM FOR AGRICULTURE.
FOR THIS IT WAS NECESSARY TO MOVE THEM CLOSER TO OUR SUN.
YOU USED ROBOT SHIPS, OF COURSE.
OF COURSE, BUT OUR CIVILIZATION WAS DYING IN ITS OWN WASTE HEAT, MAKING OUR WORLD UNINHABITABLE.
WHY DIDN'T YOU LEAVE?
WHO WOULD TRUST HIS LIFE TO THE MANY DEATHS OF SPACE? ONLY SUCH A ONE AS ME. SHOULD WE SETTLE OUR WORLDS WITH OUR INSANE?

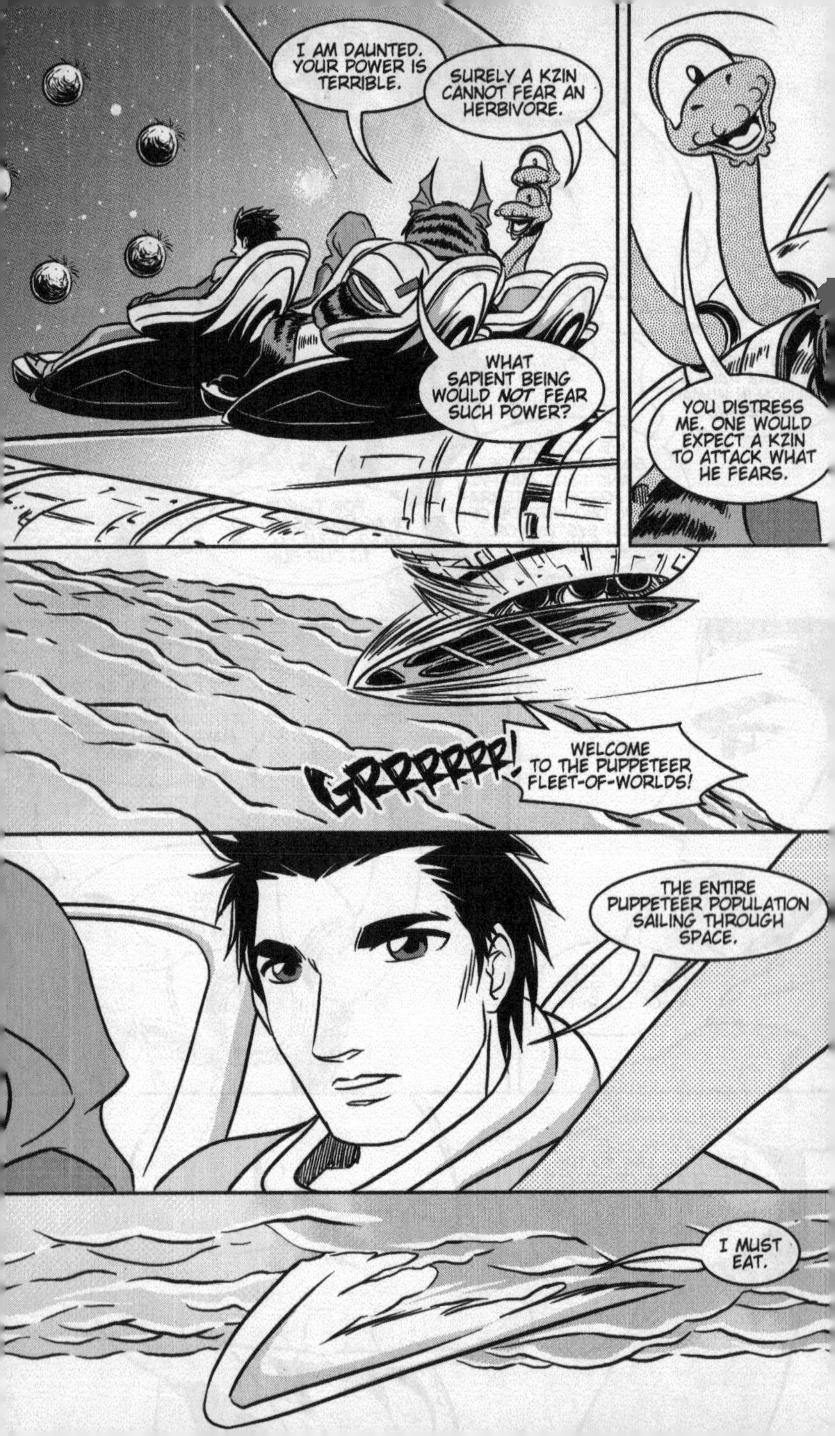
I AM DAUNTED. YOUR POWER IS TERRIBLE.
SURELY A KZIN CANNOT FEAR AN HERBIVORE.
WHAT SAPIENT BEING WOULD *NOT* FEAR SUCH POWER?
YOU DISTRESS ME. ONE WOULD EXPECT A KZIN TO ATTACK WHAT HE FEARS.
GRRRRRR!
WELCOME TO THE PUPPETEER FLEET-OF-WORLDS!
THE ENTIRE PUPPETEER POPULATION SAILING THROUGH SPACE.
I MUST EAT.

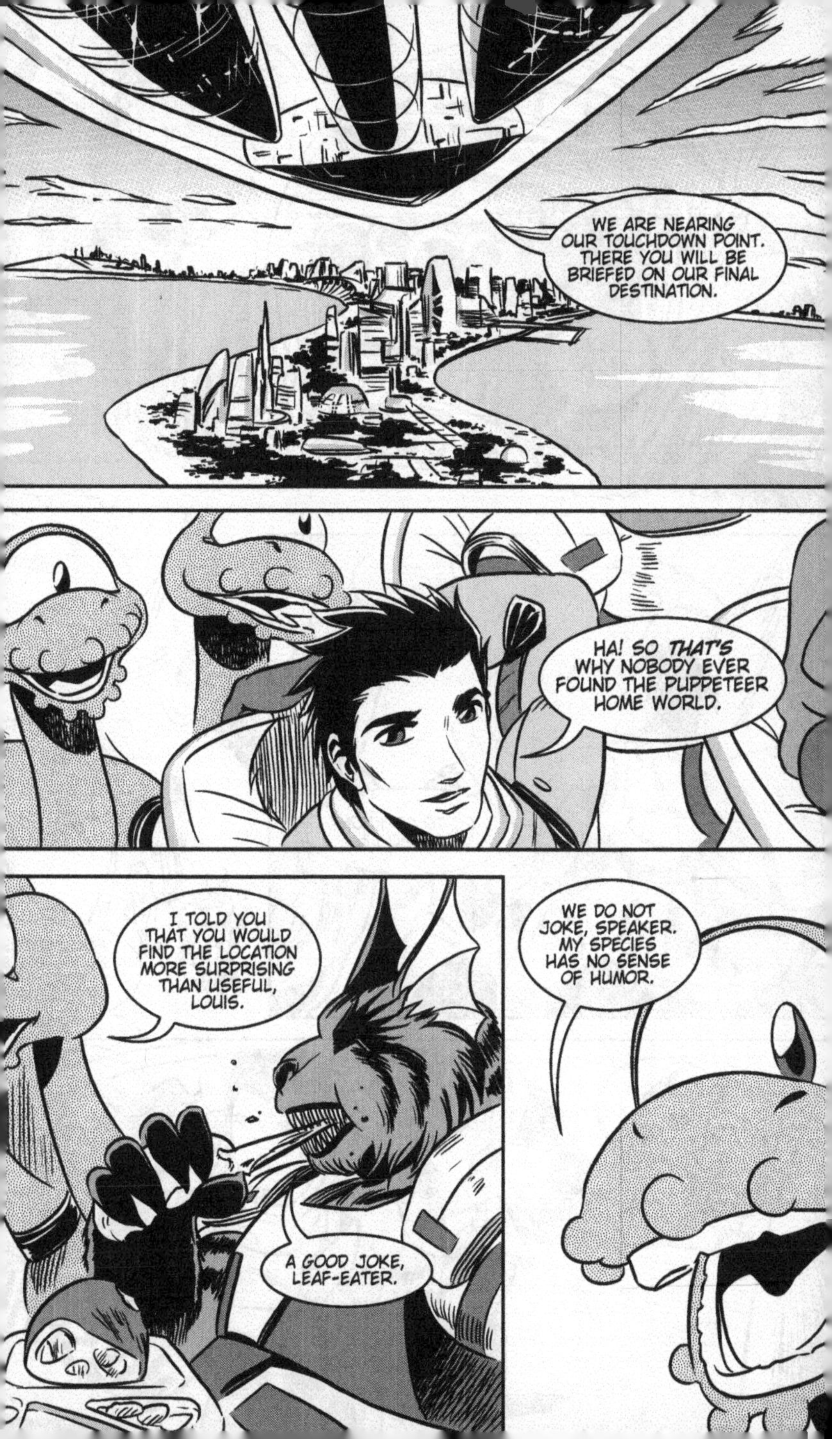
WE ARE NEARING OUR TOUCHDOWN POINT. THERE YOU WILL BE BRIEFED ON OUR FINAL DESTINATION.
HA! SO *THAT'S* WHY NOBODY EVER FOUND THE PUPPETEER HOME WORLD.
I TOLD YOU THAT YOU WOULD FIND THE LOCATION MORE SURPRISING THAN USEFUL, LOUIS.
A GOOD JOKE, LEAF-EATER.
WE DO NOT JOKE, SPEAKER. MY SPECIES HAS NO SENSE OF HUMOR.

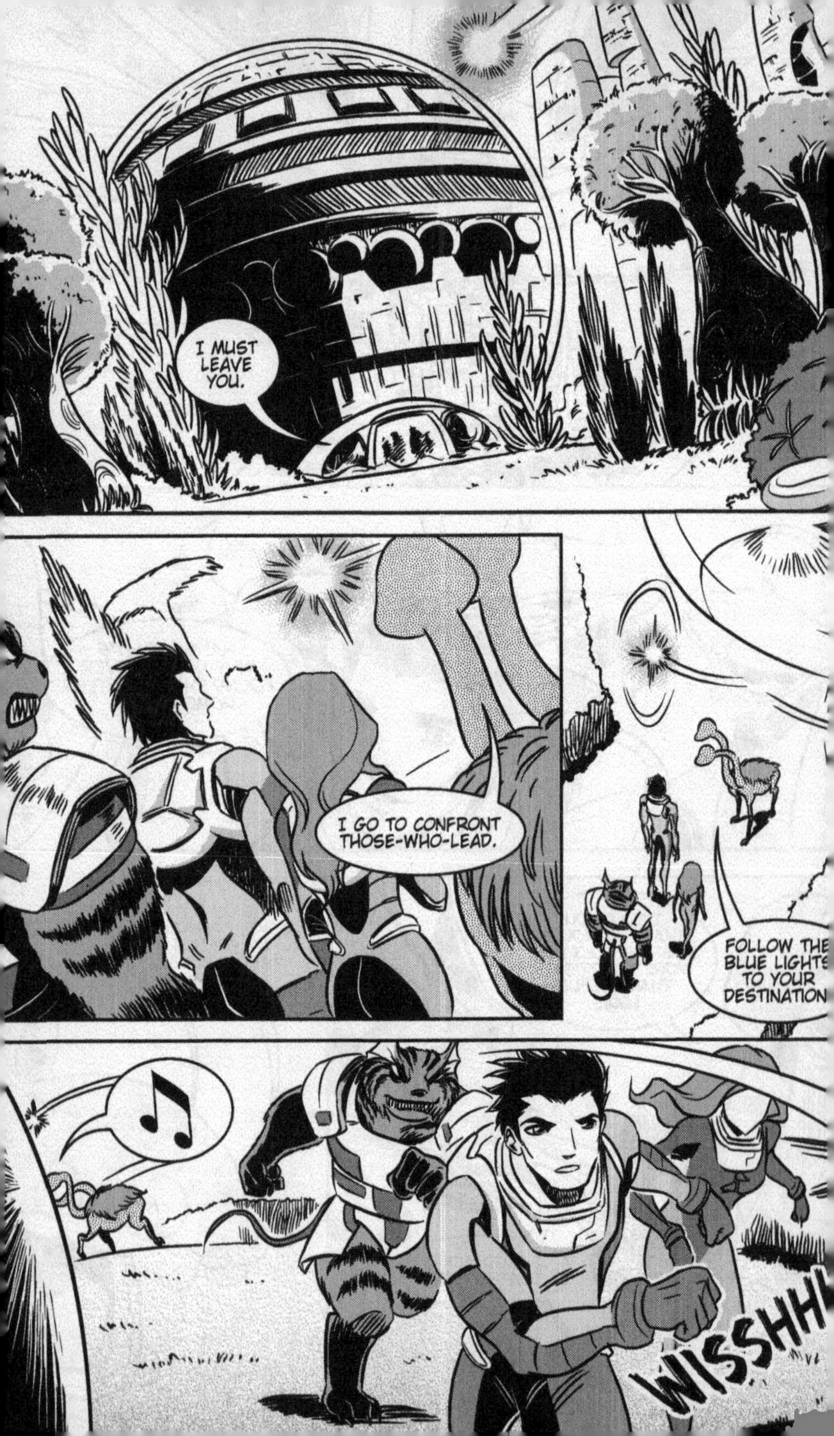
I MUST LEAVE YOU.
I GO TO CONFRONT THOSE-WHO-LEAD.
FOLLOW THE BLUE LIGHTS TO YOUR DESTINATION
♫
WISSHH

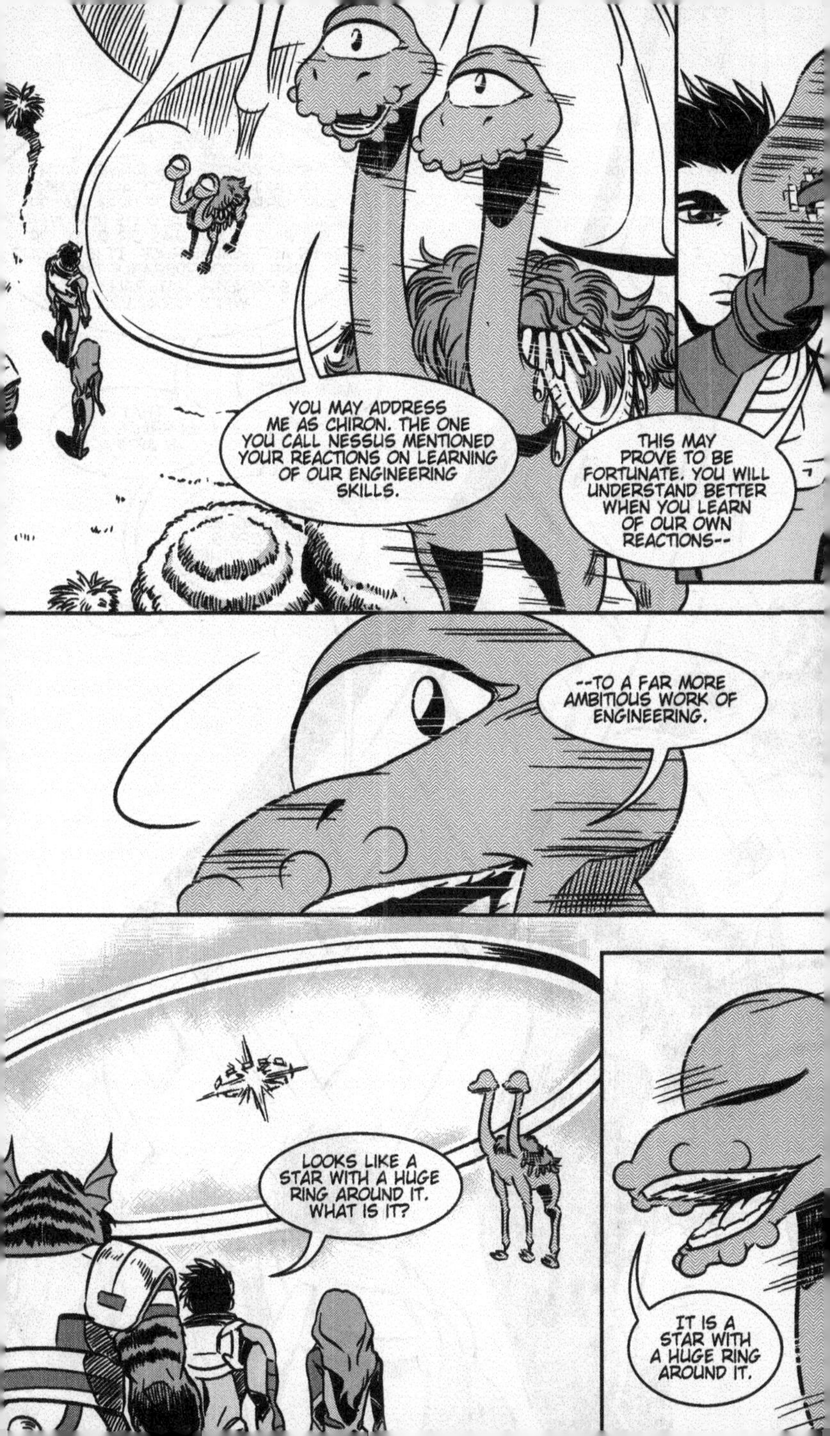
YOU MAY ADDRESS ME AS CHIRON. THE ONE YOU CALL NESSUS MENTIONED YOUR REACTIONS ON LEARNING OF OUR ENGINEERING SKILLS.
THIS MAY PROVE TO BE FORTUNATE. YOU WILL UNDERSTAND BETTER WHEN YOU LEARN OF OUR OWN REACTIONS--
--TO A FAR MORE AMBITIOUS WORK OF ENGINEERING.
LOOKS LIKE A STAR WITH A HUGE RING AROUND IT. WHAT IS IT?
IT IS A STAR WITH A HUGE RING AROUND IT.

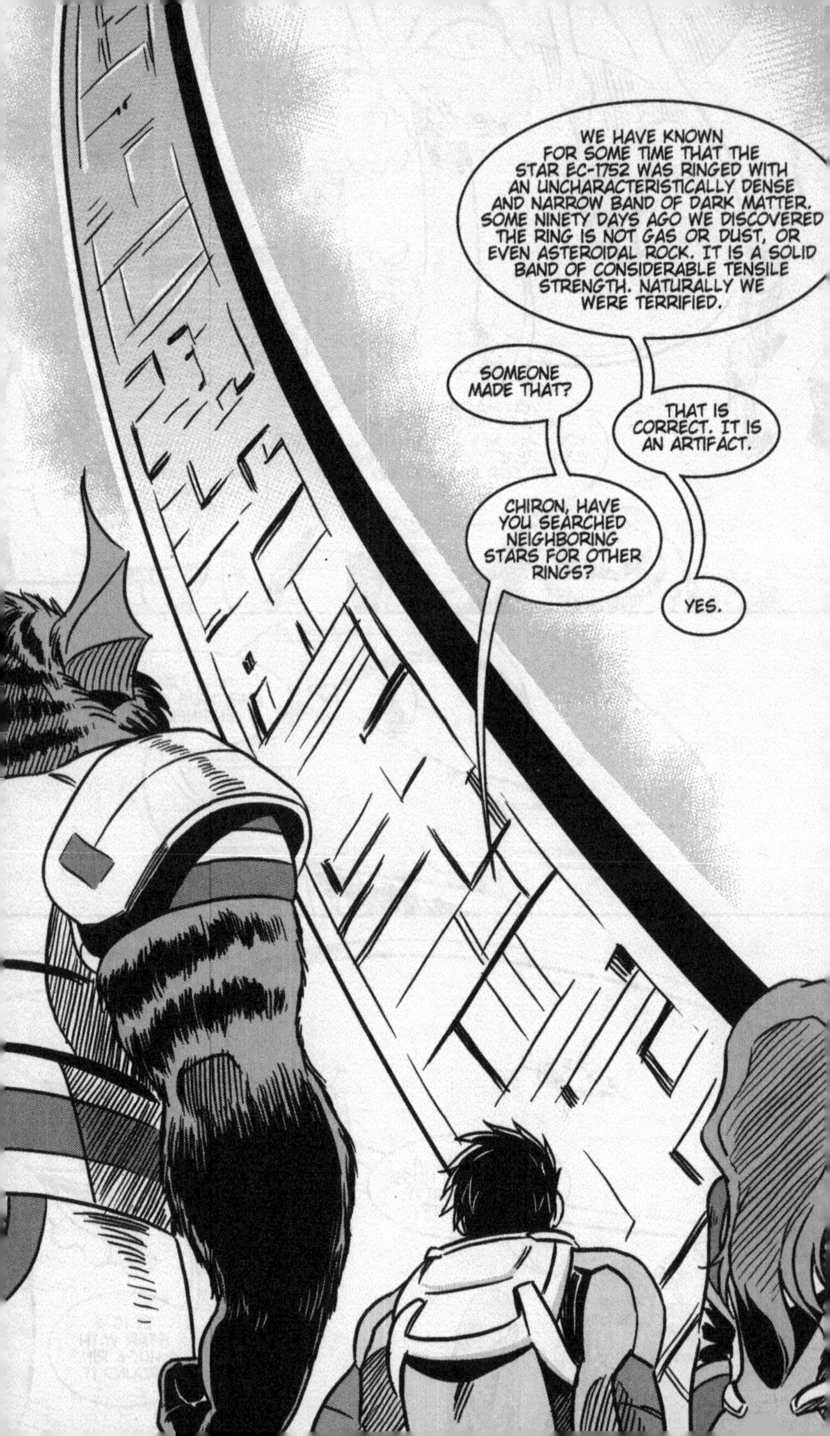
WE HAVE KNOWN FOR SOME TIME THAT THE STAR EC-1752 WAS RINGED WITH AN UNCHARACTERISTICALLY DENSE AND NARROW BAND OF DARK MATTER. SOME NINETY DAYS AGO WE DISCOVERED THE RING IS NOT GAS OR DUST, OR EVEN ASTEROIDAL ROCK. IT IS A SOLID BAND OF CONSIDERABLE TENSILE STRENGTH. NATURALLY WE WERE TERRIFIED.
SOMEONE MADE THAT?
THAT IS CORRECT. IT IS AN ARTIFACT.
CHIRON, HAVE YOU SEARCHED NEIGHBORING STARS FOR OTHER RINGS?
YES.

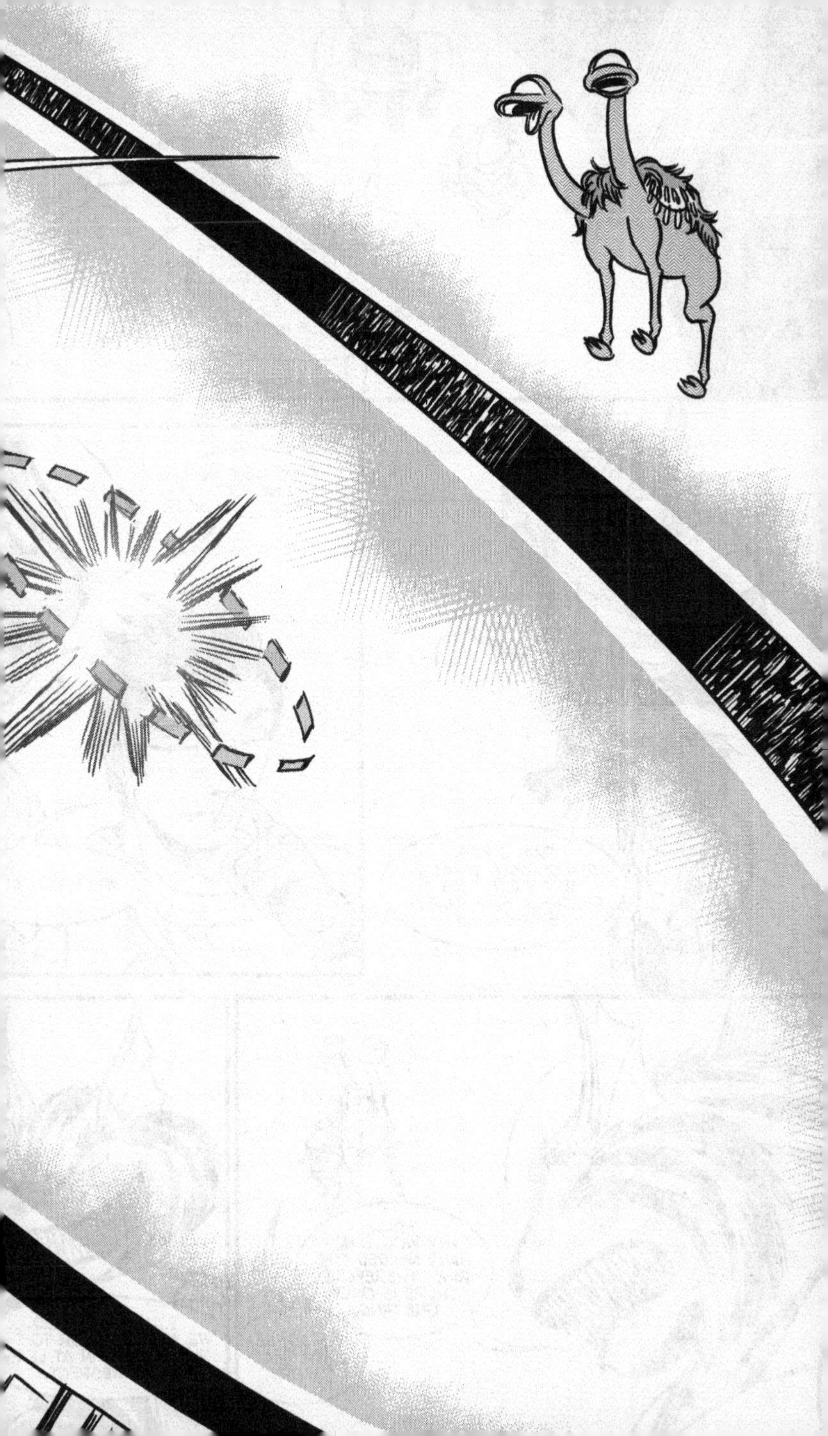

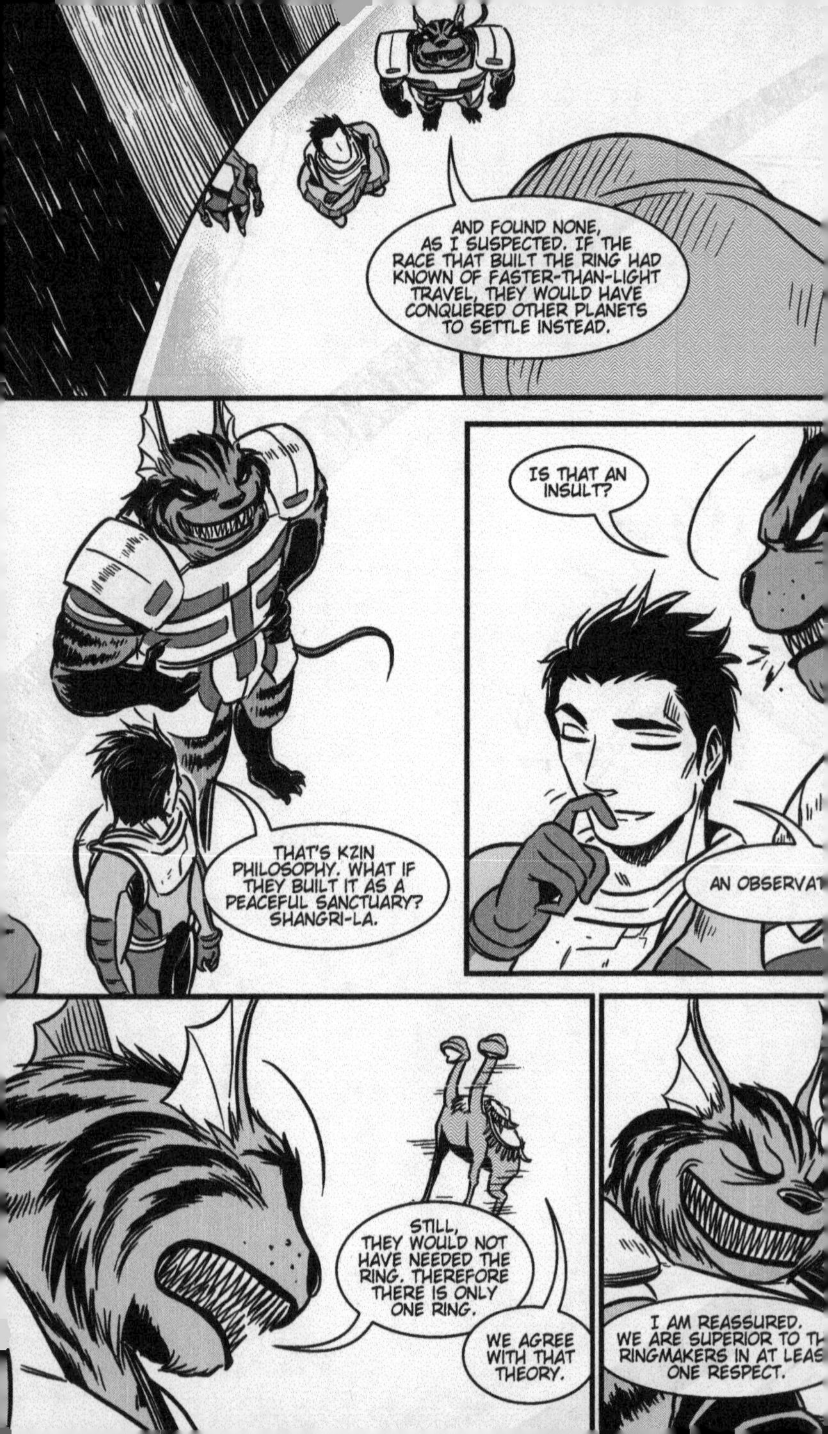
AND FOUND NONE, AS I SUSPECTED. IF THE RACE THAT BUILT THE RING HAD KNOWN OF FASTER-THAN-LIGHT TRAVEL, THEY WOULD HAVE CONQUERED OTHER PLANETS TO SETTLE INSTEAD.
THAT'S KZIN PHILOSOPHY. WHAT IF THEY BUILT IT AS A PEACEFUL SANCTUARY? SHANGRI-LA.
IS THAT AN INSULT?
AN OBSERVAT
STILL, THEY WOULD NOT HAVE NEEDED THE RING. THEREFORE THERE IS ONLY ONE RING.
WE AGREE WITH THAT THEORY.
I AM REASSURED. WE ARE SUPERIOR TO TH RINGMAKERS IN AT LEAS ONE RESPECT.

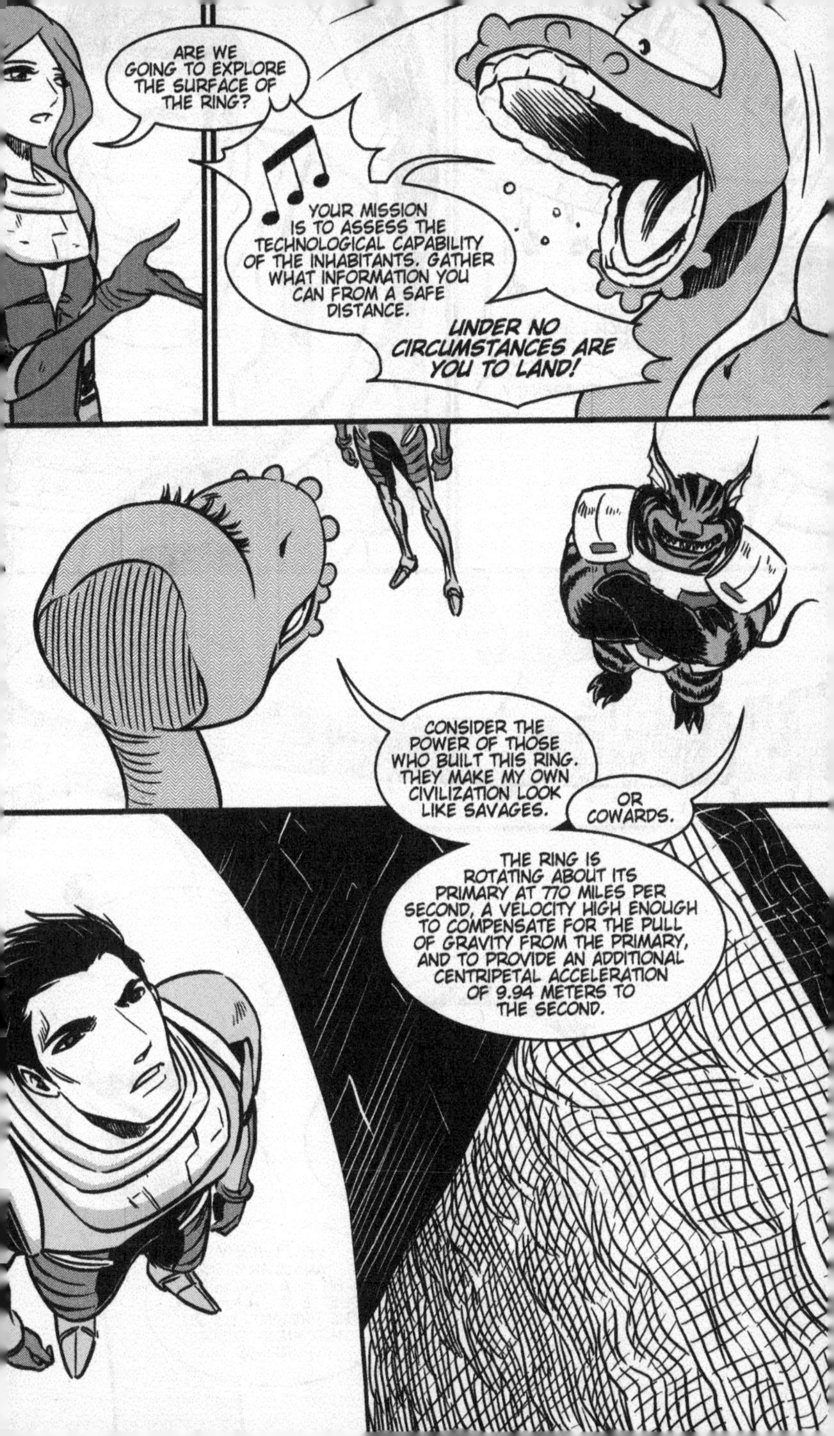
ARE WE GOING TO EXPLORE THE SURFACE OF THE RING?
YOUR MISSION IS TO ASSESS THE TECHNOLOGICAL CAPABILITY OF THE INHABITANTS. GATHER WHAT INFORMATION YOU CAN FROM A SAFE DISTANCE.
UNDER NO CIRCUMSTANCES ARE YOU TO LAND!
CONSIDER THE POWER OF THOSE WHO BUILT THIS RING. THEY MAKE MY OWN CIVILIZATION LOOK LIKE SAVAGES.
OR COWARDS.
THE RING IS ROTATING ABOUT ITS PRIMARY AT 770 MILES PER SECOND, A VELOCITY HIGH ENOUGH TO COMPENSATE FOR THE PULL OF GRAVITY FROM THE PRIMARY, AND TO PROVIDE AN ADDITIONAL CENTRIPETAL ACCELERATION OF 9.94 METERS TO THE SECOND.

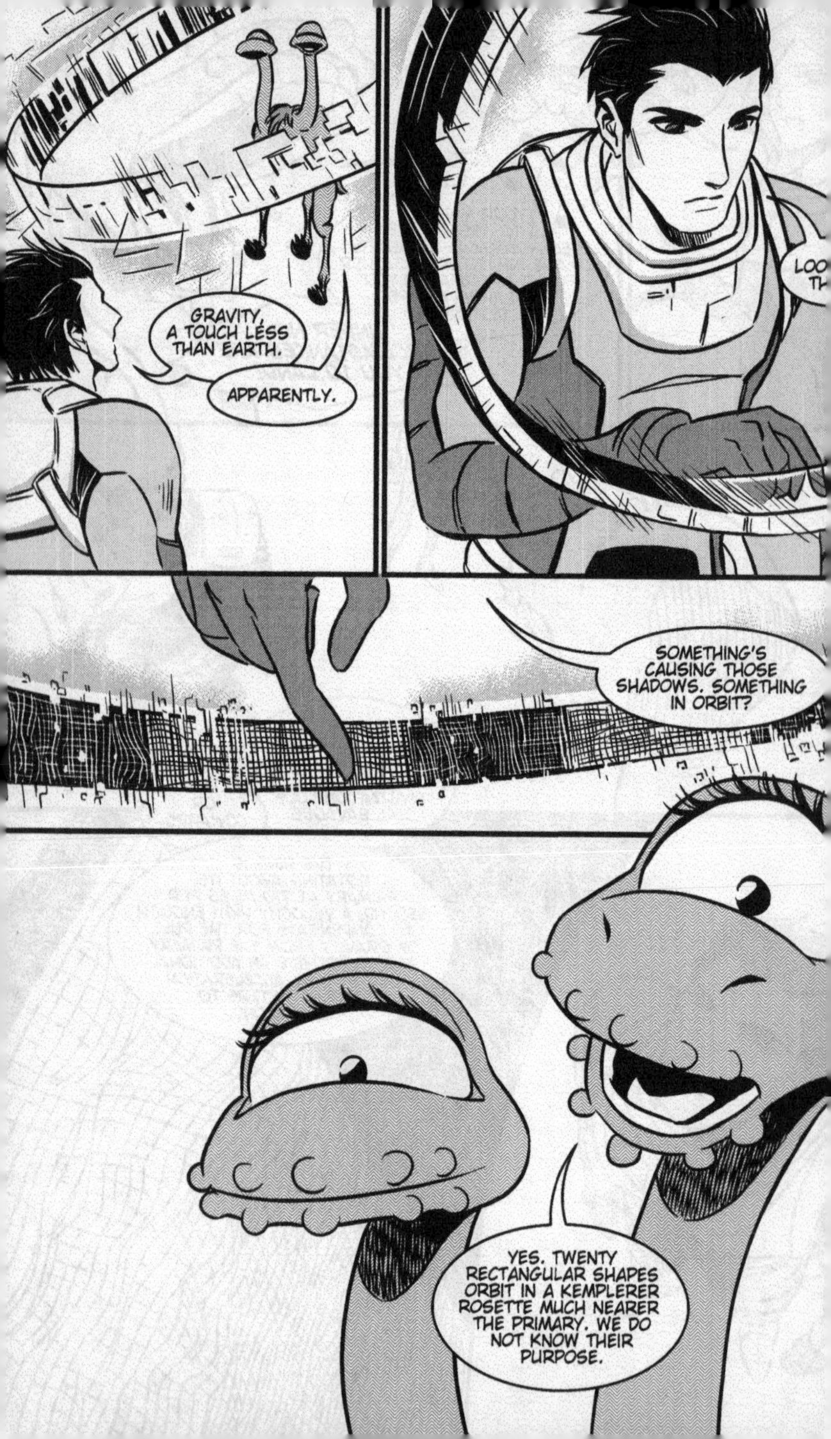
GRAVITY, A TOUCH LESS THAN EARTH.
APPARENTLY.
SOMETHING'S CAUSING THOSE SHADOWS. SOMETHING IN ORBIT?
YES. TWENTY RECTANGULAR SHAPES ORBIT IN A KEMPLERER ROSETTE MUCH NEARER THE PRIMARY. WE DO NOT KNOW THEIR PURPOSE.

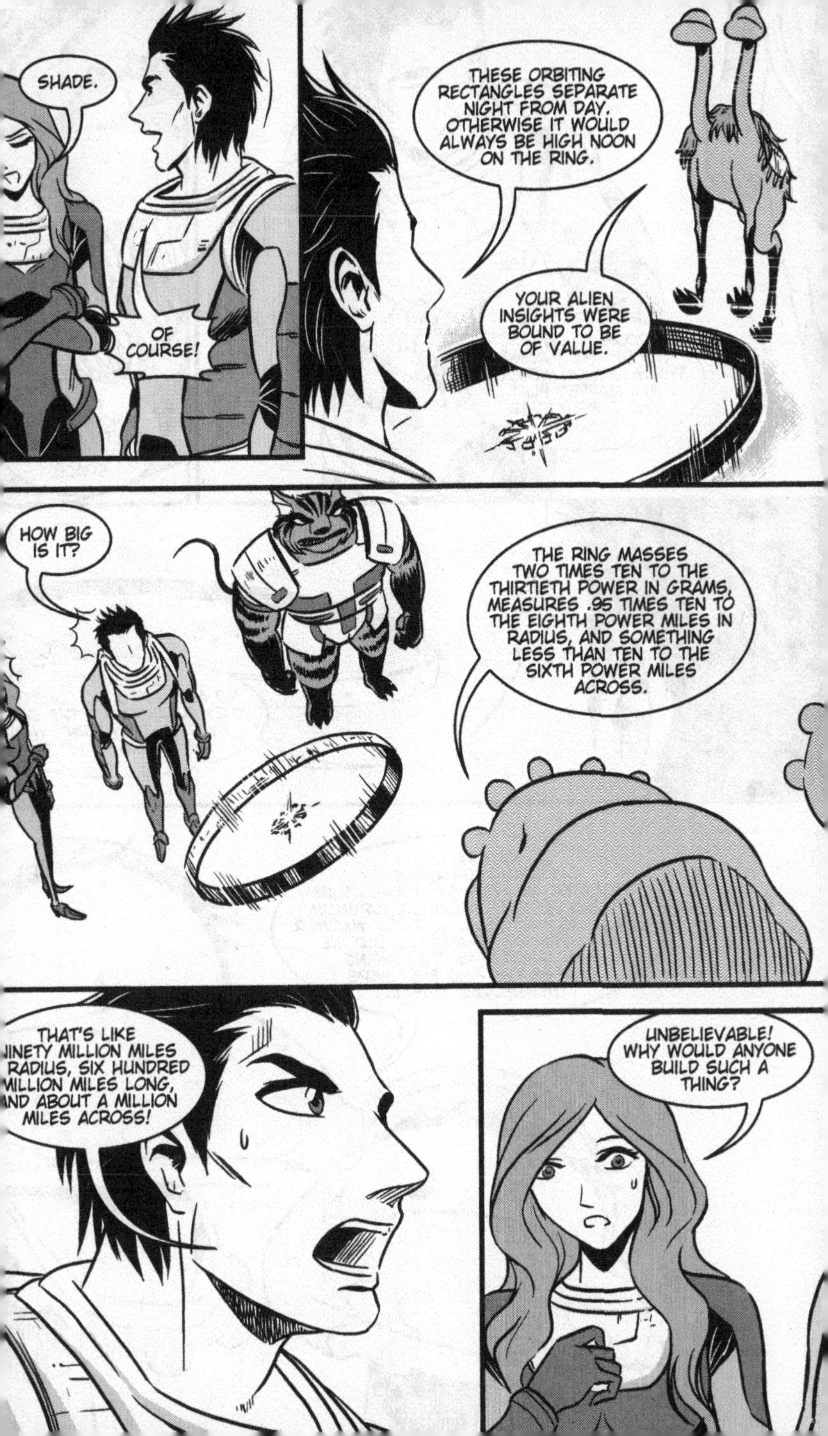
SHADE.
OF COURSE!
THESE ORBITING RECTANGLES SEPARATE NIGHT FROM DAY. OTHERWISE IT WOULD ALWAYS BE HIGH NOON ON THE RING.
YOUR ALIEN INSIGHTS WERE BOUND TO BE OF VALUE.
HOW BIG IS IT?
THE RING MASSES TWO TIMES TEN TO THE THIRTIETH POWER IN GRAMS, MEASURES .95 TIMES TEN TO THE EIGHTH POWER MILES IN RADIUS, AND SOMETHING LESS THAN TEN TO THE SIXTH POWER MILES ACROSS.
THAT'S LIKE INETY MILLION MILES RADIUS, SIX HUNDRED MILLION MILES LONG, ND ABOUT A MILLION MILES ACROSS!
UNBELIEVABLE! WHY WOULD ANYONE BUILD SUCH A THING?

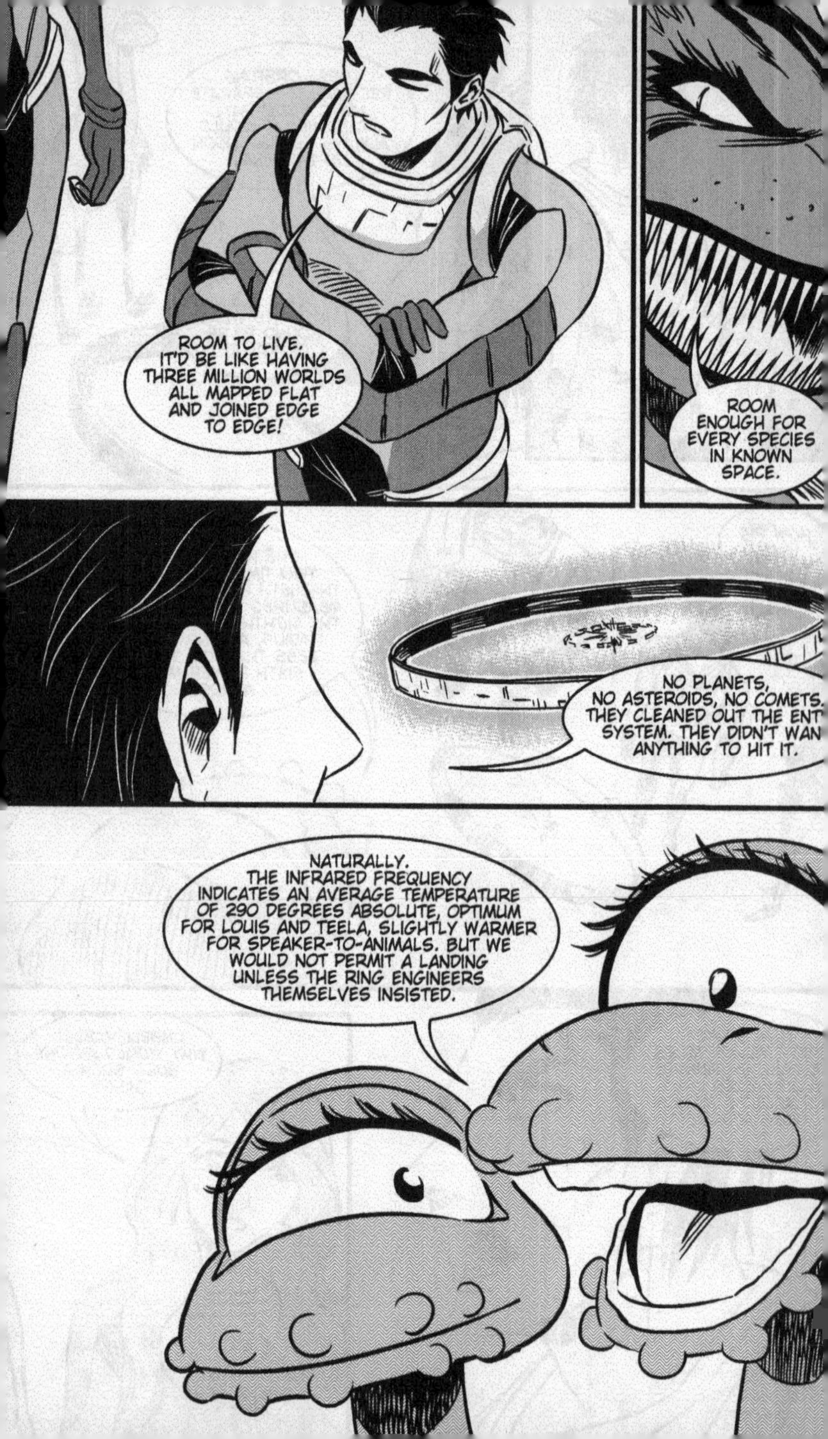
ROOM TO LIVE. IT'D BE LIKE HAVING THREE MILLION WORLDS ALL MAPPED FLAT AND JOINED EDGE TO EDGE!
ROOM ENOUGH FOR EVERY SPECIES IN KNOWN SPACE.
NO PLANETS, NO ASTEROIDS, NO COMETS. THEY CLEANED OUT THE ENT SYSTEM. THEY DIDN'T WAN ANYTHING TO HIT IT.
NATURALLY. THE INFRARED FREQUENCY INDICATES AN AVERAGE TEMPERATURE OF 290 DEGREES ABSOLUTE, OPTIMUM FOR LOUIS AND TEELA, SLIGHTLY WARMER FOR SPEAKER-TO-ANIMALS. BUT WE WOULD NOT PERMIT A LANDING UNLESS THE RING ENGINEERS THEMSELVES INSISTED.

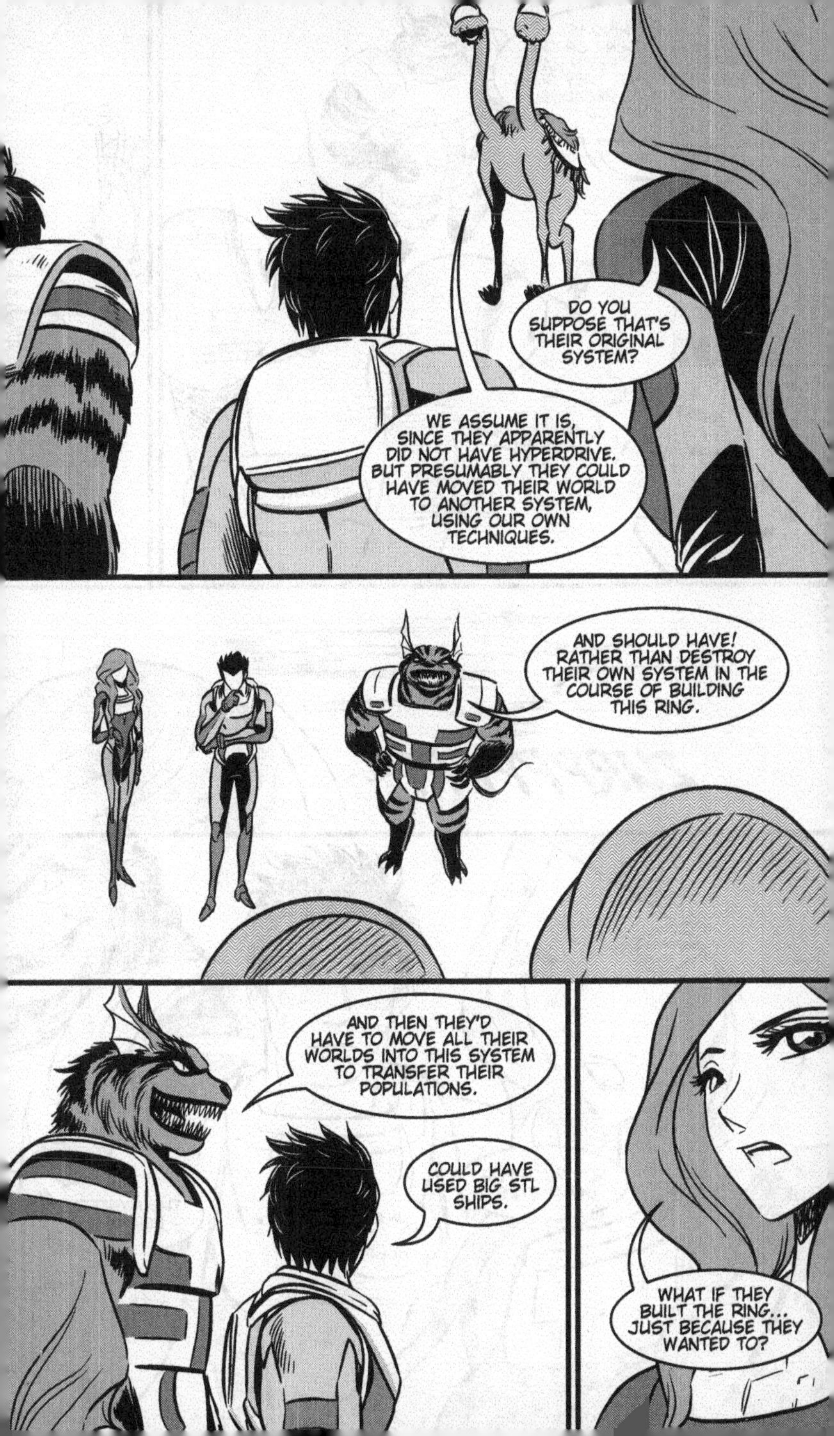
DO YOU SUPPOSE THAT'S THEIR ORIGINAL SYSTEM?
WE ASSUME IT IS, SINCE THEY APPARENTLY DID NOT HAVE HYPERDRIVE. BUT PRESUMABLY THEY COULD HAVE MOVED THEIR WORLD TO ANOTHER SYSTEM, USING OUR OWN TECHNIQUES.
AND SHOULD HAVE! RATHER THAN DESTROY THEIR OWN SYSTEM IN THE COURSE OF BUILDING THIS RING.
AND THEN THEY'D HAVE TO MOVE ALL THEIR WORLDS INTO THIS SYSTEM TO TRANSFER THEIR POPULATIONS.
COULD HAVE USED BIG STL SHIPS.
WHAT IF THEY BUILT THE RING... JUST BECAUSE THEY WANTED TO?

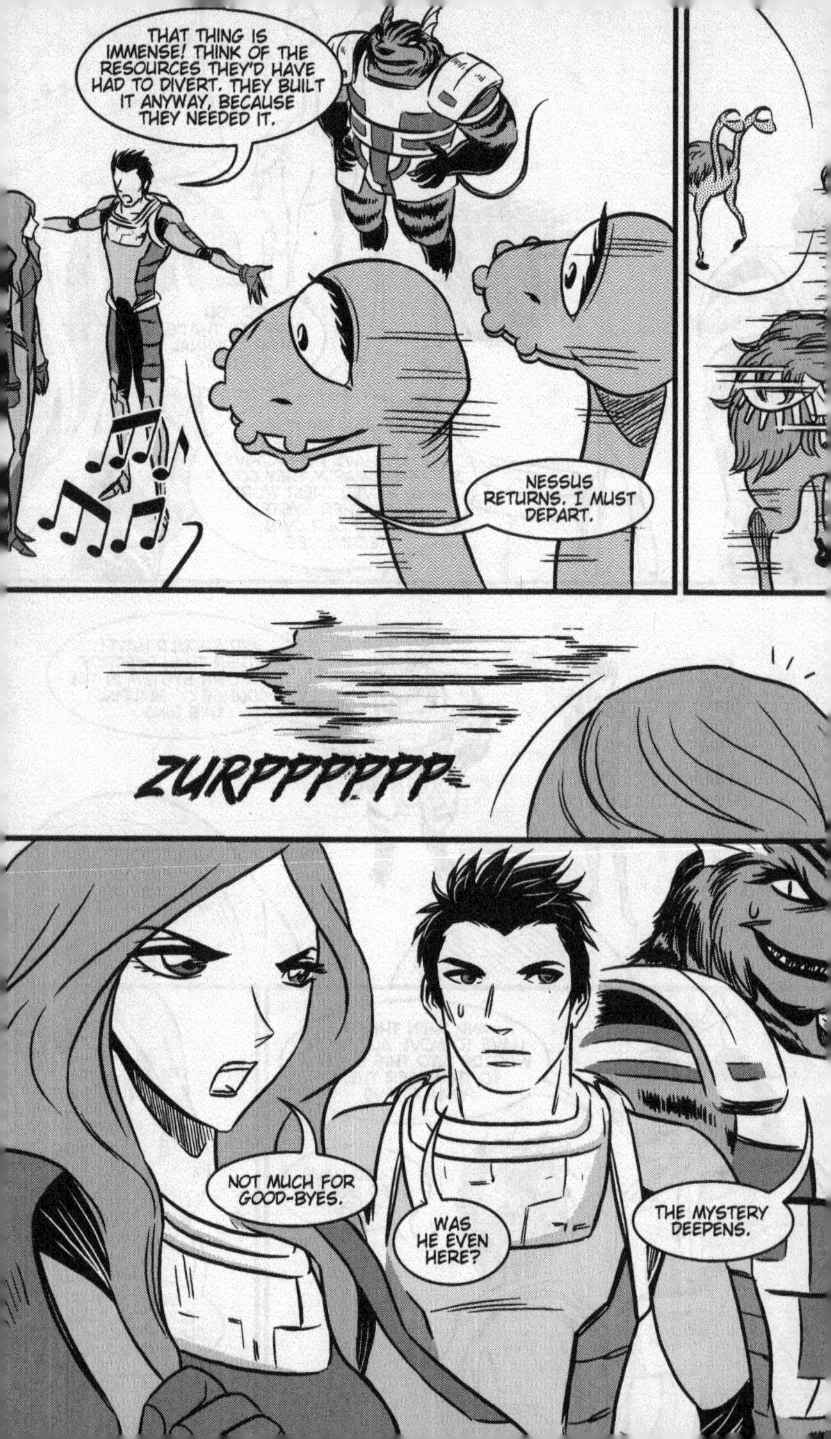
THAT THING IS IMMENSE! THINK OF THE RESOURCES THEY'D HAVE HAD TO DIVERT. THEY BUILT IT ANYWAY, BECAUSE THEY NEEDED IT.
NESSUS RETURNS. I MUST DEPART.
ZURPPPPPPP
NOT MUCH FOR GOOD-BYES.
WAS HE EVEN HERE?
THE MYSTERY DEEPENS.

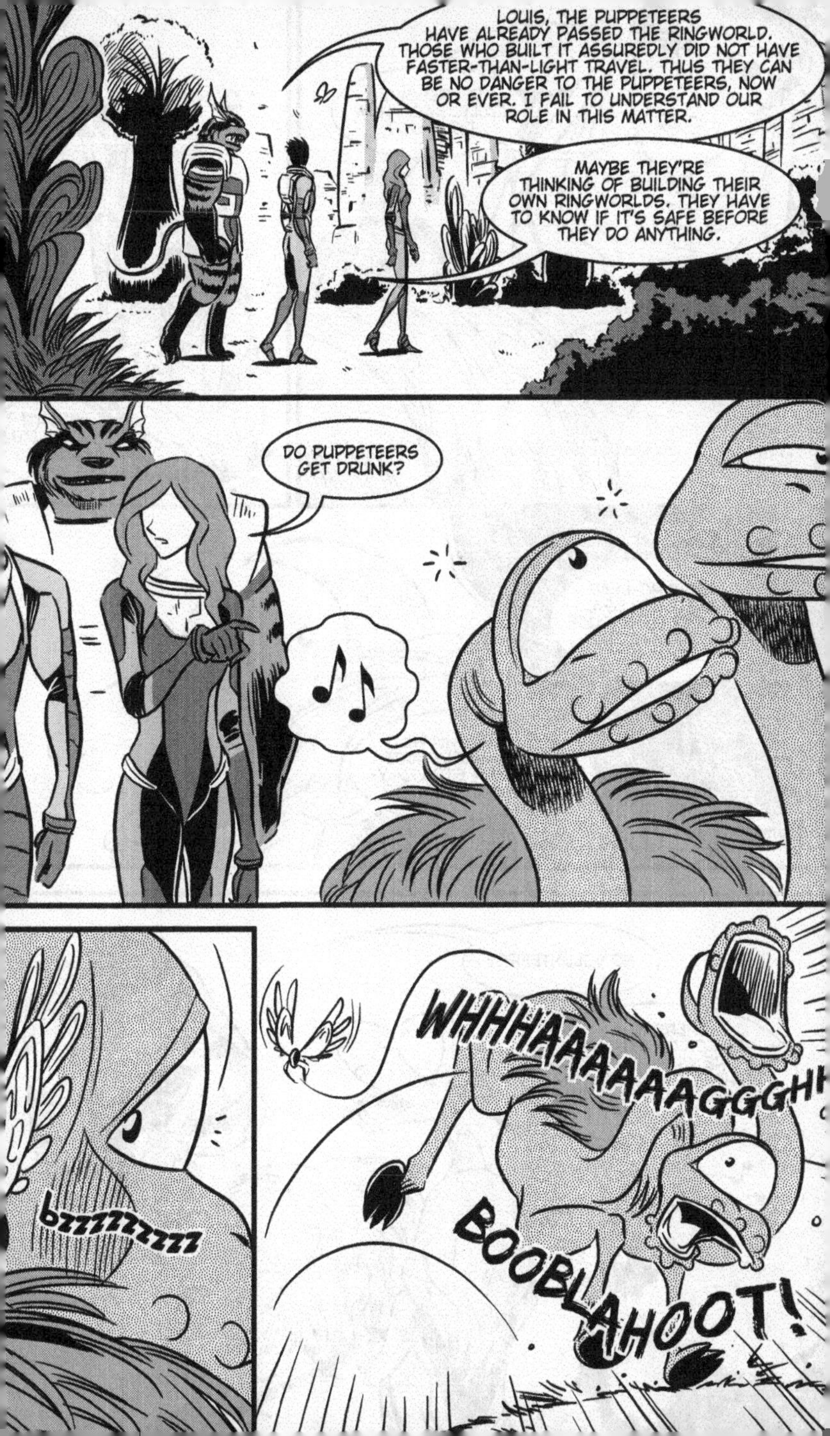
LOUIS, THE PUPPETEERS HAVE ALREADY PASSED THE RINGWORLD. THOSE WHO BUILT IT ASSUREDLY DID NOT HAVE FASTER-THAN-LIGHT TRAVEL. THUS THEY CAN BE NO DANGER TO THE PUPPETEERS, NOW OR EVER. I FAIL TO UNDERSTAND OUR ROLE IN THIS MATTER.
MAYBE THEY'RE THINKING OF BUILDING THEIR OWN RINGWORLDS. THEY HAVE TO KNOW IF IT'S SAFE BEFORE THEY DO ANYTHING.
DO PUPPETEERS GET DRUNK?
♪ ♪
bzzzzzzzzz
WHHHAAAAAAAAGGGGH!
BOOBLAHOOT!

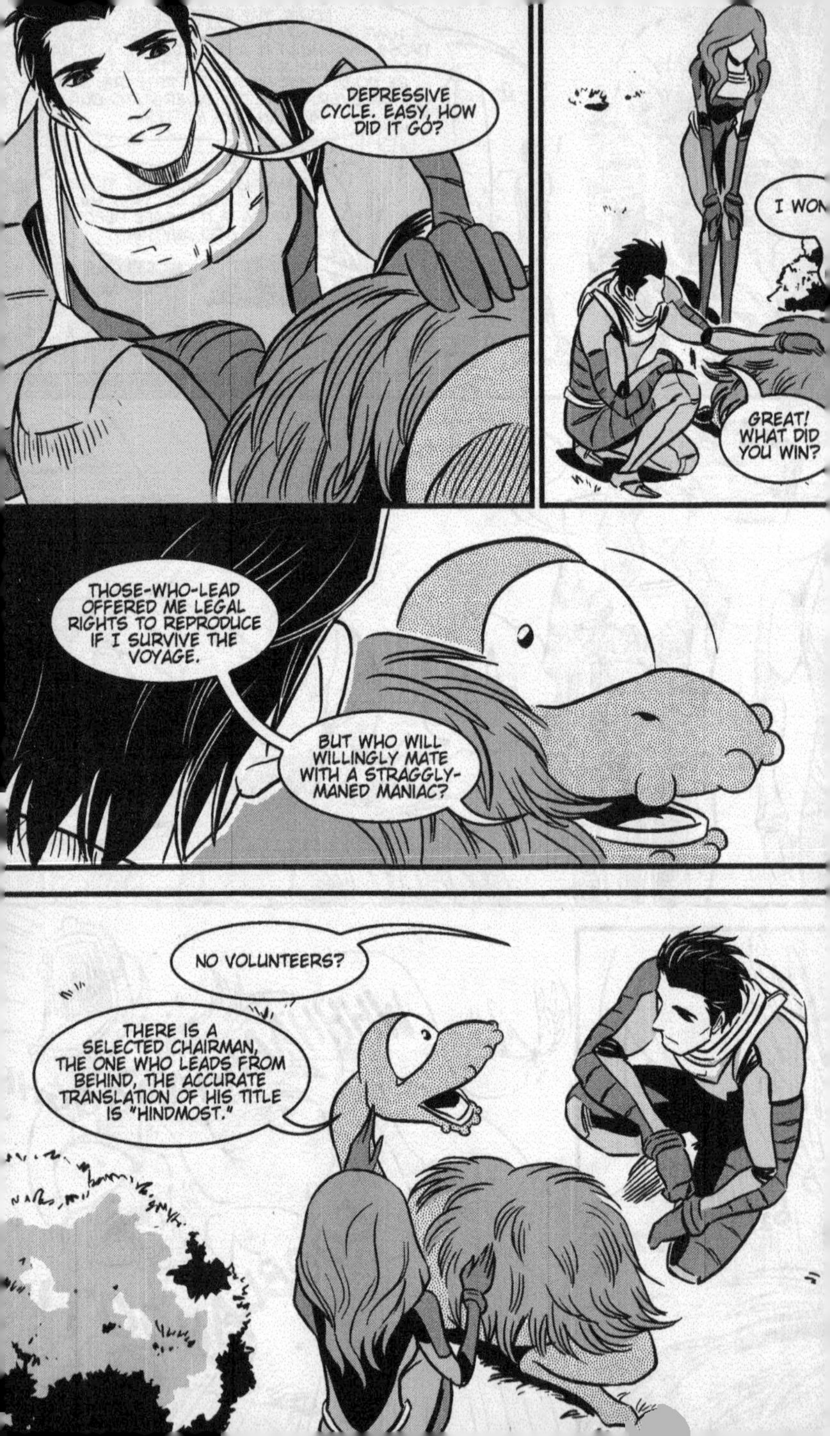
DEPRESSIVE CYCLE. EASY, HOW DID IT GO?
I WON
GREAT! WHAT DID YOU WIN?
THOSE-WHO-LEAD OFFERED ME LEGAL RIGHTS TO REPRODUCE IF I SURVIVE THE VOYAGE.
BUT WHO WILL WILLINGLY MATE WITH A STRAGGLY-MANED MANIAC?
NO VOLUNTEERS?
THERE IS A SELECTED CHAIRMAN, THE ONE WHO LEADS FROM BEHIND, THE ACCURATE TRANSLATION OF HIS TITLE IS "HINDMOST."

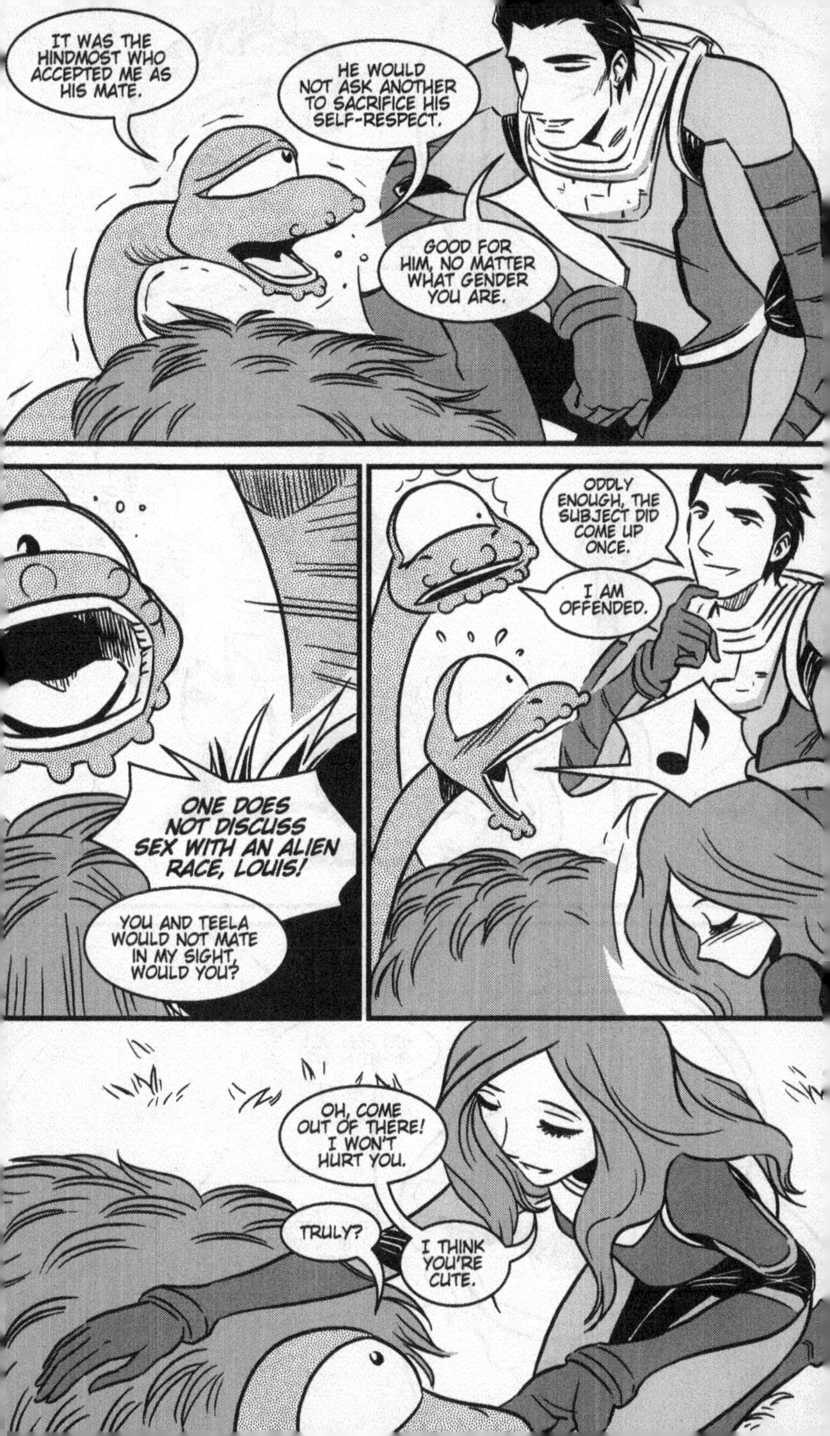
IT WAS THE HINDMOST WHO ACCEPTED ME AS HIS MATE.
HE WOULD NOT ASK ANOTHER TO SACRIFICE HIS SELF-RESPECT.
GOOD FOR HIM, NO MATTER WHAT GENDER YOU ARE.
ONE DOES NOT DISCUSS SEX WITH AN ALIEN RACE, LOUIS!
YOU AND TEELA WOULD NOT MATE IN MY SIGHT, WOULD YOU?
ODDLY ENOUGH, THE SUBJECT DID COME UP ONCE.
I AM OFFENDED.
OH, COME OUT OF THERE! I WON'T HURT YOU.
TRULY?
I THINK YOU'RE CUTE.

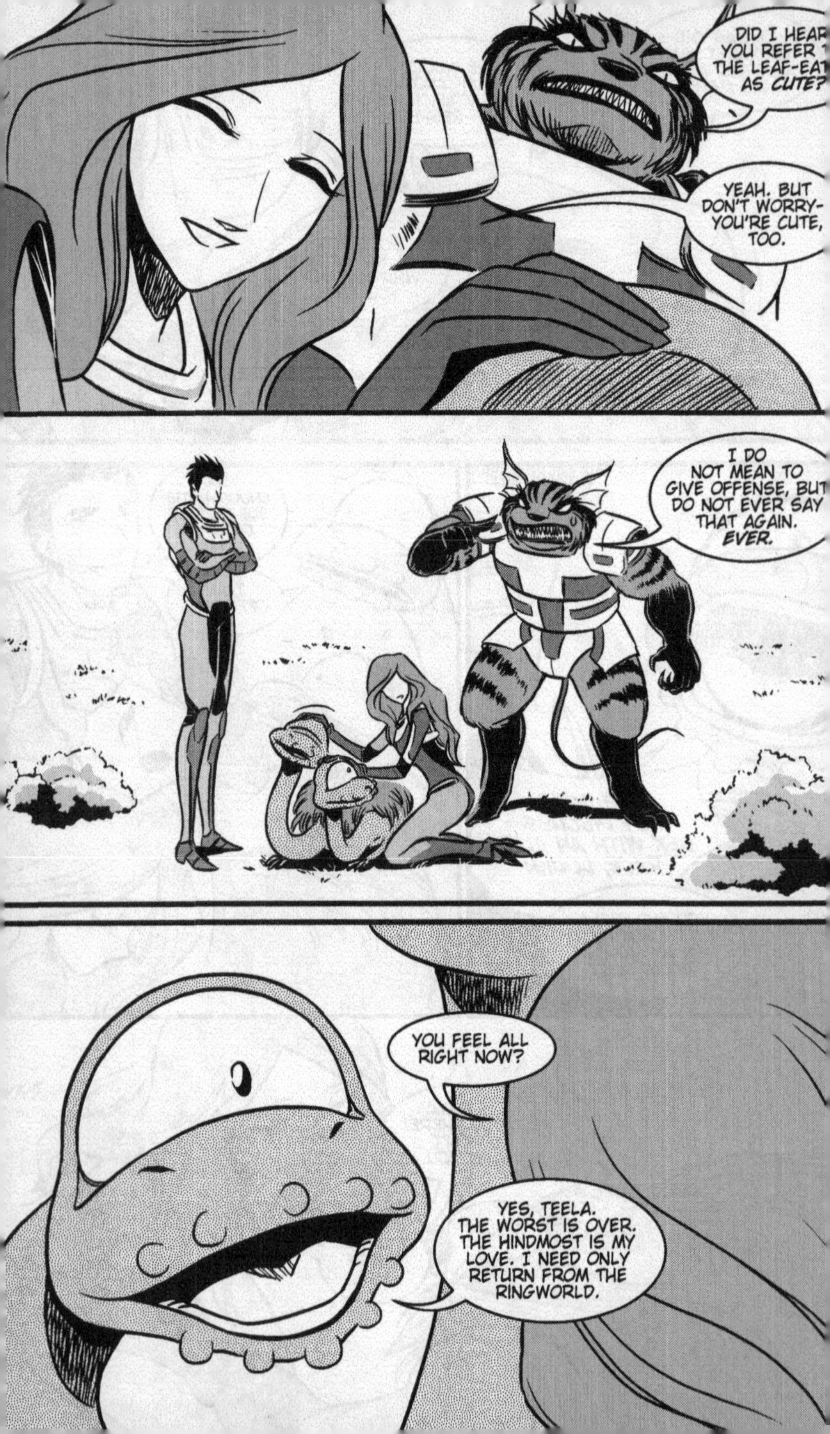
DID I HEAR YOU REFER T THE LEAF-EAT AS *CUTE?*
YEAH. BUT DON'T WORRY-YOU'RE CUTE, TOO.
I DO NOT MEAN TO GIVE OFFENSE, BUT DO NOT EVER SAY THAT AGAIN. *EVER.*
YOU FEEL ALL RIGHT NOW?
YES, TEELA. THE WORST IS OVER. THE HINDMOST IS MY LOVE. I NEED ONLY RETURN FROM THE RINGWORLD.

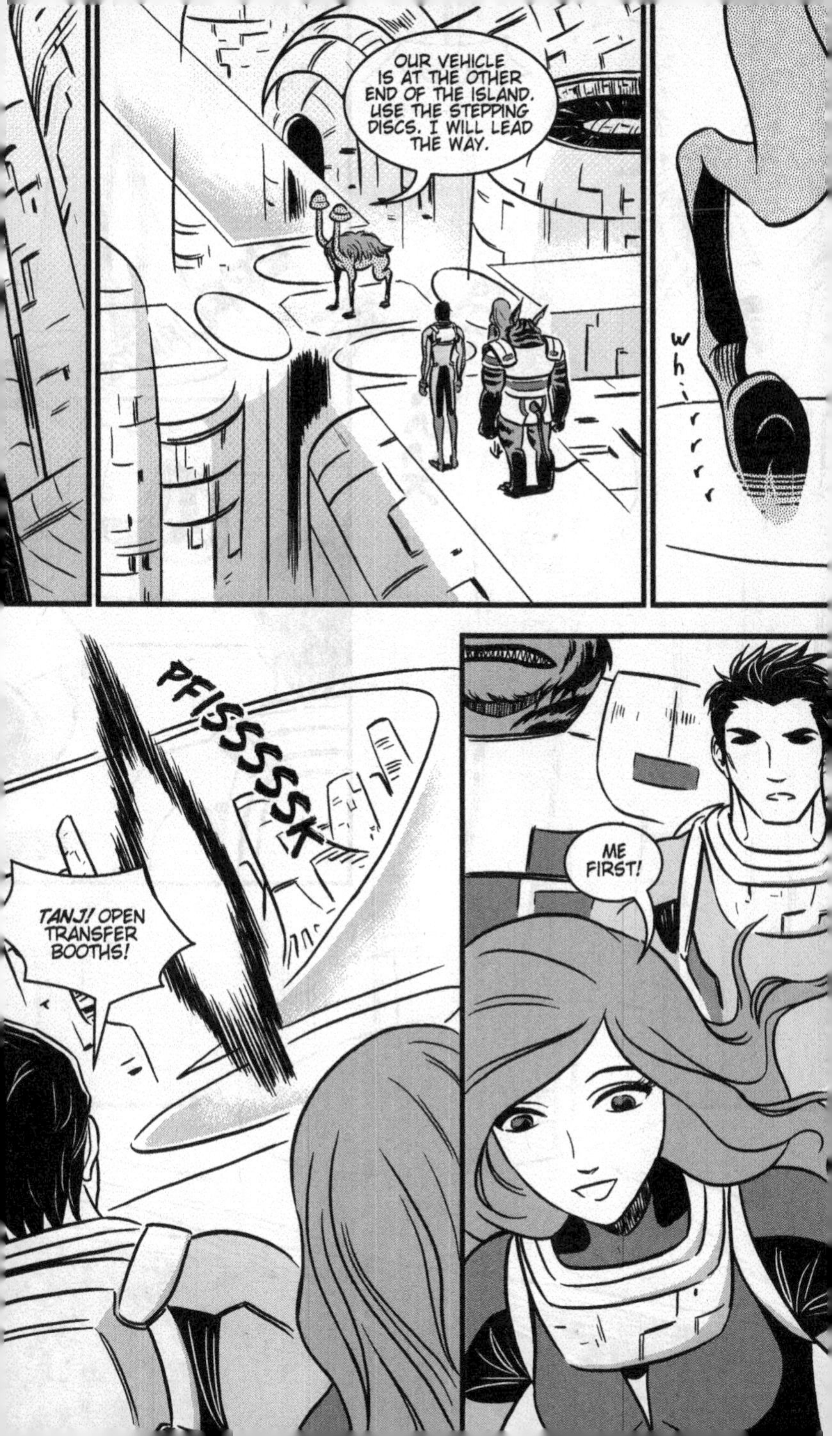
OUR VEHICLE IS AT THE OTHER END OF THE ISLAND. USE THE STEPPING DISCS. I WILL LEAD THE WAY.
whirrrr
PFISSSSSK
TANJ! OPEN TRANSFER BOOTHS!
ME FIRST!

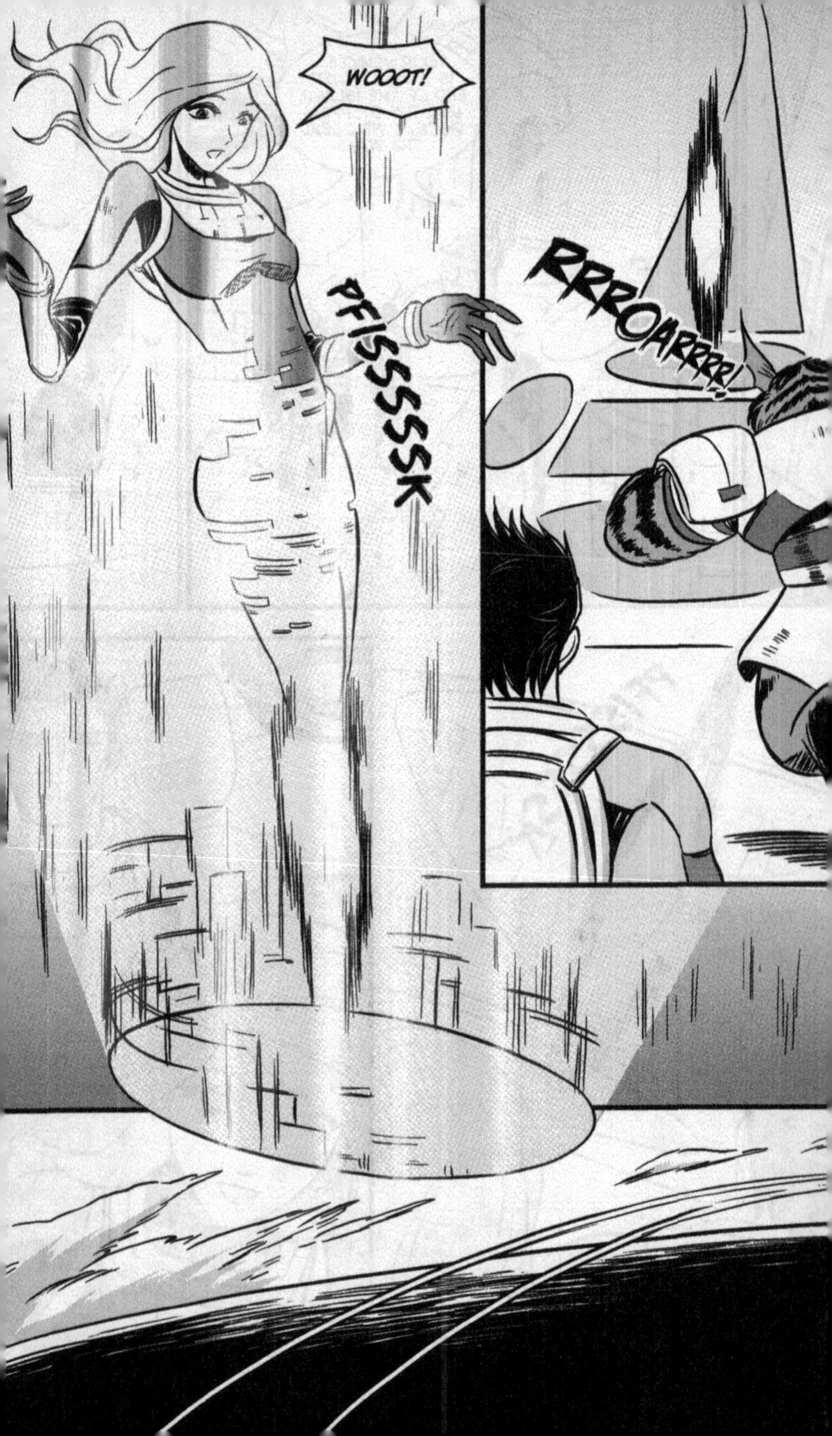
WOOOT!
PFISSSSSK
RRRROARRRR!

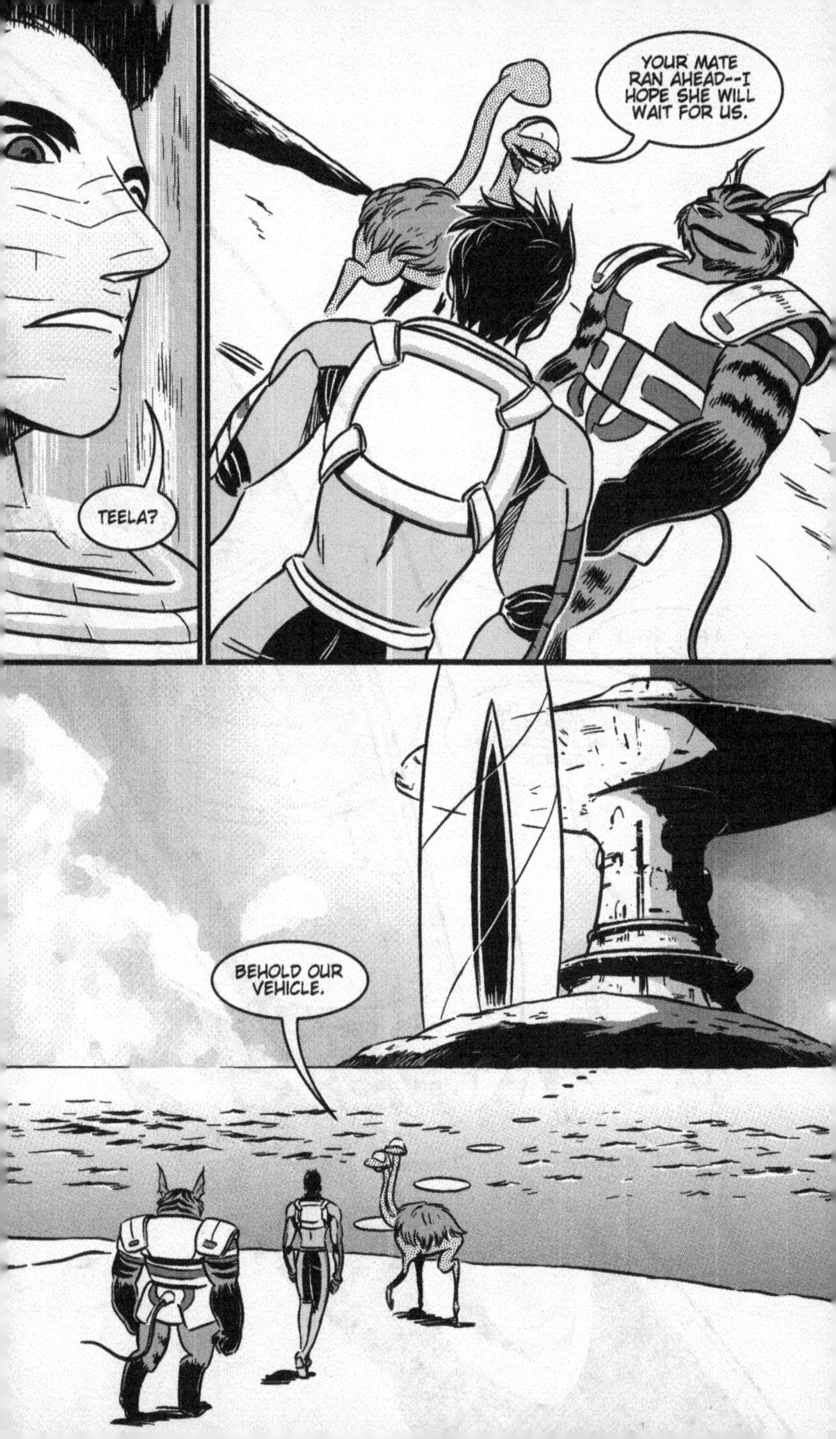
TEELA?
YOUR MATE RAN AHEAD--I HOPE SHE WILL WAIT FOR US.
BEHOLD OUR VEHICLE.

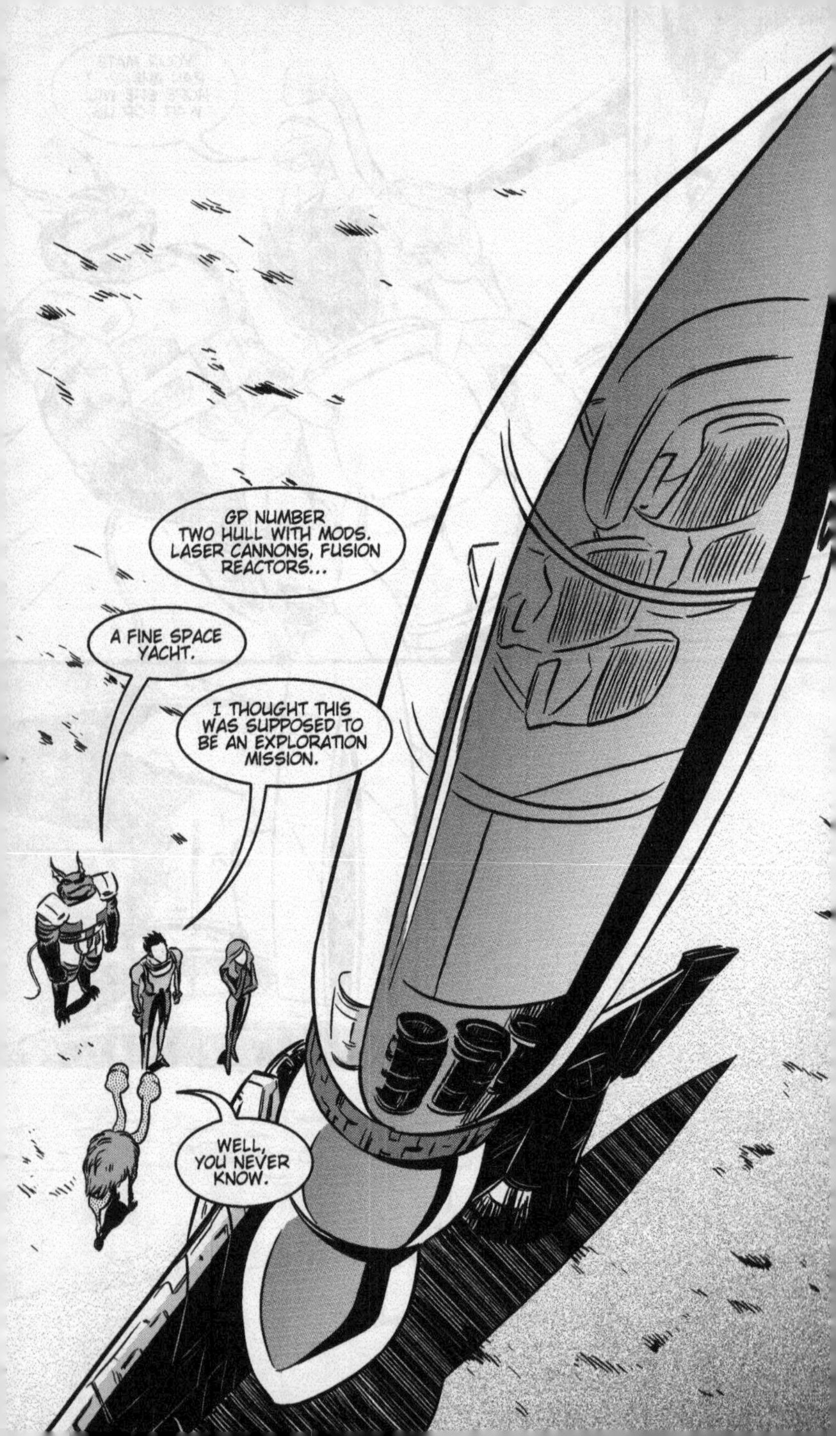
GP NUMBER TWO HULL WITH MODS. LASER CANNONS, FUSION REACTORS...
A FINE SPACE YACHT.
I THOUGHT THIS WAS SUPPOSED TO BE AN EXPLORATION MISSION.
WELL, YOU NEVER KNOW.

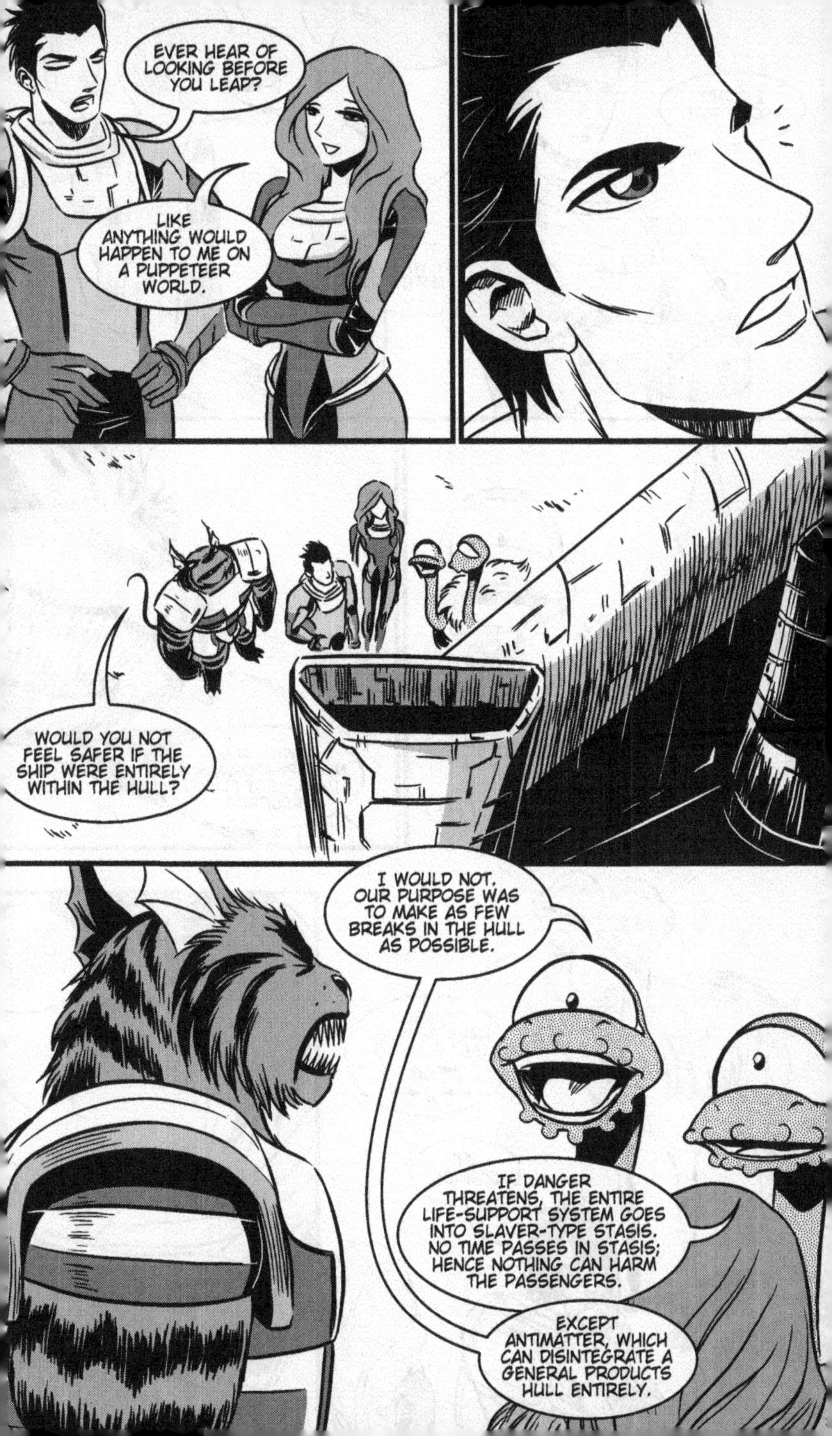
EVER HEAR OF LOOKING BEFORE YOU LEAP?
LIKE ANYTHING WOULD HAPPEN TO ME ON A PUPPETEER WORLD.
WOULD YOU NOT FEEL SAFER IF THE SHIP WERE ENTIRELY WITHIN THE HULL?
I WOULD NOT. OUR PURPOSE WAS TO MAKE AS FEW BREAKS IN THE HULL AS POSSIBLE.
IF DANGER THREATENS, THE ENTIRE LIFE-SUPPORT SYSTEM GOES INTO SLAVER-TYPE STASIS. NO TIME PASSES IN STASIS; HENCE NOTHING CAN HARM THE PASSENGERS.
EXCEPT ANTIMATTER, WHICH CAN DISINTEGRATE A GENERAL PRODUCTS HULL ENTIRELY.

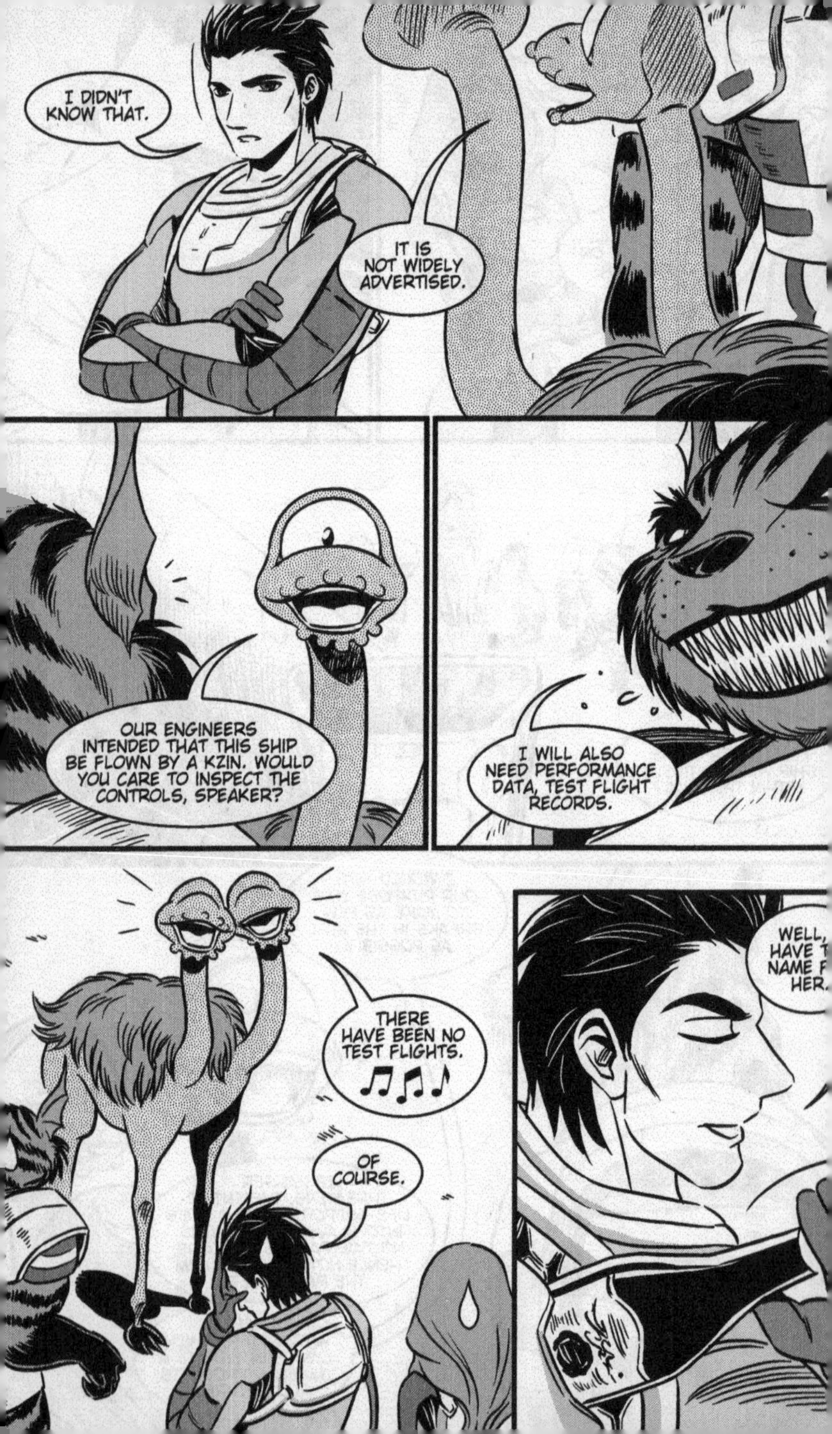
I DIDN'T KNOW THAT.
IT IS NOT WIDELY ADVERTISED.
OUR ENGINEERS INTENDED THAT THIS SHIP BE FLOWN BY A KZIN. WOULD YOU CARE TO INSPECT THE CONTROLS, SPEAKER?
I WILL ALSO NEED PERFORMANCE DATA, TEST FLIGHT RECORDS.
THERE HAVE BEEN NO TEST FLIGHTS. ♫♫♪
OF COURSE.

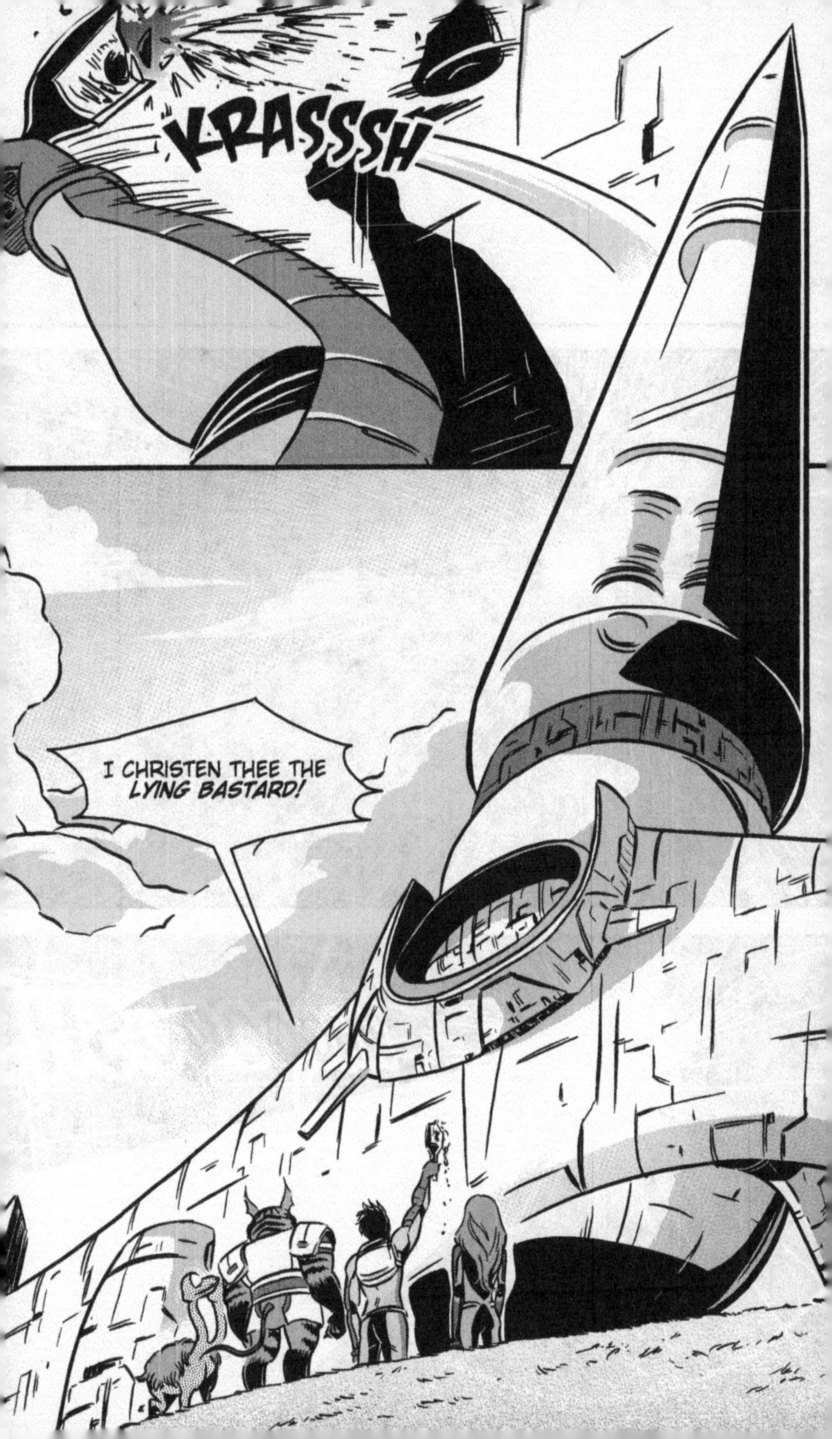
KRASSSH
I CHRISTEN THEE THE *LYING BASTARD!*

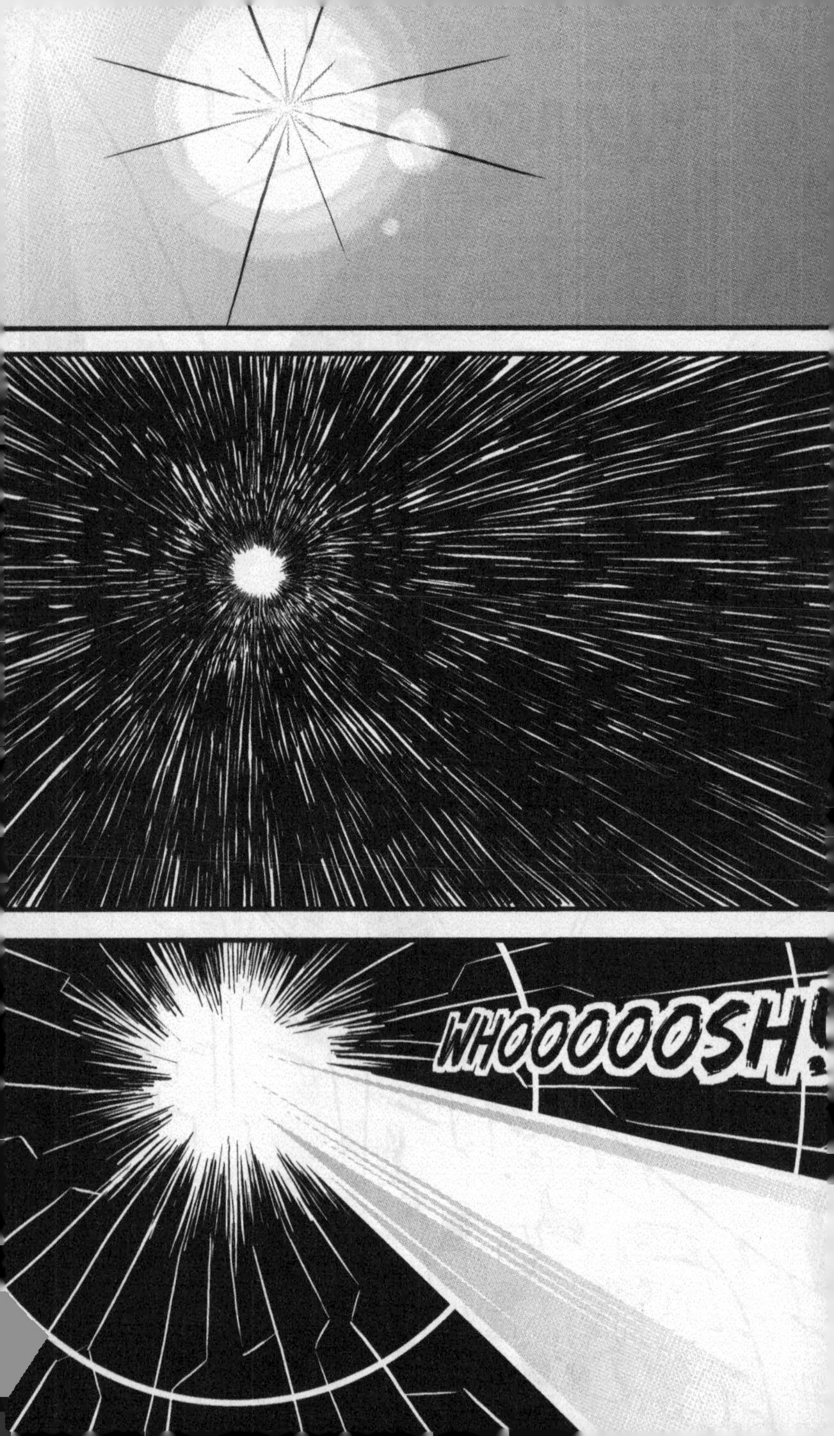
WHOOOOOOSH!

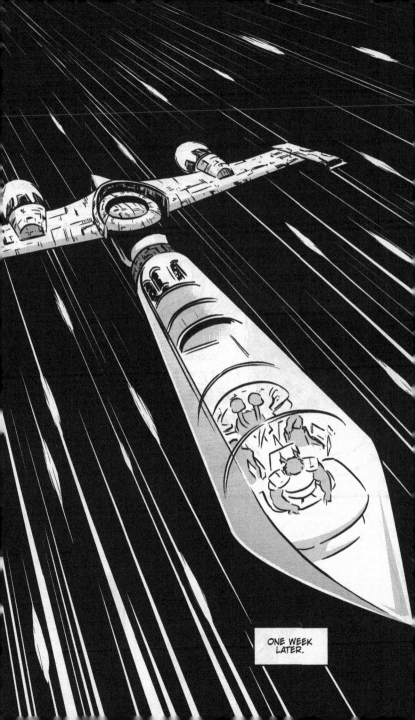

ONE WEEK
LATER.

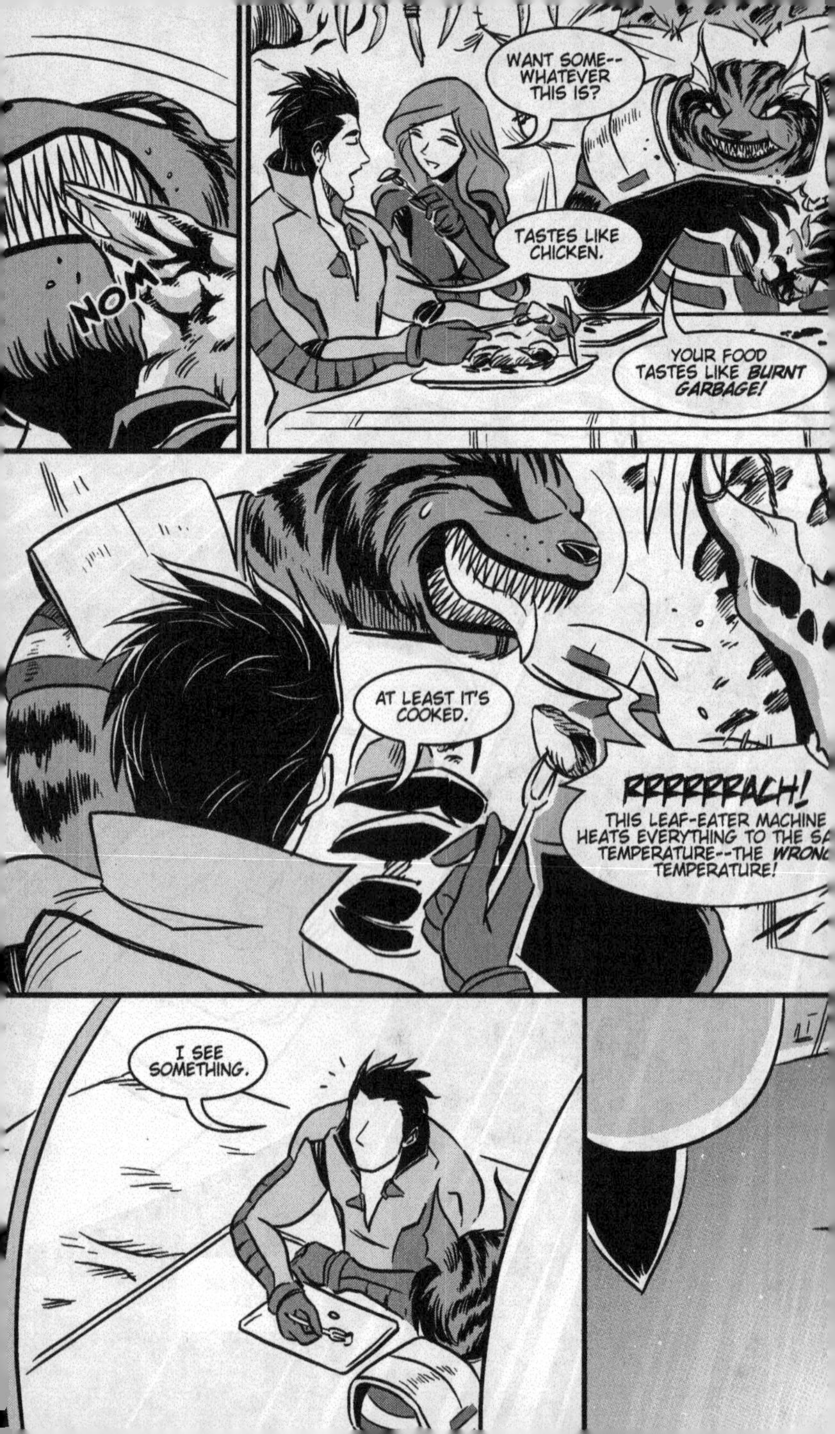
NOM
WANT SOME--WHATEVER THIS IS?
TASTES LIKE CHICKEN.
YOUR FOOD TASTES LIKE BURNT GARBAGE!
AT LEAST IT'S COOKED.
RRRRRRACH!
THIS LEAF-EATER MACHINE HEATS EVERYTHING TO THE SA
TEMPERATURE--THE WRONG TEMPERATURE!
I SEE SOMETHING.

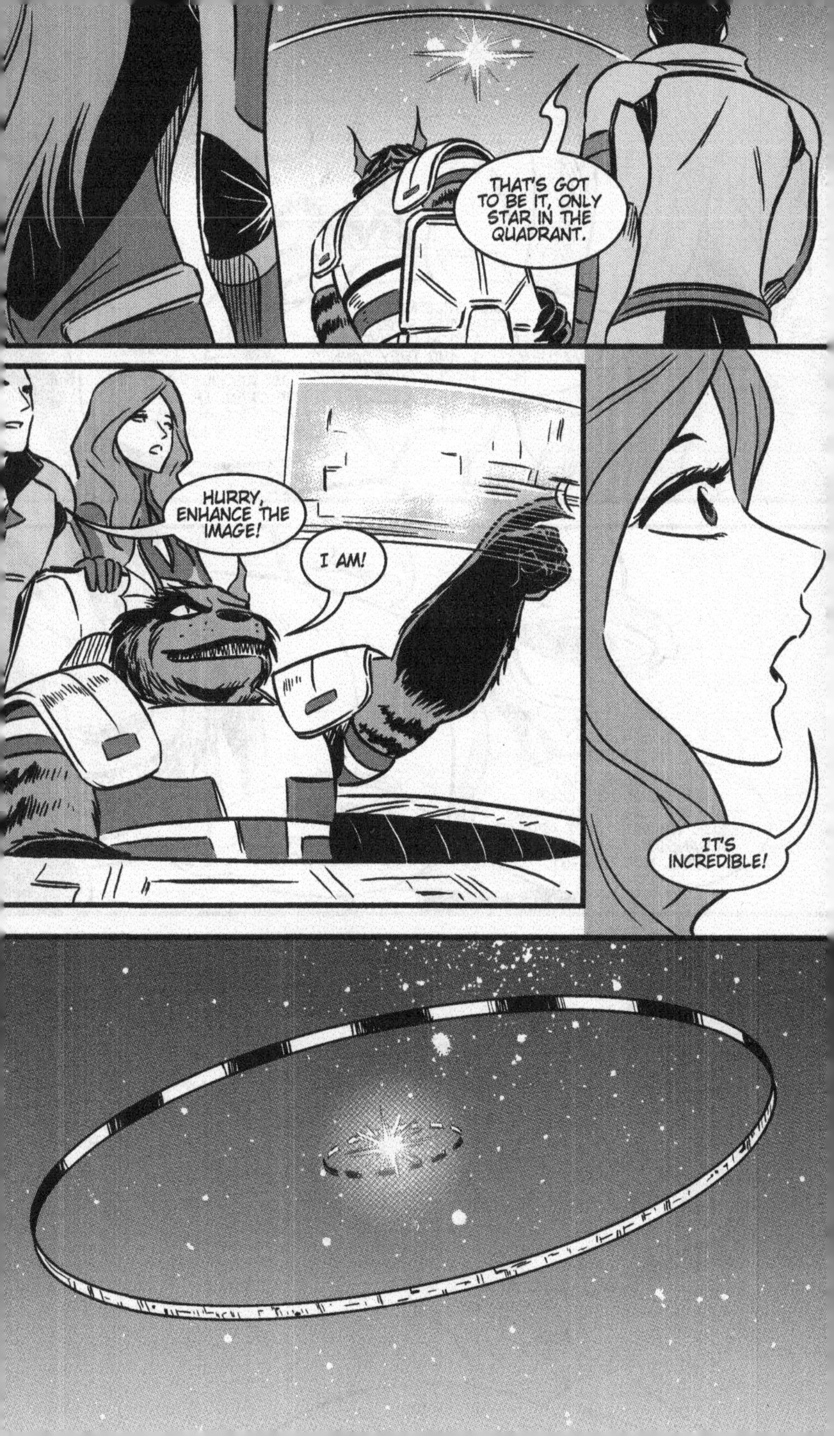
THAT'S GOT TO BE IT, ONLY STAR IN THE QUADRANT.
HURRY, ENHANCE THE IMAGE!
I AM!
IT'S INCREDIBLE!

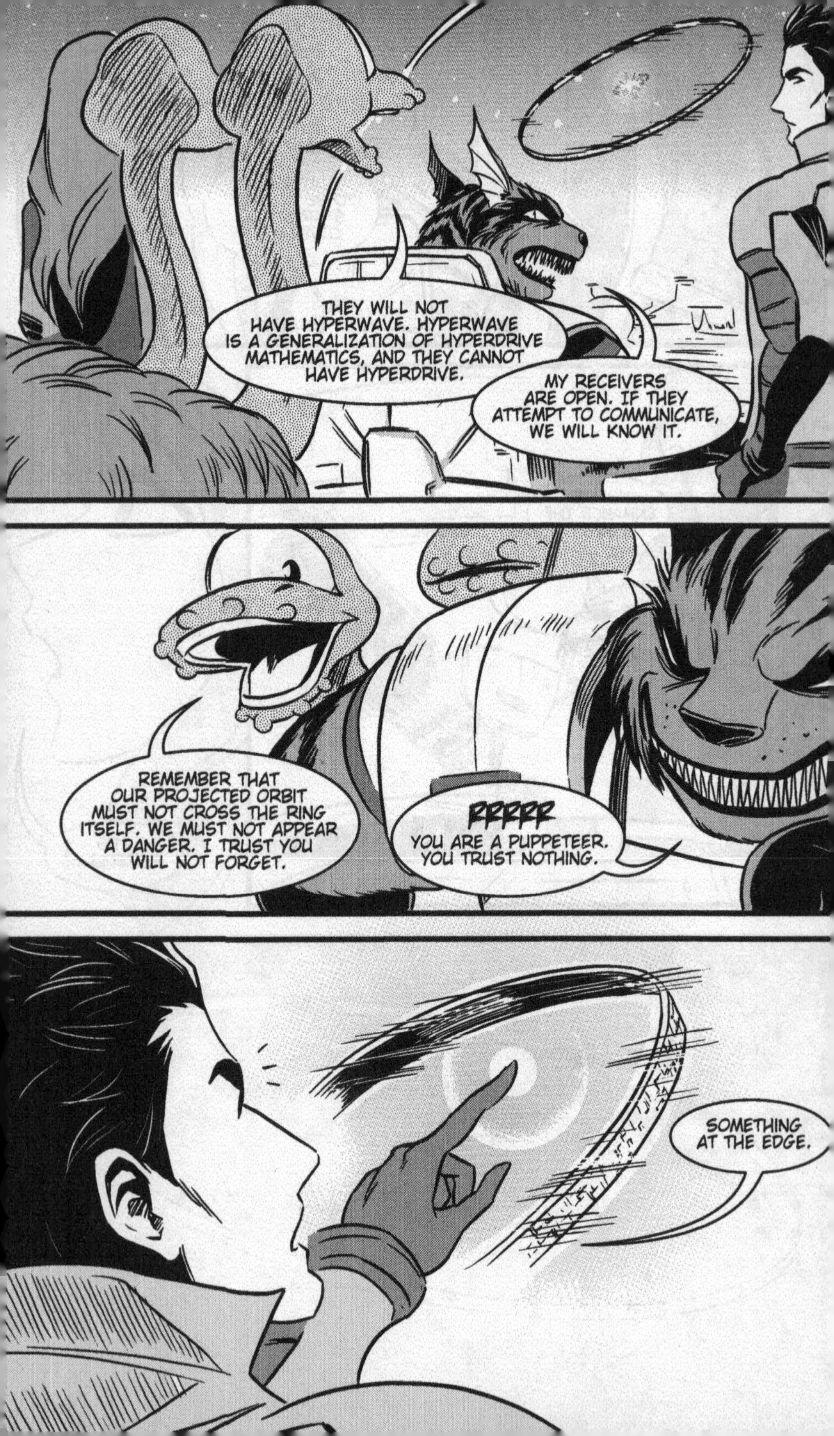
THEY WILL NOT HAVE HYPERWAVE. HYPERWAVE IS A GENERALIZATION OF HYPERDRIVE MATHEMATICS, AND THEY CANNOT HAVE HYPERDRIVE.
MY RECEIVERS ARE OPEN. IF THEY ATTEMPT TO COMMUNICATE, WE WILL KNOW IT.
REMEMBER THAT OUR PROJECTED ORBIT MUST NOT CROSS THE RING ITSELF. WE MUST NOT APPEAR A DANGER. I TRUST YOU WILL NOT FORGET.
RRRRR
YOU ARE A PUPPETEER. YOU TRUST NOTHING.
SOMETHING AT THE EDGE.

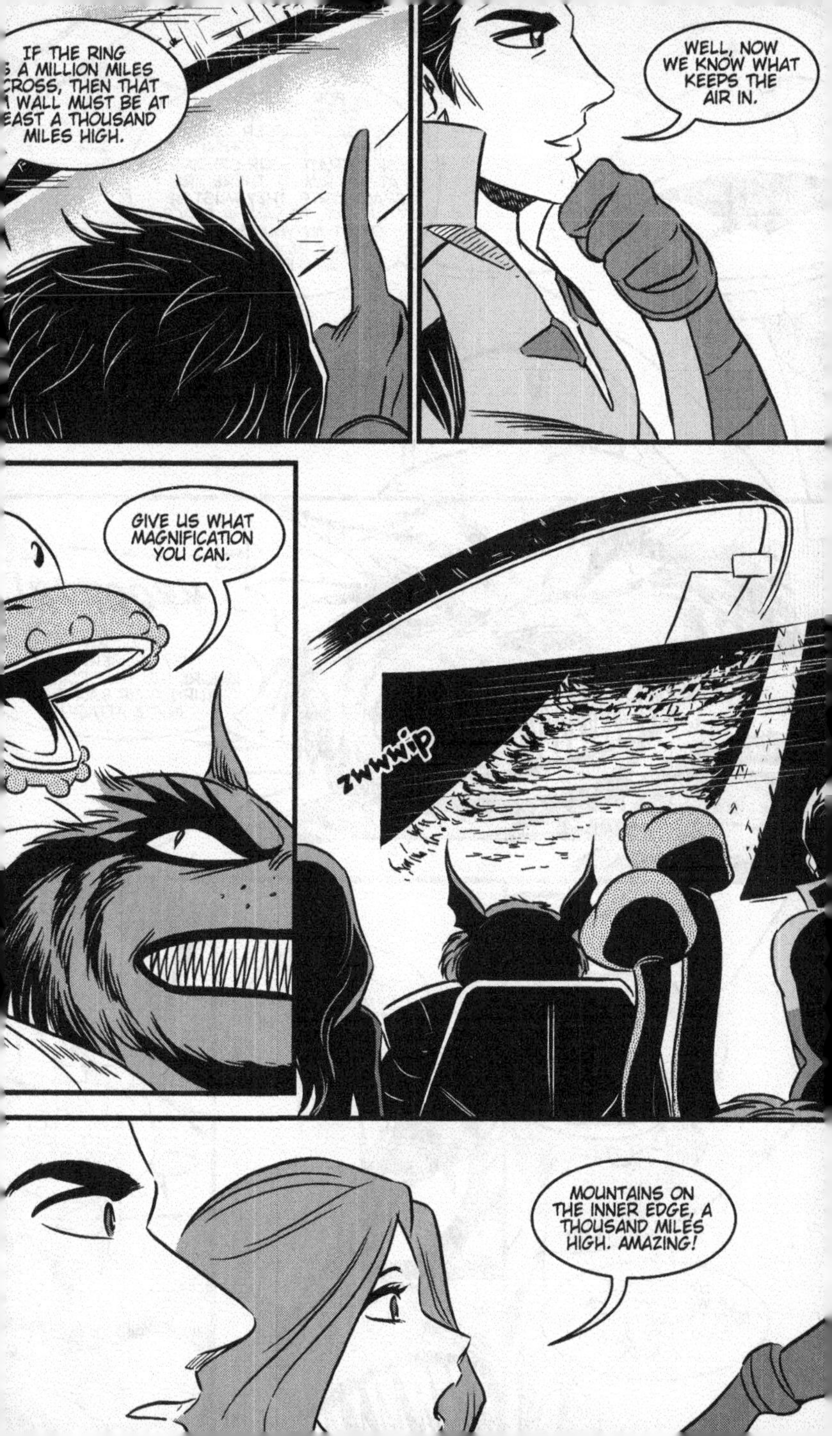
IF THE RING
S A MILLION MILES
CROSS, THEN THAT
WALL MUST BE AT
EAST A THOUSAND
MILES HIGH.
WELL, NOW WE KNOW WHAT KEEPS THE AIR IN.
GIVE US WHAT MAGNIFICATION YOU CAN.
ZWWWIP
MOUNTAINS ON THE INNER EDGE, A THOUSAND MILES HIGH. AMAZING!

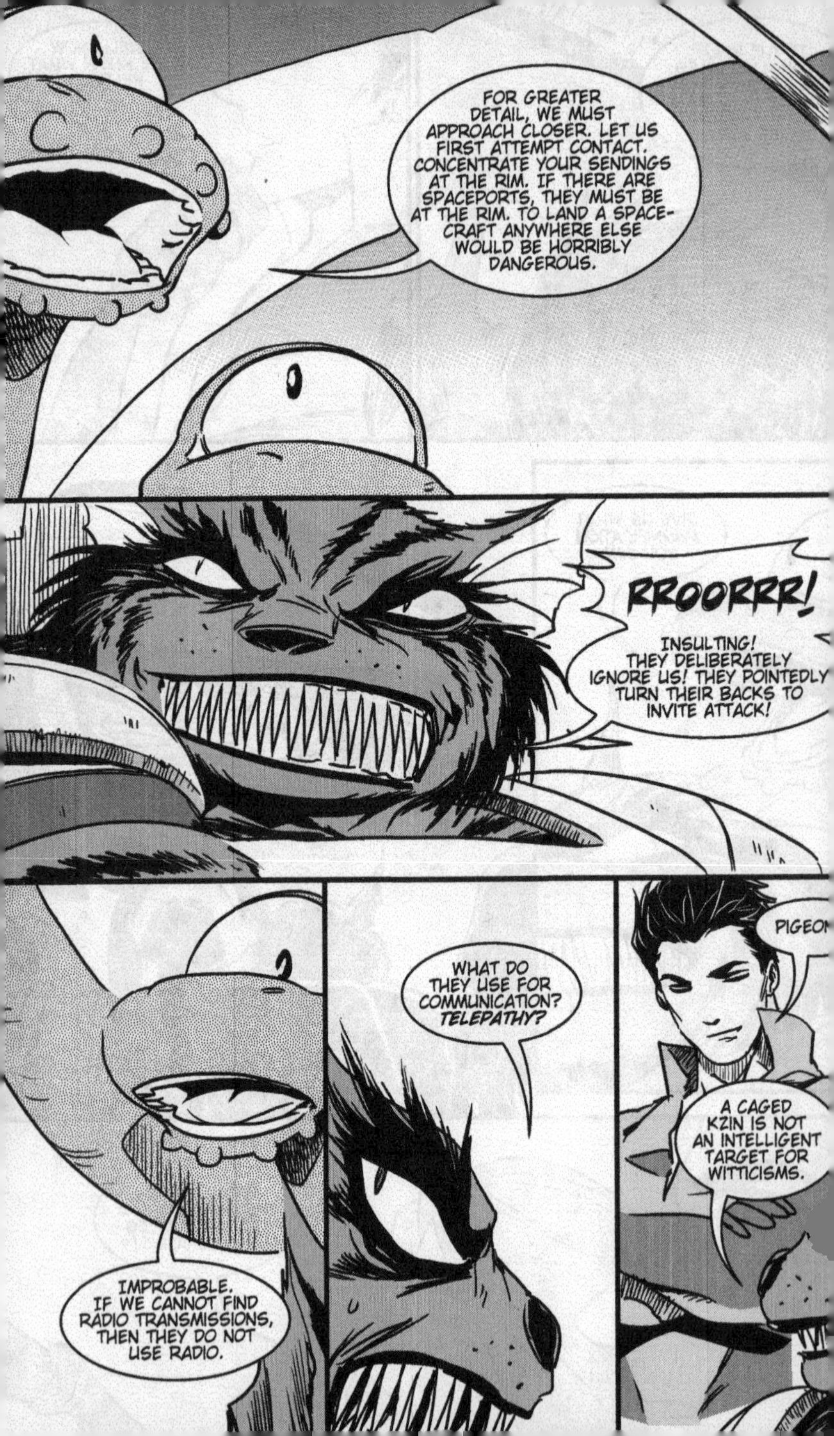
FOR GREATER DETAIL, WE MUST APPROACH CLOSER. LET US FIRST ATTEMPT CONTACT. CONCENTRATE YOUR SENDINGS AT THE RIM. IF THERE ARE SPACEPORTS, THEY MUST BE AT THE RIM. TO LAND A SPACE-CRAFT ANYWHERE ELSE WOULD BE HORRIBLY DANGEROUS.
RROORRR!
INSULTING! THEY DELIBERATELY IGNORE US! THEY POINTEDLY TURN THEIR BACKS TO INVITE ATTACK!
IMPROBABLE. IF WE CANNOT FIND RADIO TRANSMISSIONS, THEN THEY DO NOT USE RADIO.
WHAT DO THEY USE FOR COMMUNICATION? *TELEPATHY?*
PIGEON
A CAGED KZIN IS NOT AN INTELLIGENT TARGET FOR WITTICISMS.

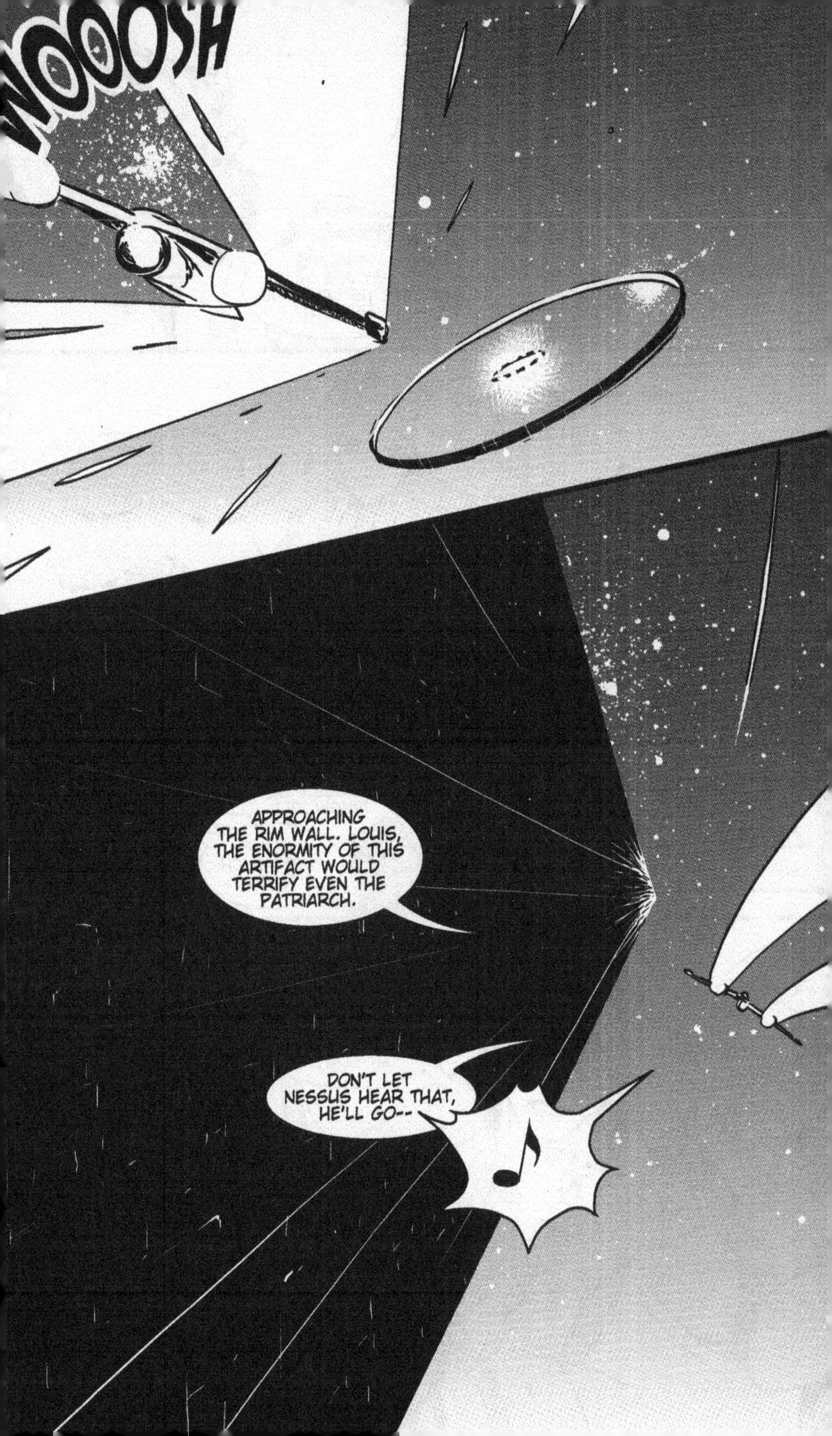
WOOOSH
APPROACHING THE RIM WALL. LOUIS, THE ENORMITY OF THIS ARTIFACT WOULD TERRIFY EVEN THE PATRIARCH.
DON'T LET NESSUS HEAR THAT, HE'LL GO--

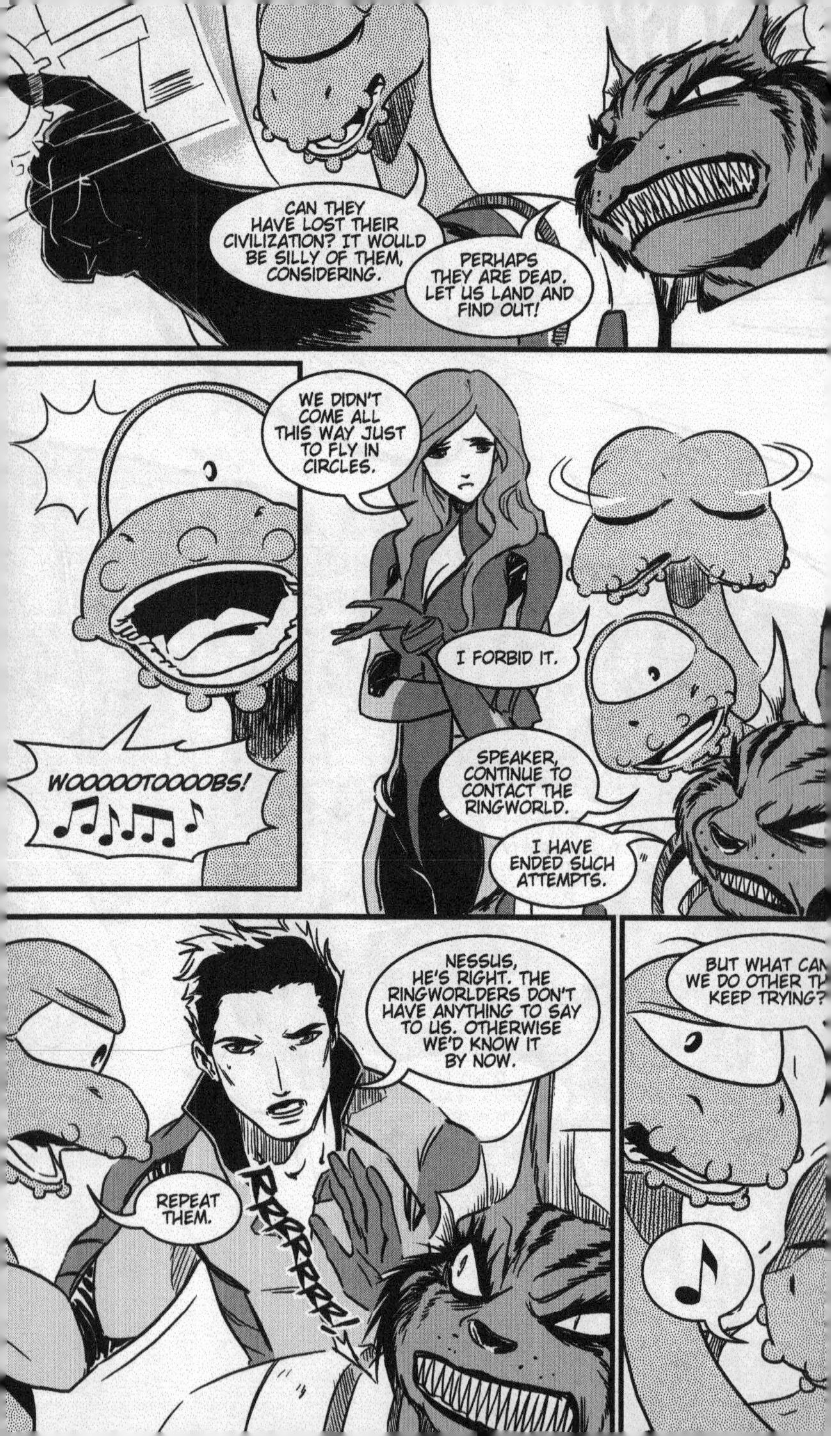

CAN THEY HAVE LOST THEIR CIVILIZATION? IT WOULD BE SILLY OF THEM, CONSIDERING.
PERHAPS THEY ARE DEAD. LET US LAND AND FIND OUT!
WOOOOOTOOOOBS!
WE DIDN'T COME ALL THIS WAY JUST TO FLY IN CIRCLES.
I FORBID IT.
SPEAKER, CONTINUE TO CONTACT THE RINGWORLD.
I HAVE ENDED SUCH ATTEMPTS.
NESSUS, HE'S RIGHT. THE RINGWORLDERS DON'T HAVE ANYTHING TO SAY TO US. OTHERWISE WE'D KNOW IT BY NOW.
REPEAT THEM.
RRRRRRRR!
BUT WHAT CAN WE DO OTHER TH KEEP TRYING?

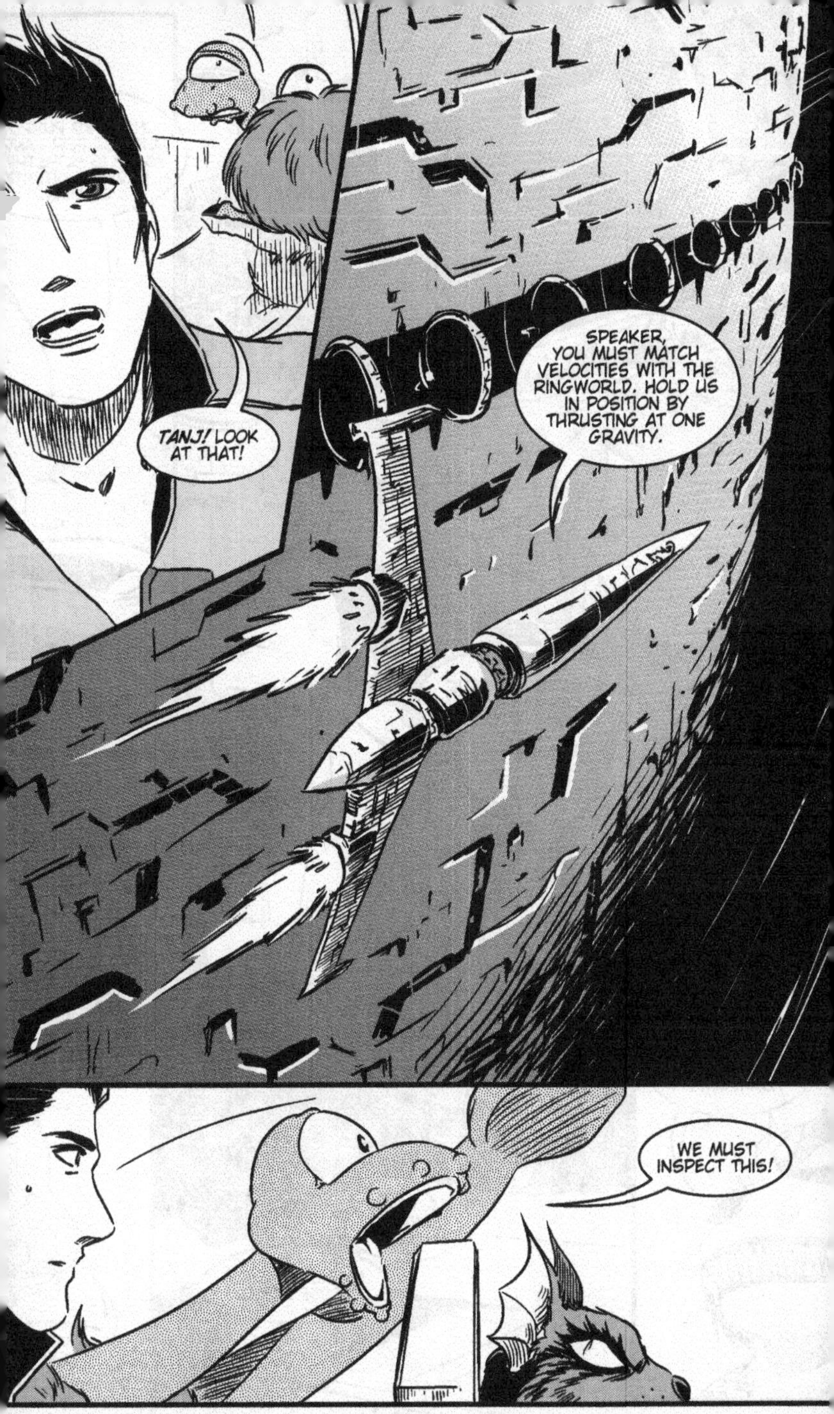
TANJ! LOOK AT THAT!
SPEAKER, YOU MUST MATCH VELOCITIES WITH THE RINGWORLD. HOLD US IN POSITION BY THRUSTING AT ONE GRAVITY.
WE MUST INSPECT THIS!

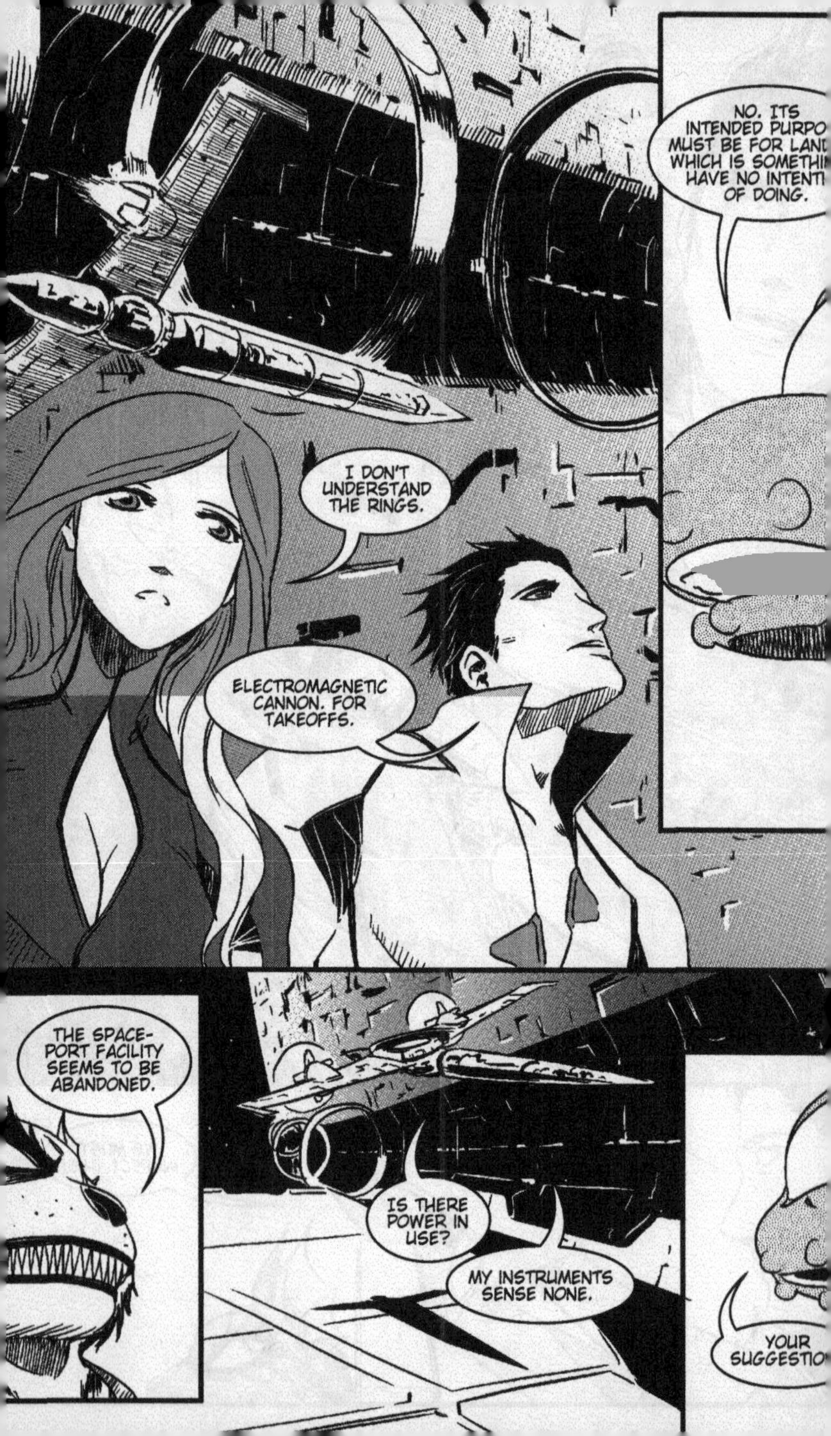
I DON'T UNDERSTAND THE RINGS.
ELECTROMAGNETIC CANNON. FOR TAKEOFFS.
NO. ITS INTENDED PURPO
MUST BE FOR LAND
WHICH IS SOMETHI
HAVE NO INTENT
OF DOING.
THE SPACE-PORT FACILITY SEEMS TO BE ABANDONED.
IS THERE POWER IN USE?
MY INSTRUMENTS SENSE NONE.
YOUR SUGGESTIO

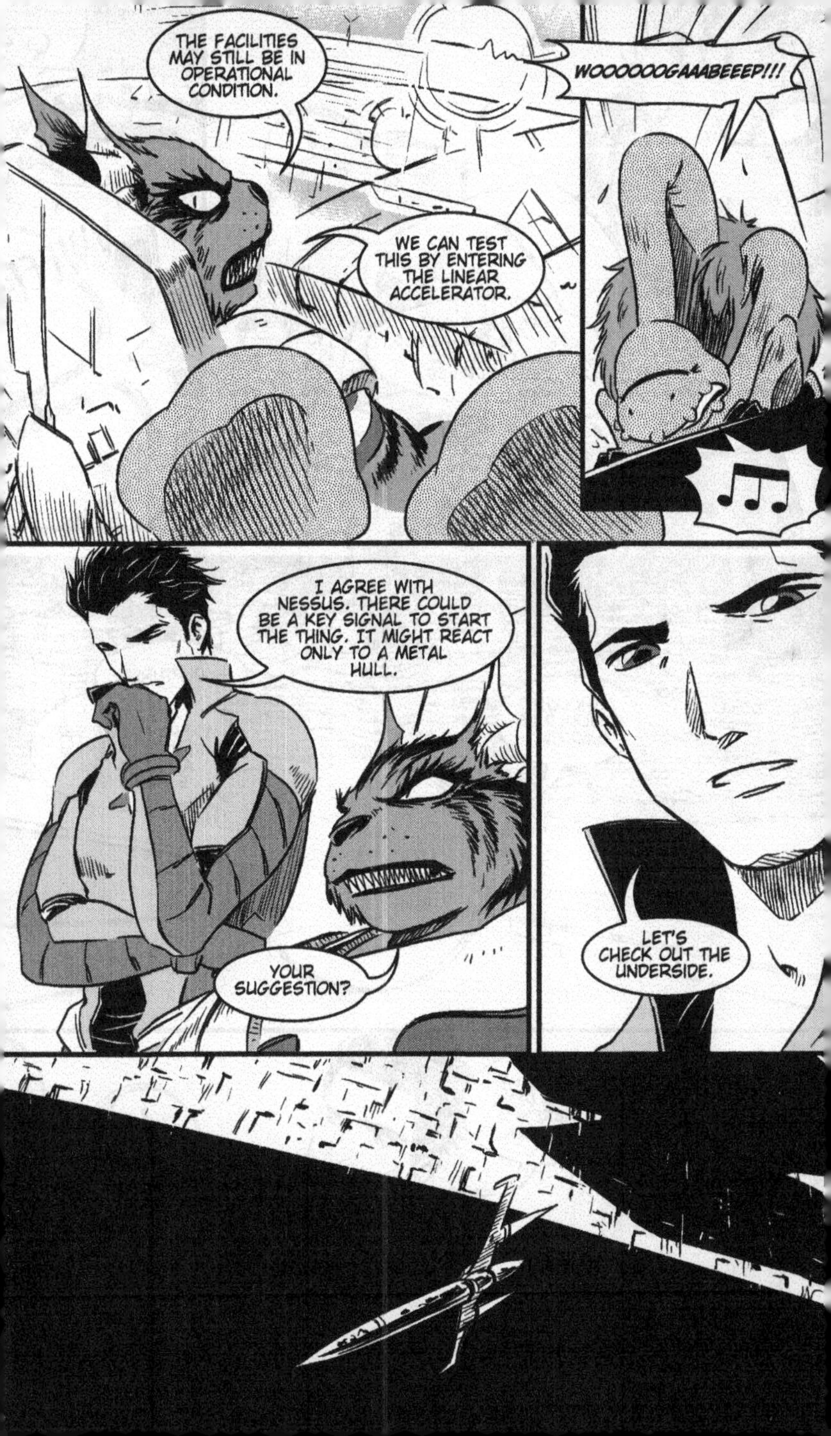
THE FACILITIES MAY STILL BE IN OPERATIONAL CONDITION.
WE CAN TEST THIS BY ENTERING THE LINEAR ACCELERATOR.
WOOOOOOGAAABEEEP!!!
I AGREE WITH NESSUS. THERE COULD BE A KEY SIGNAL TO START THE THING. IT MIGHT REACT ONLY TO A METAL HULL.
YOUR SUGGESTION?
LET'S CHECK OUT THE UNDERSIDE.

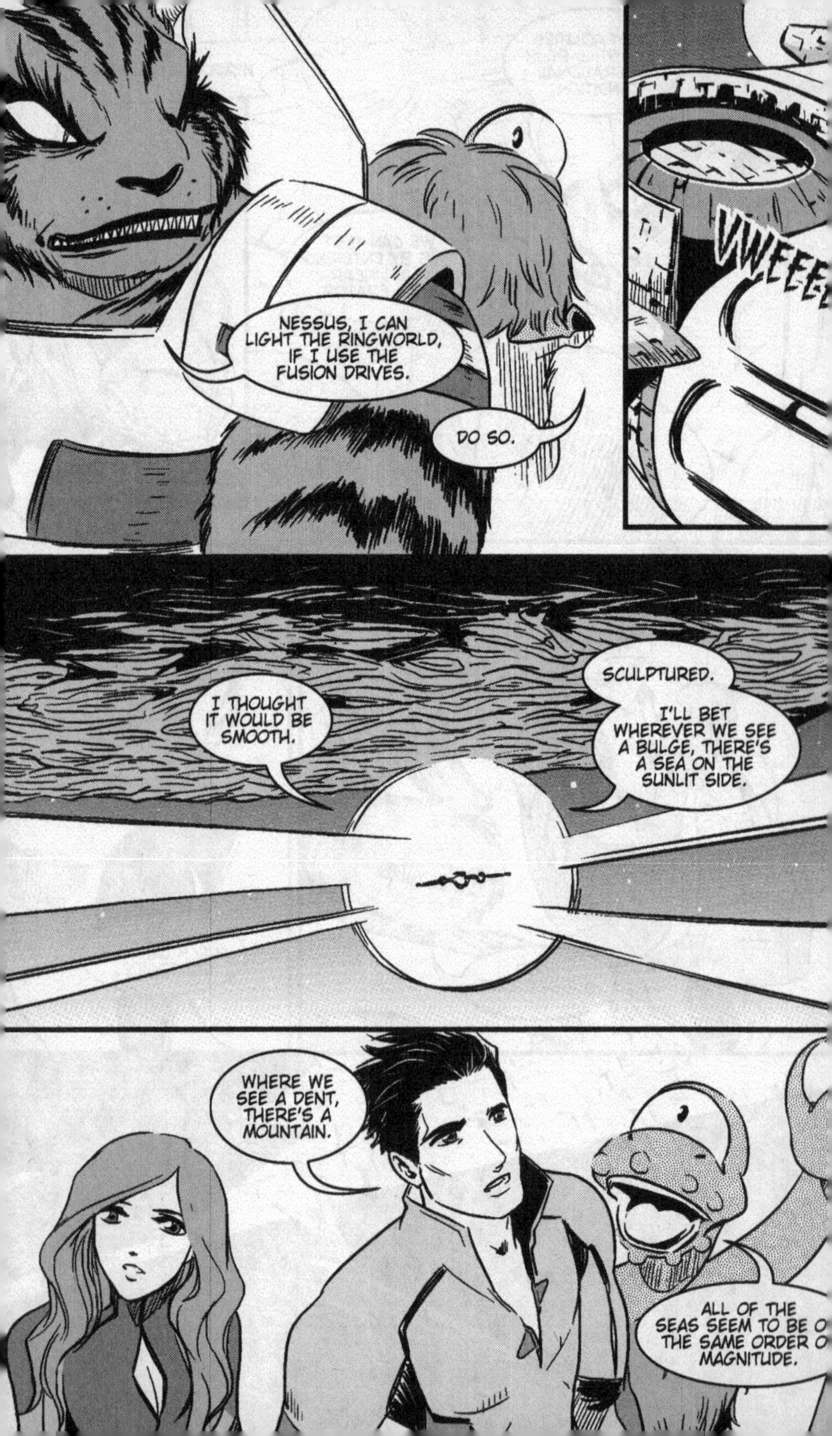
NESSUS, I CAN LIGHT THE RINGWORLD, IF I USE THE FUSION DRIVES.
DO SO.
VWEEEE
I THOUGHT IT WOULD BE SMOOTH.
SCULPTURED.
I'LL BET WHEREVER WE SEE A BULGE, THERE'S A SEA ON THE SUNLIT SIDE.
WHERE WE SEE A DENT, THERE'S A MOUNTAIN.
ALL OF THE SEAS SEEM TO BE O THE SAME ORDER O MAGNITUDE.

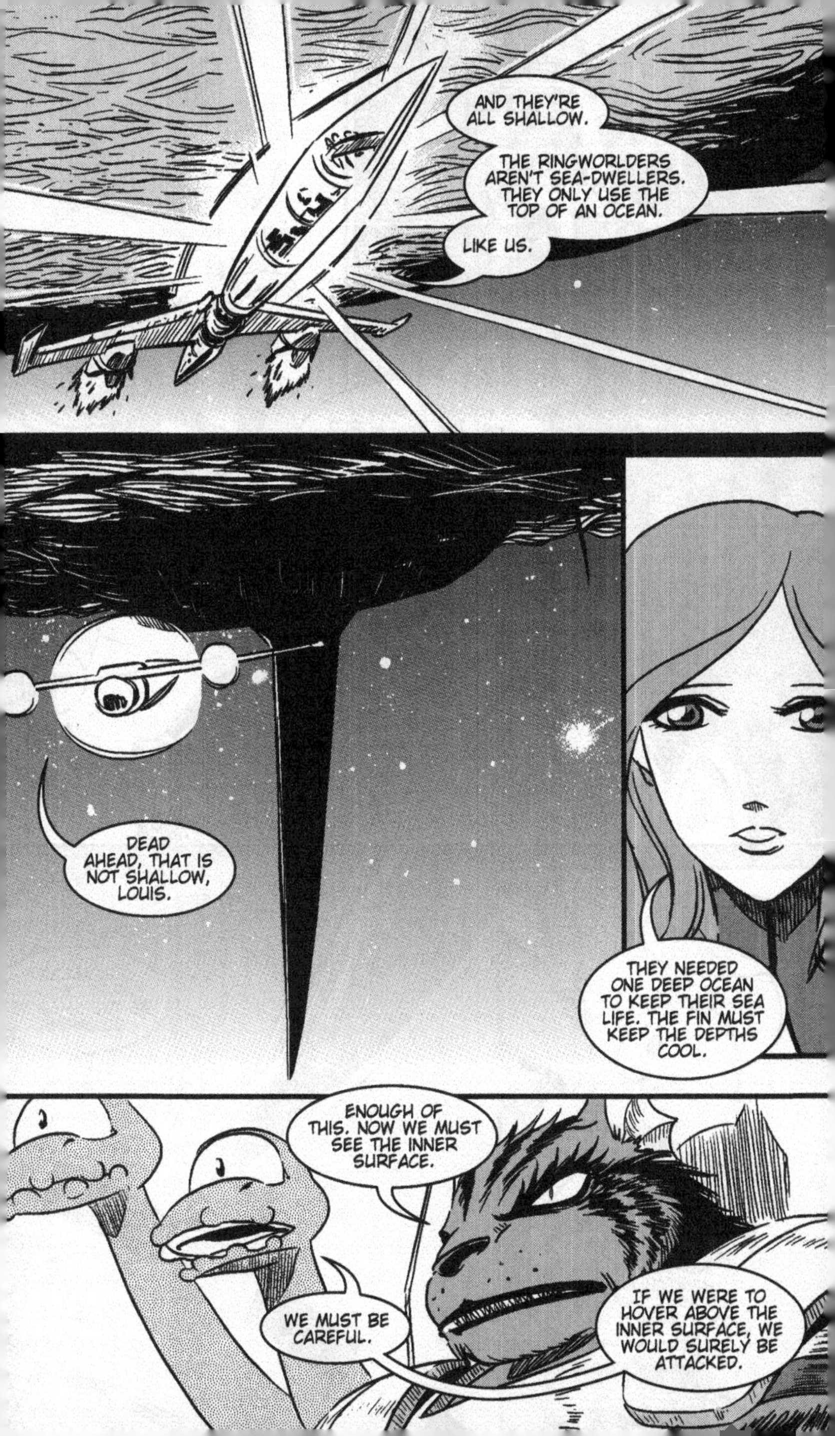
AND THEY'RE ALL SHALLOW.
THE RINGWORLDERS AREN'T SEA-DWELLERS. THEY ONLY USE THE TOP OF AN OCEAN.
LIKE US.
DEAD AHEAD, THAT IS NOT SHALLOW, LOUIS.
THEY NEEDED ONE DEEP OCEAN TO KEEP THEIR SEA LIFE. THE FIN MUST KEEP THE DEPTHS COOL.
ENOUGH OF THIS. NOW WE MUST SEE THE INNER SURFACE.
WE MUST BE CAREFUL.
IF WE WERE TO HOVER ABOVE THE INNER SURFACE, WE WOULD SURELY BE ATTACKED.

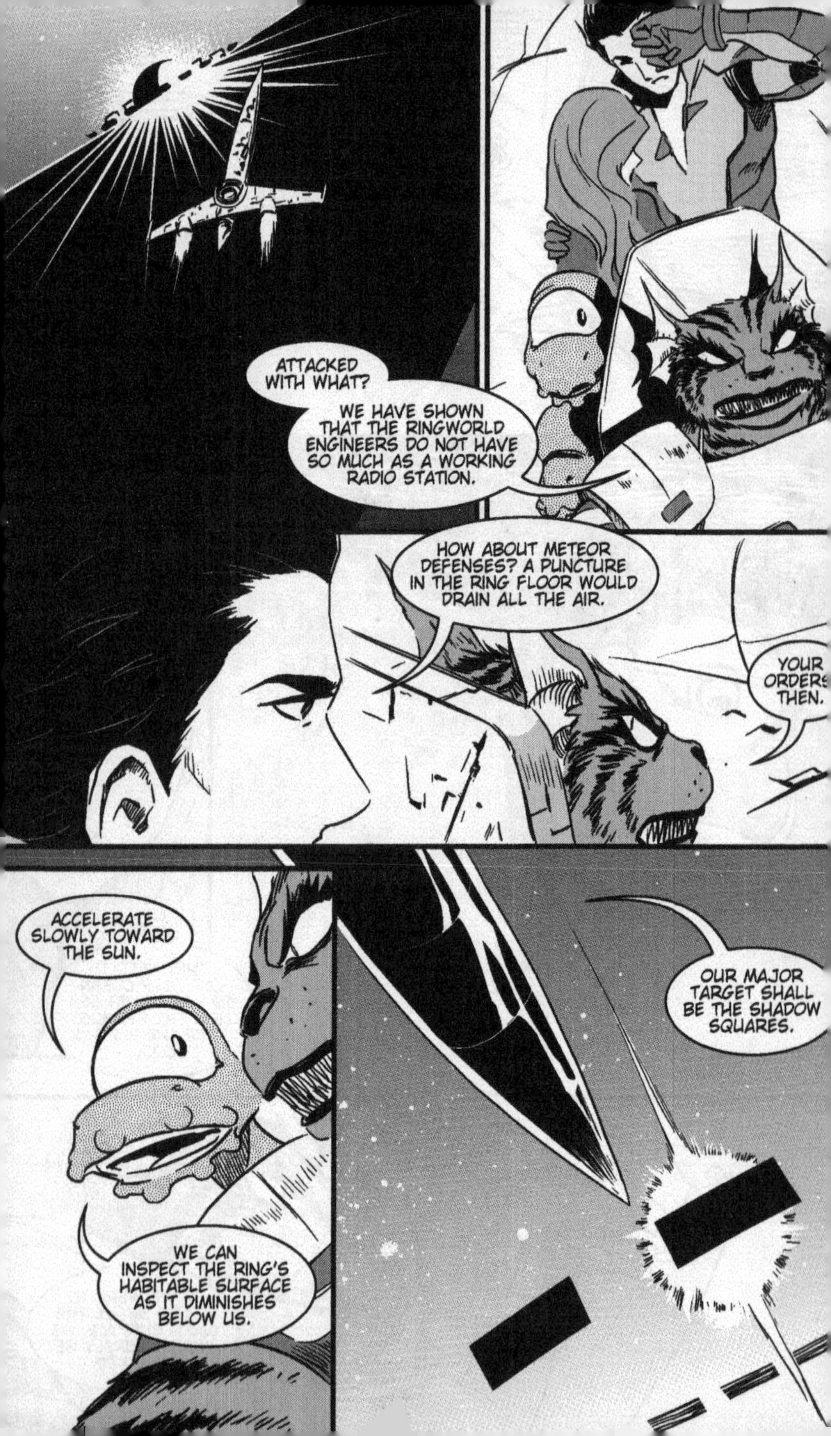
ATTACKED WITH WHAT?
WE HAVE SHOWN THAT THE RINGWORLD ENGINEERS DO NOT HAVE SO MUCH AS A WORKING RADIO STATION.
HOW ABOUT METEOR DEFENSES? A PUNCTURE IN THE RING FLOOR WOULD DRAIN ALL THE AIR.
YOUR ORDERS THEN.
ACCELERATE SLOWLY TOWARD THE SUN.
WE CAN INSPECT THE RING'S HABITABLE SURFACE AS IT DIMINISHES BELOW US.
OUR MAJOR TARGET SHALL BE THE SHADOW SQUARES.

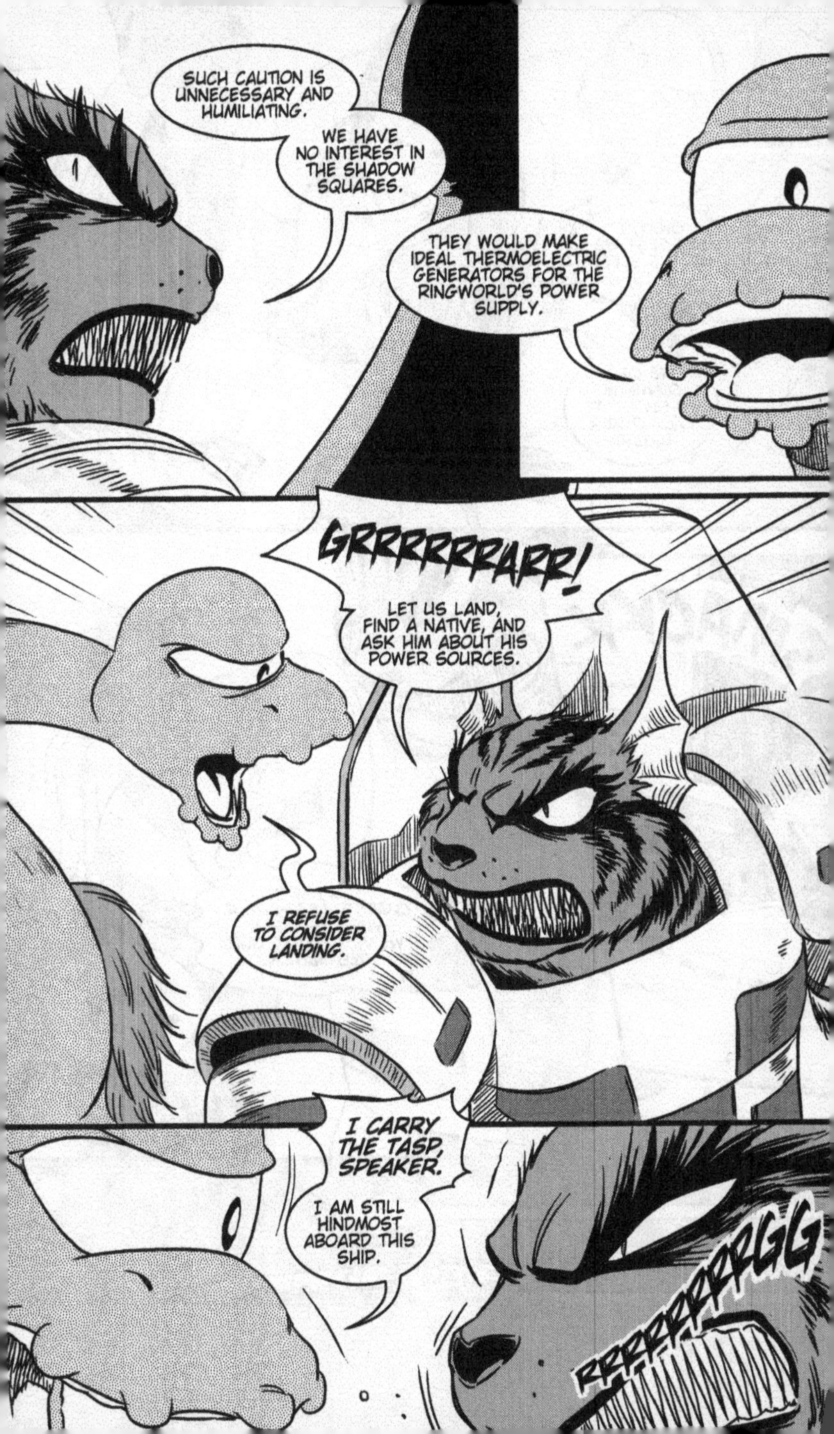
SUCH CAUTION IS UNNECESSARY AND HUMILIATING.
WE HAVE NO INTEREST IN THE SHADOW SQUARES.
THEY WOULD MAKE IDEAL THERMOELECTRIC GENERATORS FOR THE RINGWORLD'S POWER SUPPLY.
GRRRRRRARR!
LET US LAND, FIND A NATIVE, AND ASK HIM ABOUT HIS POWER SOURCES.
I REFUSE TO CONSIDER LANDING.
I CARRY THE TASP, SPEAKER.
I AM STILL HINDMOST ABOARD THIS SHIP.
RRRRRRRRRGG

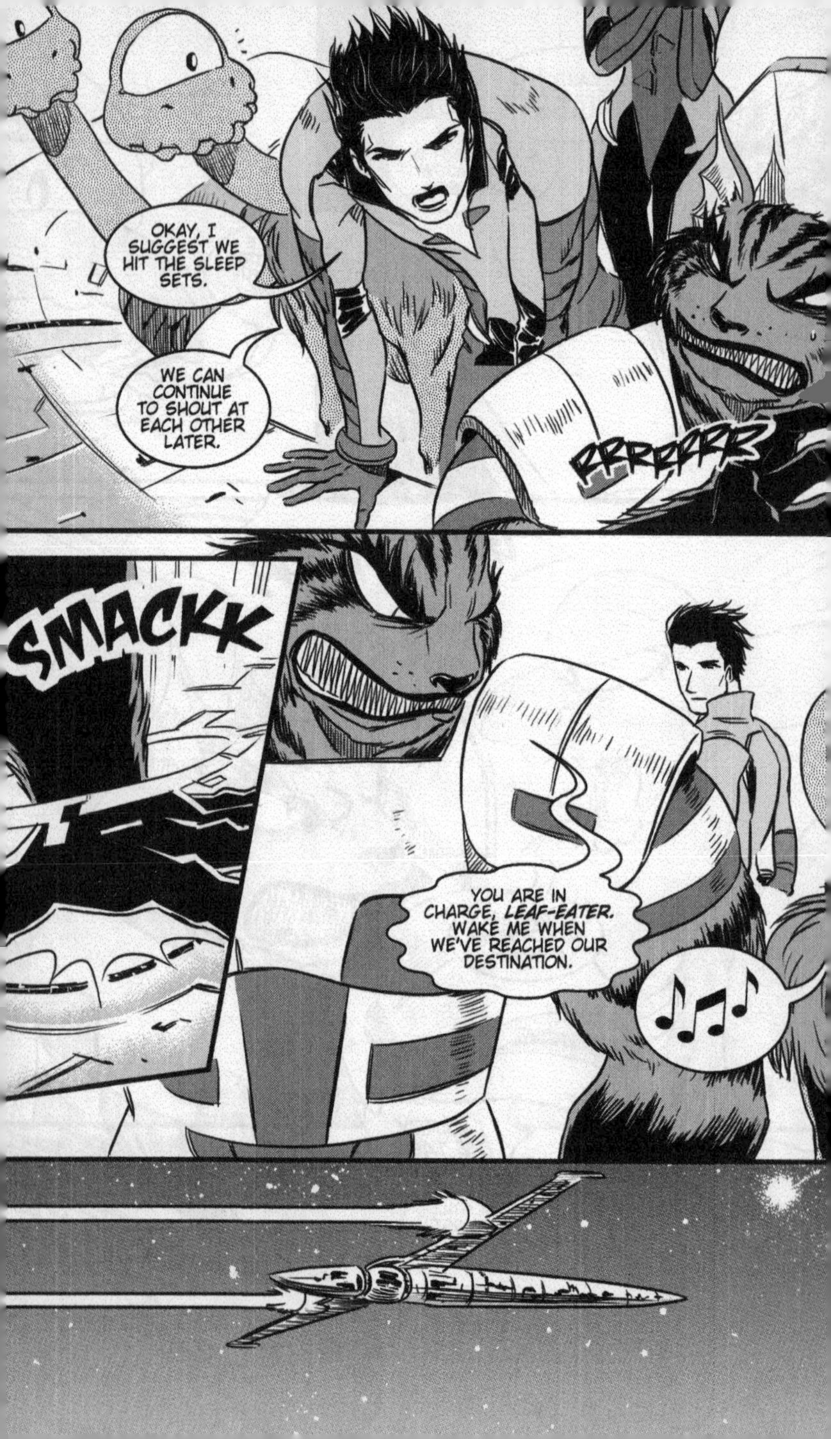
OKAY, I SUGGEST WE HIT THE SLEEP SETS.
WE CAN CONTINUE TO SHOUT AT EACH OTHER LATER.
RRRRRRR
SMACKK
YOU ARE IN CHARGE, *LEAF-EATER.* WAKE ME WHEN WE'VE REACHED OUR DESTINATION.

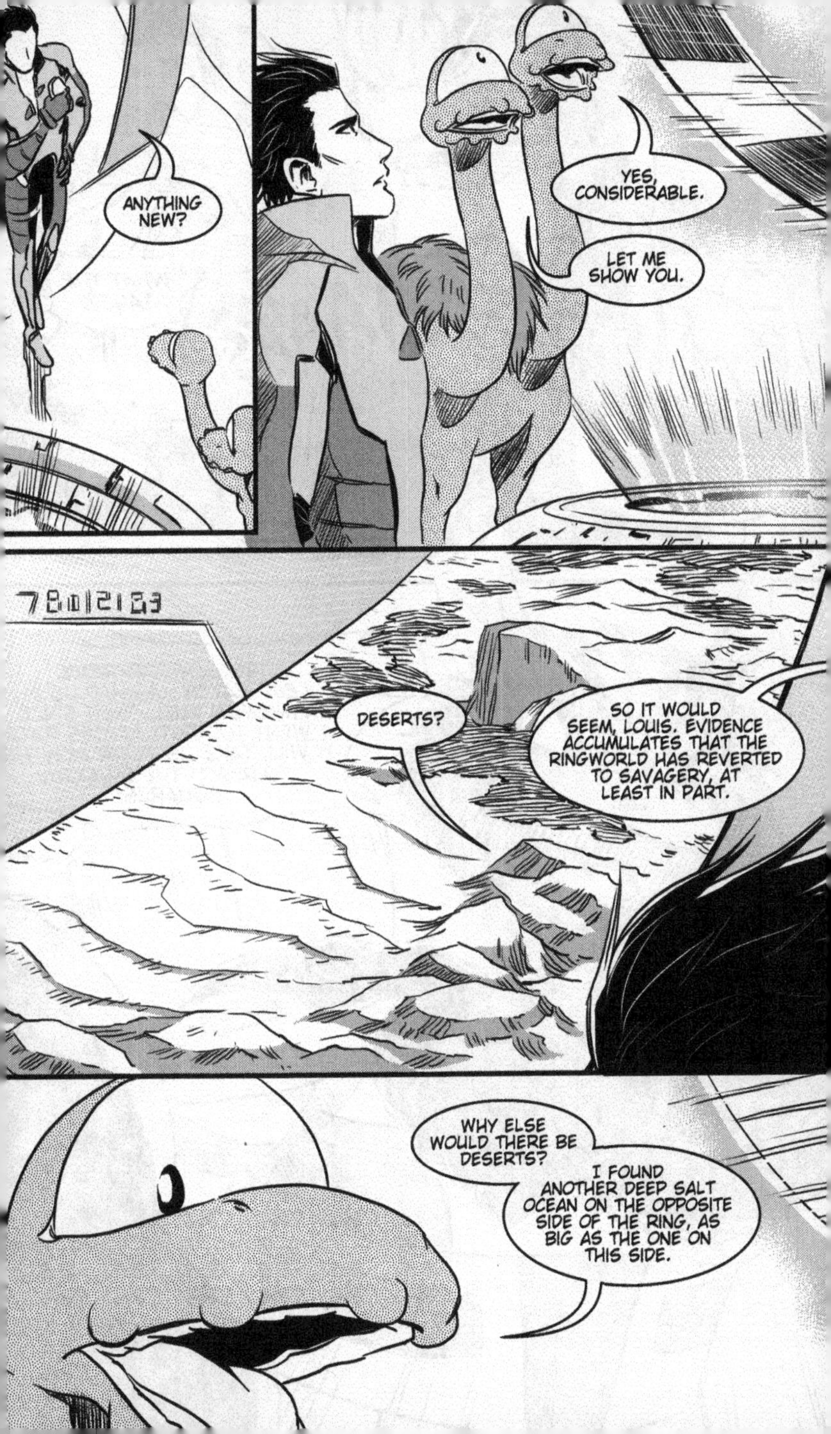
ANYTHING NEW?
YES, CONSIDERABLE.
LET ME SHOW YOU.
78012183
DESERTS?
SO IT WOULD SEEM, LOUIS. EVIDENCE ACCUMULATES THAT THE RINGWORLD HAS REVERTED TO SAVAGERY, AT LEAST IN PART.
WHY ELSE WOULD THERE BE DESERTS?
I FOUND ANOTHER DEEP SALT OCEAN ON THE OPPOSITE SIDE OF THE RING, AS BIG AS THE ONE ON THIS SIDE.

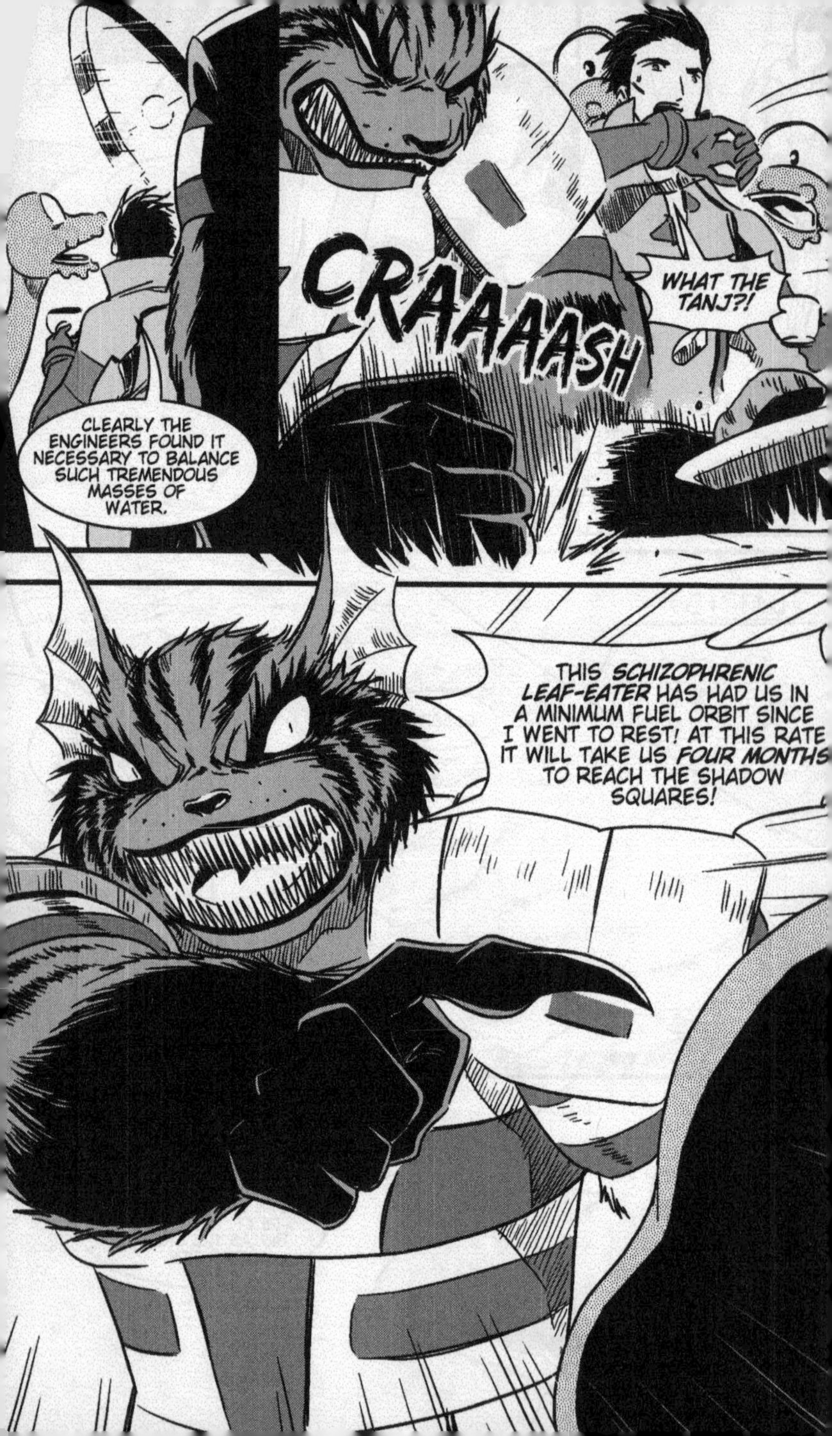
CLEARLY THE ENGINEERS FOUND IT NECESSARY TO BALANCE SUCH TREMENDOUS MASSES OF WATER.
CRAAAAASH
WHAT THE TANJ?!
THIS *SCHIZOPHRENIC LEAF-EATER* HAS HAD US IN A MINIMUM FUEL ORBIT SINCE I WENT TO REST! AT THIS RATE IT WILL TAKE US *FOUR MONTHS* TO REACH THE SHADOW SQUARES!

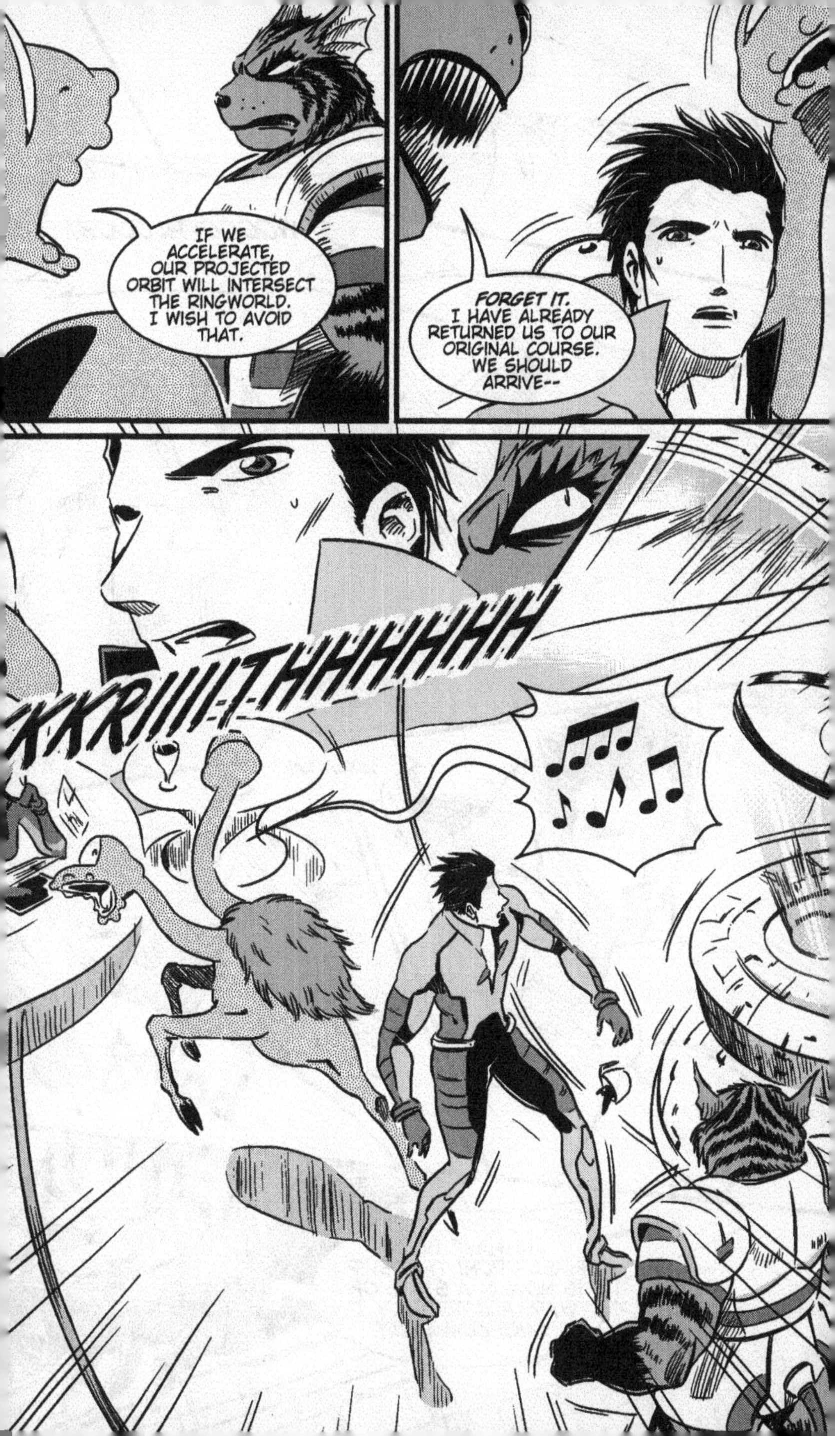

IF WE ACCELERATE, OUR PROJECTED ORBIT WILL INTERSECT THE RINGWORLD. I WISH TO AVOID THAT.
FORGET IT. I HAVE ALREADY RETURNED US TO OUR ORIGINAL COURSE. WE SHOULD ARRIVE--
KKRIIIII-I-THHHHHHHH

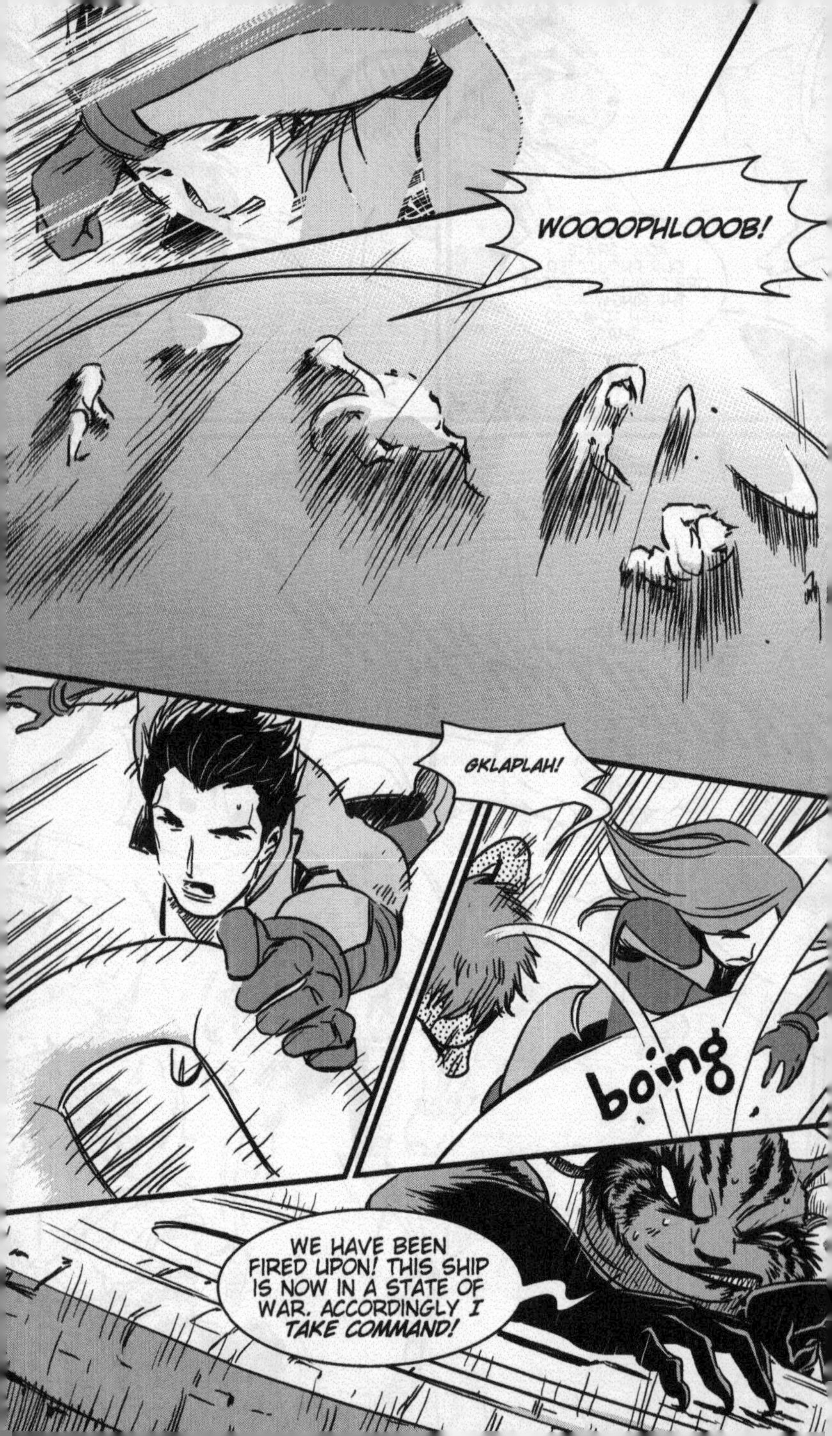
WOOOOPHLOOOB!
GKLAPLAH!
boing
WE HAVE BEEN FIRED UPON! THIS SHIP IS NOW IN A STATE OF WAR. ACCORDINGLY *I TAKE COMMAND!*

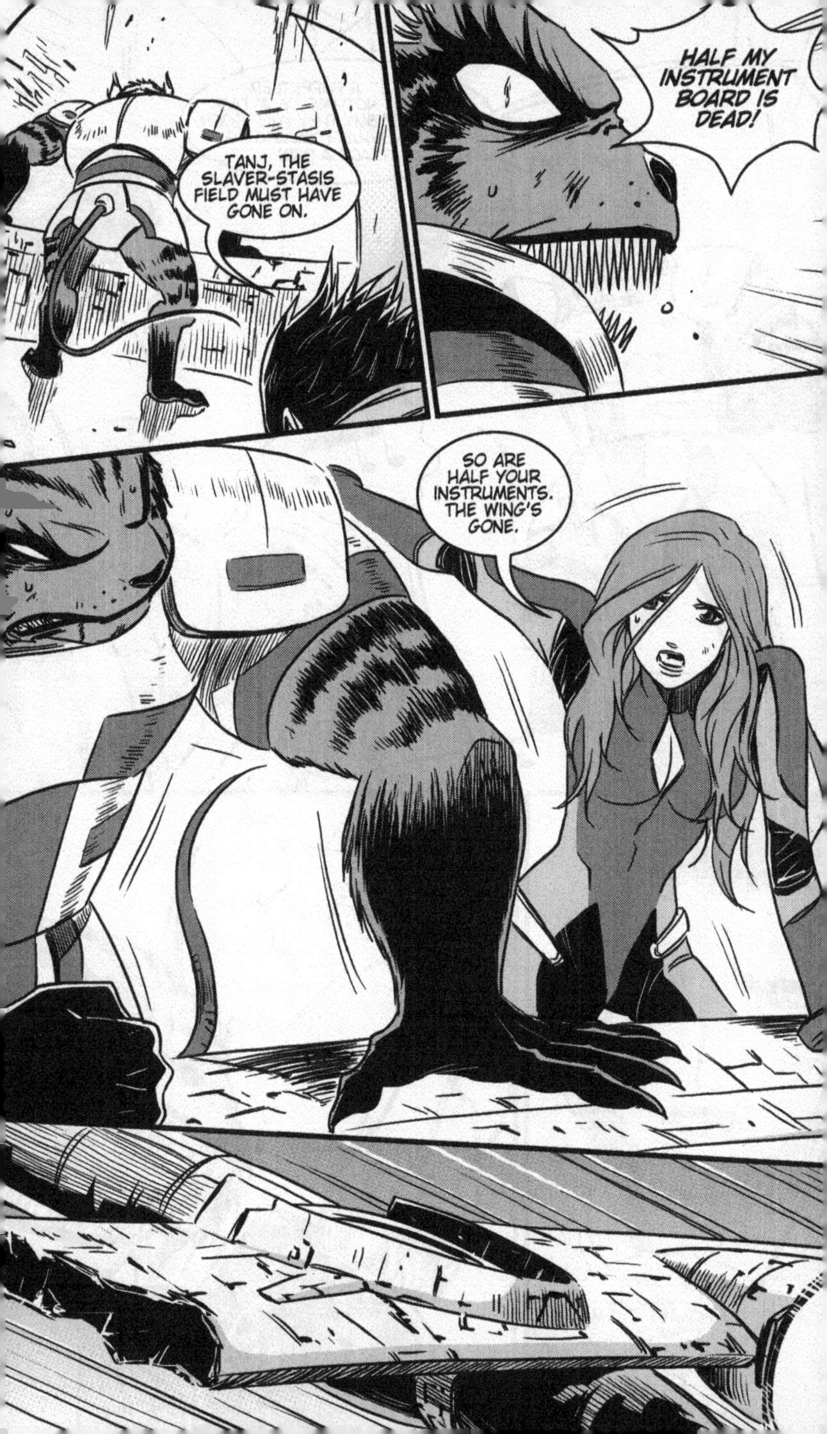
TANJ, THE SLAVER-STASIS FIELD MUST HAVE GONE ON.
HALF MY INSTRUMENT BOARD IS DEAD!
SO ARE HALF YOUR INSTRUMENTS. THE WING'S GONE.

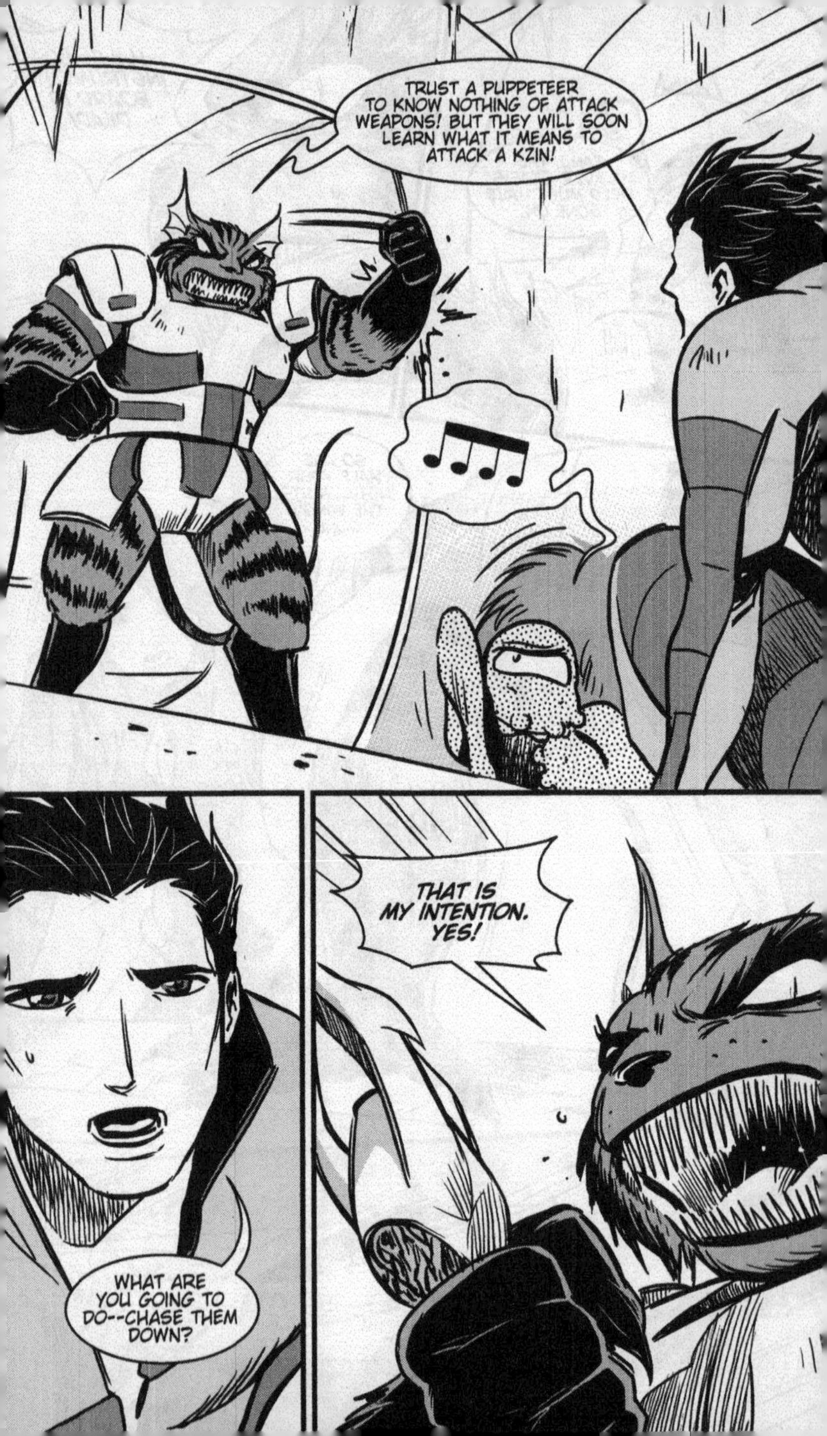
TRUST A PUPPETEER TO KNOW NOTHING OF ATTACK WEAPONS! BUT THEY WILL SOON LEARN WHAT IT MEANS TO ATTACK A KZIN!
WHAT ARE YOU GOING TO DO--CHASE THEM DOWN?
THAT IS MY INTENTION. YES!

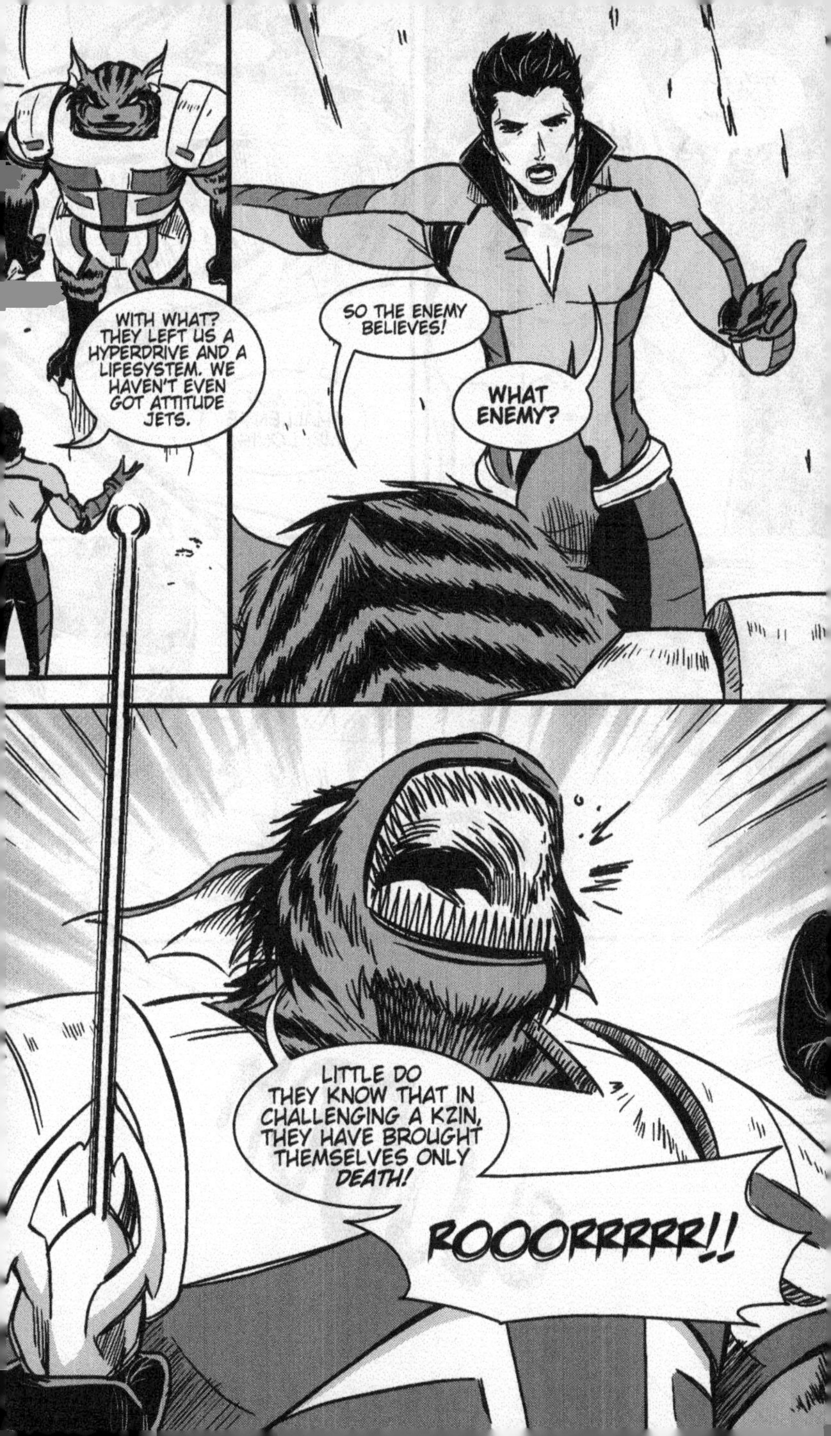
WITH WHAT? THEY LEFT US A HYPERDRIVE AND A LIFESYSTEM. WE HAVEN'T EVEN GOT ATTITUDE JETS.
SO THE ENEMY BELIEVES!
WHAT ENEMY?
LITTLE DO THEY KNOW THAT IN CHALLENGING A KZIN, THEY HAVE BROUGHT THEMSELVES ONLY *DEATH!*
ROOORRRRR!!

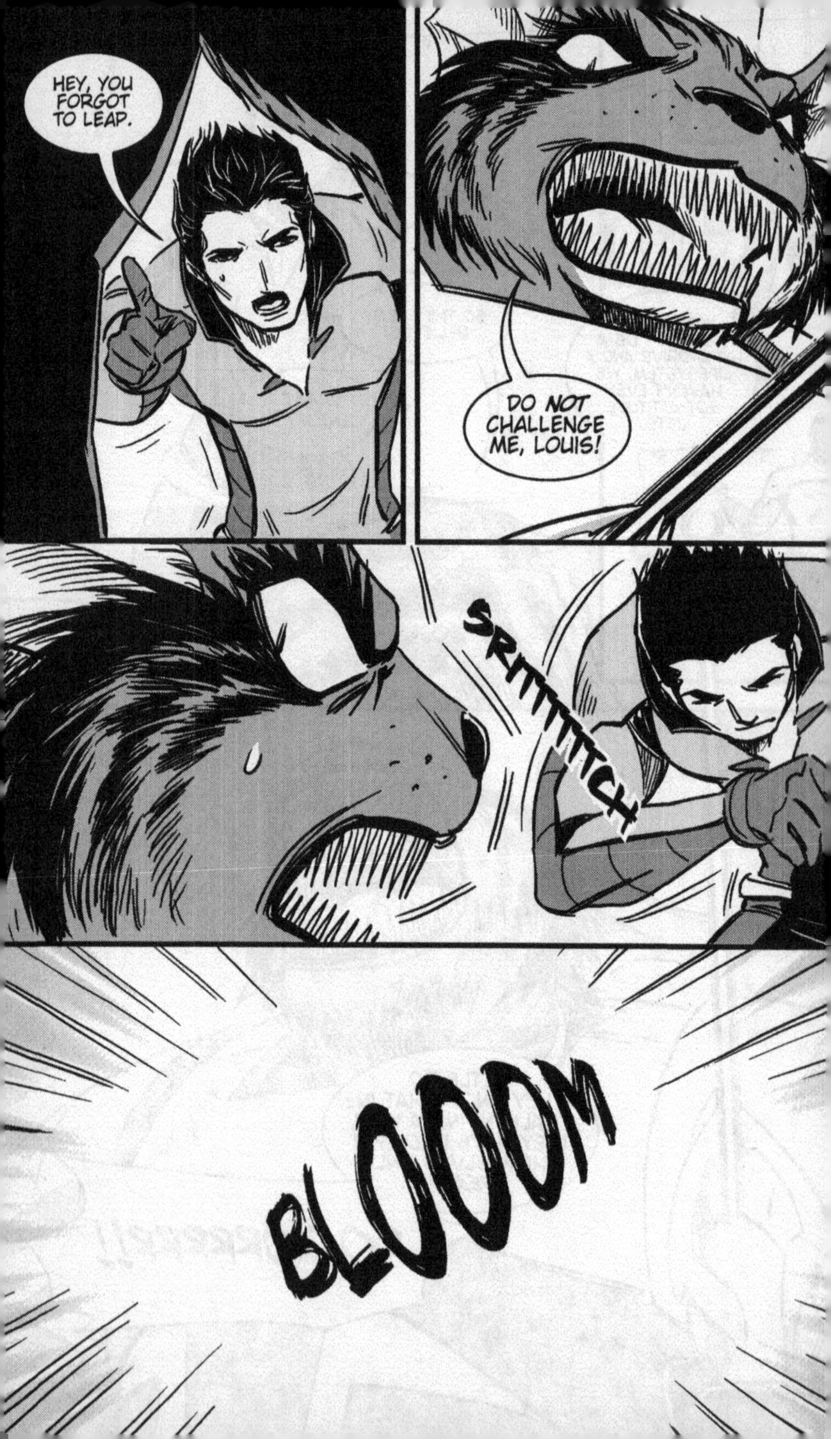
HEY, YOU FORGOT TO LEAP.
DO NOT CHALLENGE ME, LOUIS!
SRITTTTTCH
BLOOOM

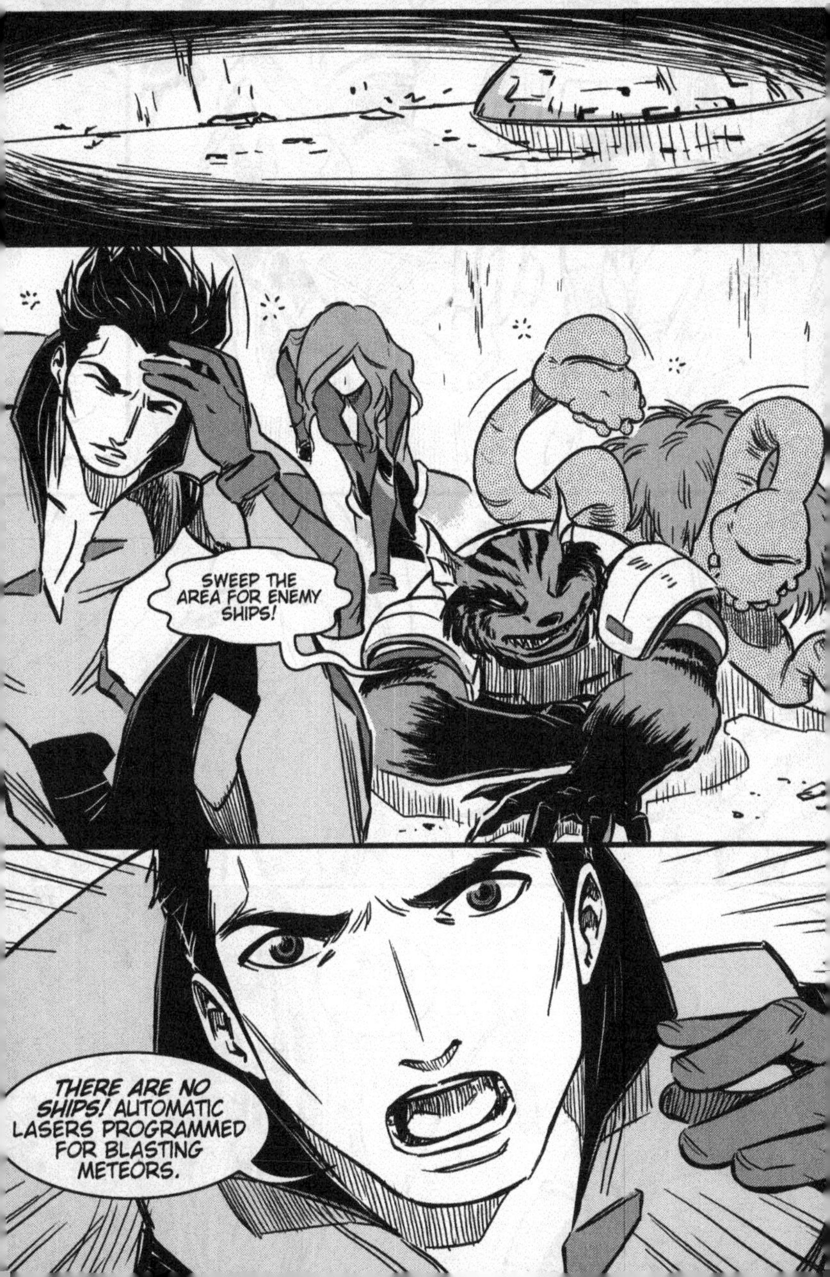
SWEEP THE AREA FOR ENEMY SHIPS!
THERE ARE NO SHIPS! AUTOMATIC LASERS PROGRAMMED FOR BLASTING METEORS.

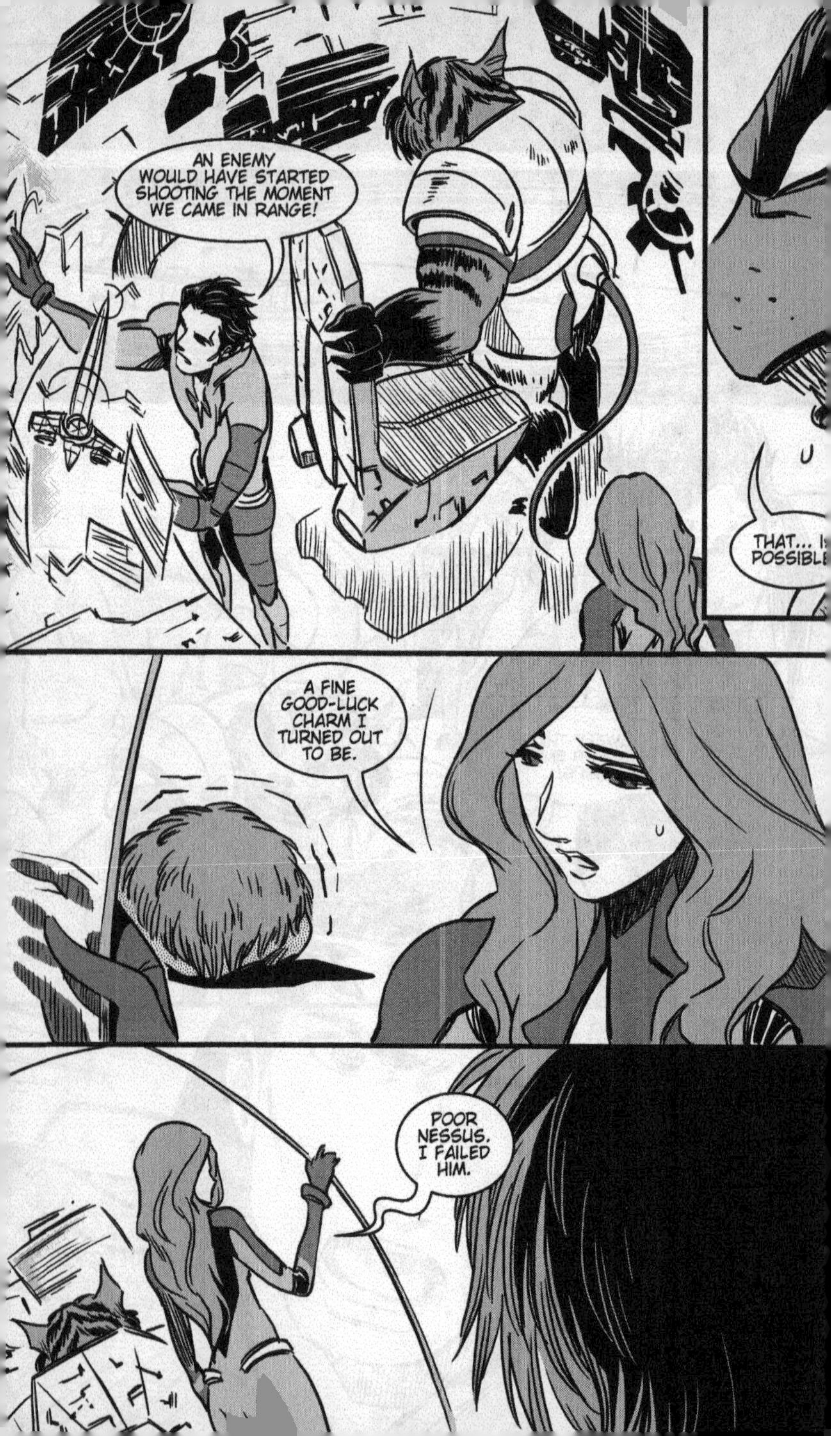
AN ENEMY WOULD HAVE STARTED SHOOTING THE MOMENT WE CAME IN RANGE!
THAT... IS POSSIBLE
A FINE GOOD-LUCK CHARM I TURNED OUT TO BE.
POOR NESSUS. I FAILED HIM.

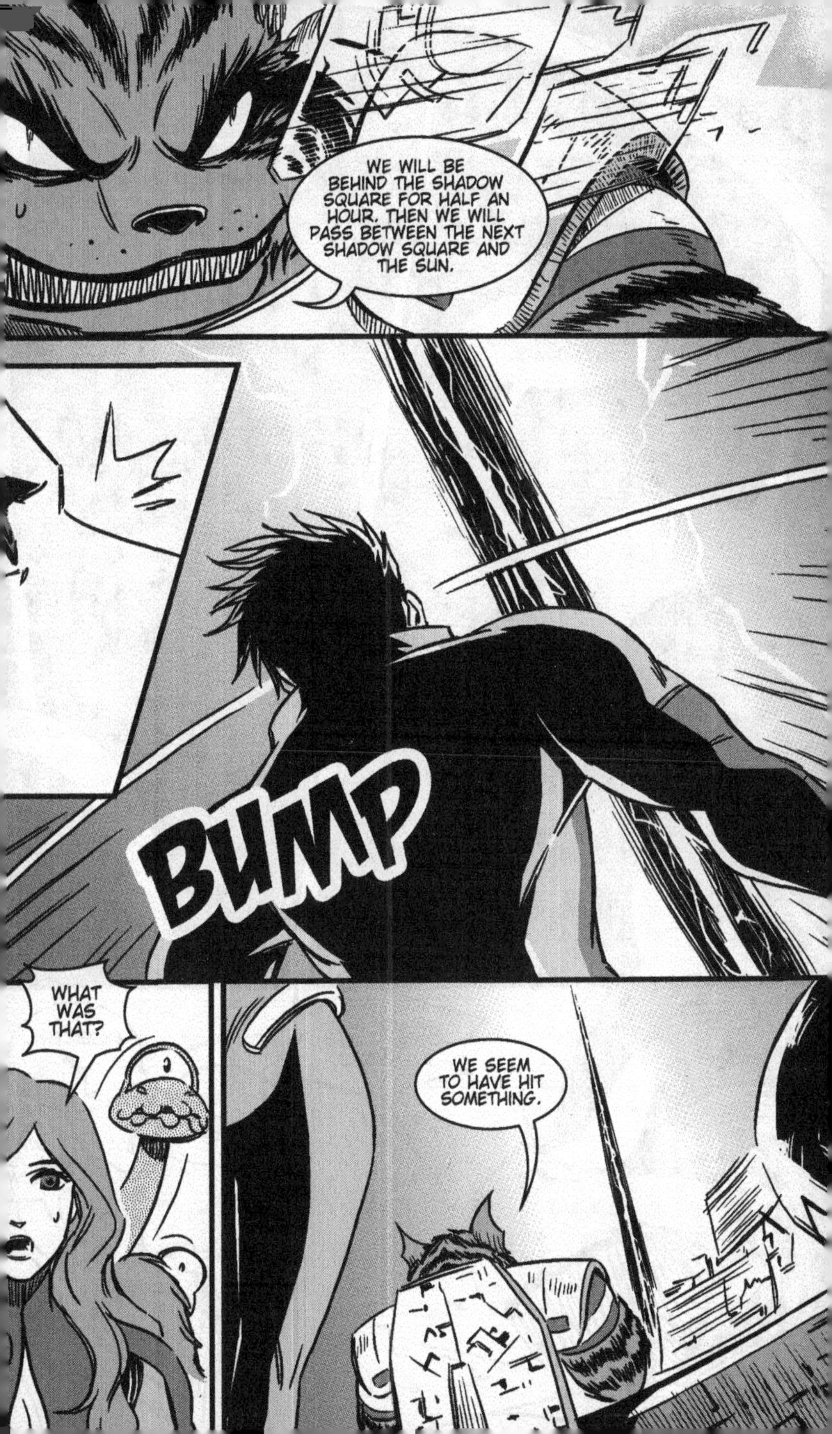
WE WILL BE BEHIND THE SHADOW SQUARE FOR HALF AN HOUR. THEN WE WILL PASS BETWEEN THE NEXT SHADOW SQUARE AND THE SUN.
BUMP
WHAT WAS THAT?
WE SEEM TO HAVE HIT SOMETHING.

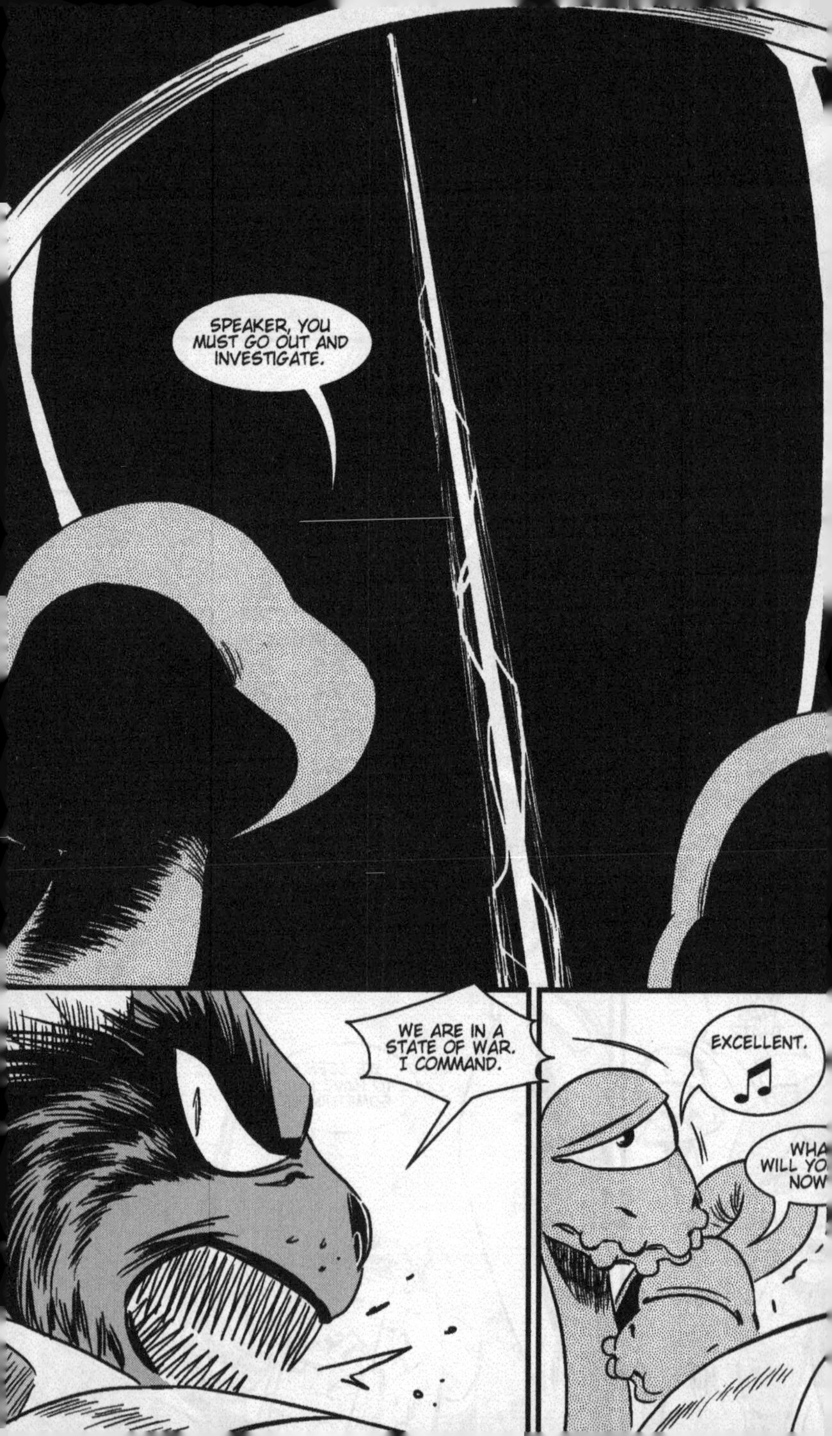
SPEAKER, YOU MUST GO OUT AND INVESTIGATE.
WE ARE IN A STATE OF WAR. I COMMAND.
EXCELLENT. ♫
WHA WILL YO NOW

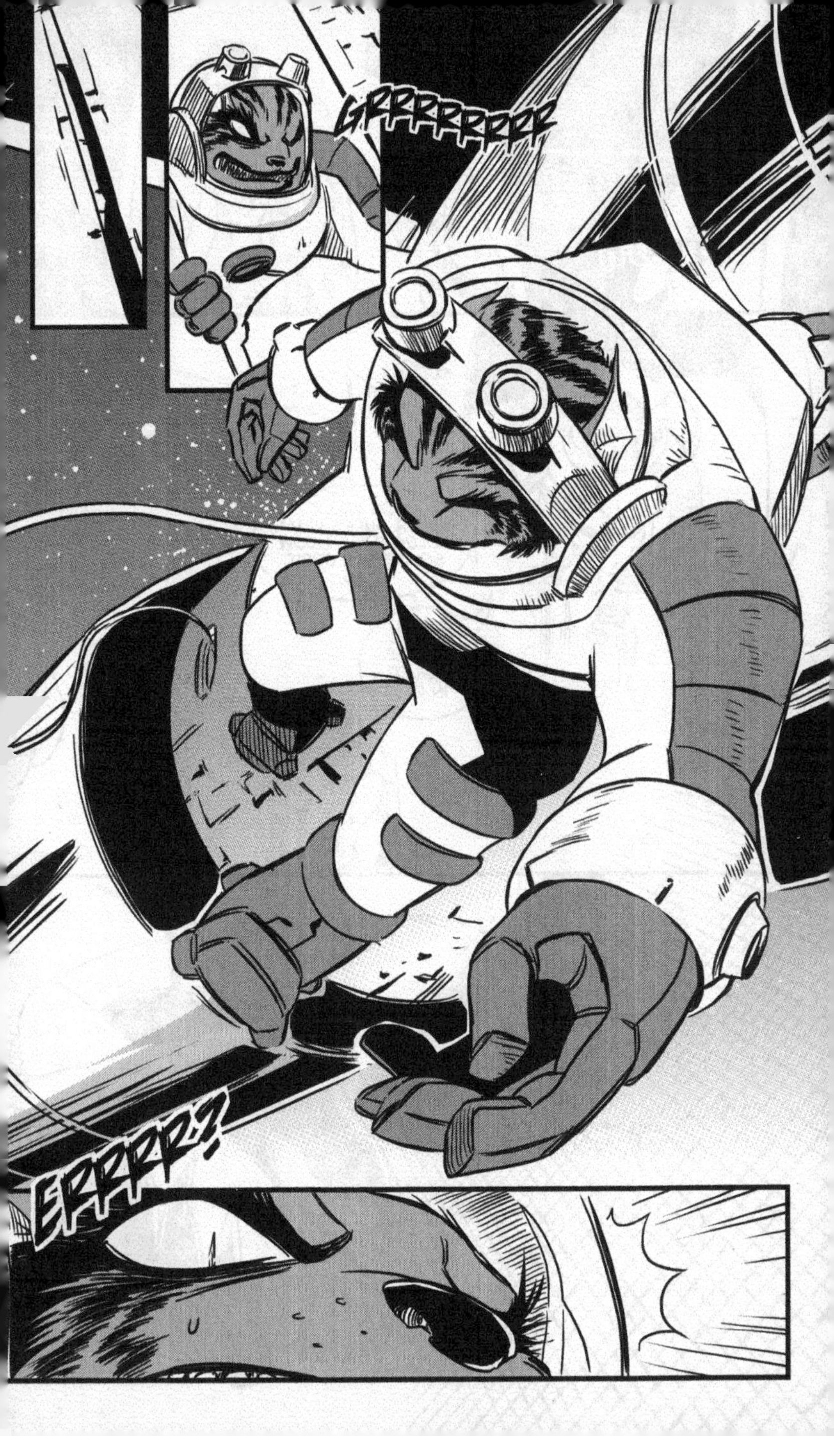
GRRRRRRRRR
ERRRRZ

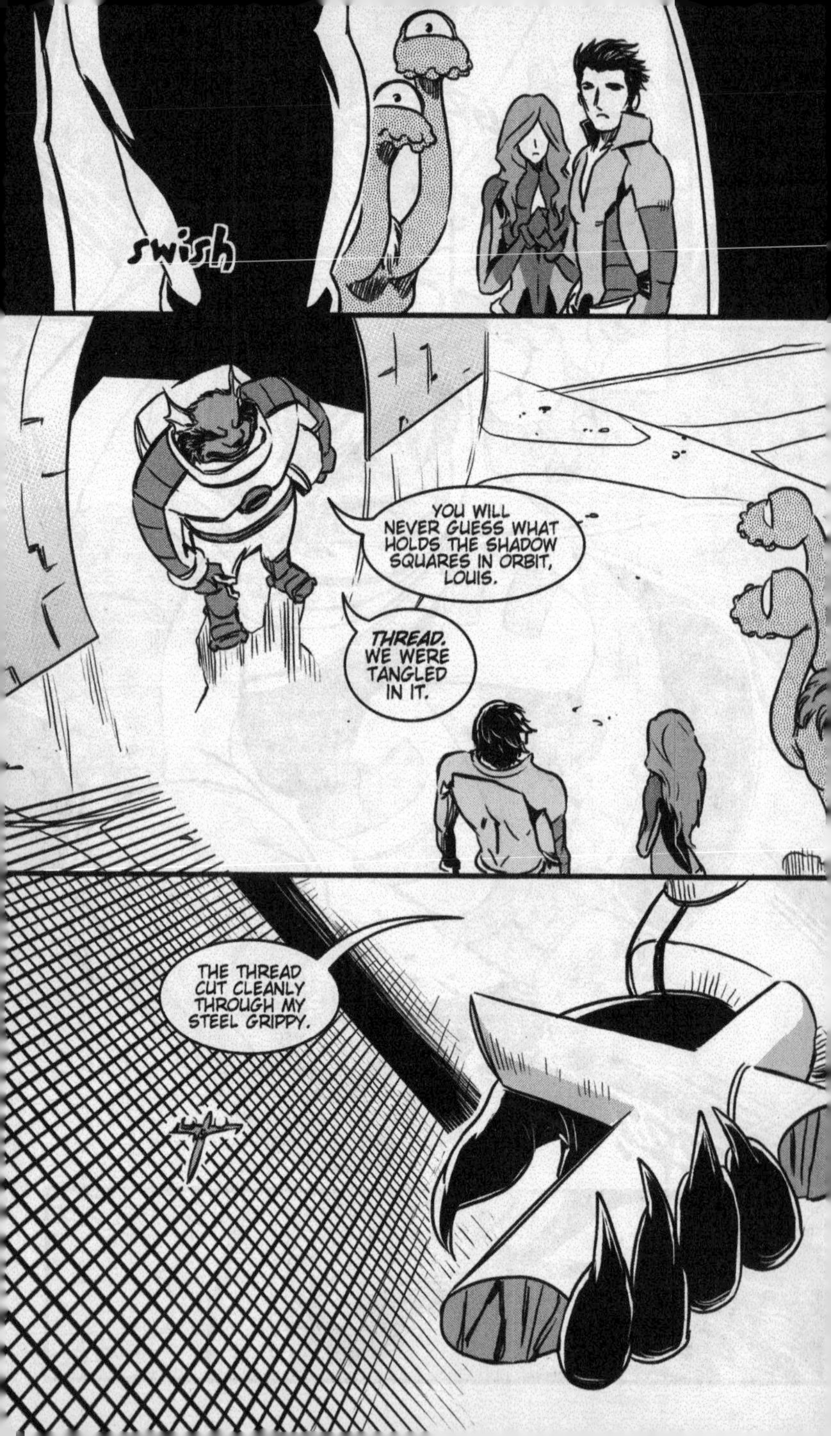
swish
YOU WILL NEVER GUESS WHAT HOLDS THE SHADOW SQUARES IN ORBIT, LOUIS.
THREAD. WE WERE TANGLED IN IT.
THE THREAD CUT CLEANLY THROUGH MY STEEL GRIPPY.

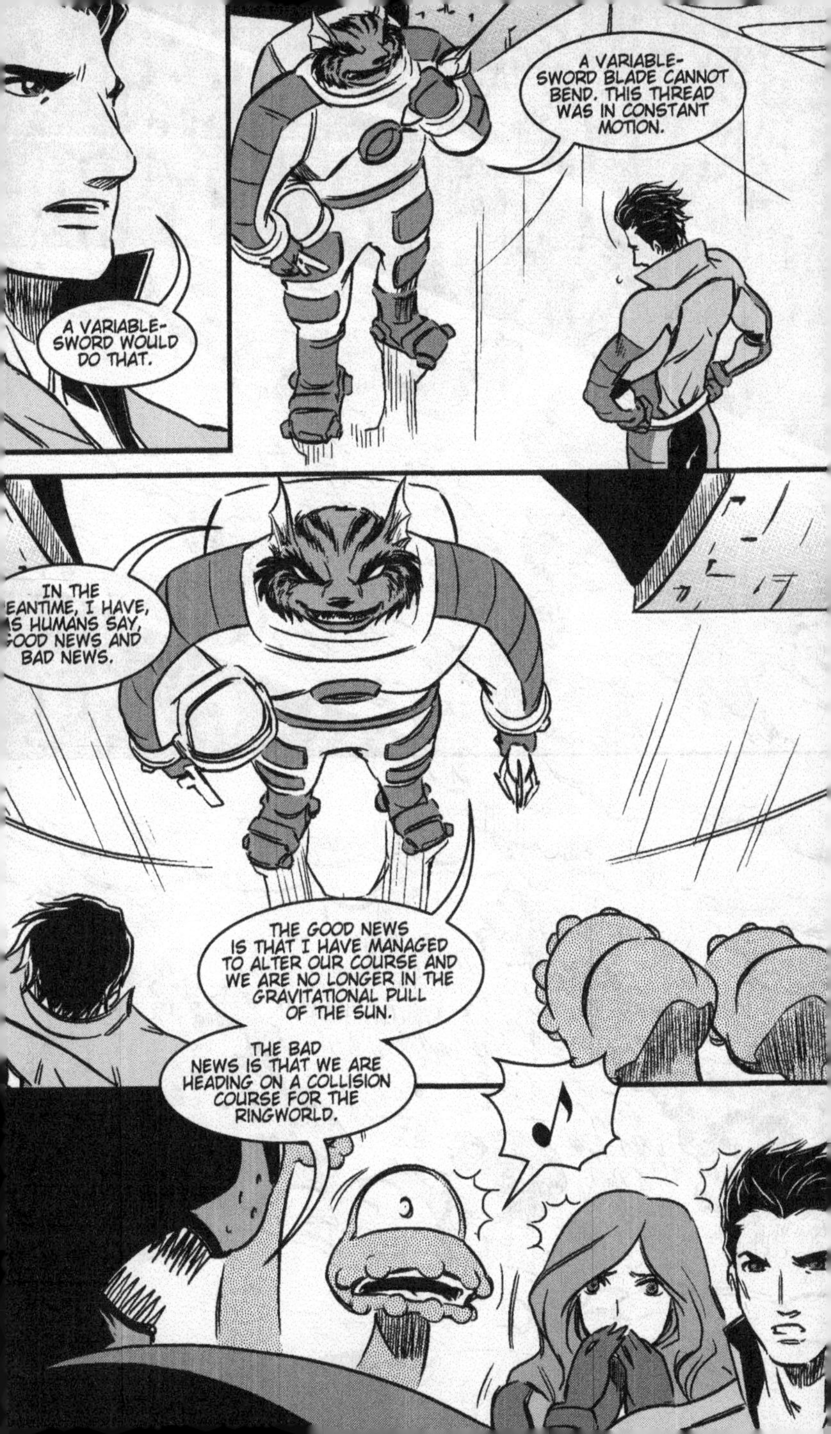
A VARIABLE-SWORD WOULD DO THAT.
A VARIABLE-SWORD BLADE CANNOT BEND. THIS THREAD WAS IN CONSTANT MOTION.
IN THE EANTIME, I HAVE, S HUMANS SAY, OOD NEWS AND BAD NEWS.
THE GOOD NEWS IS THAT I HAVE MANAGED TO ALTER OUR COURSE AND WE ARE NO LONGER IN THE GRAVITATIONAL PULL OF THE SUN.
THE BAD NEWS IS THAT WE ARE HEADING ON A COLLISION COURSE FOR THE RINGWORLD.
♪

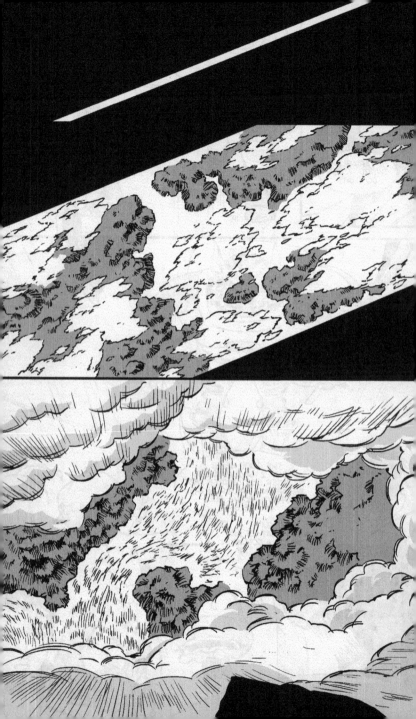

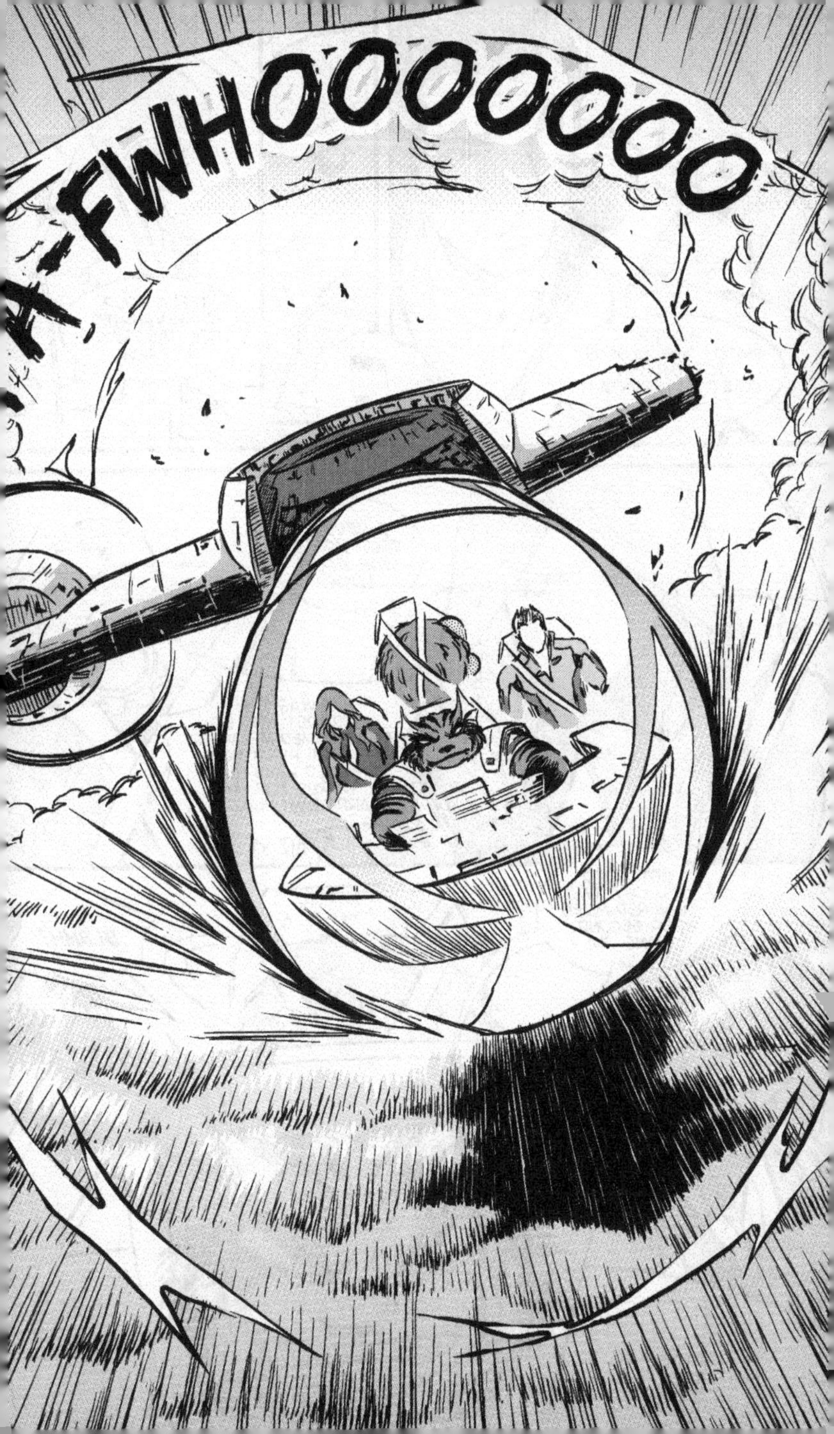
FWHOOOOOOOO

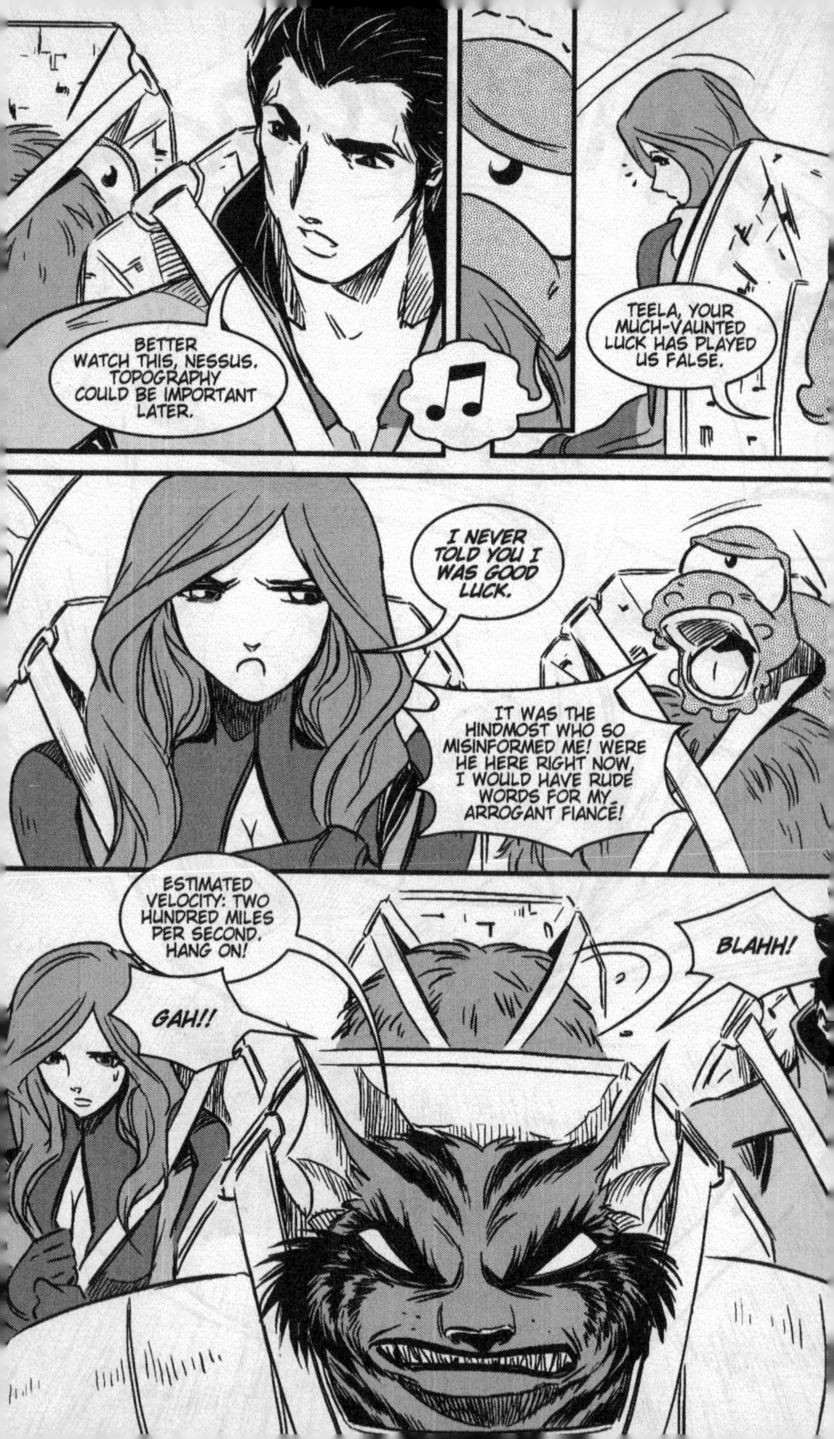
BETTER WATCH THIS, NESSUS. TOPOGRAPHY COULD BE IMPORTANT LATER.
♪
TEELA, YOUR MUCH-VAUNTED LUCK HAS PLAYED US FALSE.
I NEVER TOLD YOU I WAS GOOD LUCK.
IT WAS THE HINDMOST WHO SO MISINFORMED ME! WERE HE HERE RIGHT NOW, I WOULD HAVE RUDE WORDS FOR MY ARROGANT FIANCÉ!
ESTIMATED VELOCITY: TWO HUNDRED MILES PER SECOND. HANG ON!
GAH!!
BLAHH!

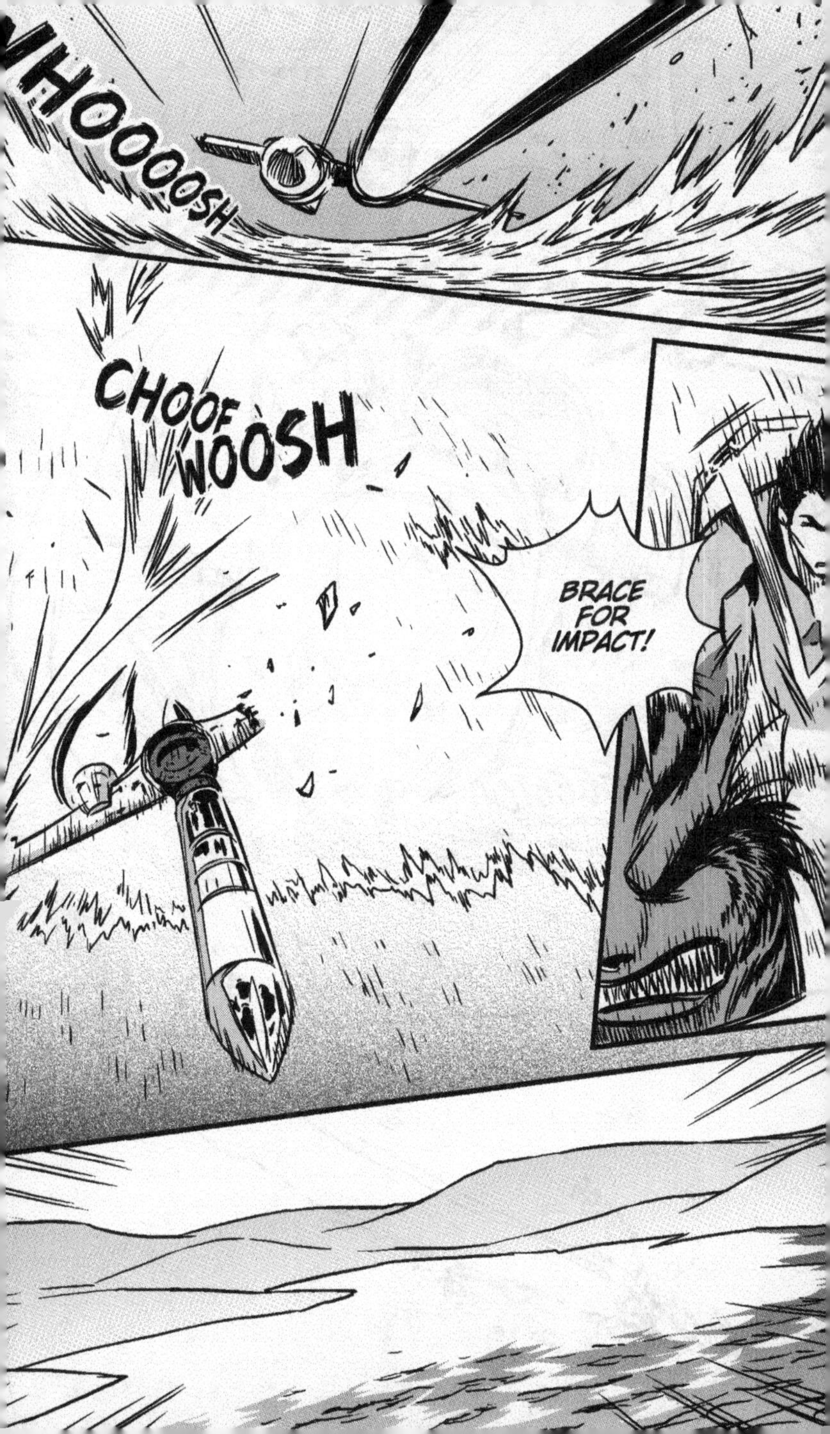
WHOOOOSH
CHOOF
WOOSH
BRACE FOR IMPACT!

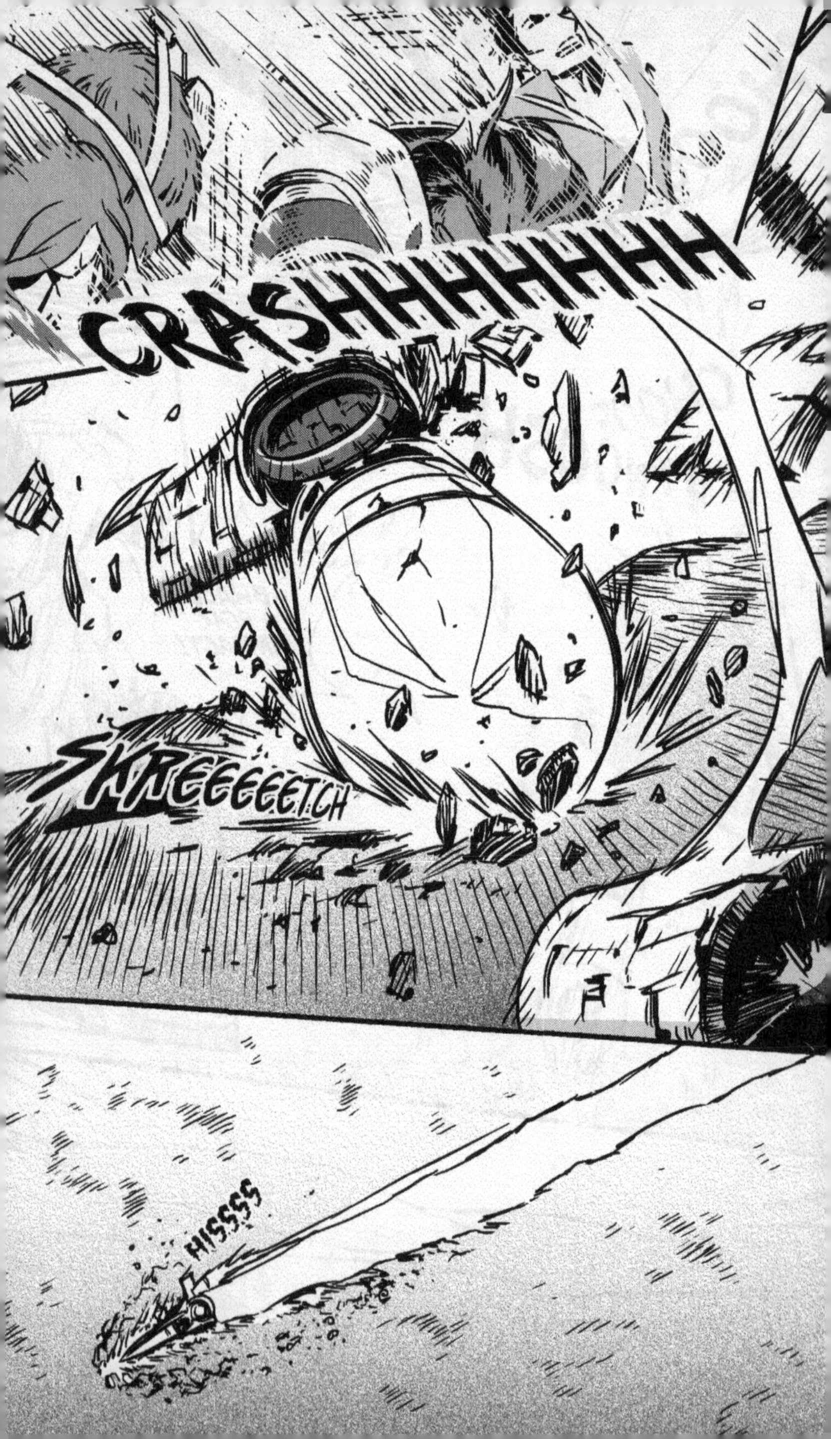
CRASHHHHHHHH
SKREEEEEETCH
HISSSS

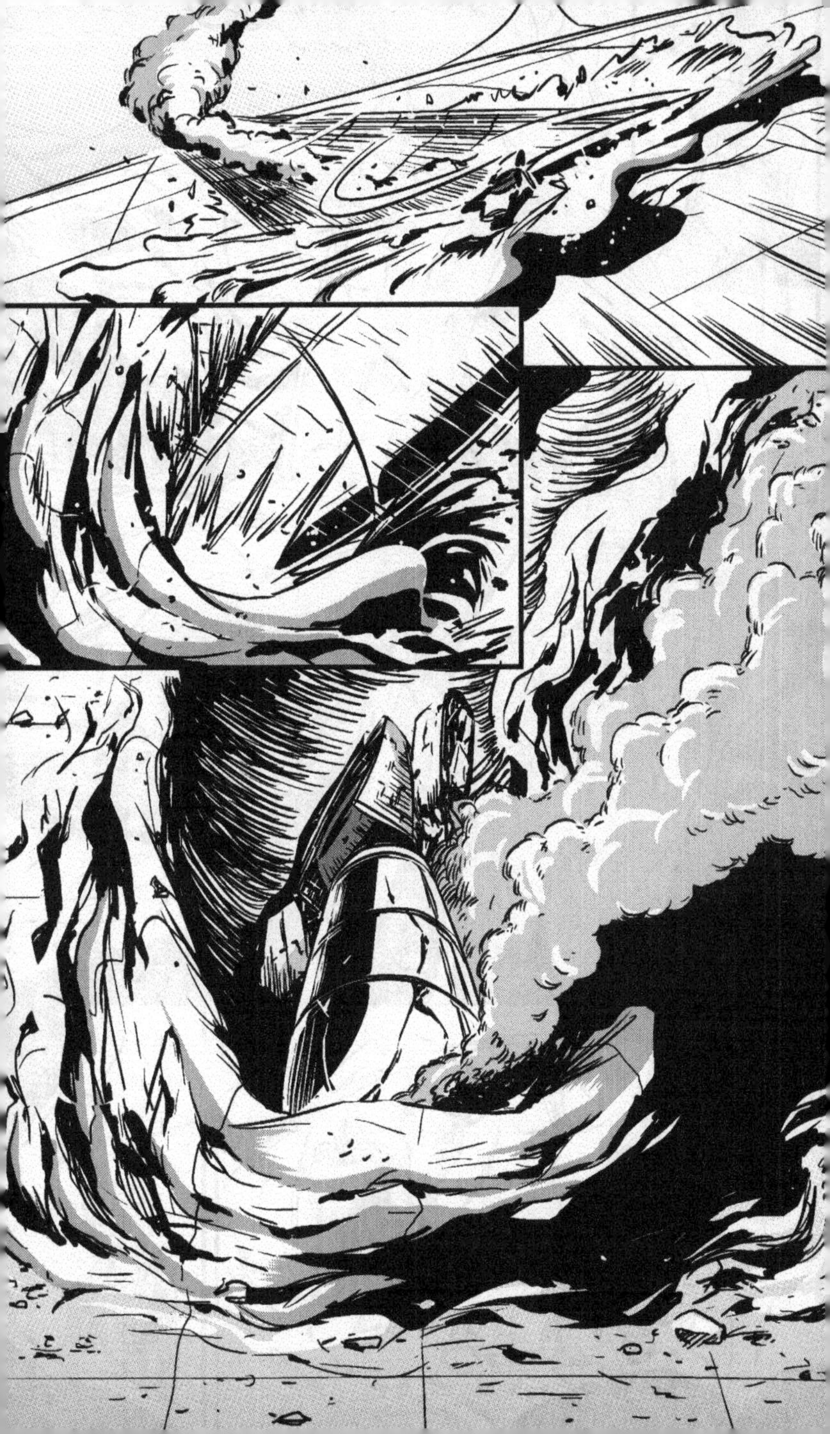

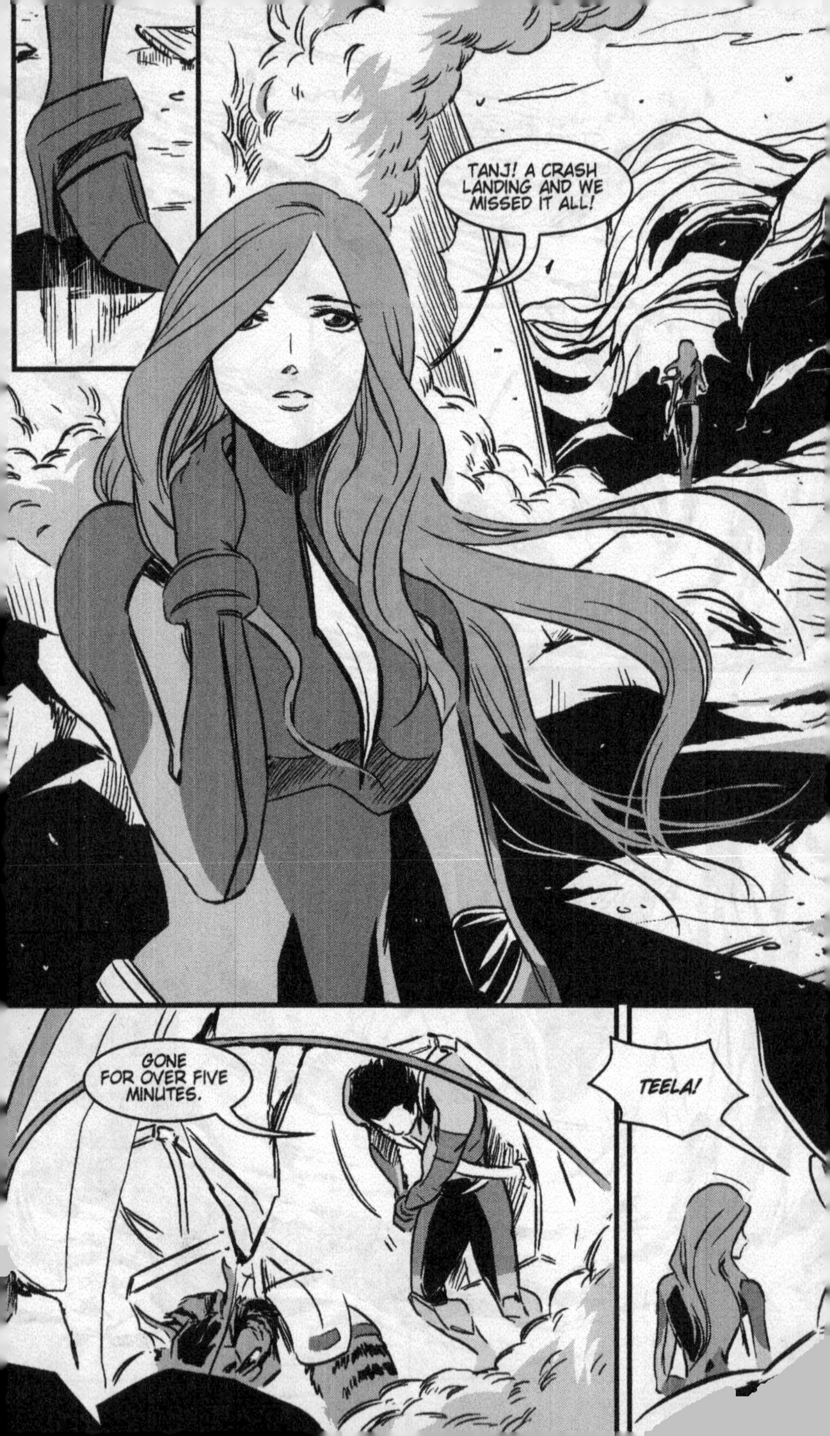
TANJ! A CRASH LANDING AND WE MISSED IT ALL!
GONE FOR OVER FIVE MINUTES.
TEELA!

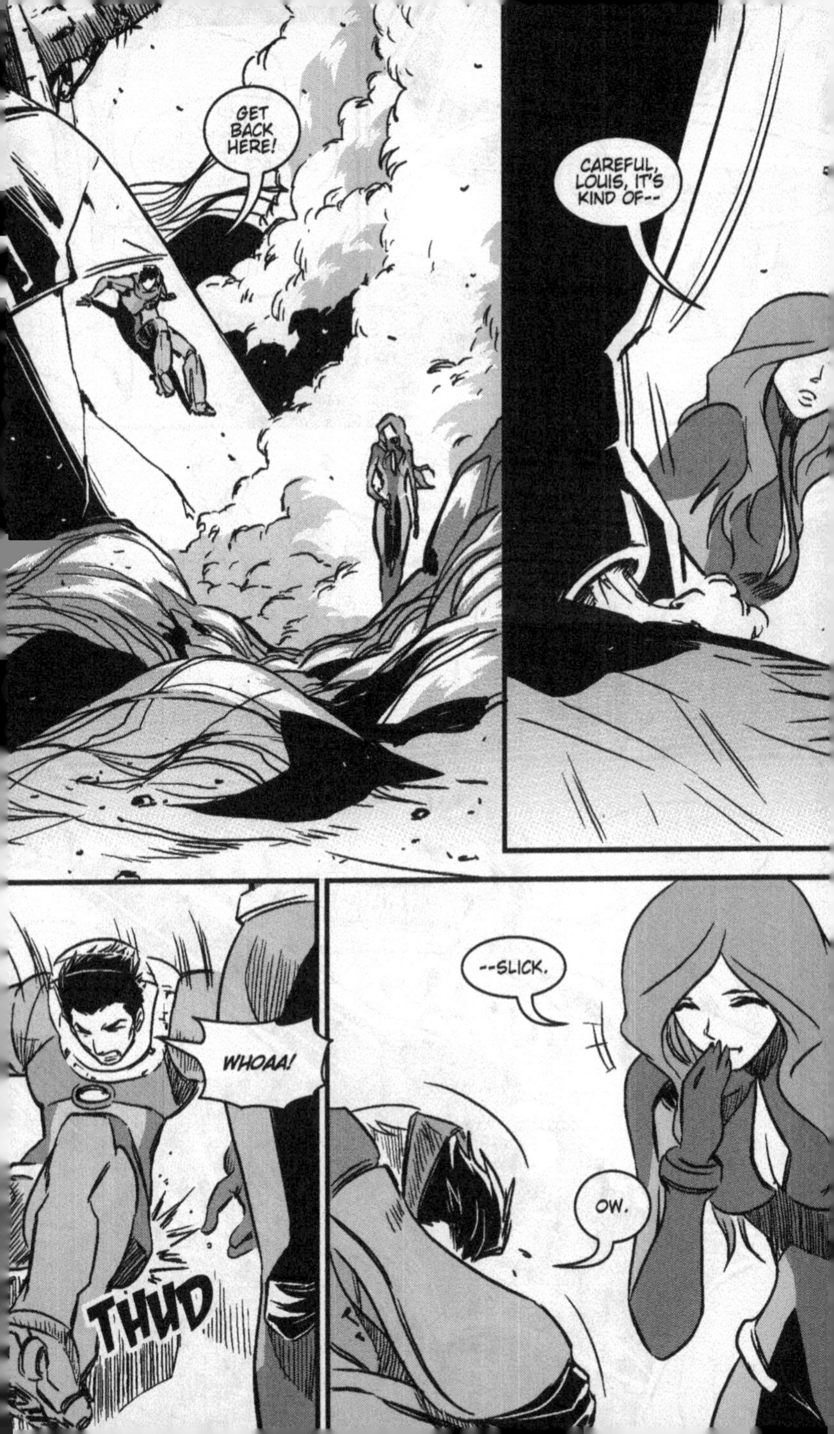
GET BACK HERE!
CAREFUL, LOUIS, IT'S KIND OF--
WHOAA!
THUD
--SLICK.
OW.

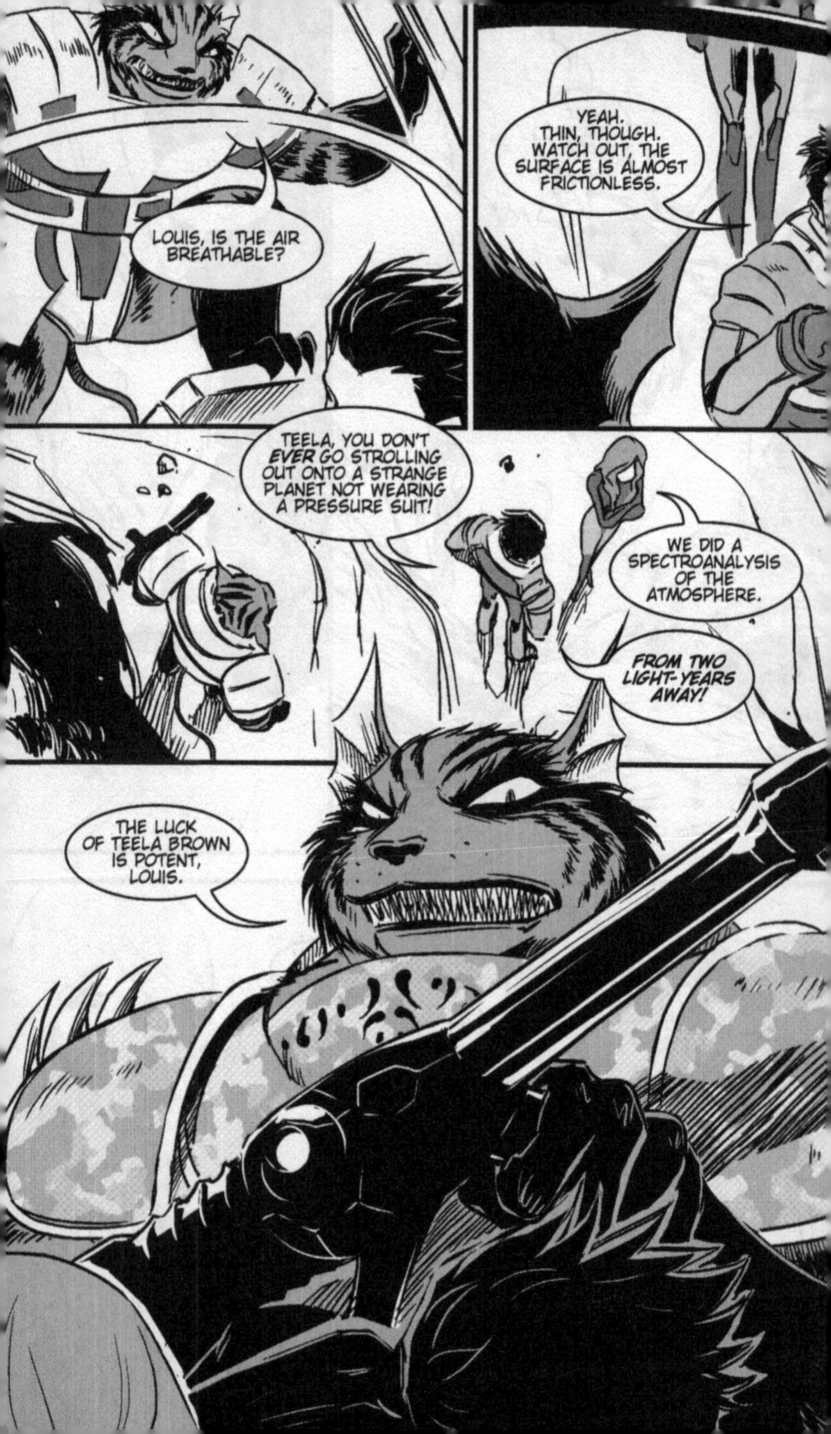
LOUIS, IS THE AIR BREATHABLE?
YEAH. THIN, THOUGH. WATCH OUT, THE SURFACE IS ALMOST FRICTIONLESS.
TEELA, YOU DON'T *EVER* GO STROLLING OUT ONTO A STRANGE PLANET NOT WEARING A PRESSURE SUIT!
WE DID A SPECTROANALYSIS OF THE ATMOSPHERE.
FROM TWO LIGHT-YEARS AWAY!
THE LUCK OF TEELA BROWN IS POTENT, LOUIS.

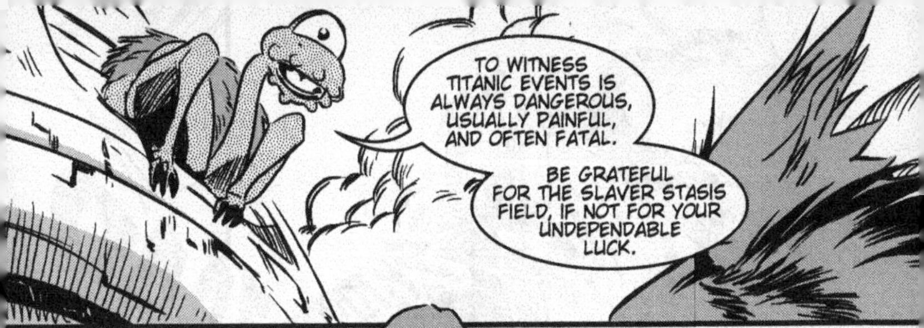
TO WITNESS TITANIC EVENTS IS ALWAYS DANGEROUS, USUALLY PAINFUL, AND OFTEN FATAL.
BE GRATEFUL FOR THE SLAVER STASIS FIELD, IF NOT FOR YOUR UNDEPENDABLE LUCK.

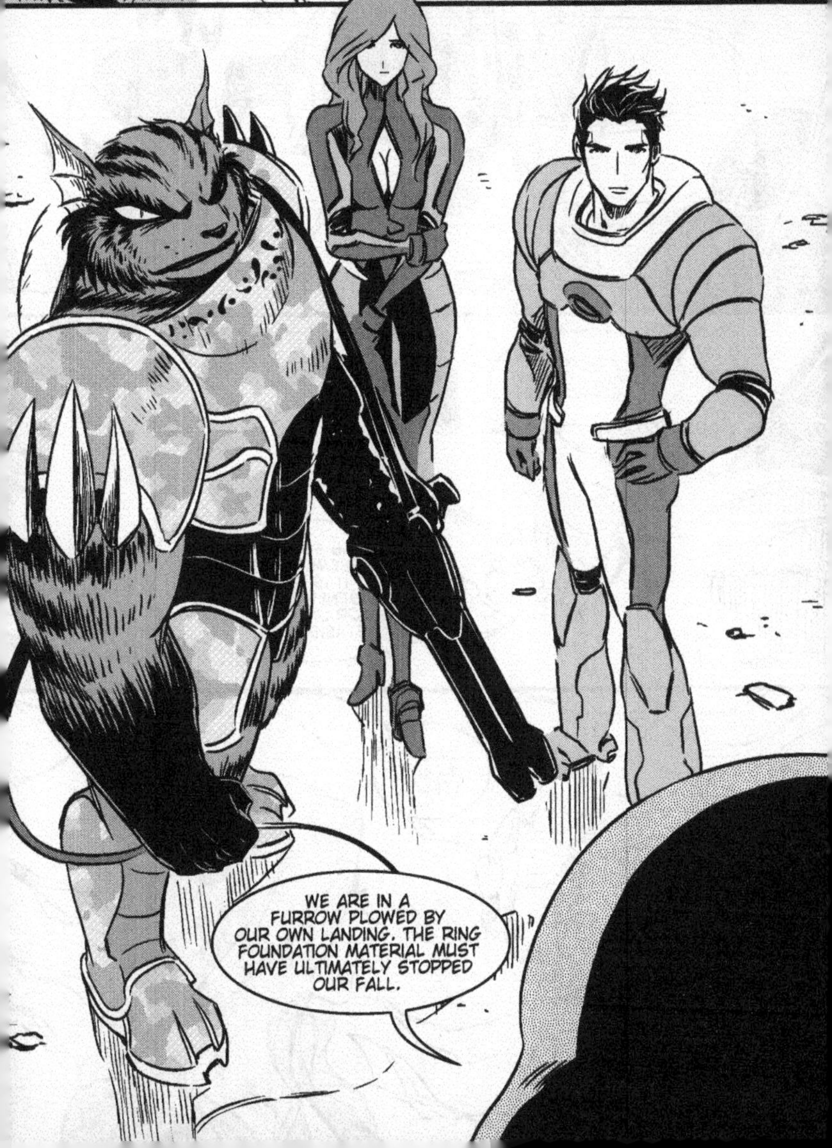
WE ARE IN A FURROW PLOWED BY OUR OWN LANDING. THE RING FOUNDATION MATERIAL MUST HAVE ULTIMATELY STOPPED OUR FALL.

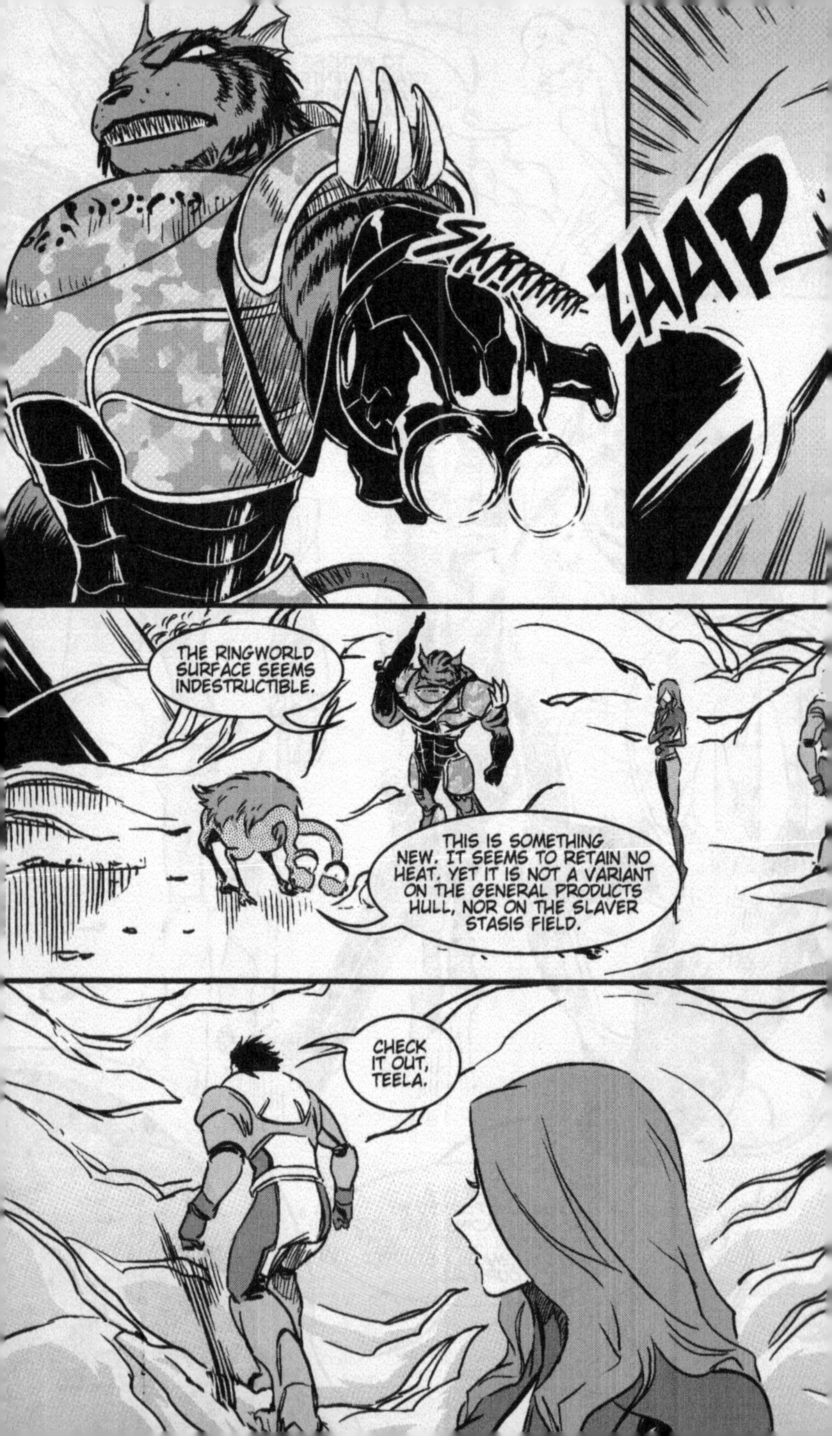
SKRRRRRRR-
ZAAP
THE RINGWORLD SURFACE SEEMS INDESTRUCTIBLE.
THIS IS SOMETHING NEW. IT SEEMS TO RETAIN NO HEAT. YET IT IS NOT A VARIANT ON THE GENERAL PRODUCTS HULL, NOR ON THE SLAVER STASIS FIELD.
CHECK IT OUT, TEELA.

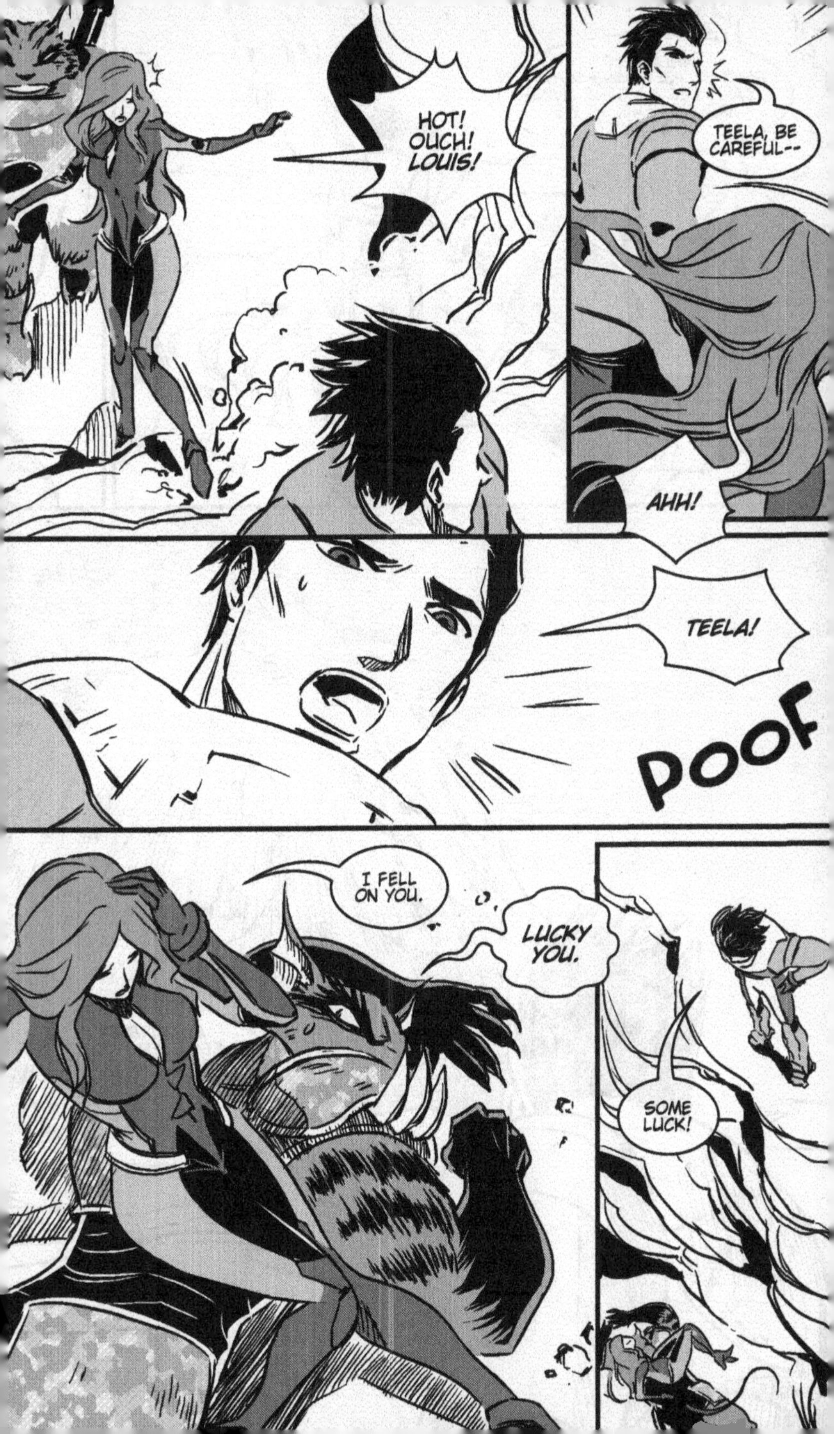
HOT! OUCH! LOUIS!
TEELA, BE CAREFUL--
AHH!
TEELA!
POOF
I FELL ON YOU.
LUCKY YOU.
SOME LUCK!

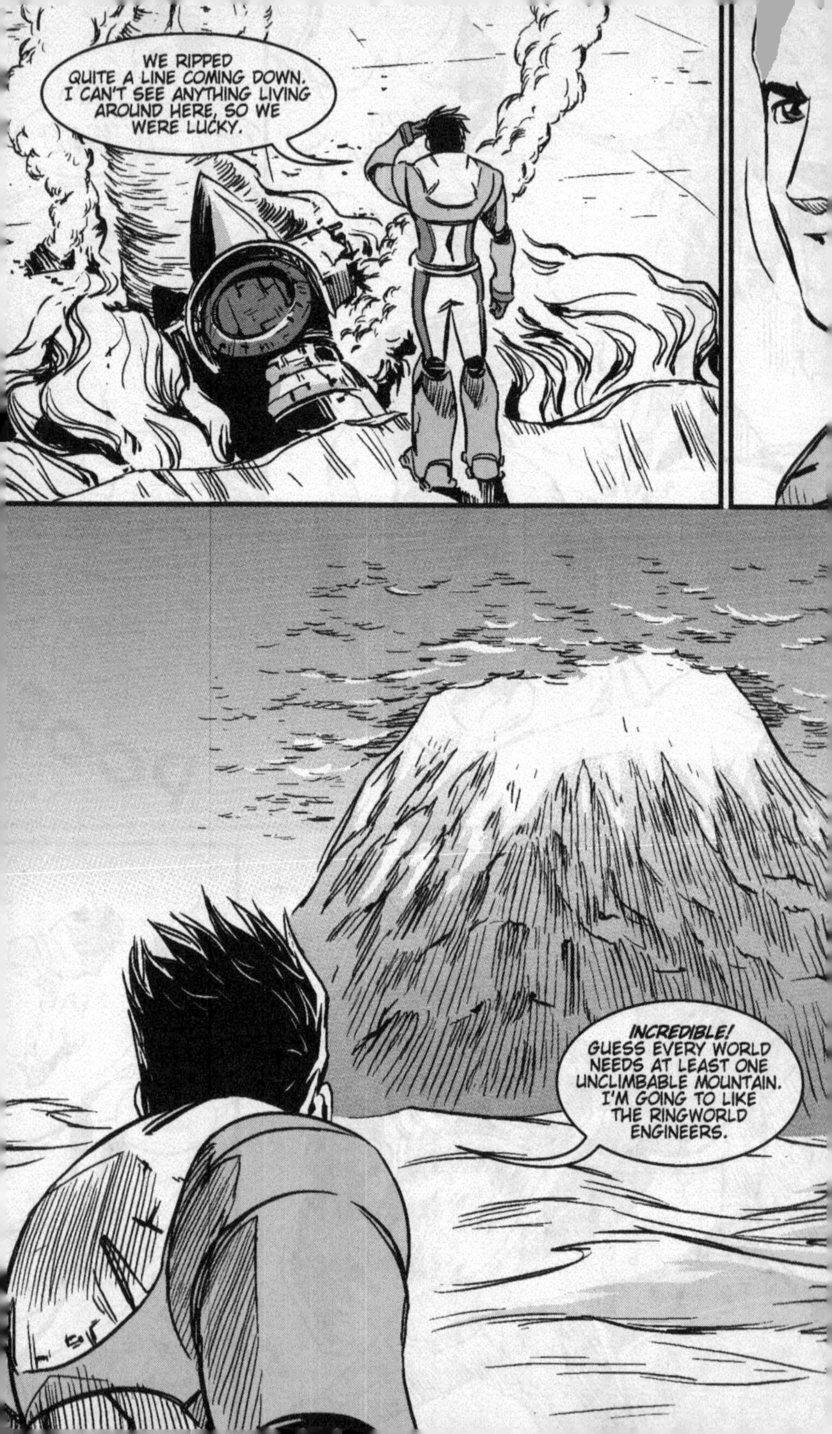
WE RIPPED QUITE A LINE COMING DOWN. I CAN'T SEE ANYTHING LIVING AROUND HERE, SO WE WERE LUCKY.
INCREDIBLE! GUESS EVERY WORLD NEEDS AT LEAST ONE UNCLIMBABLE MOUNTAIN. I'M GOING TO LIKE THE RINGWORLD ENGINEERS.

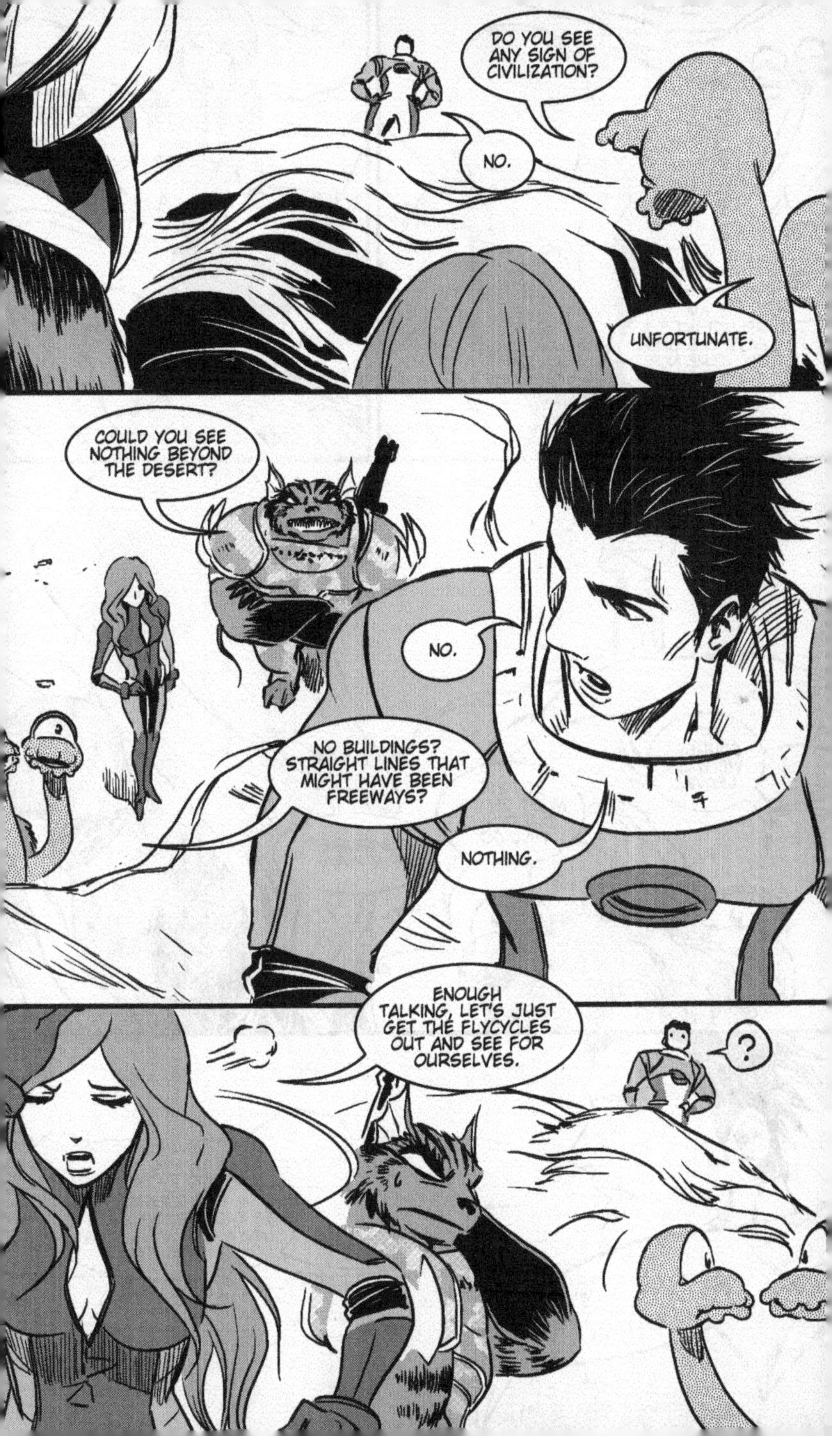
DO YOU SEE ANY SIGN OF CIVILIZATION?
NO.
UNFORTUNATE.
COULD YOU SEE NOTHING BEYOND THE DESERT?
NO.
NO BUILDINGS? STRAIGHT LINES THAT MIGHT HAVE BEEN FREEWAYS?
NOTHING.
ENOUGH TALKING, LET'S JUST GET THE FLYCYCLES OUT AND SEE FOR OURSELVES.
?

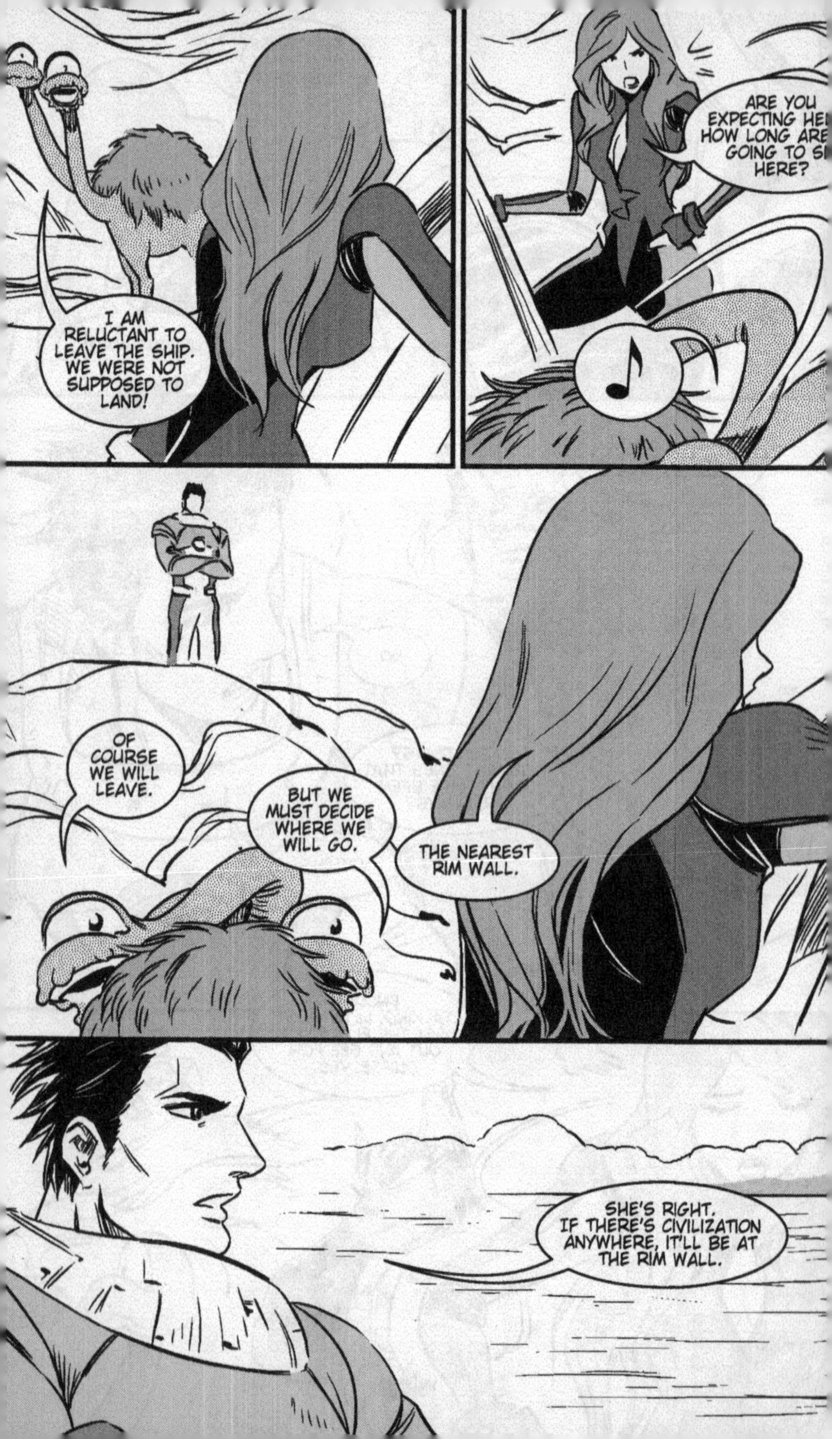
I AM RELUCTANT TO LEAVE THE SHIP. WE WERE NOT SUPPOSED TO LAND!
ARE YOU EXPECTING HE
HOW LONG ARE
GOING TO S
HERE?
♪
OF COURSE WE WILL LEAVE.
BUT WE MUST DECIDE WHERE WE WILL GO.
THE NEAREST RIM WALL.
SHE'S RIGHT. IF THERE'S CIVILIZATION ANYWHERE, IT'LL BE AT THE RIM WALL.

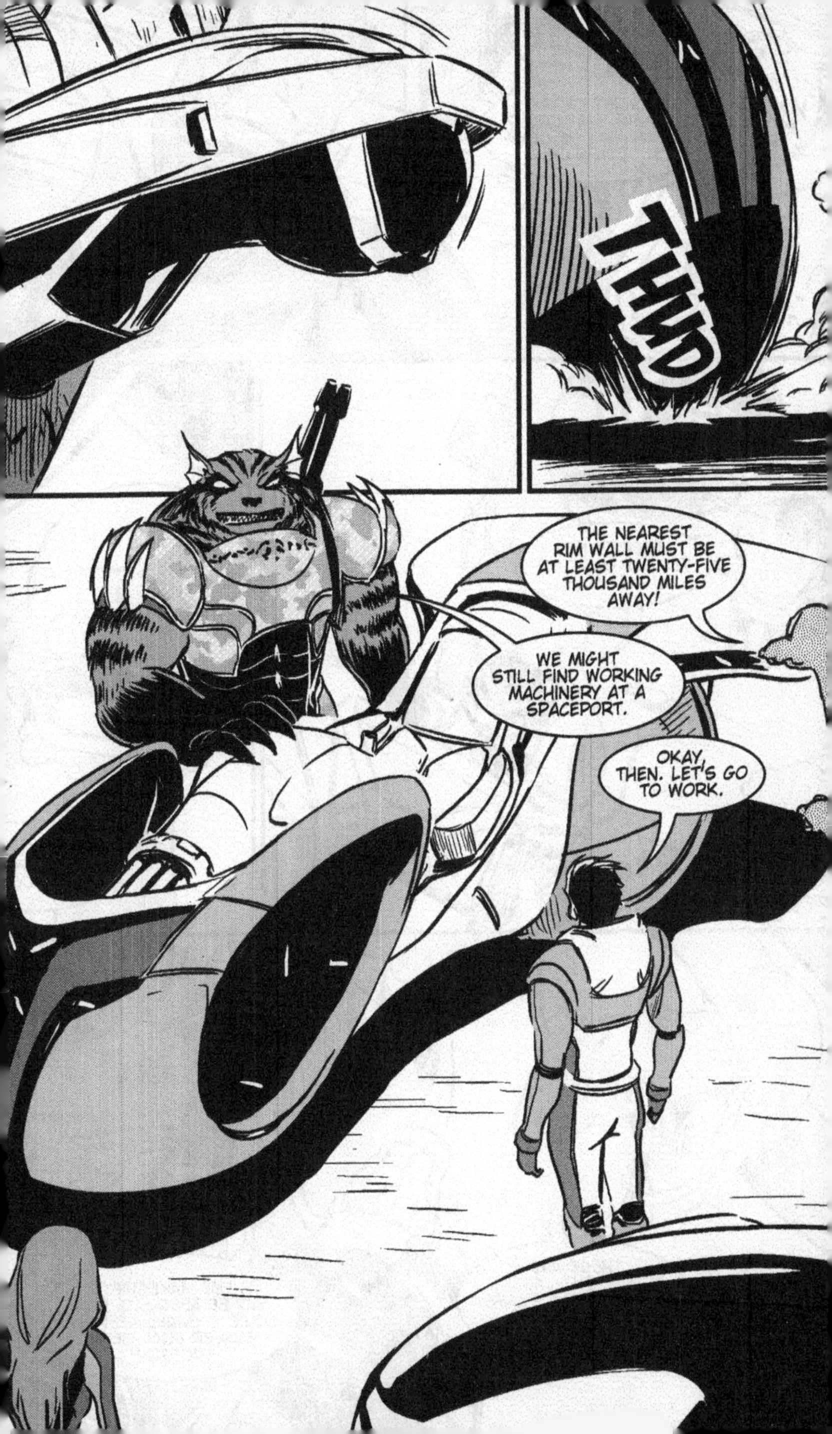
THWD
THE NEAREST RIM WALL MUST BE AT LEAST TWENTY-FIVE THOUSAND MILES AWAY!
WE MIGHT STILL FIND WORKING MACHINERY AT A SPACEPORT.
OKAY, THEN. LET'S GO TO WORK.

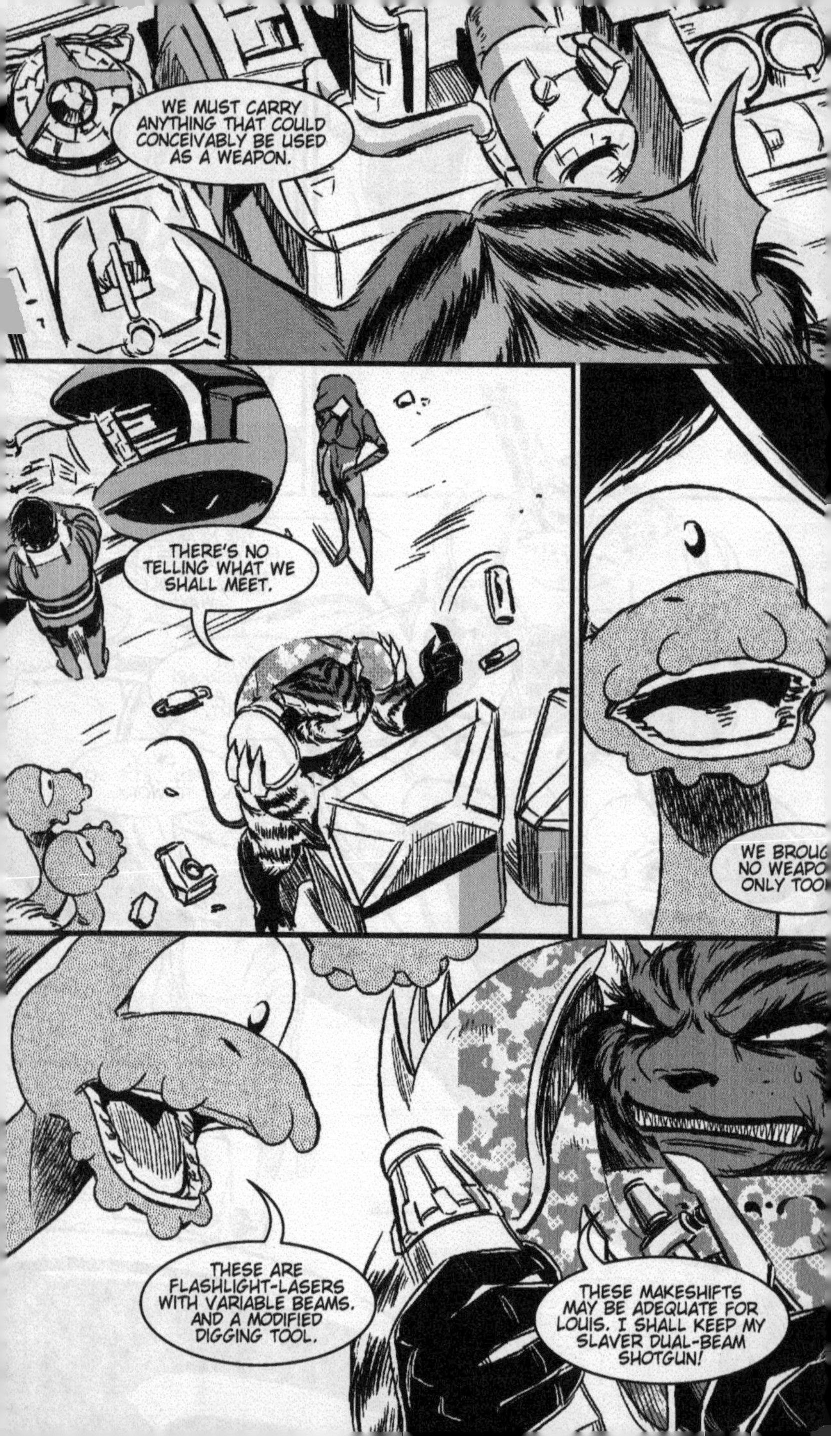
WE MUST CARRY ANYTHING THAT COULD CONCEIVABLY BE USED AS A WEAPON.
THERE'S NO TELLING WHAT WE SHALL MEET.
WE BROUG NO WEAPO ONLY TOO
THESE ARE FLASHLIGHT-LASERS WITH VARIABLE BEAMS. AND A MODIFIED DIGGING TOOL.
THESE MAKESHIFTS MAY BE ADEQUATE FOR LOUIS. I SHALL KEEP MY SLAVER DUAL-BEAM SHOTGUN!

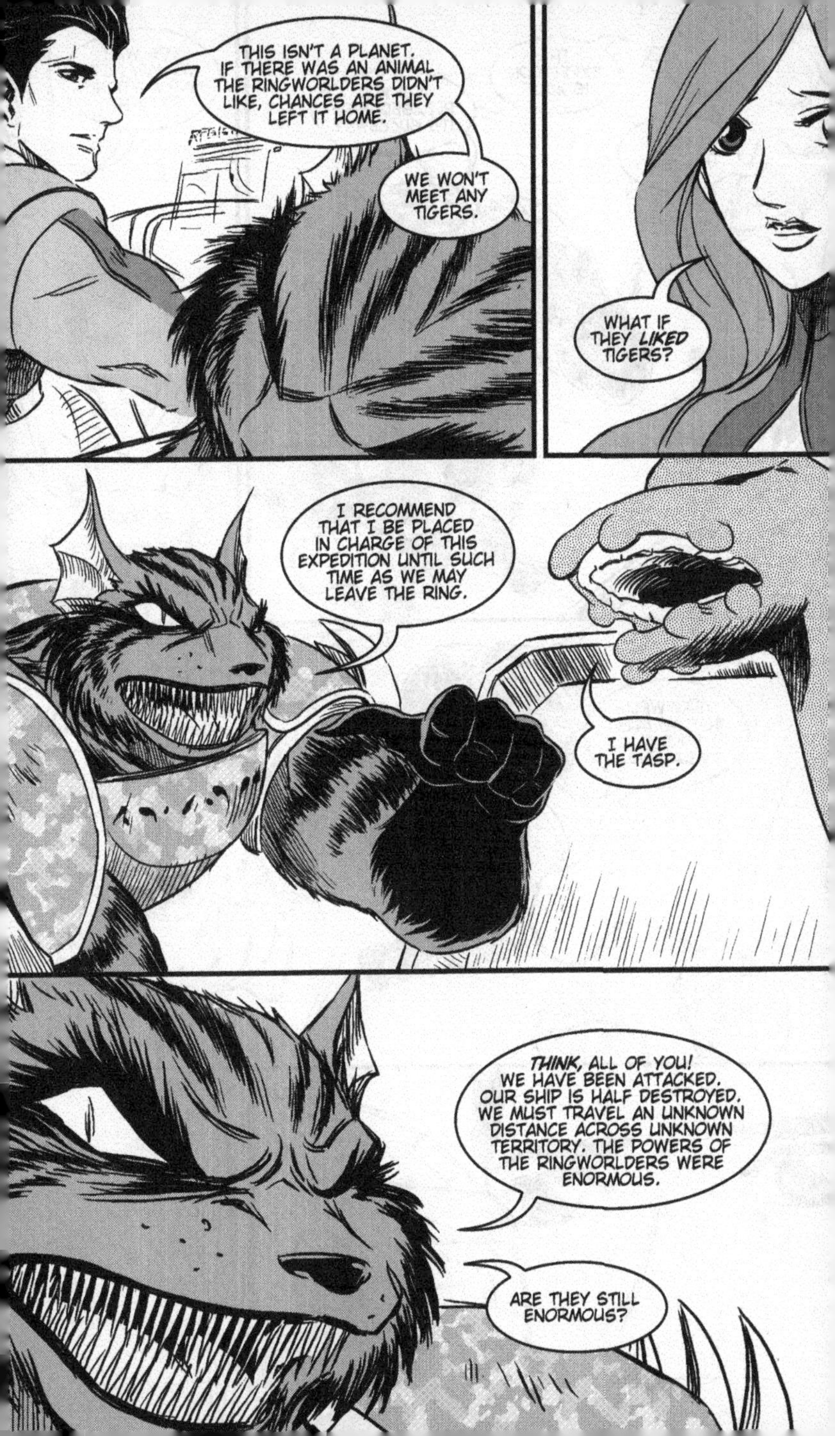
THIS ISN'T A PLANET. IF THERE WAS AN ANIMAL THE RINGWORLDERS DIDN'T LIKE, CHANCES ARE THEY LEFT IT HOME.
WE WON'T MEET ANY TIGERS.
WHAT IF THEY *LIKED* TIGERS?
I RECOMMEND THAT I BE PLACED IN CHARGE OF THIS EXPEDITION UNTIL SUCH TIME AS WE MAY LEAVE THE RING.
I HAVE THE TASP.
THINK, ALL OF YOU! WE HAVE BEEN ATTACKED. OUR SHIP IS HALF DESTROYED. WE MUST TRAVEL AN UNKNOWN DISTANCE ACROSS UNKNOWN TERRITORY. THE POWERS OF THE RINGWORLDERS WERE ENORMOUS.
ARE THEY STILL ENORMOUS?

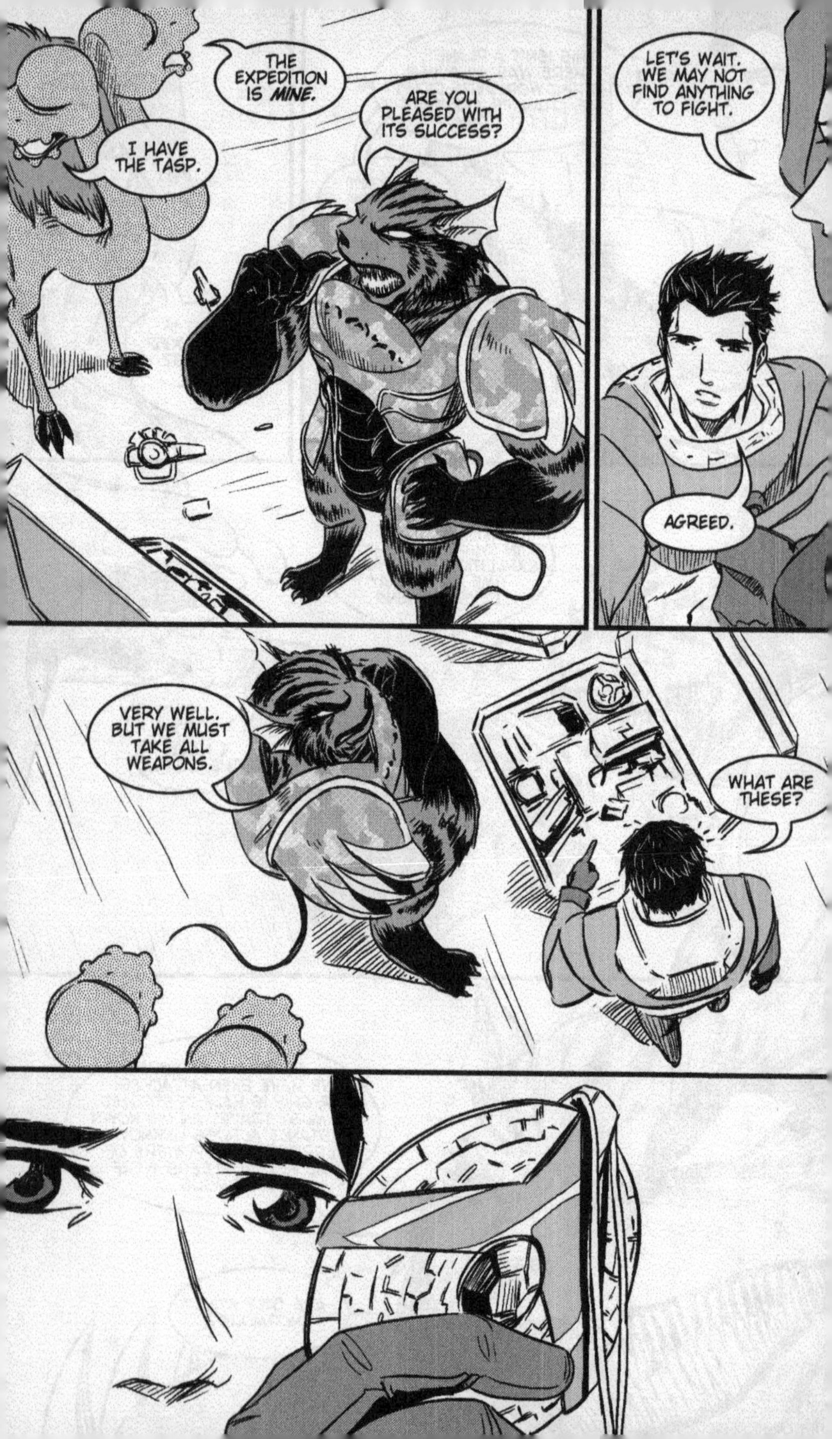
THE EXPEDITION IS *MINE.*
I HAVE THE TASP.
ARE YOU PLEASED WITH ITS SUCCESS?
LET'S WAIT. WE MAY NOT FIND ANYTHING TO FIGHT.
AGREED.
VERY WELL. BUT WE MUST TAKE ALL WEAPONS.
WHAT ARE THESE?

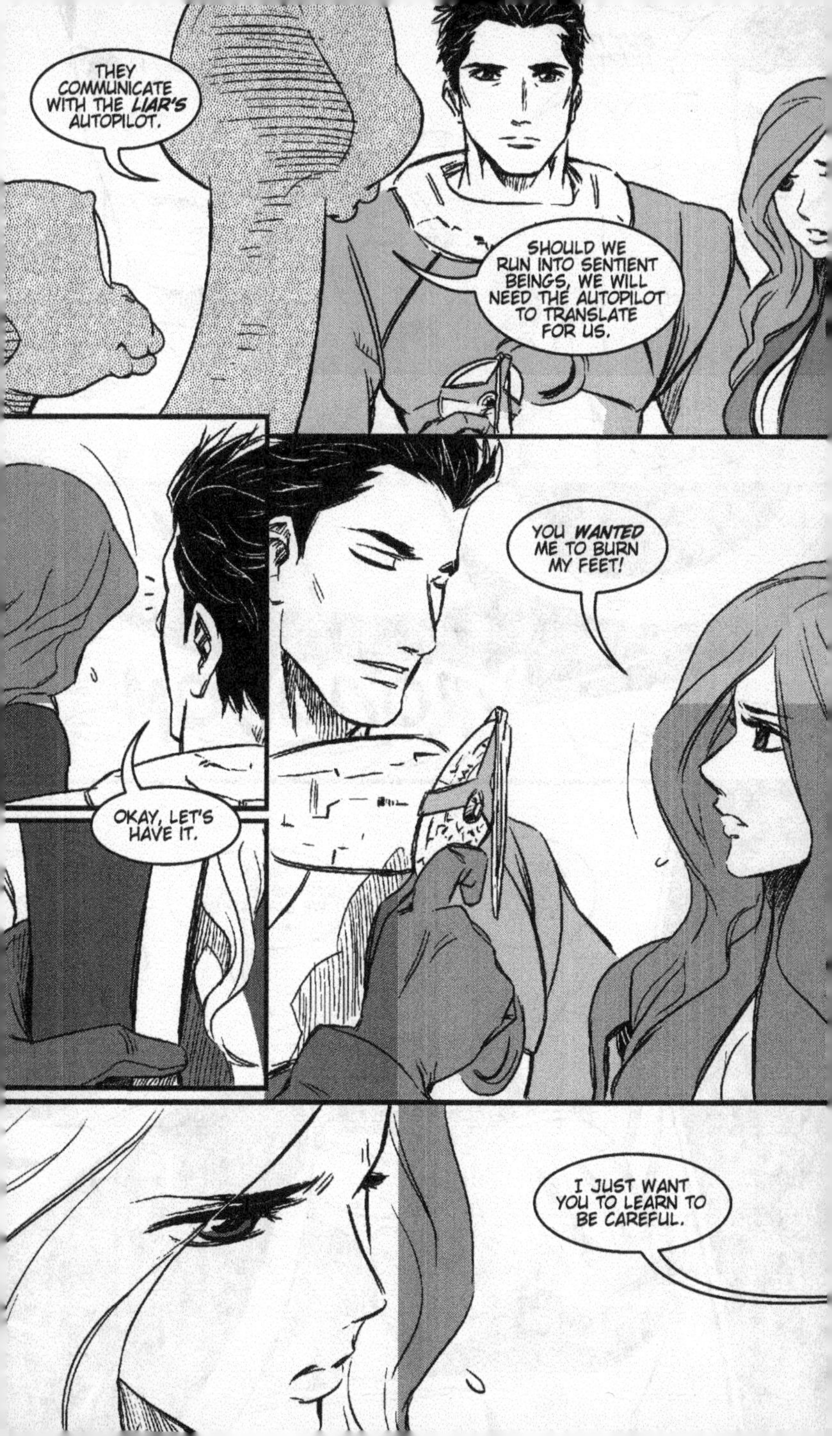
THEY COMMUNICATE WITH THE *LIAR'S* AUTOPILOT.
SHOULD WE RUN INTO SENTIENT BEINGS, WE WILL NEED THE AUTOPILOT TO TRANSLATE FOR US.
OKAY, LET'S HAVE IT.
YOU *WANTED* ME TO BURN MY FEET!
I JUST WANT YOU TO LEARN TO BE CAREFUL.

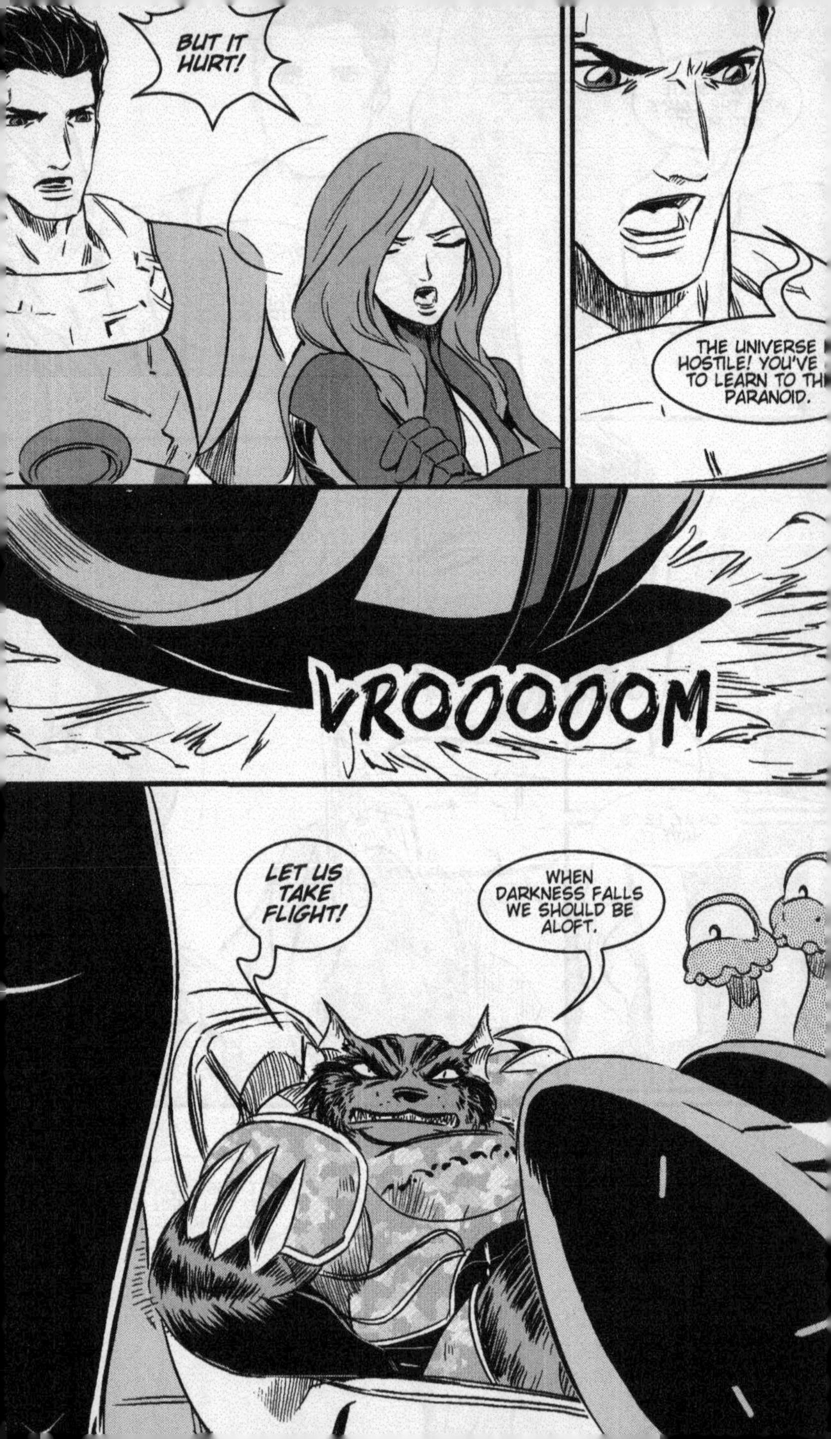
BUT IT HURT!
THE UNIVERSE HOSTILE! YOU'VE TO LEARN TO TH PARANOID.
VROOOOOM
LET US TAKE FLIGHT!
WHEN DARKNESS FALLS WE SHOULD BE ALOFT.

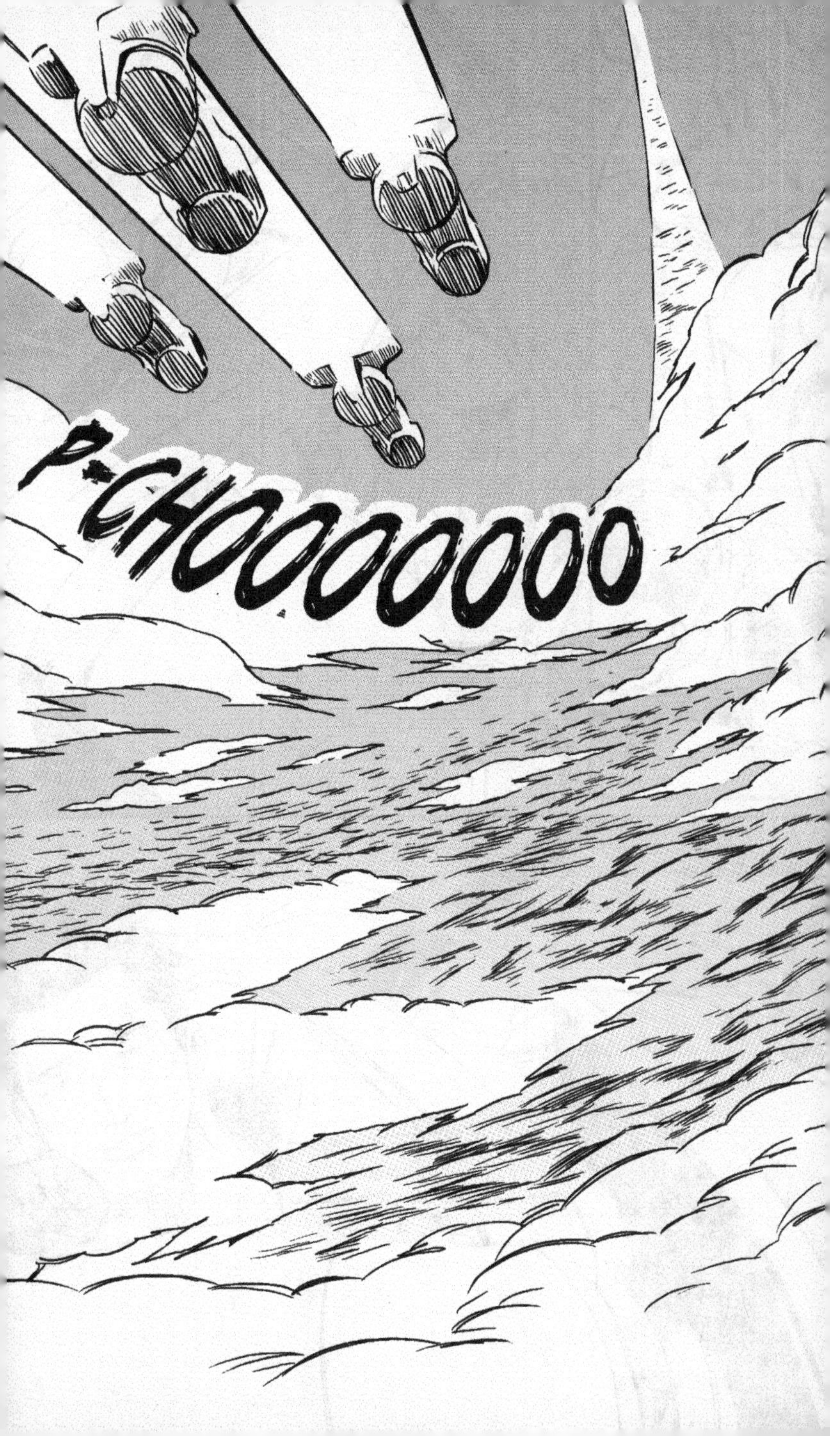
P-CHOOOOOOOO

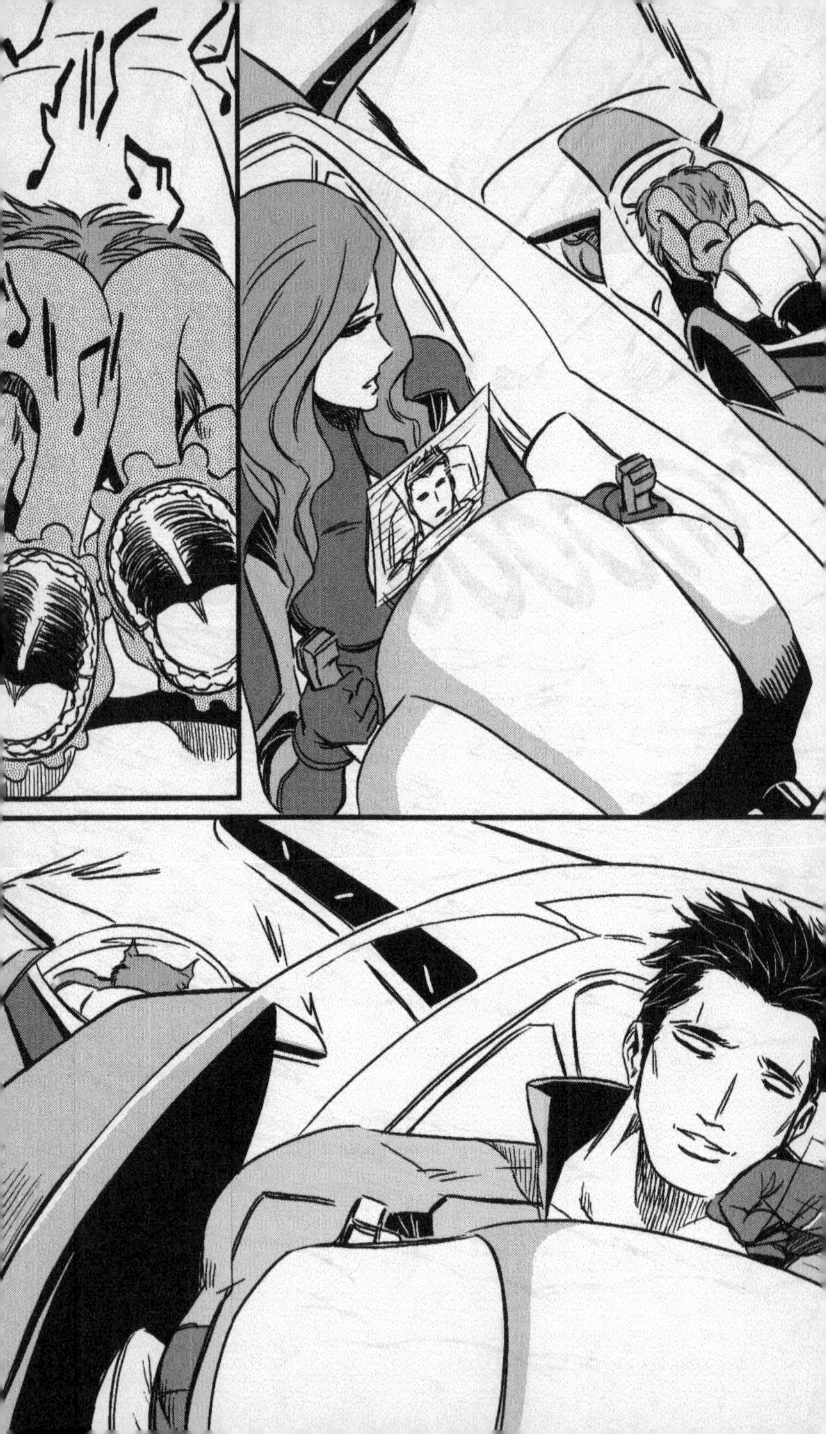

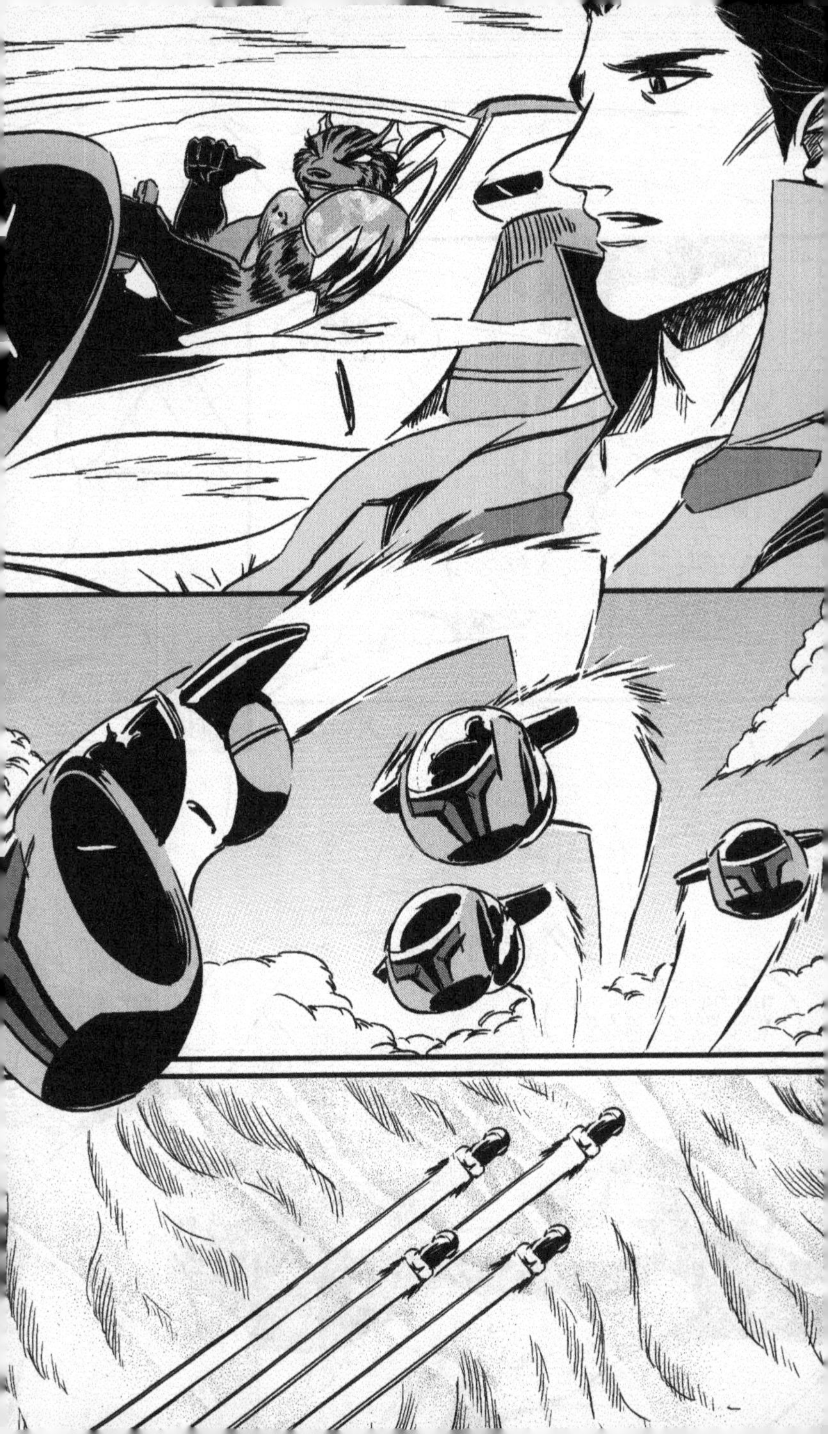

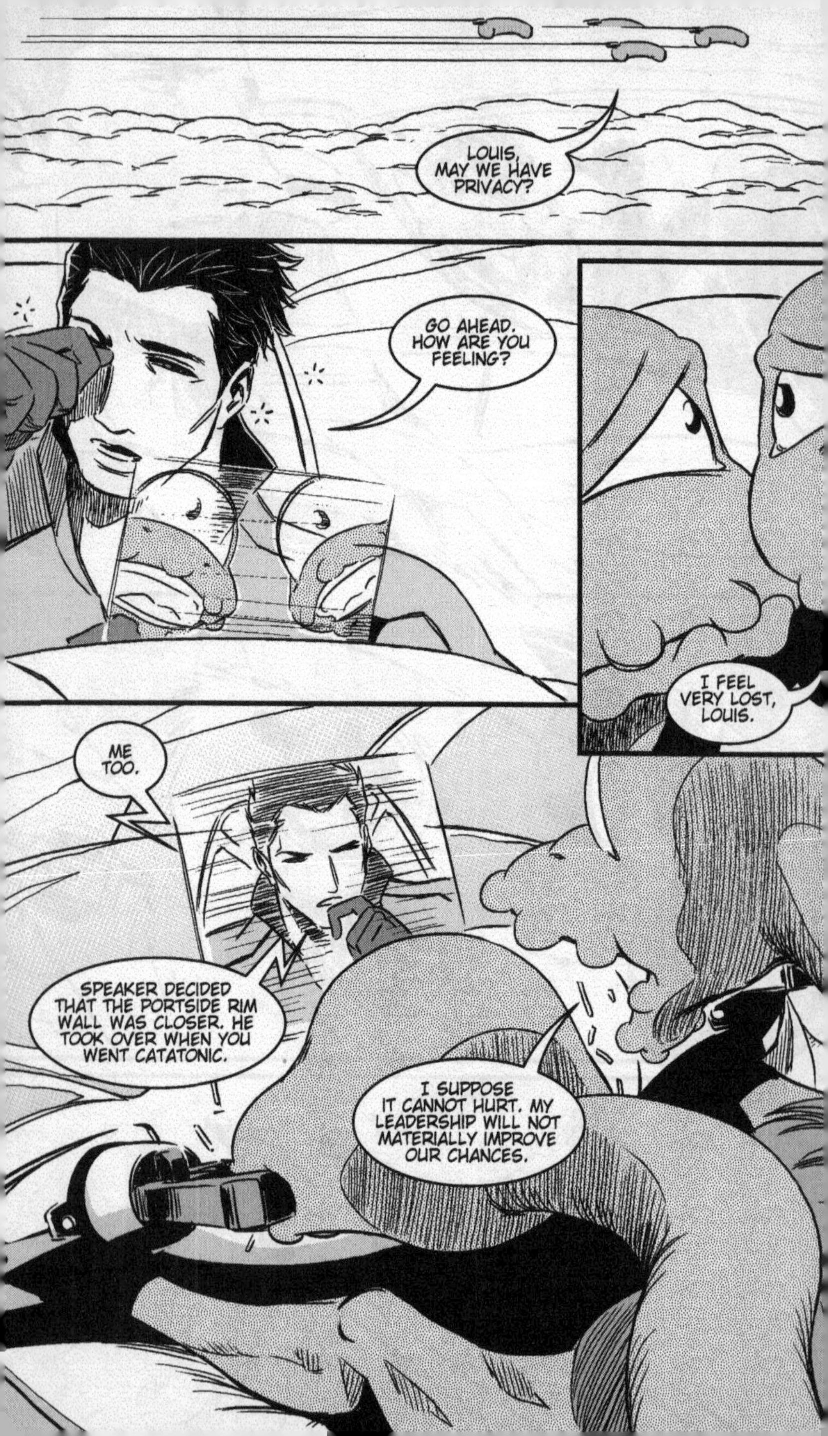
LOUIS, MAY WE HAVE PRIVACY?
GO AHEAD. HOW ARE YOU FEELING?
I FEEL VERY LOST, LOUIS.
ME TOO.
SPEAKER DECIDED THAT THE PORTSIDE RIM WALL WAS CLOSER. HE TOOK OVER WHEN YOU WENT CATATONIC.
I SUPPOSE IT CANNOT HURT. MY LEADERSHIP WILL NOT MATERIALLY IMPROVE OUR CHANCES.

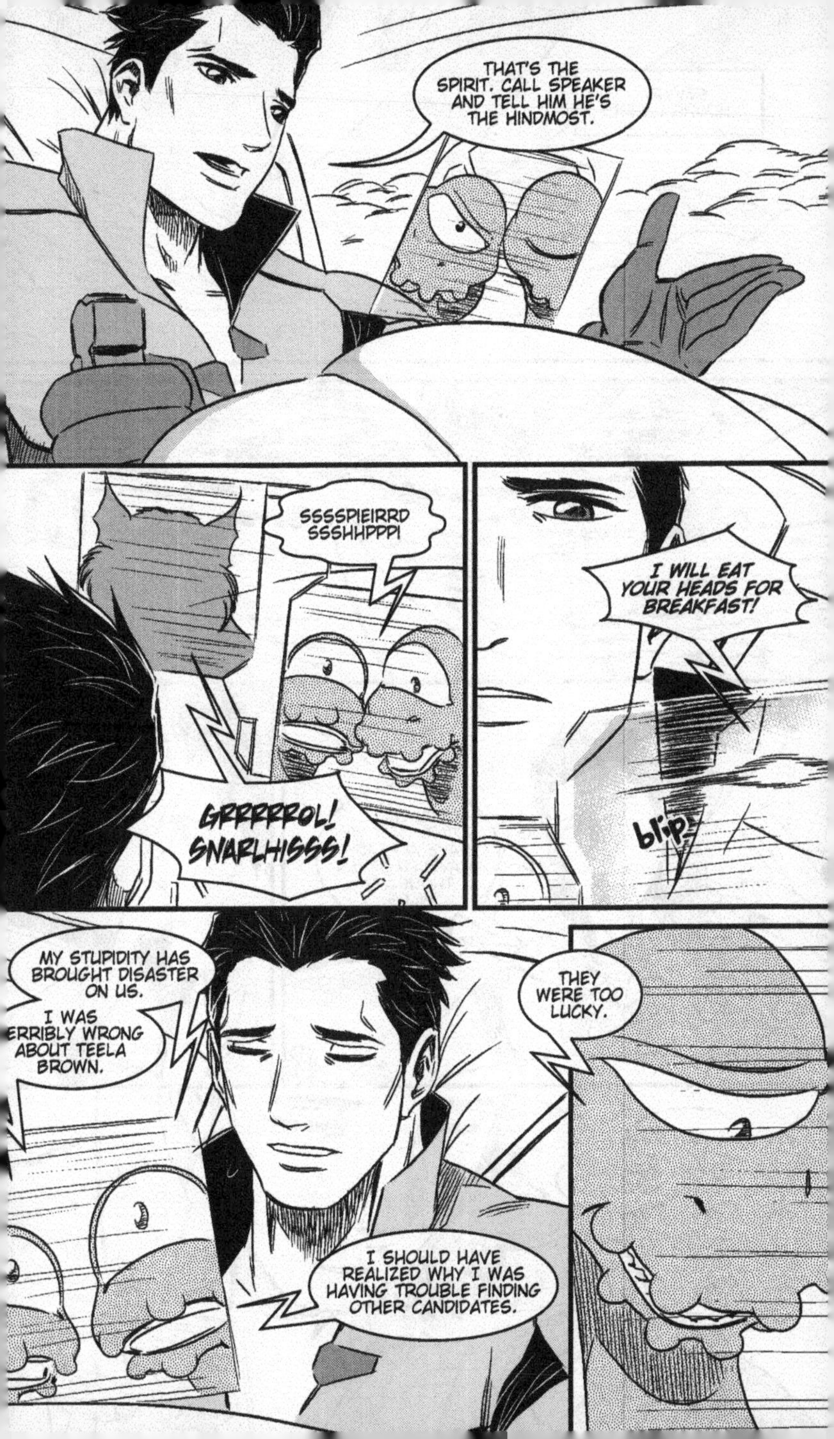

THAT'S THE SPIRIT. CALL SPEAKER AND TELL HIM HE'S THE HINDMOST.
SSSSPIEIRRD SSSHHPPP!
GRRRRROL! SNARLHISSS!
I WILL EAT YOUR HEADS FOR BREAKFAST!
blip
MY STUPIDITY HAS BROUGHT DISASTER ON US.
I WAS ERRIBLY WRONG ABOUT TEELA BROWN.
I SHOULD HAVE REALIZED WHY I WAS HAVING TROUBLE FINDING OTHER CANDIDATES.
THEY WERE TOO LUCKY.

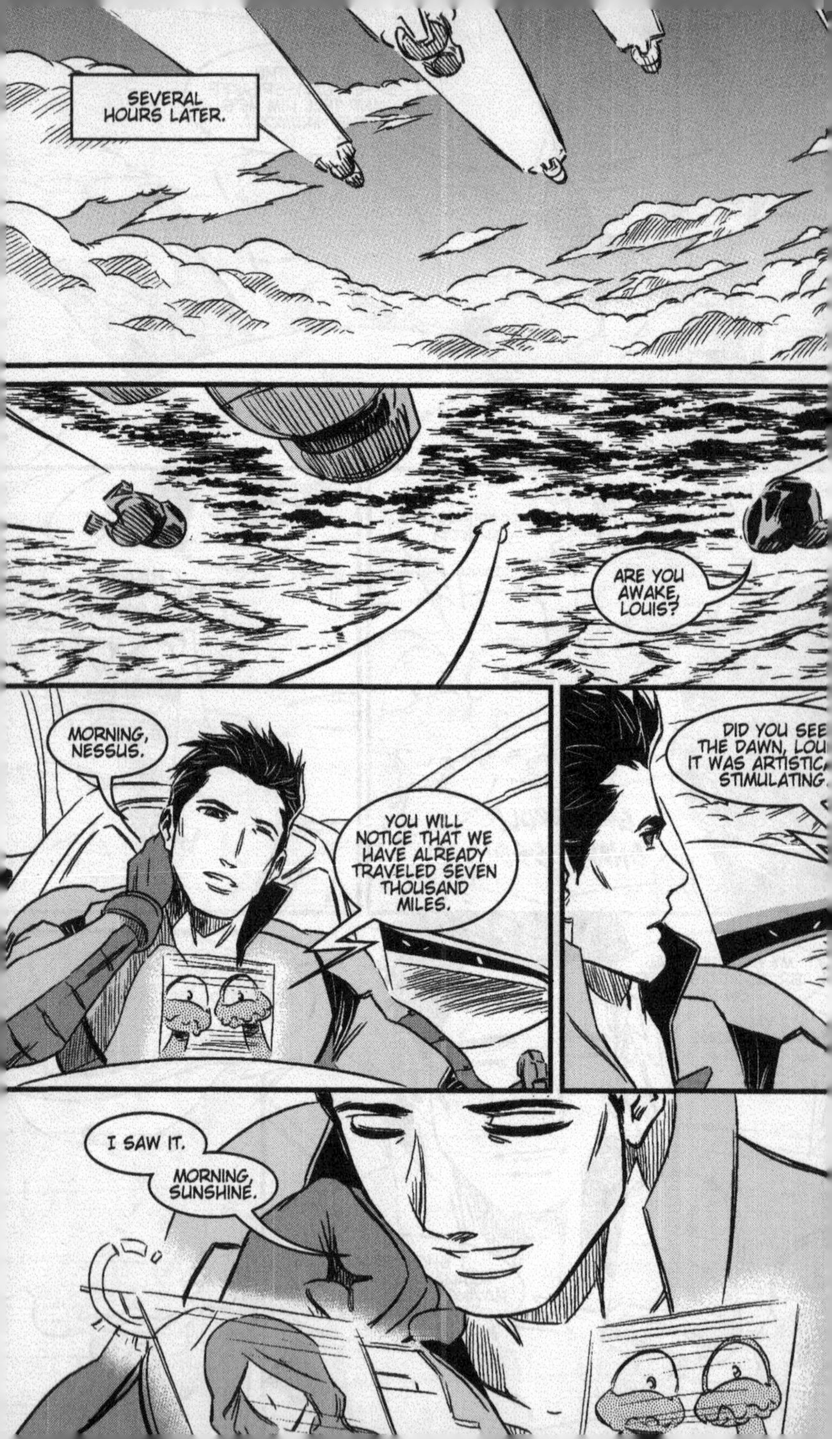
SEVERAL HOURS LATER.
ARE YOU AWAKE, LOUIS?
MORNING, NESSUS.
YOU WILL NOTICE THAT WE HAVE ALREADY TRAVELED SEVEN THOUSAND MILES.
DID YOU SEE THE DAWN, LOU IT WAS ARTISTIC STIMULATING.
I SAW IT.
MORNING, SUNSHINE.

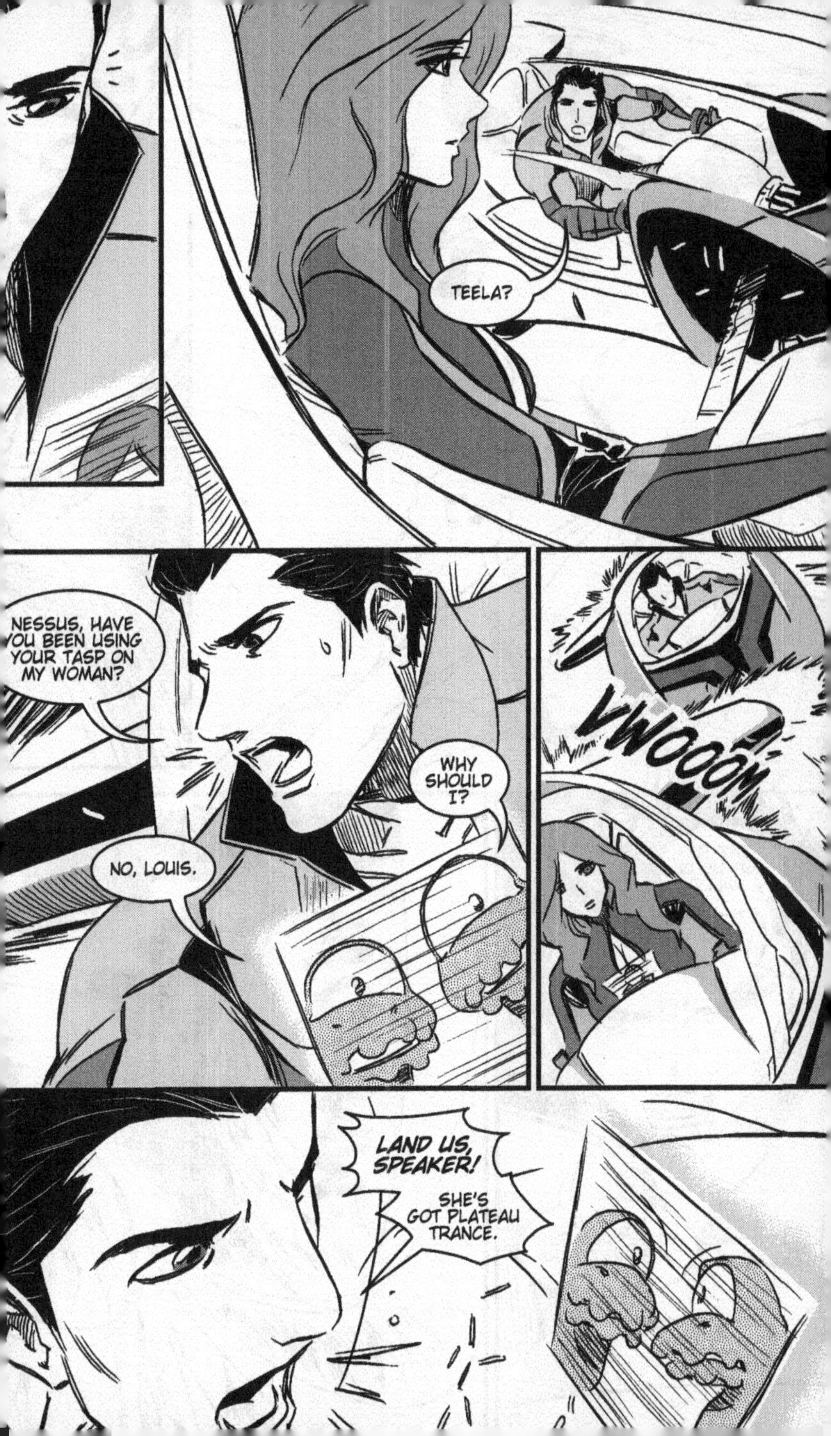
TEELA?
NESSUS, HAVE YOU BEEN USING YOUR TASP ON MY WOMAN?
WHY SHOULD I?
NO, LOUIS.
VWOOOM
LAND US, SPEAKER!
SHE'S GOT PLATEAU TRANCE.

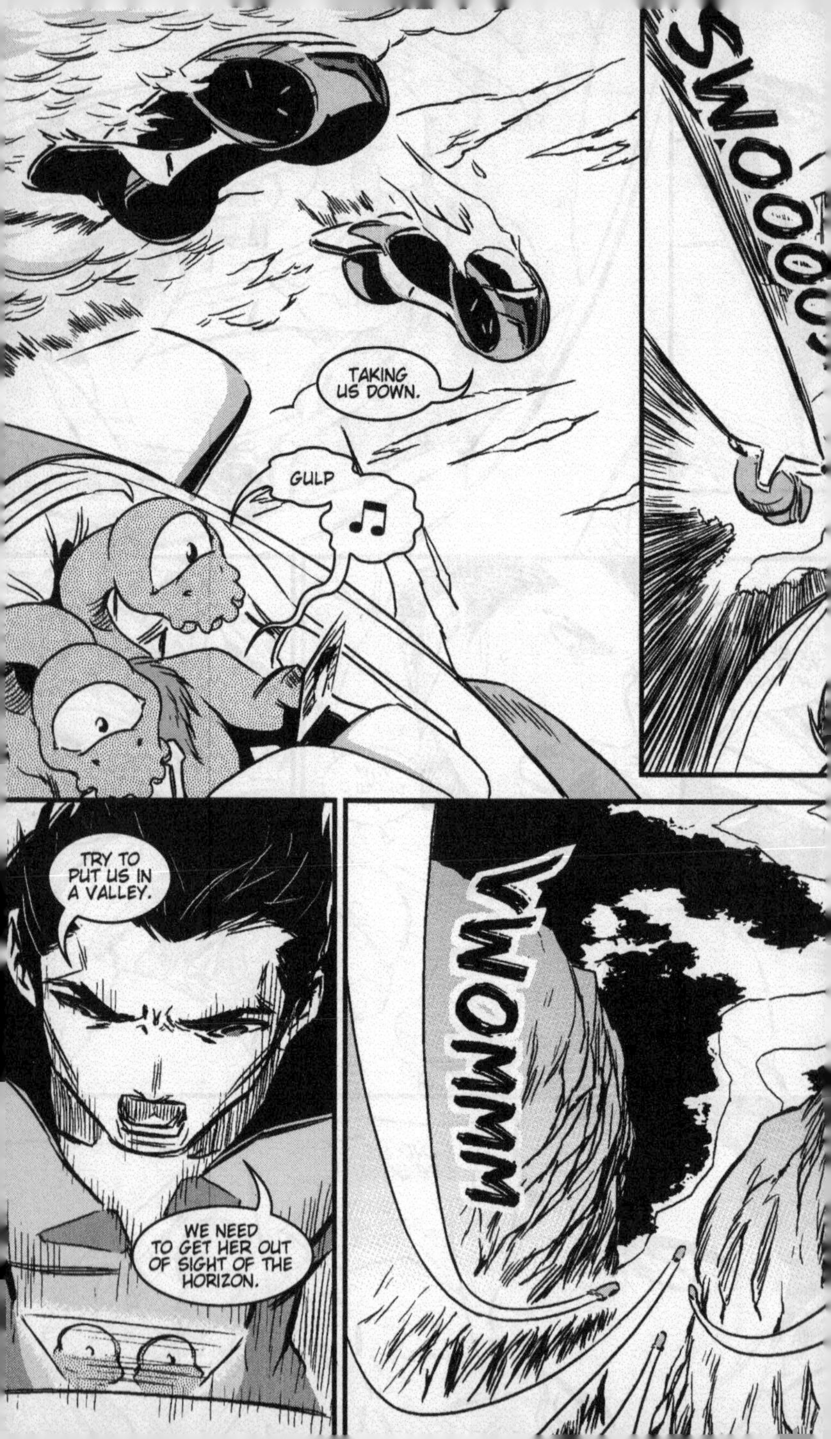
TAKING US DOWN.
GULP
♪
SWOOOOO
TRY TO PUT US IN A VALLEY.
WE NEED TO GET HER OUT OF SIGHT OF THE HORIZON.
VWOMM

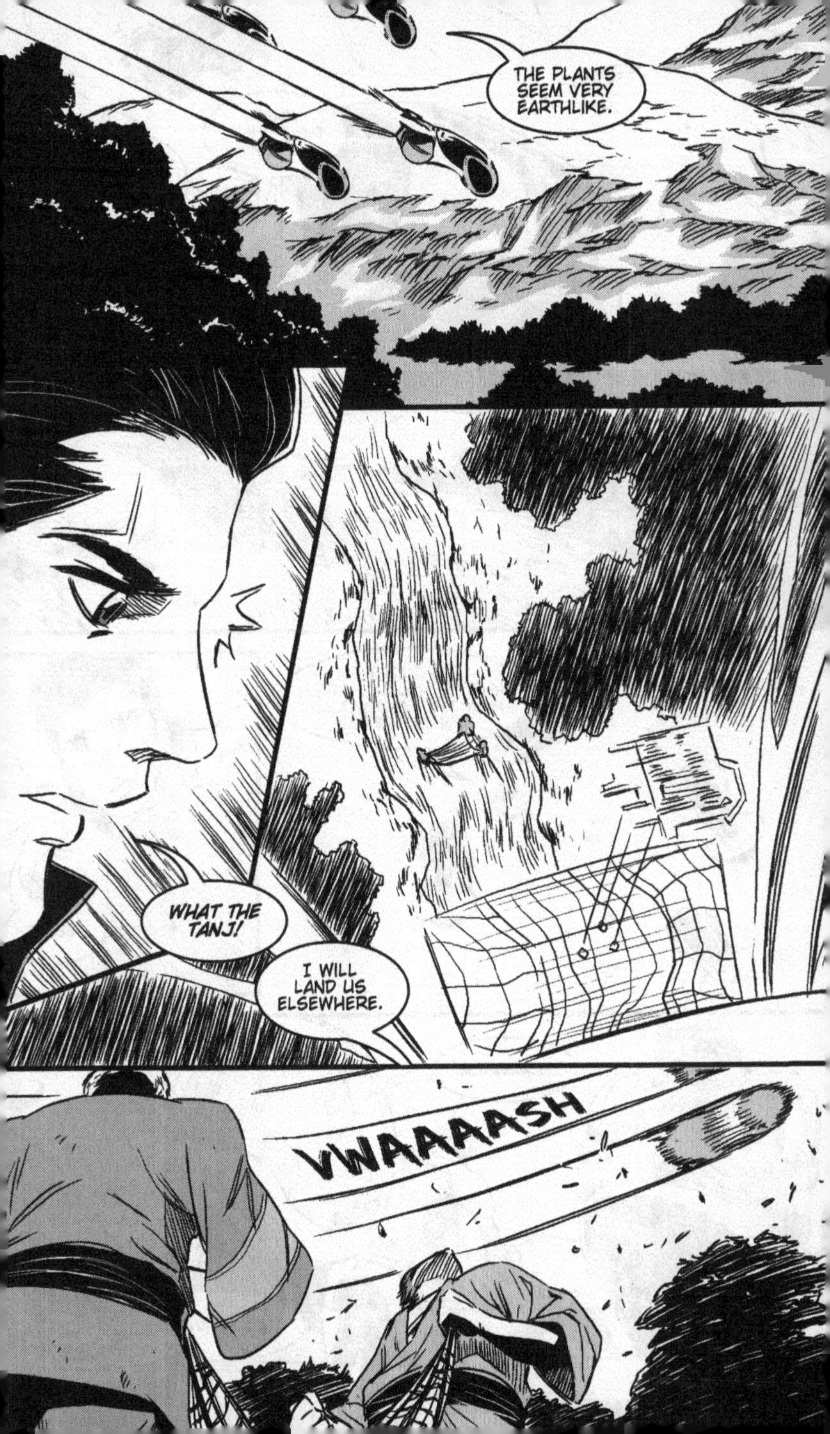
THE PLANTS SEEM VERY EARTHLIKE.
WHAT THE TANJ!
I WILL LAND US ELSEWHERE.
VWAAAAASH

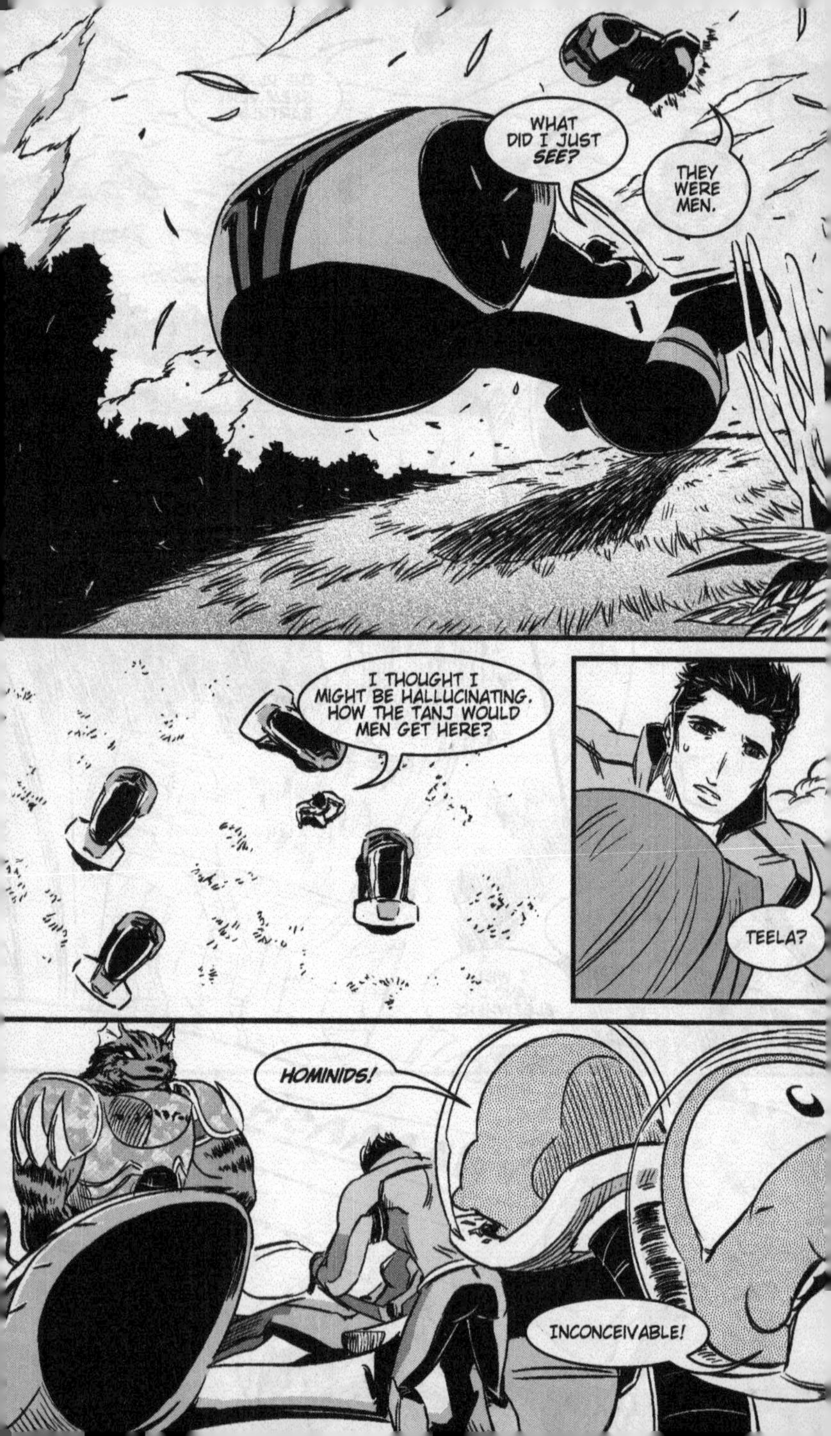
WHAT DID I JUST SEE?
THEY WERE MEN.
I THOUGHT I MIGHT BE HALLUCINATING. HOW THE TANJ WOULD MEN GET HERE?
TEELA?
HOMINIDS!
INCONCEIVABLE!

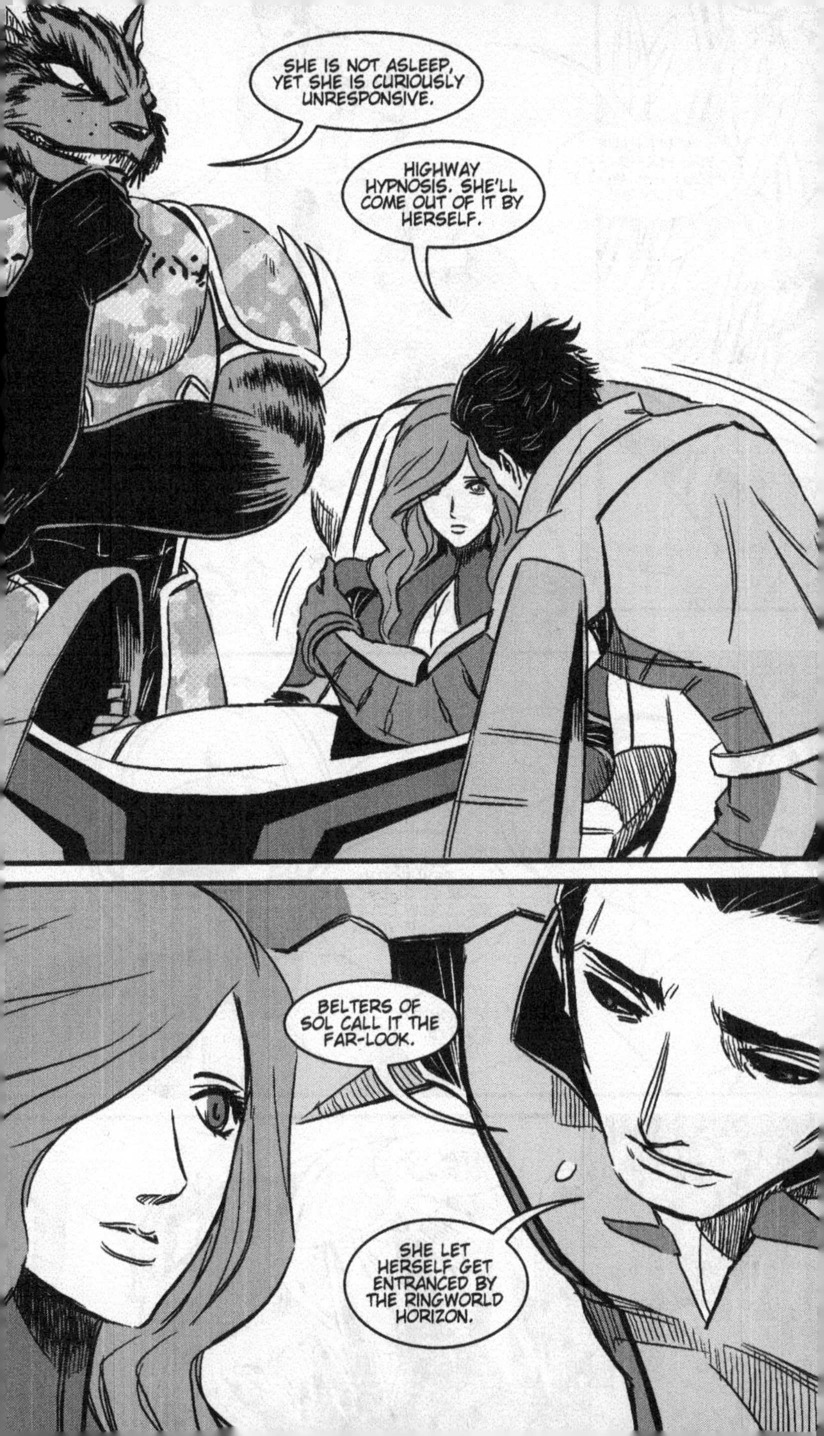
SHE IS NOT ASLEEP, YET SHE IS CURIOUSLY UNRESPONSIVE.
HIGHWAY HYPNOSIS. SHE'LL COME OUT OF IT BY HERSELF.
BELTERS OF SOL CALL IT THE FAR-LOOK.
SHE LET HERSELF GET ENTRANCED BY THE RINGWORLD HORIZON.

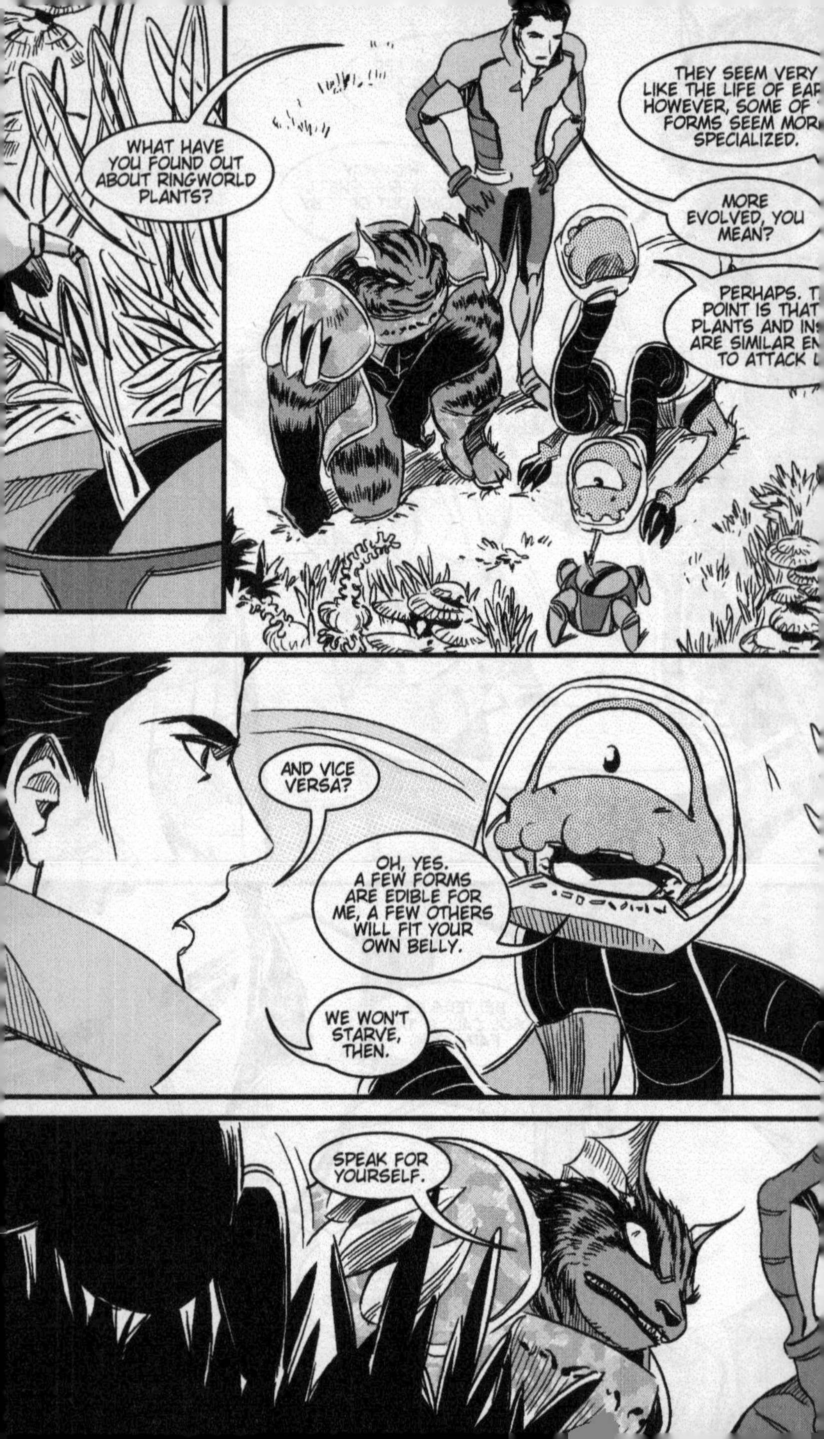
WHAT HAVE YOU FOUND OUT ABOUT RINGWORLD PLANTS?
THEY SEEM VERY LIKE THE LIFE OF EAR HOWEVER, SOME OF FORMS SEEM MOR SPECIALIZED.
MORE EVOLVED, YOU MEAN?
PERHAPS. T POINT IS THAT PLANTS AND INS ARE SIMILAR EN TO ATTACK U
AND VICE VERSA?
OH, YES. A FEW FORMS ARE EDIBLE FOR ME, A FEW OTHERS WILL FIT YOUR OWN BELLY.
WE WON'T STARVE, THEN.
SPEAK FOR YOURSELF.

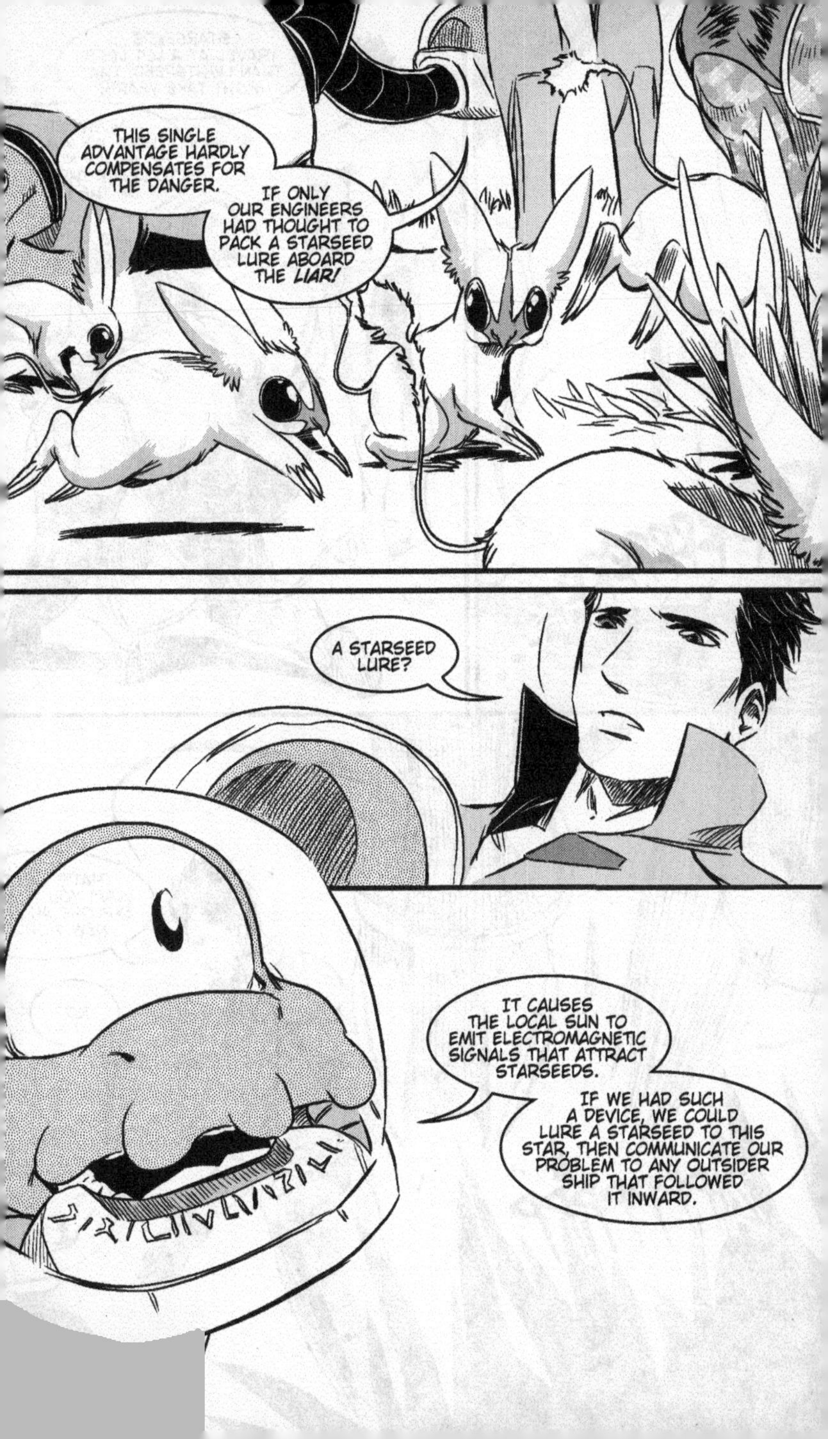
THIS SINGLE ADVANTAGE HARDLY COMPENSATES FOR THE DANGER.
IF ONLY OUR ENGINEERS HAD THOUGHT TO PACK A STARSEED LURE ABOARD THE *LIAR!*
A STARSEED LURE?
IT CAUSES THE LOCAL SUN TO EMIT ELECTROMAGNETIC SIGNALS THAT ATTRACT STARSEEDS.
IF WE HAD SUCH A DEVICE, WE COULD LURE A STARSEED TO THIS STAR, THEN COMMUNICATE OUR PROBLEM TO ANY OUTSIDER SHIP THAT FOLLOWED IT INWARD.

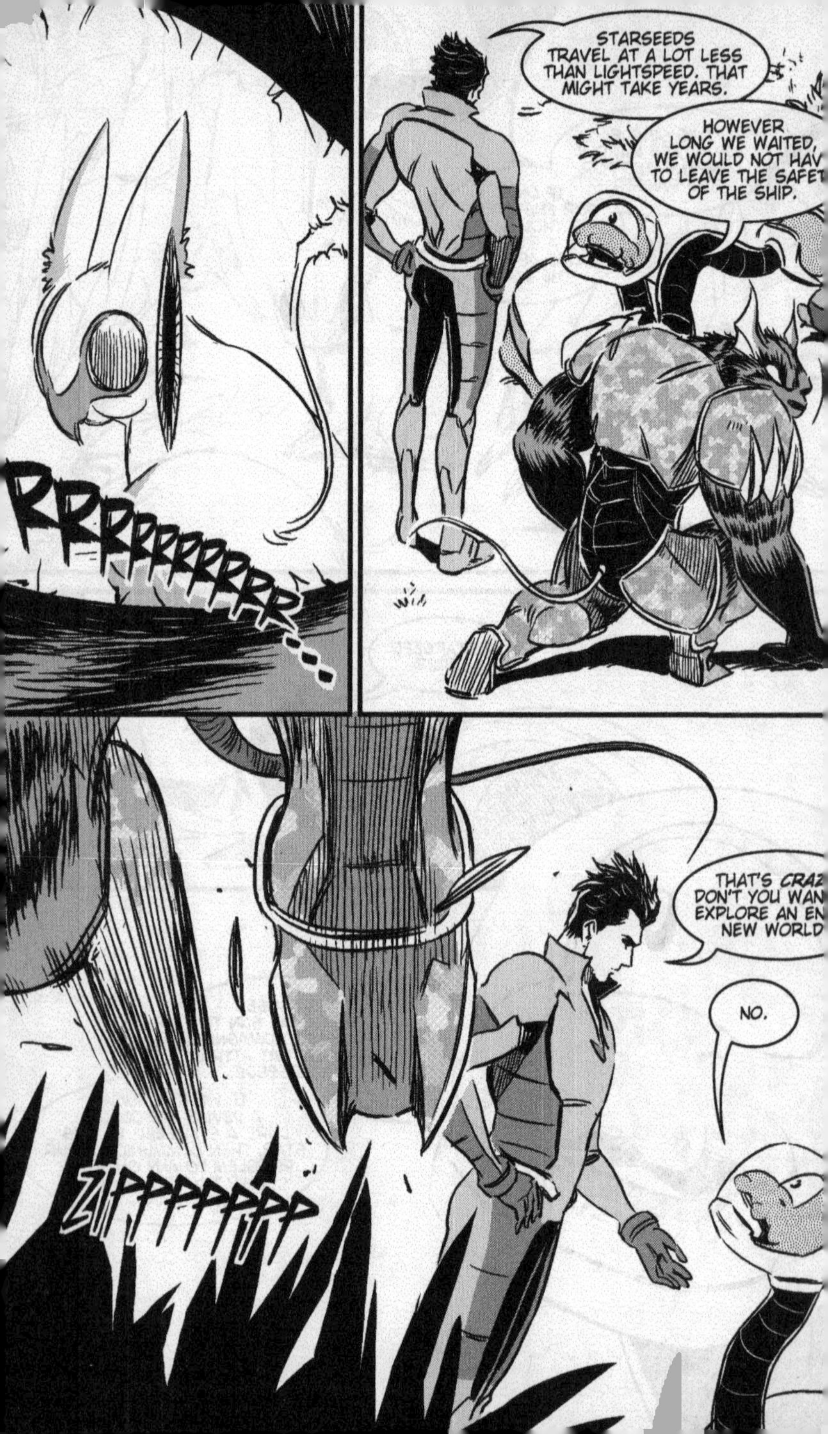
RRRRRRRRRRRRR...
STARSEEDS TRAVEL AT A LOT LESS THAN LIGHTSPEED. THAT MIGHT TAKE YEARS.
HOWEVER LONG WE WAITED, WE WOULD NOT HAV TO LEAVE THE SAFET OF THE SHIP.
ZIPPPPPPPPP
THAT'S *CRAZ* DON'T YOU WAN EXPLORE AN EN NEW WORLD
NO.

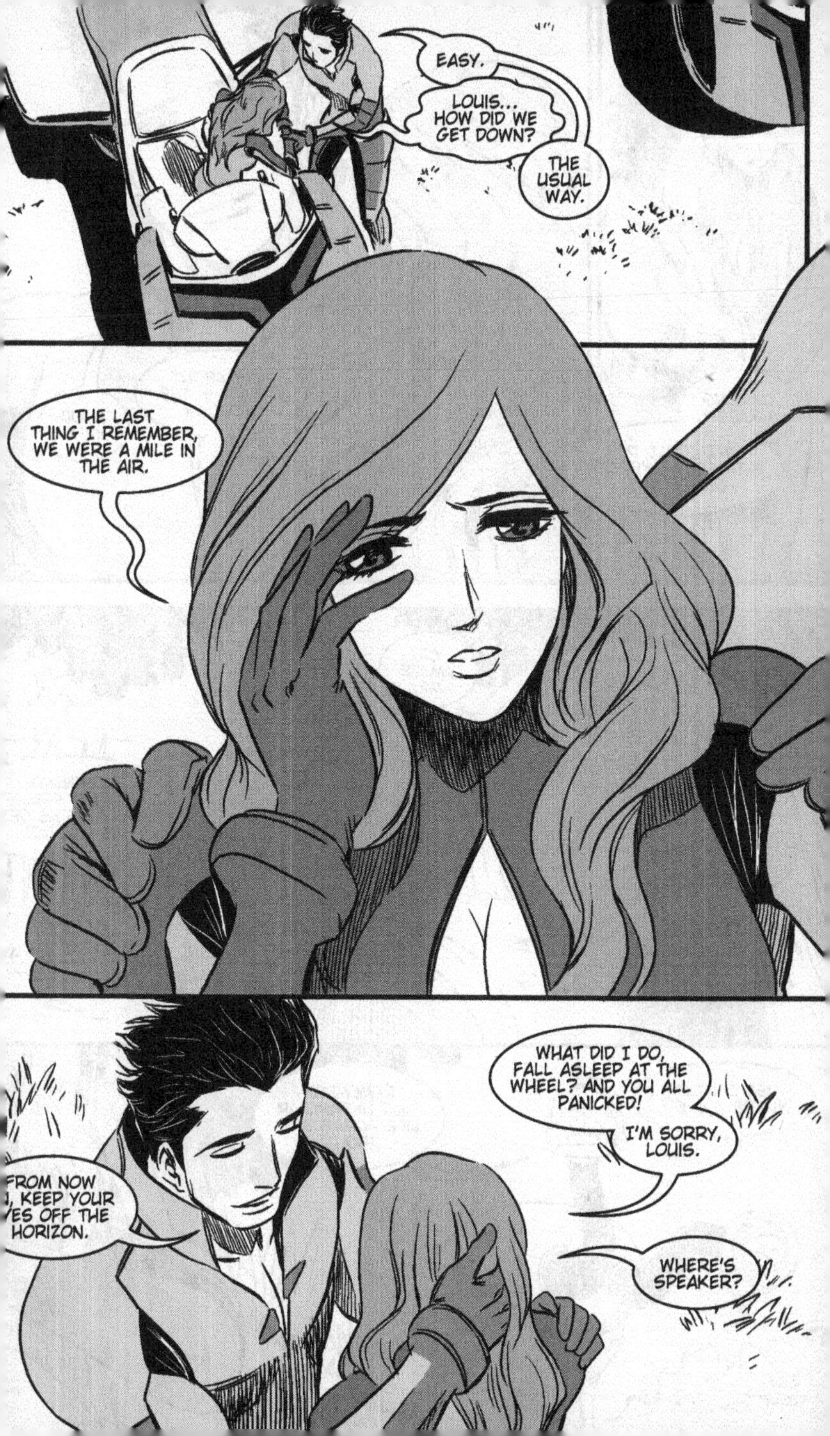
EASY.
LOUIS... HOW DID WE GET DOWN?
THE USUAL WAY.
THE LAST THING I REMEMBER, WE WERE A MILE IN THE AIR.
FROM NOW
, KEEP YOUR
ES OFF THE
HORIZON.
WHAT DID I DO, FALL ASLEEP AT THE WHEEL? AND YOU ALL PANICKED!
I'M SORRY, LOUIS.
WHERE'S SPEAKER?

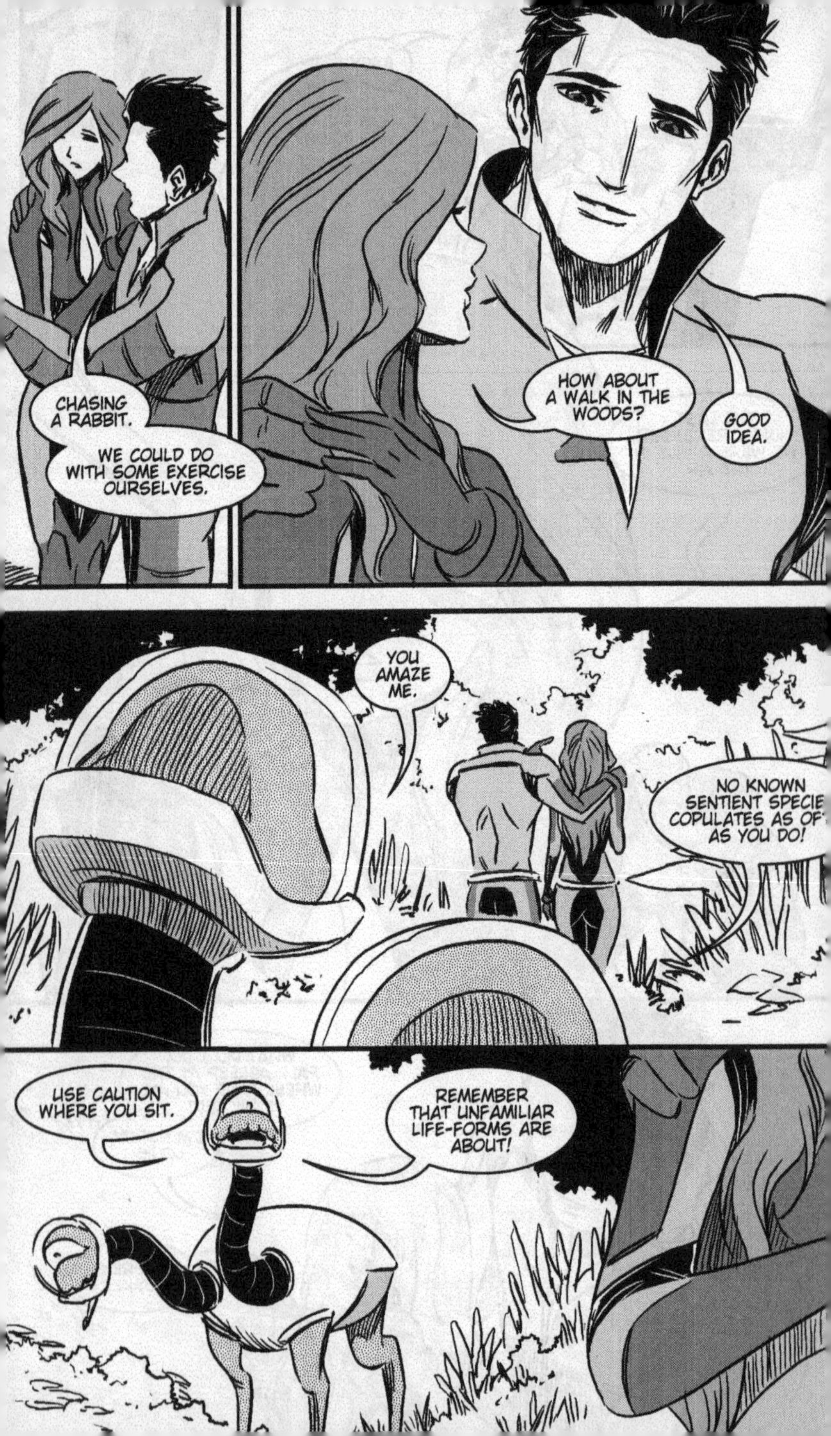
CHASING A RABBIT.
WE COULD DO WITH SOME EXERCISE OURSELVES.
HOW ABOUT A WALK IN THE WOODS?
GOOD IDEA.
YOU AMAZE ME.
NO KNOWN SENTIENT SPECIE COPULATES AS OF AS YOU DO!
USE CAUTION WHERE YOU SIT.
REMEMBER THAT UNFAMILIAR LIFE-FORMS ARE ABOUT!

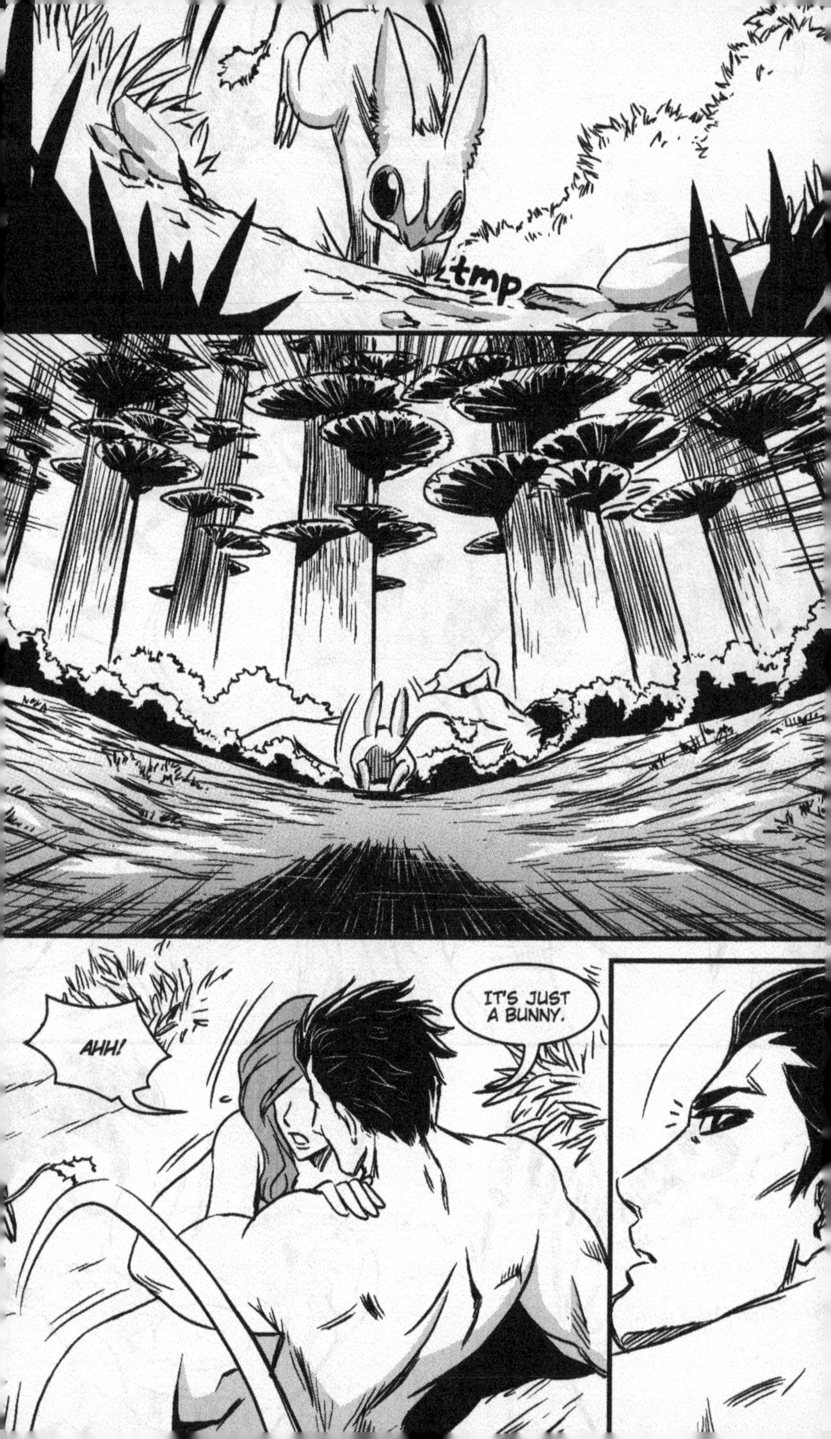
tmp
AHH!
IT'S JUST A BUNNY.

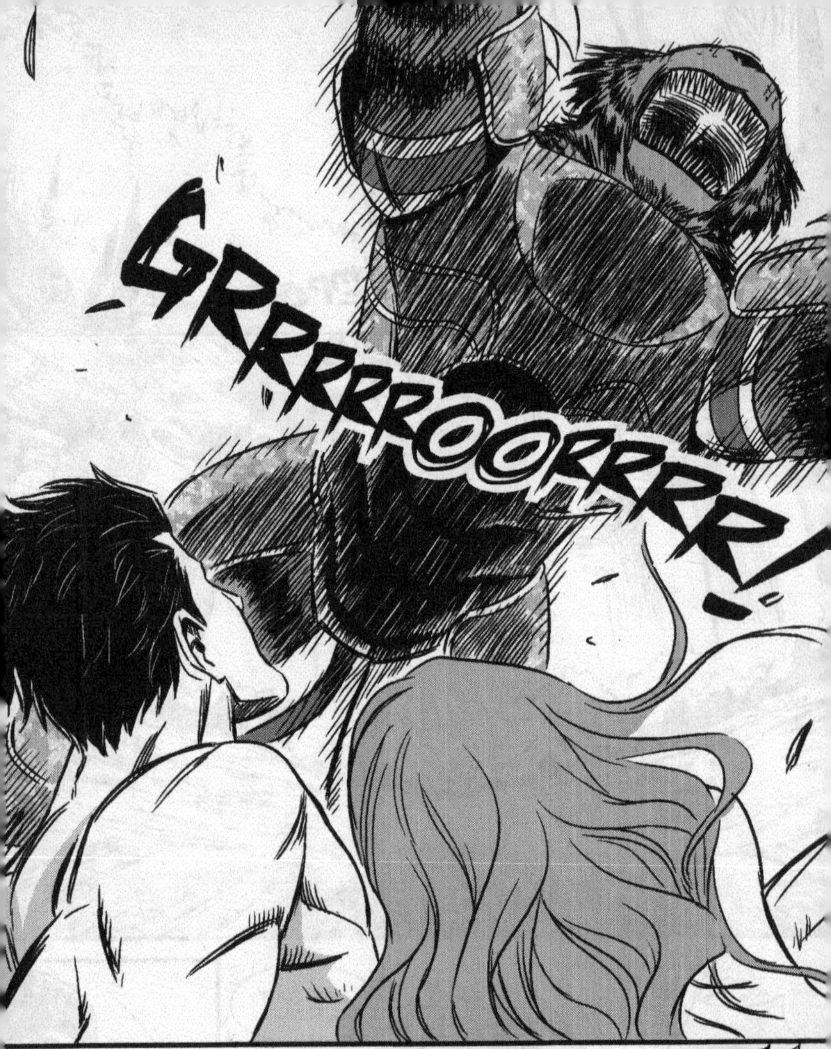
GRRRRROOORRRRR!
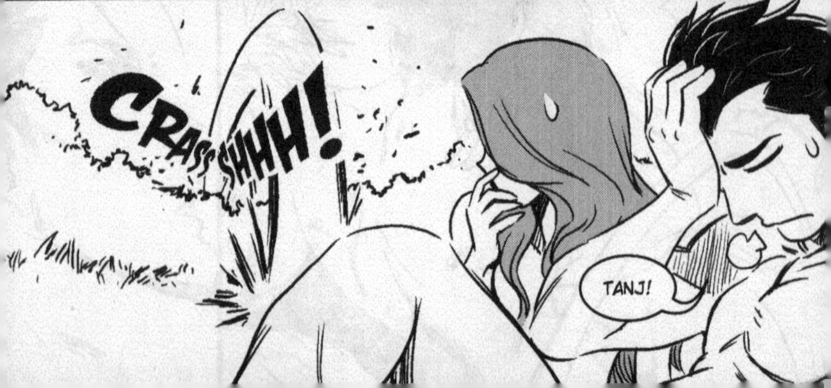
CRASSSHHH!
TANJ!

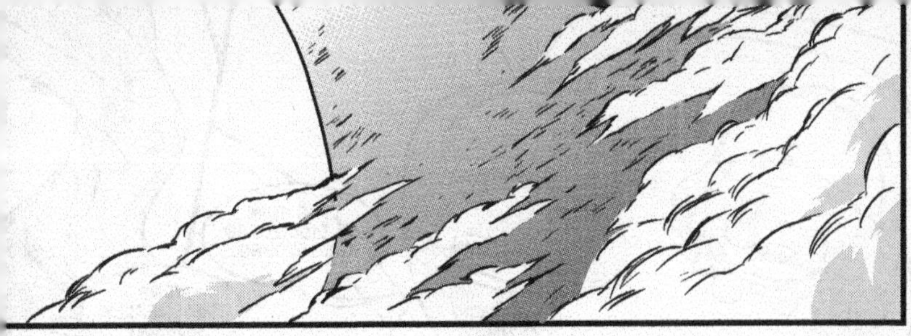

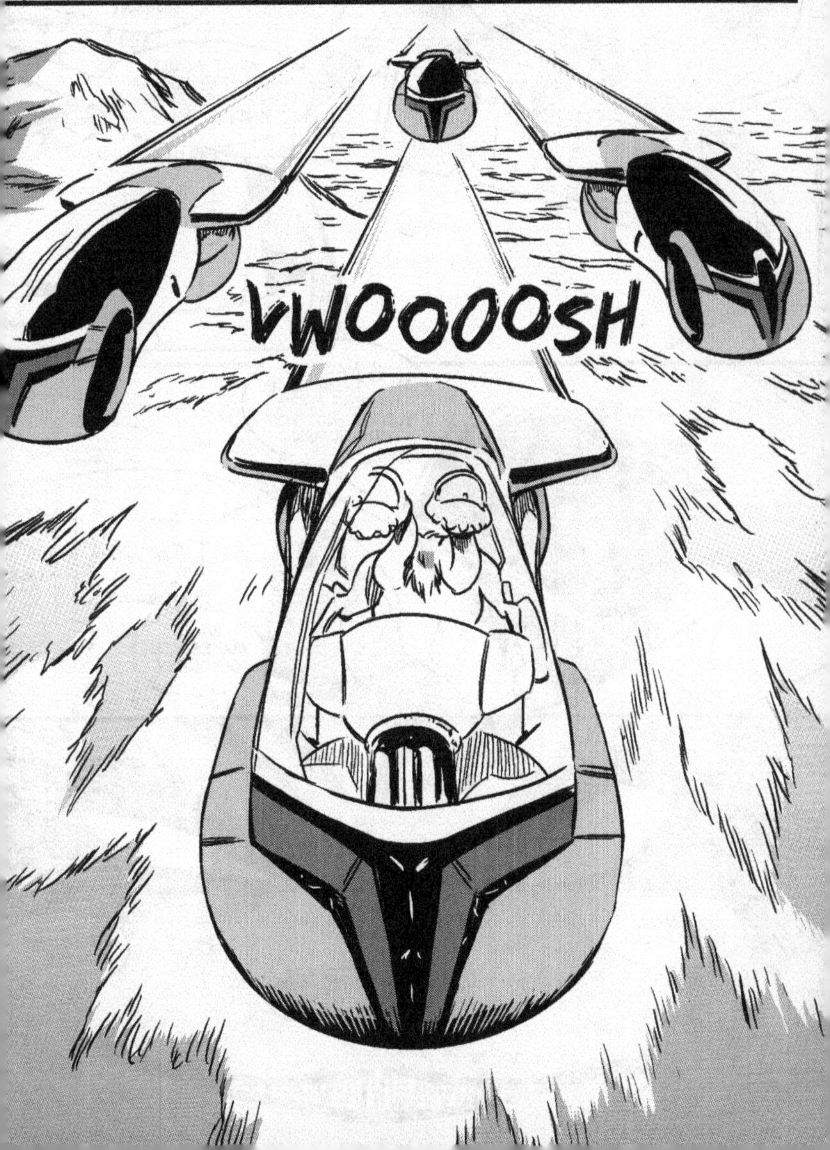
VWOOOOOSH

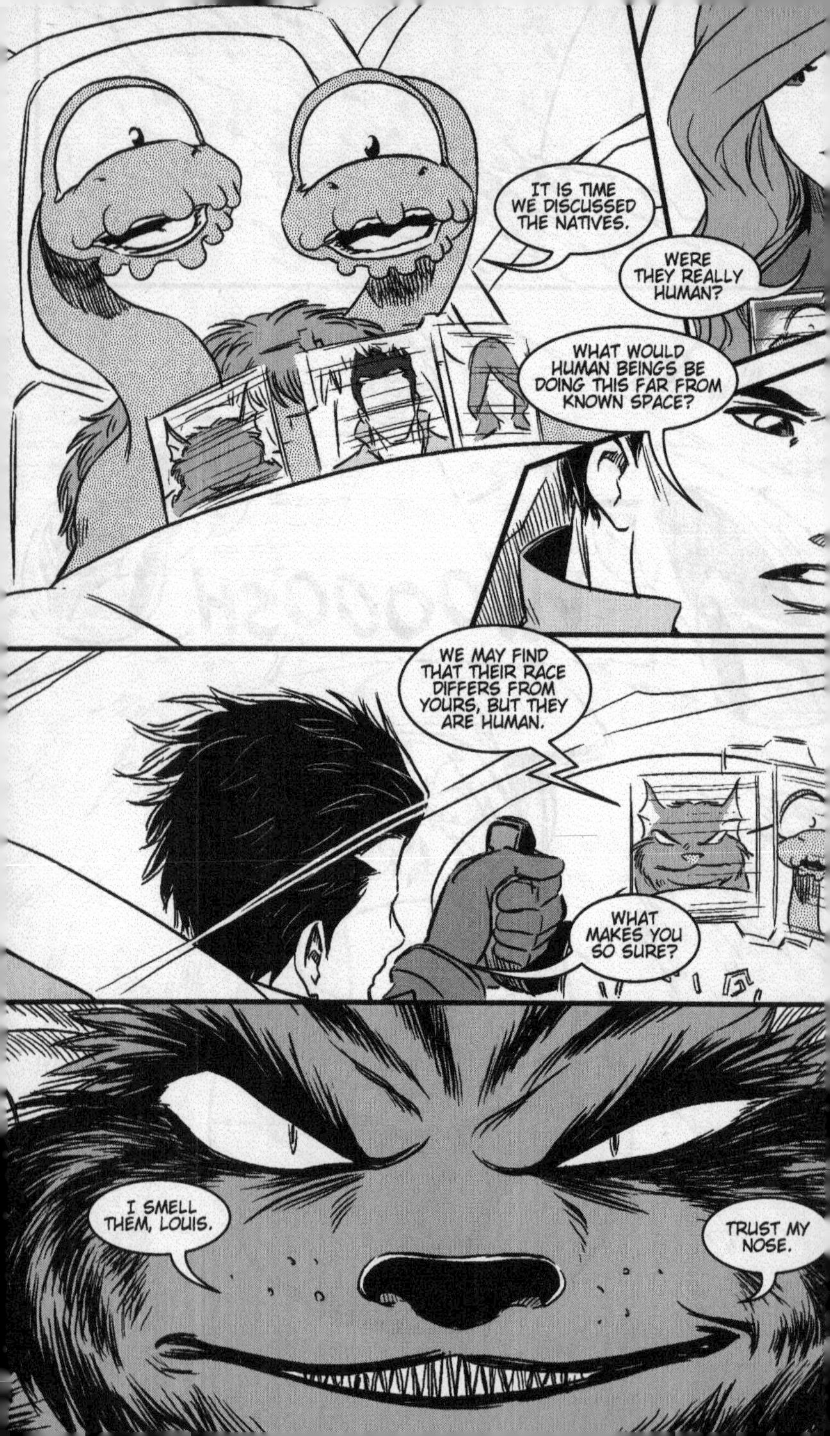
IT IS TIME WE DISCUSSED THE NATIVES.
WERE THEY REALLY HUMAN?
WHAT WOULD HUMAN BEINGS BE DOING THIS FAR FROM KNOWN SPACE?
WE MAY FIND THAT THEIR RACE DIFFERS FROM YOURS, BUT THEY ARE HUMAN.
WHAT MAKES YOU SO SURE?
I SMELL THEM, LOUIS.
TRUST MY NOSE.

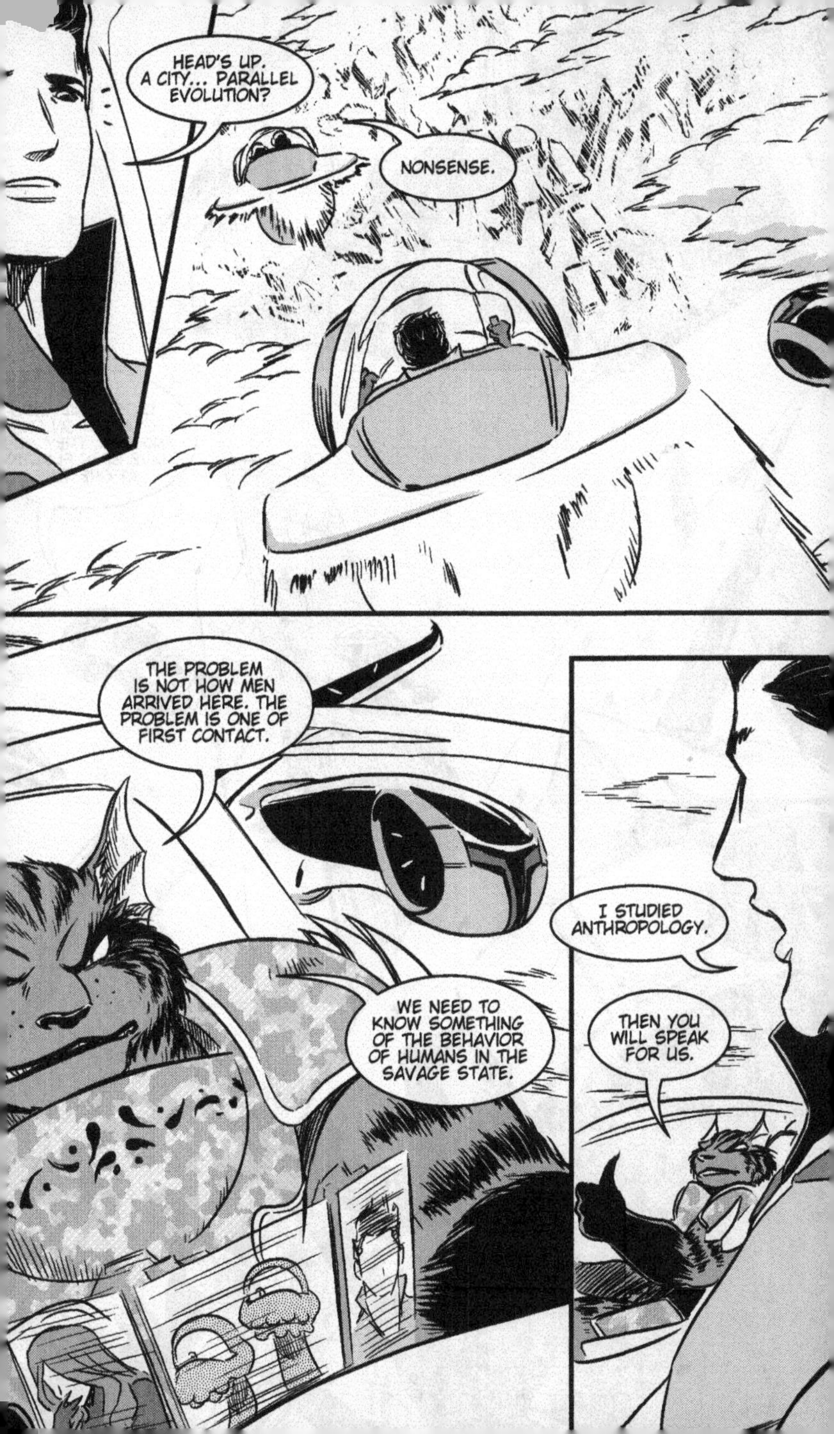
HEAD'S UP. A CITY... PARALLEL EVOLUTION?
NONSENSE.
THE PROBLEM IS NOT HOW MEN ARRIVED HERE. THE PROBLEM IS ONE OF FIRST CONTACT.
WE NEED TO KNOW SOMETHING OF THE BEHAVIOR OF HUMANS IN THE SAVAGE STATE.
I STUDIED ANTHROPOLOGY.
THEN YOU WILL SPEAK FOR US.

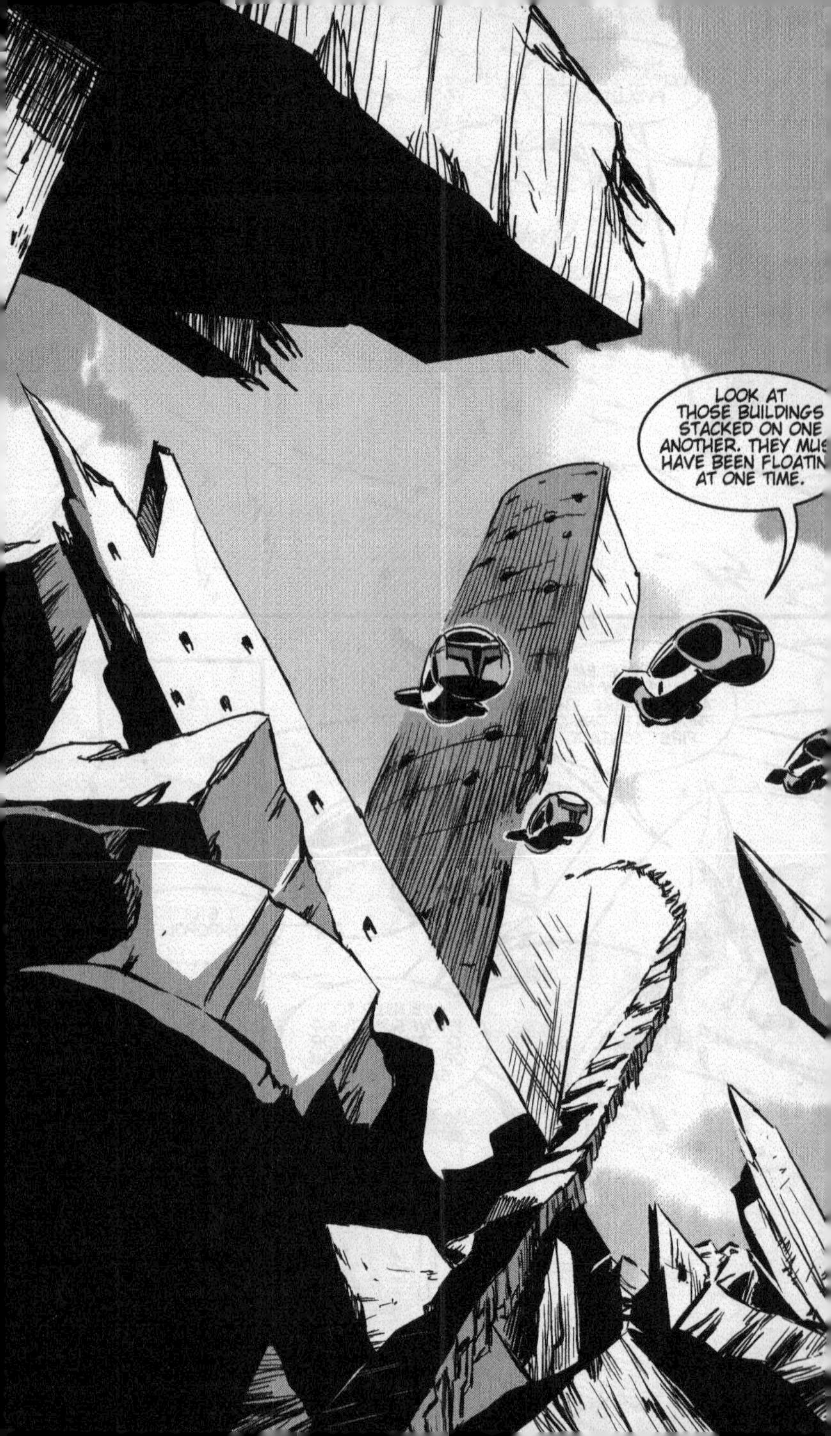
LOOK AT THOSE BUILDINGS STACKED ON ONE ANOTHER. THEY MUS HAVE BEEN FLOATIN AT ONE TIME.

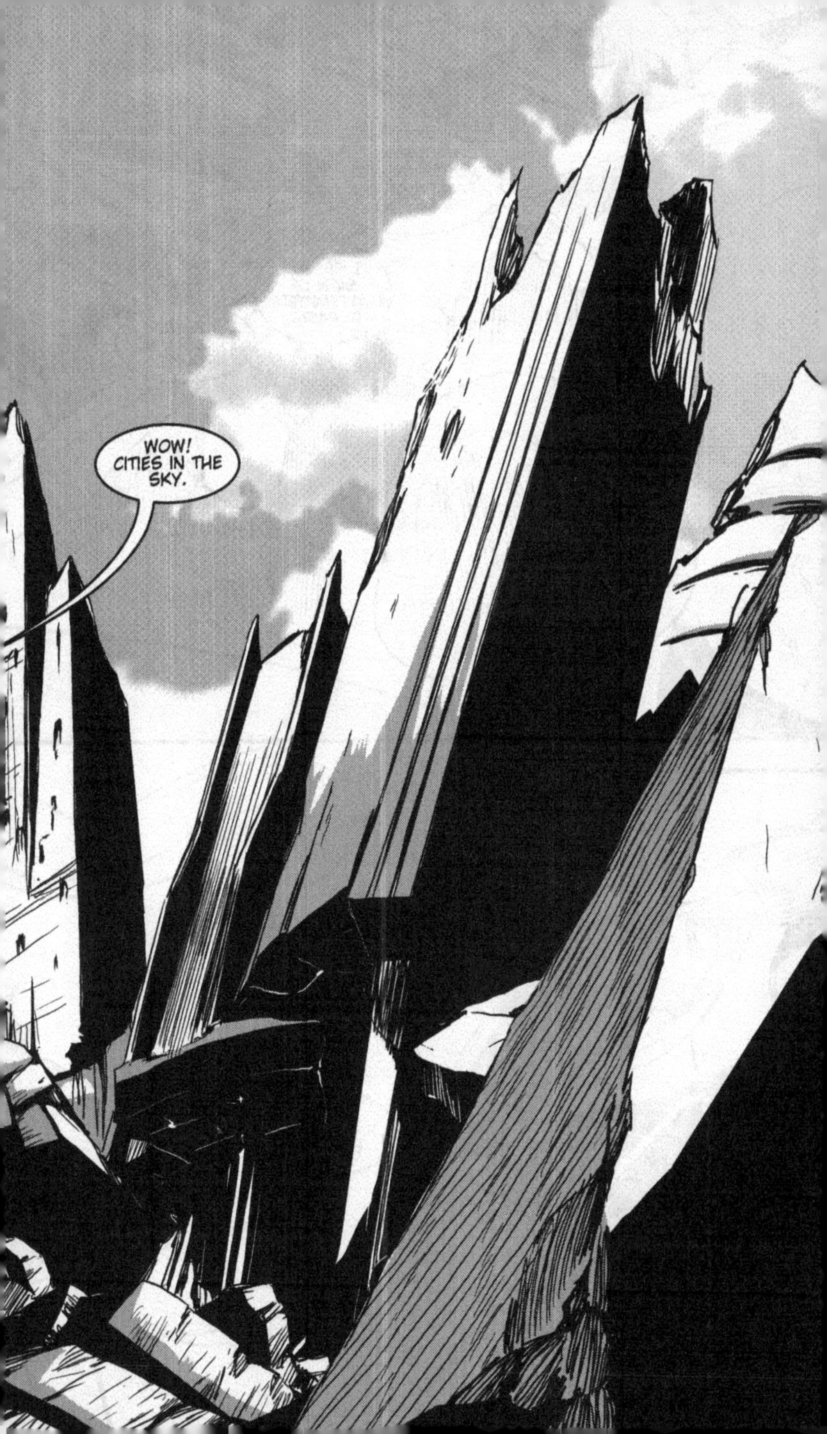
WOW! CITIES IN THE SKY.

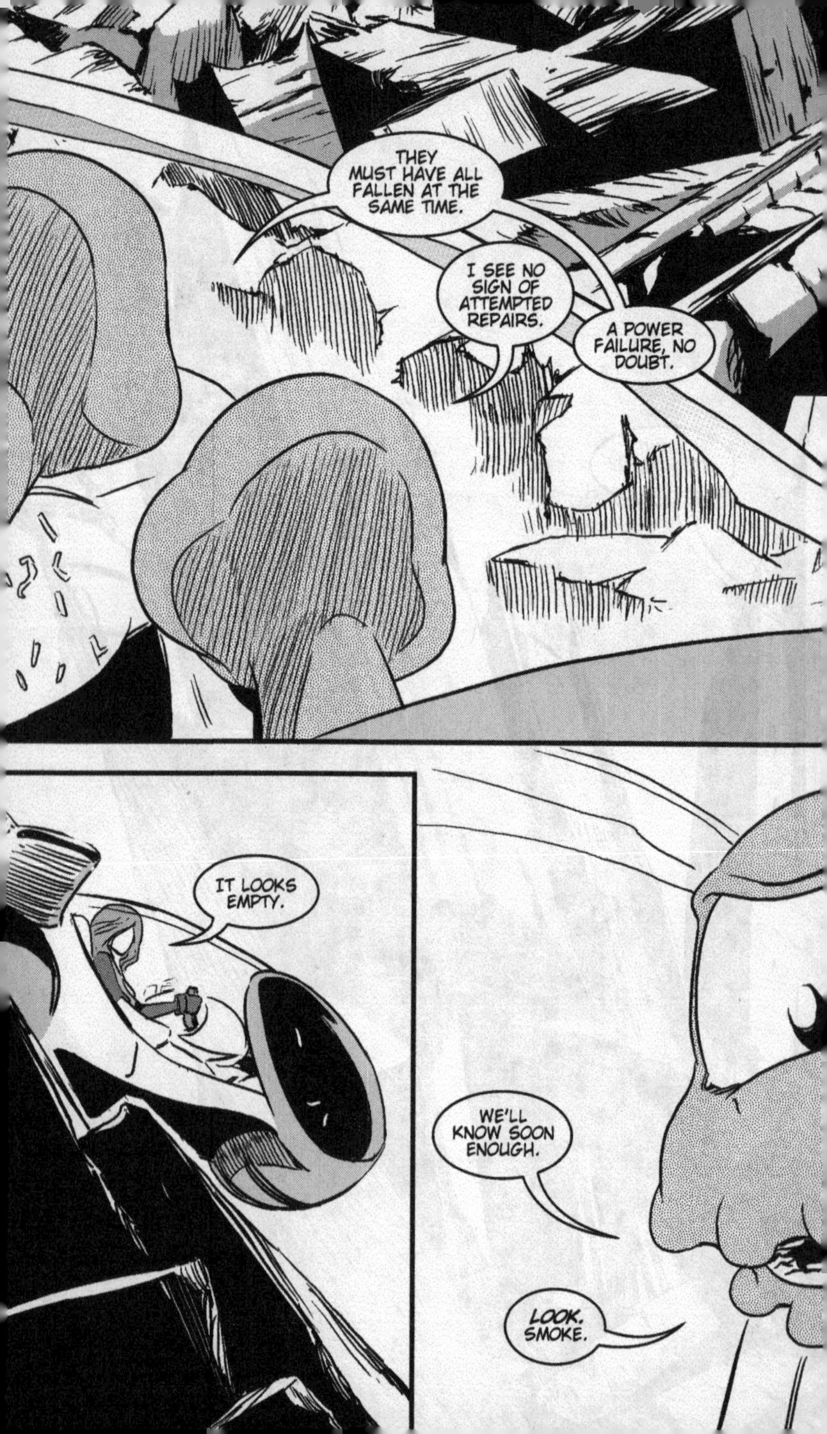
THEY MUST HAVE ALL FALLEN AT THE SAME TIME.
I SEE NO SIGN OF ATTEMPTED REPAIRS.
A POWER FAILURE, NO DOUBT.
IT LOOKS EMPTY.
WE'LL KNOW SOON ENOUGH.
LOOK. SMOKE.

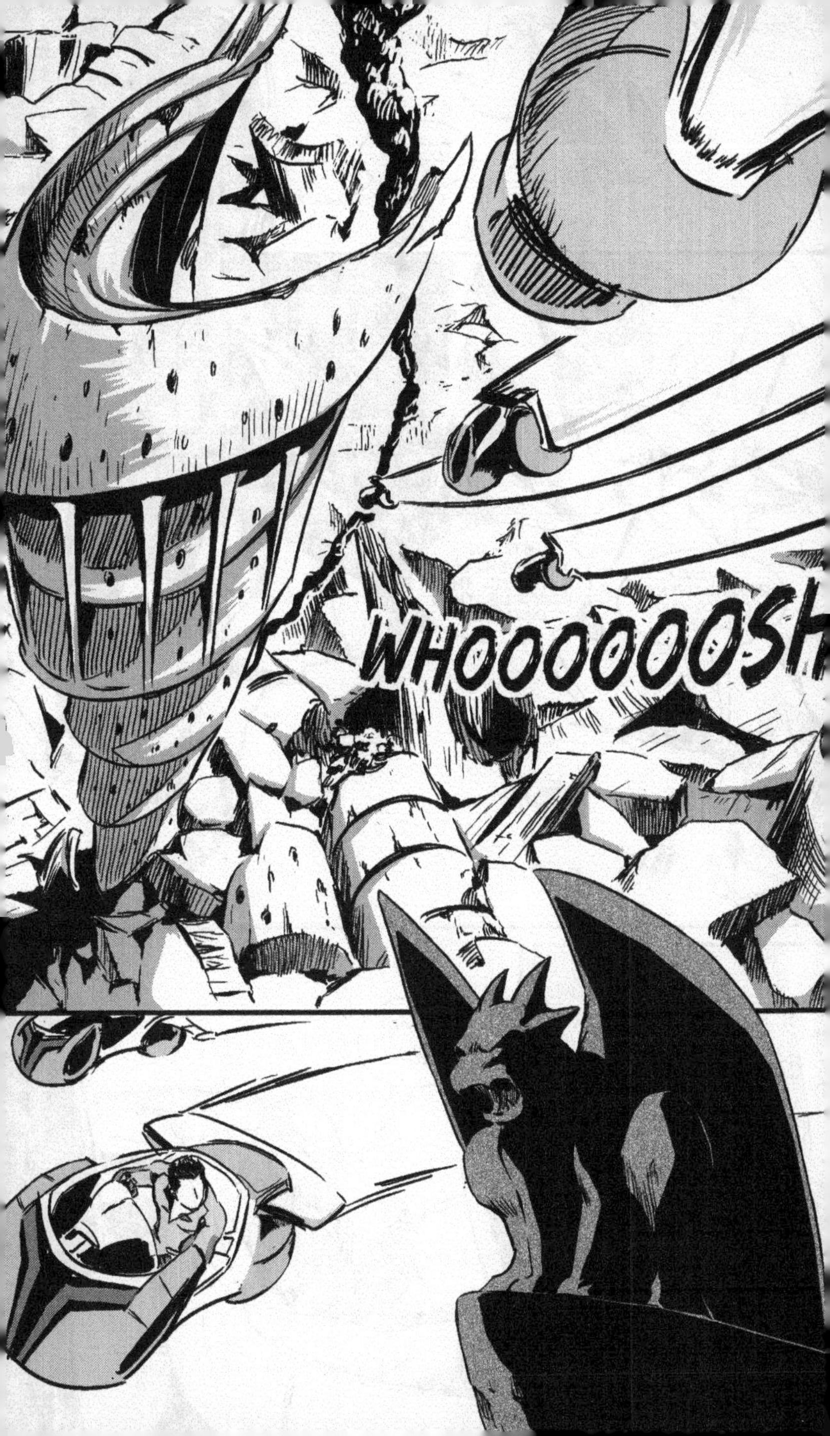
WHOOOOOOOSH

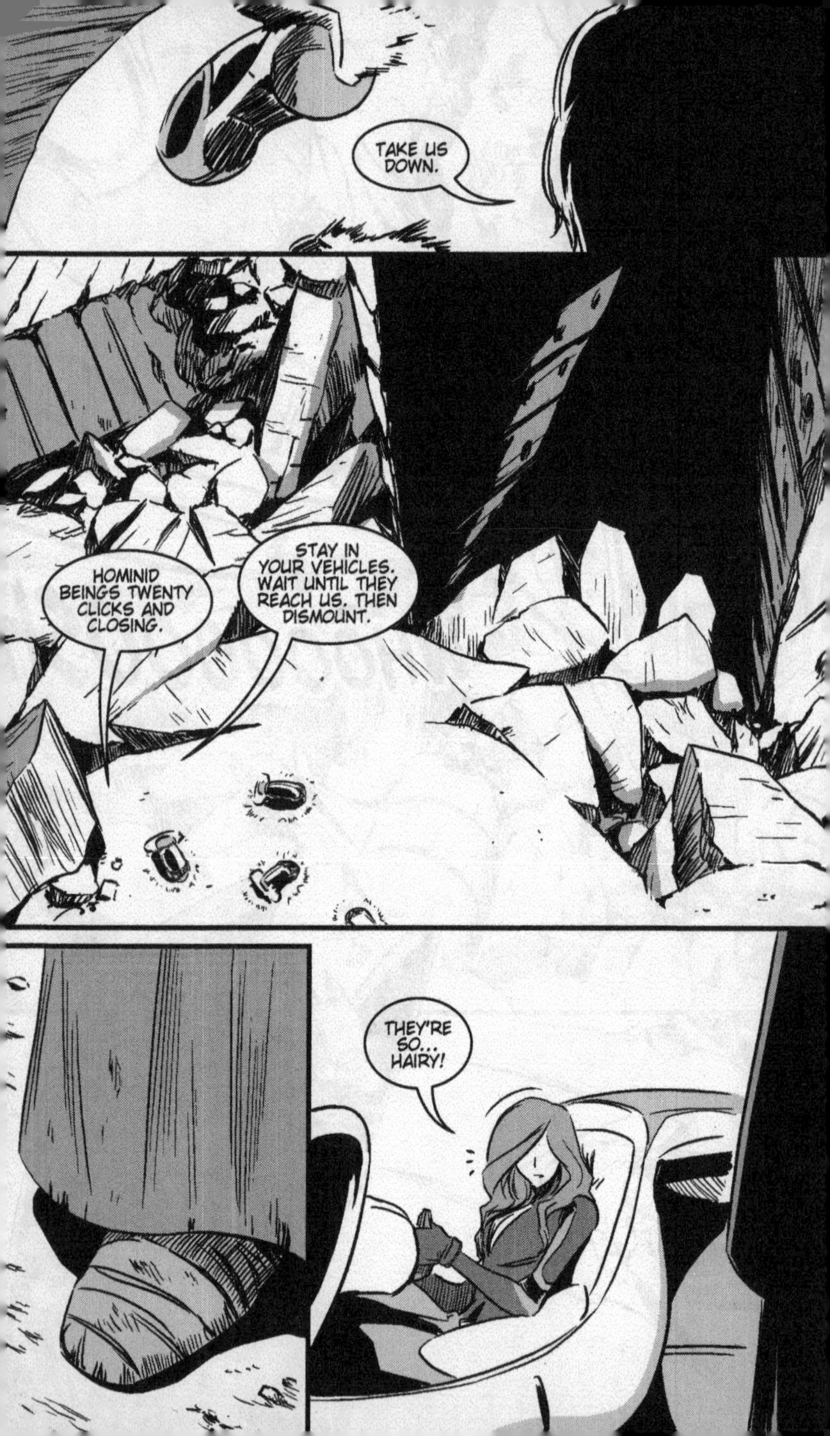
TAKE US DOWN.
HOMINID BEINGS TWENTY CLICKS AND CLOSING.
STAY IN YOUR VEHICLES. WAIT UNTIL THEY REACH US. THEN DISMOUNT.
THEY'RE SO... HAIRY!

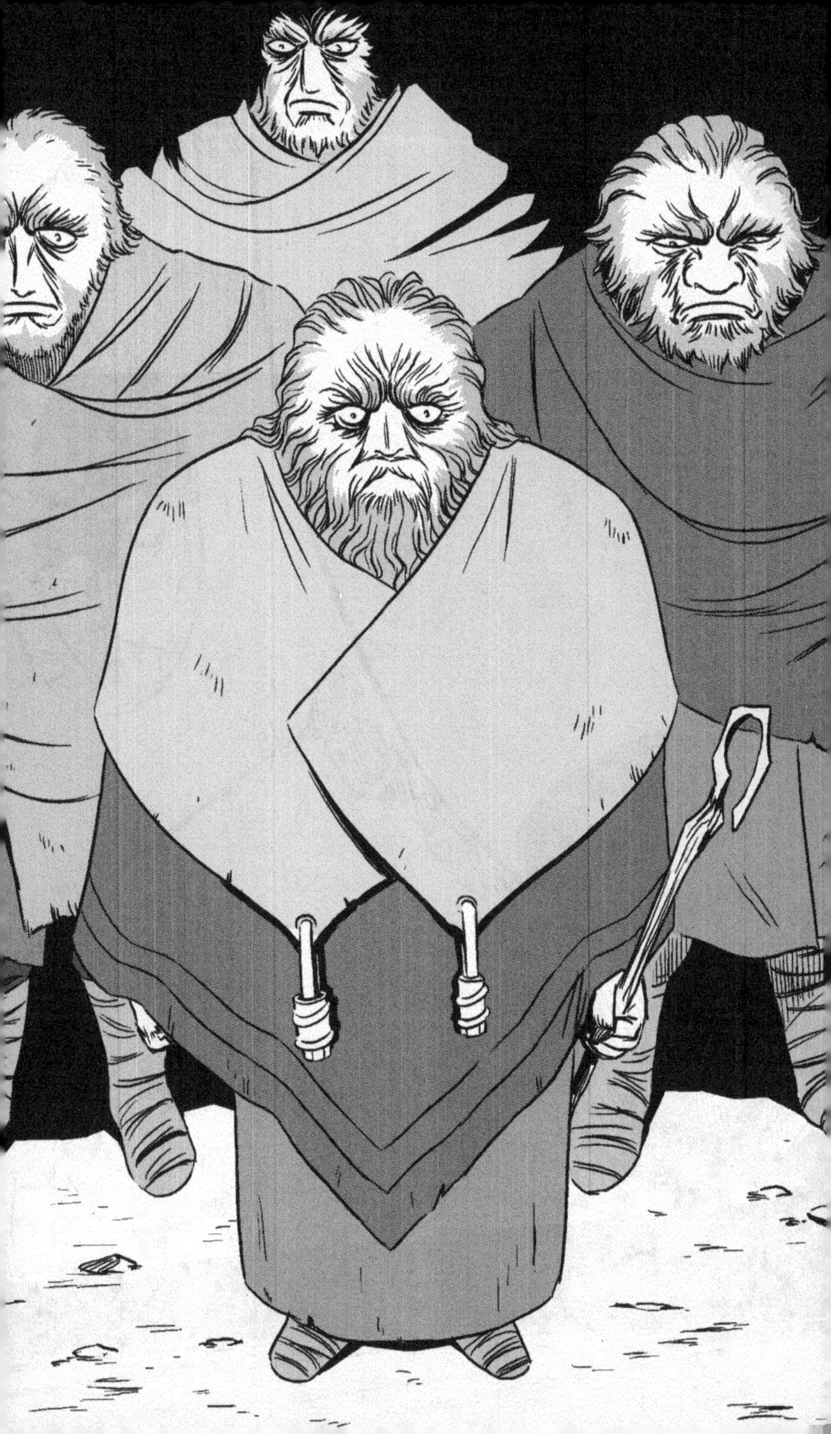

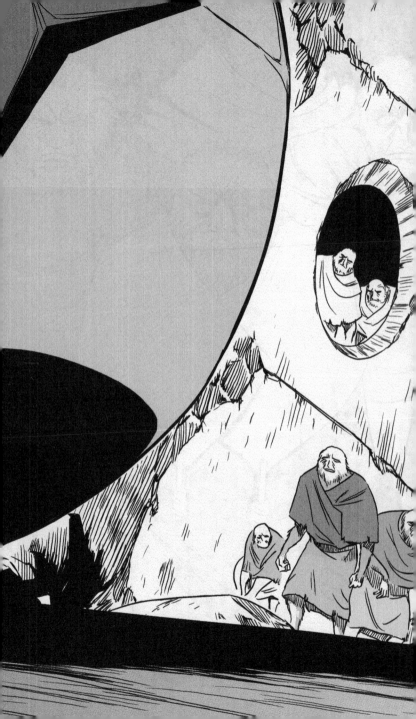

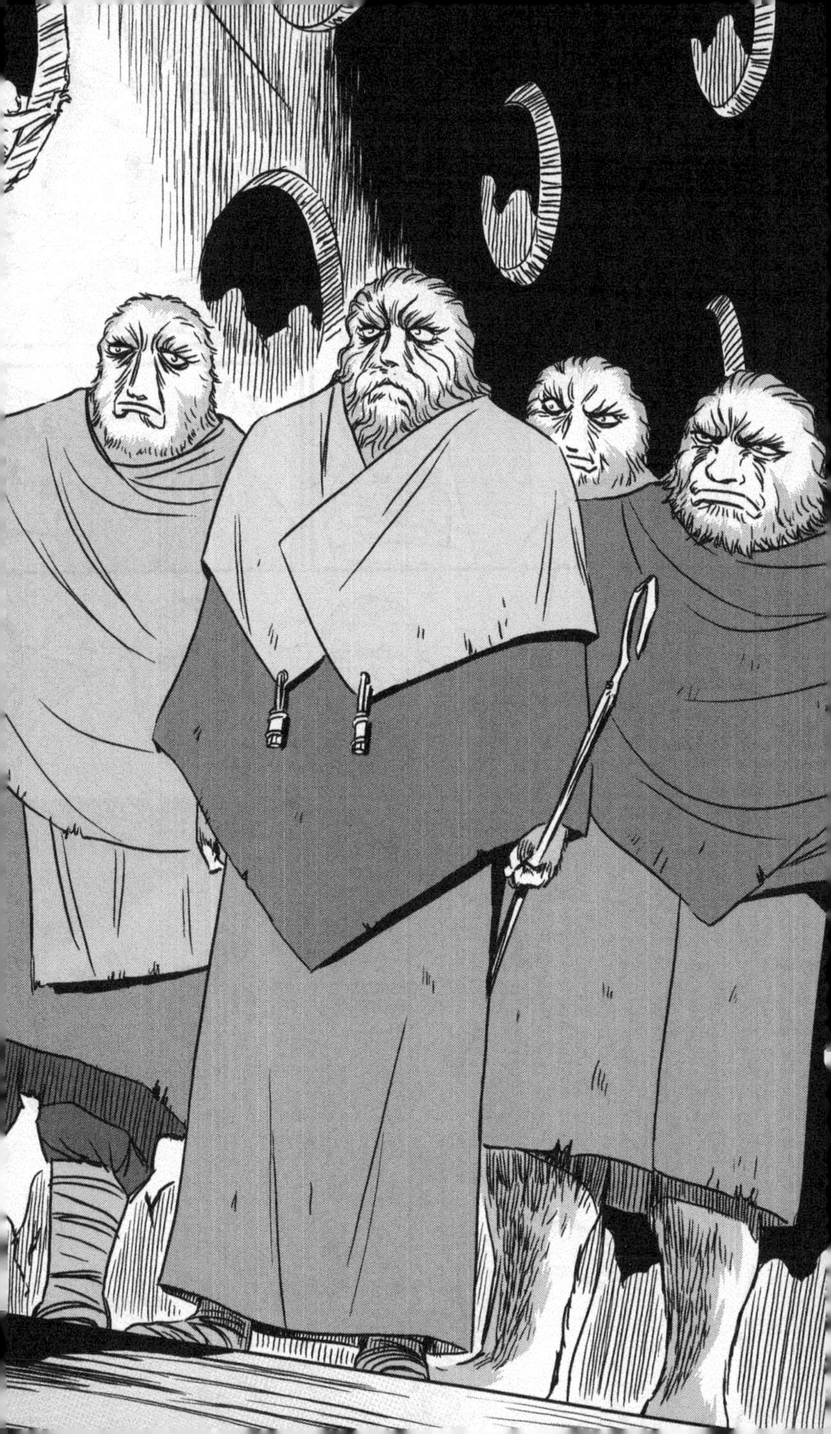

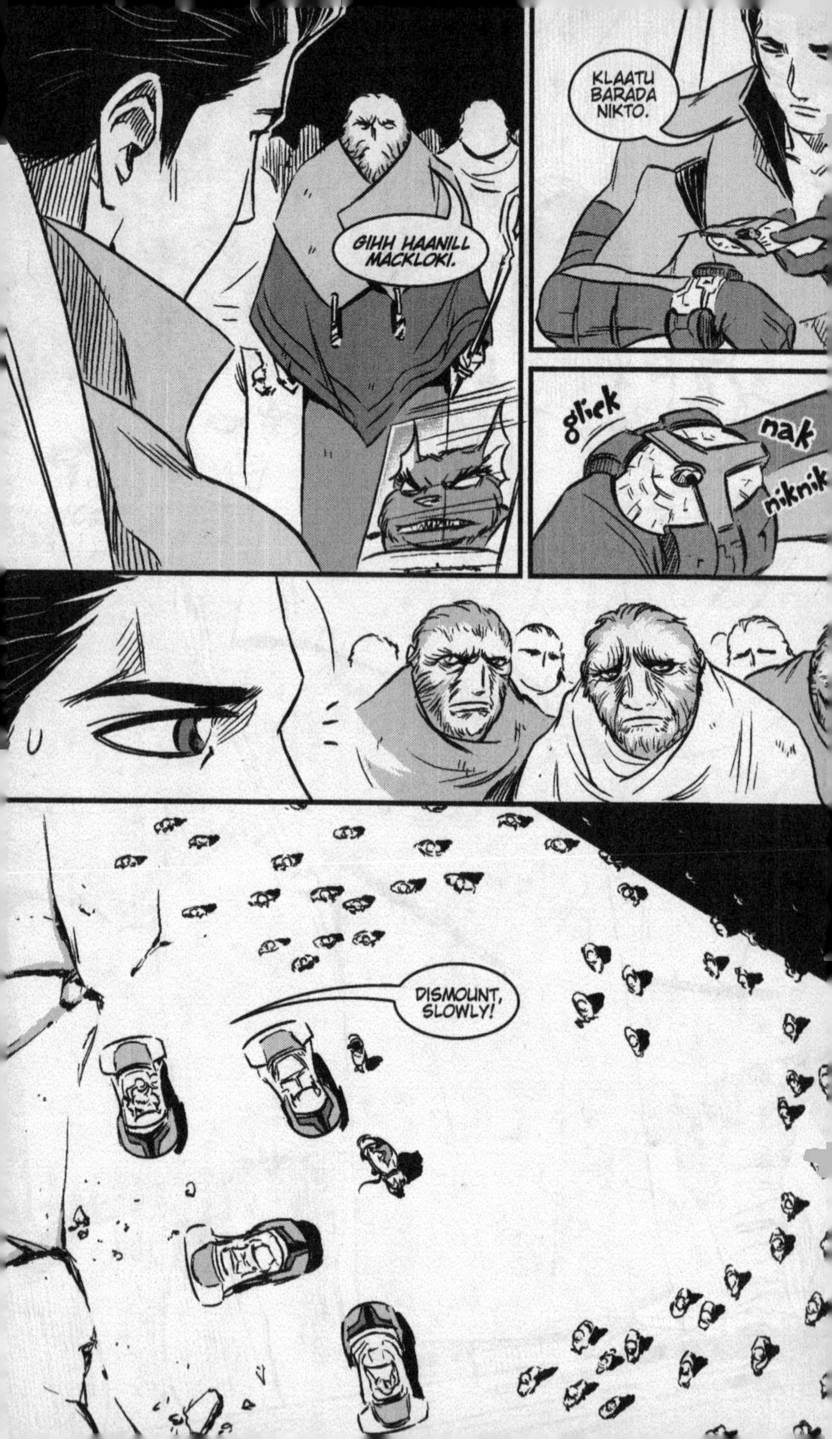
GIHH HAANILL MACKLOKI.
KLAATU BARADA NIKTO.
glick
nak
niknik
DISMOUNT, SLOWLY!

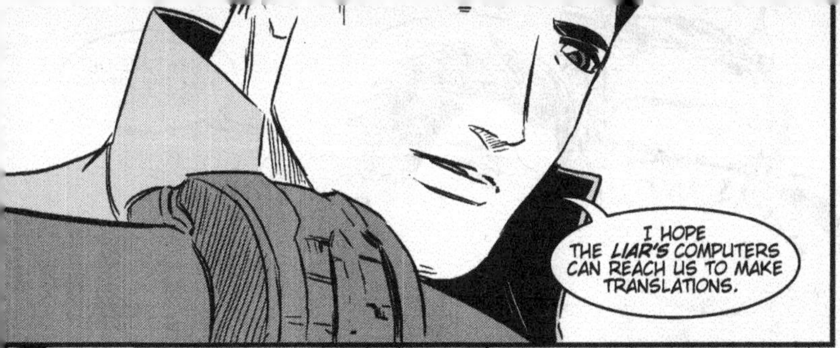
I HOPE THE LIAR'S COMPUTERS CAN REACH US TO MAKE TRANSLATIONS.
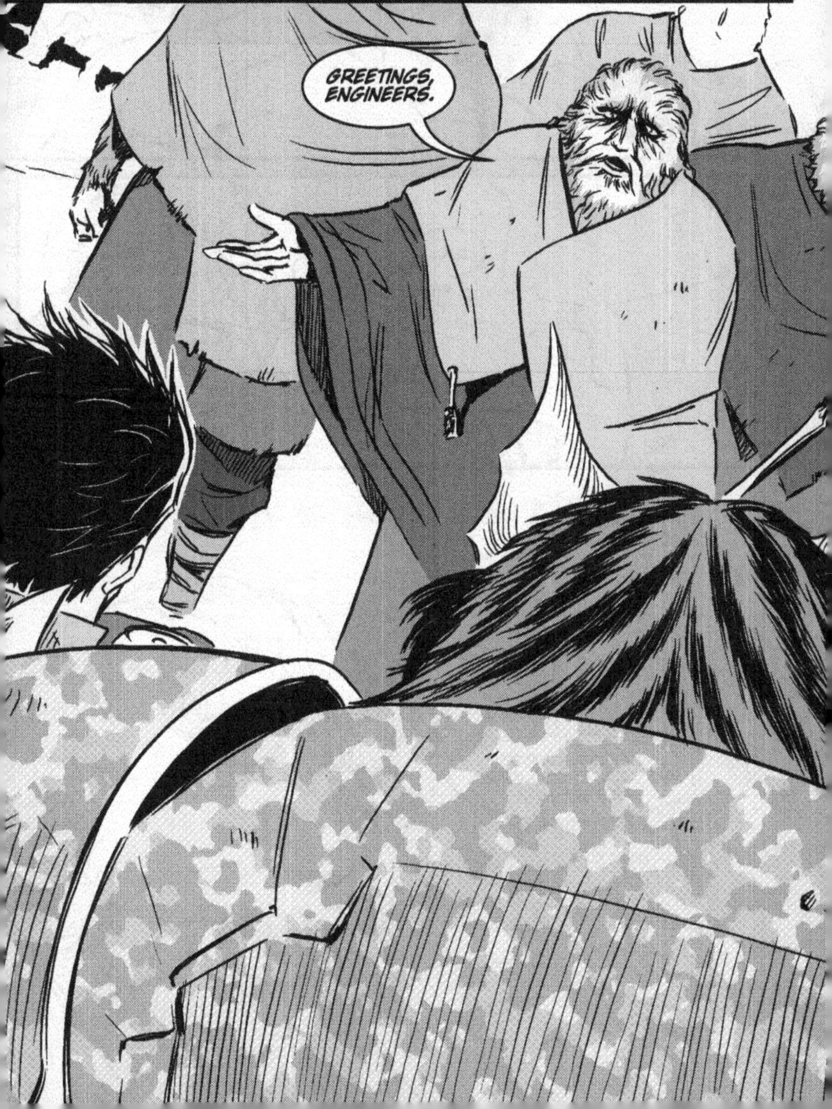
GREETINGS, ENGINEERS.

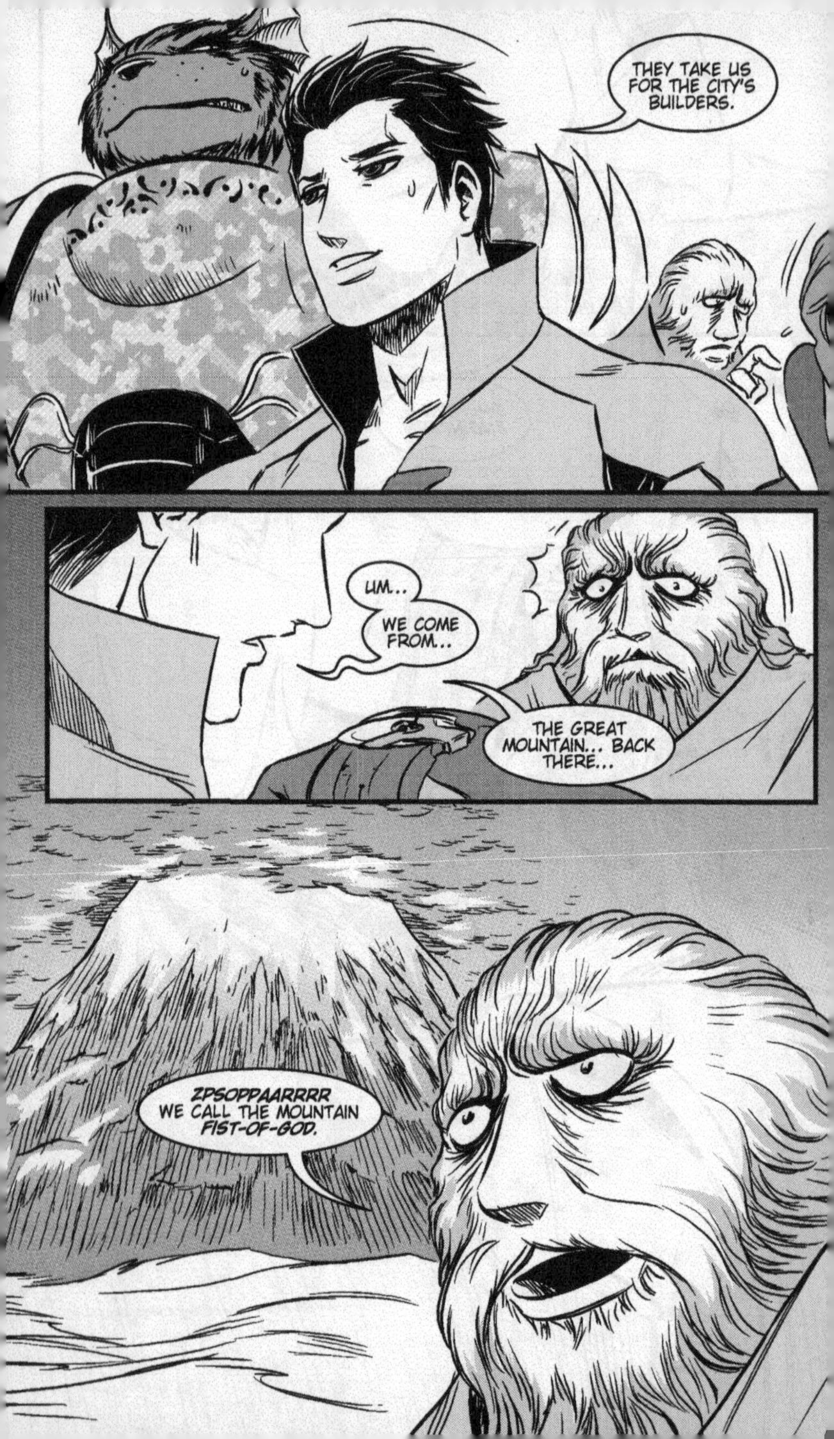
THEY TAKE US FOR THE CITY'S BUILDERS.
UM...
WE COME FROM...
THE GREAT MOUNTAIN... BACK THERE...
ZPSOPPAARRRR WE CALL THE MOUNTAIN FIST-OF-GOD.

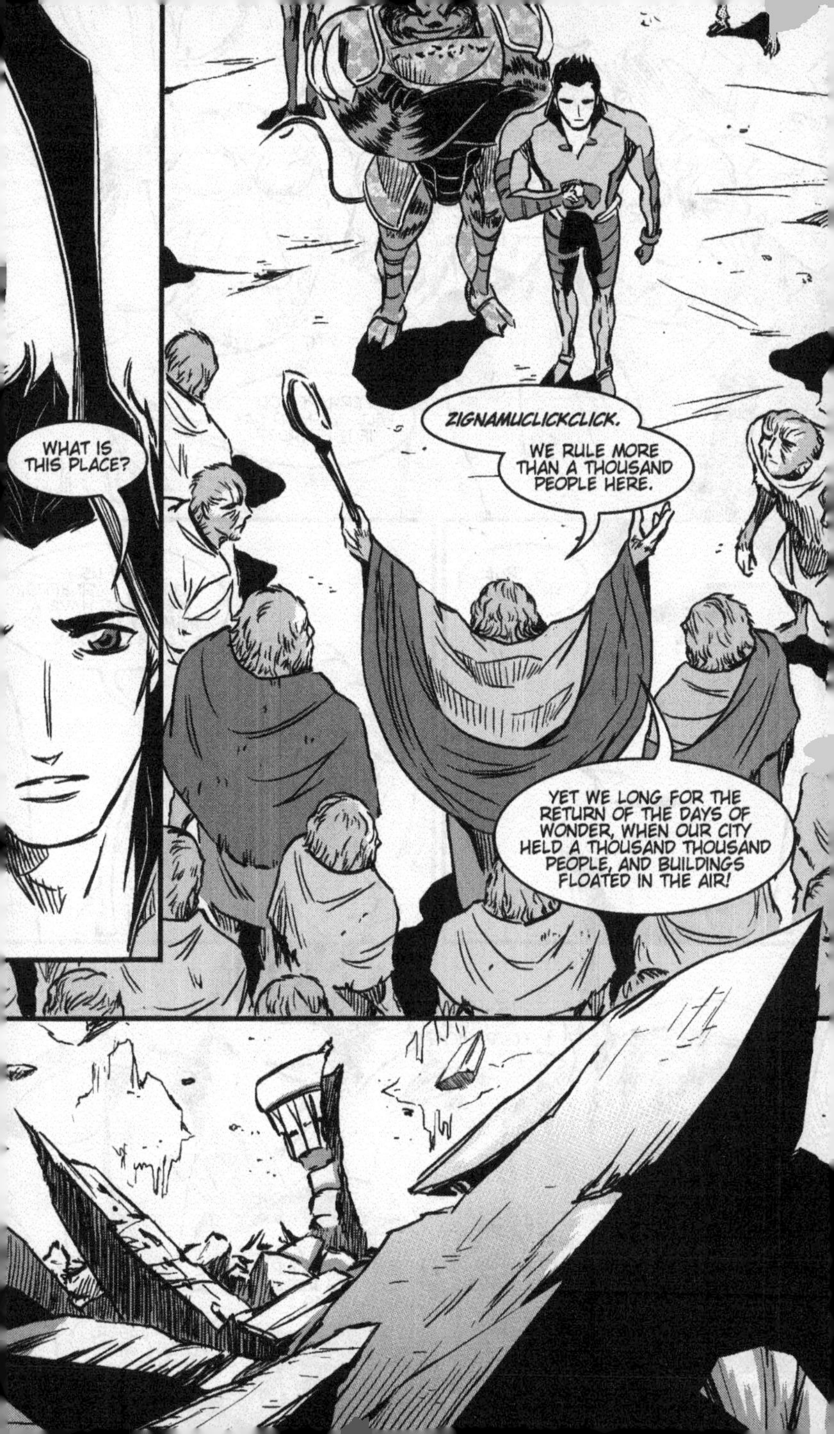
WHAT IS THIS PLACE?
ZIGNAMUCLICKCLICK.
WE RULE MORE THAN A THOUSAND PEOPLE HERE.
YET WE LONG FOR THE RETURN OF THE DAYS OF WONDER, WHEN OUR CITY HELD A THOUSAND THOUSAND PEOPLE, AND BUILDINGS FLOATED IN THE AIR!

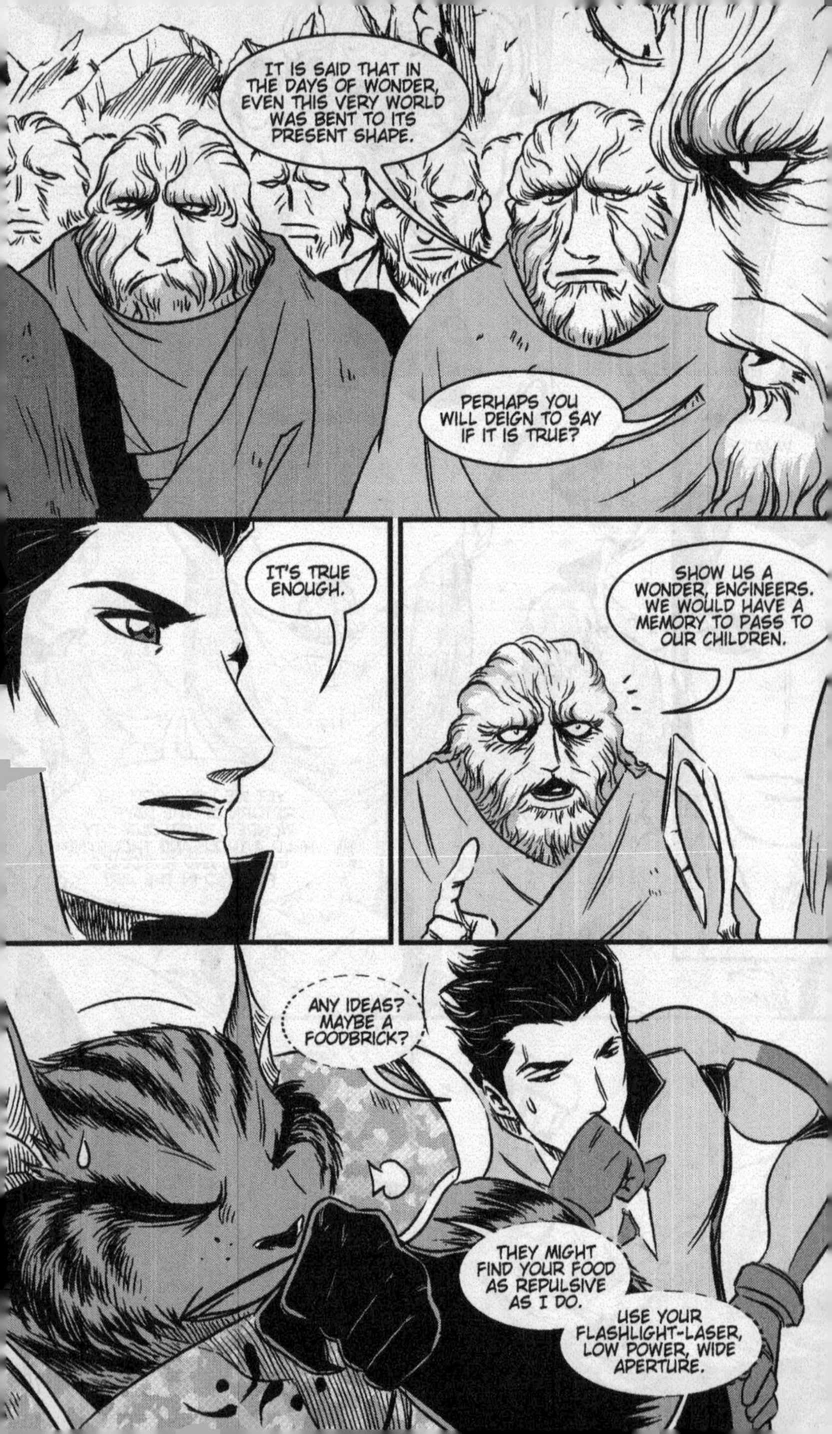

IT IS SAID THAT IN THE DAYS OF WONDER, EVEN THIS VERY WORLD WAS BENT TO ITS PRESENT SHAPE.
PERHAPS YOU WILL DEIGN TO SAY IF IT IS TRUE?
IT'S TRUE ENOUGH.
SHOW US A WONDER, ENGINEERS. WE WOULD HAVE A MEMORY TO PASS TO OUR CHILDREN.
ANY IDEAS? MAYBE A FOODBRICK?
THEY MIGHT FIND YOUR FOOD AS REPULSIVE AS I DO.
USE YOUR FLASHLIGHT-LASER, LOW POWER, WIDE APERTURE.

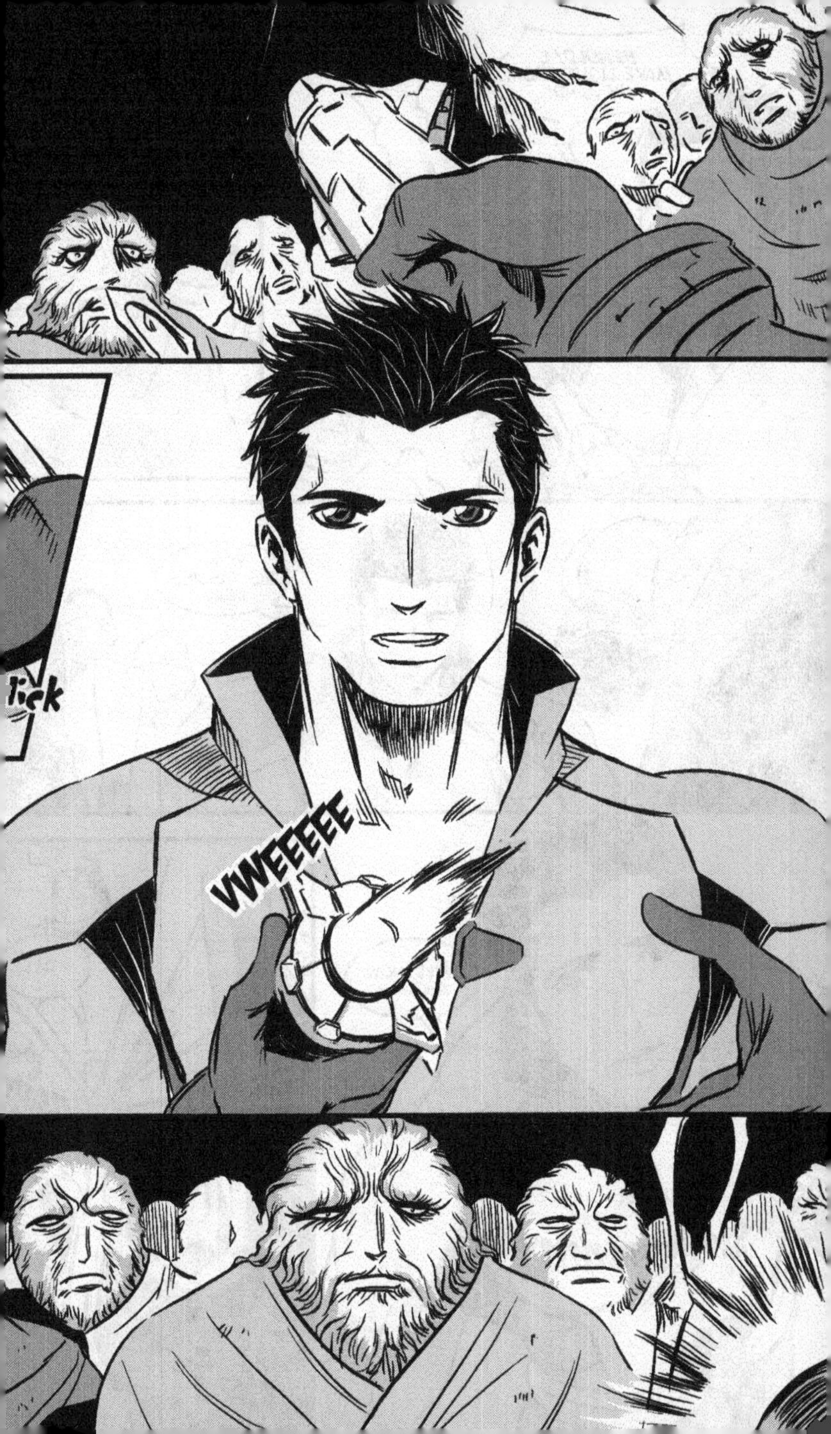
VWEEEEE

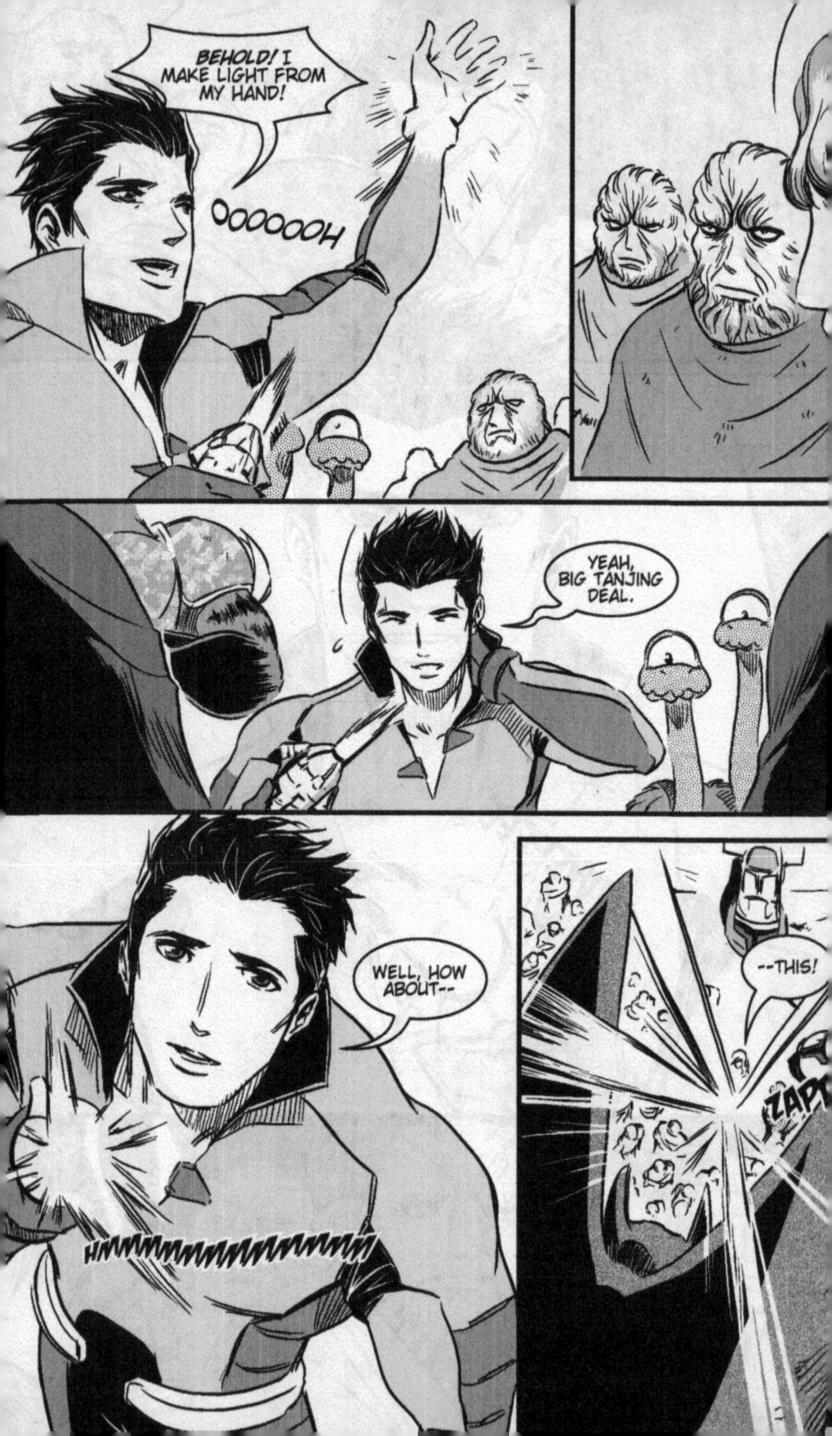
BEHOLD! I MAKE LIGHT FROM MY HAND!
OOOOOOOH
YEAH, BIG TANJING DEAL.
WELL, HOW ABOUT--
HMMMMMMMMMMMM
--THIS!
ZAP

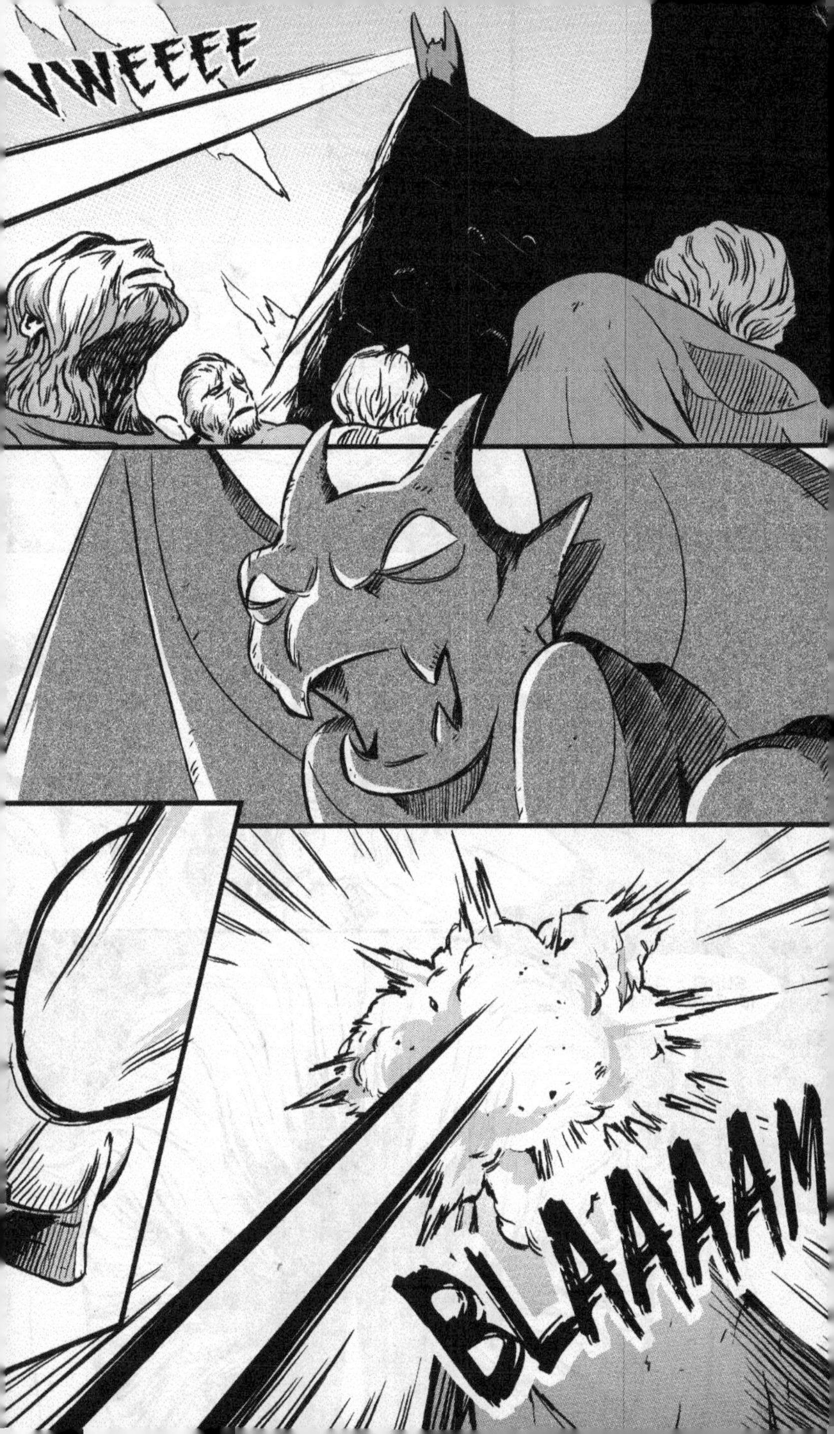
VWEEEE
BLAAAAM

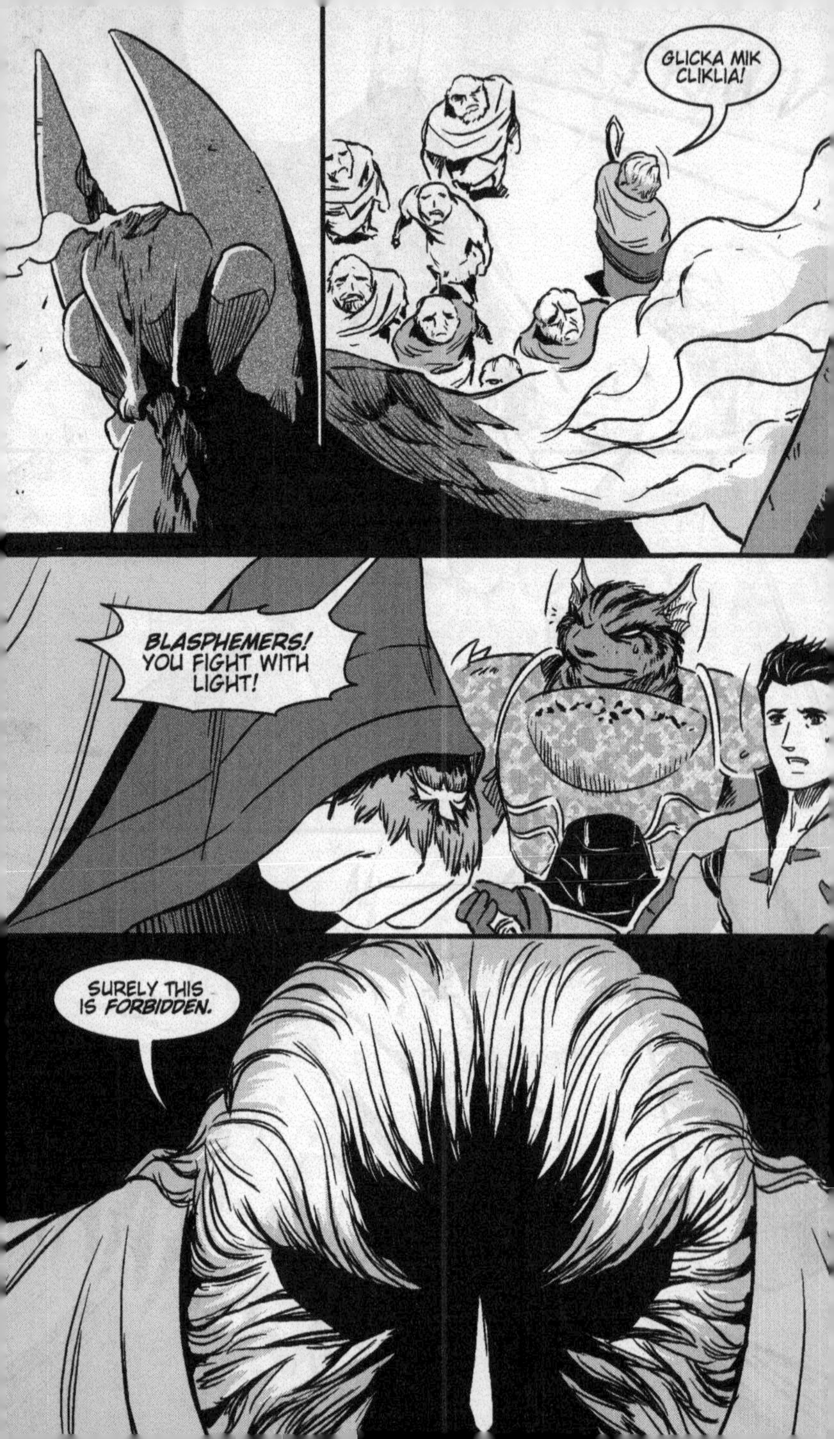
GLICKA MIK CLIKLIA!
BLASPHEMERS! YOU FIGHT WITH LIGHT!
SURELY THIS IS FORBIDDEN.

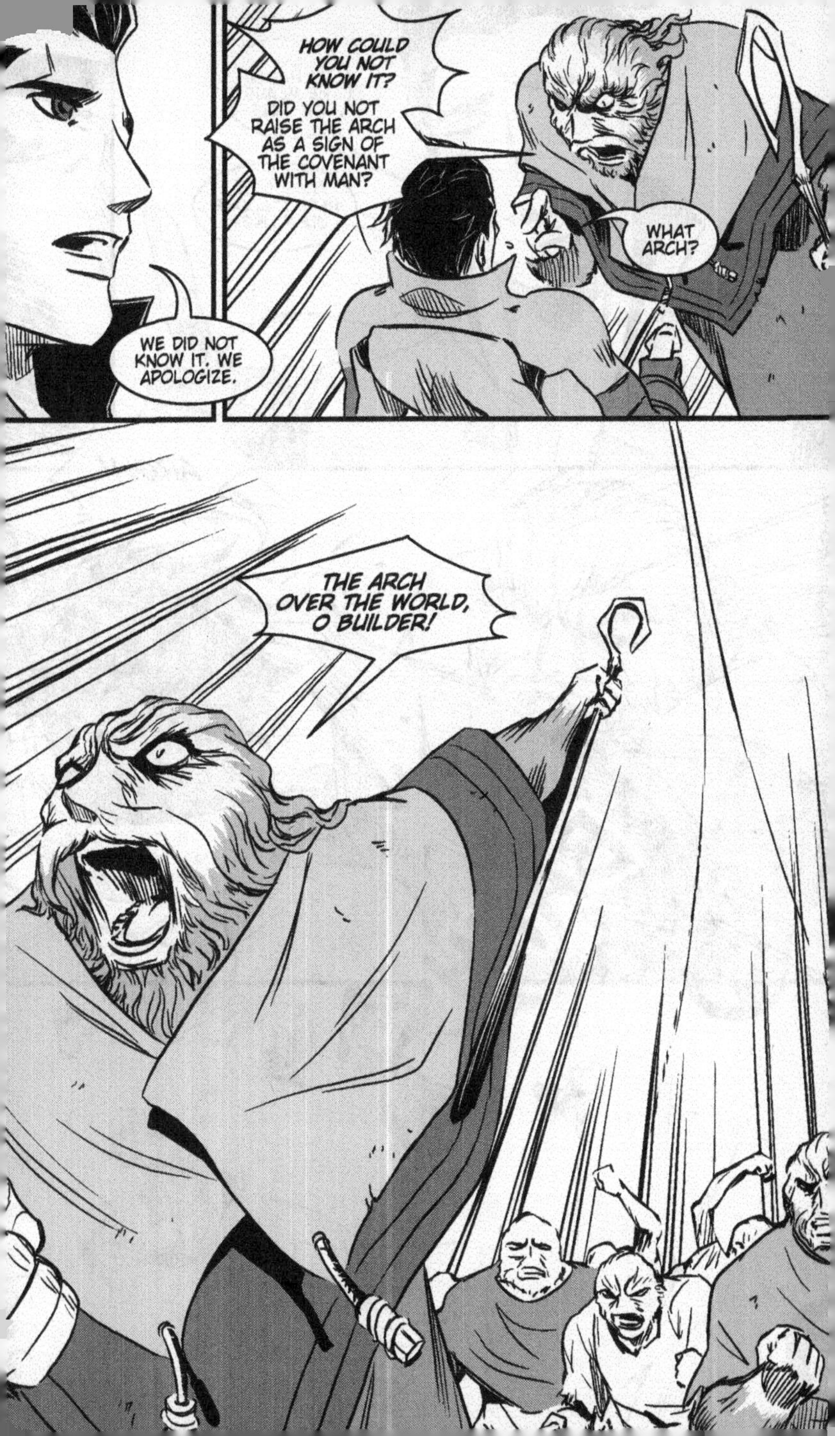
WE DID NOT KNOW IT. WE APOLOGIZE.
HOW COULD YOU NOT KNOW IT?
DID YOU NOT RAISE THE ARCH AS A SIGN OF THE COVENANT WITH MAN?
WHAT ARCH?
THE ARCH OVER THE WORLD, O BUILDER!

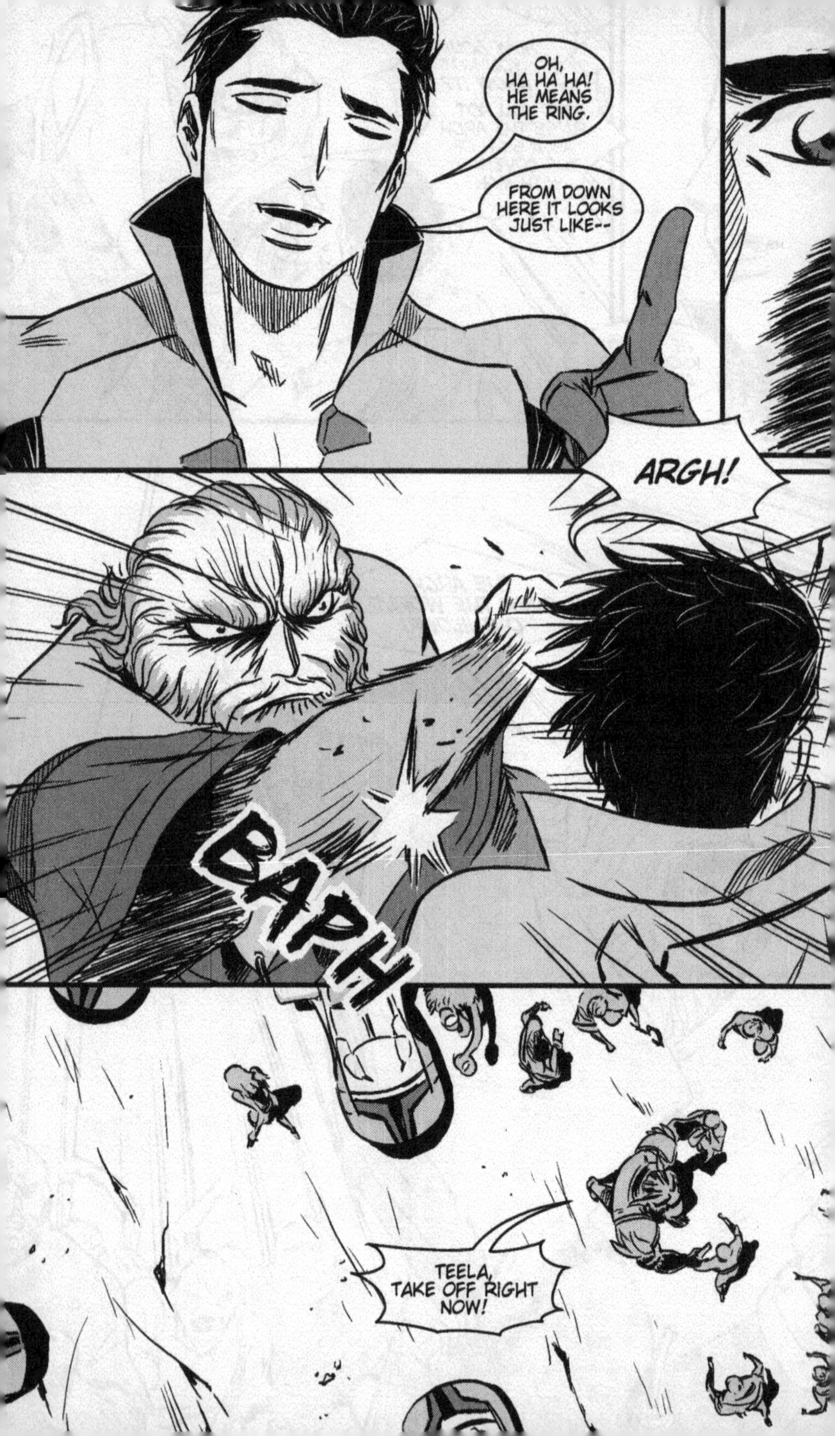
OH, HA HA HA! HE MEANS THE RING.
FROM DOWN HERE IT LOOKS JUST LIKE--
ARGH!
BAPH
TEELA, TAKE OFF RIGHT NOW!

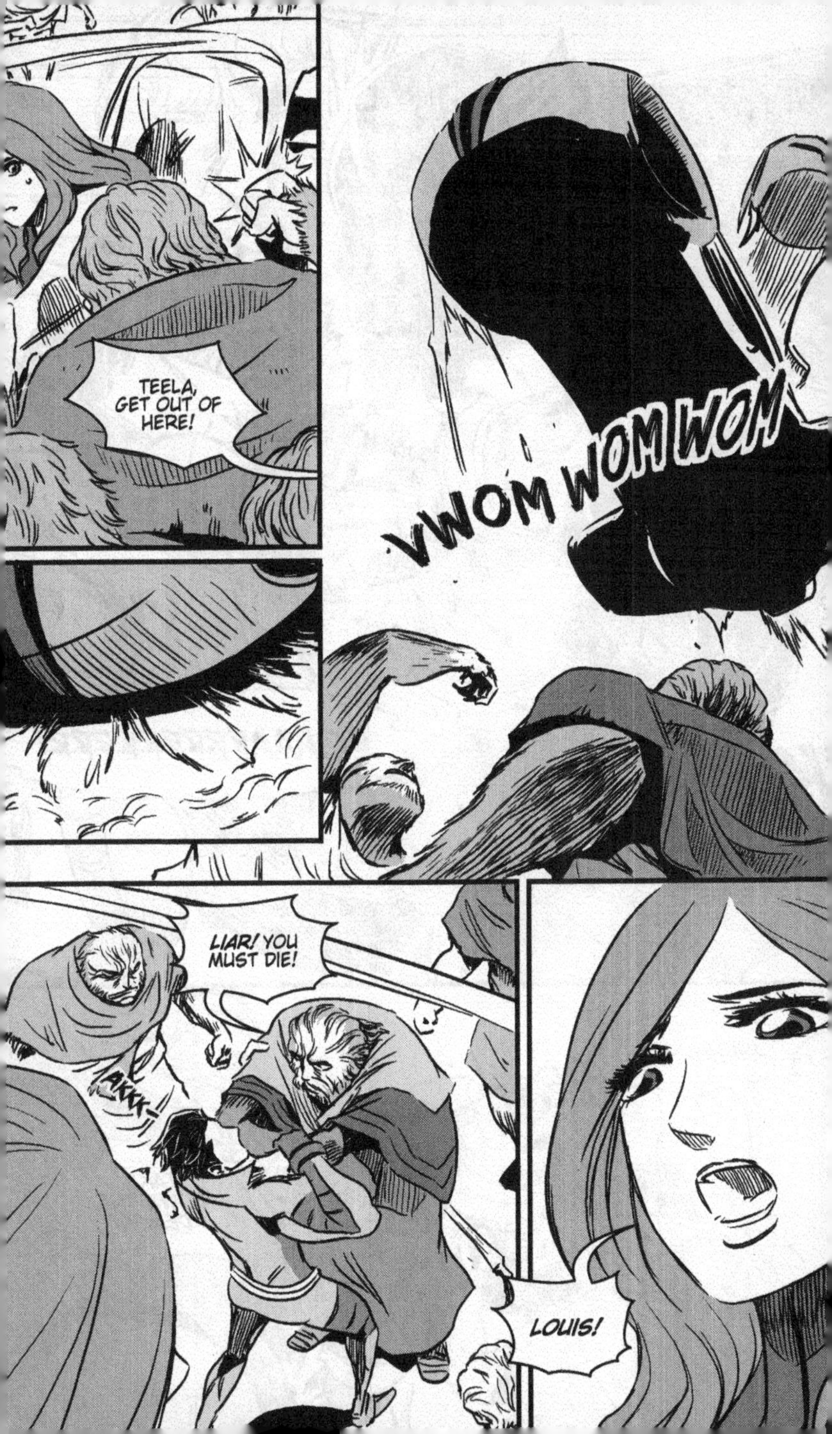

TEELA, GET OUT OF HERE!
VWOM WOM WOM
LIAR! YOU MUST DIE!
AKKK–
LOUIS!

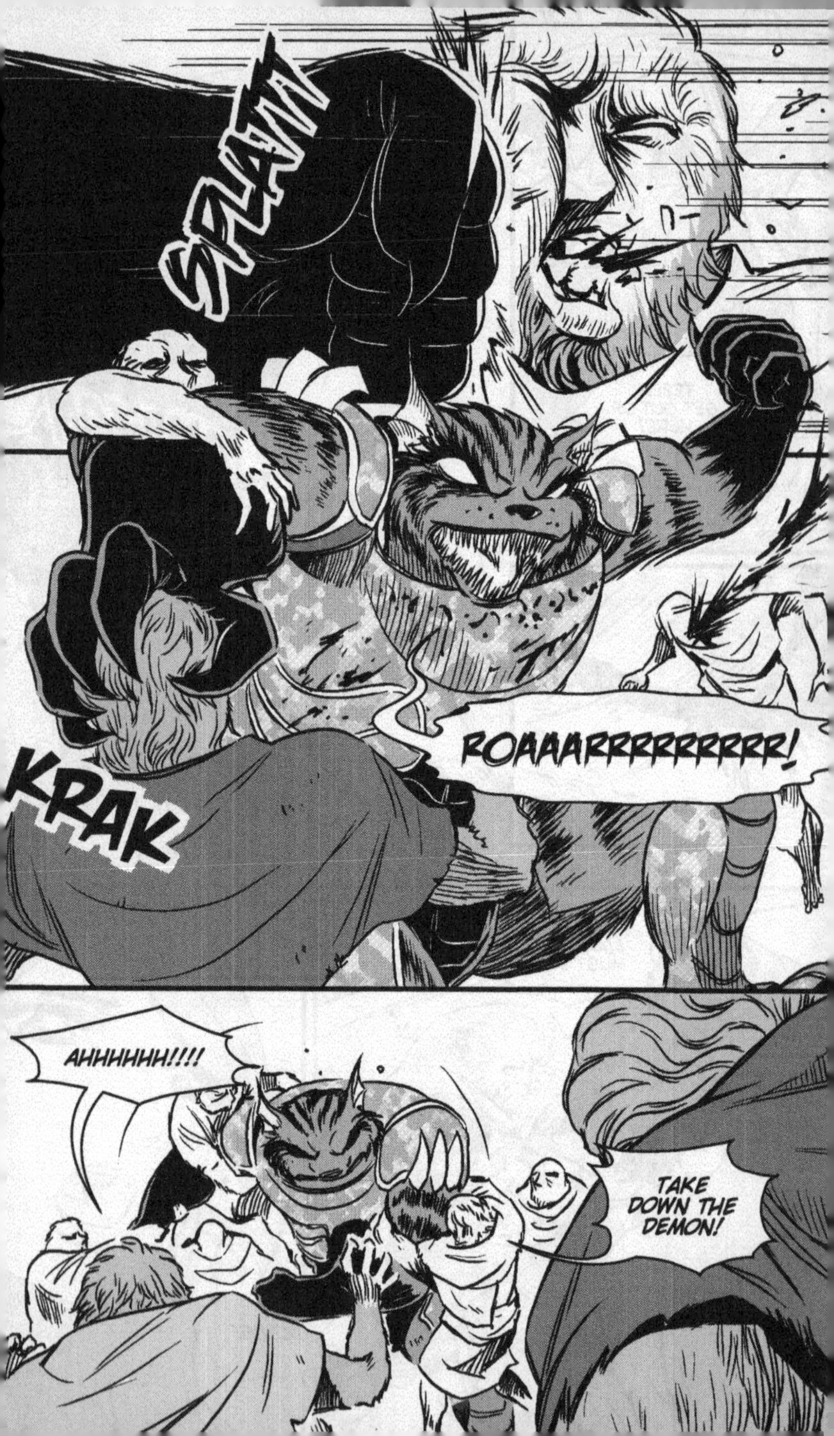
SPLATT
KRAK
ROAAARRRRRRRRR!
AHHHHHH!!!!
TAKE DOWN THE DEMON!

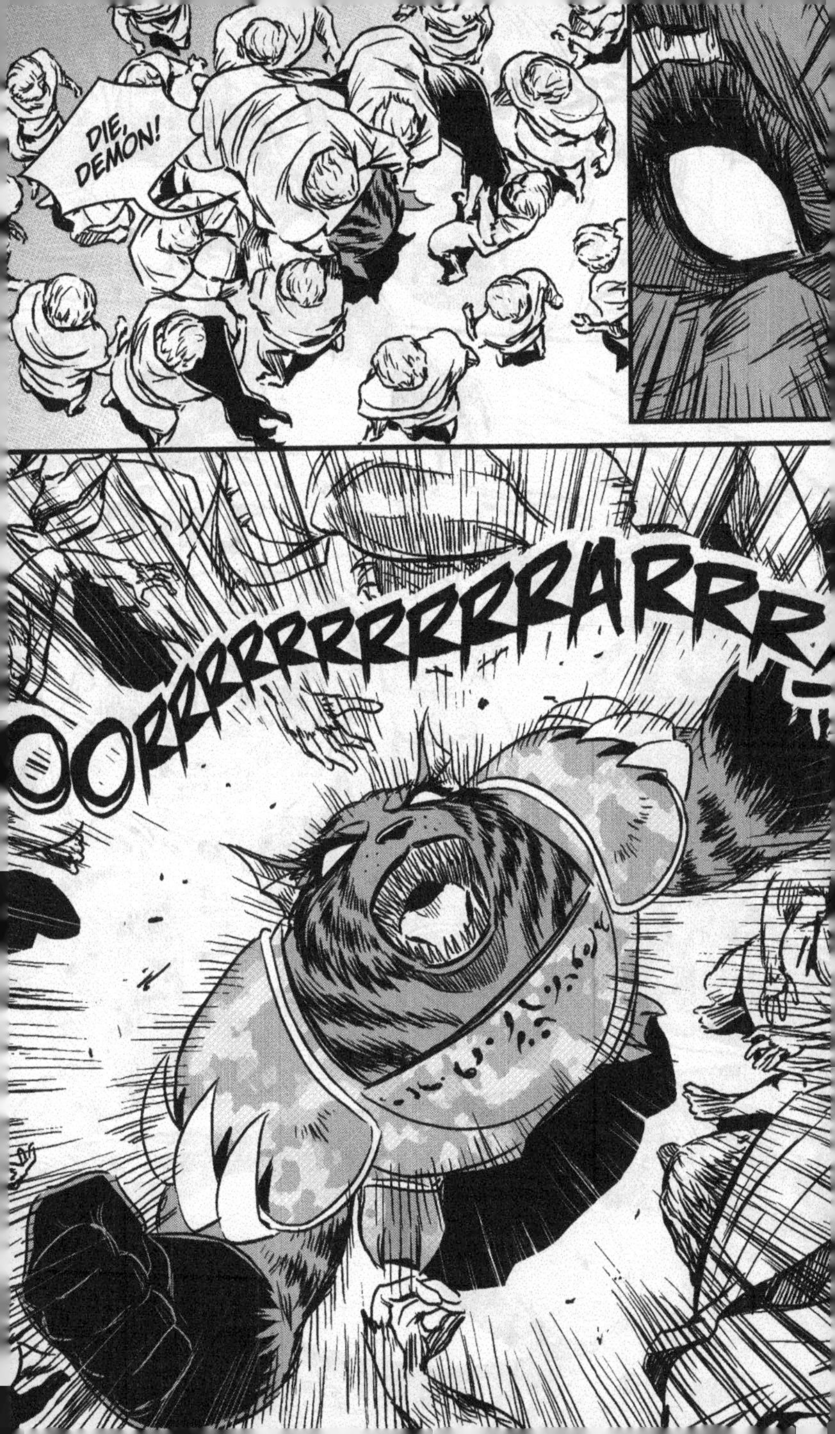
DIE, DEMON!
OORRRRRRRRRRARRR

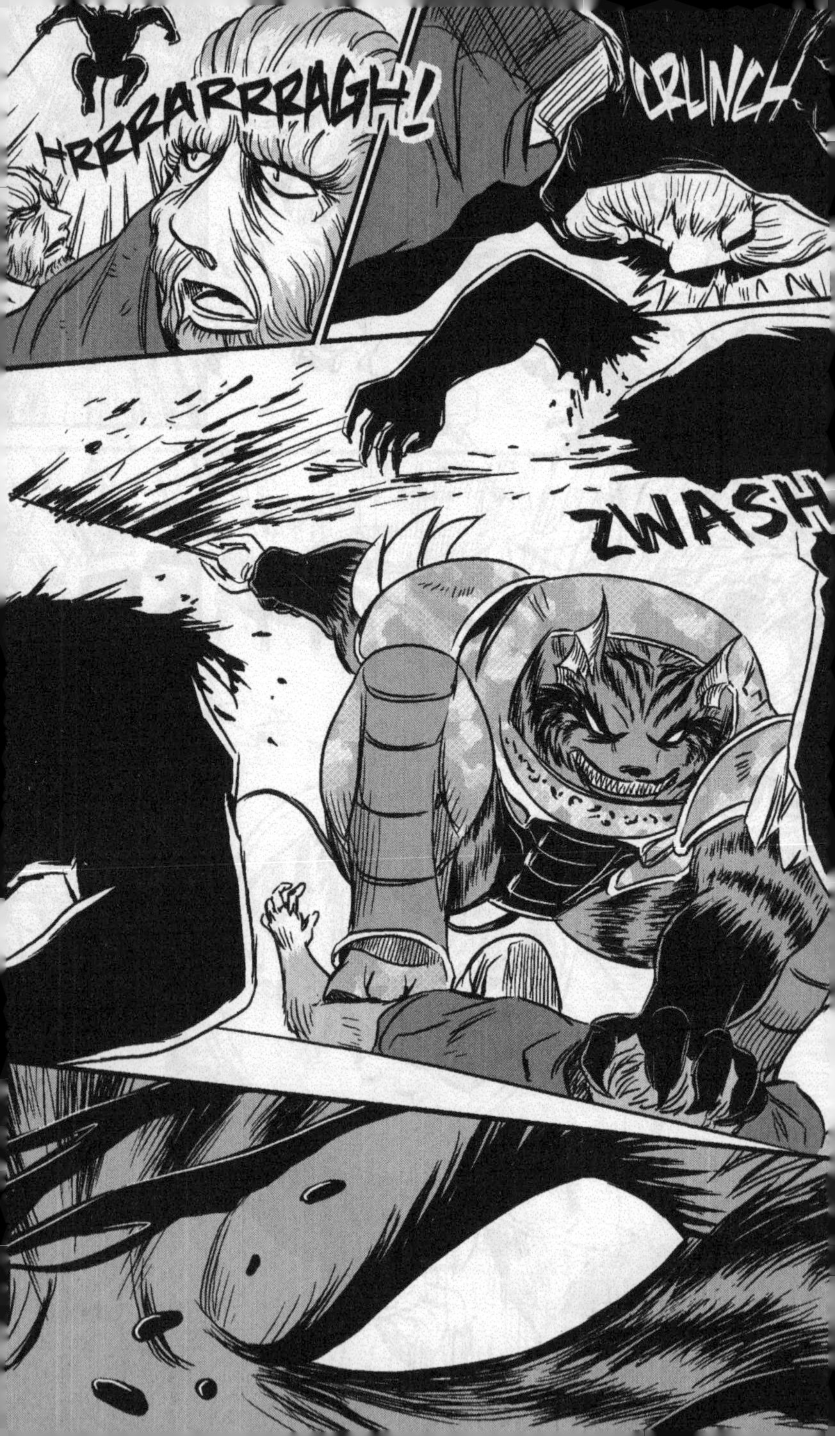
HRRRARRRRAGH!
CRUNCH
ZWASH

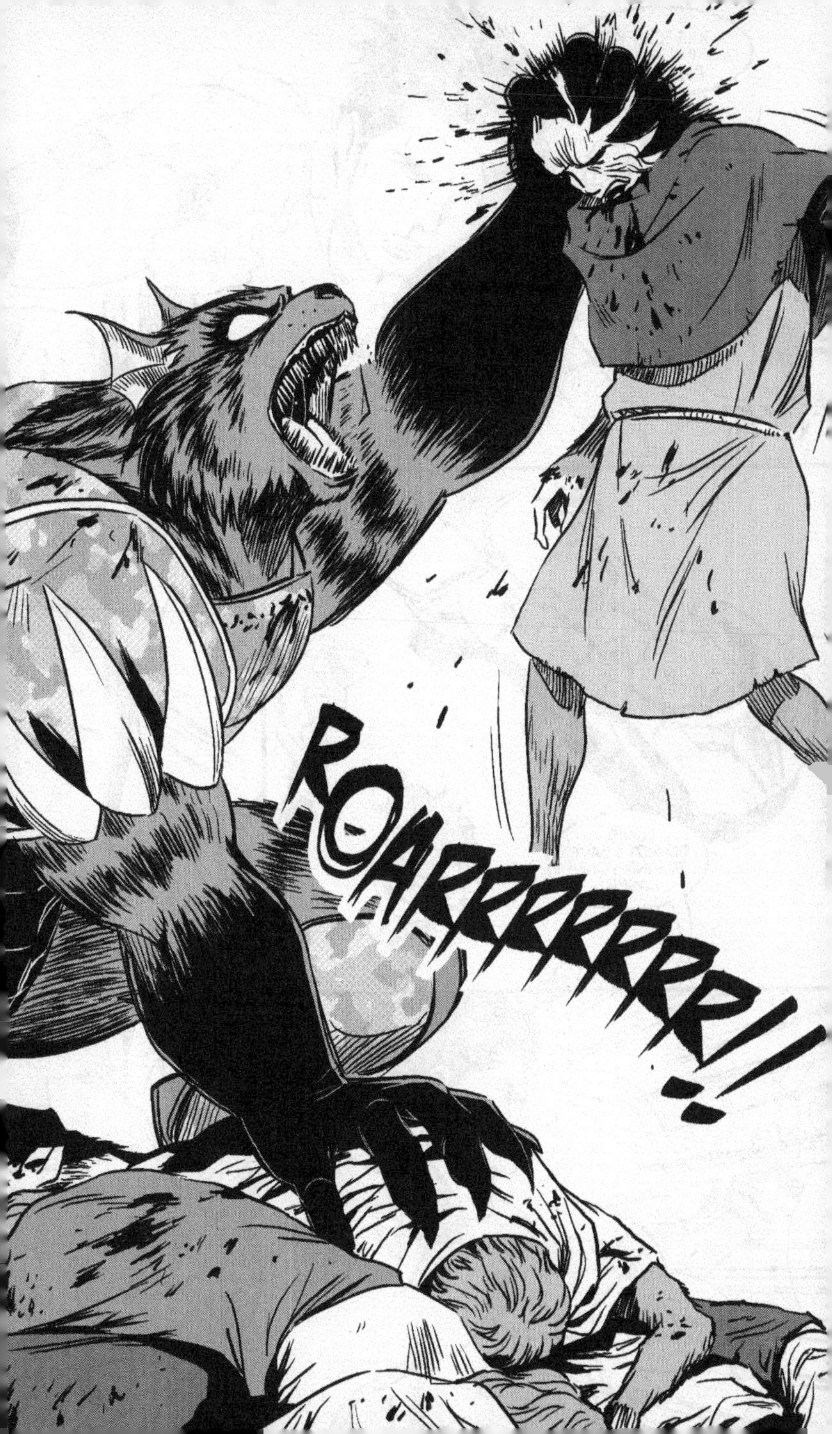
ROARRRRRRR!!

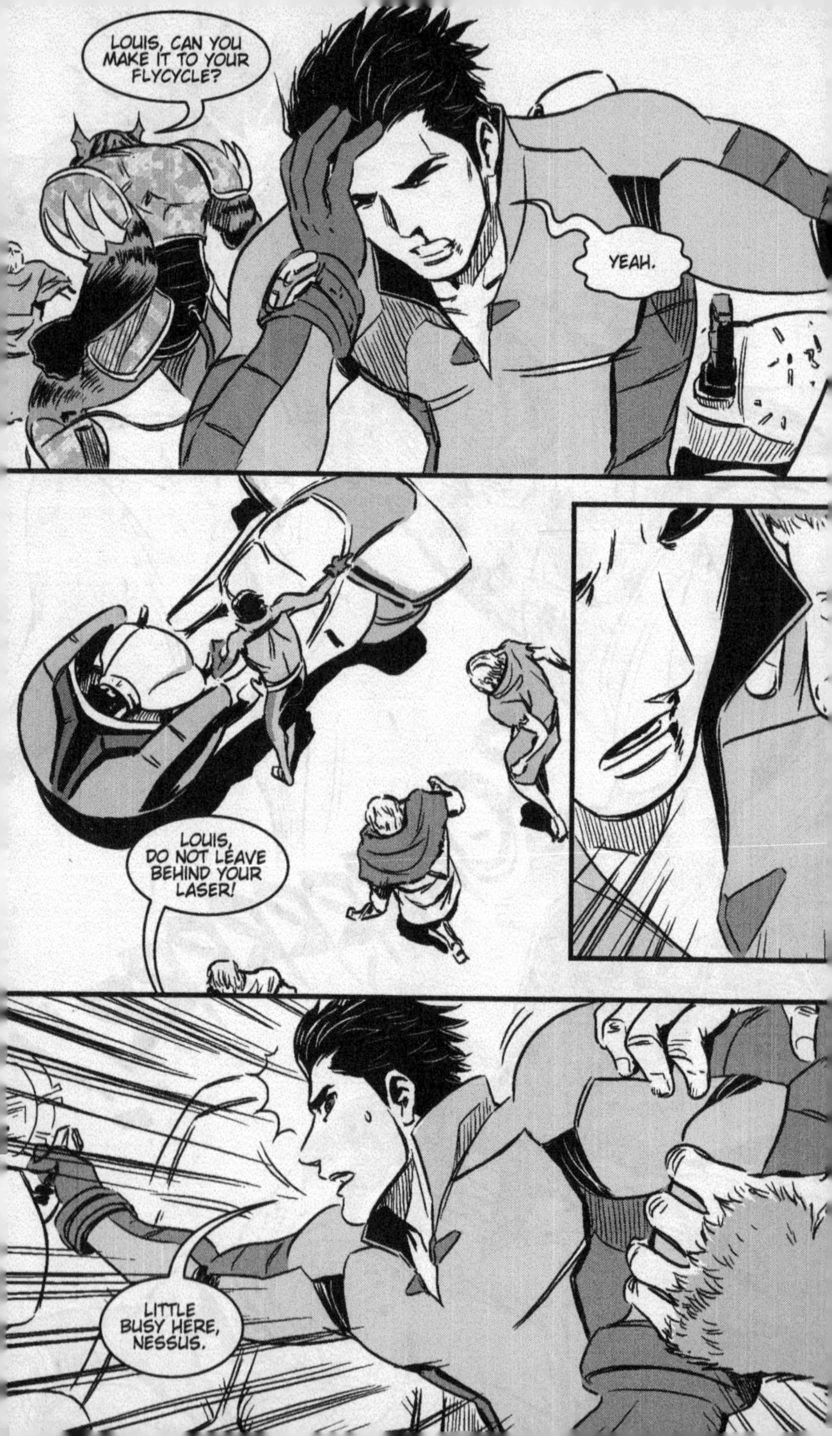
LOUIS, CAN YOU MAKE IT TO YOUR FLYCYCLE?
YEAH.
LOUIS, DO NOT LEAVE BEHIND YOUR LASER!
LITTLE BUSY HERE, NESSUS.

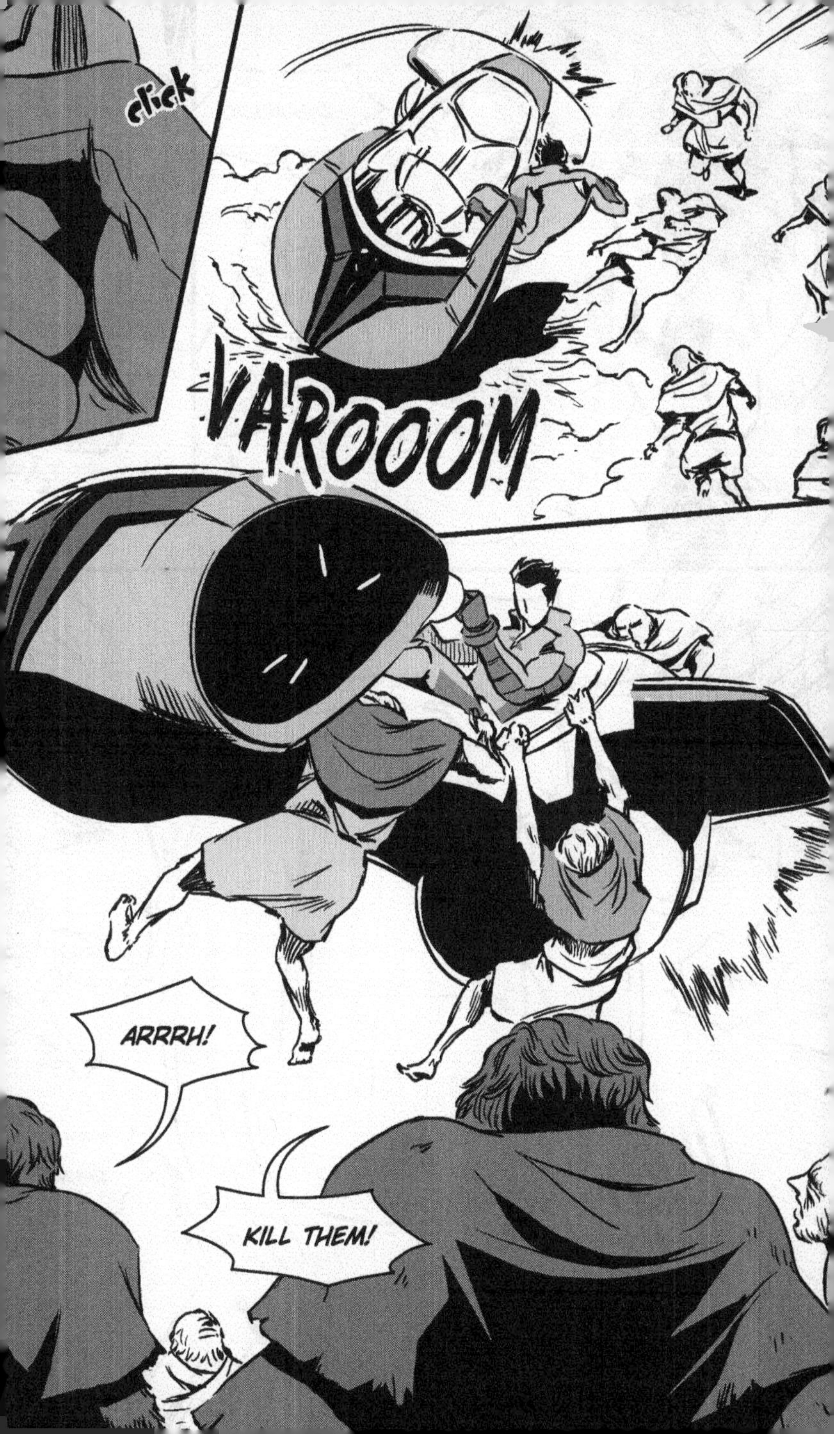
click
VAROOOM
ARRRH!
KILL THEM!

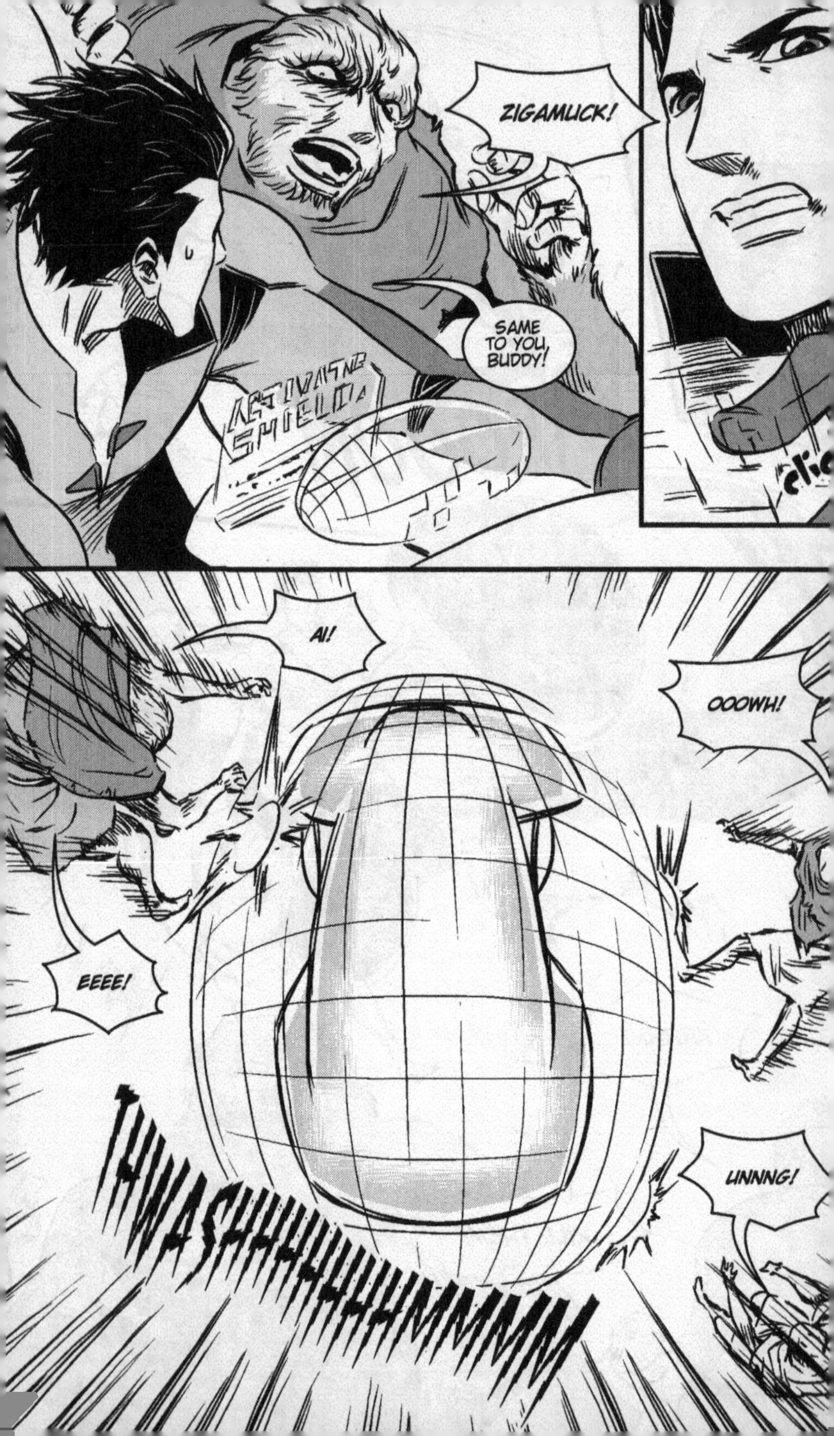
ZIGAMUCK!
SAME TO YOU, BUDDY!
AI!
OOOWH!
EEEE!
THWASHHHHHHMMMM
UNNNG!

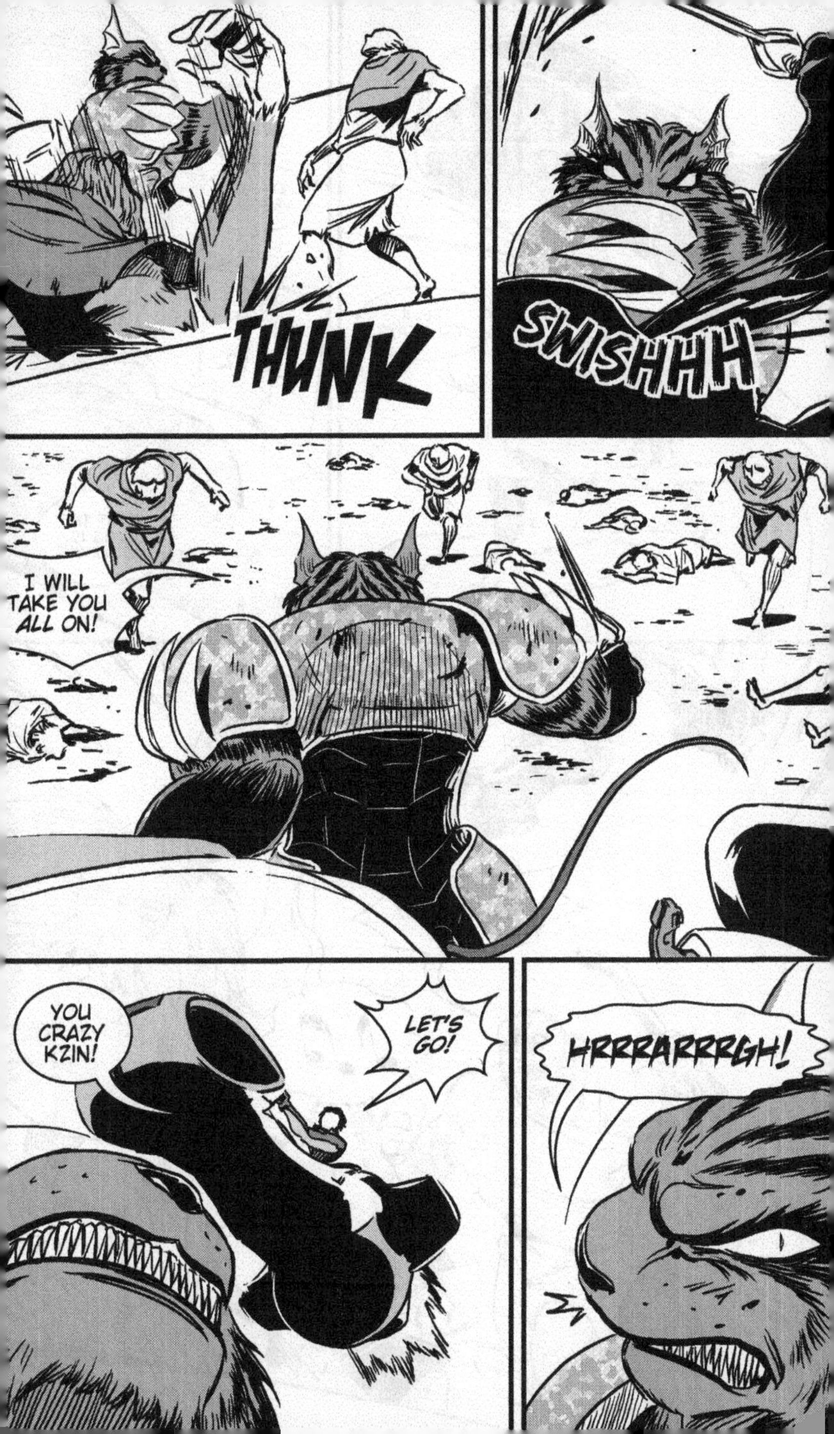
THUNK
SWISHHH
I WILL TAKE YOU ALL ON!
YOU CRAZY KZIN!
LET'S GO!
HRRRARRRGH!

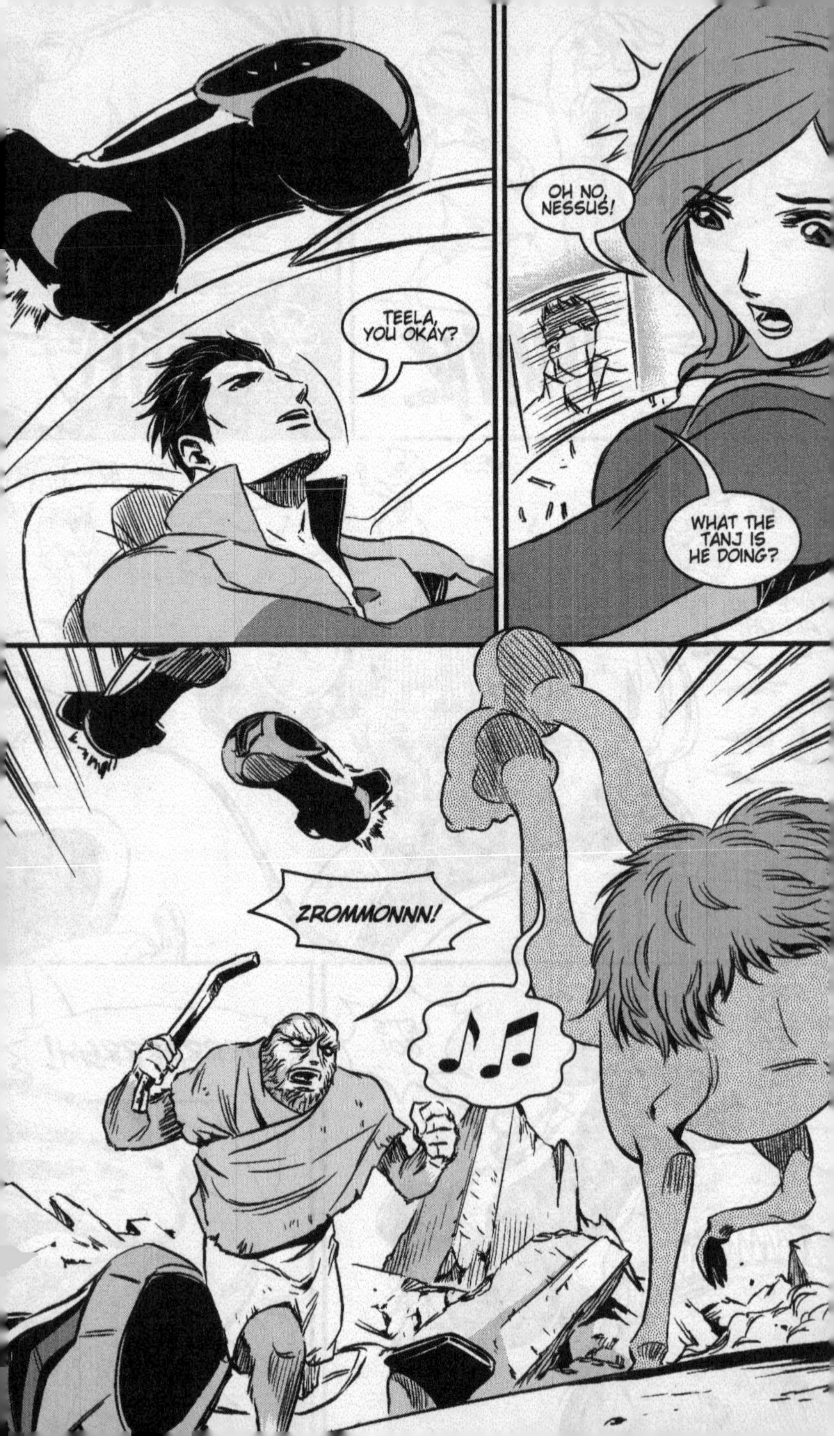
TEELA, YOU OKAY?
OH NO, NESSUS!
WHAT THE TANJ IS HE DOING?
ZROMMONNN!

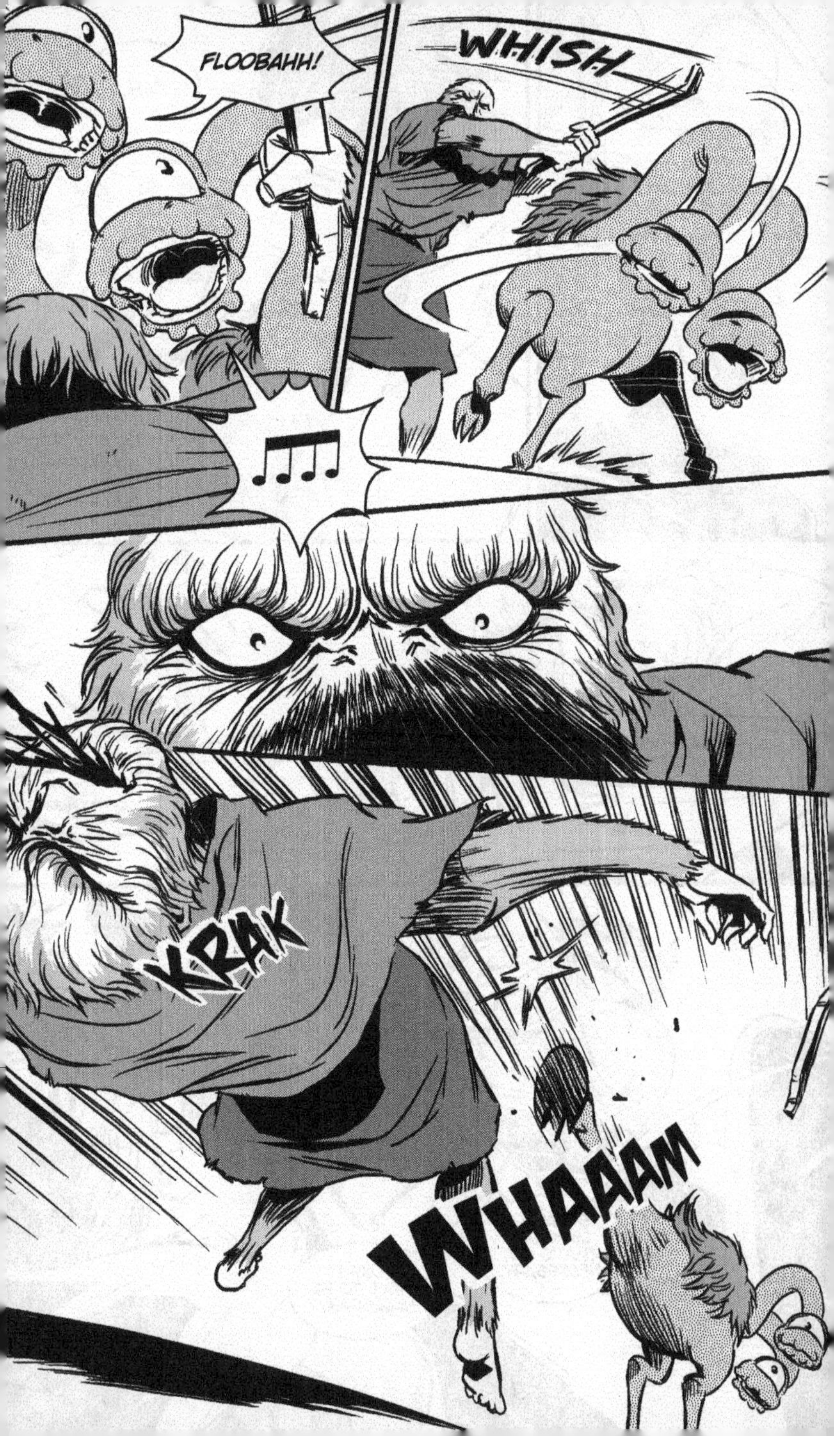
FLOOBAHH!
WHISH
KRAK
WHAAAM

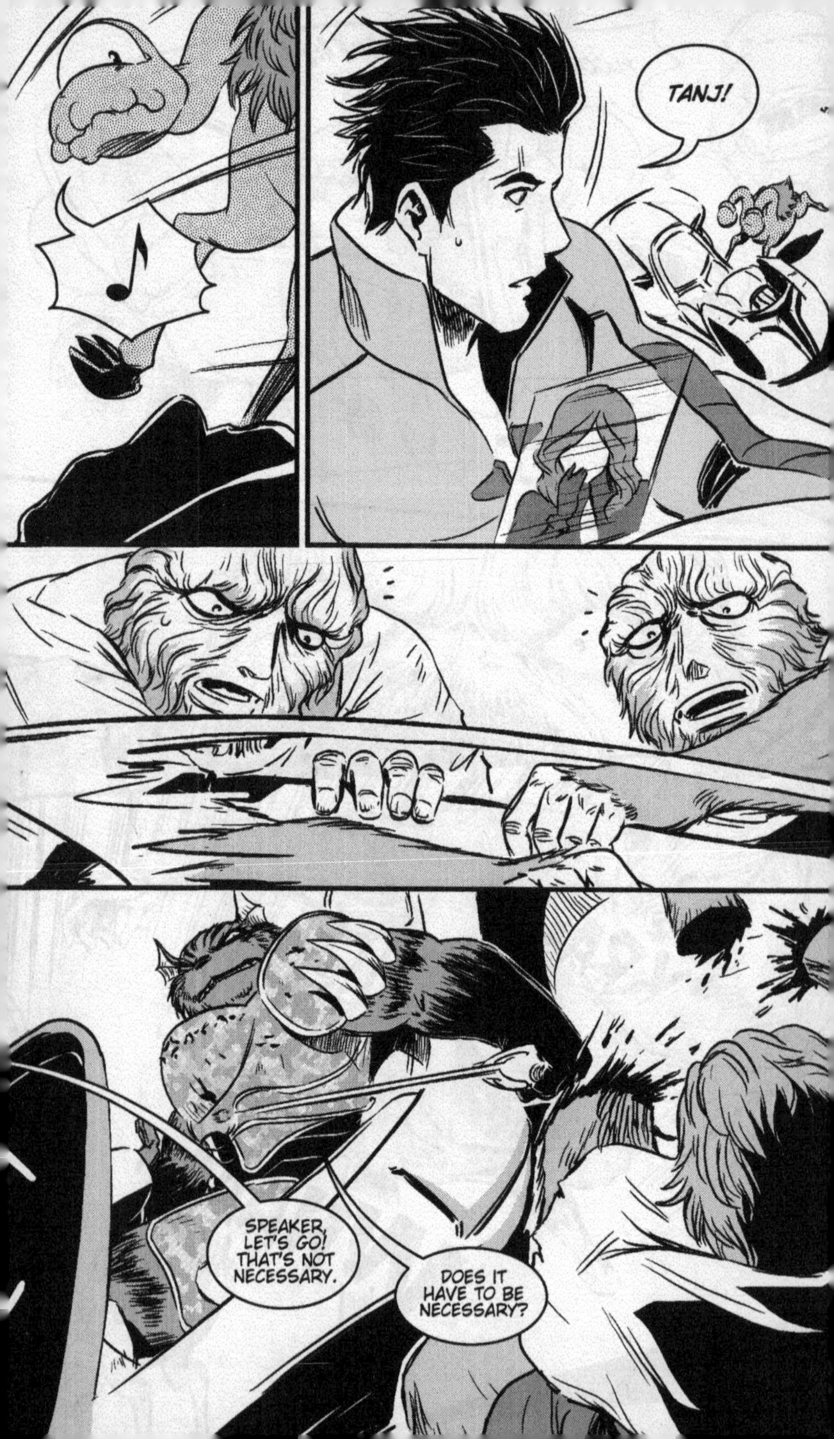
TANJ!
SPEAKER, LET'S GO! THAT'S NOT NECESSARY.
DOES IT HAVE TO BE NECESSARY?

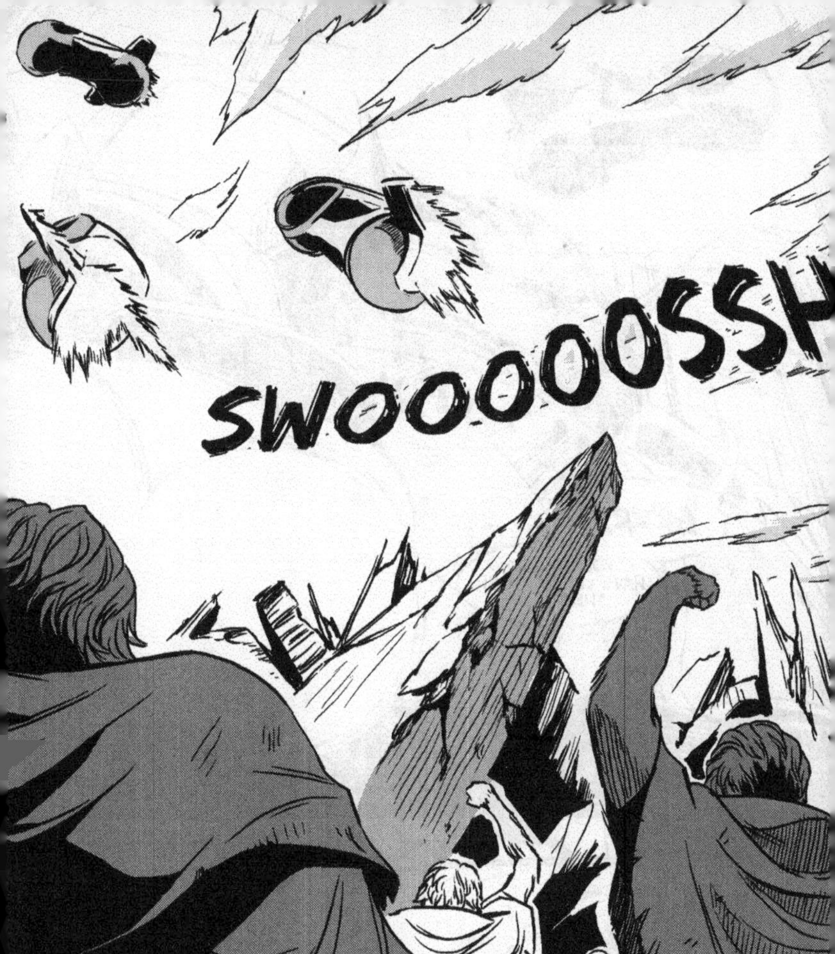
SWOOOOOOSSH

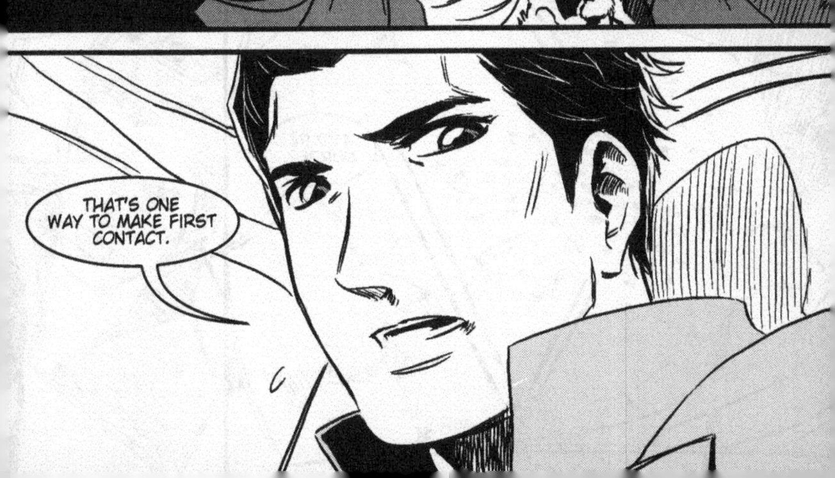
THAT'S ONE WAY TO MAKE FIRST CONTACT.

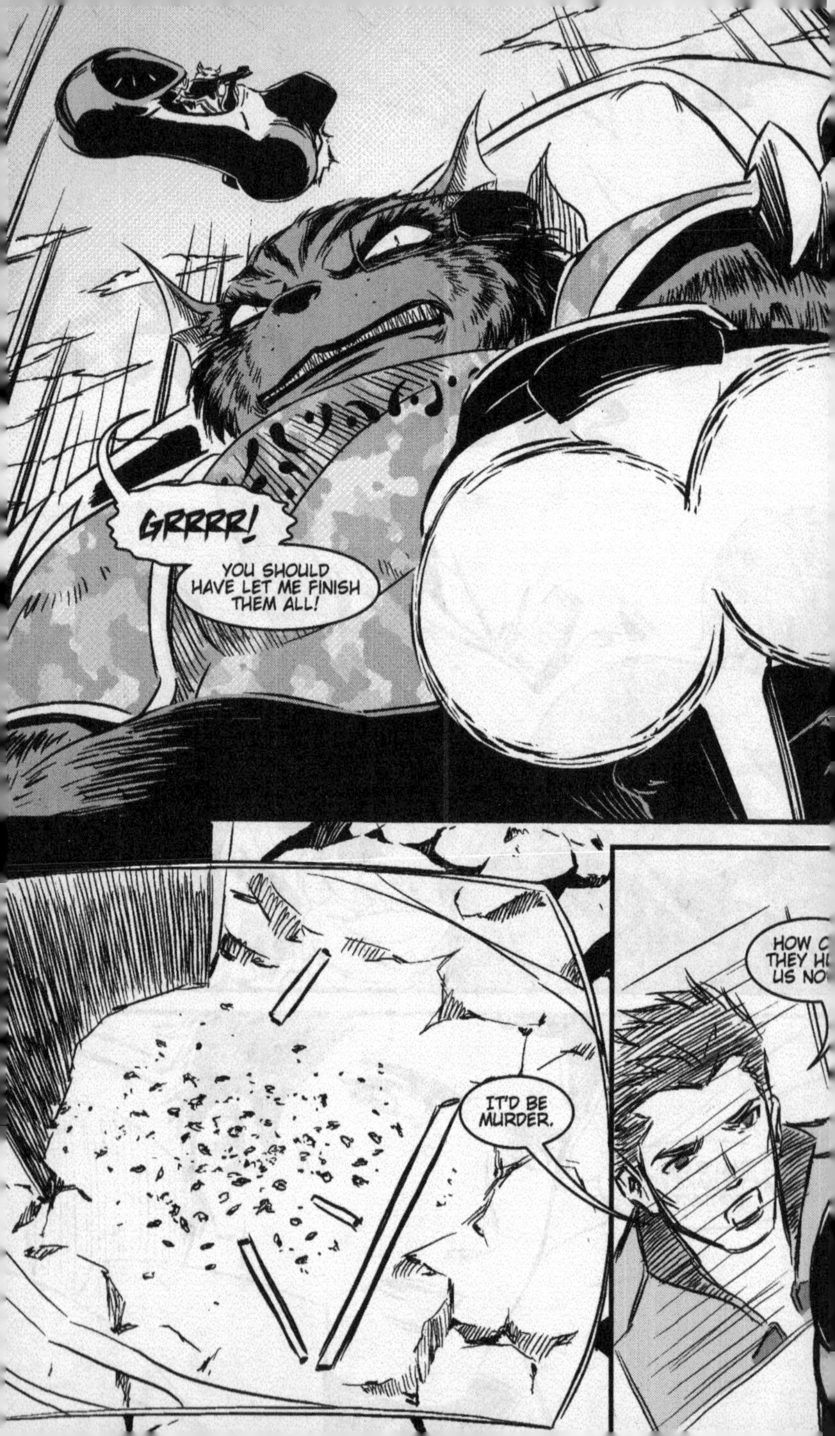
GRRRR!
YOU SHOULD HAVE LET ME FINISH THEM ALL!
IT'D BE MURDER.
HOW C THEY H US NO

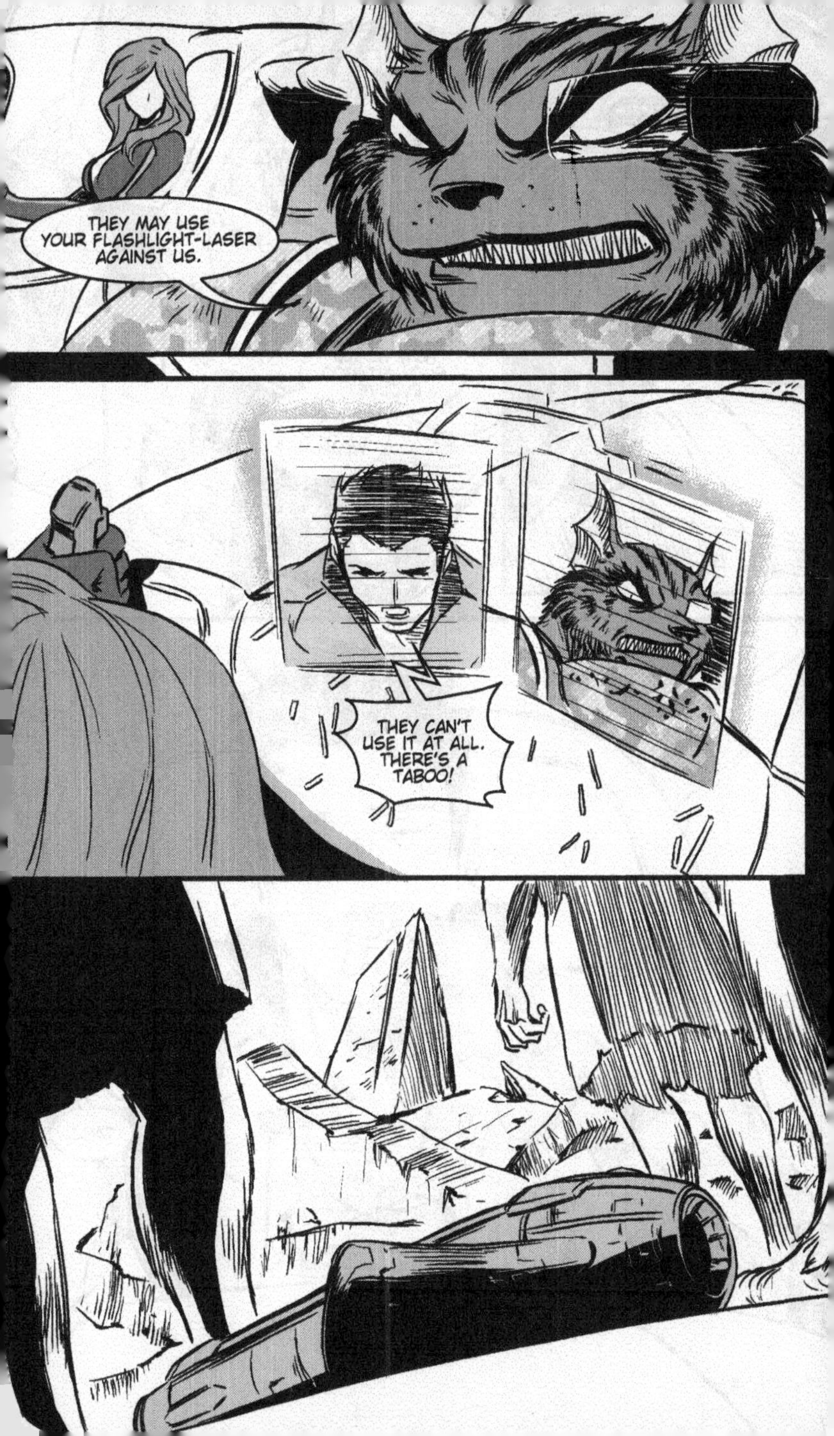
THEY MAY USE YOUR FLASHLIGHT-LASER AGAINST US.
THEY CAN'T USE IT AT ALL. THERE'S A TABOO!

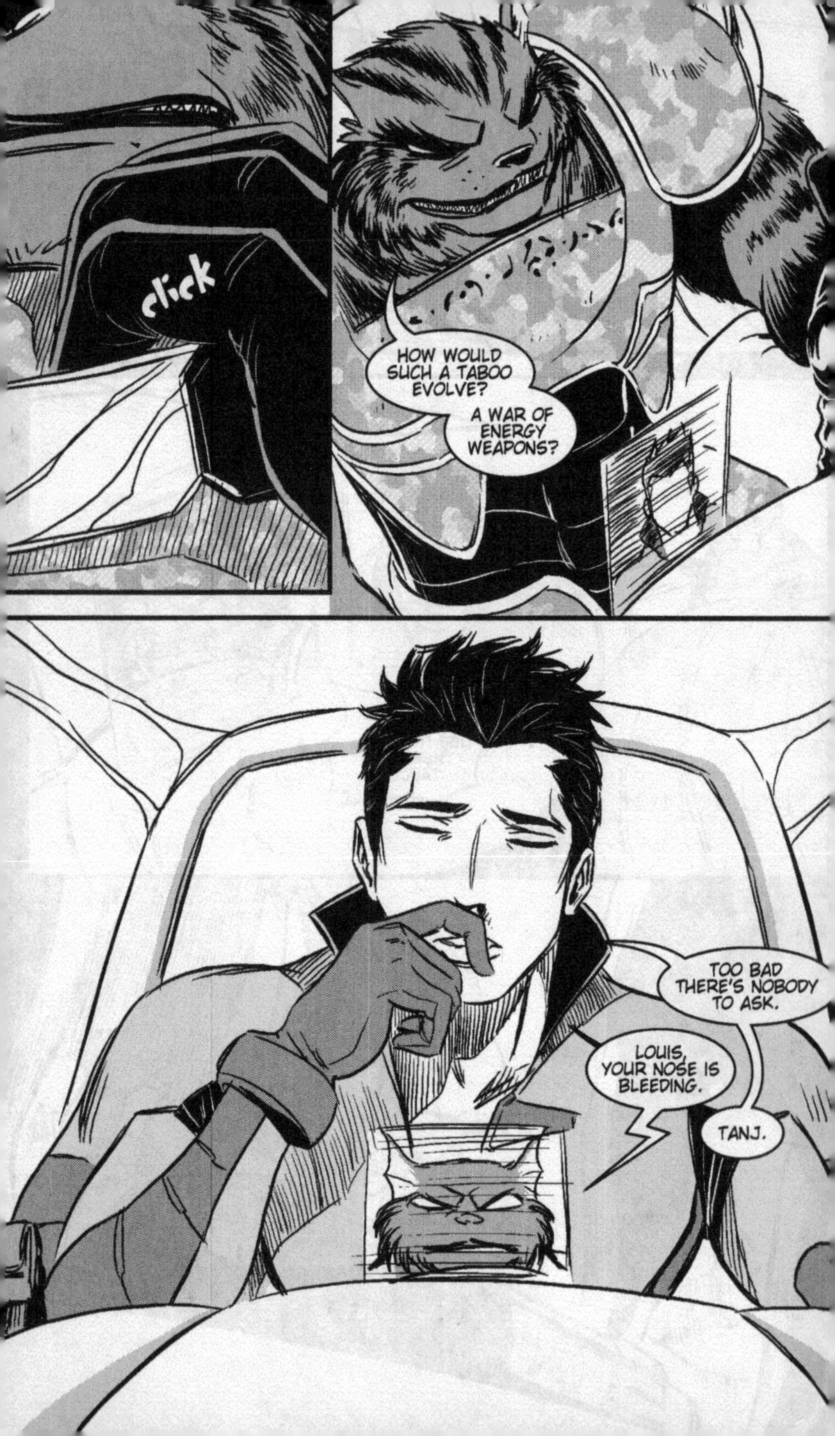
click
HOW WOULD SUCH A TABOO EVOLVE?
A WAR OF ENERGY WEAPONS?
TOO BAD THERE'S NOBODY TO ASK.
LOUIS, YOUR NOSE IS BLEEDING.
TANJ.

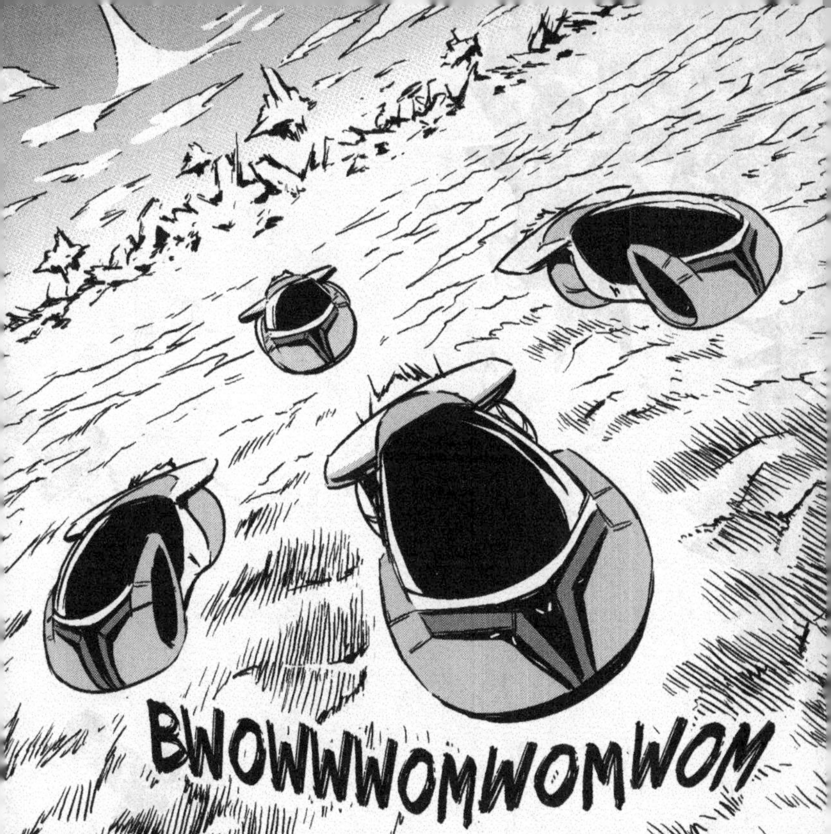
BWOWWWOMWOMWOM
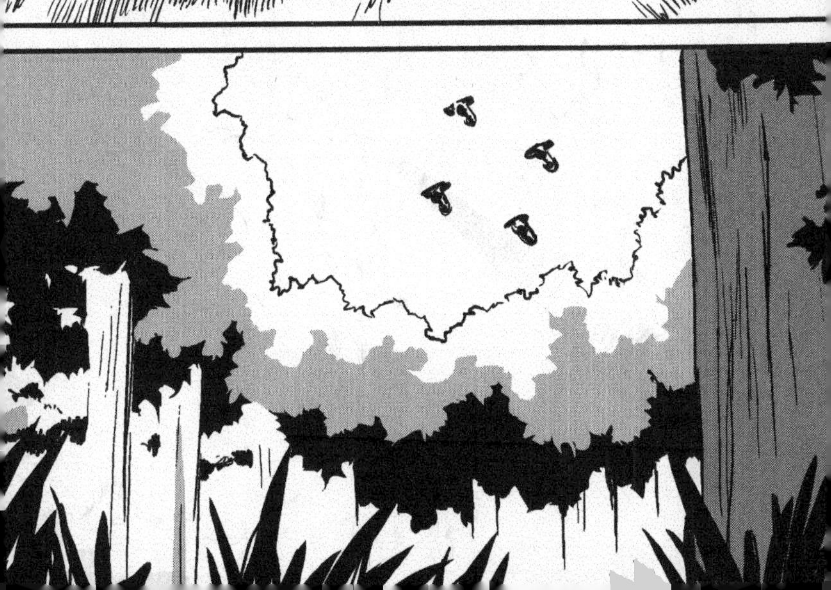

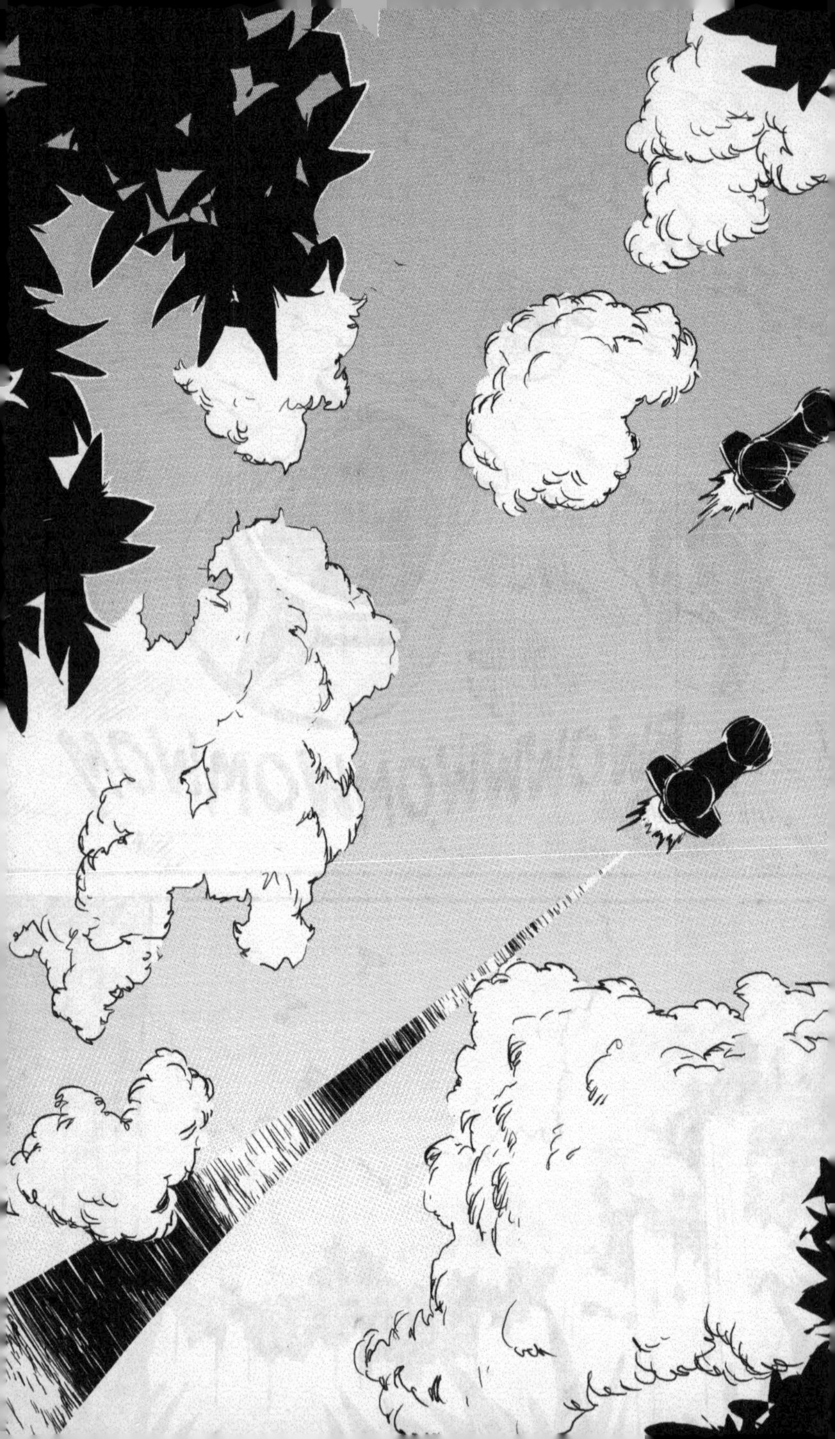

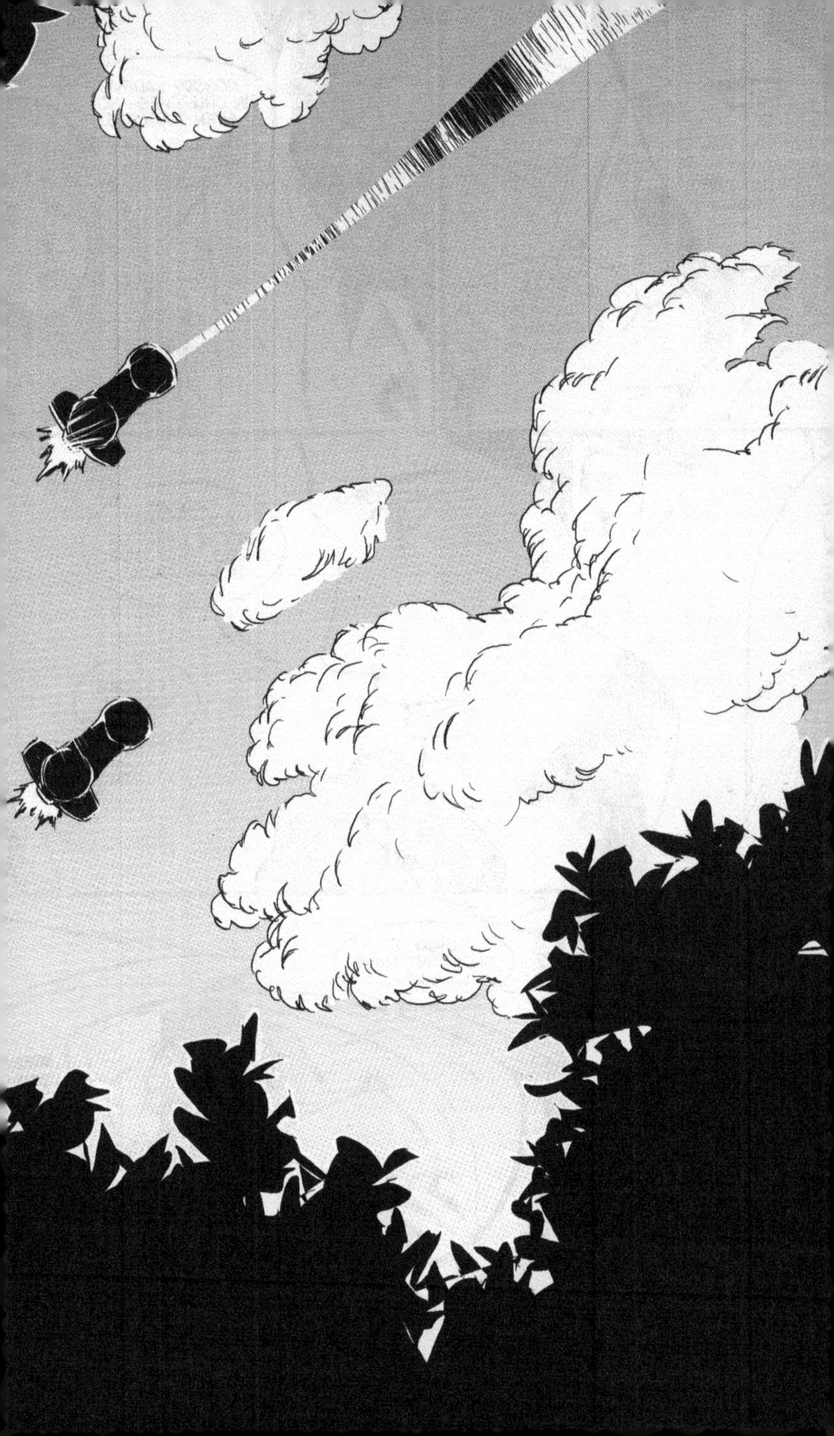

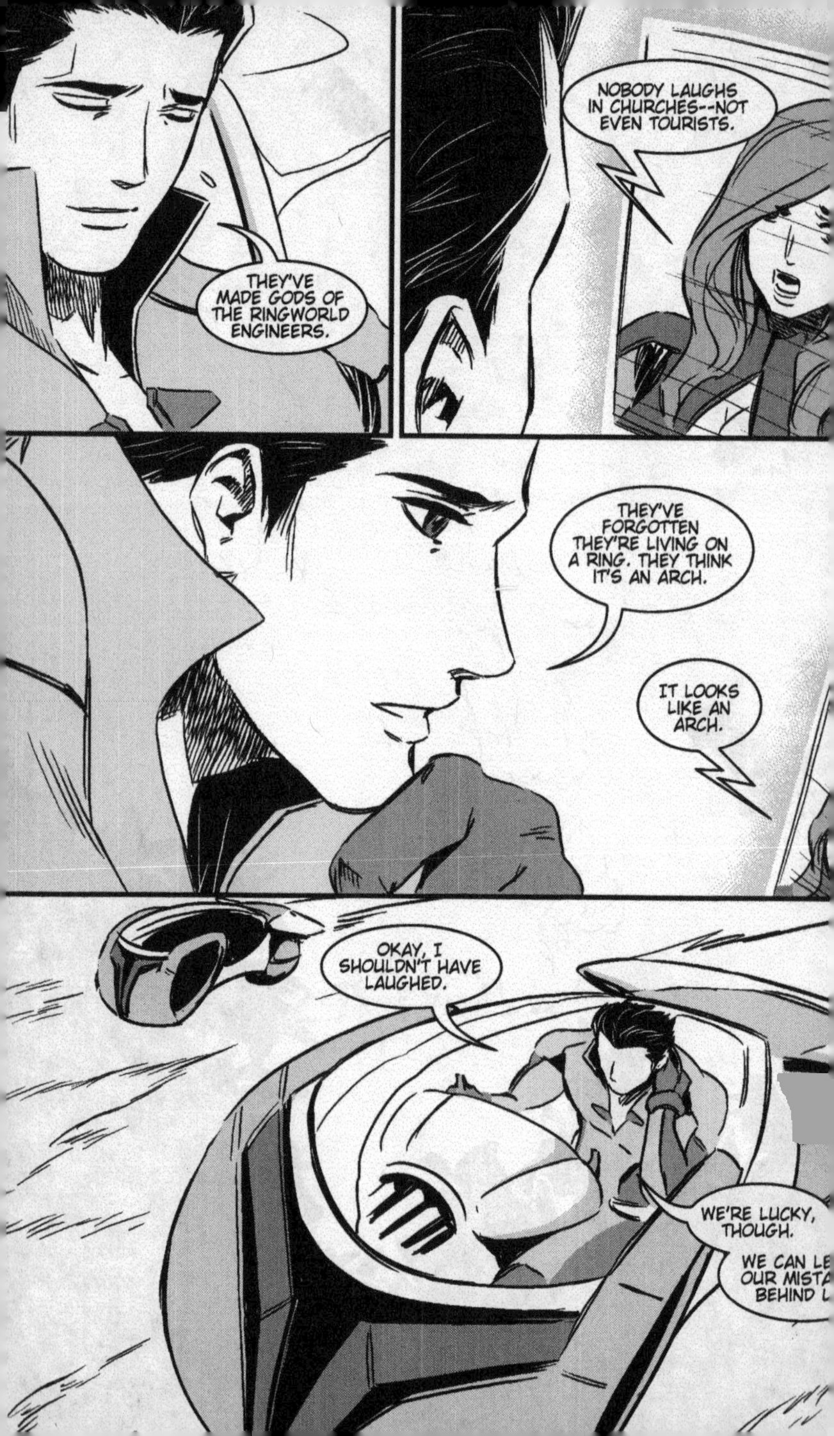
THEY'VE MADE GODS OF THE RINGWORLD ENGINEERS.
NOBODY LAUGHS IN CHURCHES--NOT EVEN TOURISTS.
THEY'VE FORGOTTEN THEY'RE LIVING ON A RING. THEY THINK IT'S AN ARCH.
IT LOOKS LIKE AN ARCH.
OKAY, I SHOULDN'T HAVE LAUGHED.
WE'RE LUCKY, THOUGH.

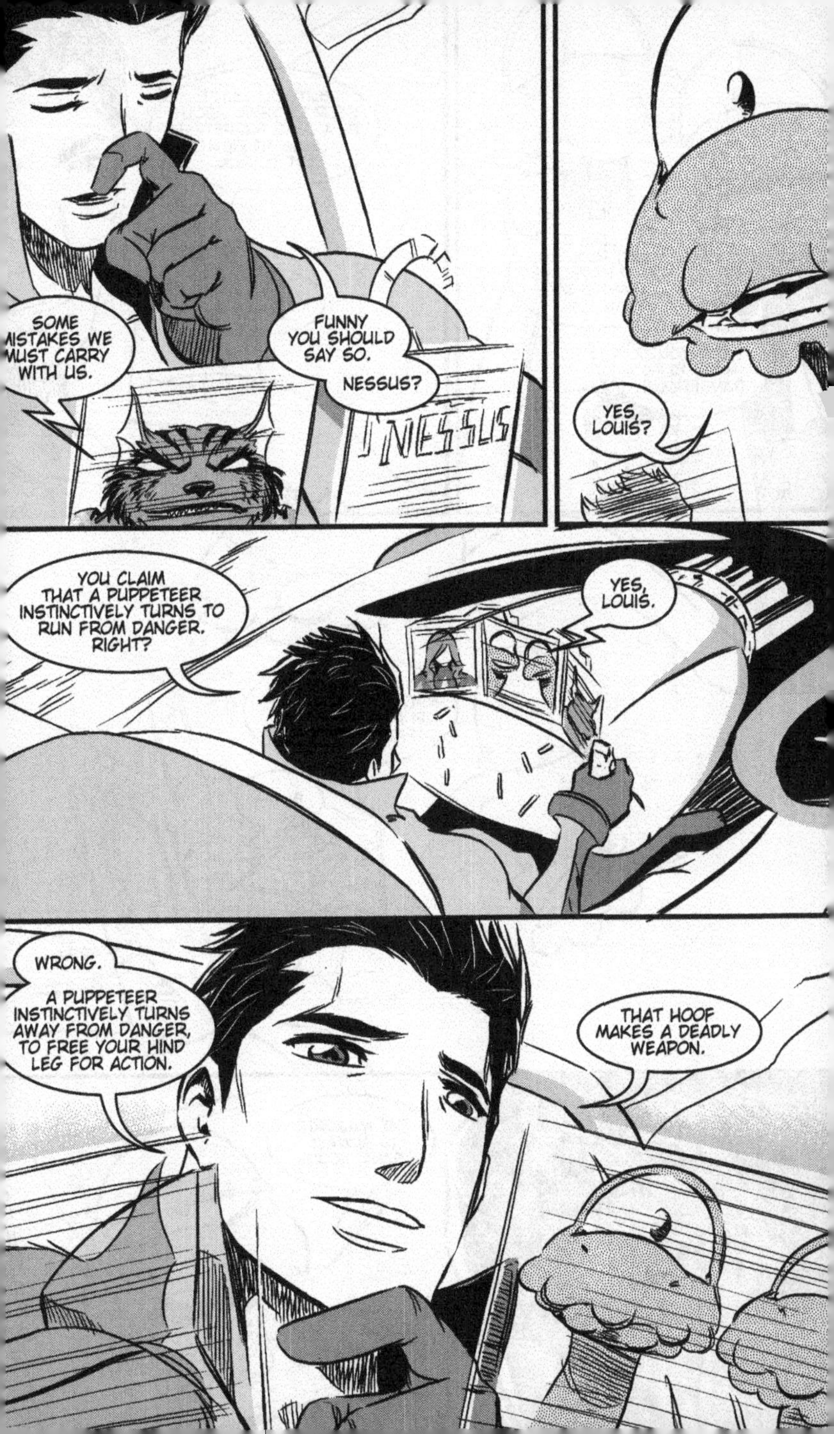
SOME MISTAKES WE MUST CARRY WITH US.
FUNNY YOU SHOULD SAY SO.
NESSUS?
NESSUS
YES, LOUIS?
YOU CLAIM THAT A PUPPETEER INSTINCTIVELY TURNS TO RUN FROM DANGER. RIGHT?
YES, LOUIS.
WRONG.
A PUPPETEER INSTINCTIVELY TURNS AWAY FROM DANGER, TO FREE YOUR HIND LEG FOR ACTION.
THAT HOOF MAKES A DEADLY WEAPON.

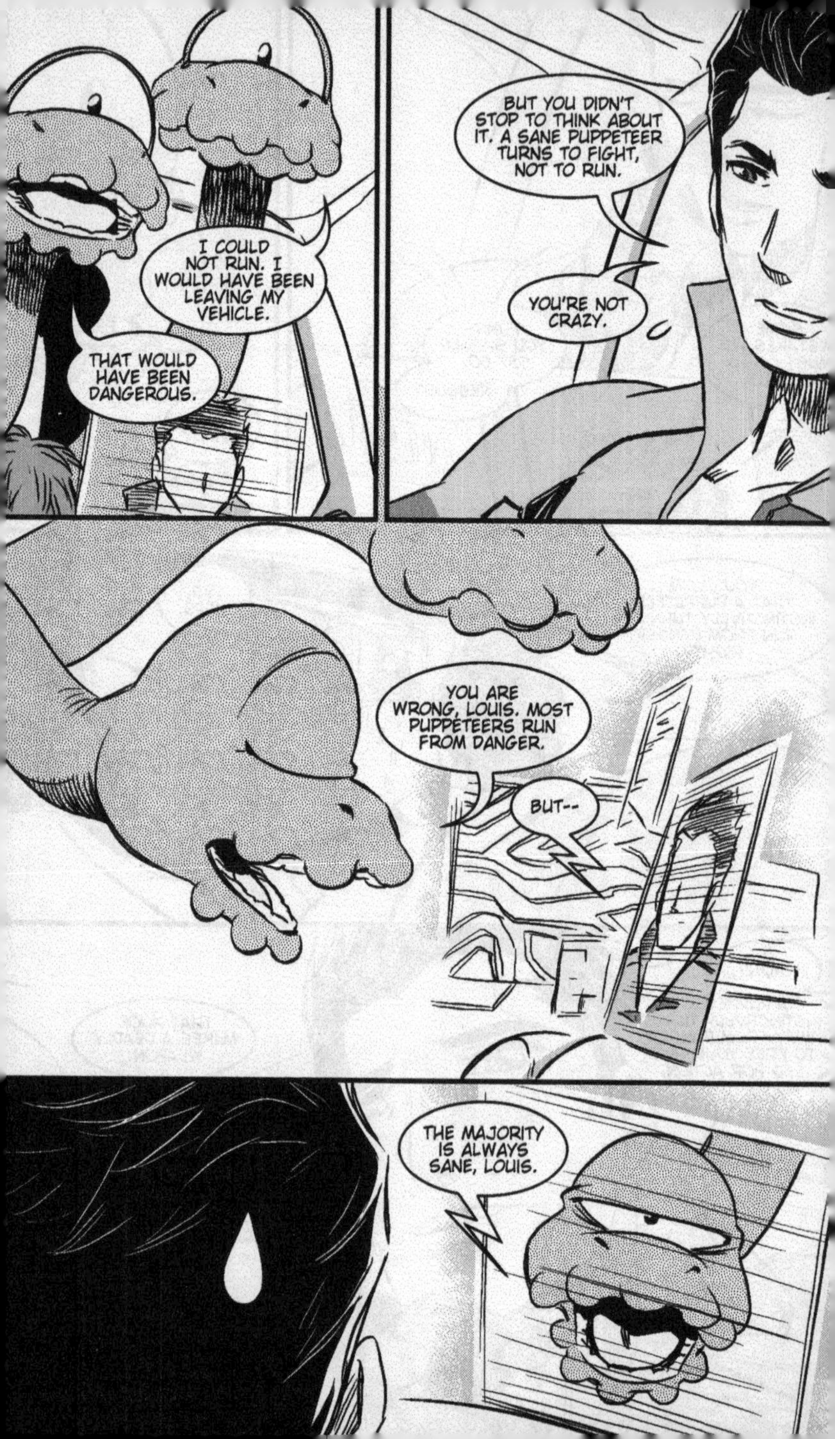
I COULD NOT RUN. I WOULD HAVE BEEN LEAVING MY VEHICLE.
THAT WOULD HAVE BEEN DANGEROUS.
BUT YOU DIDN'T STOP TO THINK ABOUT IT. A SANE PUPPETEER TURNS TO FIGHT, NOT TO RUN.
YOU'RE NOT CRAZY.
YOU ARE WRONG, LOUIS. MOST PUPPETEERS RUN FROM DANGER.
BUT--
THE MAJORITY IS ALWAYS SANE, LOUIS.

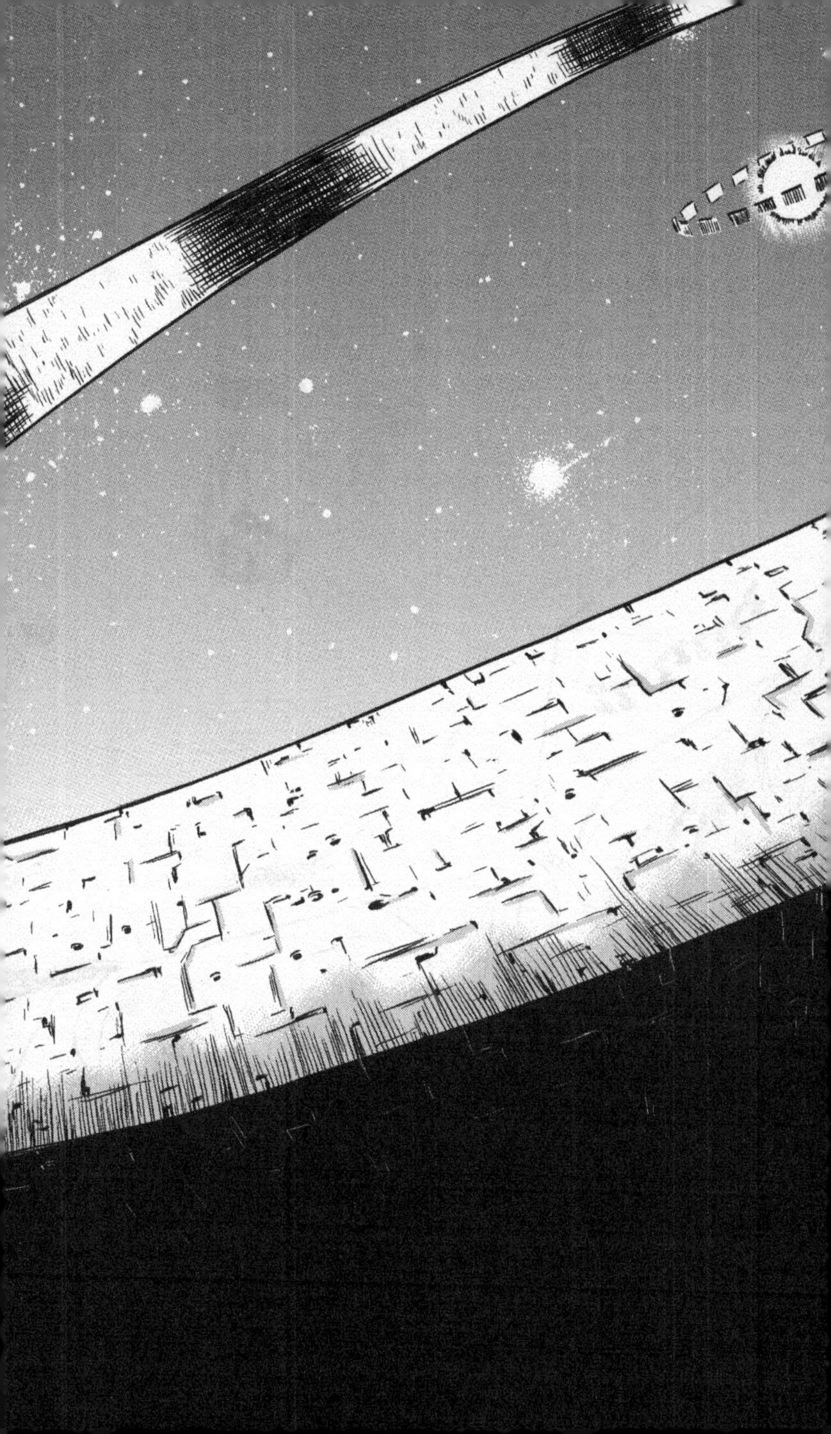

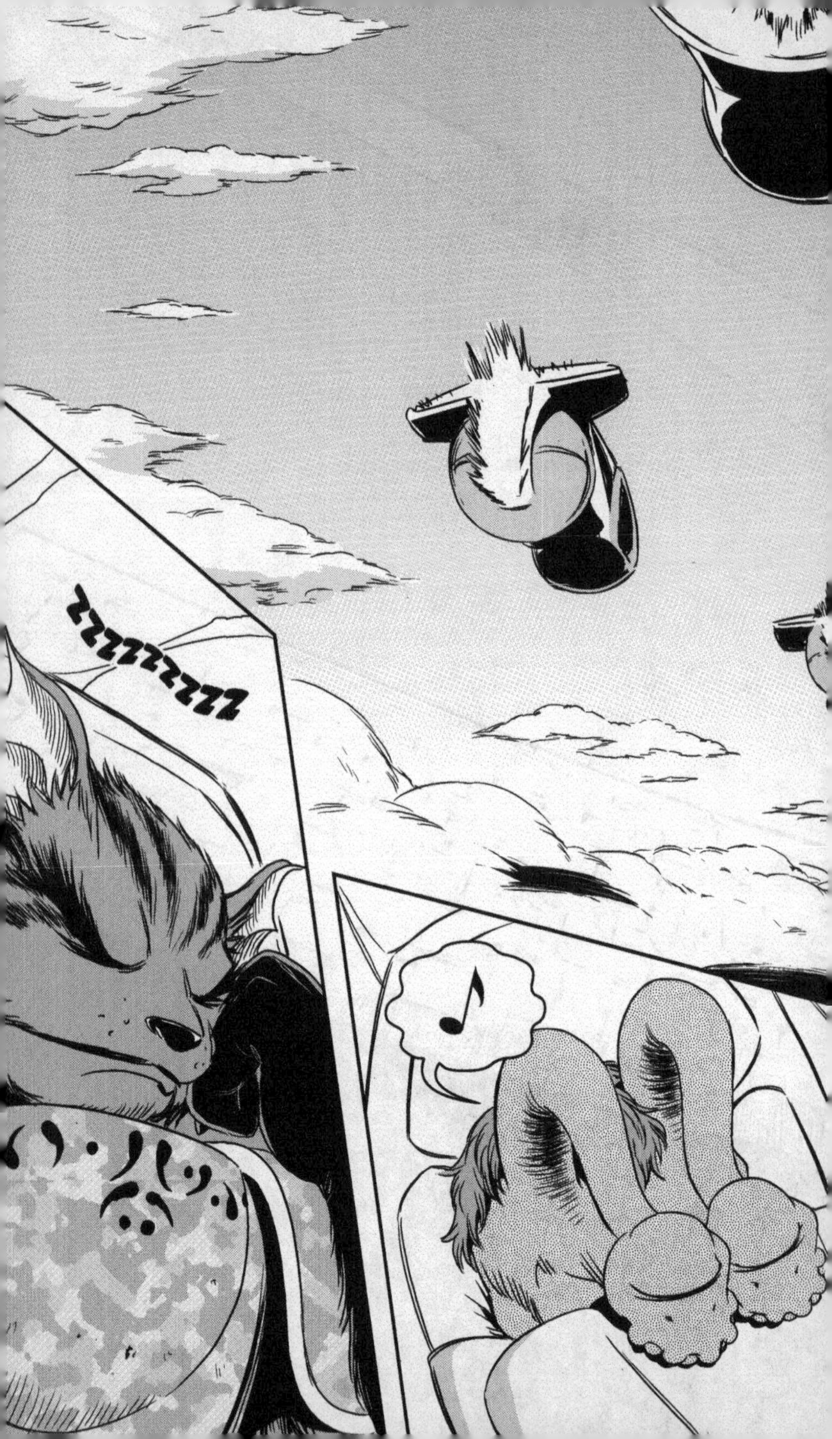
ZZZZZZZZZZ
♪

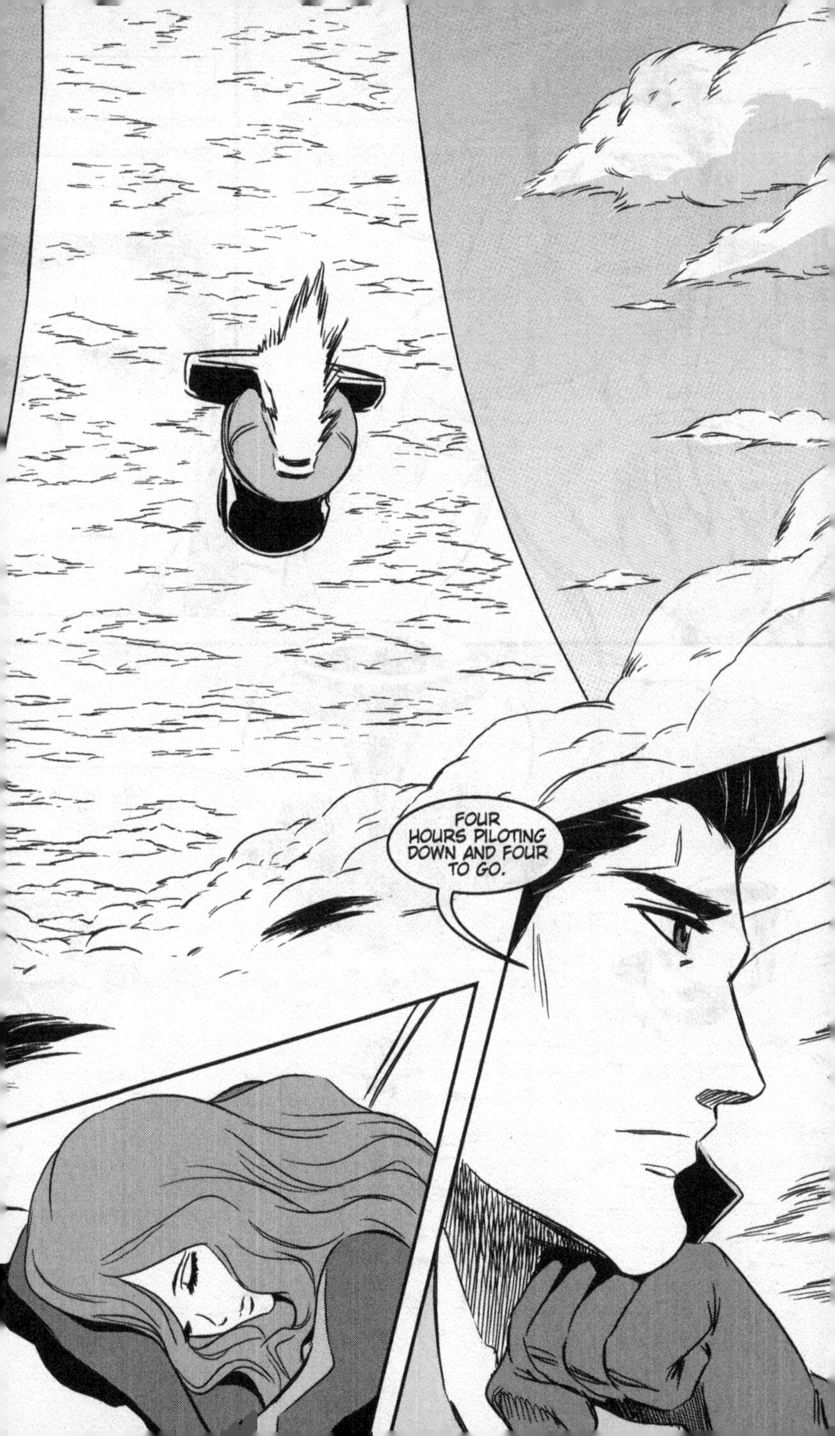
FOUR HOURS PILOTING DOWN AND FOUR TO GO.

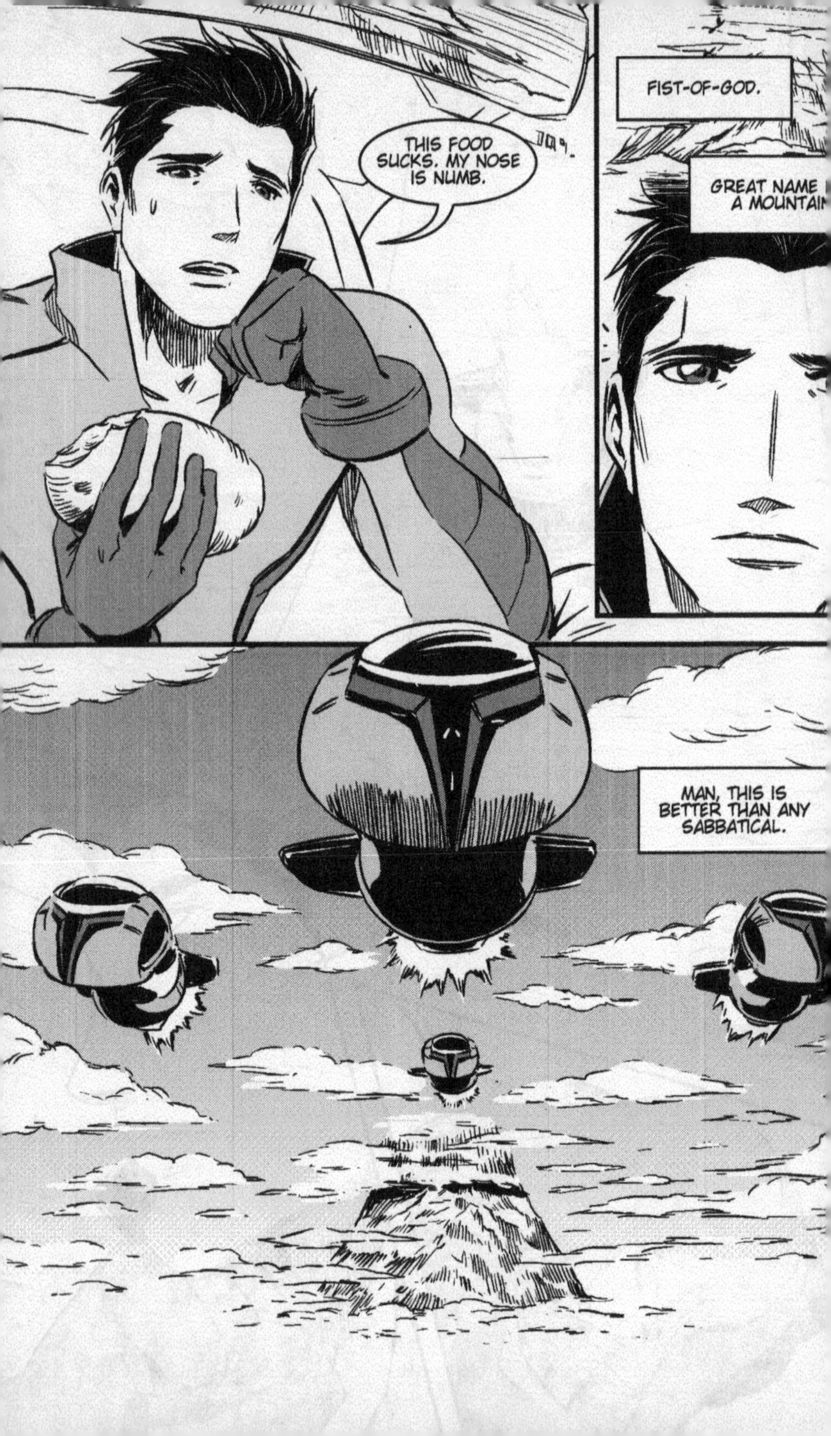

THIS FOOD SUCKS. MY NOSE IS NUMB.
FIST-OF-GOD.
GREAT NAME A MOUNTAI
MAN, THIS IS BETTER THAN ANY SABBATICAL.

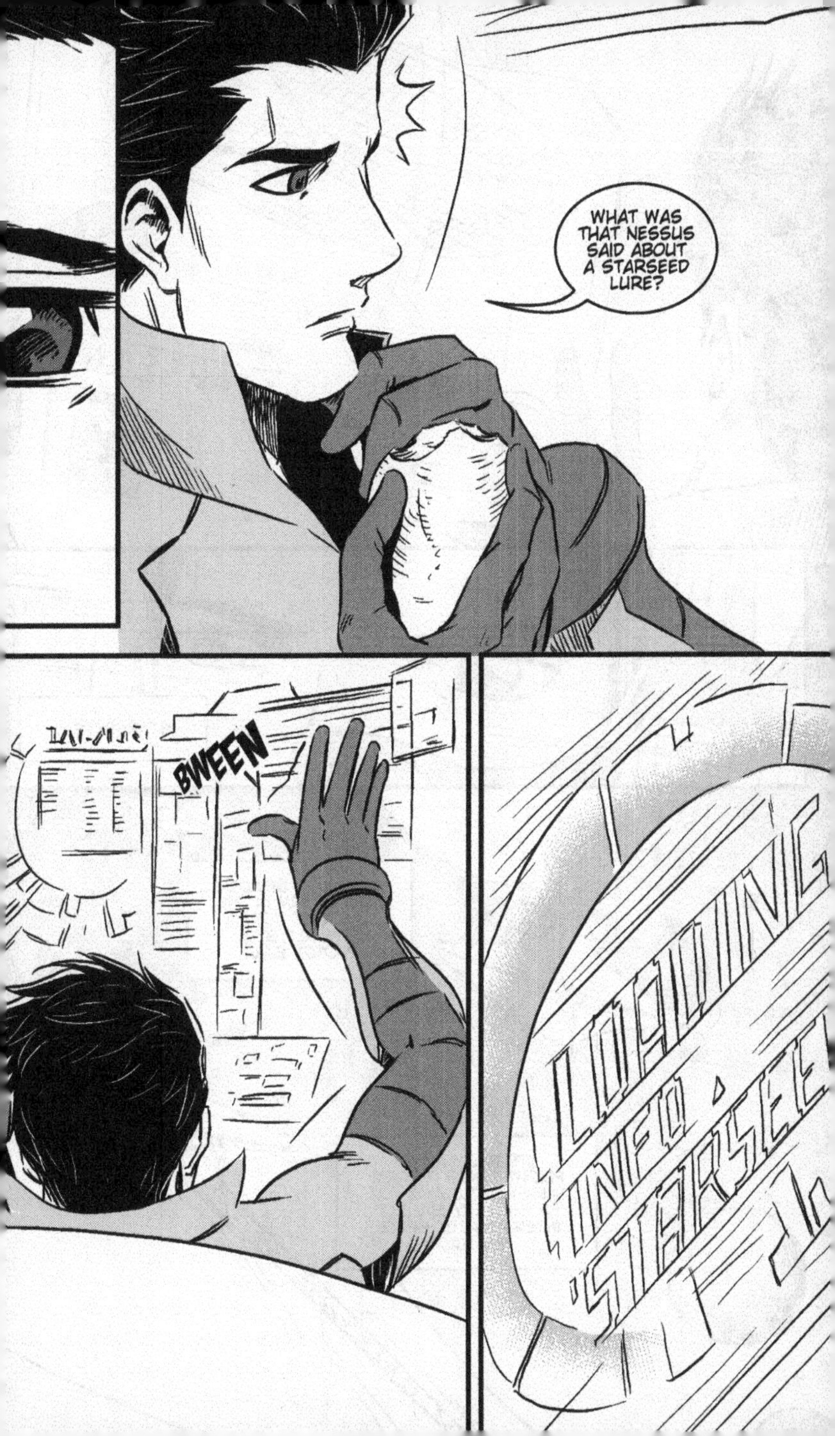
WHAT WAS THAT NESSUS SAID ABOUT A STARSEED LURE?
BWEEN
LOADING
INFO
STARSEE

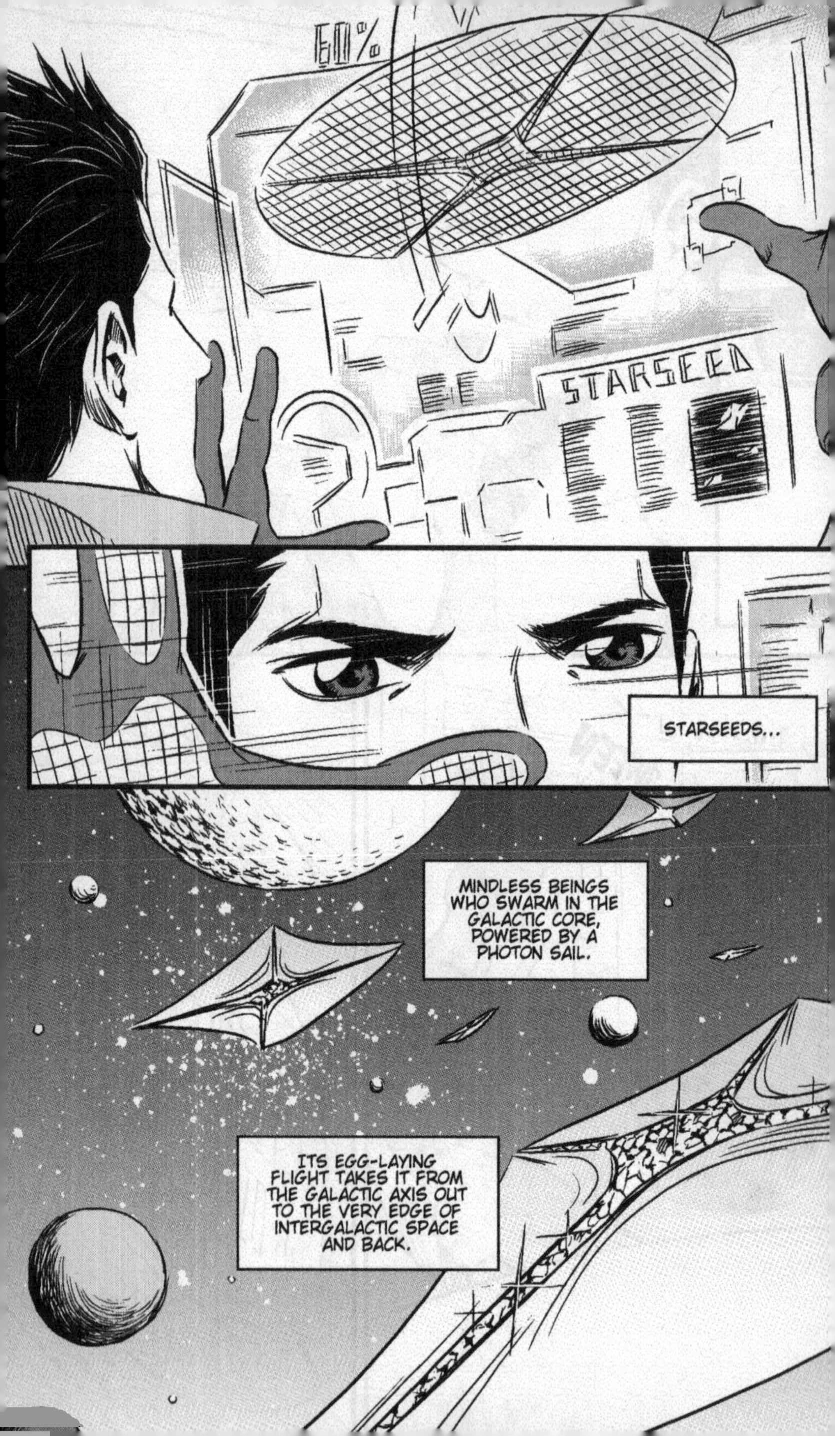

60%
STARSEED
STARSEEDS...
MINDLESS BEINGS WHO SWARM IN THE GALACTIC CORE, POWERED BY A PHOTON SAIL.
ITS EGG-LAYING FLIGHT TAKES IT FROM THE GALACTIC AXIS OUT TO THE VERY EDGE OF INTERGALACTIC SPACE AND BACK.

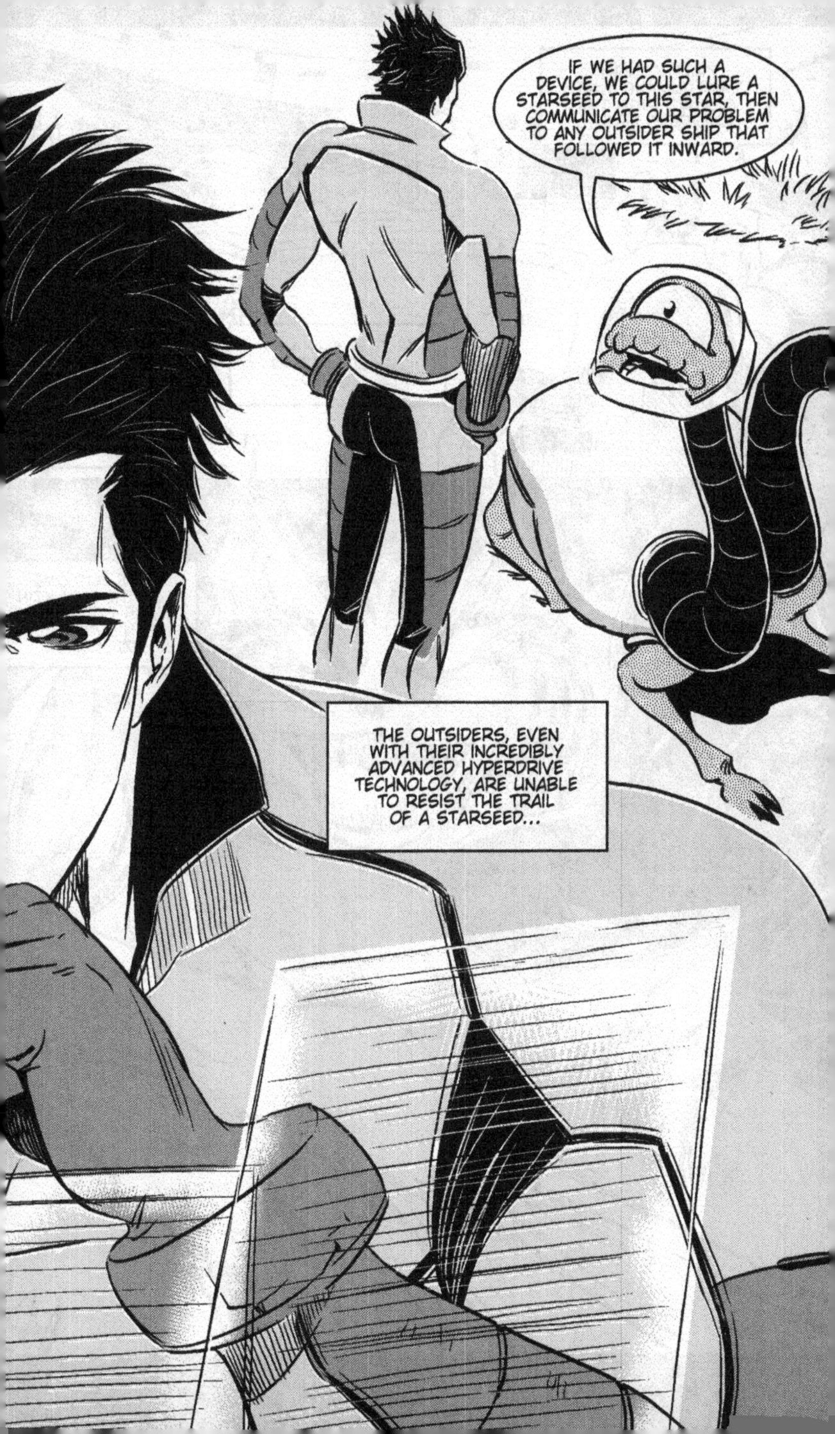
IF WE HAD SUCH A DEVICE, WE COULD LURE A STARSEED TO THIS STAR, THEN COMMUNICATE OUR PROBLEM TO ANY OUTSIDER SHIP THAT FOLLOWED IT INWARD.
THE OUTSIDERS, EVEN WITH THEIR INCREDIBLY ADVANCED HYPERDRIVE TECHNOLOGY, ARE UNABLE TO RESIST THE TRAIL OF A STARSEED...

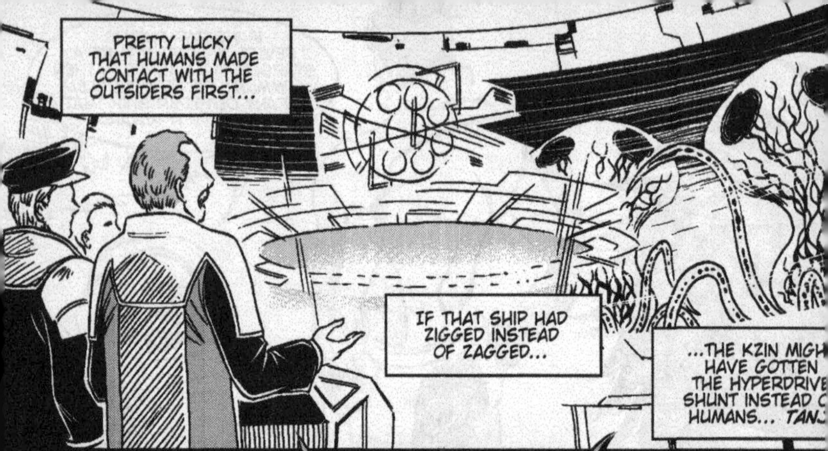
PRETTY LUCKY THAT HUMANS MADE CONTACT WITH THE OUTSIDERS FIRST...
IF THAT SHIP HAD ZIGGED INSTEAD OF ZAGGED...
...THE KZIN MIGH HAVE GOTTEN THE HYPERDRIVE SHUNT INSTEAD O HUMANS... *TAN*

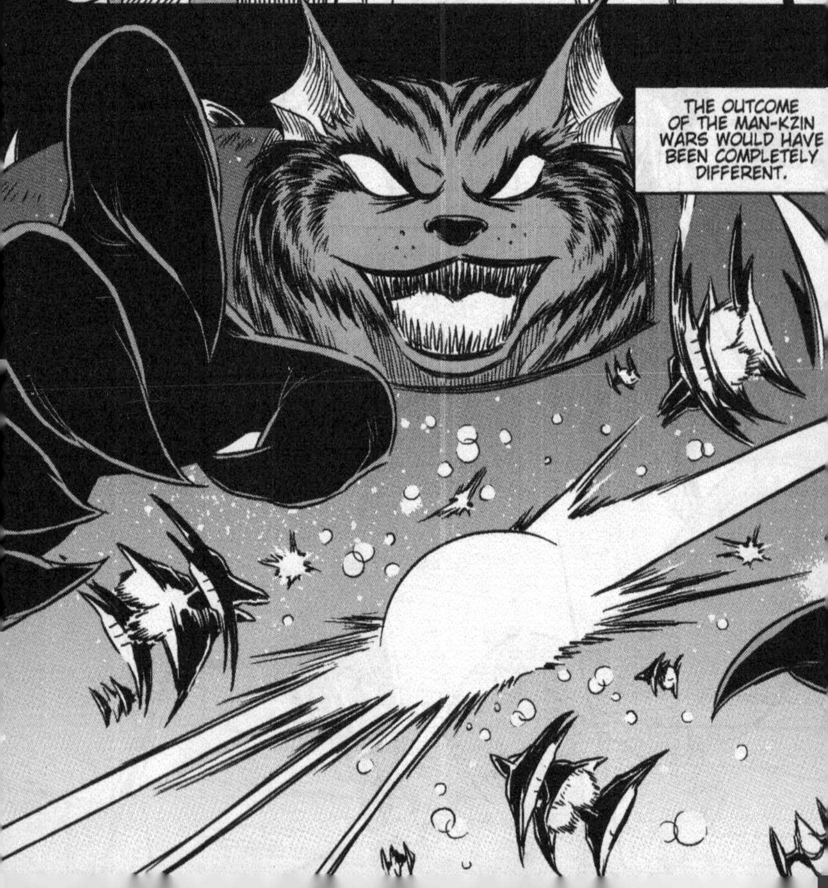
THE OUTCOME OF THE MAN-KZIN WARS WOULD HAVE BEEN COMPLETELY DIFFERENT.

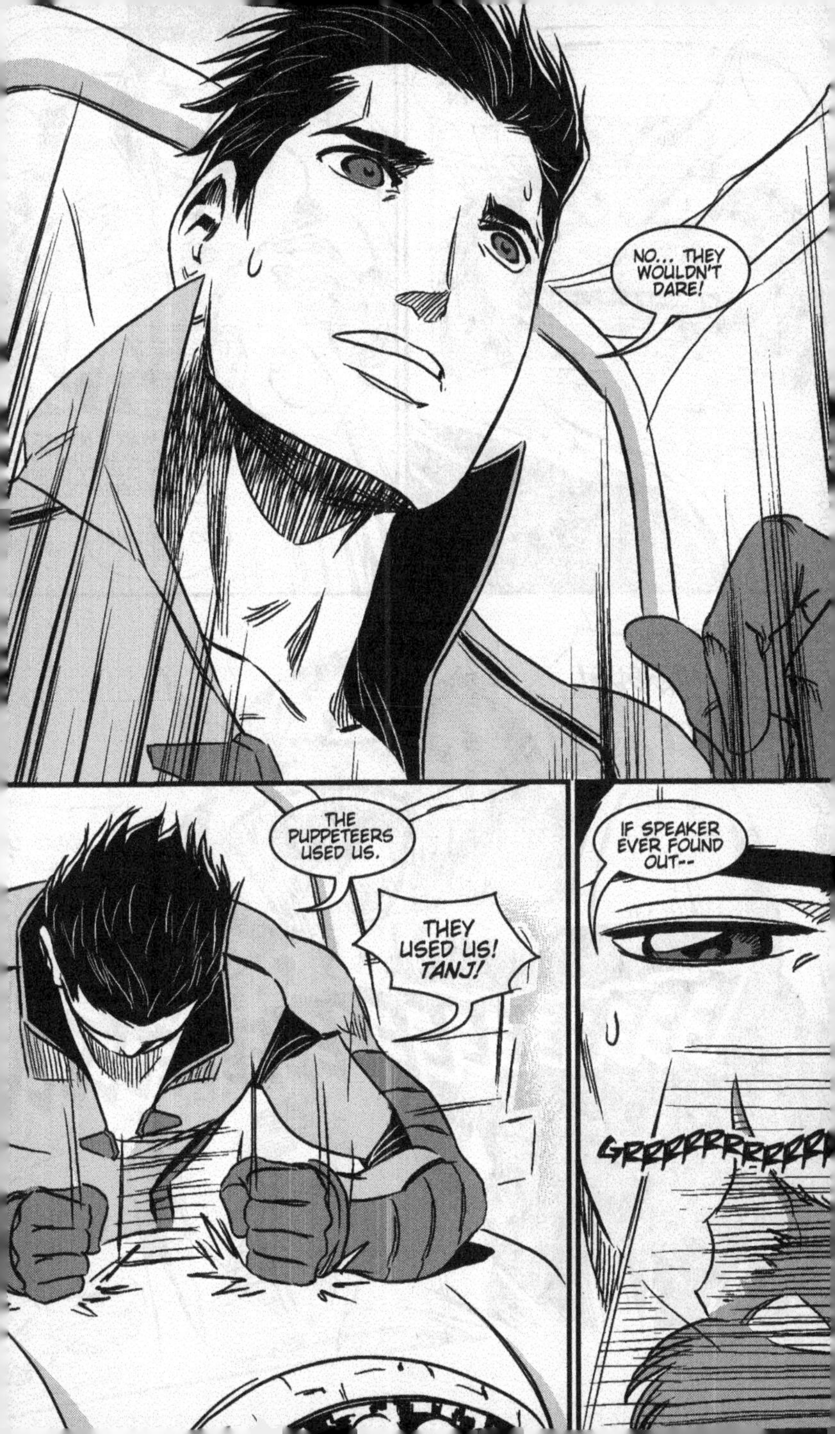
NO... THEY WOULDN'T DARE!
THE PUPPETEERS USED US.
THEY USED US! *TANJ!*
IF SPEAKER EVER FOUND OUT--
GRRRRRRRRRRR

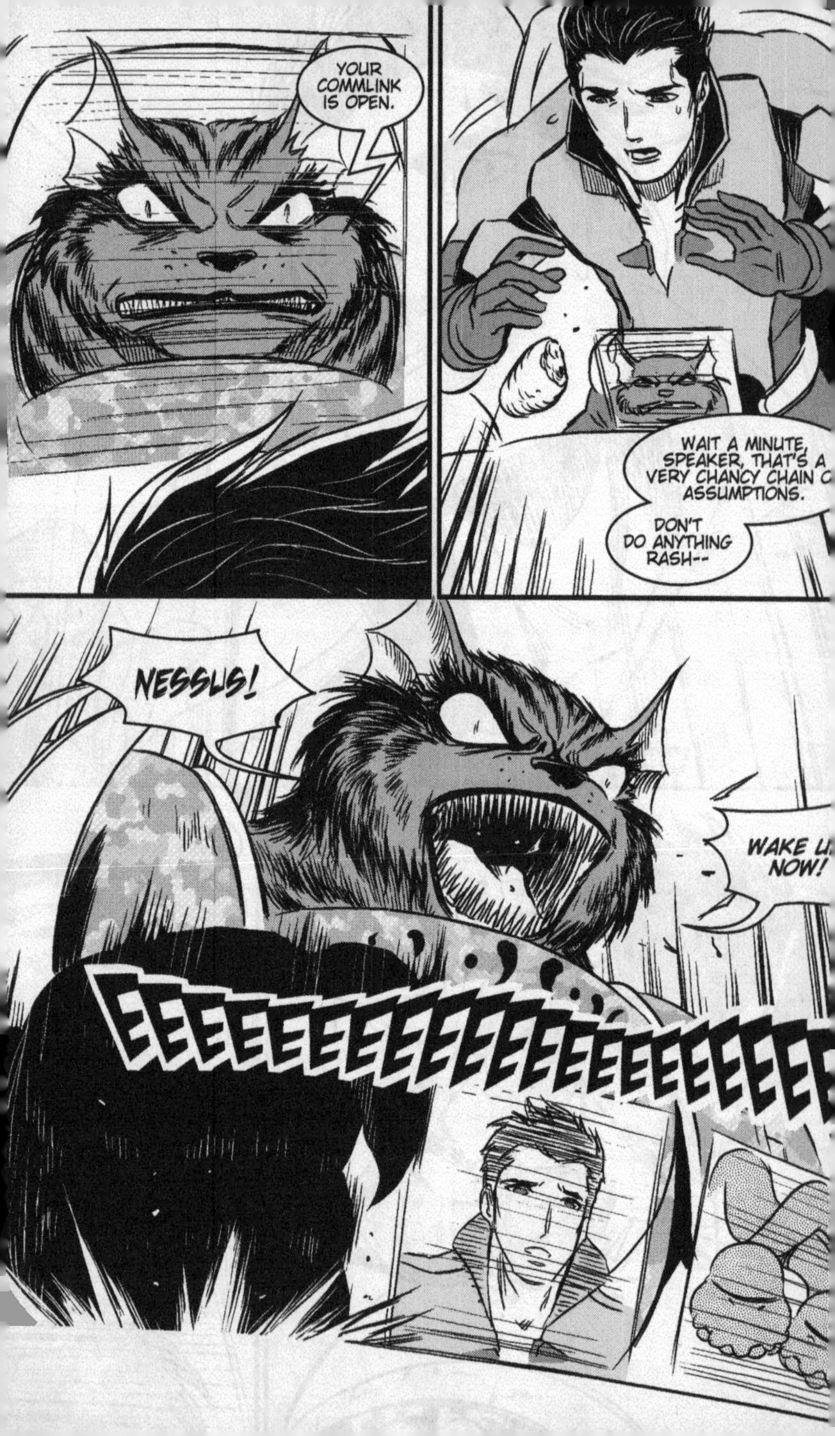

YOUR COMMLINK IS OPEN.
WAIT A MINUTE, SPEAKER, THAT'S A VERY CHANCY CHAIN O ASSUMPTIONS.
DON'T DO ANYTHING RASH--
NESSUS!
WAKE U NOW!
EEEEEEEEEEEEEEEEEEEEEEEEEEEEE

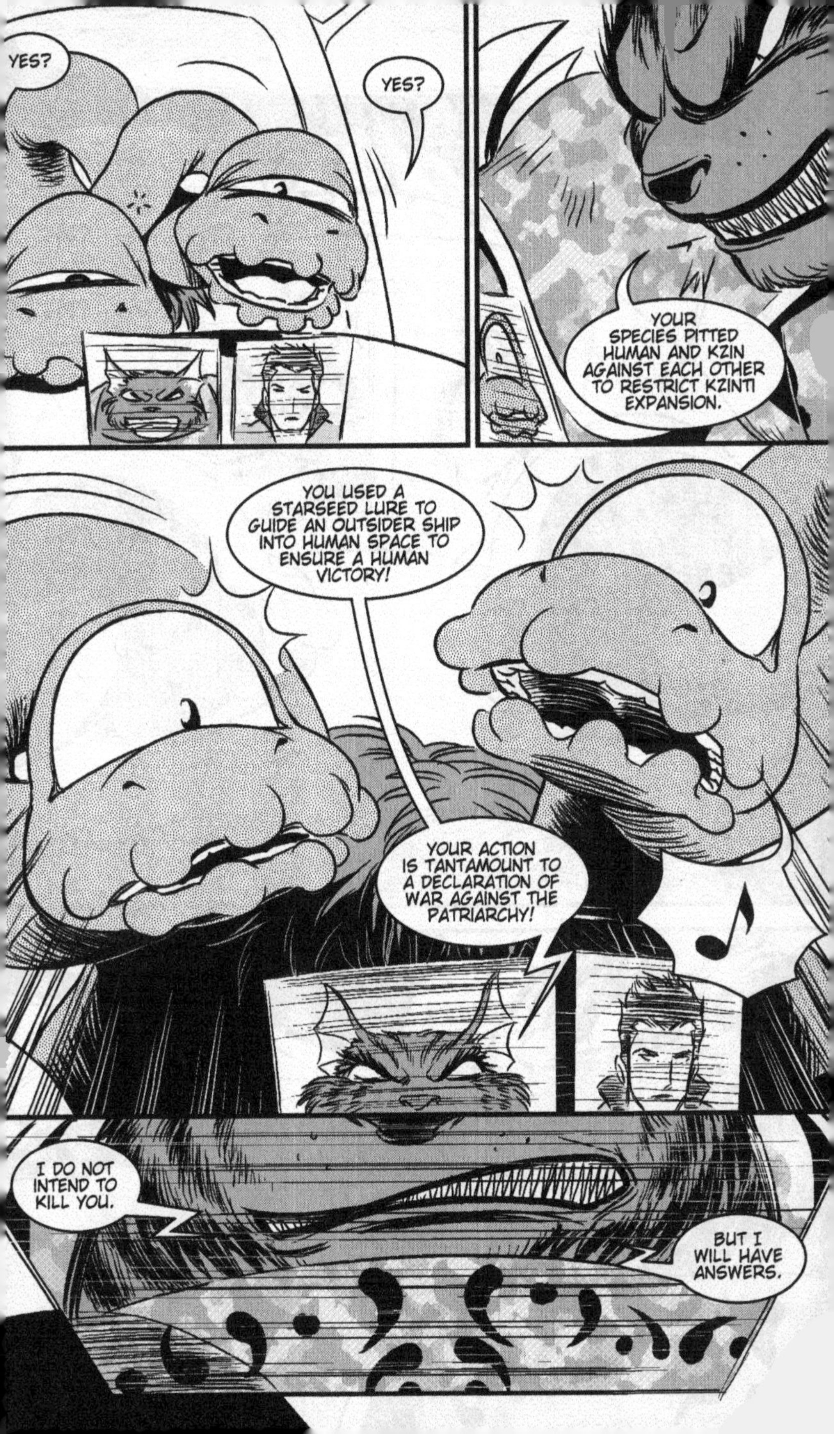
YES?
YES?
YOUR SPECIES PITTED HUMAN AND KZIN AGAINST EACH OTHER TO RESTRICT KZINTI EXPANSION.
YOU USED A STARSEED LURE TO GUIDE AN OUTSIDER SHIP INTO HUMAN SPACE TO ENSURE A HUMAN VICTORY!
YOUR ACTION IS TANTAMOUNT TO A DECLARATION OF WAR AGAINST THE PATRIARCHY!
I DO NOT INTEND TO KILL YOU.
BUT I WILL HAVE ANSWERS.

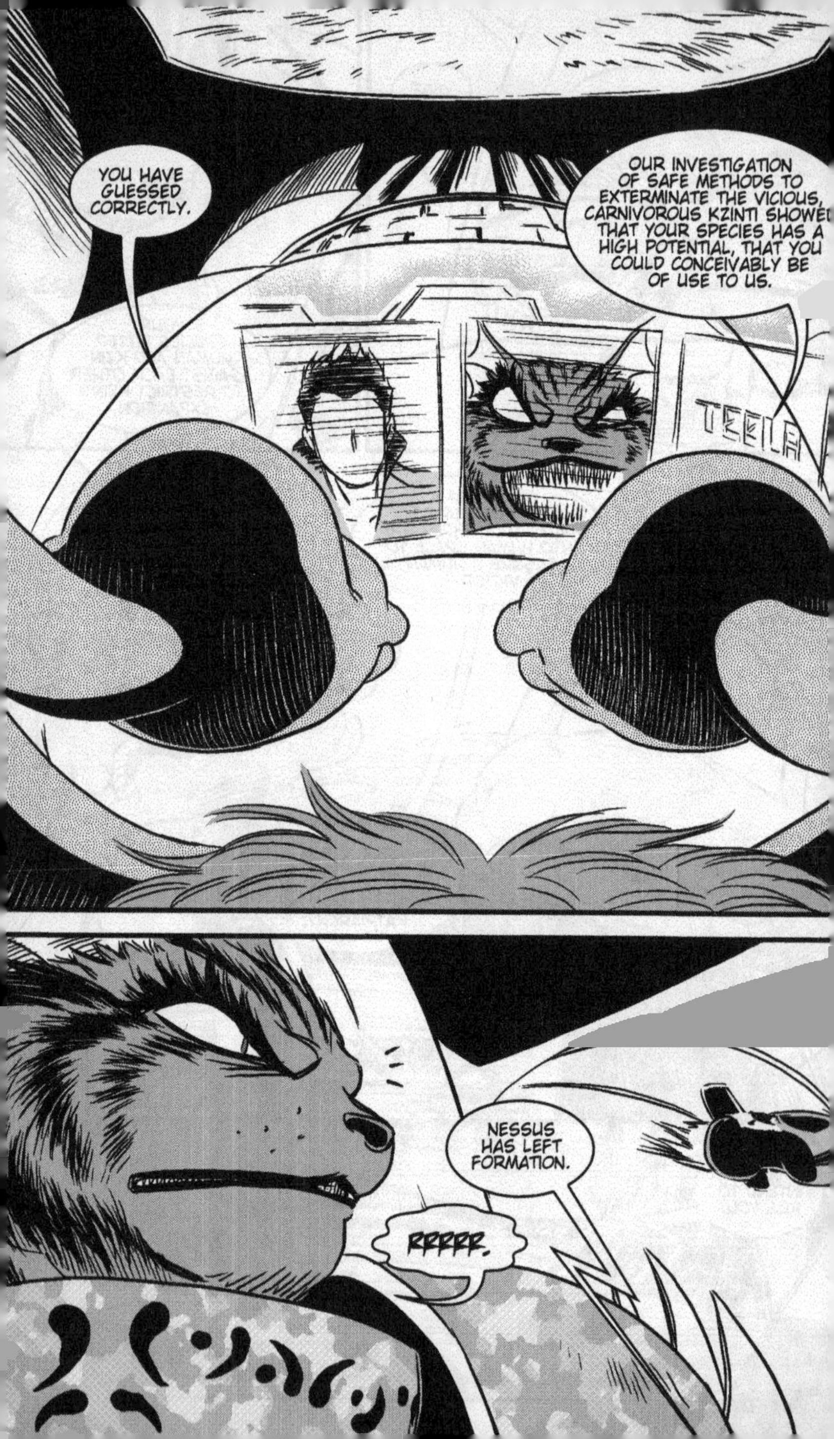
YOU HAVE GUESSED CORRECTLY.
OUR INVESTIGATION OF SAFE METHODS TO EXTERMINATE THE VICIOUS, CARNIVOROUS KZINTI SHOWED THAT YOUR SPECIES HAS A HIGH POTENTIAL, THAT YOU COULD CONCEIVABLY BE OF USE TO US.
TEELA
NESSUS HAS LEFT FORMATION.
RRRRR.

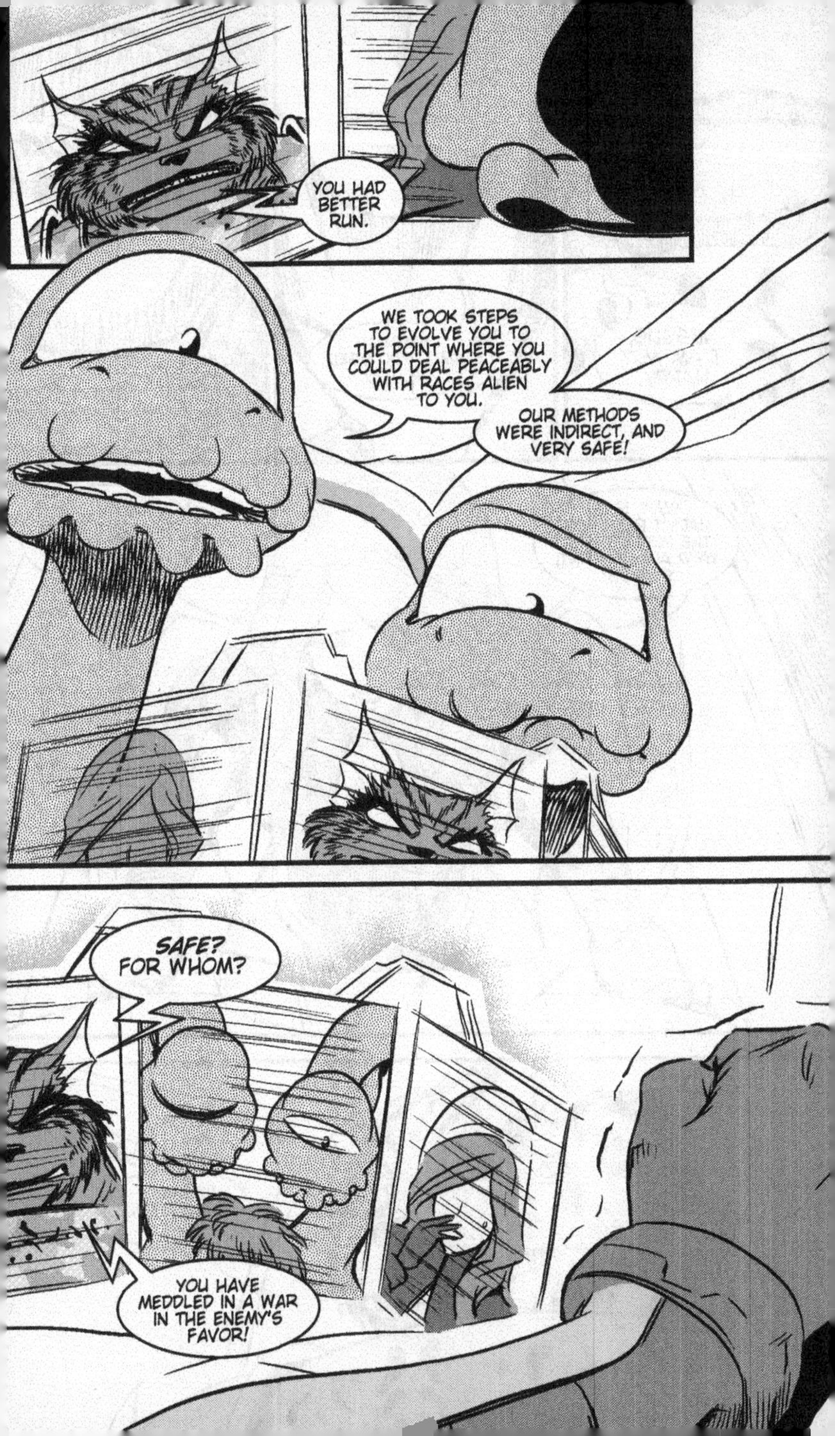
YOU HAD BETTER RUN.
WE TOOK STEPS TO EVOLVE YOU TO THE POINT WHERE YOU COULD DEAL PEACEABLY WITH RACES ALIEN TO YOU.
OUR METHODS WERE INDIRECT, AND VERY SAFE!
SAFE? FOR WHOM?
YOU HAVE MEDDLED IN A WAR IN THE ENEMY'S FAVOR!

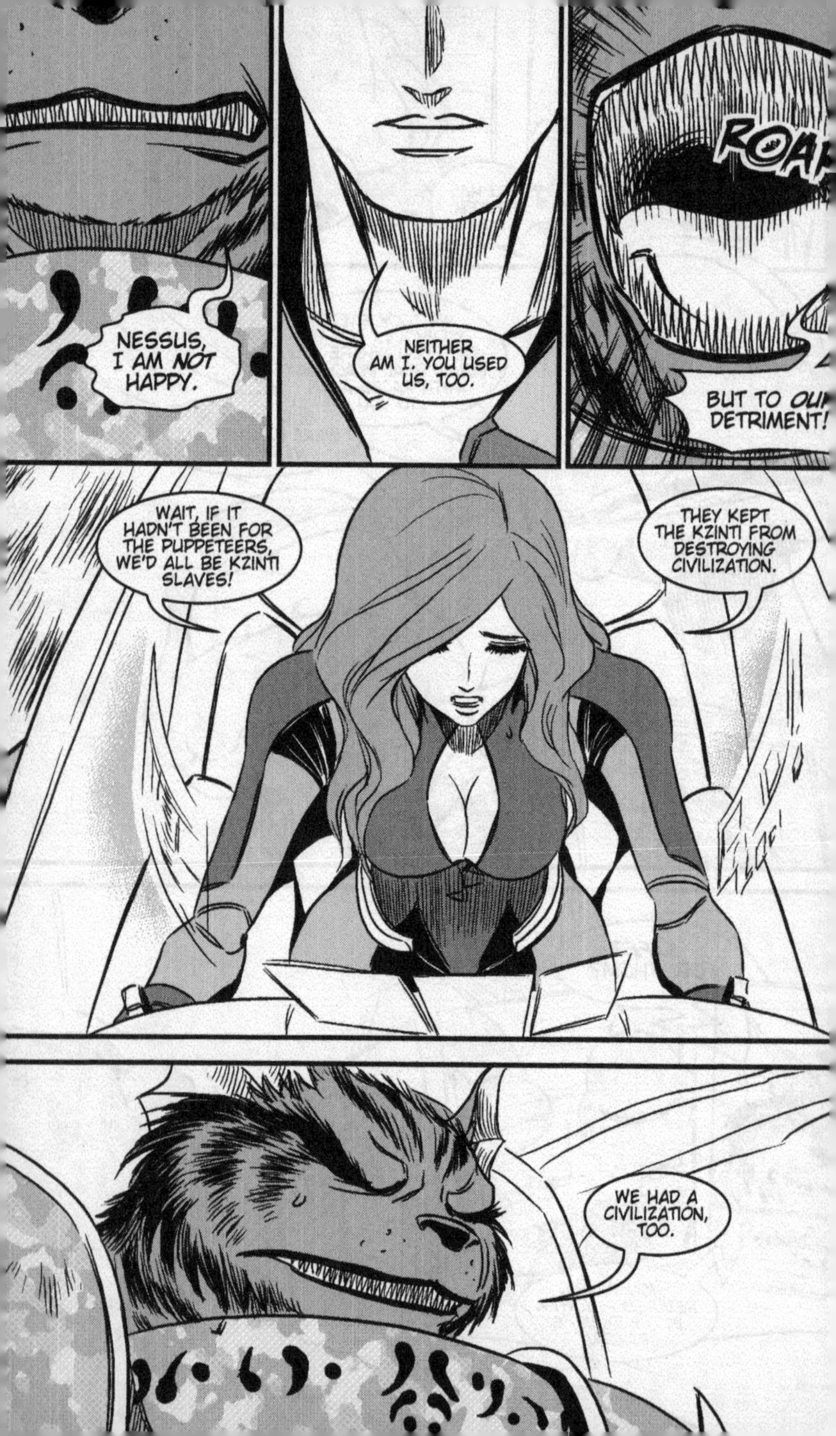
NESSUS, I AM *NOT* HAPPY.
NEITHER AM I. YOU USED US, TOO.
ROAR
BUT TO *OUR* DETRIMENT!
WAIT, IF IT HADN'T BEEN FOR THE PUPPETEERS, WE'D ALL BE KZINTI SLAVES!
THEY KEPT THE KZINTI FROM DESTROYING CIVILIZATION.
WE HAD A CIVILIZATION, TOO.

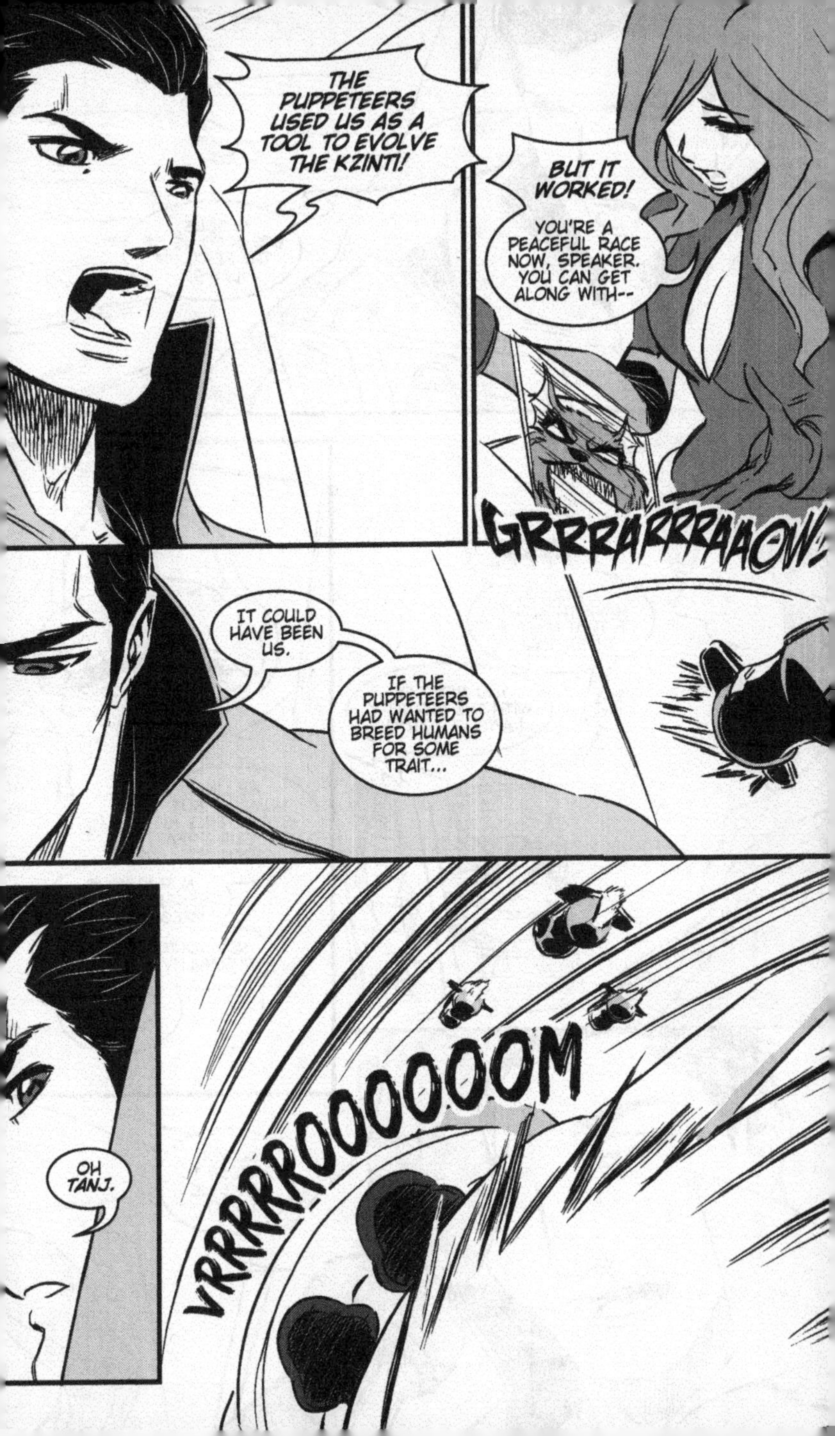
THE PUPPETEERS USED US AS A TOOL TO EVOLVE THE KZINTI!
BUT IT WORKED!
YOU'RE A PEACEFUL RACE NOW, SPEAKER. YOU CAN GET ALONG WITH--
GRRRARRRAAOW!
IT COULD HAVE BEEN US.
IF THE PUPPETEERS HAD WANTED TO BREED HUMANS FOR SOME TRAIT...
OH TANJ.
VRRRRROOOOOOOM

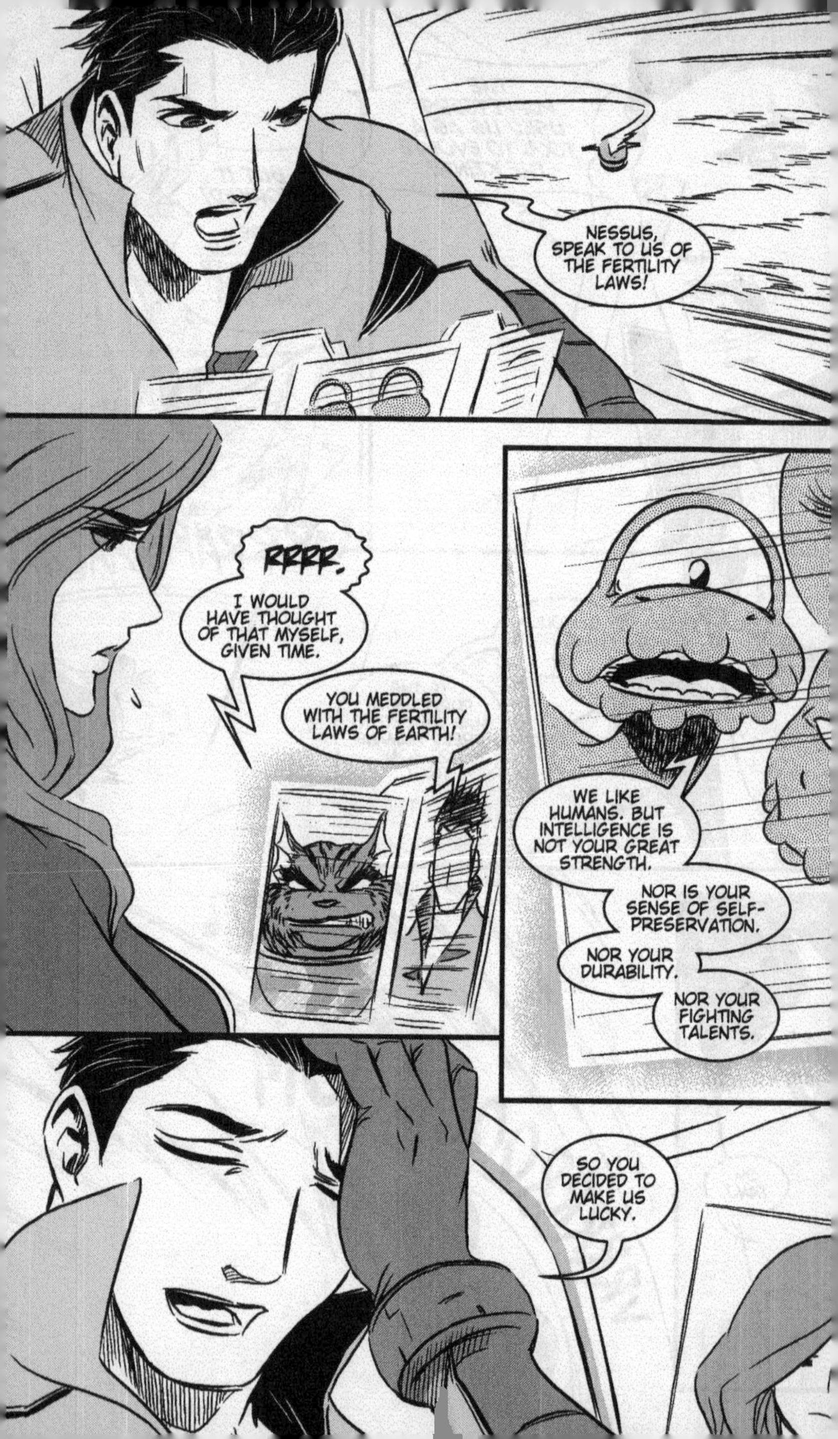
NESSUS, SPEAK TO US OF THE FERTILITY LAWS!
RRRR.
I WOULD HAVE THOUGHT OF THAT MYSELF, GIVEN TIME.
YOU MEDDLED WITH THE FERTILITY LAWS OF EARTH!
WE LIKE HUMANS. BUT INTELLIGENCE IS NOT YOUR GREAT STRENGTH.
NOR IS YOUR SENSE OF SELF-PRESERVATION.
NOR YOUR DURABILITY.
NOR YOUR FIGHTING TALENTS.
SO YOU DECIDED TO MAKE US LUCKY.

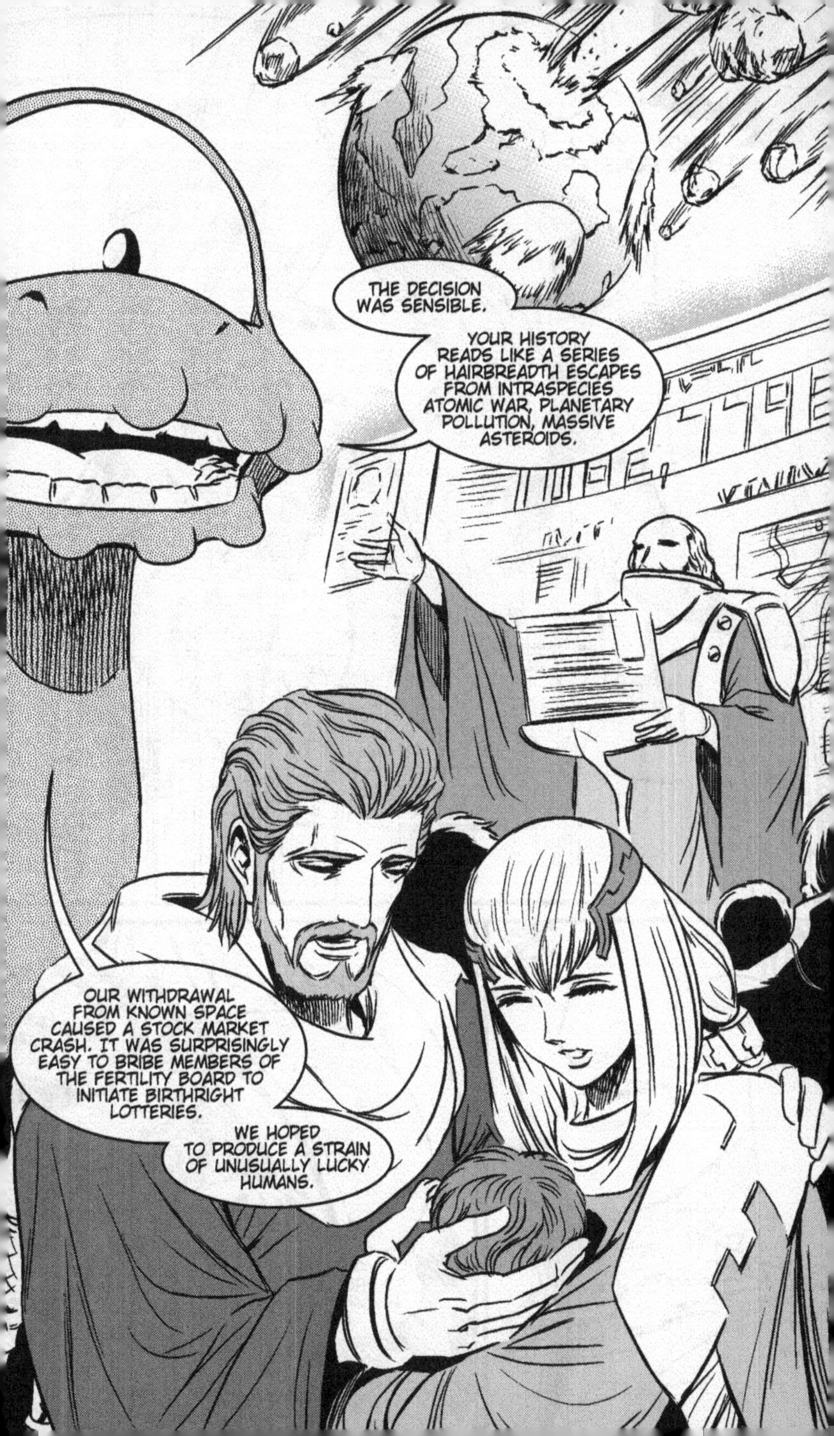
THE DECISION WAS SENSIBLE.
YOUR HISTORY READS LIKE A SERIES OF HAIRBREADTH ESCAPES FROM INTRASPECIES ATOMIC WAR, PLANETARY POLLUTION, MASSIVE ASTEROIDS.
OUR WITHDRAWAL FROM KNOWN SPACE CAUSED A STOCK MARKET CRASH. IT WAS SURPRISINGLY EASY TO BRIBE MEMBERS OF THE FERTILITY BOARD TO INITIATE BIRTHRIGHT LOTTERIES.
WE HOPED TO PRODUCE A STRAIN OF UNUSUALLY LUCKY HUMANS.

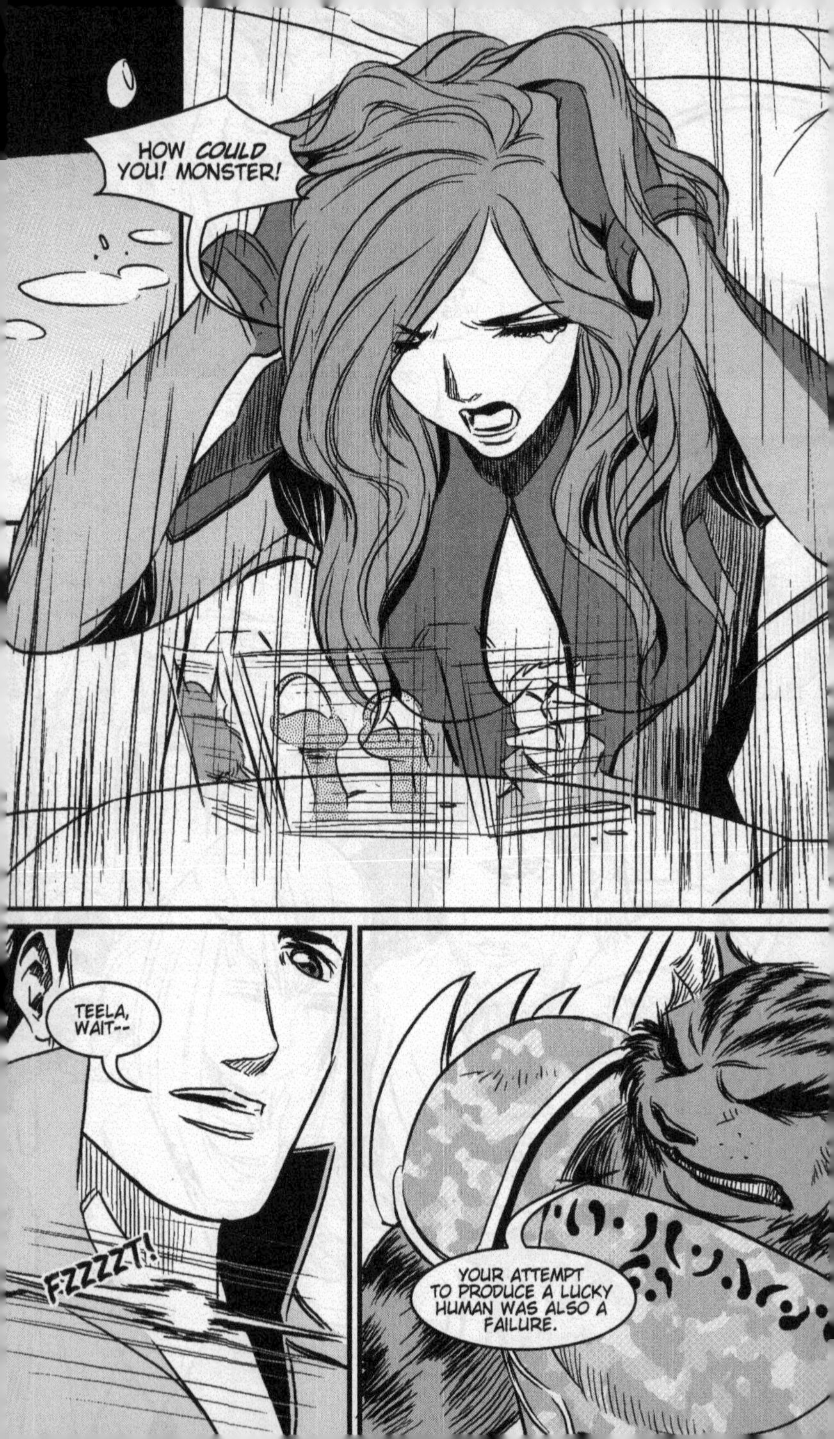
HOW COULD YOU! MONSTER!
TEELA, WAIT--
FZZZZT!
YOUR ATTEMPT TO PRODUCE A LUCKY HUMAN WAS ALSO A FAILURE.

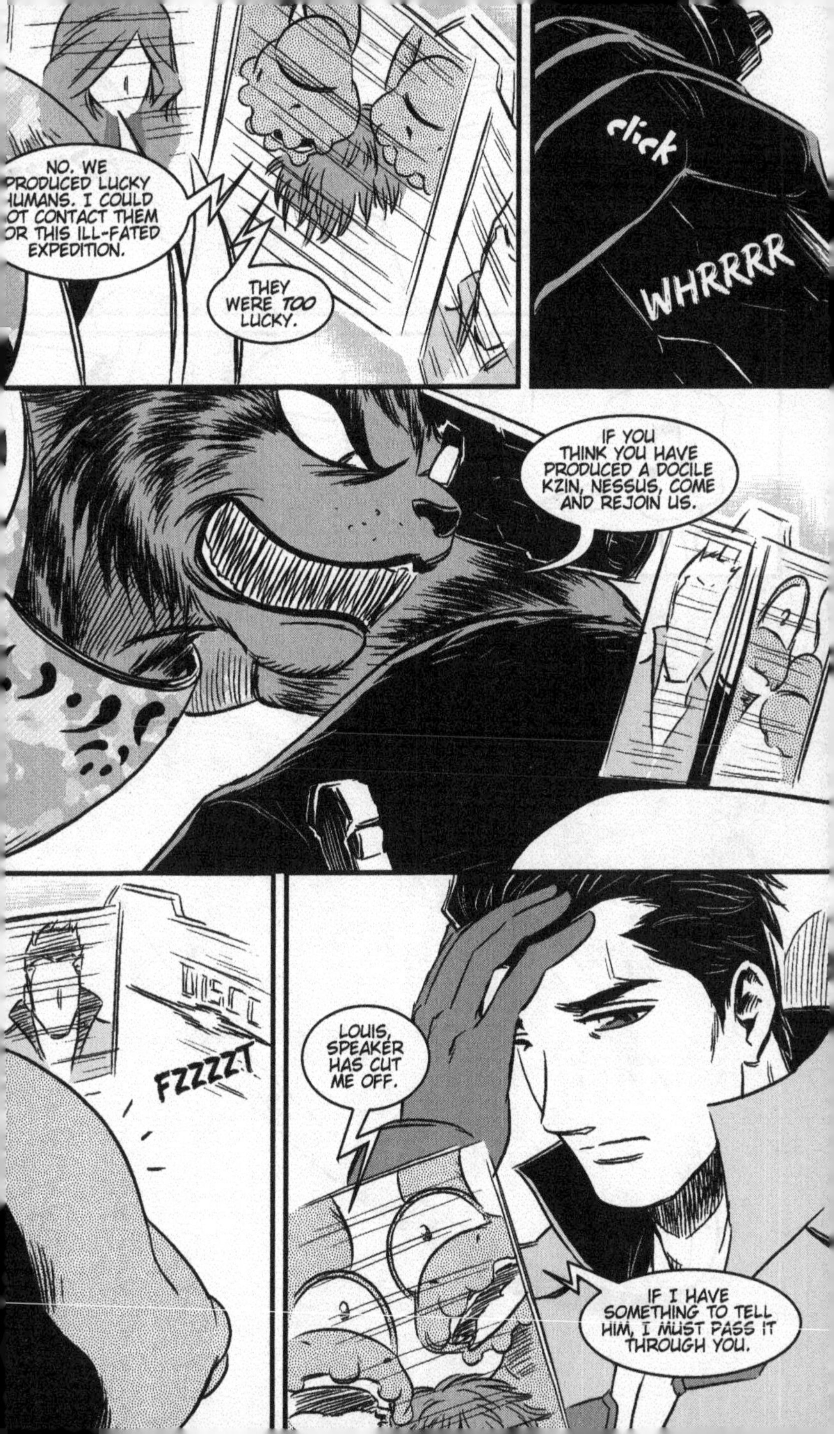
NO. WE PRODUCED LUCKY HUMANS. I COULD NOT CONTACT THEM FOR THIS ILL-FATED EXPEDITION.
THEY WERE *TOO* LUCKY.
click
WHRRRR
IF YOU THINK YOU HAVE PRODUCED A DOCILE KZIN, NESSUS, COME AND REJOIN US.
FZZZZT
LOUIS, SPEAKER HAS CUT ME OFF.
IF I HAVE SOMETHING TO TELL HIM, I MUST PASS IT THROUGH YOU.

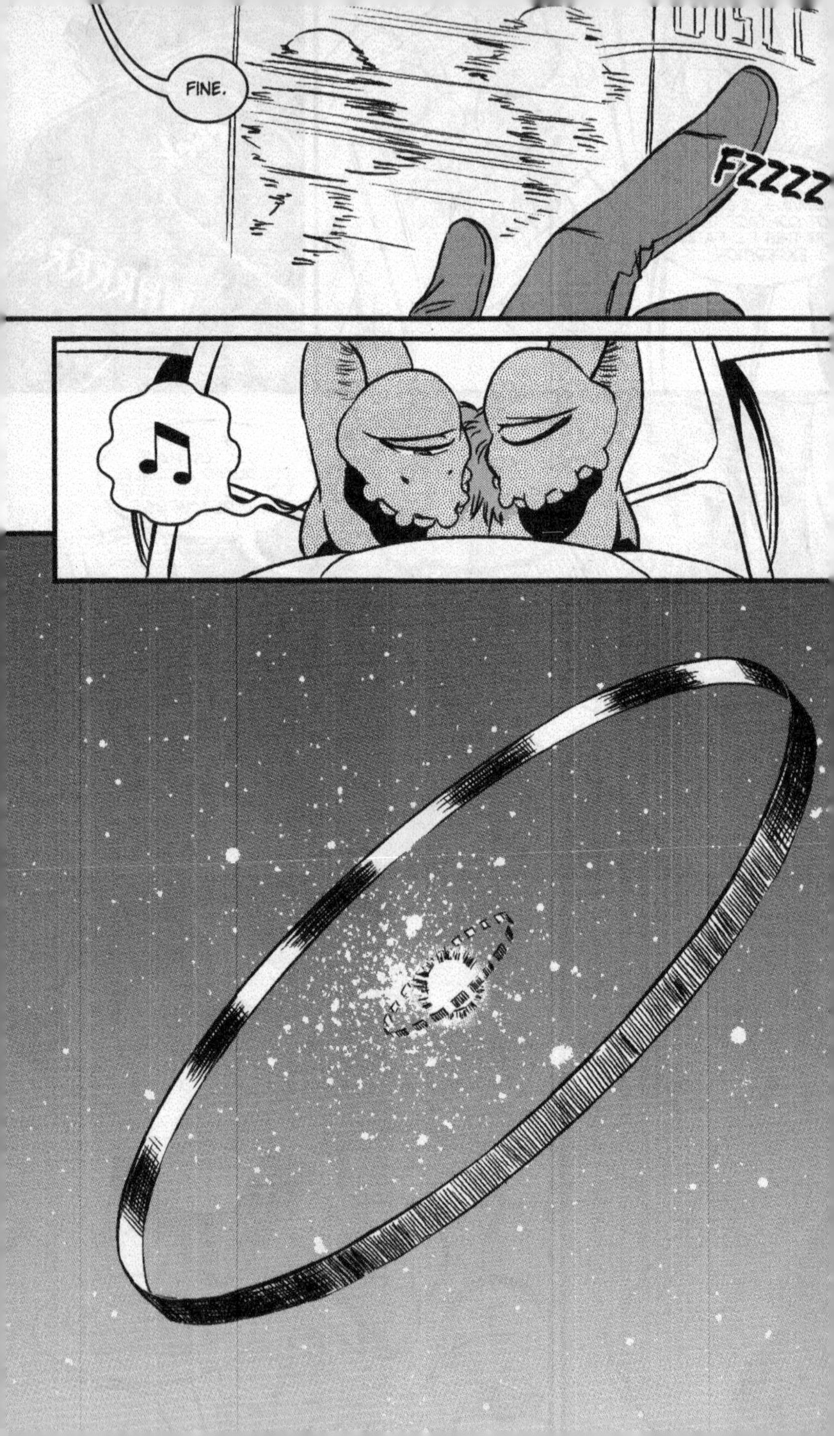
FINE.
FZZZZZ

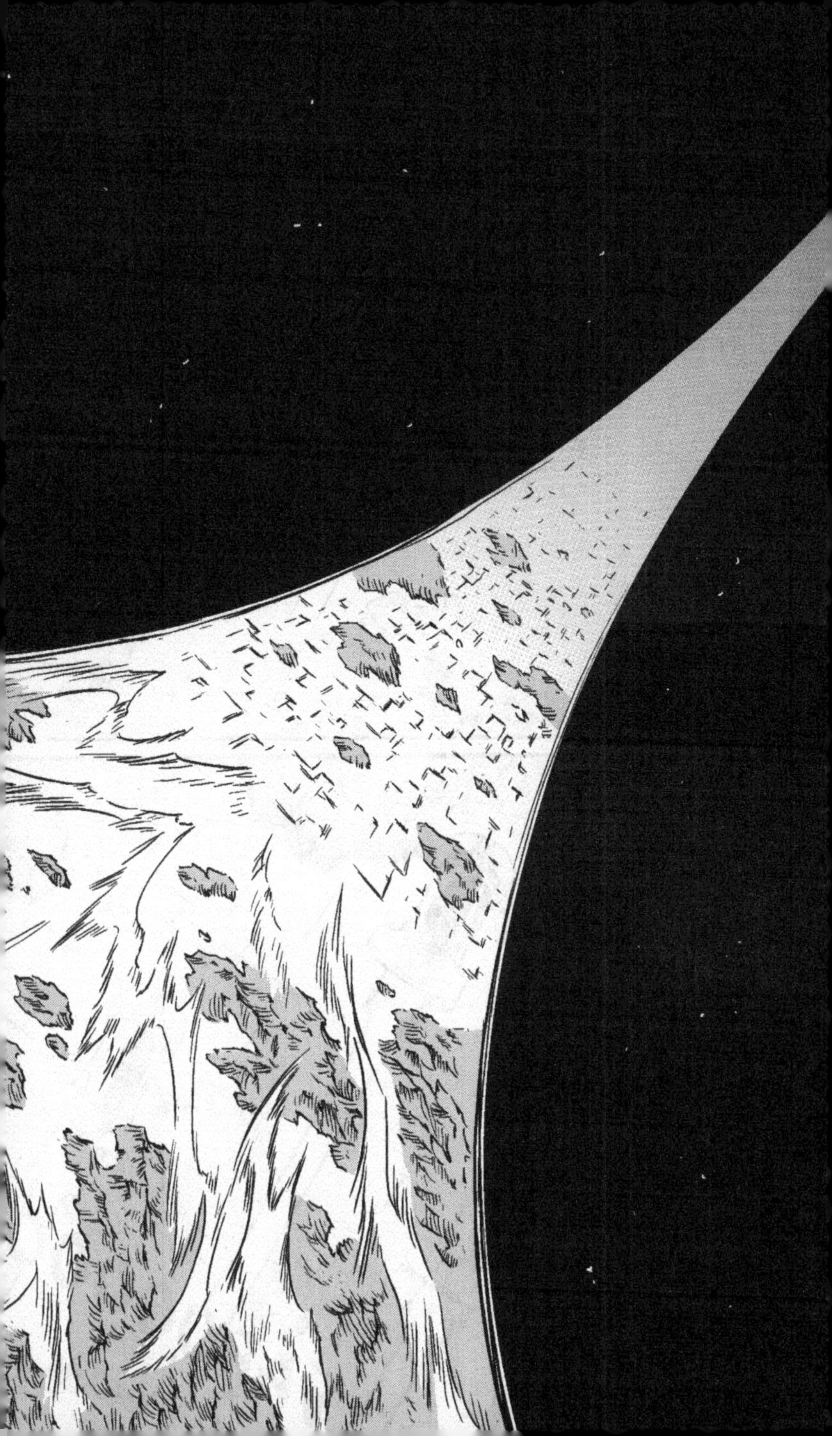

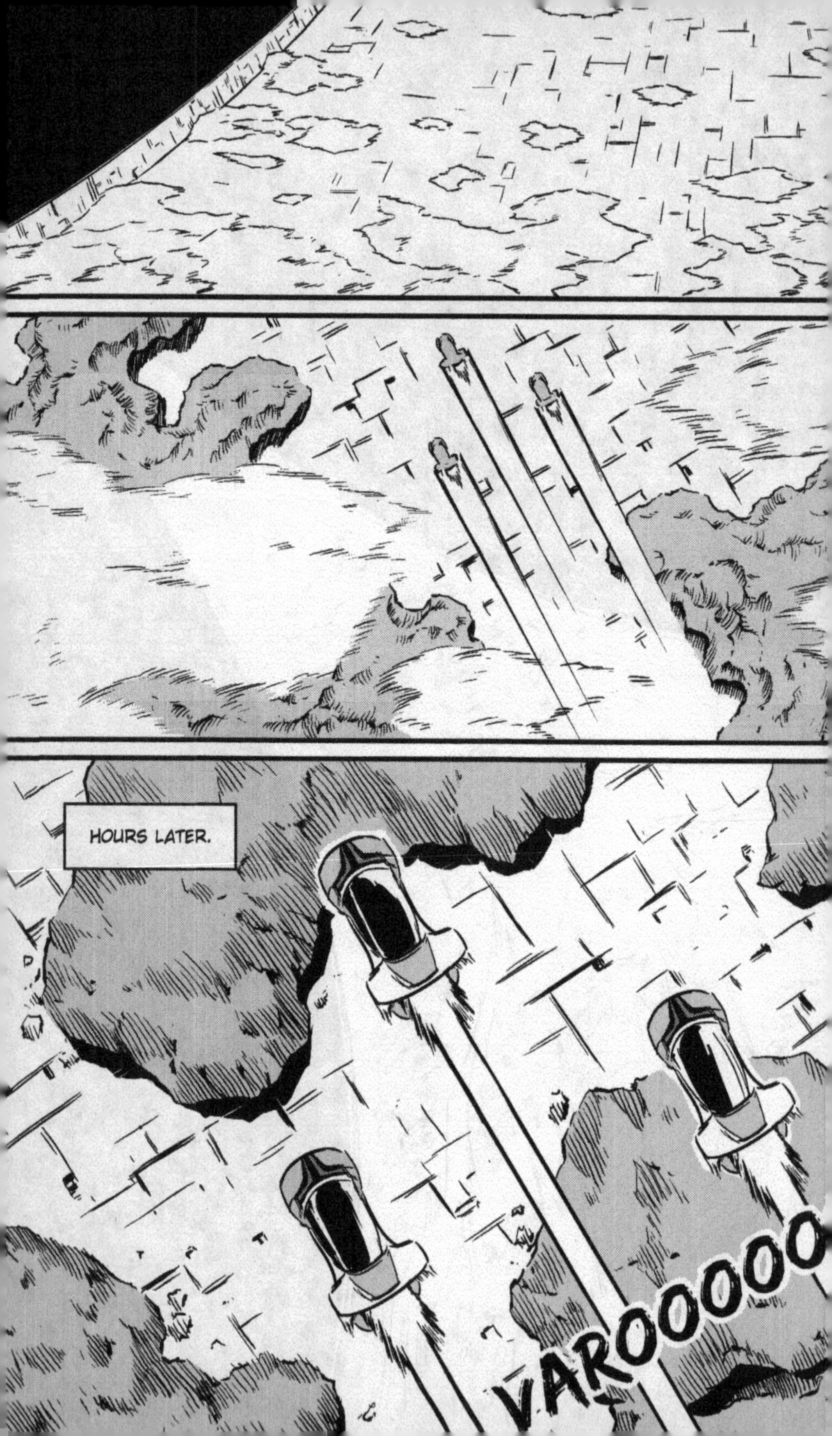
HOURS LATER.
VAROOOOOO

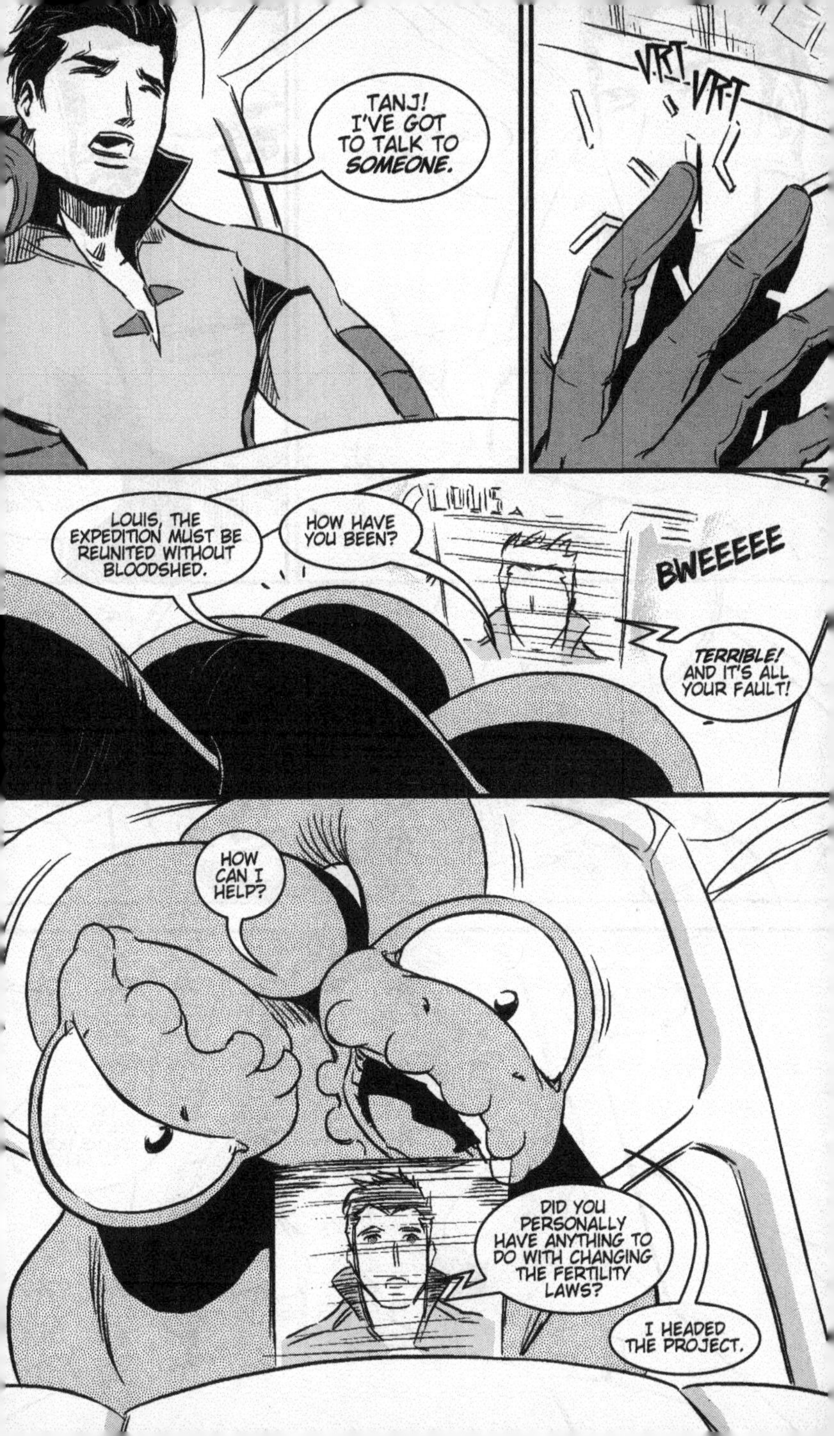
TANJ! I'VE GOT TO TALK TO SOMEONE.
V-R-T V-R-T
LOUIS
LOUIS, THE EXPEDITION MUST BE REUNITED WITHOUT BLOODSHED.
HOW HAVE YOU BEEN?
BWEEEEE
TERRIBLE! AND IT'S ALL YOUR FAULT!
HOW CAN I HELP?
DID YOU PERSONALLY HAVE ANYTHING TO DO WITH CHANGING THE FERTILITY LAWS?
I HEADED THE PROJECT.

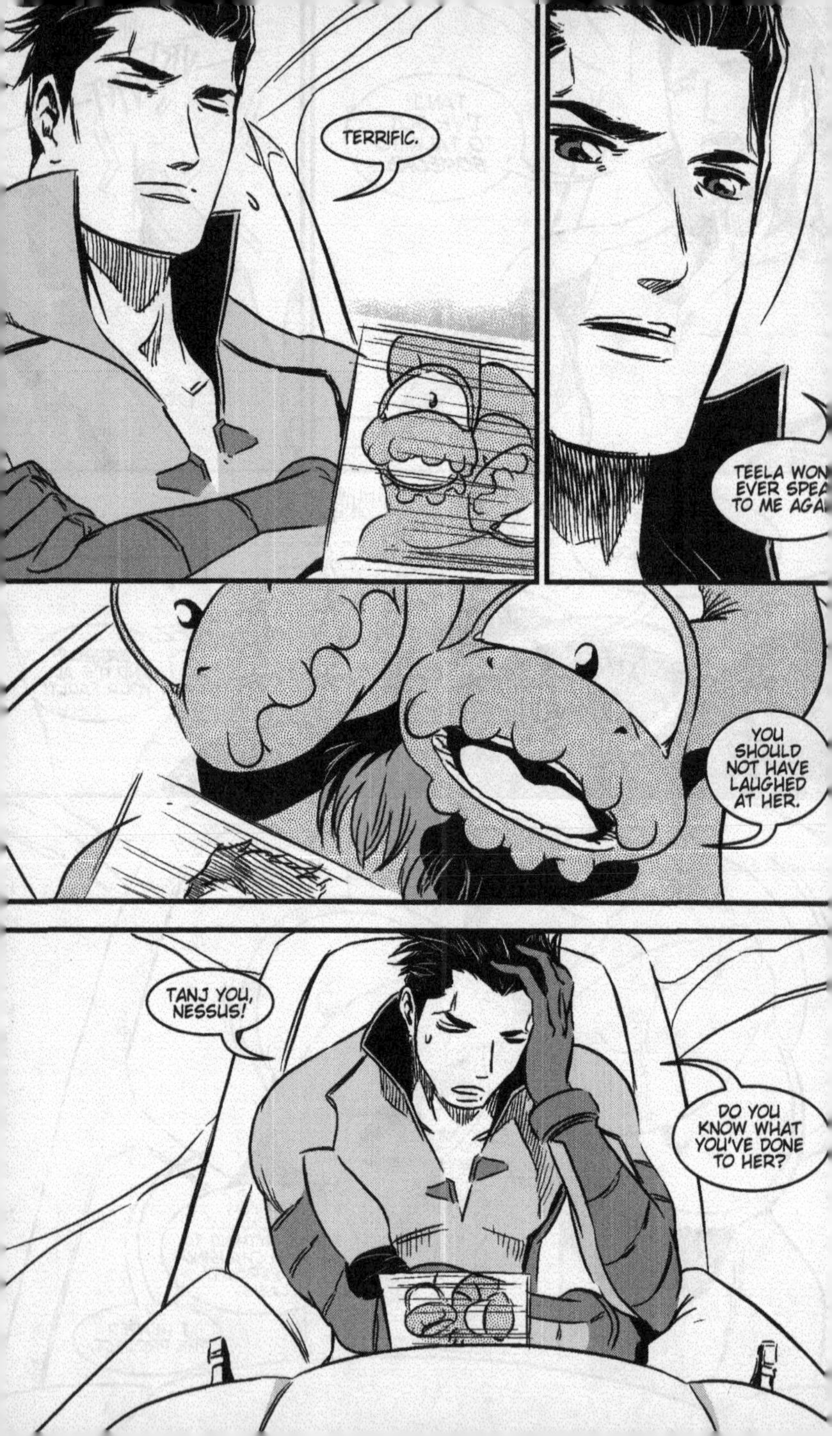
TERRIFIC.
TEELA WON EVER SPEA TO ME AGA
YOU SHOULD NOT HAVE LAUGHED AT HER.
TANJ YOU, NESSUS!
DO YOU KNOW WHAT YOU'VE DONE TO HER?

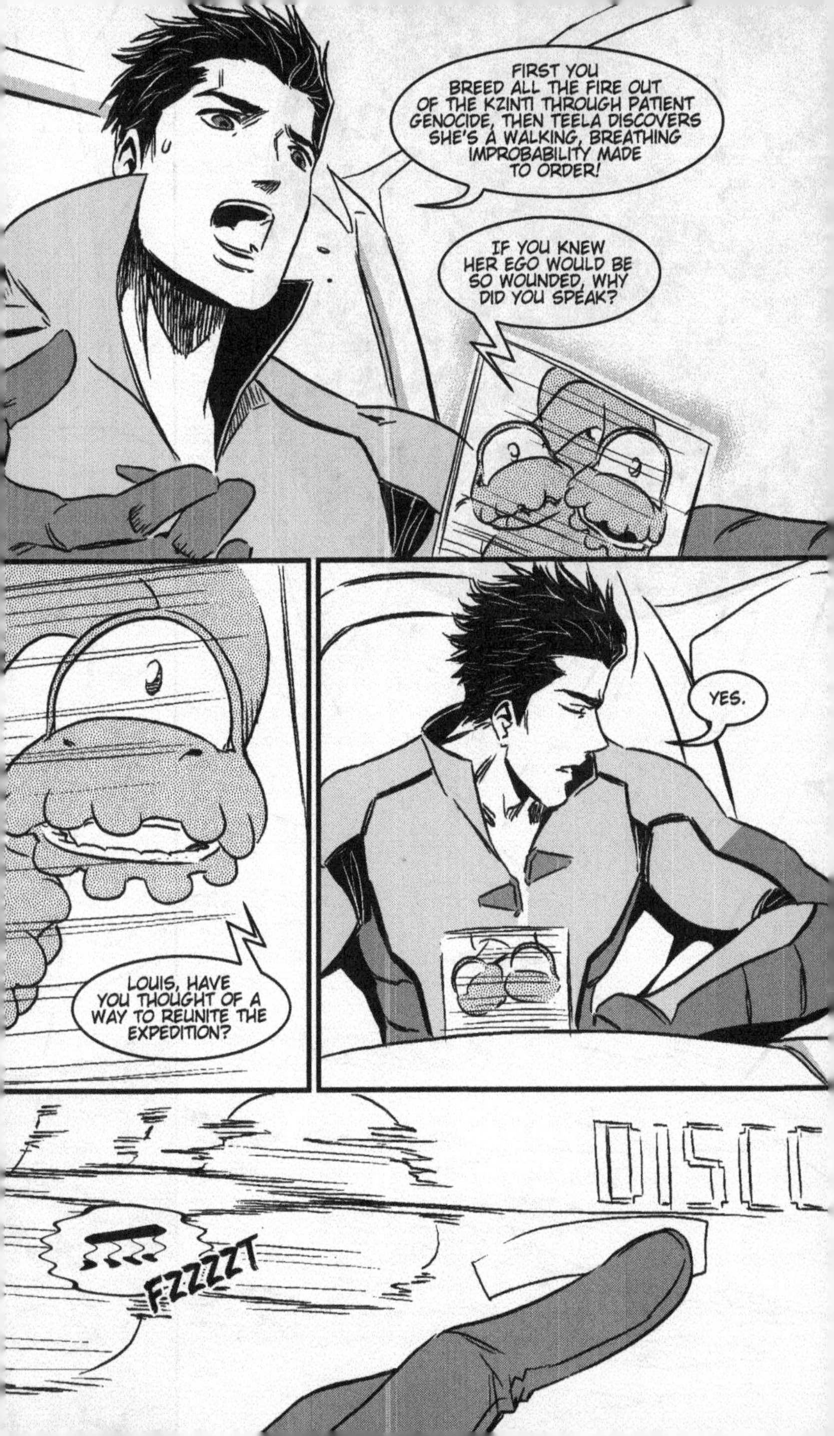
FIRST YOU BREED ALL THE FIRE OUT OF THE KZINTI THROUGH PATIENT GENOCIDE, THEN TEELA DISCOVERS SHE'S A WALKING, BREATHING IMPROBABILITY MADE TO ORDER!
IF YOU KNEW HER EGO WOULD BE SO WOUNDED, WHY DID YOU SPEAK?
LOUIS, HAVE YOU THOUGHT OF A WAY TO REUNITE THE EXPEDITION?
YES.
DISCO
FZZZZT

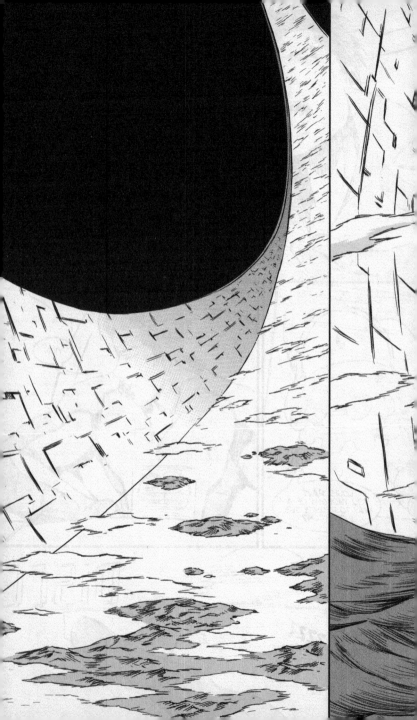

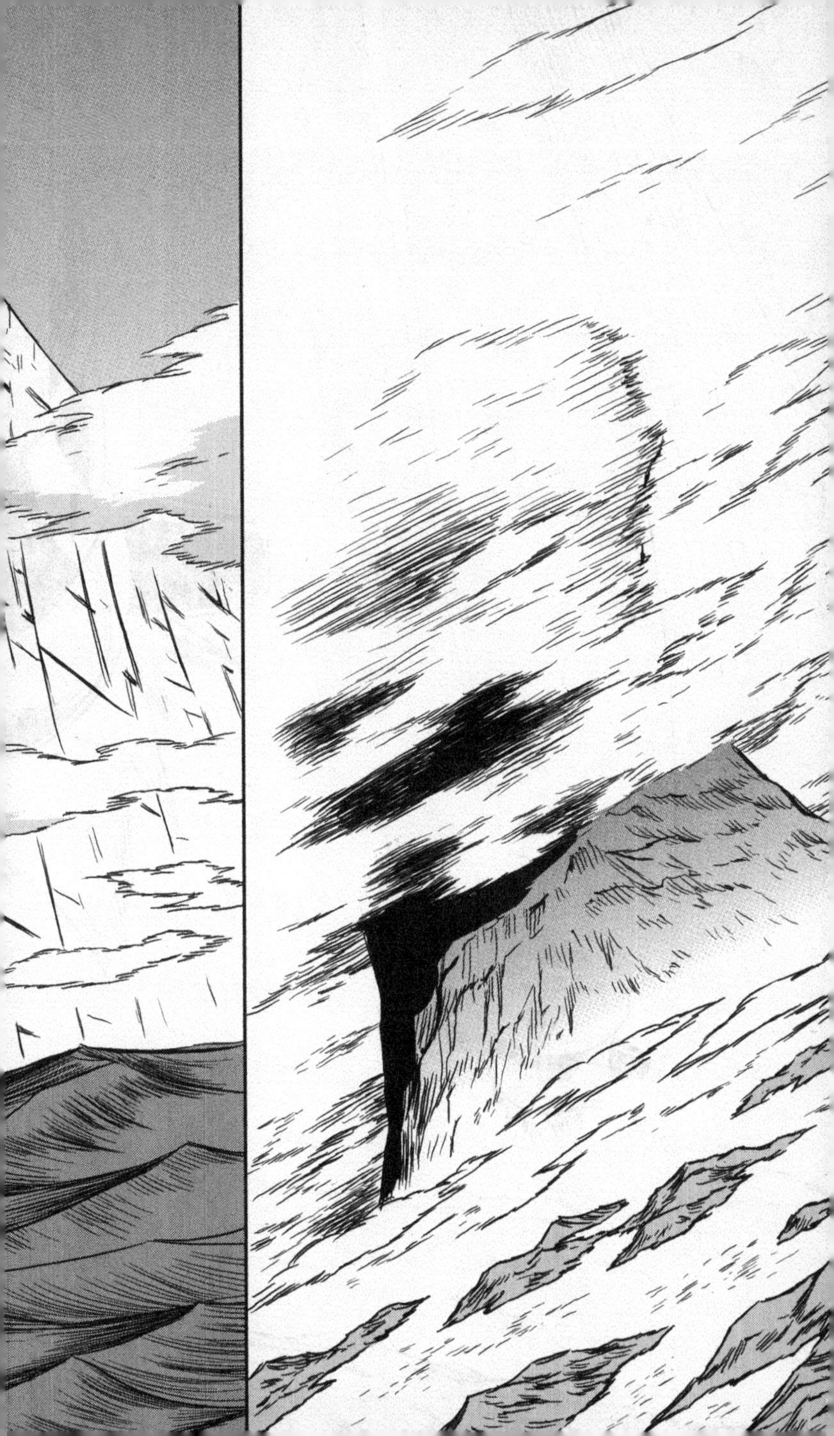

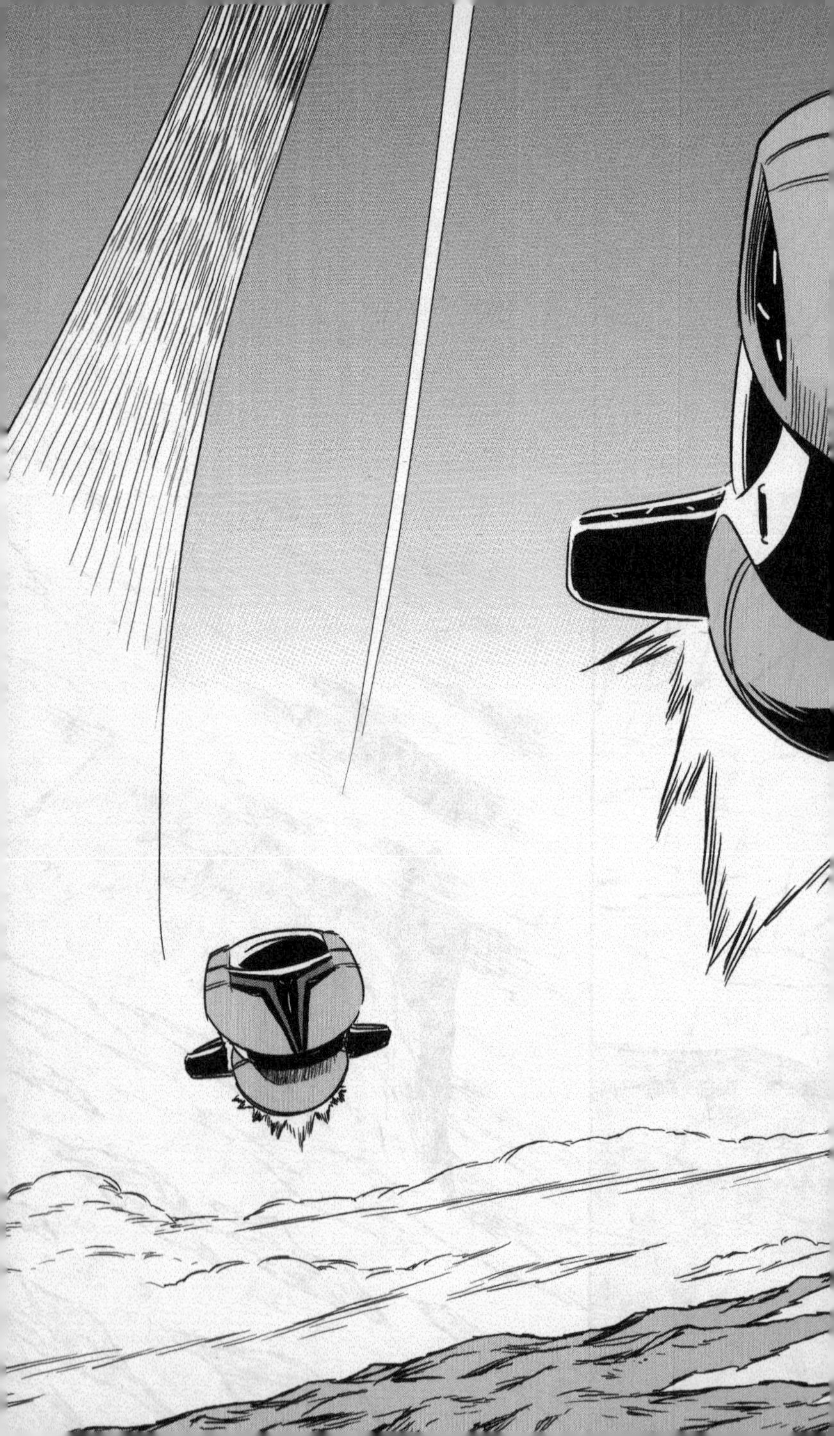

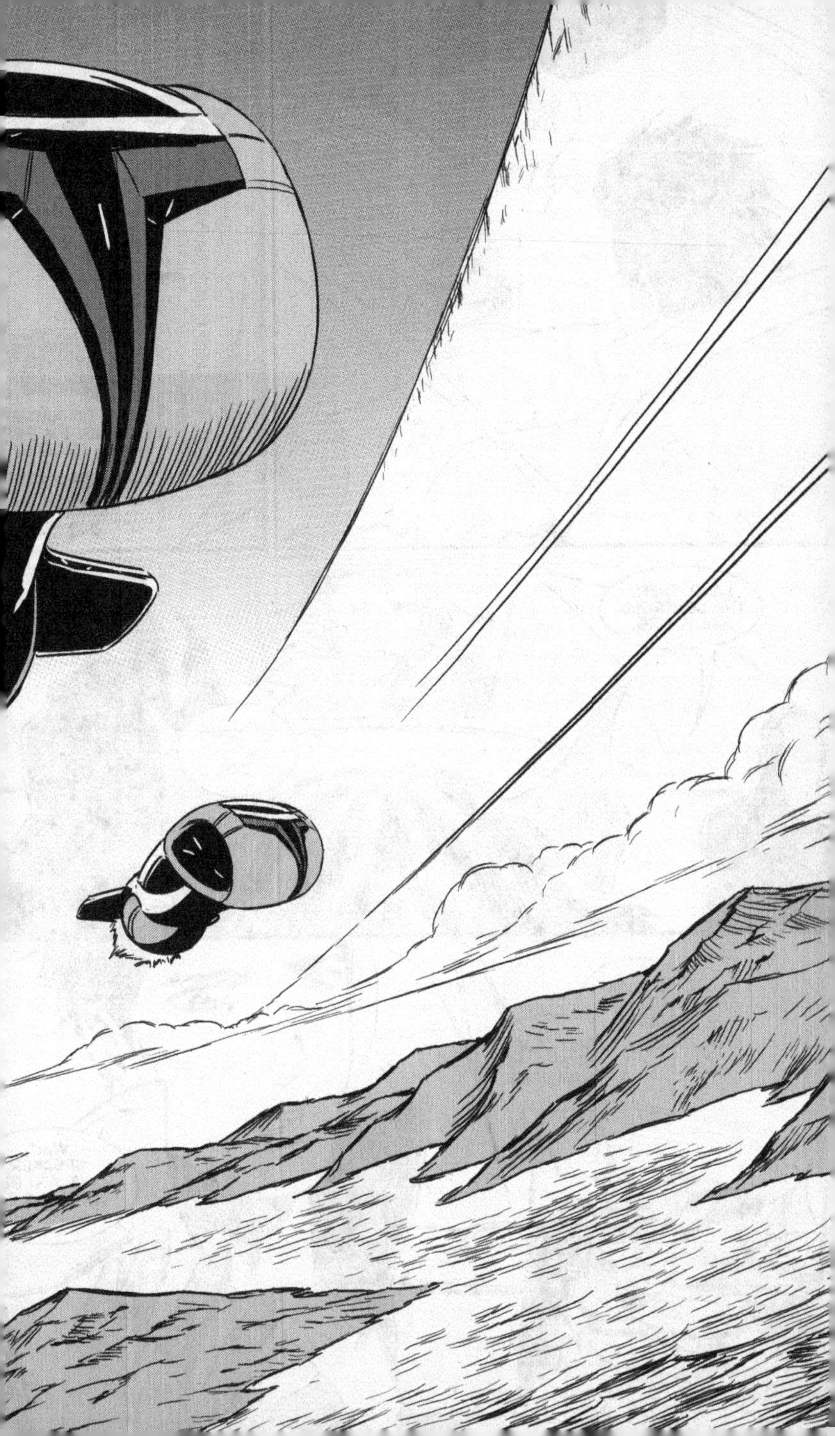

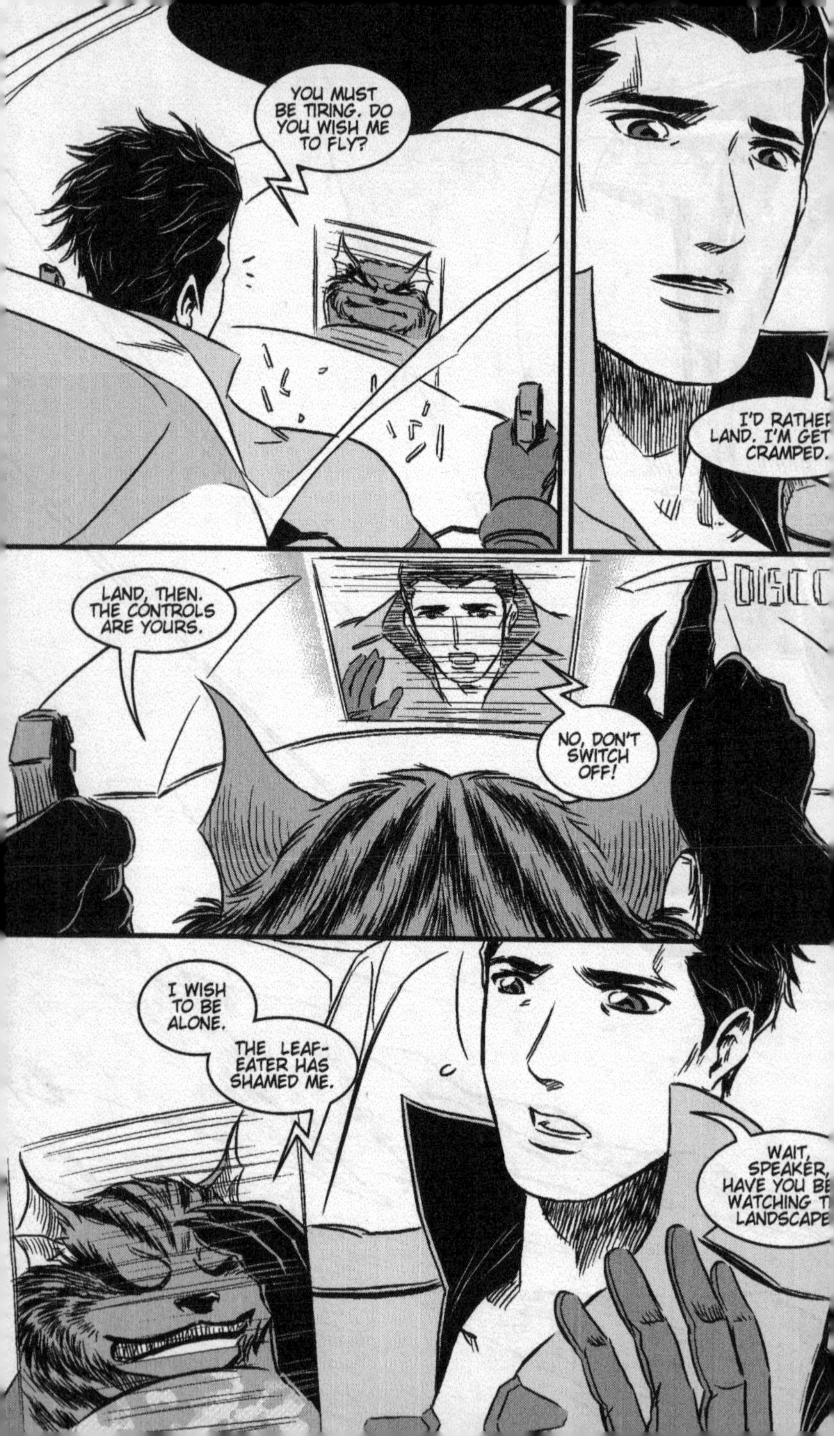
YOU MUST BE TIRING. DO YOU WISH ME TO FLY?
I'D RATHER LAND. I'M GET CRAMPED.
LAND, THEN. THE CONTROLS ARE YOURS.
DISCO
NO, DON'T SWITCH OFF!
I WISH TO BE ALONE.
THE LEAF-EATER HAS SHAMED ME.
WAIT, SPEAKER, HAVE YOU BE WATCHING T LANDSCAPE

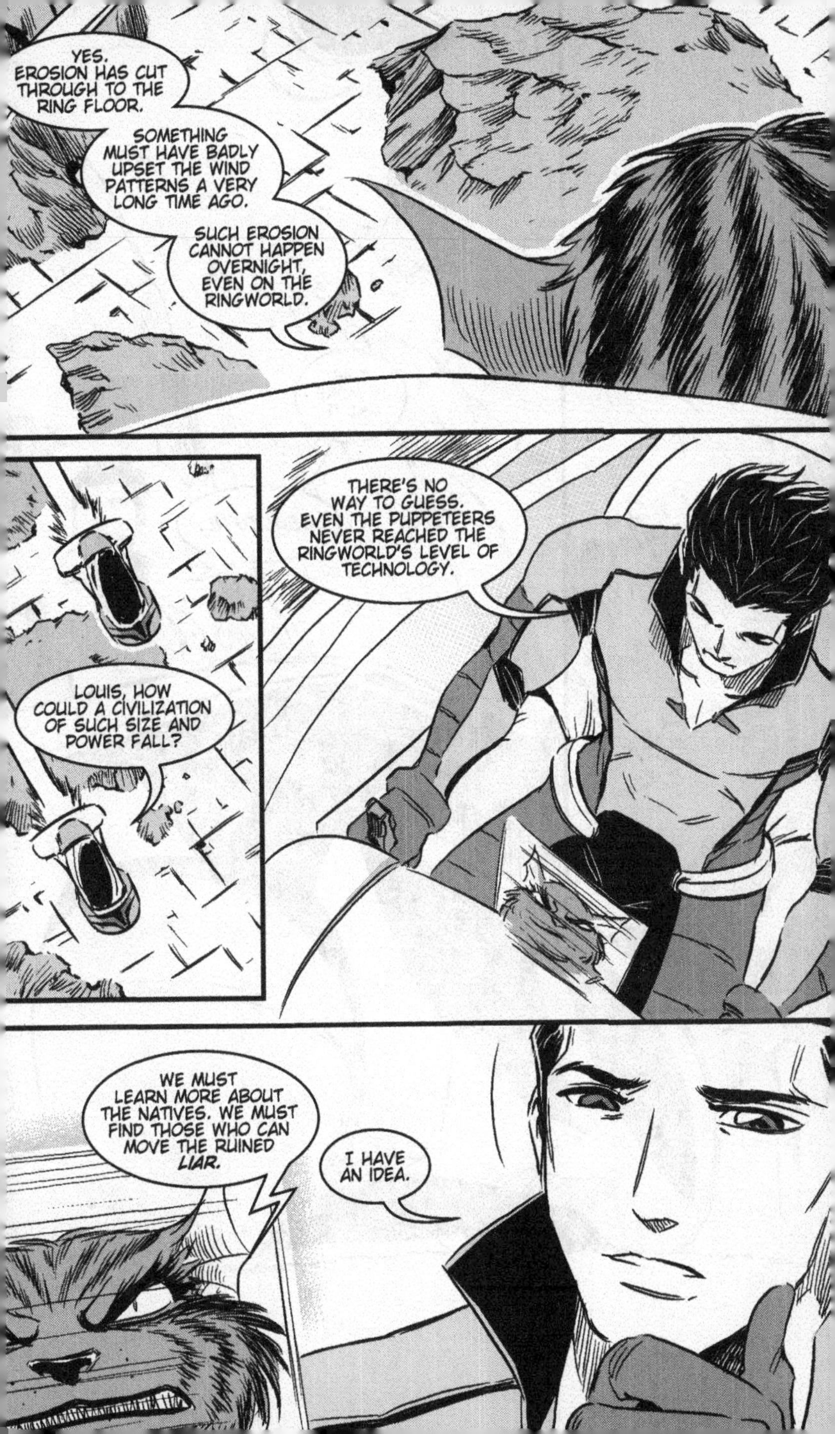
YES. EROSION HAS CUT THROUGH TO THE RING FLOOR.
SOMETHING MUST HAVE BADLY UPSET THE WIND PATTERNS A VERY LONG TIME AGO.
SUCH EROSION CANNOT HAPPEN OVERNIGHT, EVEN ON THE RINGWORLD.
LOUIS, HOW COULD A CIVILIZATION OF SUCH SIZE AND POWER FALL?
THERE'S NO WAY TO GUESS. EVEN THE PUPPETEERS NEVER REACHED THE RINGWORLD'S LEVEL OF TECHNOLOGY.
WE MUST LEARN MORE ABOUT THE NATIVES. WE MUST FIND THOSE WHO CAN MOVE THE RUINED *LIAR*.
I HAVE AN IDEA.

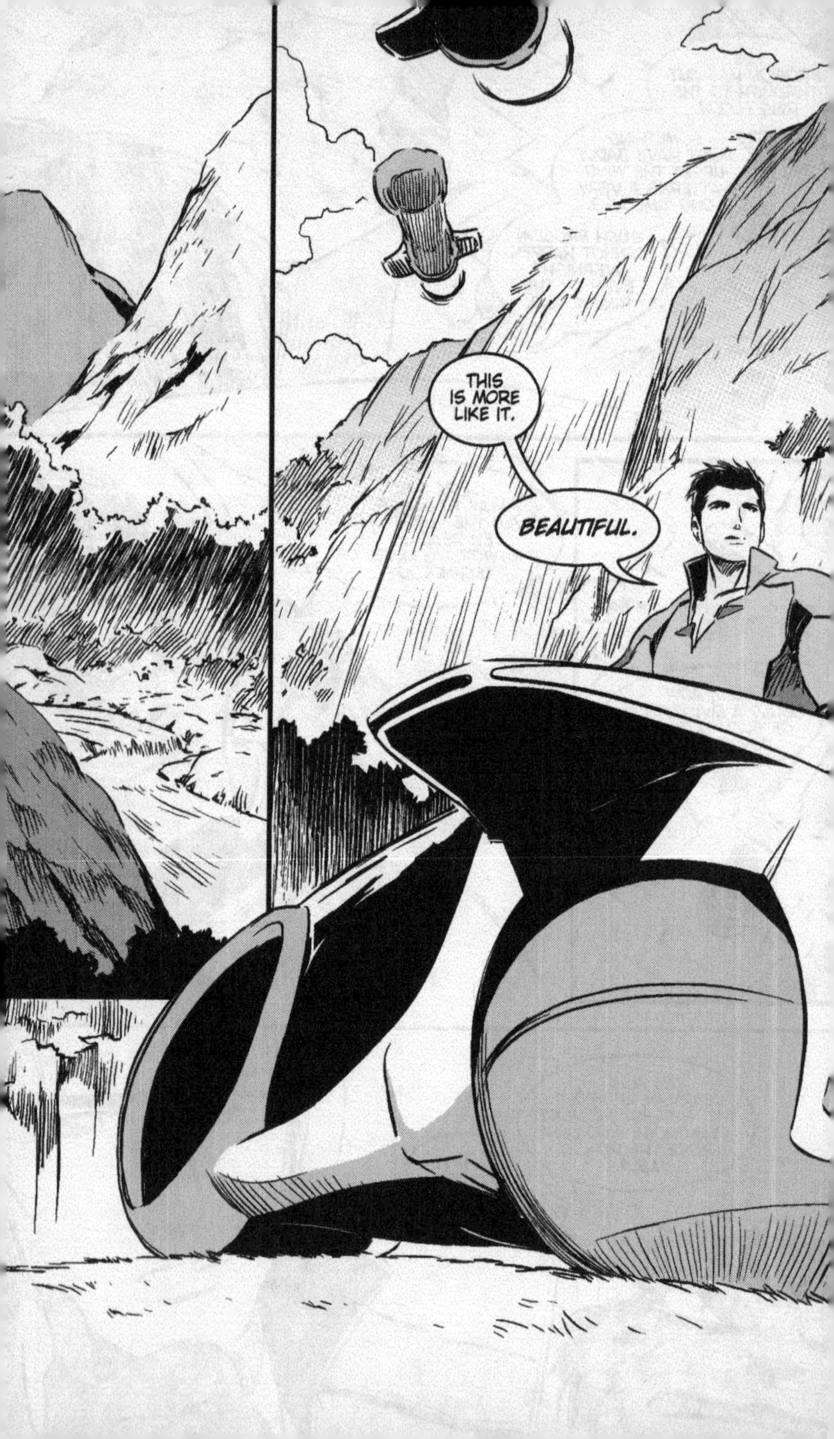
THIS IS MORE LIKE IT.
BEAUTIFUL.

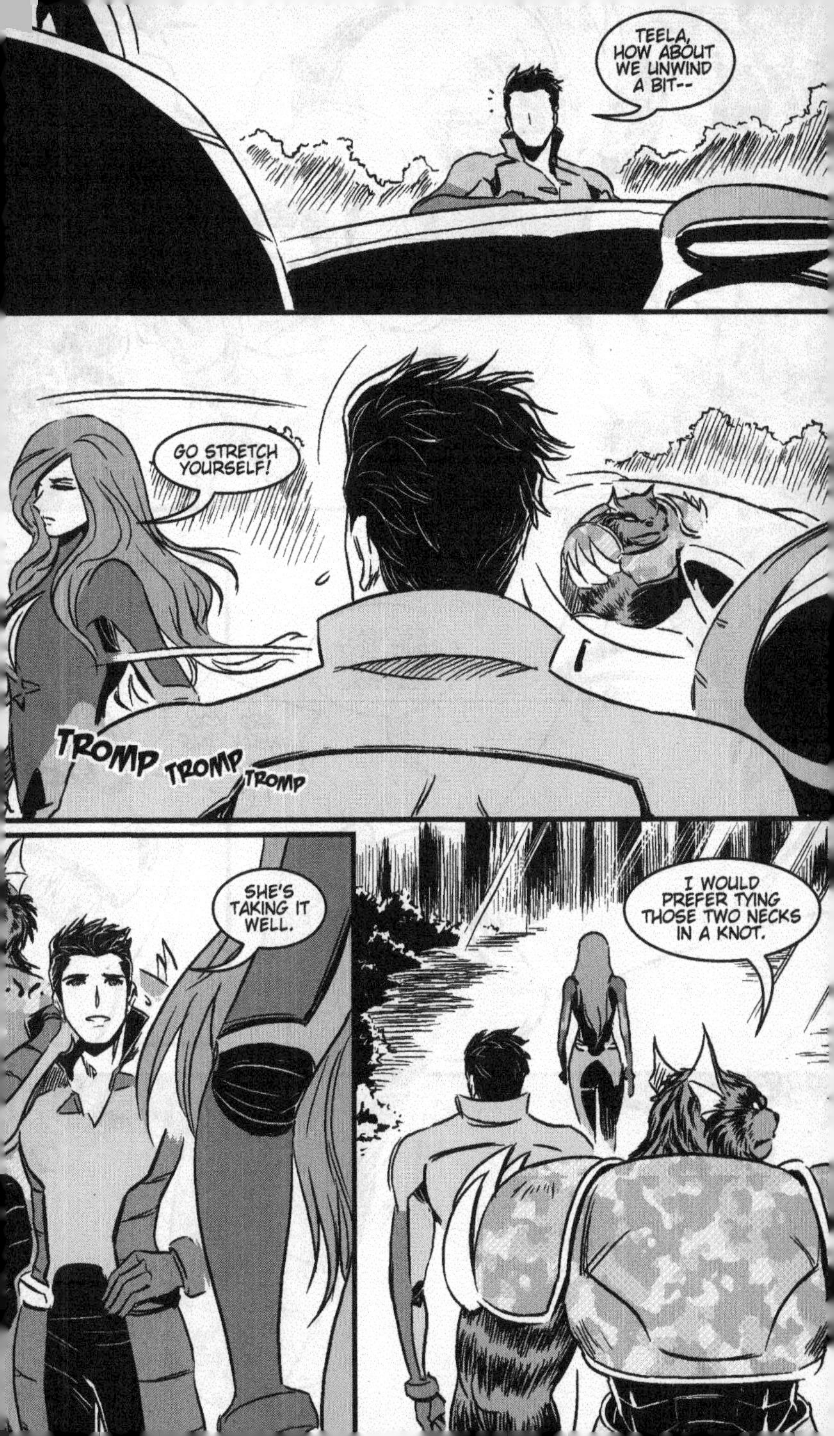
TEELA, HOW ABOUT WE UNWIND A BIT--
GO STRETCH YOURSELF!
TROMP TROMP TROMP
SHE'S TAKING IT WELL.
I WOULD PREFER TYING THOSE TWO NECKS IN A KNOT.

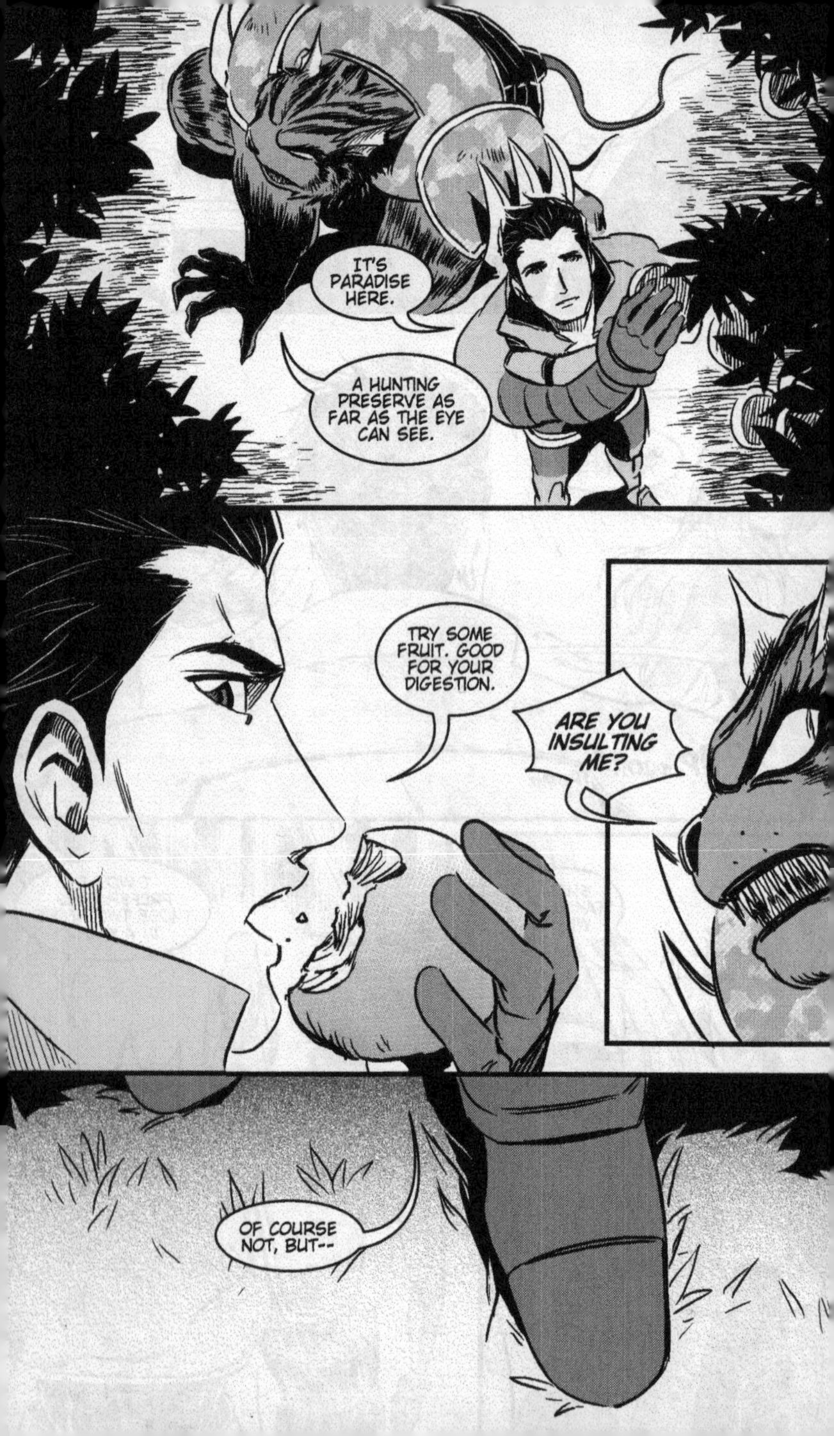
IT'S PARADISE HERE.
A HUNTING PRESERVE AS FAR AS THE EYE CAN SEE.
TRY SOME FRUIT. GOOD FOR YOUR DIGESTION.
ARE YOU INSULTING ME?
OF COURSE NOT, BUT--

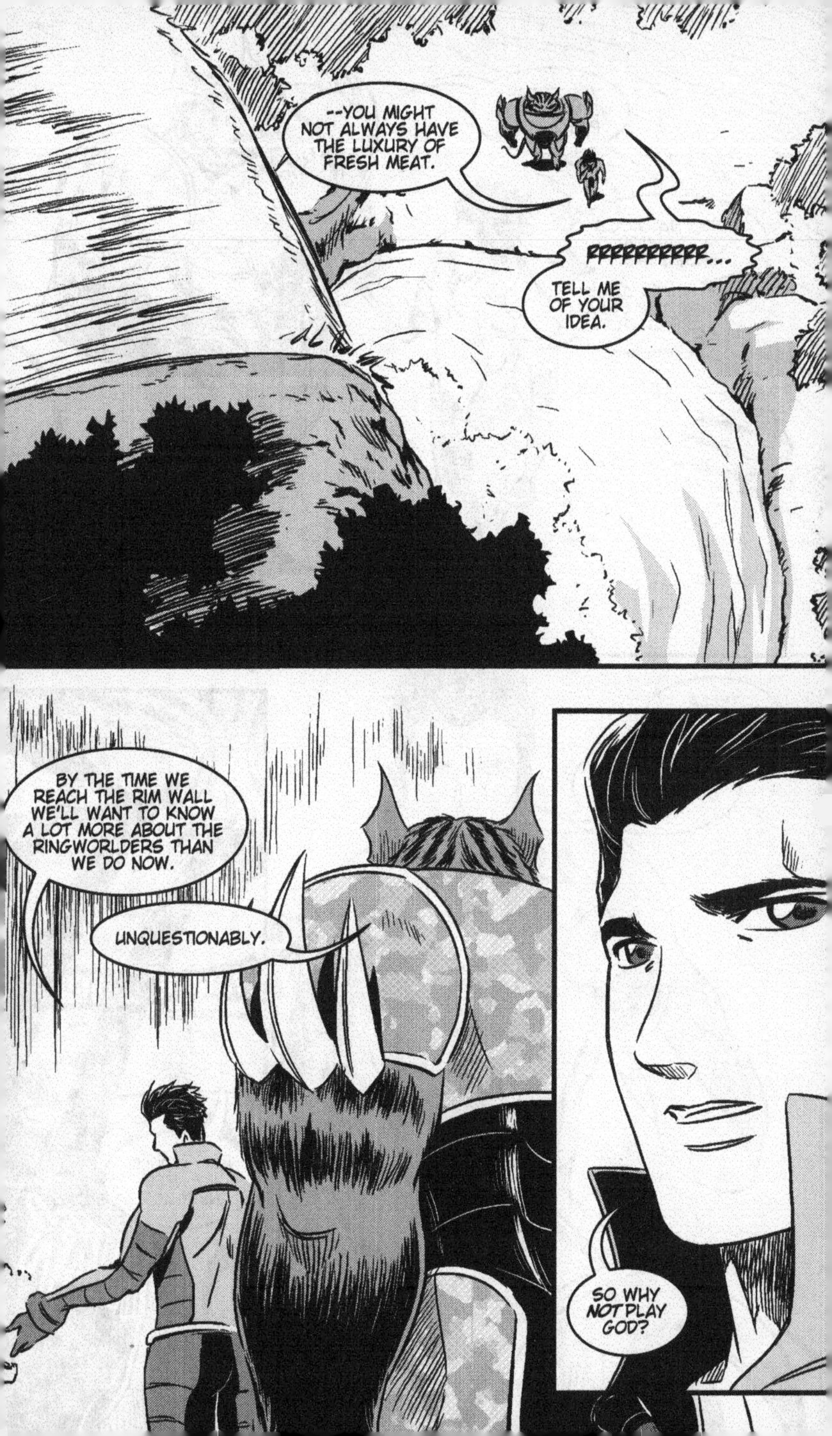
--YOU MIGHT NOT ALWAYS HAVE THE LUXURY OF FRESH MEAT.
RRRRRRRRRR...
TELL ME OF YOUR IDEA.
BY THE TIME WE REACH THE RIM WALL WE'LL WANT TO KNOW A LOT MORE ABOUT THE RINGWORLDERS THAN WE DO NOW.
UNQUESTIONABLY.
SO WHY *NOT* PLAY GOD?

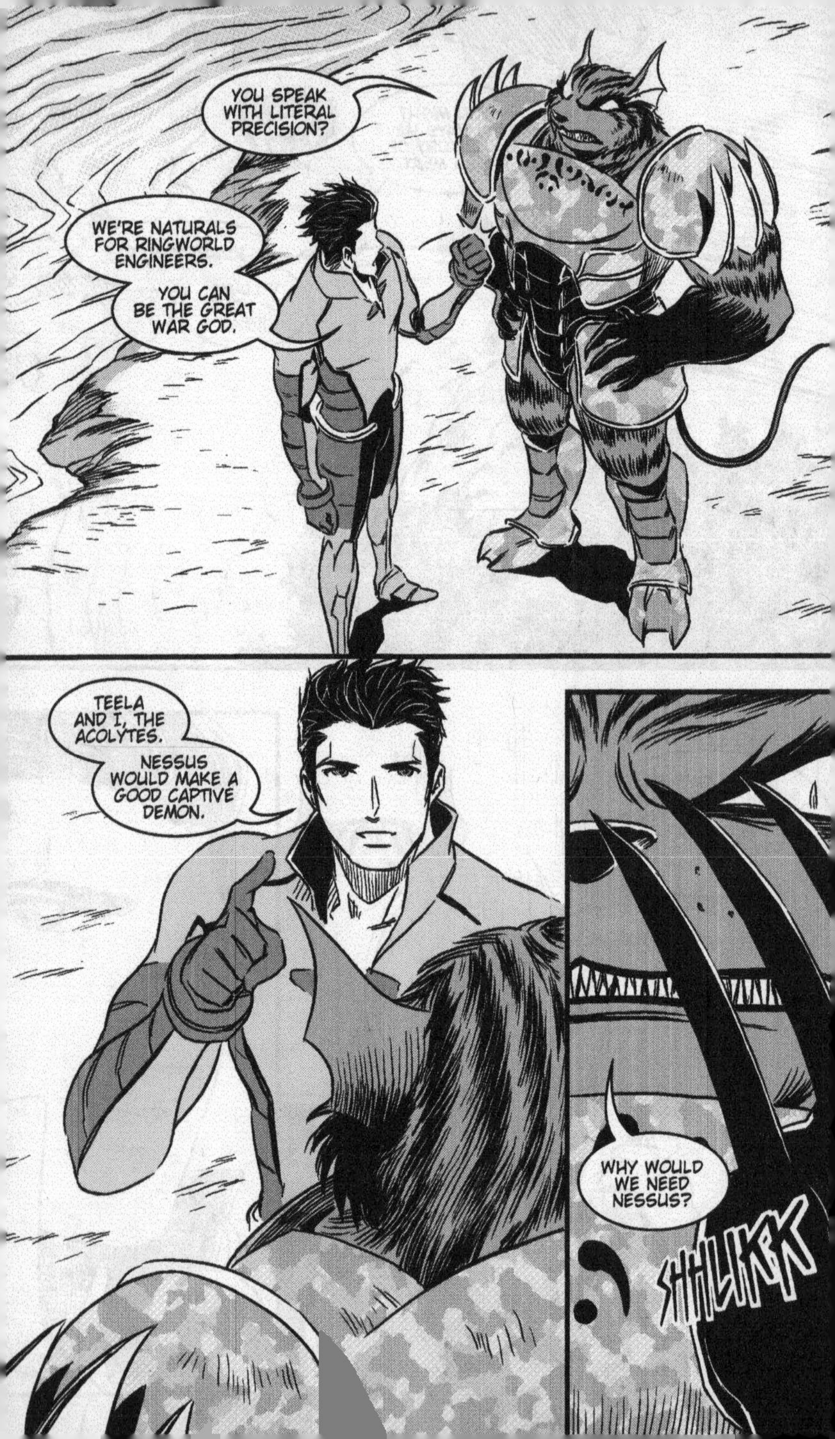
YOU SPEAK WITH LITERAL PRECISION?
WE'RE NATURALS FOR RINGWORLD ENGINEERS.
YOU CAN BE THE GREAT WAR GOD.
TEELA AND I, THE ACOLYTES.
NESSUS WOULD MAKE A GOOD CAPTIVE DEMON.
WHY WOULD WE NEED NESSUS?
SHHLIKKK

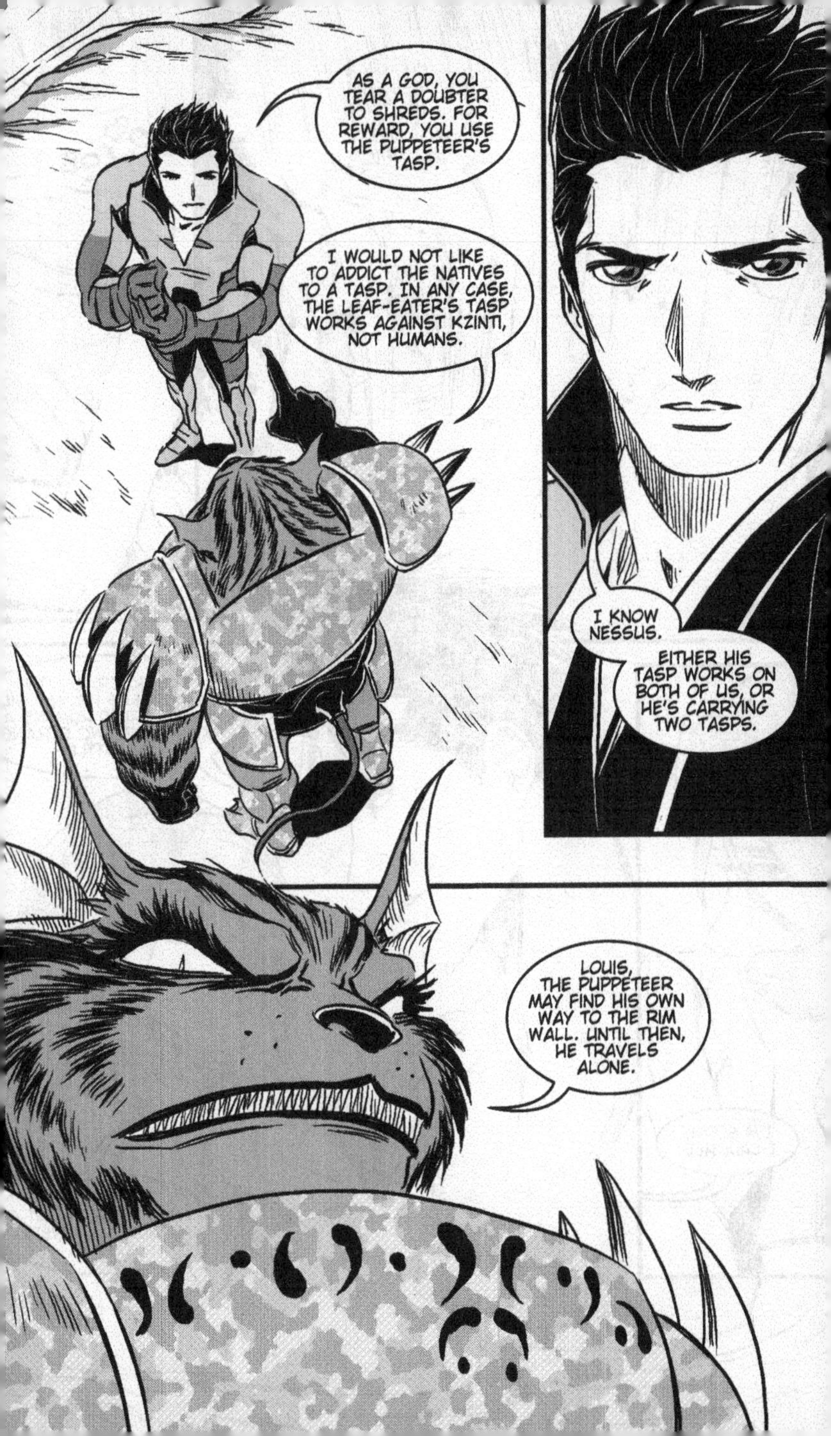
AS A GOD, YOU TEAR A DOUBTER TO SHREDS. FOR REWARD, YOU USE THE PUPPETEER'S TASP.
I WOULD NOT LIKE TO ADDICT THE NATIVES TO A TASP. IN ANY CASE, THE LEAF-EATER'S TASP WORKS AGAINST KZINTI, NOT HUMANS.
I KNOW NESSUS.
EITHER HIS TASP WORKS ON BOTH OF US, OR HE'S CARRYING TWO TASPS.
LOUIS, THE PUPPETEER MAY FIND HIS OWN WAY TO THE RIM WALL. UNTIL THEN, HE TRAVELS ALONE.

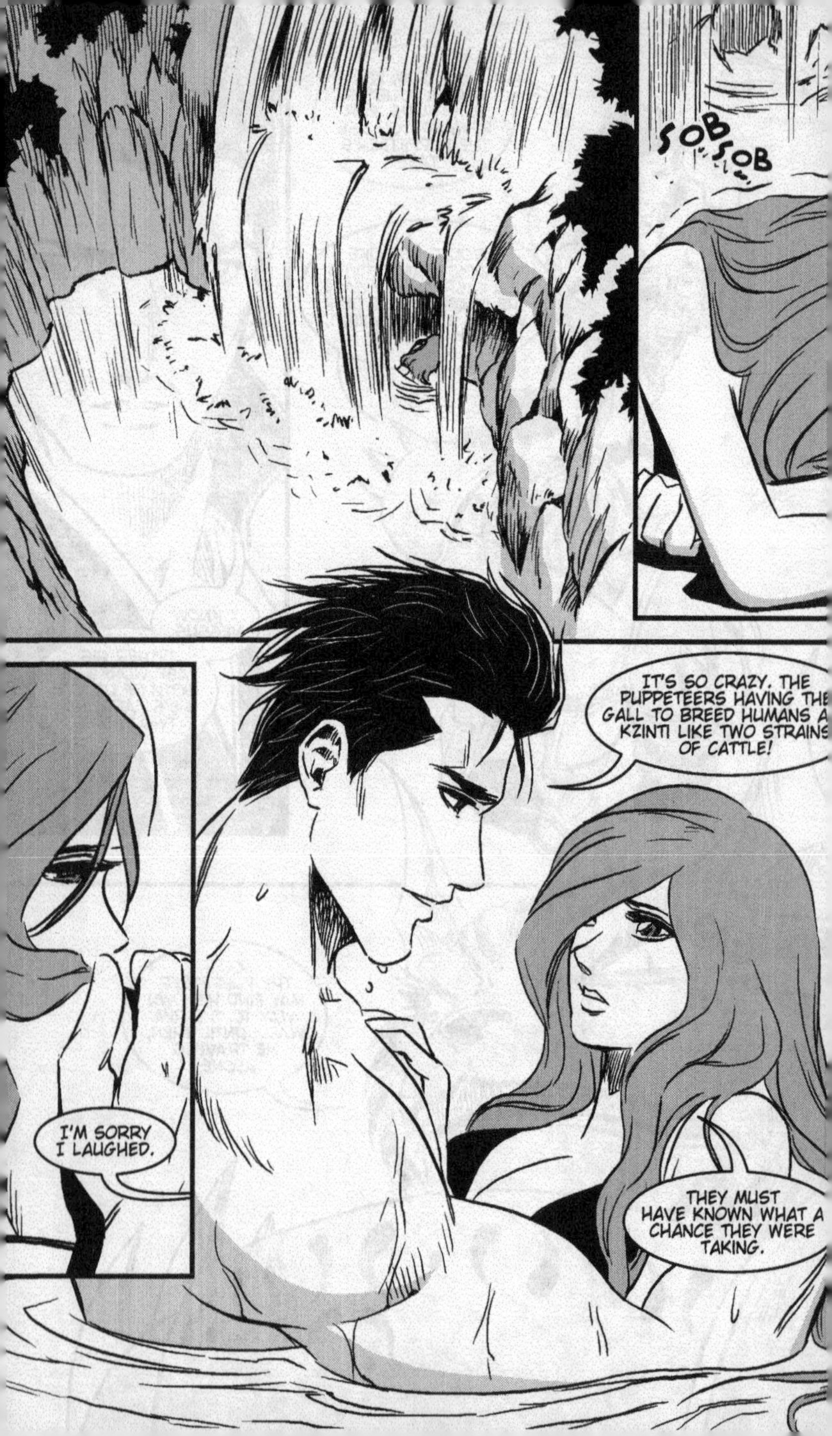
SOB SOB
I'M SORRY I LAUGHED.
IT'S SO CRAZY. THE PUPPETEERS HAVING THE GALL TO BREED HUMANS A KZINTI LIKE TWO STRAINS OF CATTLE!
THEY MUST HAVE KNOWN WHAT A CHANCE THEY WERE TAKING.

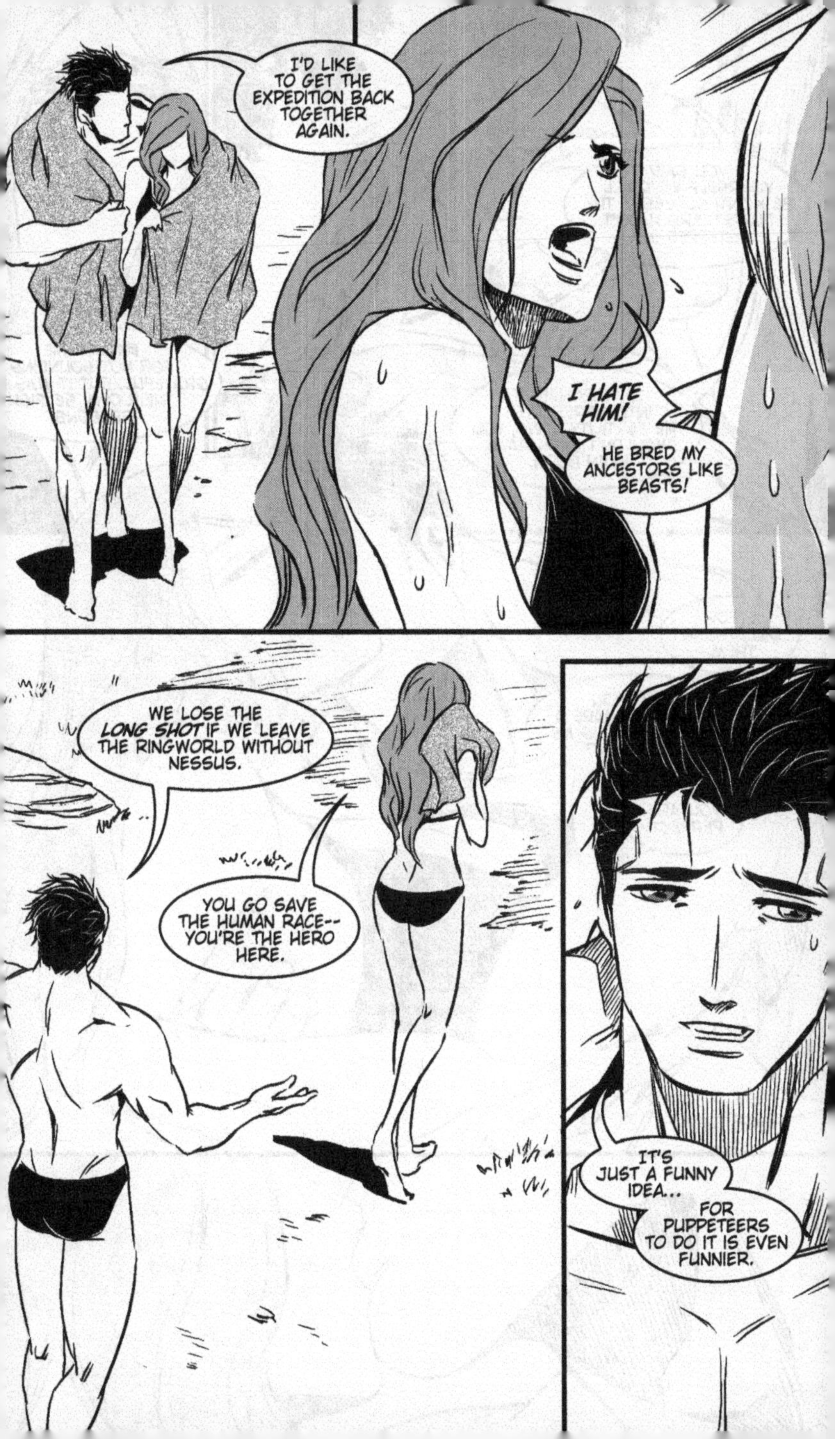
I'D LIKE TO GET THE EXPEDITION BACK TOGETHER AGAIN.
I HATE HIM!
HE BRED MY ANCESTORS LIKE BEASTS!
WE LOSE THE *LONG SHOT* IF WE LEAVE THE RINGWORLD WITHOUT NESSUS.
YOU GO SAVE THE HUMAN RACE-- YOU'RE THE HERO HERE.
IT'S JUST A FUNNY IDEA...
FOR PUPPETEERS TO DO IT IS EVEN FUNNIER.

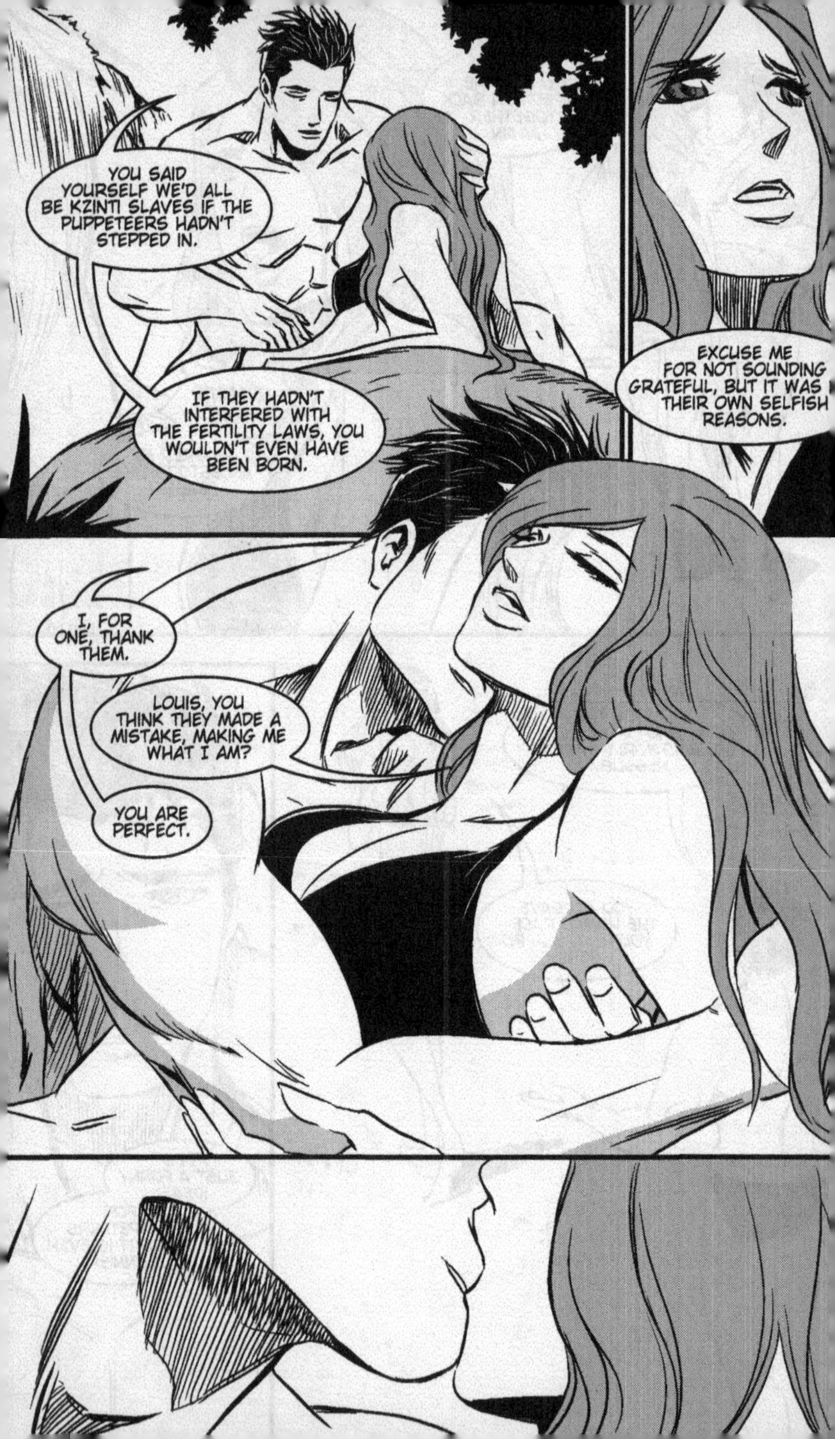
YOU SAID YOURSELF WE'D ALL BE KZINTI SLAVES IF THE PUPPETEERS HADN'T STEPPED IN.
IF THEY HADN'T INTERFERED WITH THE FERTILITY LAWS, YOU WOULDN'T EVEN HAVE BEEN BORN.
EXCUSE ME FOR NOT SOUNDING GRATEFUL, BUT IT WAS FOR THEIR OWN SELFISH REASONS.
I, FOR ONE, THANK THEM.
LOUIS, YOU THINK THEY MADE A MISTAKE, MAKING ME WHAT I AM?
YOU ARE PERFECT.

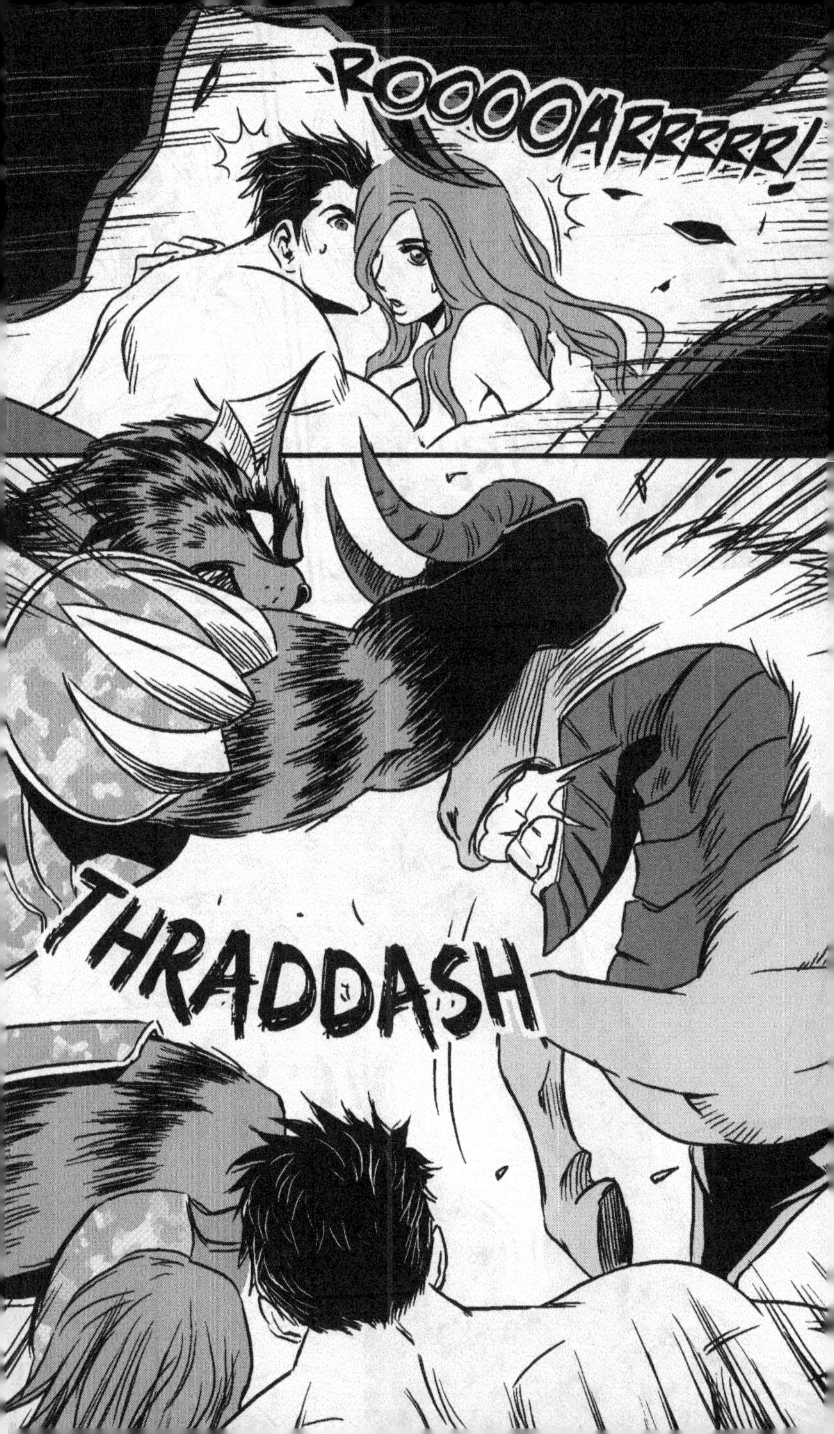
ROOOOOARRRRR!
THRADDASH

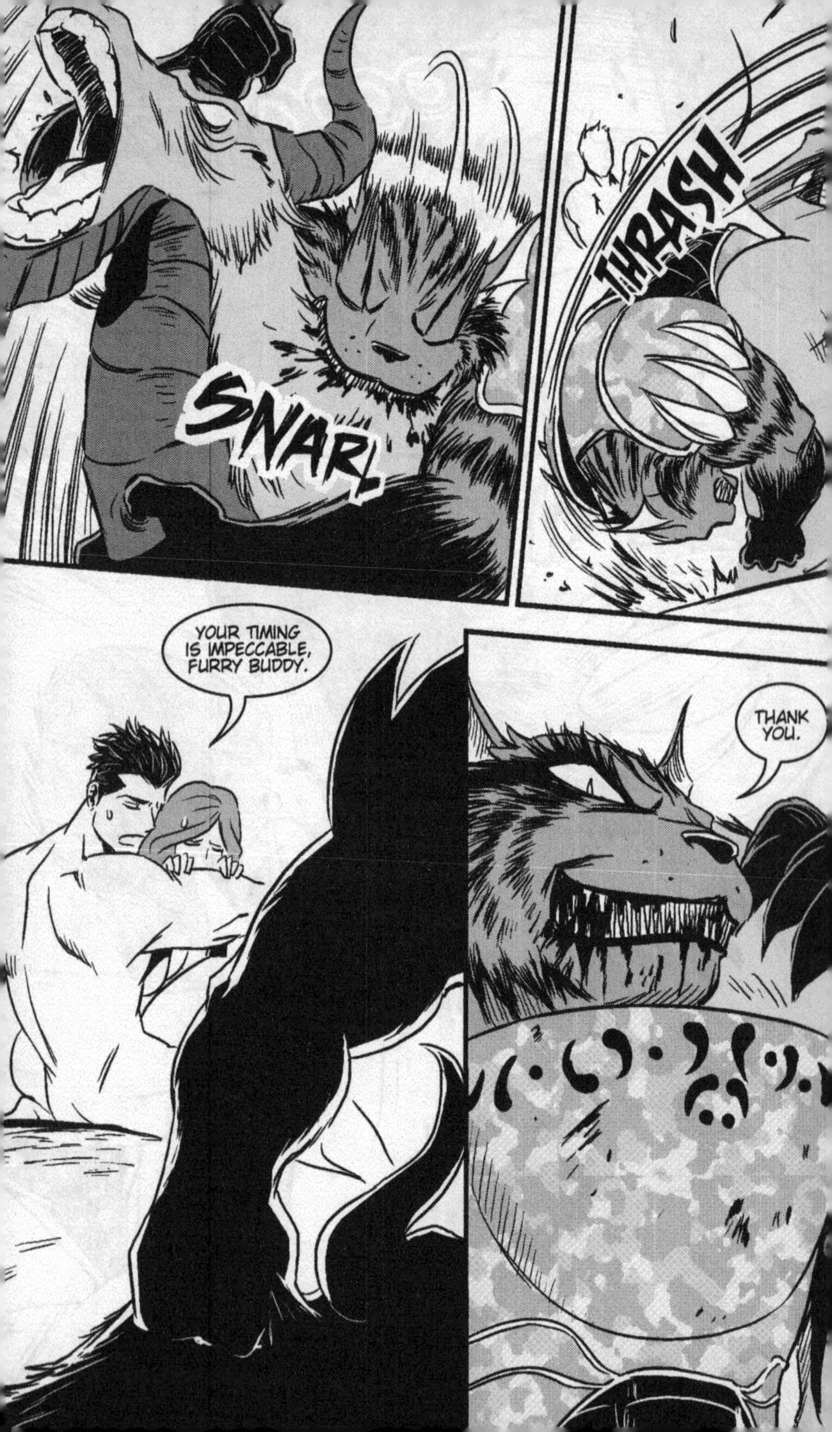
SNARL
THRASH
YOUR TIMING IS IMPECCABLE, FURRY BUDDY.
THANK YOU.

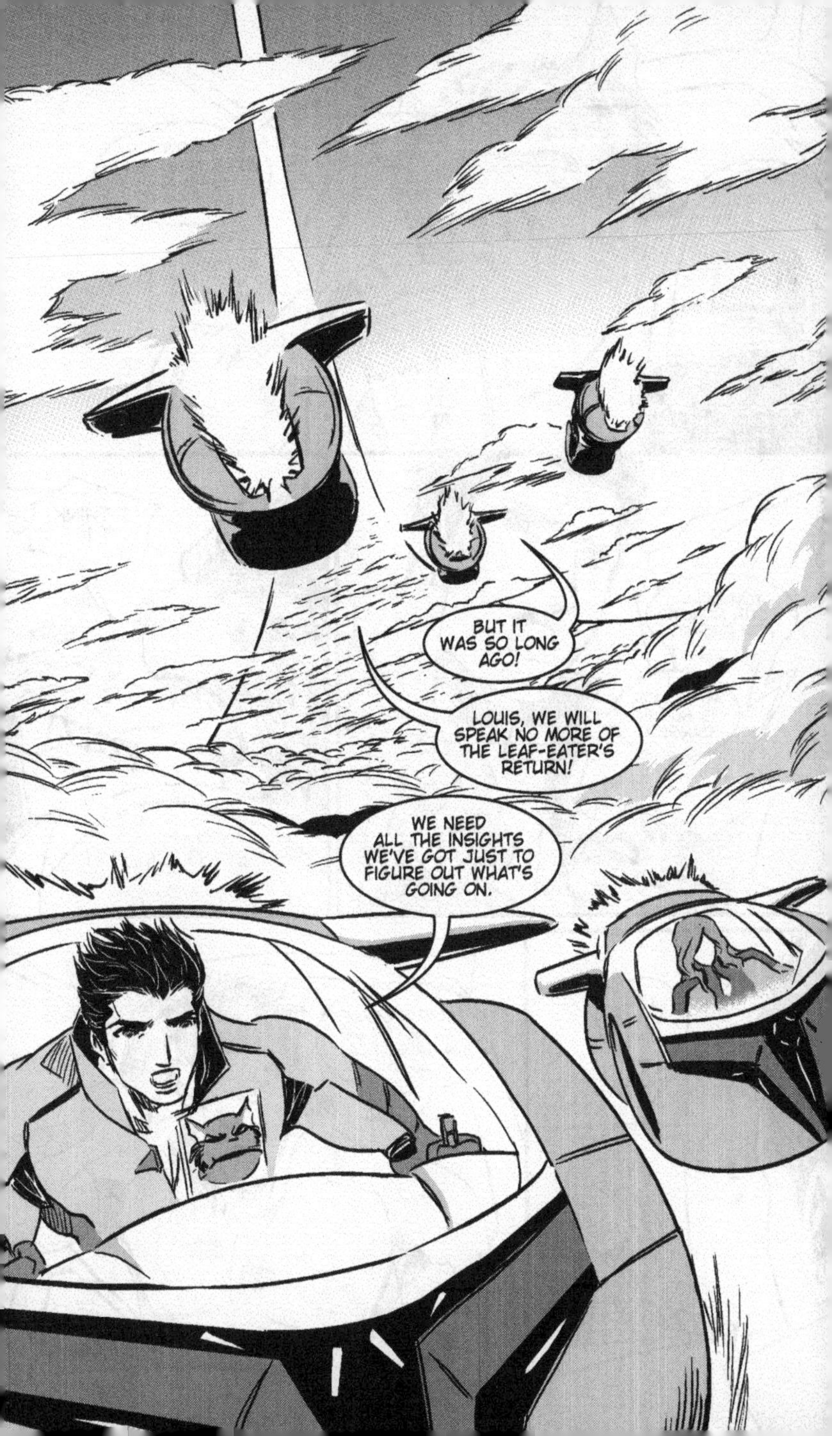
BUT IT WAS SO LONG AGO!
LOUIS, WE WILL SPEAK NO MORE OF THE LEAF-EATER'S RETURN!
WE NEED ALL THE INSIGHTS WE'VE GOT JUST TO FIGURE OUT WHAT'S GOING ON.

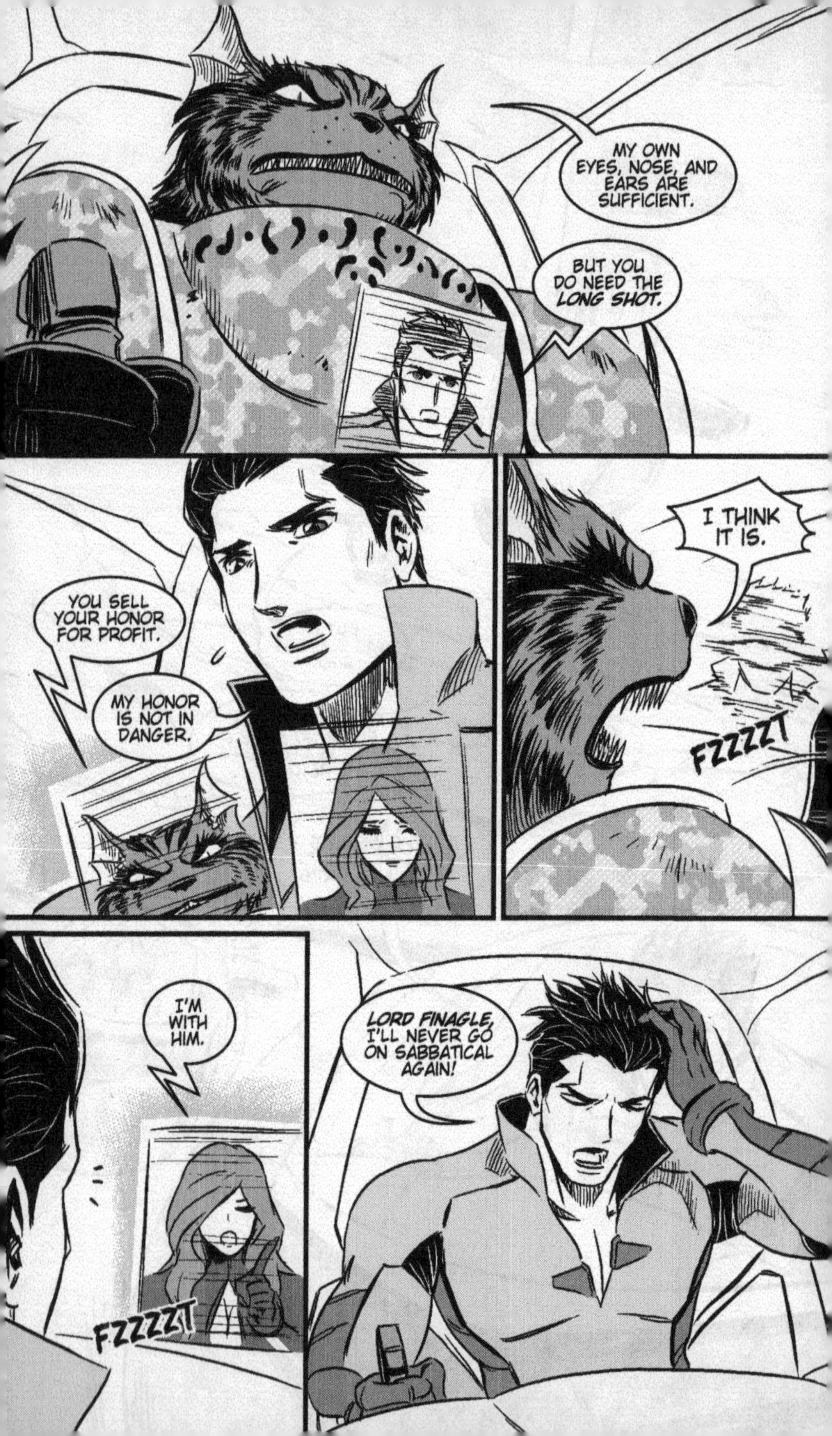
MY OWN EYES, NOSE, AND EARS ARE SUFFICIENT.
BUT YOU DO NEED THE *LONG SHOT.*
YOU SELL YOUR HONOR FOR PROFIT.
MY HONOR IS NOT IN DANGER.
I THINK IT IS.
FZZZZT
I'M WITH HIM.
FZZZZT
LORD FINAGLE, I'LL NEVER GO ON SABBATICAL AGAIN!

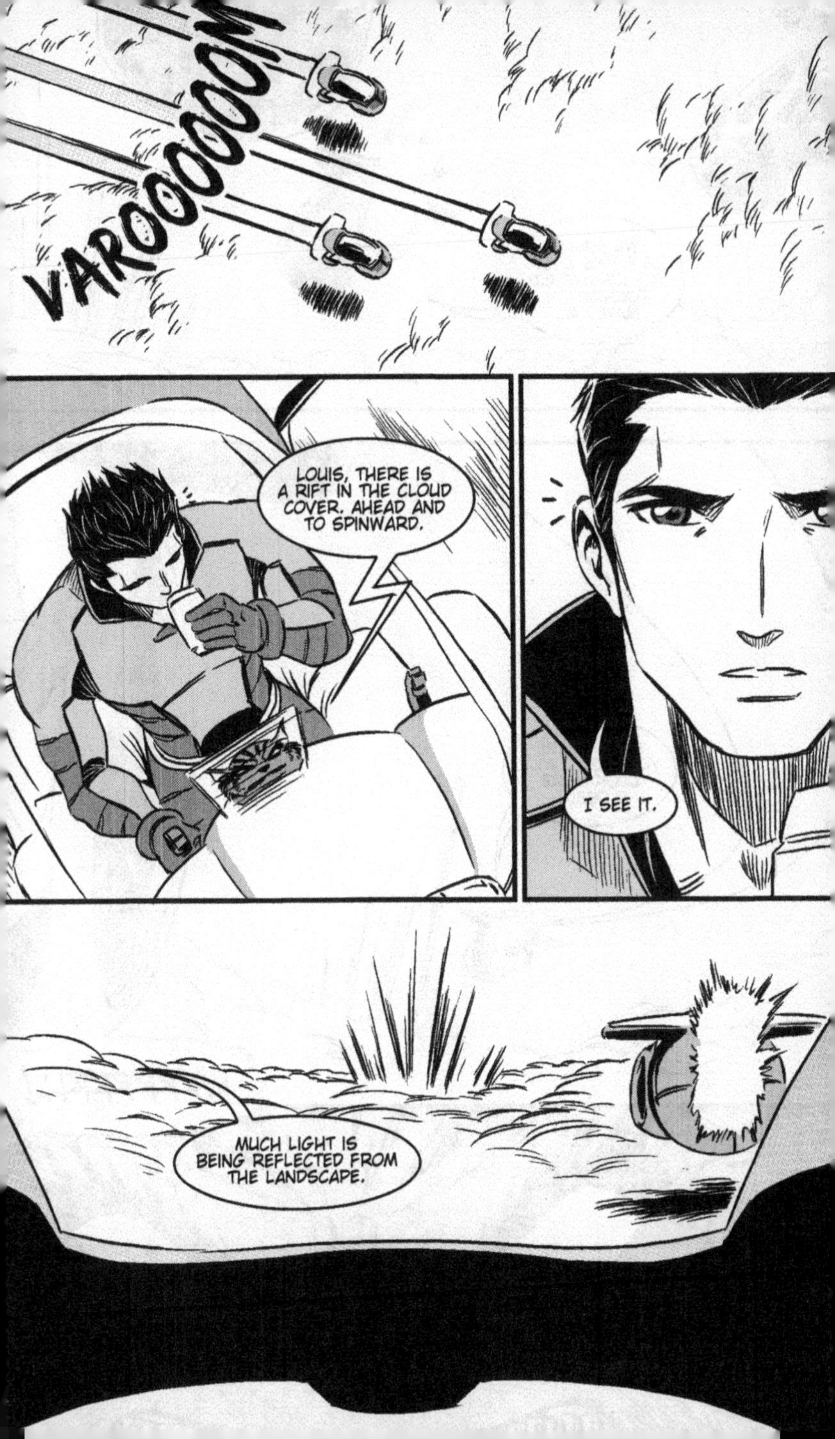
VAROOOOOOM
LOUIS, THERE IS A RIFT IN THE CLOUD COVER. AHEAD AND TO SPINWARD.
I SEE IT.
MUCH LIGHT IS BEING REFLECTED FROM THE LANDSCAPE.

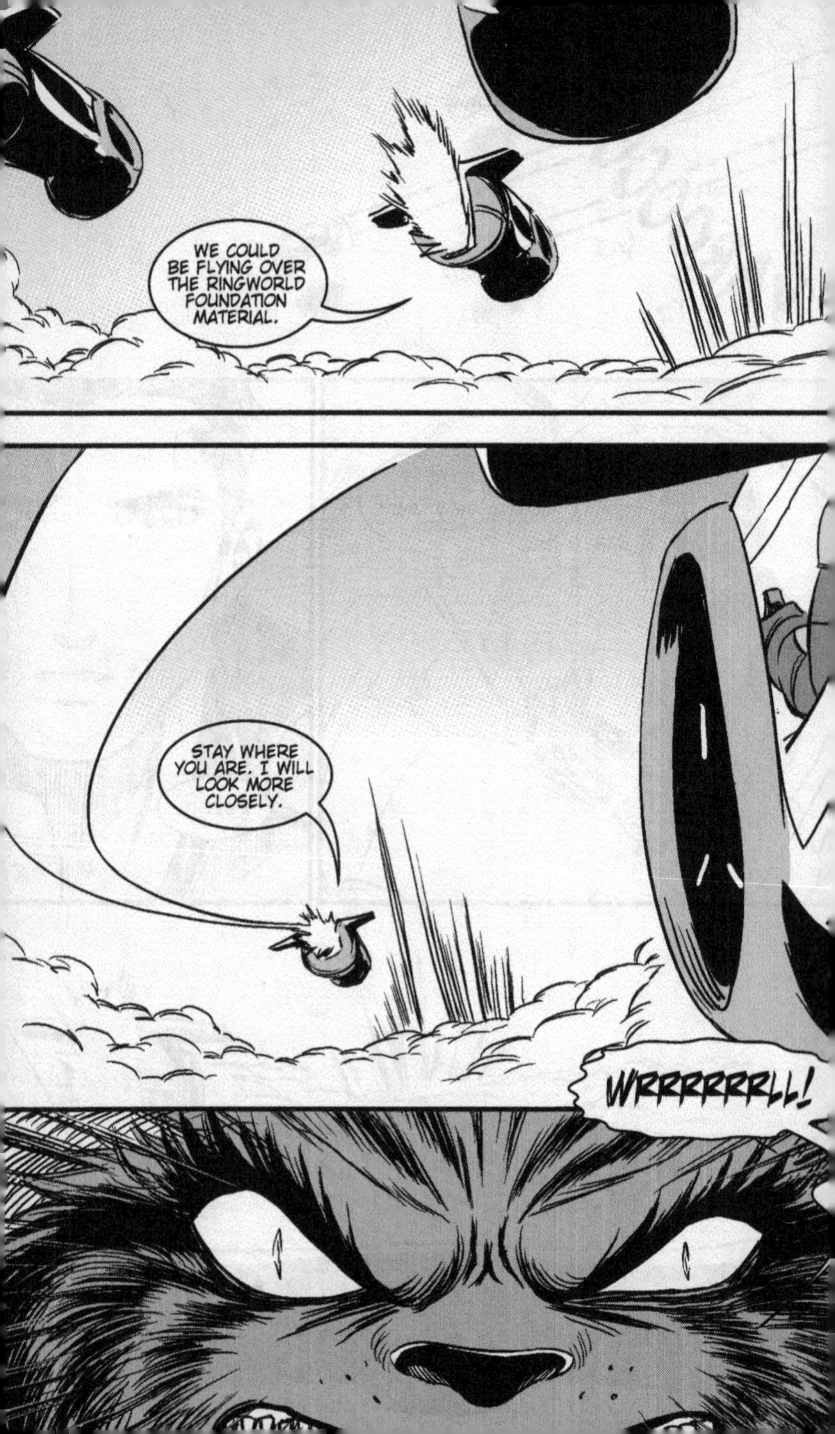
WE COULD BE FLYING OVER THE RINGWORLD FOUNDATION MATERIAL.
STAY WHERE YOU ARE. I WILL LOOK MORE CLOSELY.
WRRRRRRLL!

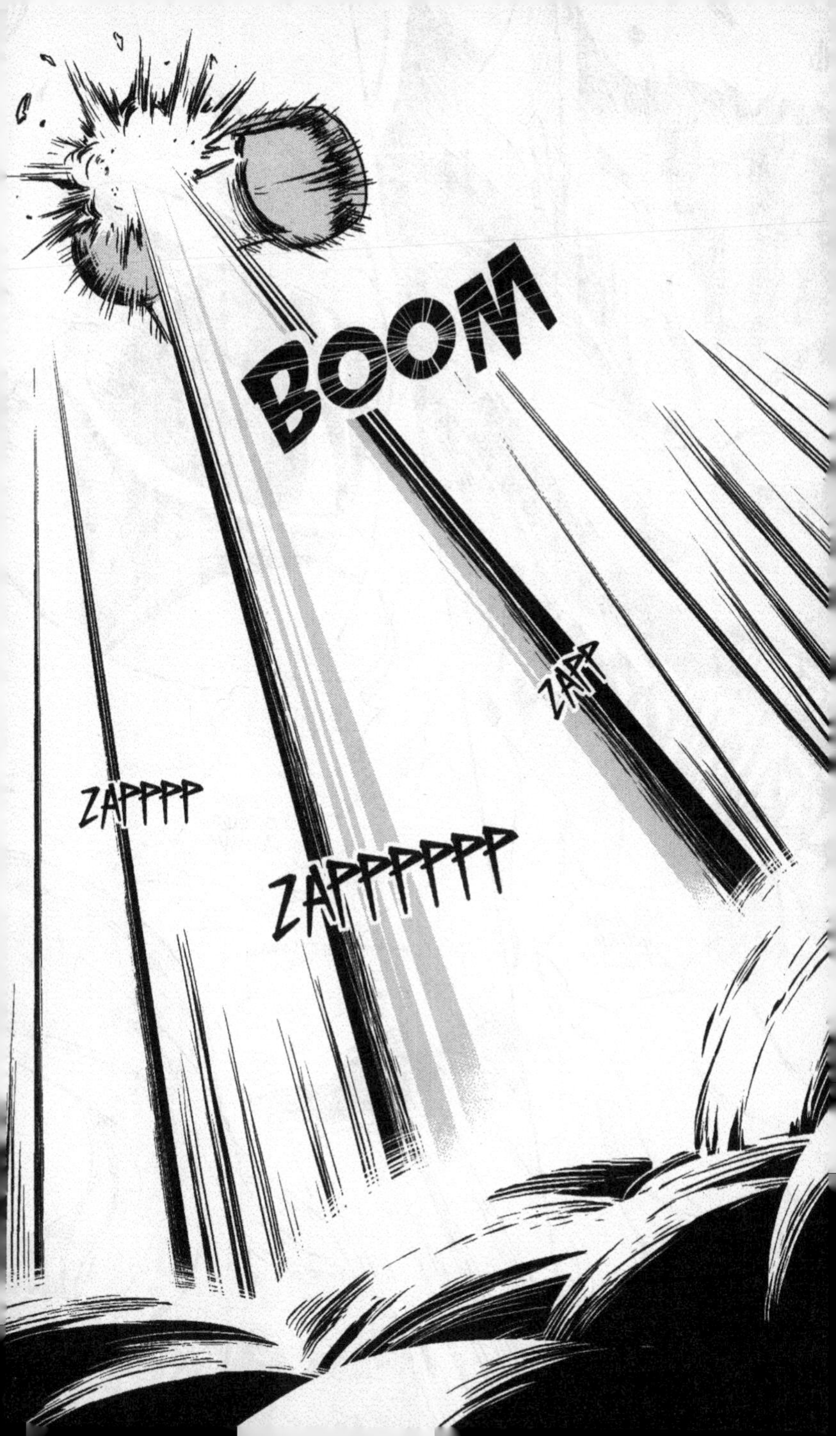
BOOM
ZAPP
ZAPPPP
ZAPPPPPP

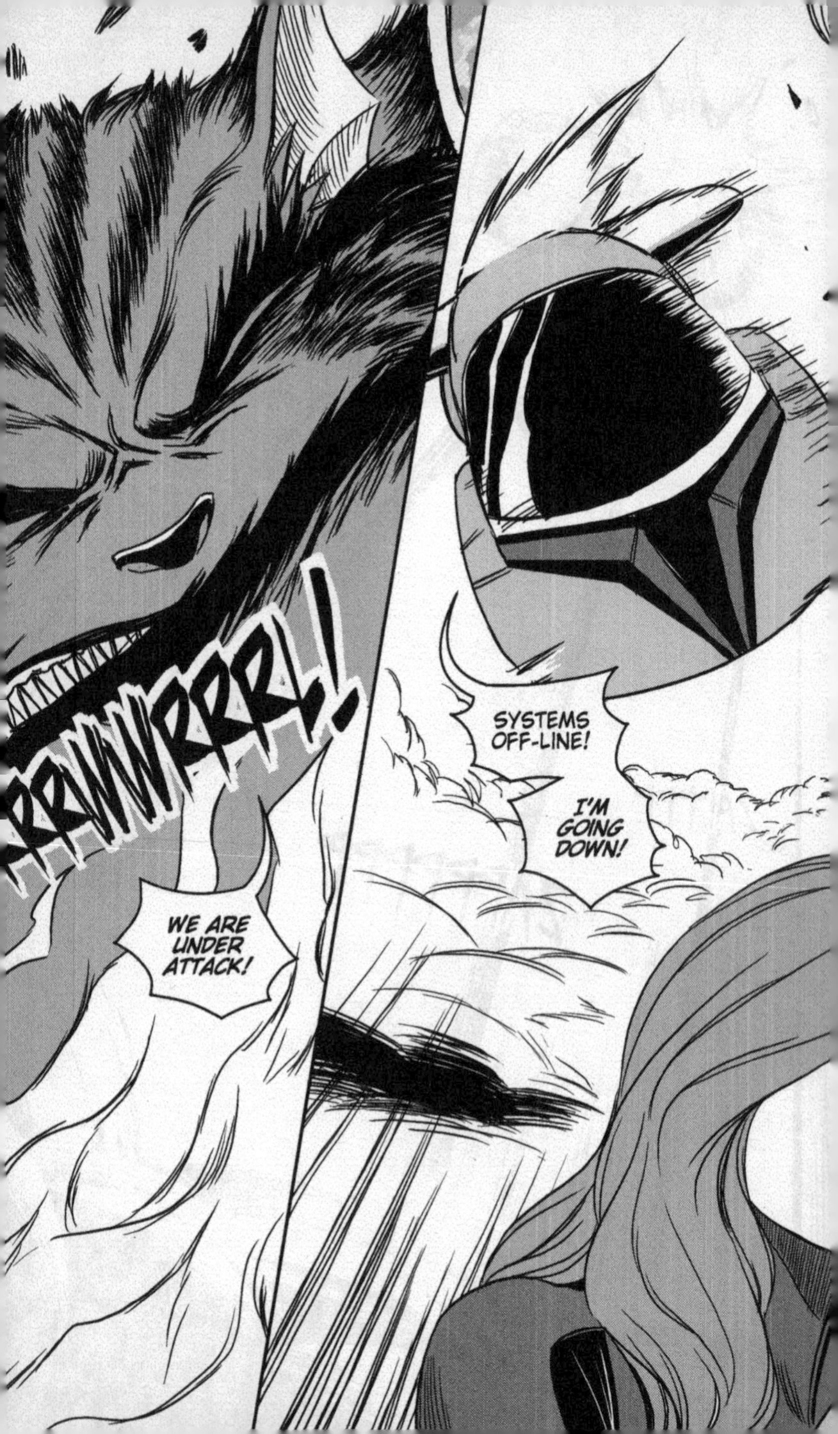
RRWWRRL!!
WE ARE UNDER ATTACK!
SYSTEMS OFF-LINE!
I'M GOING DOWN!

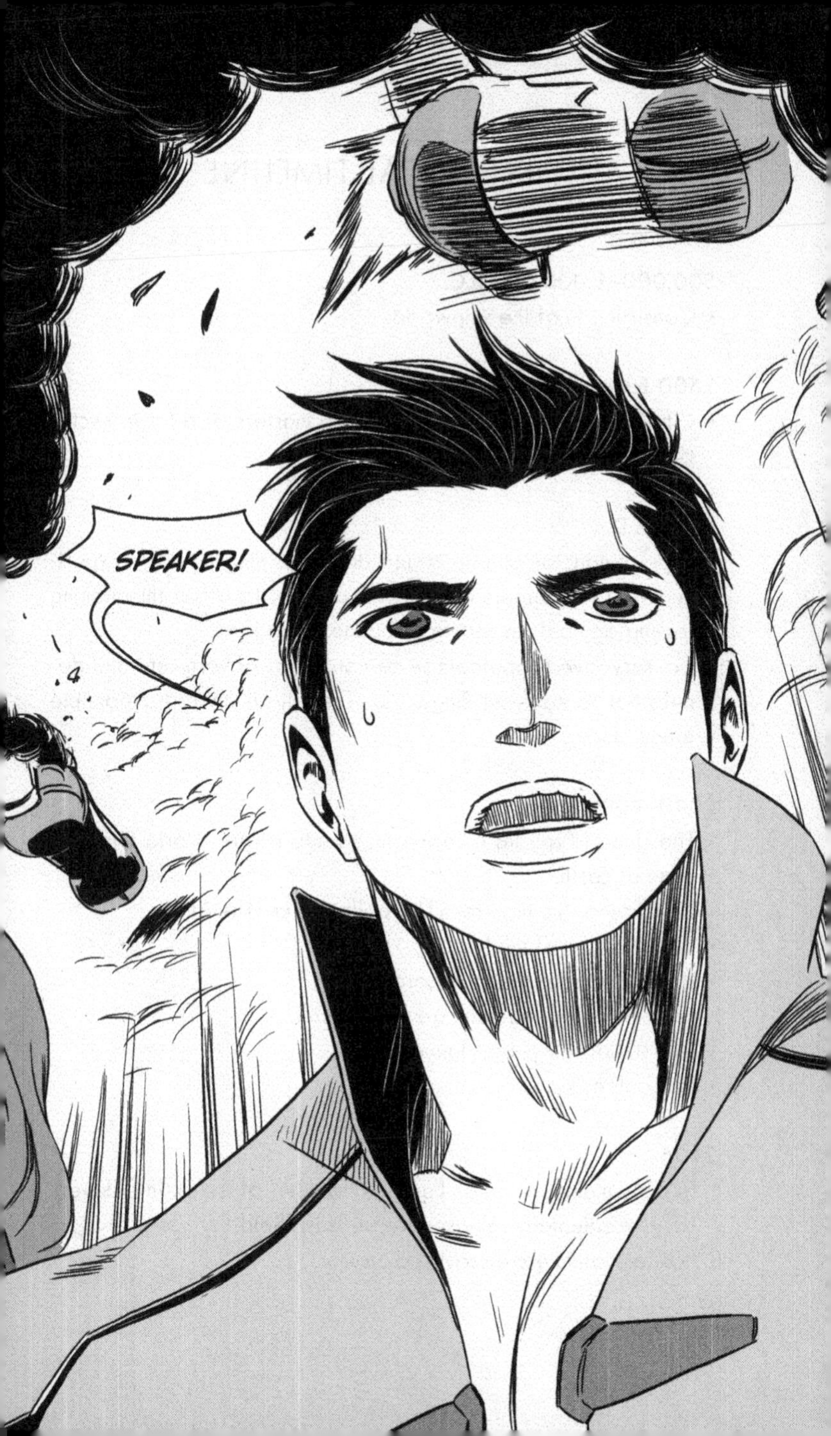
SPEAKER!

HISTORICAL TIMELINE

500,000–1,000,000 B.C.
- Construction of the Ringworld.

1500 B.C.
- City Builders became the undisputed masters of a large sector of Ringworld.

1733 A.D.
- Superconductor plague is introduced to Ringworld by Experimentalist Puppeteers in a shrewd attempt to offset threatening technology before setting up business relations.
- Conservative Puppeteers seize control of government and decide not to confront Ringworld. They file it away for possible future study.

2040–2099
- The United Nations is reorganized into a true World Government of Earth.
- Creation of the high-tech UN police force, The ARM.
- Colonization of the belt.
- UN-Belt Cooperation Accord.
- Belt sets up independent government.
- Interstellar ram robots launched.
- First colony slowboats launched.

2106
- First alien discovered on Earth—a member of the Thrint (Slaver) race, accidentally released from a stasis field.
- Bandersnatchi are discovered on Jinx.

2125

- Phssthpok the Pak arrives in the Sol system after traveling 30,000 light-years to save humanity.

2135

- Human colony worlds established on Jinx, We Made It, and Wunderland.

2189

- Human colony established on Home.

2150–2360

- The Golden Age on Earth.

2200

- Jinx proclaims independence from UN controls.

2351

- The Home catastrophe.

2360

- First contact with the Kzin.
- Experimentalists regain control of Puppeteer government.

2367

- Kzin attack Alpha Centauri, subjugating Wunderland.
- Institute of Knowledge on Jinx invents Boosterspice.

2410

- Humans on We Made It buy hyperdrive engine from Outsider merchants, ensuring a string of victories by humans over Kzin.

2420

- End of the first Man-Kzin War.
- Down is liberated.
- Puppeteers reveal themselves to humanity.

2449–2475

- Second Man-Kzin War.

2491–2531

- Third Man-Kzin War.
- The Kzinti military command planet Canyon is annexed.

2560–2584

- Fourth Man-Kzin War.

2589

- Home is recolonized.

2590

- Puppeteers expand their business empire into Human and Kzin space, controlling an ample portion of Known Space commerce.

2640

- Puppeteer development of the Quantum II hyperdrive.
- Puppeteer sponsored test flight of the *Long Shot*, the first ship to utilize the Quantum II hyperdrive, piloted by Beowolf Schaffer. Schaffer takes the craft to the galactic core and discovers the Galactic core explosion is expanding and a cloud of deadly radiation will engulf Known Space in 20,000 years.
- The Puppeteer Exodus.
- Stock market crash in human space.

2650

- Louis Gridley Wu is born.
- Puppeteer influence amends Fertility Laws by introducing Birth-right Lotteries in an attempt to "breed" lucky humans.

2830

- Contact with Trinocs.

2850

- First expedition to Ringworld, sponsored by the Experimentalist Hindmost.

2851

- Conservative Puppeteer party denounces the Ringworld expedition as a total disaster and tosses out the Experimentalist Hindmost. The Conservatives take control of the Puppeteer Fleet-of-Worlds.

2870

- Second expedition to Ringworld—a secret mission led by the deposed Experimentalist Hindmost to discover secrets that would reinstate its former status.

2895

- Third expedition to Ringworld. After the second expedition mysteriously disappears, Webbster, an insane Experimentalist Puppeteer, sponsors a secret expedition to Ringworld to discover what happened.

WORLDS OF KNOWN SPACE

Canyon

Canyon marks the southernmost contour of Kzin Space, and has been of invaluable strategic importance historically in enforcing the UN restrictions on Kzinti expansionism. Formerly a Kzinti world with a substantial military-industrial complex, it was annexed at the close of the Third Man-Kzin War (2531) by the use of an awesome energy weapon called the "Wunderland Treatymaker." This weapon virtually annihilated the Kzinti top military command when the military installation, protected by stasis fields, was swallowed by molten lava in the center of a twelve-mile-deep gash before the rock congealed. Officially, the Kzin Patriarchy recognizes Earth's dominion, but many of the old-guard Patriarchy regard Canyon as an outpost within their territory. They know that buried within the lava, great Kzinti military leaders are still alive in frozen time with their secret plans for galactic dominance.

System: e Eridani A
Distance from sol: 22 light-years
Size: small, not much bigger than Mars
Surface gravity: 0.45 gee
Day: 27.1 hours
Moons: none
Distance from primary: 70.7 million miles
Chief industries: mining of rich radioactives and high-grade heavy-metal ores
Atmosphere: air pressure and oxygen content too low for humans and Kzin
Human population: 8.5 million, spread out in comfortable high-density habitats and domed cities

Down

Down is the home world of the Grogs, disturbing but docile aliens who possess heightened mind-control abilities. Down once had a long-established Kzin military outpost that maintained a fleet of Kzinti warships within easy striking distance of all Earth's developing interstellar colonies. Down was liberated after the first Man-Kzin War. In the present day, humans and Grogs work harmoniously in all fields of mutual interest. Safeguards against Grog mind control are no longer necessary.

System: L5 1668
Distance from sol: 12.3 light-years
Size: slightly larger than Earth
Surface gravity: 1.15 gee
Day: 28.7 hours
Moons: none
Distance from primary: 13 million miles
Chief industries: Major fish-farming industries run by Dolphins
Atmosphere: tranquil red-desert world with dusty but breathable air
Human population: about 360 million living in high-density wheeled space colonies in orbit around Down; some 30 million live on the surface in widely separated urban oases

Home

Home has a mysterious history. First settled in 2189, the colonists thought they had discovered Eden. By the mid-twenty-fourth century they had developed a healthy industrial civilization. Then in 2351, something happened that catastrophically wiped out every last man, woman, and child on the planet. They completely disappeared. It was thought to be a virulent plague of uncertain origin but no proof was ever conclusive. The Kzin were wrongly accused of having obliterated the Home colony. Kzinti legends describe horrible parasitic creatures that emerged from a cycle of deep slumber and devoured the colonists but no evidence has ever been found. For two centuries the planet was judged unsafe for human habitation. Home was officially recolonized in 2589. Growth and development has proceeded cautiously since.

System: Epsilon Indi
Distance from sol: 11.4 light-years
Size: slightly larger than Earth
Surface gravity: 1.08 gee
Day: 23.2 hours
Moons: one
Distance from primary: 80 million miles
Chief industries: Extensive mining operations, farms, aquaculture
Atmosphere: Earthlike
Human population: 51 million

Jinx

Jinx is the largest, most technologically advanced, and most highly industrialized human colony world. Jinx is the major moon of the third planet from Sirius A, Binary, a banded orange gas giant more massive than Jupiter. General Products maintains a major regional facility on Jinx and it is home to the Institute of Knowledge, the finest museum and research complex in human space. Since Jinx proclaimed itself independent of UN control in 2200, it has truly become an interstellar melting pot with alien populations sometimes equaling humans. Certain sections have gained reputations as safe havens for outlaws, smugglers, and pirates. The ARM maintains an outpost here per an agreement between the UN and Jinx to police alien relations.

System: Sirius A
Distance from sol: 8.7 light-years
Size: egg shaped with colorful bands, six times denser than Earth
Surface gravity: 1.78 gee

Day: 96 hours—the same face, the East End, is always turned to
the gas giant planet, Binary
Distance from primary: 397 million miles
Chief industries: high-technology and research, alien studies
Atmosphere: habitable Earthlike bands; bands of seas and low-
lands are thick and dense with temperatures higher than 200
degrees F
Human population: over 2.1 billion

Plateau

In 2090 an Earth colony ship arrived at Tau Ceti following reports
from an earlier ram robot that one planet in the system was Earthlike. The closest they could find was a Venus-type world with a poisonous, corrosive atmosphere lethal to humans. There would be no
rescue and no escape. Finally the radar picked out what the ram
robot had found: a vast multiplateaued mountain, the size of Cali-
fornia, projecting above the deadly lower atmosphere. The atmosphere on the mountain was surprisingly Earthlike. The pilot gasped,
"Lookitthat!" christening the great peak forever.

Surrounding the great plateaus are spectacular waterfalls at
the Void Edge. The colony quickly adapted to the mountainous en-
vironment and Lookitthat! became a panorama resembling twen-
tieth-century Europe. Many quaint mountain villages and resort
towns spread about the various levels. Today tourism is the major
business and tourists flock to Plateau for sightseeing and a variety
of entertainment and leisure activities. Fabulous hotels, casinos,
spas, gambling clubs, and ski resorts are major attractions perched
high above the fabulous views over the Void's Edge.

System: Tau Ceti
Distance from sol: 11.8 light-years
Size: smaller than Earth, and less dense
Surface gravity: .81 gee
Day: 29.4 hours

Distance from primary: 100 million miles

Chief industries: Tourism

Atmosphere: The plateaus of Mt. Lookitthat vary little in its pleasantly moderate climate and seasons. The rest of the planet is covered in swirling poisonous mist.

Human population: permanent population is 105 million. Three orbital stations hold a million more.

We Made It

We Made It was settled when a ram robot landed on a rare mild spring day near one of the planet's viscous, algae-chocked "oceans." Reporting favorable conditions, colonists arrived and found a planet whose odd axis of rotation cause perpetual daylight summers and winters of eternal night. Hurricane-force winds scour the surface throughout the year. The landscape is flat, sandblasted desert and utterly lifeless. The colonists that made it were nicknamed "crashlanders" and the struggle to build a civilization endured and developed underground. The savage power of the surface winds helped transform the colonies into respectable buried cities. Refineries for processing the rich algae oceans soon developed into municipal utilities. We Made It's severe isolation ended in 2046 when an Outsider merchant ship arrived and offered the sale of the Quantum I hyperdrive engine, resulting in a sudden industrial revolution. In the present day, We Made It has a booming, highly industrialized economy with immense underground factories.

System: Procyon

Distance from sol: 11.3 light-years

Size: small

Surface gravity: .59 gee

Day: 20.4 UNS hours

Distance from primary: 195 million miles

Chief industries: soft sciences, creative arts, synthetic food stuffs, manufacturing

Atmosphere: fairly dense, often dusty oxygen atmosphere
Human population: 950 million

Wunderland

The first of the human interstellar colonies was established on a beautiful, idyllic, Earthlike world called Wunderland in 2091. Originally settled by elite, aristocratic families whose resources had financed the settlement, Wunderland's society is the closest thing to royalty in Human Space. City-states grow around the sites of magnificent estates, plantations, and baronial villas of the rich and powerful. Its infamy as the home to so much interstellar wealth has made Wunderland's history rife with political intrigue and conflict. The Kzin discovered Wunderland and conquered it in 2367, initiating the first Man-Kzin war. During the years of Kzinti occupation, the aristocracy suffered terribly, many becoming servants to the "rat-cats" and many simply were killed or eaten. To this day many Wunderland families maintain strong anti-Kzin alliances.

System: Alpha Centauri
Distance from sol: 4.3 light-years
Size: smaller than Earth
Surface gravity: .61 gee
Day: 26.7 UNS hours
Distance from primary: 123 million miles
Moons: one
Chief industries: farming, zero-gee manufacturing
Atmosphere: Earthlike with pastoral and comfortable temperatures
Human population: 3.25 billion

ABOUT THE AUTHORS

Robert Mandell created and is the cowriter for the bestselling series Avalon: Web of Magic, in addition to the Heavy Metal Pulp novels, the Hollywood mystery series Angela Harris: Hollywood Detective, the action adventure series Web Warriors, the graphic novel series The 3rd Degree, and the brand-new series Sky Rider with partner and cowriter Rachel Roberts.

Mandell served as executive producer of *The King and I* animated motion picture for Warner Brothers Family Entertainment and executive producer of *Ace Ventura: Pet Detective*, the animated series for CBS and Nickelodeon. He was also creator, writer, and director of the animated series *Princess Gwenevere and the Jewel Riders* and cult fan-favorite series *The Adventures of the Galaxy Rangers* and *Thunderbirds: 2086*.

Sean Lam is the artist of *It Takes A Wizard*, published by Seven Seas Entertainment, and several instructional art books, where he was lead artist. A graduate in graphic design from Nanyang Academy of Fine Arts in Singapore, Sean worked in advertising as a creative and art director before pursuing his passion for illustrating.